JEAN RHYS

THE COMPLETE NOVELS

Jean Rhys

WITH AN INTRODUCTION BY DIANA ATHILL
AND PHOTOGRAPHS BY BRASSAÏ

THE COMPLETE NOVELS

Voyage in the Dark ◆ Quartet ◆ After Leaving Mr Mackenzie
Good Morning, Midnight ◆ Wide Sargasso Sea

W. W. NORTON & COMPANY
NEW YORK ◆ LONDON

JEAN RHYS: THE COMPLETE NOVELS
First published 1985 by W.W. Norton & Company, Inc.
500 Fifth Avenue · New York, N.Y. 10110

Library of Congress Cataloging in Publication Data

Rhys, Jean.
Jean Rhys, the complete novels.

I. Title.
PR 6035.H96A15   1985   823'.912   85–4996
ISBN 0–393–02226–9

Quartet, After Leaving Mr Mackenzie, and Good Morning,
Midnight are reprinted by permission of Harper & Row, Publishers, Inc.

The first four novels in this collection appeared as Jean Rhys:
The Early Novels, published 1984 by André Deutsch Limited, London.

Quartet: First published Chatto & Windus, London, 1928
(under the title Postures) and Simon & Schuster, New York, 1929.

After Leaving Mr Mackenzie: First published Jonathan Cape,
London, 1930, and Alfred A. Knopf, New York, 1931.

Voyage in the Dark: First published Constable,
London, 1934, and William Morrow, New York, 1935.

Good Morning, Midnight: First published Constable,
London, 1939, and Harper & Row, New York, 1970.

Wide Sargasso Sea: First published André Deutsch,
London, 1966, and W.W. Norton, New York, 1967.

Frontispiece: Pont Neuf, © Brassaï 1949

CONTENTS

INTRODUCTION

DIANA ATHILL

The life of an artist . . . differs from the lives of other persons in that its events are becoming artistic sources even as they command his present attention. Instead of allowing each day, pushed back by the next, to lapse into imprecise memory, he shapes again the experiences which have shaped him. He is at once the captive and the liberator.

— RICHARD ELLMANN, *James Joyce*

In the years when I knew Jean Rhys — the last fifteen of her life — she often spoke about how much she wanted to "get things right": to be as true as possible in her writing to place, speech, mood, the taste and texture of experience, and to achieve this precision without — as she once said in a letter — "any stunts". "I didn't want to use any stunts and haven't. . . . "*

The "stuntlessness" of her style is its great beauty. She fell in love with words when she was a child, but she never used them rhetorically, to show them off. I have sometimes thought that the way she wrote resembled the way a cat moves (she liked cats). Her language does what it needs to do with an elegance and economy which is perfectly natural and easy . . . or rather, easy-seeming. Even a writer with an instinct for her craft as strong as hers has to work hard to break through to such an easiness. And over and over again place, speech, mood, the taste and texture of experience are "got right".

You cannot get something right unless you have a thorough knowledge of it. Jean Rhys was a conscious and dedicated artist who wrote novels, not a woman displaying, or brooding over, her own experience in the form of autobiography, but she never denied that the material for her novels came from her own life. In a

*In a letter to Evelyn Scott, February 1934, from *The Letters of Jean Rhys*, selected and edited by Francis Wyndham and Diana Melly, published by André Deutsch, London, 1984, and Viking, New York, 1984.

diary which she kept during the 'forties* she imagined herself being cross-examined:

> *It is in myself.*
> What is?
> *All. Good, evil, love, hate, life, death, beauty, ugliness.*
> And in everyone?
> *I do not know everyone. I only know myself.*
> And others?
> *I do not know them. I see them as trees walking.*
> COUNSEL FOR THE PROSECUTION: There you are! Didn't take long, did it?

Those lines say everything about Jean's use of her own experience in her novels. She thought — or said — that she *chose* to use it because it was the only thing she knew well, but she was not really choosing, she was following her nature. She could not have done anything else, being a deeply self-absorbed person who was also honest. And having accepted the necessity of following her nature, she was able to avoid the traps which can beset the path of the novelist who uses autobiographical material, because she commanded the necessary detachment. The Counsel for the Prosecution was there in her head.

In a novel the smallest touch of autobiographical special pleading, whether it takes the form of self-pity or exhibitionism, will destroy the reader's confidence. To avoid such touches the writer must be able to stand back from the experience far enough to see the whole of it and must concentrate with a self-purging intensity on the process of reproducing it in words. Jean Rhys could stand back, and her concentration on the process was as intense as that of a tight-rope walker. As a result her novels do not say "This is what happened to me", but "This is how things happen".

Her career fell into two parts. She published her first book in 1927: a collection of stories called *The Left Bank*. This was followed by the novels *Quartet* (1928 in London, under the title *Postures*; 1929 in New York), *After Leaving Mr Mackenzie* (1930 in London; 1931 in New York), *Voyage in the Dark* (1934 in London; 1935 in New York), and *Good Morning, Midnight* (1939 in London). Then Jean Rhys "disappeared", and was almost forgotten. The second part of her career began in 1966 with the publication in London of *Wide Sargasso Sea†*. The success of this novel led to the republication of her earlier books,

*Quoted in *Smile Please*, her autobiographical book, André Deutsch, London, 1979, and Harper & Row, Publishers, Inc., New York, 1979.
†André Deutsch, London, 1966, and W.W. Norton & Company, New York, 1967.

and was followed by the collection of stories *Sleep it off, lady** and the autobiographical *Smile Please*. Between 1966 and her death in 1979 she received — without undue excitement — plenty of the recognition which had come her way only sparsely between the wars.

In this collection of the novels, *Voyage in the Dark* has been put first, not third, for two reasons. It was written in a first version long before she wrote anything else; and its central figure, Anna Morgan, is very young, having been created out of experiences which her author underwent within a few years of coming to school in England in 1907. Jean came from the West Indies, where she was born in 1890. Anna shared Jean's childhood in Dominica, her life as a chorus girl in a touring company, her first love affair, and the affair's end in an abortion, and in a rejection which was humiliating as well as heartbreaking because the helpless girl could see no alternative to accepting the allowance which her lover offered as conscience-money.

In its first version this story was rawly autobiographical. Jean describes in *Smile Please* how as soon as she finished writing it she stuffed it into a suitcase and didn't touch it again for years: we cannot be sure how many years, because she was always vague about dates, but it was probably about ten. Then she found herself stranded in Paris in a desperate plight, her first husband in prison, no money. . . . She thought she might raise some cash by translating stories written in French by her husband, and selling them to an English newspaper. An acquaintance — a Mrs Adam — told her the stories would not sell and asked whether she herself had ever written anything, and Jean remembered the script in the suitcase.

Mrs Adam liked the script. She offered to edit it for publication, and introduced Jean to the novelist Ford Madox Ford, who was in Paris at the time, editing *Transatlantic Review*. Grateful though Jean was, she disliked the editing and put the script away again; and almost ten more years would pass before she herself began to work on it. Which was lucky for Anna Morgan, since she finally came to wonderfully vivid life as the creation of a conscious and experienced artist, instead of existing as part of a therapeutic outpouring by an unhappy girl.

But, although it makes sense to talk first about *Voyage in the Dark* when considering the use Jean Rhys made of her own experience in her work, doing so is to jump ahead of events as they unfolded for Jean in the 'twenties. It was stories that she began to write with the encouragement of Ford Madox Ford, who published a few of them in his review and wrote an introduction to them when they appeared as a

*André Deutsch, London, 1976, and Harper & Row, Publishers, Inc., New York, 1976.

book. He also gave her something less respectable than encouragement, but finally no less valuable: the subject of her first novel, *Quartet*. Ford rapidly absorbed Jean into a ménage à trois with himself and his wife-like mistress, Stella Bowen (Jean was lonely and frightened, and Ford — she used to say — was "a very comforting man"). Marya Zelli, in *Quartet*, who also had a husband in prison, was absorbed in a ménage à trois with the art-dealer H.J. Heidler and his wife, Lois.

Marya's story is less well realized than Anna's, partly, no doubt, because it was Jean's first novel, and partly because Jean was much nearer in time to the set of experiences on which she built it than she was to be to the experiences behind *Voyage in the Dark*. *Quartet* is the only one of her books in which her detachment falters. There are moments — not many, but some — when the reader feels puzzled by Marya's reactions; and I believe that Jean once gave me a clue to the reason for this.

She told me that while the sadness in *Quartet* is "love sadness" (those were her words), the sadness in her life at that time was more that of anxiety, loneliness, and "my husband being in prison and all that". Ford, she said, had never been in love with her, nor she with him. "But you had an affair?" — "Well . . . yes. But not nearly so much of one". It was enough of one to agitate Stella Bowen, as she revealed in her autobiography,* but it could still have resulted from impulses a good deal more tangled than straight falling in love. Anyone who reads Jean's letters will suspect that her invariable and almost pathological inertia in the face of trouble, and the recklessness which emerged when she tried to overcome inertia with drink, are likely to have played as large a part in the story as attraction, or as greed or deviousness on the part of Ford and Stella. If this were so, it would not be strange if Jean had decided to try for something more "novel-like" and less hard on herself than getting her own behaviour exactly right, and had attempted to make Marya's behaviour result from the comparatively simple fact that she had fallen in love with Heidler. The feeling of puzzlement creeps in through a crack between what is supposed to be Marya's infatuation and the events which surround it. Jean could make Marya more in love with H.J. than she herself had been with Ford, but she could not prevent herself from getting a great deal of the surrounding picture true to her own more complicated experience.

None of this prevents the novel from being enjoyable. Its "magic carpet" powers are great, transporting the reader to Paris in the 'twenties in the most satisfying way, and it abounds in subtle and

Drawn from Life, Collins, London, 1940.

ironic observation; and the slightly disreputable extra interest which comes from knowing that these strange goings-on really happened is undeniable. But in her next book, *After Leaving Mr Mackenzie*, Jean Rhys came nearer the achievement she aimed for.

Marya Zelli is about ten years older than Anna Morgan. Julia Martin, in *After Leaving Mr Mackenzie*, is ten years older again . . . and Mr Mackenzie is not Ford, as people sometimes assume from the order of the novels' publication. (It was an assumption that greatly annoyed Jean: "The *fools!*" I heard her exclaim once, on coming across it in some article.) This is a novel about being an outsider rather than about a relationship. Mr Mackenzie embodies not a particular man, but one half of a situation: that in which a woman depends for money on men who desire her without love — or who feel guilty at desiring her no longer. Jean had experienced this before she knew Ford, and was out of it by the time she wrote *Mackenzie*. By that time Leslie Tilden Smith had come into her life, although they were not married until 1932, when her divorce from her first husband came through; and — perhaps even more important — she had found herself as a writer. She was no more Julia than Ford was Mackenzie.

But an outsider Jean had been, and at heart would always remain, and the unsparing gaze she turns on Julia (this is the most severe of her novels) sees everything about the woman and her condition. When Julia visits her dying mother and her sister Norah — the good sister, the one who has stayed at home and sacrificed her youth to caring for their mother — she confronts the life into which she cannot or will not fit more directly than any of the other "Jean Rhys women". The sisters regard each other with hostile eyes — their hostility complicated by threads of envy and even of pity, though they are both too exhausted by their own troubles to spare much energy for that. We see all that happens from Julia's point of view, we feel it with her nerves; yet we are clearly shown why this lonely, unhappy woman alarms people, and that Norah's life has been as cruelly "smashed" by the pressures of conformity as Julia's has been by the buffeting she has received for breaking out.

Jean Rhys holds the scales steady between the two women — until finally she tips them, very slightly, *against* Julia. She does it in an uncharacteristically symbolic passage. Julia remembers catching butterflies when she was a child: how desperately she longed for their beauty, and how it was unfair of the grown-ups to scold her for damaging them when all she had intended was to keep them safe and happy in her jar. Julia remembers no more than her longing and her sense of injustice, but the reader is free to see that the butterflies died because the child's desire was blindly selfish. This passage of symbolism seems to me a flaw; but it does suggest that the reader who judges Julia severely is not doing so against the will of Jean Rhys. The cold gaze of the Counsel for the Prosecution can be felt throughout *After Leaving Mr Mackenzie*.

Sasha Jansen, in *Good Morning, Midnight*, is brought to confrontation not with society, but with her inner self. It is the finest of these first four extraordinary novels. Jean Rhys's detachment from Sasha is so complete that she can temper severity with compassion without the least danger of the compassion's verging on self-pity. The woman in the novel feels persecuted. The woman writing simply shows what such an experience is like.

Armed with a precarious irony, Sasha, revisiting Paris, cautiously calls up her past. As she does so we learn the mixture of vulnerability and recklessness which, she tells us, finally reduced her to cowering in a London bedsitter, trying to drink herself to death. A friend has come to her rescue, lent her money, and packed her off on this holiday. At the Dôme she is picked up by René, the young man she calls "the gigolo".

No meeting could be less romantic or more poignant. They recognize each other: both of them outsiders, both wounded, both defiant of the respectable world, both naughty . . . it is the naughty child that they seem to be recognizing in each other as they swap dirty jokes over their drinks and walk hand in hand. She doesn't mean to like him — indeed she means to take advantage of the fact that he doesn't frighten her and have the fun, for once, of hurting instead of being hurt. But he is still young and optimistic. He sees at once that they could curl up in bed together for at least one night in trust and liking; that, for a moment, they could *rest* together. She begins to hover on the edge of responding. She begins to yearn to trust him in return. But finally she cannot do it. By the time she feels able to let him see her although her face has been made ugly by weeping, and to say "Now I am simple and not afraid; now I am myself", it is too late. He has gone because she, cruelly, has driven him away. And Sasha understands what a tragic and shameful thing it is to lose simplicity and courage — to become set in the role of victim, of the woman hopelessly "smashed" by "them", instead of being what, at that moment, she knows herself to be: just "another poor devil of a human being".

Jean Rhys used to say that she was proud of the end of *Good Morning, Midnight*, because finding it had been such a struggle: she had been forced to "make it up" because a novel must have a shape and life does not provide shapes. She may once have come across a young man like René (for what a guess is worth, I think that she did), but no man in a white dressing-gown ever played the role she imagined for

Sasha's neighbour in the hotel until she conjured him up. Nevertheless it was in life that she found her novel's end — Sasha's recognition of herself in others and of others in herself: in life at a deeper level than that of any particular incident, down in the "all" which Jean Rhys knew she held within her.

After *Good Morning, Midnight* came Jean Rhys's "disappearance", which used to be seen as mysterious. Now the facts are known, and her *Letters* have revealed what it was like to live through them. Her third husband had proved almost as impractical as she was, they were desperately poor, and he — foolish rather than dishonest — allowed an acquaintance to persuade him that he could save them by a piece of financial misconduct. He was caught, and sent to prison. The long build-up to this disaster, and the disaster itself, came near to destroying Jean, and life was not much easier after her husband had served his sentence and they had crept into the obscurity of meagre lodgings, first in Cornwall, then in Devonshire. There was still almost no money, her husband's health gave way, and the pressure she was under caused Jean to be (as she said in a letter to an old friend) almost always "two days drunk, one day hungover".

For nearly thirty years the literary world saw nothing of her, and the misery of those years was profound. But all the time, inch by slow and painful inch, her next book was growing within her.

Charlotte Brontë's *Jane Eyre* had always disturbed Jean. She may not be the only reader of that novel to dislike its heroine, but is probably the only one to identify with Mr Rochester's mad wife from the West Indies. Ever since Jean had come to school in England she had felt that the English misunderstood and despised West Indians, and here was a West Indian woman so totally misunderstood and despised that she was presented as a monster. Impoverished English gentlemen had, in fact, married West Indian heiresses from time to time during the eighteenth and nineteenth centuries, and Jean thought it likely that Charlotte Brontë had known of one such marriage and had based her novel on it. What had really happened to that unhappy bride onto whom Brontë had projected such a cruel — such (in Jean's eyes) a typically English — version of the story?

From that question grew *Wide Sargasso Sea*, the novel created over so many years, against such heavy odds, with which she made her come-back in 1966.

It works faultlessly as a reinterpretation of events imagined by another writer, and also as an evocation of life among the white planters of the West Indies soon after the emancipation of the slaves on whom their fortunes had depended; but the reason why it is unforgettable is that it has the intensity of a story which has been lived.

On the surface it seems the least autobiographical of Jean Rhys's novels, because the only obviously personal experience in it is that of the Caribbean, in which it is steeped; but it appears to me to be as closely linked to her life as her other work, though on a different level. By approaching experience obliquely, through the medium of *Jane Eyre*, she distanced herself from it more successfully than ever before, and could therefore look into it even more clearly. Nowhere else did she write with more poignancy about what it is like to be rejected, and nowhere else did she go so deeply into something which filled her with a special terror because (or so I believe) there had been times when she felt it happening to herself: what it is like to be driven beyond your psychic strength, and go mad. At a hidden level the story of Antoinette and her mother is that of Jean and her own mother, and the story of Antoinette and Mr Rochester is that of Jean and England; and it is from this hidden level that its vibrancy springs.

To wring out of herself things so painful, in circumstances so cruel, and finally to hand us a novel so lovely and haunting, which seems to alight on the page as easily as a bird on a branch: if she had done nothing else but this, Jean Rhys would still be one of the most remarkable writers of the century.

Voyage in the Dark

Overleaf: The wall of La Santé Prison,
Boulevard Arago, © Brassaï 1932

PART ONE

1

It was as if a curtain had fallen, hiding everything I had ever known. It was almost like being born again. The colours were different, the smells different, the feeling things gave you right down inside yourself was different. Not just the difference between heat, cold; light, darkness; purple, grey. But a difference in the way I was frightened and the way I was happy. I didn't like England at first. I couldn't get used to the cold. Sometimes I would shut my eyes and pretend that the heat of the fire, or the bed-clothes drawn up round me, was sun-heat; or I would pretend I was standing outside the house at home, looking down Market Street to the Bay. When there was a breeze the sea was millions of spangles; and on still days it was purple as Tyre and Sidon. Market Street smelt of the wind, but the narrow street smelt of niggers and wood-smoke and salt fishcakes fried in lard. (When the black women sell fishcakes on the savannah they carry them in trays on their heads. They call out, 'Salt fishcakes, all sweet an' charmin', all sweet an' charmin'.') It was funny, but that was what I thought about more than anything else — the smell of the streets and the smells of frangipani and lime juice and cinnamon and cloves, and sweets made of ginger and syrup, and incense after funerals or Corpus Christi processions, and the patients standing outside the surgery next door, and the smell of the sea-breeze and the different smell of the land-breeze.

Sometimes it was as if I were back there and as if England were a dream. At other times England was the real thing and out there was the dream, but I could never fit them together.

After a while I got used to England and I liked it all right; I got used to everything except the cold and that the towns we went to always looked so exactly alike. You were perpetually moving to another place which was perpetually the same. There was always a little grey street leading to the stage-door of the theatre and another little grey street where your lodgings were, and rows of little houses with chimneys like the funnels of dummy steamers and smoke the same colour as the sky; and a grey stone promenade running hard, naked and straight by the side of the grey-brown or grey-green sea; or a Corporation Street or High Street or Duke Street or Lord Street where you walked about and looked at the shops.

Southsea, this place was.

We had good rooms. The landlady had said, 'No, I don't let to professionals.' But she didn't bang the door in our faces, and after Maudie had talked for a while, making her voice sound as ladylike as possible, she had said, 'Well, I might make an exception for this time.' Then the second day we were there she made a row because we both got up late and Maudie came downstairs in her nightgown and a torn kimono.

'Showing yourself at my sitting-room window 'alf naked like that,' the landlady said. 'And at three o'clock in the afternoon too. Getting my house a bad name.'

'It's all right, Ma,' Maudie said. 'I'm going up to get dressed in a minute. I had a shocking headache this morning.'

'Well, I won't 'ave it,' the landlady said. 'When you come downstairs for your dinner you've got to be decent. Not in your nightclothes.'

She slammed the door.

'I ask you,' Maudie said, 'I ask you. That old goat's starting to get on my nerves. I'll tell her off if she says another word to me.'

'Don't take any notice of her,' I said.

I was lying on the sofa, reading *Nana*. It was a paper-covered book with a coloured picture of a stout, dark woman brandishing a wine-glass. She was sitting on the knee of a bald-headed man in evening dress. The print was very small, and the endless procession of words gave me a curious feeling — sad, excited and frightened. It wasn't what 1 was reading, it was the look of the dark, blurred words going on endlessly that gave me that feeling.

There was a glass door behind the sofa. You could see into a small, unfurnished room, and then another glass door led into the walled-in garden. The tree by the back wall was lopped so that it looked like a man with stumps instead of arms and legs. The washing hung limp, without moving, in the grey-yellow light.

'I'll get dressed,' Maudie said, 'and then we'd better go out and get some air. We'll go to the theatre and see if there are any letters. That's a dirty book, isn't it?'

'Bits of it are all right,' I said.

Maudie said, 'I know; it's about a tart. I think it's disgusting. I

4

bet you a man writing a book about a tart tells a lot of lies one way and another. Besides, all books are like that — just somebody stuffing you up.'

Maudie was tall and thin, and her nose made a straight line with her forehead. She had pale yellow hair and a very white, smooth skin. When she smiled a tooth was missing on one side. She was twenty-eight years old and all sorts of things had happened to her. She used to tell me about them when we came back from the theatre at night. 'You've only got to learn how to swank a bit, then you're all right,' she would say. Lying in bed with her, her hair in two long yellow plaits on either side of her long white face.

'Swank's the word,' she would say.

There were no letters for us at the theatre.

Maudie said she knew a shop where I could get a pair of stockings I wanted. 'The street just before you get on to the front,' she said.

Somebody was playing the piano in one of the houses we passed — a tinkling sound like water running. I began to walk very slowly because I wanted to listen. But it got farther and farther away and then I couldn't hear it any more. 'Gone for ever,' I thought. There was a tight feeling in my throat as if I wanted to cry.

'There's one thing about you,' Maudie said. 'You always look ladylike.'

'Oh God,' I said, 'who wants to look ladylike?'

We walked on.

'Don't look round,' Maudie said. 'Two men are following us. I think they're trying to get off with us.'

The two men went past and walked ahead very slowly. One of them had his hands in his pockets; I liked the way he walked. It was the other one, the taller one, who looked back and smiled.

Maudie giggled.

'Good afternoon,' he said. 'Are you going for a walk? Nice day, isn't it? Very warm for October.'

'Yes, we're taking the air,' Maudie said. 'Not all of it, of course.'

Everybody laughed. We paired off. Maudie went on ahead with the tall man. The other looked at me sideways once or twice — very quickly up and down, in that way they have — and then asked where we were going.

'I was going to this shop to buy a pair of stockings,' I said.

They all came into the shop with me. I said I wanted two pairs —lisle thread with clocks up the sides — and took a long time choosing them. The man I had been walking with offered to pay for them and I let him.

When we got outside Maudie said, 'Gone quite chilly, hasn't it? Why don't you two come back to our rooms and have some tea? We live quite near by.'

The tall man seemed rather anxious to get away, but the other one said they would like to; and they bought two bottles of port and some cakes on the way back.

We had no latch-key. I thought the landlady would be sure to be rude when she let us in. However, when she opened the door she only glared, without speaking.

The fire was laid in the sitting-room. Maudie put a match to it and lit the gas. On the mantelpiece two bronze horses pawed the air with their front legs on either side of a big, dark clock. Blue plates hung round the walls at regular intervals.

'Make yourselves at home, you blokes,' Maudie said. 'And allow me to introduce Miss Anna Morgan and Miss Maudie Beardon, now appearing in *The Blue Waltz*. What about opening the port? I'll get you a corkscrew, Mr What's-your-name. What is your name, by the way?'

The tall man didn't answer. He stared over her shoulder, his eyes round and opaque. The other one coughed.

Maudie said in cockney, 'I was speaking to you, 'Orace. You 'eard. You ain't got clorf ears. I asked what your name was.'

'Jones,' the tall man said. 'Jones is my name.'

'Go on,' Maudie said.

He looked annoyed.

'That's rather funny,' the other one said, starting to laugh.

'What's funny?' I said.

'You see, Jones is his name.'

'Oh, is it?' I said.

He stopped laughing. 'And my name's Jeffries.'

'Is it really?' I said. 'Jeffries, is it?'

'Jones and Jeffries,' Maudie said. 'That's not hard to remember.'

I hated them both. You pick up people and then they are rude to you. This business of picking up people and then they always imagine they can be rude to you.

But when I had had a glass of port I began to laugh too and after that I couldn't stop. I watched myself in the glass over the mantelpiece, laughing.

'How old are you?' Mr Jeffries said.

'I'm eighteen. Did you think I was older?'

'No,' he said. 'On the contrary.'

Mr Jones said, 'He knew you'd be either eighteen or twenty-two. You girls only have two ages. You're eighteen and so of course your friend's twenty-two. Of course.'

'You're one of those clever people, aren't you?' Maudie said, sticking her chin out. She always did that when she was vexed. 'You know everything.'

'Well, I am eighteen,' I said. 'I can show you my birth certificate if you like.'

'No, my dear child, no. That would be excessive,' Mr Jones said.

He brought the bottle of port over and filled my glass again. When he touched my hand he pretended to shiver. He said, 'Oh God, cold as ice. Cold and rather clammy.'

'She's always cold,' Maudie said. 'She can't help it. She was born in a hot place. She was born in the West Indies or somewhere, weren't you, kid? The girls call her the Hottentot. Isn't it a shame?'

'Why the Hottentot?' Mr Jeffries said. 'I hope you call them something worse back.'

He spoke very quickly, but with each word separated from the other. He didn't look at my breasts or my legs, as they usually do. Not that I saw. He looked straight at me and listened to everything I said with a polite and attentive expression, and then he looked away and smiled as if he had sized me up.

He asked how long I had been in England, and I told him, 'Two years,' and then we talked about the tour. The company was going on to Brighton, then Eastbourne, and then we finished in London.

'London?' Mr Jones said, lifting his eyebrows.

'Well, Holloway. Holloway's London, isn't it?'

'Of course it is,' Mr Jeffries said.

'That's enough about the show,' Maudie said. She still looked vexed. 'Tell us about yourselves for a change. Tell us how old you are and what you do for a living. Just for a change.'

Mr Jeffries said, 'I work in the City. I work very hard.'

'You mean somebody else works hard for you,' Maudie said. 'And what does Daniel-in-the-lions'-den do? But it's no use asking him. He won't tell us. Cheer up, Daniel, d'you know the one about the snake-charmer?'

'No, I don't think I know that one,' Mr Jones said stiffly.

Maudie told the one about the snake-charmer. They didn't laugh much, and then Mr Jones coughed and said they had to go.

'I wish we could have seen your show tonight,' Mr Jeffries said, 'but I'm afraid it's not possible. We must meet again when you come up to London; yes, certainly we must meet again.'

'Perhaps you would dine with me one evening, Miss Morgan,' he said. 'Will you give me an address that'll find you, so that we can fix it up?'

I said, 'We'll be at Holloway in a fortnight, but this is my permanent address.' I wrote down:

Miss Anna Morgan,
c/o Mrs Hester Morgan,
118, Fellside Road,
Ilkley,
Yorks.

'Is that your mother?'

'No, Hester's my stepmother.'

'We must fix it up,' he said. 'I shall look forward to it.'

We went out into the street to say good-bye to them. I was thinking it was funny I could giggle like that because in my heart I was always sad, with the same sort of hurt that the cold gave me in my chest.

We went back into the sitting-room. We heard the landlady coming along the passage outside.

'She's going to make another row,' Maudie said.

We listened. But she passed the door without coming in.

Maudie said, 'What I'd like to know is this: why they think they've got the right to insult you for nothing at all? That's what I'd like to know.'

I got very close to the fire. I was thinking, 'It's October. Winter's coming.'

'You got off with your bloke,' Maudie said. 'Mine was a bit of no good. Did you hear what he said about my being twenty-two and sort of sneering?'

'I didn't like either of them,' I said.

'You gave your address pretty quick, though,' Maudie said. 'And quite right too. You go out with him if he asks you. Those men have money; you can tell that in a minute, can't you? Anybody can. Men who have money and men who haven't are perfectly different.

'I've never seen anybody shiver like you do,' she said. 'It's awful. Do you do it on purpose or what? Get on the sofa and I'll put my big coat over you if you like.'

The coat had a warm animal smell and a cheap scent smell.

'Viv gave me that coat,' Maudie said. 'He's like that. He doesn't give much but what he gives is good stuff, not shoddy.'

'Like a Jew,' I said. 'Is he a Jew?'

'Of course he isn't. I told you.'

She went on talking about the man who gave her the coat. His name was Vivian Roberts and she had been in love with him for a long time. She still saw him when she was up in London between tours, but only very occasionally. She said she was sure he was breaking it off, but doing it gradually because he was cautious and he did everything gradually.

She went on talking about him. I didn't listen.

Thinking how cold the street would be outside and the dressing-room cold too, and that my place was by the door in the draught. It always was. A damned shame. And about Laurie Gaynor, who was dressing next me that week. The virgin, she calls me, or sometimes the silly cow. ('Can't you manage to keep the door shut, Virgin, you silly cow?') But I like her better than any of the others. She's a fine girl. She's the only one I really like. And the cold nights; and the way my collar-bones stick out in my first-act dress. There's something you can buy that makes your neck fat. Venus Carnis. 'No fascination without curves. Ladies, realize your charms.' But it costs three guineas and where can I get three guineas? And the cold nights, the damned cold nights.

Lying between 15° 10' and 15° 40' N. and 61° 14' and 61° 30' W. 'A goodly island and something highland, but all overgrown with woods,' that book said. And all crumpled into hills and mountains as you would crumple a piece of paper in your hand — rounded green hills and sharply-cut mountains.

A curtain fell and then I was here.

. . . This is England Hester said and I watched it through the train-window divided into squares like pocket-handkerchiefs; a small tidy look it had everywhere fenced off from everywhere else — what are those things — those are haystacks — oh are those haystacks — I had read about England ever since I could read —smaller meaner everything is never mind — this is London — hundreds thousands of white people white people rushing along and the dark houses all alike frowning down one after the other all alike all stuck together — the streets like smooth shut-in ravines and the dark houses frowning down — oh I'm not going to like this place I'm not going to like this place I'm not going to like this place — you'll get used to it Hester kept saying I expect you feel like a fish out of water but you'll soon get used to it — now don't look like Dying Dick and Solemn Davy as your poor father used to say you'll get used to it . . .

Maudie said, 'Let's finish the port.' She poured out two glasses and we drank slowly. She watched herself in the mirror.

'I'm getting lines under my eyes, aren't I?'

I said, 'I've got a cousin out home, quite a kid. And she's never seen snow and she's awfully curious about it. She keeps writing and asking me to tell her what it's like. I wanted to see snow, too. That was one of the things I was longing to see.'

'Well,' Maudie said, 'you've seen it now, haven't you? How much do you suppose our bill's going to be this week?'

'About fifteen bob, I suppose.'

We reckoned up.

I had saved six pounds and Hester had promised to send me five pounds for Christmas, or earlier if I wanted it. So I had decided to find a cheap room somewhere instead of going to the chorus-girls' hostel in Maple Street. A ghastly place, that was.

'Only three more weeks of this damned tour, T.G.,' Maudie said. 'It's no life, not in winter it isn't.'

When we were coming home from the theatre that night it began to rain and in Brighton it rained all the time. We got to Holloway and it was winter and the dark streets round the theatre made me think of murders.

I gave Maudie the letter to read and she said, 'I told you so. I told you he had money. That's an awfully swanky club. The four swankiest clubs in London are . . .'

All the girls started arguing about which was the swankiest club in London.

I wrote and said I couldn't dine with him on Monday, because I had a previous engagement. ('Always say you have a previous engagement.') But I said I could on Wednesday, the 17th of November, and I gave him the address of the room I had taken in Judd Street.

Laurie Gaynor said, 'Tell him to borrow the club tin-opener. Say "P.S. Don't forget the tin-opener".'

'Oh, leave her alone,' Maudie said.

'That's all right,' Laurie said. 'I'm not troubling her. I'm teaching her etiquette.'

'She knows I'm a good old cow,' Laurie said. 'A lot better than most of the other old cows. Aren't I, what's-your-name — Anna?'

2

I looked down at my hands and the nails shone as bright as brass. At least, the left hand did — the right wasn't so good.

'Do you always wear black?' he said. 'I remember you were wearing a black dress when I saw you before.'

'Wait a minute,' he said. 'Don't drink that.'

The waiter knocked a long, elaborate knock and came in to take away the soup.

'This wine is corked,' Mr Jeffries said.

'Corked, sir?' the waiter said in a soft, incredulous and horror-stricken voice. He had a hooked nose and a pale, flat face.

'Yes, corked. Smell that.'

The waiter sniffed. Then Mr Jeffries sniffed. Their noses were exactly alike, their faces very solemn. The Brothers Slick and Slack, the Brothers Pushmeofftheearth. I thought, 'Now then, you mustn't laugh. He'll know you're laughing at him. You can't laugh.'

There was a red-shaded lamp on the table, and heavy pink silk curtains over the windows. There was a hard, straight-backed sofa, and two chairs with curved legs against the wall — all upholstered in red. The Hoffner Hotel and Restaurant, the place was called. The Hoffner Hotel and Restaurant, Hanover Square.

The waiter finished apologizing and went out. Then he came in again with the fish and another bottle of wine and filled up our glasses. I drank mine quickly because all day I had been feeling as if I had caught a cold. I had a pain in my throat.

'How's your friend — Maisie?'

'Maudie.'

'Yes, Maudie. How's Maudie?'

'Oh, she's all right,' I said. 'She's very well.'

'What's become of her? Is she still with you?'

'No,' I said. 'Between tours she stays with her mother in Kilburn.'

He said, 'She stays with her mother in Kilburn, does she?' and looked at me as if he were trying to size me up. 'What do you do between tours as a rule? Do you stay with the lady whose address you gave me?'

'My stepmother?' I said. 'Hester? No, I don't see much of her. She's not often in London.'

'Do you always stay at those rooms in Judd Street?'

'Room,' I said, 'room. There's only one. No. I've never been there before and I don't like it much. But it's better than the Cats' Home, anyway. That's where I was last summer — the chorus-girls' hostel in Maple Street. It got on my nerves because they make you come down to prayers every morning before breakfast.'

I drank some more wine and stared at the table-cloth, seeing the matron praying with uplifted face and shut eyes. And her little, short nose and her long, moving lips. Just like a rabbit, she was, like a blind rabbit. There was something horrible about that sort of praying. I thought, 'I believe there's something horrible about any sort of praying.'

I saw her and I saw the shadows of the carnations that were on the table and we talked about touring and he asked me how much I was getting. I told him, 'Thirty-five bob a week, and of course extra for extra matinées.'

'Good God,' he said. 'You surely can't manage on that, can you?'

'I'm getting along all right,' I thought. But the waiter coming in and out, bringing us things to eat, bothered me.

We had another bottle of wine and I felt it warm and happy in my stomach. I heard my voice going on and on, answering his questions, and all the time I was talking he kept looking at me in a funny sort of way, as if he didn't believe what I was saying.

'So you don't see much of your stepmother? Doesn't she approve of your gadding about on tour? Does she think you've disgraced the family or something?'

I looked at him, and he was smiling as if he were laughing at me. I stopped talking. I thought, 'Oh God, he's the sneering sort. I wish I hadn't come.'

But when the waiter brought in coffee and liqueurs and shut the door as if he wasn't coming back and we went over to the fire, I felt all right again. I liked the room and the red carnations on the table and the way he talked and his clothes — especially his clothes. It was a pity about my clothes, but anyway they were black. 'She wore black. Men delighted in that sable colour, or lack of colour.' A man called 'Coronet' wrote that, or was it a man called 'A Peer'?

He said, 'You've got the loveliest teeth. You're sweet. You

looked awfully pathetic when you were choosing those horrible stockings so anxiously.' And then he started kissing me and all the time he was kissing me I was thinking about the man at that supper-party at the Greyhound, Croydon, when he told me, 'You don't know how to kiss. I'll show you how to kiss. This is what you do.'

I felt giddy. I twisted my head away and got up.

There was a door behind the sofa, but I hadn't noticed it before because a curtain hung over it. I turned the handle. 'Oh,' I said, 'it's a bedroom.' My voice went high.

'So it is,' he said. He laughed. I laughed too, because I felt that that was what I ought to do. *You can now and you can see what it's like, and why not?*

My arms hung straight down by my sides awkwardly. He kissed me again, and his mouth was hard, and I remembered him smelling the glass of wine and I couldn't think of anything but that, and I hated him.

'Look here, let me go,' I said. He said something I didn't hear. 'Do you think I was born yesterday, or what?' I said, talking very loud. I pushed him away as hard as I could. I could feel the sharp points of his collar against my hand. I kept saying, 'Damn you, let me go, damn you. Or I'll make a hell of a row.' But as soon as he let me go I stopped hating him.

'I'm very sorry,' he said. 'That was extremely stupid of me.' Looking at me with his eyes narrow and close together, as if he hated me, as if I wasn't there; and then he turned away and looked at himself in the glass.

There were the red carnations on the table and the fire leaping up. I thought, 'If it could go back and be just as it was before it happened and then happen differently.'

I took up my coat and hat and went into the bedroom. I pushed the door shut after me.

There was a fire but the room was cold. I walked up to the looking-glass and put the lights on over it and stared at myself. It was as if I were looking at somebody else. I stared at myself for a long time, listening for the door to open. But I didn't hear a sound from the next room. There wasn't a sound from anywhere. When I listened I could only hear a noise like when you hold a shell up to your ear, like something rushing past you.

In this room too the lights were shaded in red; and it had a secret feeling — quiet, like a place where you crouch down when you are playing hide-and-seek.

I sat down on the bed and listened, then I lay down. The bed was soft; the pillow was as cold as ice. I felt as if I had gone out of myself, as if I were in a dream.

Soon he'll come in again and kiss me, but differently. He'll be different and so I'll be different. It'll be different. I thought, 'It'll be different, different. It must be different.'

I lay there for a long while, listening. The fire was like a painted fire; no warmth came from it. When I put my hand against my face it was very cold and my face was hot. I began to shiver. I got up and went back into the next room.

'Hullo,' he said, 'I thought you'd gone to sleep.'

He smiled at me, as cool as a cucumber. 'Cheer up,' he said. 'Don't look so sad. What's the matter? Have another kümmel.'

'No, thank you,' I said. 'I don't want anything.' My chest hurt.

We stood there looking at each other. He said, 'Come on, let's go, for God's sake,' and held my coat up for me. I got into it and put my hat on.

We went down the stairs.

I was thinking, 'The girls would shriek with laughter if I were to tell them this. Simply shriek.'

We went out into the street and walked to the corner and he stopped a taxi. 'Let's see — Judd Street, isn't it?'

I got into the taxi. He gave the driver some money.

'Well, good night.'

'Good night,' I said.

It was early when I got back, not twelve o'clock. I had a little room on the second floor. Ten-and-six a week I paid for it.

I undressed and got into bed, but I couldn't get warm. The room had a cold, close smell. It was like being in a small, dark box.

Somebody went past in the street, singing. Bawling:

> *Bread, bread, bread,*
> *Standard bread,*
> *A little bit er Standard bread,*
> *Pom, pom,*

over and over again.

I thought, 'What a song! Mad as a hatter that song is. It's the tune that's so awful; it's like blows.' But the words went over and over again in my head and I began to breathe in time to them.

When I thought about my clothes I was too sad to cry.

About clothes, it's awful. Everything makes you want pretty clothes like hell. People laugh at girls who are badly dressed. Jaw, jaw, jaw . . . 'Beautifully dressed woman . . .' As if it isn't enough that you want to be beautiful, that you want to have pretty clothes, that you want it like hell. As if that isn't enough. But no, it's jaw, jaw and sneer all the time. And the shop-windows sneering and smiling in your face. And then you look at the skirt of your costume, all crumpled at the back. And your hideous underclothes. You look at your hideous underclothes and you think, 'All right, I'll do anything for good clothes. Anything — anything for clothes.'

'But it isn't always going to be like this, is it?' I thought. 'It would be too awful if it were always going to be like this. It isn't possible. Something must happen to make it different.' And then I thought, 'Yes, that's all right. I'm poor and my clothes are cheap and perhaps it will always be like this. And that's all right too.' It was the first time in my life I'd thought that.

The ones without any money, the ones with beastly lives. Perhaps I'm going to be one of the ones with beastly lives. They swarm like woodlice when you push a stick into a woodlice-nest at home. And their faces are the colour of woodlice.

I felt ill when I woke up. I had pains all over me. I lay there and after a while I heard the landlady coming up the stairs. She was thin and younger than most landladies. She had black hair and little red eyes. I kept my head turned away so as not to see her.

'It's gone ten,' she said. 'I'm a bit late this morning with your breakfast but my clock stopped. This came for you; a messenger-boy brought it.'

There was a letter on the breakfast-tray, and a big bunch of violets. I took them up; they smelt like rain.

The landlady was watching me with her little red eyes. I said, 'Can I have my hot water?' and she went out.

I opened the letter and there were five five-pound notes inside.

'My dear Anna, I wish I could tell you how sweet you are. I'm worried about you. Will you buy yourself some stockings with this? And don't look anxious when you are buying them, please. Always yours, Walter Jeffries.'

When I heard the landlady coming back I put the money under my pillow. It crackled. She put the can of hot water down outside and went away.

The bunch of violets was too big for the tooth-glass. I put it in the water-jug.

I took the money from under my pillow and put it into my handbag. I was accustomed to it already. It was as if I had always had it. Money ought to be everybody's. It ought to be like water. You can tell that because you get accustomed to it so quickly.

All the time I was dressing I was thinking what clothes I would buy. I didn't think of anything else at all, and I forgot about feeling ill.

Outside it smelt of melted snow.

The landlady was washing the steps. She plunged her hands into a pail of filthy water, wrung out the cloth and started to rub again. There she was on her knees.

'Will you lay a fire in my room, please?' I said. My voice sounded round and full instead of small and thin. 'That's because of the money,' I thought.

'You'll have to wait,' she said. 'I've got something else to do besides running up and down stairs laying fires.'

'I shan't be in again till this afternoon,' I said.

I looked back and she was kneeling upright staring after me. I thought, 'All right — stare.'

A dress and a hat and shoes and underclothes.

I got a taxi and told the driver to go to Cohen's in Shaftesbury Avenue.

There were two Miss Cohens and they really were sisters because their noses were the same and their eyes — opaque and shining — and their insolence that was only a mask. I knew the shop; I had been there with Laurie during rehearsals.

It was warm and it smelt of fur. There were two long mirrors and a sliding cupboard with the doors pushed back so that you could see the rows of dresses on hangers. The dresses, all colours, hanging there, waiting. The hats, except one or two on stands, were in a smaller room at the back.

The two Miss Cohens stared — one small and round, the other thin with a yellow face.

I said, 'Can I try on the dark blue dress and coat in the window, please?' And the thin one advanced smiling. Her red lips smiled and her heavy lids drooped over her small, shiny eyes.

This is a beginning. Out of this warm room that smells of fur I'll go to all the lovely places I've ever dreamt of. This is the beginning.

The fat Miss Cohen went into the back room. I held my arms up and the thin one put on the dress as if I were a doll. The skirt was long and tight so that when I moved in it I saw the shape of my thighs.

'It's perfect,' she said. 'You could walk right out in it just as it is.'

I said, 'Yes, I like this. I'll keep it on.' But my face in the glass looked small and frightened.

The dress and coat cost eight guineas.

When I took out the money to pay the thin Miss Cohen said, 'I have a very pretty little evening dress that would just suit you.' 'Not today,' I said. 'If you like the dress,' she said, 'you needn't pay at once.' I shook my head.

The fat one smiled and said, 'I remember you now. I thought I knew your face. Didn't you come in when Miss Gaynor was fitting her costume? Miss Laurie Gaynor?' 'That's right,' the thin one said, 'I remember. You were in the same company. How is Miss Gaynor?' The fat Miss Cohen said, 'We're having some new dresses in next week. Paris models. Come in and look at them and if you can't pay at once I daresay we can make an arrangement.'

The streets looked different that day, just as a reflection in the looking-glass is different from the real thing.

I went across the road to Jacobus and bought shoes. And then I bought underclothes and silk stockings. Then I had seven pounds left.

I began to feel ill again. When I breathed my side hurt. I got a taxi and went back to Judd Street.

The fire wasn't laid. I spread the underclothes I had bought on the bed and I was looking at them when the landlady came in with a scuttle of coals and sticks and paper.

I said, 'I'll be glad of the fire. I don't feel very well. Could you make me some tea?

'You seem to think I'm here to wait on you,' she said.

When she had gone I got the letter out of my bag and read it through very carefully, sentence by sentence, to find out what each sentence meant. 'He doesn't say anything about seeing me again,' I thought.

'Here's your tea, Miss Morgan,' the landlady said. 'And I must ask you to find another room on Saturday. This room is reserved after Saturday.'

'Why didn't you tell me that when you let it to me?' I said.

She began to bawl. 'I don't hold with the way you go on, if you want to know, and my 'usband don't neither. Crawling up the stairs at three o'clock in the morning. And then today dressed up to the nines. I've got eyes in my head.'

'It wasn't three o'clock,' I said. 'What a lie!'

'I won't 'ave you calling me a liar,' she said. 'You and your drawly voice. And if you give me any of your lip I'll 'ave my 'usband up to you.'

At the door she turned round and said, 'I don't want no tarts in my house, so now you know.'

I didn't answer. My heart was beating like hell. I lay down and started thinking about the time when I was ill in Newcastle, and the room I had there, and that story about the walls of a room getting smaller and smaller until they crush you to death. *The Iron Shroud*, it was called. It wasn't Poe's story; it was more frightening than that. 'I believe this damned room's getting smaller and smaller,' I thought. And about the rows of houses outside, gimcrack, rotten-looking, and all exactly alike.

After a while I got a sheet of paper and wrote, 'Thank you for your letter. I've gone and got an awful cold. Would you come and see me, please? Would you come as soon as you get this? I mean if you care to. My landlady won't want to let you up, but she'll have to if you tell her that you're a relation and please do come.'

I went out and posted the letter and got some ammoniated quinine. It was nearly three o'clock. But when I had taken the quinine and had lain down again I felt too ill to care whether he came or not.

This is England, and I'm in a nice, clean English room with all the dirt swept under the bed.

It got dark, but I couldn't get up to light the gas. I felt as if there were weights on my legs so that I couldn't move. Like that time at home when I had fever and it was afternoon and the jalousies were down and yellow light came in through the slats and lay on the floor in bars. The room wasn't painted. There were knots in the wood and on one of them a cockroach, waving its feelers slowly backwards and forwards. I couldn't move. I lay watching it. I thought, 'If it flies on to the bed or if it flies on to my face I shall go mad.' I watched it and I thought, 'Is it going to fly?' and the bandage on my head was hot. Then Francine came in and she saw it and got a shoe and killed it. She changed the bandage round my head and it was ice-cold and she started fanning me with a palm-leaf fan. And then night outside and the voices of people passing in the street — the forlorn sound of voices, thin and sad. And the heat pressing down on you as if it were something alive. I wanted to be black, I always wanted to be black. I was happy because Francine was there, and I watched her hand waving the fan backward and forwards and the beads of sweat that rolled from underneath her handkerchief. Being black is warm and gay, being white is cold and sad. She used to sing:

> *Adieu, sweetheart, adieu,*
> *Salt beef and sardines too,*
> *And all good times I leave behind,*
> *Adieu, sweetheart, adieu.*

That was her only English song.

— It was when I looked back from the boat and saw the lights of the town bobbing up and down that was the first time I really knew I was going. Uncle Bob said well you're off now and I turned my head so that nobody would see me crying — it ran down my face and splashed into the sea like the rain was splashing — Adieu sweetheart adieu — And I watched the lights heaving up and down —

He was standing in the doorway. I could see him against the light in the passage.

'What's the time?' I said.

He said, 'It's half-past five. I came as soon as I got your letter.'

He came up to the bed and put his hand on mine. He said, 'But you're burning hot. You really are ill.'

'I should shay sho,' I said.

He took a box of matches out of his pocket and lit the gas. 'My God, this isn't very cheerful.'

'It's like they all are,' I said.

The underclothes I had bought were heaped up on a chair.

'I got a lot of clothes,' I said.

'Good.'

'And I've got to clear out of here.'

'That's a pretty good thing too, I should say,' he said. 'This really is an awful place.'

'It's so cold,' I said. 'That's the worst thing about it. But where are you going?' Not that it mattered. I felt too ill to care.

'I'll be back in ten minutes,' he said.

He came in again with a lot of parcels — an eiderdown and a bottle of burgundy and some grapes and Brand's essence of beef and a cold chicken.

He kissed me and his face felt cool and smooth against mine. But the heat and the cold of the fever were running up and down my back. When you have fever you are heavy and light, you are small and swollen, you climb endlessly a ladder which turns like a wheel.

I said, 'Take care. You'll catch my 'flu.'

'I expect I shall,' he said. 'It can't be helped.'

He sat down and smoked a cigarette, but I couldn't smoke. I liked watching him, though. It was as if I had always known him.

He said, 'Listen. Tomorrow I've got to go away, but I'll be back next week. I'm going to send my doctor in to see you tonight or tomorrow morning. Ames is his name. He's a nice chap, you'll like him. Just get well and don't worry, and write and tell me how you get on.'

'I've got to go out and look for another room tomorrow,' I said.

'Oh no,' he said. 'I'll speak to your landlady and I'll tell Ames to speak to her too. You'll find that'll be all right. Don't you worry about her.'

'I'd better take the food downstairs with me,' he said.

He went out. The room looked different, as if it had grown bigger.

After a while the landlady came in and put the opened bottle of wine and the soup on the table without speaking. I ate the soup, and then I drank two glasses of wine, and then went to sleep.

3

There was a black table with curly legs in the hall in that house, and on it a square-faced clock, stopped at five minutes past twelve, and a plant made of rubber with shiny, bright red leaves, five-pointed. I couldn't take my eyes off it. It looked proud of itself, as if it knew that it was going on for ever and ever, as if it knew that it fitted in with the house and the street and the spiked iron railings outside.

The landlady came up from the kitchen.

'You'll be well enough to leave tomorrow, won't you, Miss Morgan?'

'Yes,' I said.

'That's all I wanted to know,' she said. But she stayed there staring at me, so I went outside and finished putting on my gloves standing on the doorstep. (A lady always puts on her gloves before going into the street.)

A man and a girl were leaning against the railings in Brunswick

Square, kissing. They stood without moving in the shadow, with their mouths glued together. They were like beetles clinging to the railings.

I got the glass out of my handbag and looked at myself every time the taxi passed a street-lamp. *It's soppy always to look sad. Funny stories – remember some, for God's sake.*

But the only story I could remember was the one about the curate. He laughed and then he said, 'You've got a hairpin sticking out on this side, spoiling your otherwise perfect appearance.'

When he pushed the hairpin back his hand touched my face and I tried to catch hold of myself and remember that the first time I had met him I hadn't liked him. But it seemed too long ago, so I stopped trying.

'Dr Ames was nice,' I said. 'He shut my landlady up like anything.'

I could still feel it on my face where his hand had touched me.

'Are you often ill like that in the winter?' he said. 'Last winter, yes,' I said. 'Not the first winter I was here. I was all right then; I didn't even think it very cold. They say it's always like that — it takes a year before the cold really gets you. But last winter I got pleurisy and the company had to leave me behind in Newcastle.' 'By yourself?' he said. 'How wretched!' 'Yes,' I said, 'it was. Three weeks I was there. It seemed like for ever.'

I didn't taste anything I ate. The orchestra played Puccini and the sort of music that you always know what's going to come next, that you can listen to ahead, as it were; and I could still feel it on my face where his hand had touched me. I kept trying to imagine his life.

When we went out the taxis and the lights and the people passing looked swollen, as if I were drunk. We got to his house in Green Street and it was quiet and watching and not friendly to me.

'I was expecting to have a letter from you all last week,' he said, 'and you never wrote. Why didn't you?'

'I wanted to see if you would,' I said.

The sofa was soft and fat, covered in chintz with a pattern of small blue flowers. He put his hand on my knee and I thought, 'Yes . . . yes . . . yes . . .' Sometimes it's like that — everything drops away except the one moment.

'When I sent you that money I never meant — I never thought I should see you again,' he said.

'I know, but I wanted to see you again,' I said.

Then he started talking about my being a virgin and it all went — the feeling of being on fire — and I was cold.

'Why did you start about that?' I said. 'What's it matter? Besides, I'm not a virgin if that's what's worrying you.'

'You oughtn't to tell lies about that.'

'I'm not telling lies, but it doesn't matter, anyway,' I said. 'People have made all that up.'

'Oh yes, it matters. It's the only thing that matters.'

'It's not the only thing that matters,' I said. 'All that's made up.'

He stared at me and then he laughed. 'You're quite right,' he said.

But I felt cold, as if someone had thrown cold water over me. When he kissed me I began to cry.

'I must go,' I thought. 'Where's the door? I can't see the door. What's happened?' It was as if I were blind.

He wiped my eyes very gently with his handkerchief, but I kept saying, 'I must go, I must go.' Then we were going up another flight of stairs and I walked softly. *'Crawling up the stairs at three o'clock in the morning,' she said. Well, I'm crawling up the stairs.*

I stopped. I wanted to say, 'No, I've changed my mind.' But he laughed and squeezed my hand and said, 'What's the matter? Come on, be brave,' and I didn't say anything, but I felt cold and as if I were dreaming.

When I got into bed there was warmth coming from him and I got close to him. *Of course you've always known, always remembered, and then you forget so utterly, except that you've always known it. Always – how long is always?*

The things spread out on the dressing-table shone in the light of the fire, and I thought, 'When I shut my eyes I'll be able to see this room all my life.'

I said, 'I must go now. What's the time?'

'It's half-past three,' he said.

'I must go,' I said again, whispering.

He said, 'You mustn't be sad, you mustn't worry. My darling mustn't be sad.'

I lay quite still, thinking, 'Say it again. Say "darling" again like that. Say it again.'

But he didn't speak and I said, 'I'm not sad. Why have you got this soppy idea that I'm always sad?'

I got up and started to dress. The ribbons in my chemise looked silly.

'I don't like your looking-glass,' I said.

'Don't you?' he said.

'Have you ever noticed how different some looking-glasses make you look?' I said.

I went on dressing without looking at myself again in the glass. I thought that it had been just like the girls said, except that I hadn't known it would hurt so much.

'Can I have a drink?' I said. 'I'm awfully thirsty.'

He said, 'Yes, have some more wine. Or would you like something else?'

'I'd like a whisky-and-soda,' I said.

There was a tray with drinks on the table. He poured one out for me.

He said, 'Now, wait a bit. I'll come with you to get a taxi.'

There was a telephone over by the bed. I thought, 'Why doesn't he telephone for a taxi?' but I didn't say anything.

He went into the bathroom. I was still very thirsty. I filled the glass up again with soda-water and drank it in small sips, not thinking of anything. It was as if everything in my head had stopped.

He came into the room again and I watched him in the glass. My handbag was on the table. He took it up and put some money into it. Before he did it he looked towards me but he thought I couldn't see him. I got up. I meant to say, 'What are you doing?' But when I went up to him, instead of saying, 'Don't do that,' I said. 'All right, if you like — anything you like, any way you like.' And I kissed his hand.

'Don't,' he said. 'It's I who ought to kiss your hand, not you mine.'

I felt miserable suddenly and utterly lost. 'Why did I do that?' I thought.

But as soon as we were out in the street I felt happy again, and calm and peaceful. We walked along in the fog and he was holding my hand.

I could feel the pulse in his wrist.

We got a taxi in Park Lane.

'Well, good-bye,' I said.

He said, 'I'll write to you tomorrow.'

'Will you write to me so that I get it early?' I said.

'Yes, I'll send it by messenger. You'll get it when you wake up.'

'You've got my new address, haven't you? You won't go and lose it?'

'Yes, yes, I've got it,' he said. 'I won't lose it.'

'I'm awfully sleepy,' I said. 'I bet I'll go to sleep in this taxi.'

When I paid the man he winked at me. I looked over his head and pretended not to notice.

4

My new rooms were in Adelaide Road, not far from Chalk Farm Tube station. There wasn't anything much to do all day. I would get up late and then go out for a walk and then go back home and have something to eat and watch out of the window for a telegraph-boy or a messenger. Every time the postman knocked I would think, 'Is that a letter for me?'

There was always some old man trailing along singing hymns — 'Nearer, my God, to Thee' or 'Abide with me' — and people making up their minds ten yards off that they were not going to see them and others not seeing them at all. Invisible men, they were. But the oldest one of all played 'The Girl I Left Behind Me' on a penny whistle.

There was a moulding round the walls of the sitting-room — grapes, pineapples and acanthus leaves, all very dirty. The light in the middle hung from more acanthus leaves. It was a large, square room, high-ceilinged, with four chairs placed against the walls, a piano, a sofa, one armchair and a table in the middle. It reminded me of a restaurant, that's why I liked it.

I would think about when he made love to me and walk up and down thinking about it; and that I hated the looking-glass in his room — it made me look so thin and pale. And about getting up and saying, 'I must go now,' and dressing, and going down the stairs quietly, and the front door that clicked so silently, that clicked always as if it were for the last time, and there I was in the dark street.

Of course, you get used to things, you get used to anything. It was as if I had always lived like that. Only sometimes, when I had got back home and was undressing to go to bed, I would think, 'My God, this is a funny way to live. My God, how did this happen?'

Sunday was the worst day, because he was never in London and there wasn't any hope that he would send for me. That year my

birthday was on a Sunday. The seventh of January. I was nineteen.
The night before he sent me roses and said in his letter: 'Nineteen is
a great age. How old do you think I am? Never mind. Tottering, I
expect you would say if you knew.' And he said that he wanted me
to meet his cousin Vincent at dinner on Monday, and that he'd
thought of a present I'd like. 'I think I'll tell you about that.'

There had been a card from Maudie: 'Coming to see you
Sunday afternoon. Cheerio. Maudie.'

I lay in bed pretty late because there wasn't anything else to do.
When I got up I went out for a walk. It's funny how parts of London
are as empty as if they were dead. There was no sun, but there was a
glare on everything like a brass band playing.

In the afternoon it began to rain. I lay down on the sofa and tried
to sleep, but I couldn't because a church bell started with that
tinny, nagging sound they have. The feeling of Sunday is the same
everywhere, heavy, melancholy, standing still. Like when they say,
'As it was in the beginning, is now, and ever shall be, world without
end.'

I thought about home and standing by the window on Sunday
morning, dressing to go to church, and putting on a woollen vest
which had shrunk in the wash and was too small, because wool next
the skin is healthy. And white drawers tight at the knee and a white
petticoat and a white embroidered dress — everything starched
and prickly. And black ribbed-wool stockings with black shoes.
(The groom Joseph cleaning the shoes with blacking and spit. Spit
— mix — rub; spit — mix — rub. Joseph had heaps of spittle and
when he spurted a jet into the tin of blacking he never missed.) And
brown kid gloves straight from England, one size too small. 'Oh,
you naughty girl, you're trying to split those gloves; you're trying
to split those gloves on purpose.'

(While you are carefully putting on your gloves you begin to
perspire and you feel the perspiration trickling down under your
arms. The thought of having a wet patch underneath your arms —
a disgusting and a disgraceful thing to happen to a lady — makes
you very miserable.)

And the sky close to the earth. Hard, blue and close to the earth.
The mango tree was so big that all the garden was in its shadow and
the ground under it always looked dark and damp. The stable-
yard was by the side of the garden, white-paved and hot, smelling
of horses and manure. And then next to the stables was a
bathroom. And the bathroom too was always dark and damp. It
had no windows, but the door used to be hooked a little bit open.

The light was always dim, greenish. There were cobwebs on the roof.

The stone bath was half as big as a good-sized room. You went up into it by two stone steps, cool and lovely to your feet. Then you sat on the side of the bath and let your legs dangle into the dark green water.

' ". . . And all the Roy-al Fam-i-lee."

' "We beseech thee to hear us, good Lord." '

During the Litany I would bite the back of the pitch-pine pew in front, and sigh, and read bits of the marriage-service, and fan myself with an old wire fan with a picture on it in faded blues and reds of a fat Chinese woman toppling over backwards. Her little fat feet, with slippers turned up at the toes, seemed to be moving in the air; her little fat hands clutched at nothingness.

'To the Memory of Doctor Charles Le Mesurier, the Poor of this Island were Grateful for his Benevolence, the Rich Rewarded his Industry and Skill.' That gave you a peaceful and melancholy feeling. The poor do this and the rich do that, the world is so-and-so and nothing can change it. For ever and for ever turning and nothing, nothing can change it.

Red, blue, green, purple in the stained-glass windows. And saints with bare, wax-coloured feet with long, supple toes.

' "We beseech thee to hear us, good Lord." '

Always, just when I had fallen into a sort of stupor, the Litany would end.

Walking through the still palms in the churchyard. The light is gold and when you shut your eyes you see fire-colour.

'What have you done to yourself?' Maudie said. 'You look different. I'd have been round to see you before, but I've been away. You've done something to your hair, haven't you? It's lighter.' I said, 'Yes, I've had henna-shampoos. Do you like it?' 'In a way I do,' Maudie said. 'It's not bad.'

She sat down and began a long discourse. Every now and then she would giggle a nervous and meaningless giggle. When I remembered living with her it was like looking at an old photograph of myself and thinking, 'What on earth's that got to do with me?'

I had some vermouth. I got it out and we each had a drink.

'It's my birthday. Wish me many happy returns.'

'You bet I do,' Maudie said. 'Here's to us. Who's like us? Damned few. What a life!'

'You've got swanky rooms, anyway,' she said. 'A piano and everything.' 'Yes, they're all right,' I said. 'Have another.' 'Ta,' Maudie said.

When I had finished the second vermouth I felt I wanted to tell her about it.

'What, the man you got off with at Southsea?' Maudie said. 'He's got a lot of money, hasn't he? D'you know, I always knew you'd get off with somebody with money. I was saying so only the other day. I said, "It's all very well, but I bet you she gets off with somebody with money." '

'What did I talk about it for?' I thought.

'I don't know what I'm laughing at,' Maudie said. 'It's nothing to laugh about really. I like this drink. Can I have some more?'

'Only, don't get soppy about him,' she said. 'That's fatal. The thing with men is to get everything you can out of them and not care a damn. You ask any girl in London — or any girl in the whole world if it comes to that — who really knows, and she'll tell you the same thing.' 'I've heard all that a million times,' I said. 'I'm sick of hearing it.' 'Oh, I needn't talk,' Maudie said, 'the fool I made of myself over Viv! Though it was a bit different with me, you understand. We were going to be married.'

'What a life!' she said.

We went into the bedroom. 'Cherry Ripe' over the washstand and facing it another picture of a little girl in a white dress with a blue sash fondling a woolly dog.

Maudie stared at the bed, which was small and narrow.

'He never comes here,' I said. 'We go to his house or different places. He's never been here at all.' 'Oh, that's the sort he is,' Maudie said, 'the cautious sort, is he? Viv was awfully cautious too. It's not such a good sign when they're like that.'

Then she started telling me that I ought to swank as much as I could.

'I don't want to interfere, kid, but really you ought. The more you swank the better. If you don't swank a bit nothing's any use. If he's a rich man and he's keeping you, you ought to make him get you a nice flat up West somewhere and furnish it for you. Then you'd have something. I remember — he said he worked in the City. Is he one of these Stock Exchange blokes?' 'Yes,' I said, 'but he's something to do with an insurance company too. I don't know; he doesn't talk much about himself.' 'There you are — the cautious sort,' Maudie said.

She looked at my dresses and kept saying, 'Very ladylike. I call that one very ladylike indeed. And you've got a fur coat. Well, if a girl has a lot of good clothes and a fur coat she has something, there's no getting away from that.'

'My dear, I had to laugh,' she said. 'D'you know what a man said to me the other day? It's funny, he said, have you ever thought that a girl's clothes cost more than the girl inside them?'

'What a swine of a man!' I said.

'Yes, that's what I told him,' Maudie said. ' "That isn't the way to talk," I said. And he said, "Well, it's true, isn't it? You can get a very nice girl for five pounds, a very nice girl indeed; you can even get a very nice girl for nothing if you know how to go about it. But you can't get a very nice costume for her for five pounds. To say nothing of underclothes, shoes, etcetera and so on." And then I had to laugh, because after all it's true, isn't it? People are much cheaper than things. And look here! Some dogs are more expensive than people, aren't they? And as to some horses . . .'

'Oh, shut up,' I said. 'You're getting on my nerves. Let's go back into the sitting-room; it's cold in here.'

'What about your stepmother?' Maudie said. 'What'll she think if you chuck the tour? Are you going to chuck it?' 'I don't know what she'll think,' I said. 'I don't suppose she'll think anything.' 'Well, I call that funny,' Maudie said. 'I will say that for your stepmother. She doesn't seem to be at all inquisitive, does she?' 'I shall tell her that I'm trying for a job in London. Why should she think it funny?' I said.

Looking out at the street was like looking at stagnant water. Hester was coming up to London in February. I started wondering what I should say to her, and I began to feel depressed. I said, 'I don't like London. It's an awful place; it looks horrible sometimes. I wish I'd never come over here at all.'

'You must be potty,' Maudie said. 'Whoever heard of anybody who didn't like London?' Her eyes looked scornful.

'Well, everybody doesn't,' I said. 'You listen to this thing.' I got it out of the drawer and read:

> 'Horse faces, faces like horses,
> And grey streets, where old men wail unnoticed
> Prayers to an ignoble God.'
> There the butcher's shop stinks to the leaden sky;
> There the fish shop stinks differently, but worse.

And so on, and so on.'

Then there were a lot of dots. And then it went on:

'But where are they —
The cool arms, white as alabaster?'

'Well,' Maudie said, 'what's all that about?'
'Just listen to this one,' I said:

'Loathsome London, vile and stinking hole. . .'

'Hey,' Maudie said, 'that's enough of that.'
I began to laugh. I said, 'That's the man who had these rooms
before me. The landlady told me about him. She had to chuck him
out because he couldn't pay his rent. I found these things in a
drawer.'
'He must have been up the pole,' Maudie said. 'D'you know, I
thought there was something about this place that gave me the pip;
I'm awfully sensitive like that. Anybody funny around — I always
feel it in a minute. And besides, I hate high ceilings. And those
blasted pineapples round the walls. It isn't cosy.'
'You ought to make him give you a flat,' she said. 'Park
Mansions, that's the place. I bet he's fond of you and he will. But
don't go and wait too long before you ask him, because that's
fatal too.'
'Well, if we're going out,' I said, 'we'd better go. It'll be pitch-
dark in a minute.'
We took the Tube to Marble Arch, and walked through the
Park. Some distance away from the crowd round the speakers,
there was a man standing on a box, bawling something about God.
Nobody was listening to him. You could only hear 'God . . . God . . .
The wrath of God. . . . Wah, wah, wah, wah. . . .'
We got up close to him. I could see the Adam's apple jumping up
and down in his throat. Maudie began to laugh, and he got wild
and shrieked after us, 'Laugh! Your sins will find you out. Already
the fear of death and hell is in your hearts, already the fear of God is
like fire in your hearts.'
'Well, the dirty tyke!' Maudie said. 'Insulting us just because we
haven't got a man with us. I know these people, they're careful who
they're rude to. They're damned careful who they try to convert.
Have you ever noticed? He wouldn't have said a word if we'd had a
man with us.'
We heard his voice after us, *'God,* wah, wah, wah. . . . *God,* wah,
wah, wah. . . .'
He was thin and he looked cold. He had little, sad eyes. But
Maudie was very vexed. She walked faster than usual, swinging

her arms and saying, 'Dirty little tyke, dirty little tyke. . . . They're damned careful who they try to convert.'

But I wanted to go back and talk to him and find out what he was really thinking of, because his eyes had a blind look, like a dog's when it sniffs something.

We took a bus at Hyde Park Corner and went to a place that Maudie knew of near Victoria Station. We had oysters and stout.

Maudie got a bus to go home.

'Well,' she said, 'look here, do write to me, kid. Let me know what happens. Take care of yourself and if you can't be good be careful. Etcetera and so on.'

I said, 'Don't be surprised if I turned up at rehearsals.'

'Oh no, I won't be surprised,' she said. 'I've given up being surprised.'

5

Next evening, we got back to Green Street about eleven o'clock. There was the light on over the sofa and the tray with drinks, and the rest of the house dark and quiet and not friendly to me. Sneering faintly, sneering discreetly, as a servant would. Who's this? Where on earth did he pick her up?

'Well,' he said, 'what did you think of Vincent? He's a good-looking boy, isn't he?'

'Yes,' I said, 'very.'

'He likes you. He thinks you're a darling.'

'Oh, does he? I thought he didn't somehow.'

'Good Lord, why?'

'I don't know,' I said. 'I just thought so.'

'Of course he likes you. He says he wants to hear you sing some time.'

'What for?' I said.

It was raining hard. When I listened I could just hear the sound of it.

'Because he could probably do something about getting you a job. He's very much in with some of these people and he might be most awfully useful to you. As a matter of fact he offered to do what he could for you off his own bat; I didn't ask him.'

'Well, I could go back on tour if it comes to that,' I said.

I was thinking about when he would start kissing me and about when we would go upstairs.

'We're going to get you something much better than that. Vincent says he doesn't see why you shouldn't get on, and I don't see why you shouldn't either. I believe it would be a good idea for you to have singing-lessons. I want to help you; I want you to get on. You want to get on, don't you?'

'I don't know,' I said.

'But, my dear, how do you mean you don't know? Good God, you must know. What would you really like to do?'

I said, 'I want to be with you. That's all I want.'

'Oh, you'll soon get sick of me.' He smiled, a bit as if he were sneering at me.

I didn't answer.

'Don't be like that,' he said. 'Don't be like a stone that I try to roll uphill and that always rolls down again.'

'Like a stone,' he said. It's funny how you think, 'It won't hurt until I move.' So you sit perfectly still. Even your face goes stiff.

He was saying, 'You're a perfect darling, but you're only a baby. You'll be all right later on. Not that it has anything to do with age. Some people are born knowing their way about; others never learn. Your predecessor — '

'My predecessor?' I said. 'Oh! my predecessor.'

'She was certainly born knowing her way about. It doesn't matter, though. Don't worry. Do believe me, you haven't got to worry.'

'Yes, of course,' I said.

'Well, look happy then. Be happy. I want you to be happy.'

'All right, I'll have a whisky,' I said. 'No, not wine — whisky.'

'You've learnt to like whisky already, haven't you?' he said.

'It's in my blood,' I said. 'All my family drink too much. You should see my Uncle Ramsay — Uncle Bo. He can drink if you like.'

'That's all very fine and large,' Walter said, 'but don't start too early.'

. . . Here's the punch Uncle Bo said welcome Hebe — this child certainly can mix a good punch Father said something to warm the cockles of your heart — the blinds on the verandah were flapping — like a sip Father said whoa he said that'll do we don't want to have you starting too early . . .

'Yes, Uncle Bo can drink if you like,' I said, 'and you wouldn't think so; it never seems to make any difference to him. He's nice. I like him much better than my other uncle.'

'You're a rum little devil, aren't you?' Walter said.

'Oh, I always was rum,' I said. 'When I was a kid I wanted to be black, and they used to say, "Your poor grandfather would turn in his grave if he heard you talking like that." '

I finished the whisky. The paralysed feeling went and I was all right again. 'Oh well,' I thought, 'I don't care. What's it matter?'

'I'm the fifth generation born out there, on my mother's side.'

'Are you really?' he said, still a bit as if he were laughing at me.

'I wish you could see Constance Estate,' I said. 'That's the old estate — my mother's family's place. It's very beautiful. I wish you could see it.'

'I wish I could,' he said. 'I'm sure it's beautiful.'

'Yes,' I said. 'On the other hand, if England is beautiful, it's not beautiful. It's some other world. It all depends, doesn't it?'

Thinking of the walls of the Old Estate house, still standing, with moss on them. That was the garden. One ruined room for roses, one for orchids, one for tree-ferns. And the honeysuckle all along the steep flight of steps that led down to the room where the overseer kept his books.

'I saw an old slave-list at Constance once,' I said. 'It was hand-written on that paper that rolls up. Parchment, d'you call it? It was in columns — the names and the ages and what they did and then General Remarks.'

... Maillotte Boyd, aged 18, mulatto, house servant. The sins of the fathers Hester said are visited upon the children unto the third and fourth generation — don't talk such nonsense to the child Father said — a myth don't get tangled up in myths he said to me ...

'All those names written down,' I said. 'It's funny, I've never forgotten it.'

I suppose it was the whisky, but I wanted to talk about it. I wanted to make him see what it was like. And it all went through my head, but too quickly. Besides, you can never tell about things.

'There was a girl at school,' I said, 'at the convent I went to. Beatrice Agostini, her name was. She came from Venezuela, she was a boarder. I liked her awfully. I wasn't a boarder, of course, except once when my father went to England for six months. When he came back he had married again; he brought Hester with him.'

'Your stepmother was all right to you, wasn't she?'

'Yes, she was all right. She was very nice — in a way.'

'We used to go for moonlight rows,' I said. 'Black Pappy was our boatman's name. We have lovely moonlight nights. You should see them. The shadows the moon makes are as dark as sun-shadows.'

Black Pappy used to wear a blue linen suit, the trousers patched behind with sacking. He had very long ears and a round gold earring in one of them. He would bawl out at you that you mustn't trail your hand in the water on account of the barracoutas. Then you would imagine the barracoutas — hundreds of them — swimming by the side of the boat, waiting to snap. Flat-headed, sharp-toothed, swimming along the cold white roads the moon makes on the water.

'I'm sure it's beautiful,' Walter said, 'but I don't like hot places much. I prefer cold places. The tropics would be altogether too lush for me, I think.'

'But it isn't lush,' I said. 'You're quite wrong. It's wild, and a bit sad sometimes. You might as well say the sun's lush.'

Sometimes the earth trembles; sometimes you can feel it breathe. The colours are red, purple, blue, gold, all shades of green. The colours here are black, brown, grey, dim-green, pale blue, the white of people's faces — like woodlice.

'Besides, it wasn't as hot as all that,' I said. 'They exaggerate about the heat. It got a bit hot in the town sometimes, but my father had a little estate called Morgan's Rest, and we were there a lot. He was a planter, my father. He had a big estate when he first went out there; then he sold it when he married Hester and we lived in the town for nearly four years and then he bought Morgan's Rest — a much smaller place. He called it that, Morgan's Rest.'

'My father was a fine man,' I said, feeling rather drunk. 'He had a red moustache and he had a most terrible temper. Not as bad as Mr Crowe's, though Mr Crowe had been out there forty years and he had such a terrible temper that one day he bit his pipe right in two — or that's what the servants said. And whenever he was at home I used to watch him and hope he'd do it again, but he never did.'

'I disliked my father,' Walter said. 'I thought most people did.'

'Oh, I didn't mine,' I said. 'Not all the time anyway.'

'I'm a real West Indian,' I kept saying. 'I'm the fifth generation on my mother's side.'

'I know, my sweet,' Walter said. 'You told me that before.'

'I don't care,' I said. 'It was a lovely place.'

'Everybody thinks the place where he was born is lovely,' Walter said.

'Well, they aren't all lovely,' I said. 'Not by a long chalk. In fact, some of them give you a shock at first, they're so ugly. Only you get used to it; you don't notice it after a while.'

He got up and pulled me up and started kissing me.

'You sound a bit tight,' he said. 'Well, let's go upstairs, you rum child, you rum little devil.'

'Champagne and whisky is a great mixture,' he said.

We went upstairs.

'Children, every day one should put aside a quarter of an hour for meditation on the Four Last Things. Every night before going to sleep — that's the best time — you should shut your eyes and try to think of one of the Four Last Things.' (*Question*: What are the Four Last Things? *Answer*: The Four Last Things are Death, Judgment, Hell and Heaven.) That was Mother St Anthony — funny old thing she was, too. She would say, 'Children, every night before you go to sleep you should lie straight down with your arms by your sides and your eyes shut and say: "One day I shall be dead. One day I shall lie like this with my eyes closed and I shall be dead."'

'Are you afraid of dying?' Beatrice would say. 'No, I don't believe I am. Are you?' 'Yes, I am, but I never think about it.'

Lying down with your arms by your sides and your eyes shut.

'Walter, will you put the light out? I don't like it in my eyes.'

Maillotte Boyd, aged 18. Maillotte Boyd, aged 18. . . . But I like it like this. I don't want it any other way but this.

'Are you asleep?'

'No, I'm not asleep.'

'You were lying so still,' he said.

Lying so still afterwards. That's what they call the Little Death.

'I must go now,' I said. 'It's getting late.'

I got up and dressed.

'I'll arrange about Vincent,' he said. 'Some afternoon next week.'

'All right,' I said.

All the way back in the taxi I was still thinking about home and when I got into bed I lay awake, thinking about it. About how sad the sun can be, especially in the afternoon, but in a different way from the sadness of cold places, quite different. And the way the bats fly out at sunset, two by two, very stately. And the smell of the store down on the Bay. ('I'll take four yards of the pink, please, Miss Jessie.') And the smell of Francine — acrid-sweet. And that hibiscus once — it was so red, so proud, and its long gold tongue hung out. It was so red that even the sky was just a background for it. And I can't believe it's dead.

. . . And the sound of rain on the galvanized-iron roof. How it would go on and on, thundering on the roof. . . .

That was when it was sad, when you lay awake at night and remembered things. That was when it was sad, when you stood by the bed and undressed, thinking, 'When he kisses me, shivers run up my back. I am hopeless, resigned, utterly happy. Is that me? I am bad, not good any longer, bad. That has no meaning, absolutely none. Just words. But something about the darkness of the streets has a meaning.'

6

Hester usually came up to London for the January sales, but it was the middle of March before she wrote to me from a boarding-house in Bayswater.

'Yes, Mrs Morgan's expecting you,' the maid said. 'She's at lunch.'

'I'm sorry I'm late,' I said, and Hester said, 'I'm glad to see you looking so well.'

She had clear brown eyes which stuck out of her head if you looked at her sideways, and an English lady's voice with a sharp, cutting edge to it. Now that I've spoken you can hear that I'm a lady. I have spoken and I suppose you now realize that I'm an English gentlewoman. I have my doubts about you. Speak up and I will place you at once. Speak up, for I fear the worst. That sort of voice.

There were two middle-aged women at our table and a young man with a newspaper which he read whenever he stopped eating. The stew tasted of nothing at all. Everybody took one mouthful and then showered salt and sauce out of a bottle on to it. Everybody did this mechanically, without a change of expression, so that you saw they knew it would taste of nothing. If it had tasted of anything they would have suspected it.

There was an advertisement at the back of the newspaper:

'What is Purity? For Thirty-five Years the Answer has been Bourne's Cocoa.'

'I've got a letter here that I want to read to you,' Hester said. 'It came just before I left Ilkley. I'm rather upset about it.'

'But not here,' she said. 'Upstairs, later on.' Then she said that the rector's daughter was getting married and that she was going to give her a present of two jumbie-beads set in gold and made into a brooch.

'The niggers say that jumbie-beads are lucky, don't they?'

'Yes, they do,' I said. 'They always say that.'

We ate tinned pears and then she said, 'Well, now we'll go to my room, I think.'

'This is the brooch,' she said, when we got upstairs. 'Don't you think it's charming?'

'Awfully pretty,' I said.

She put it back into its box and began to stroke her upper lip, as if she had an invisible moustache. She had a habit of doing that. Her hands were large with broad palms, but the fingers were long and slender and she was proud of them.

'You really are looking astonishingly well,' she said. 'What about your new engagement? Have you started rehearsing yet?'

'Well, not just yet,' I said.

She blinked and went on stroking her upper lip.

'Perhaps I'll be in a London show starting in September,' I said. 'I'm having singing-lessons now. I began them three weeks ago. With a man called Price. He's very good.'

'Really?' she said, lifting her eyebrows.

I sat there. I didn't know what to say. There wasn't anything to say. I kept on wondering whether she would ask me what I was living on. 'What is Purity? For Thirty-five Years the Answer has been Bourne's Cocoa.' Thirty-five years. . . . Fancy being thirty-five years old. What is Purity? For Thirty-five Thousand Years the Answer has been . . .

She cleared her throat. She said, 'This letter is from your Uncle Ramsay. It's in answer to one I wrote about you two months ago.'

'About me?' I said.

She said, without looking at me, 'I wrote suggesting that you should go home again. I told him that things didn't seem to be turning out as I had hoped when I brought you over here, and that I was worried about you, and that I thought this might be the best thing.'

'Oh, I see,' I said.

'Well, I *am* worried about you,' she said. 'I was shocked when I saw you after your illness in Newcastle last winter. Besides . . . I feel it's altogether too much responsibility for me.'

'And that's what Uncle Bo wrote back, is it?' I said.

'Uncle Bo!' she said. 'Uncle Bo! Uncle Boozy would be a better name for him. Yes, this is what Uncle Bo wrote back.'

She put her glasses on.

She said, 'Listen to this: "As a matter of fact I wanted to write to you about Anna some time ago when she started traipsing about the place pretending to be a chorus-girl or whatever you call it. Then I thought that as you were on the spot you were perhaps the best judge of what it was suitable for her to do. So I didn't interfere. Now you write this extraordinary letter telling me that you don't think life in England is agreeing with her very well and that you are willing to pay half her passage out here. Half her passage. But where's the other half coming from? That's what I should like to know. It's a bit late in the day for plain speaking, but better late than never. You know as well as I do that the responsibility for Anna's support is yours and I won't tolerate for a minute any attempt to shift it on to my shoulders. Poor Gerald spent the last of his capital on Morgan's Rest (much against my advice, I may say) and he meant it eventually to be his daughter's property. But, as soon as he was dead, you chose to sell the place and leave the island. You had perfect right to sell it; he left it to you. He had every faith and confidence in you, otherwise his will might have been different. Poor chap. So when you write and propose paying 'half her passage money' and sending her back out here without a penny in her pocket I can only answer that it seems to me there must be some misunderstanding, that you can't be serious. If you feel that you don't wish her to live with you in England, of course her aunt and I will have her here with us. But in that case I insist — we both insist — that she should have her proper share of the money you got from the sale of her father's estate. Anything else would be iniquitous — iniquitous is the only word. You know as well as I do that there is not the remotest chance of her ever being able to earn any money for herself out here. This is a most unpleasant letter to have to write and I can only end by saying that I am sorry it had to be written. I hope you are both well. We hardly ever hear from Anna. She's a strange child. She sent us a postcard from Blackpool or some such town and all she said on it was, 'This is a very windy place,' which doesn't tell us much about how she is getting on. Tell her from me to be a sensible girl and try to settle down. Though I must say that to give a girl the idea you're trying to get rid of her is hardly the way to make her settle down. Her Aunt Sase sends love." '

'That's an outrageous letter,' Hester said.

She began to tap on the table.

'That letter,' she said, 'was written with one solitary aim and object — it was written to hurt and grieve me. It's an outrageous thing to accuse me of cheating you out of your father's money. I got five hundred pounds for Morgan's Rest, that was all. Five hundred. And your father bamboozled into paying eight hundred and fifty. But that had nothing to do with me on the contrary if I could have stopped him I would have done so and your famous Uncle Bo had a finger in that pie too whatever he says now. The way English people are cheated into buying estates that aren't worth a halfpenny is a shame. Estate! Fancy calling a place like that an estate. Only I must say that your father ought to have known better after thirty years out there and losing touch with everybody in England. Once he said to me, "No, I never want to go back. It cost me too much last time and I didn't really enjoy it. I've got nobody there who cares a damn about me. The place stinks of hypocrites if you've got a nose," he said. "I don't care if I never see it again." When he said that I knew he was failing. And such a brilliant man poor man buried alive you might say yes it was a tragedy a tragedy. But still he ought to have known better than to have let himself be cheated in the way he was cheated first and last. Morgan's Rest! Call it Morgan's Folly I told him and you won't be far wrong. Sell it! I should think I did sell a place that lost money and always has done and always will do every penny of money that anybody is stupid enough to put into it and nothing but rocks and stones and heat and those awful doves cooing all the time. And never seeing a white face from one week's end to the other and you growing up more like a nigger every day. Enough to drive anybody mad. I should think I did sell it. And that overseer man pretending that he couldn't speak English and getting ready to rob me right and left. . . .'

I had been expecting something so different that what she was saying didn't seem to make any sense. I was looking out of the window. The leaves of the trees in the square were coming out, and there was a pigeon strutting in the street with its neck all green and gold.

'And then I had to pay your father's debts,' she said. 'When I left the island I left with under three hundred in my pocket and out of that I paid your passage to England I fitted you out to go to school you hadn't a garment that was suitable for the winter a complete outfit — everything — had to be bought and I bore your expenses for a term. And when I wrote and asked your uncle to help to keep you at school for a year because you ought to have some sort of decent education if you were going to earn your living and a term wasn't long enough to make any impression or do any real good he said he couldn't afford it because he had three children of his own to support. He sent five pounds to buy a warm dress because if he remembered England rightly you'd be shivering. And I thought three children what about the others you horrible old man what about the others all colours of the rainbow. And my income is under three hundred a year and that's *my* income and out of that last year I sent you at one time and another thirty pounds and I paid your expenses and your doctor's bill when you were ill in Newcastle and that time you had a tooth stopped I paid that too. I can't afford to give you nearly fifty pounds a year. And all the thanks I get is this outrageous charge that I've cheated you and all the responsibility for the way you're going on must be put on my shoulders. Because don't imagine that I don't guess how you're going on. Only some things must be ignored some things I refuse to be mixed up with I refuse to think about even. And your mother's family stand aside and do nothing. I shall write once more to your uncle and after that I shall have no further communication with your mother's family whatever. They always disliked me,' she said, 'and they didn't trouble to conceal it but this letter is the last straw.'

She had started talking slowly, but it now seemed as if she couldn't stop. Her face was red. 'Like a rushing river, that woman,' as Uncle Bo used to say.

'Oh, I don't suppose he meant anything,' I said. 'He's one of those people who always says much more than he means instead of the other way about.'

She said, 'I shall mean every word of the answer I send. Your uncle is not a gentleman and I shall tell him so.'

'Oh, he won't mind that,' I said. I couldn't help laughing. Thinking of Uncle Bo getting a letter which began 'Dear Ramsay, You are not a gentleman. . . .'

'I'm glad you see it's laughable,' she said. 'A gentleman! With illegitimate children wandering about all over the place called by his name — called by his name if you please. Sholto Costerus, Mildred Costerus, Dagmar. The Costeruses seem to have populated half the island in their time it's too funny. And you being told they were your cousins and giving them presents every Christmas and your father had got so slack that he said he didn't see any harm in it. He was a tragedy your father yes a tragedy and such a brilliant man poor man. But I gave Ramsay a piece of my mind one day I spoke out I said, "My idea of a gentleman an English gentleman doesn't have illegitimate children and if he does he doesn't flaunt them." "No I bet he doesn't," he said, laughing in that greasy way — exactly the laugh of a negro he had — "I should think being flaunted is the last thing that happens to the poor little devils. Not much flaunting of that sort done in England." Horrible man! How I always disliked him! . . .'

'Unfortunate propensities,' she said. 'Unfortunate propensities which were obvious to me from the first. But considering everything you probably can't help them. I always pitied you. I always thought that considering everything you were much to be pitied.'

I said, 'How do you mean, "considering everything"?'

'You know exactly what I mean, so don't pretend.'

'You're trying to make out that my mother was coloured,' I said. 'You always did try to make that out. And she wasn't.'

'I'm trying to make out nothing of the kind. You say unforgivable things sometimes — wicked and unforgivable things.'

I said, 'Well, what did you mean then?'

'I'm not going to argue with you,' she said. 'My conscience is quite clear. I always did my best for you and I never got any thanks for it. I tried to teach you to talk like a lady and behave like a lady and not like a nigger and of course I couldn't do it. Impossible to get you away from the servants. That awful sing-song voice you had! Exactly like a nigger you talked — and still do. Exactly like that dreadful girl Francine. When you were jabbering away together in the pantry I never could tell which of you was speaking. But I did think when I brought you to England that I was giving you a real chance. And now that you're beginning to turn out badly I must be made responsible for it and I must go on supporting you. And your mother's family must stand aside and do nothing. But it's always the same story. The more you do, the less thanks you get and the more you're expected to go on doing. Your uncle always pretended to be fond of you. But when it comes to parting with any money he's so stingy that rather than do it he makes up all these outrageous lies.'

'Well, you won't have to bother,' I said. 'You won't have to give me any more money. Or Uncle Bo or anybody else either. I can get all the money I want and so that's all right. Is everybody happy?

Yes, everybody's happy.'

She stared at me. Her eyes had an inquisitive look and then a cold, disgusted look.

I said, 'If you want to know, I — '

'I don't want to know,' she said. 'You tell me that you hope to get an engagement in London. That's all I want to know. I intend to write to your uncle and tell him that I refuse to be made responsible for you. If he thinks you're not living in a fit and proper way he must do something to stop it himself; I can't. I've always done my duty, and more than my duty, but there does come a time when — '

'The brooch has fallen down,' I said. I picked it up and put it on the table.

'Oh, thank you,' she said.

And I saw her getting calm. I knew that she was saying to herself, 'I'm never going to think of this again.'

'I can't discuss it any more today,' she said. 'I'm too much upset about that letter. But I believe that everything that's necessary has been said. I'm going back to Yorkshire tomorrow, but I hope you'll write and tell me how you get on. I advise you to let your uncle know that I've shown you his letter. I hope you'll get this engagement you're trying for.'

'I hope so too,' I said.

'I'll always be glad to do what I can for you. But if it's a question of money, please remember that I've already done far more than I can afford.'

'You needn't worry about that,' I said. 'I won't ask you for money.'

She didn't say anything for a bit and then she said, 'Have some tea before you go.'

'No, thanks,' I said.

She didn't kiss me when I said, 'Good-bye.'

She always hated Francine.

'What do you talk about?' she used to say.

'We don't talk about anything,' I'd say. 'We just talk.'

But she didn't believe me.

'That girl ought to be sent away,' she said to Father.

'Send Francine away?' Father said. 'What, send away a girl who can cook as well as she can. My dear Hester!'

The thing about Francine was that when I was with her I was happy. She was small and plump and blacker than most of the people out there, and she had a pretty face. What I liked was watching her eat mangoes. Her teeth would bite into the mango and her lips fasten on either side of it, and while she sucked you saw that she was perfectly happy. When she had finished she always smacked her lips twice, very loud — louder than you could believe possible. It was a ritual.

She never wore shoes and the soles of her feet were hard as leather. She could carry anything on her head — a bottleful of water, or a huge weight. Hester used to say, 'What are these people's heads made of? A white man couldn't carry a weight like that. Their heads must be like blocks of wood or something.'

She was always laughing, but when she sang it sounded sad. Even very gay, quick tunes sounded sad. She would sit for a long while singing to herself and 'beating tambou lé-lé' — a thump with the base of the hand and then five short knocks with the fingers.

I don't know how old she was and she didn't know either. Sometimes they don't. But anyhow she was a bit older than I was and when I was unwell for the first time it was she who explained to me, so that it seemed quite all right and I thought it was all in the day's work like eating or drinking. But then she went off and told Hester, and Hester came and jawed away at me, her eyes wandering all over the place. I kept saying, 'No, rather not. . . . Yes, I see. . . . Oh yes, of course. . . .' But I began to feel awfully miserable, as if everything were shutting up around me and I couldn't breathe. I wanted to die.

After she had finished talking I went on to the verandah and lay in the hammock and swung. We were up at Morgan's Rest. Hester and I were there by ourselves, for Father had gone away for a week. I can remember every minute of that day.

The ropes of the hammock creaked and there was a wind and the outer shutters kept banging, like guns. It was shut-in there, between two hills, like the end of the world. It had not rained for some time and the grass on the crête was burnt brown in the sun.

When I had swung for a bit I felt very sick. So I stopped the hammock and lay there, looking at the sea. There were white lines on it, as if ships had just passed.

At half-past twelve we had breakfast and Hester started talking about Cambridge. She was always talking about Cambridge.

She said she was sure I should like England very much and that it would be a very good thing for me if I were to go to England. And then she talked about her uncle who was fifth wrangler and people used to call him 'Dirty Watts'.

'He was rather dirty,' she said, 'but it was simply absentmindedness. And his wife, Aunt Fanny, was a beauty — a great beauty. One evening at the theatre when she entered her box everybody stood up. Spontaneously.'

'Fancy!' I said. 'My goodness!'

'Don't say my goodness,' Hester said. 'My badness, that's what you ought to say.'

'Yes, Beauty and the Beast, people used to call them,' she said. 'Beauty and the Beast. Oh, there were many stories about her. There was the young man who answered when she was annoyed at him staring at her:

> *"A cat may look at a king,*
> *So why not I at a prettier thing?"*

She was very pleased at that and she often told the story, and the young man became a great favourite — a very great favourite. Let me see — what was his name? In any case he was at King's. Was it King's or Trinity? I can't remember. However, he was quite a wit in his way and she liked witty people; she forgave them anything. People took the trouble to be witty in those days. It's all very well to cry down those days but people were wittier then.'

'Yes,' I said. 'Like Judge Bryant the other night at the dance when some fool put his arm across the door of the supper-room and said, "Nobody pass who doesn't make a rhyme, nobody pass who doesn't make a rhyme." And Judge Bryant said, as quick as lightning:

> *"Let us pass*
> *You damned old ass."*

That was pretty quick, too, don't you think?'

Hester said, 'There's a certain difference, but of course you can't be expected to see that.' In that voice as if she were talking to herself.

We ate fishcakes and sweet potatoes and then we had stewed guavas; and bread-fruit instead of bread because she liked to feel that she was eating bread-fruit.

Sitting there eating you could see the curve of a hill like the curve of a green shoulder. And there were pink roses on the table in a curly vase with gold rings.

There was a chest in the corner where the drinks were kept and a sideboard ranged with glasses. And the bookshelf with Walter Scott and a lot of old Longmans' Magazines, so old that the pages were yellow.

After breakfast I went back into the verandah and she came there too and sat down in a long canvas chair. She began to stroke Scamp and to blink her eyes, like when she asked conundrums. (Who did Hall Caine? Dorothea Baird.) Scamp fawned on her.

'I hate dogs,' I said.

'Well, really!' she said.

'Well, I do,' I said.

'I don't know what'll become of you if you go on like that,' Hester said. 'Let me tell you that you'll have a very unhappy life if you go on like that. People won't like you. People in England will dislike you very much if you say things like that.'

'I don't care,' I said. But I began to repeat the multiplication-table because I was afraid I was going to cry.

Then I got up and told her I was going to the kitchen to speak to Francine.

The kitchen was about twenty yards away — a shingled, two-roomed house. One of the rooms was Francine's bedroom. There was a bed in it, and an earthenware pitcher and basin and a chair, and above the bed a lot of pictures of Jesus with the Sacred Heart aflame with love, the Virgin Mary in blue with her arms outstretched, and so on. 'St Joseph, priez pour nous.' 'Jesus, Mary, Joseph, grant me the grace of a happy death.'

When she wasn't working Francine would sit on the doorstep and I liked sitting there with her. Sometimes she told me stories, and at the start of the story she had to say 'Timm, timm,' and I had to answer 'Bois sèche.'

You looked across a path, sometimes muddy when it had been raining, or dry, with open, gaping cracks as if the earth were thirsty, at a clump of bamboos swinging in the sun or the rain. But the kitchen was horrible. There was no chimney and it was always full of charcoal smoke.

Francine was there, washing up. Her eyes were red with the smoke and watering. Her face was quite wet. She wiped her eyes with the back of her hand and looked sideways at me. Then she said something in patois and went on washing up. But I knew that of course she disliked me too because I was white; and that I would never be able to explain to her that I hated being white. Being white and getting like Hester, and all the things you get — old and sad and everything. I kept thinking, 'No. . . . No. . . . No . . . .' And I knew that day that I'd started to grow old and nothing could stop it.

I went on without looking at her again, past the rosebeds and the big mango tree and up the hill. The doves were going all the time. It was about two o'clock, just when the sun was hottest.

It had a barren look, that place, a hot, frowning, barren look because of the big grey boulders lying about — an eruption a long time ago, they said. But I don't mean that it wasn't a beautiful place. It was good land — or my father always said it was. He grew cocoa and nutmegs. And coffee on the slopes of the hill.

When the young nutmeg trees flowered for the first time he used to take me with him to see if the tree was male or female, because the buds were so small that you had to have sharp eyes to see the difference. 'You're young and you have sharp eyes,' he would say. 'Come along.'

'I'm getting old,' he would say. 'My eyes aren't as good as they used to be.' I always felt so miserable when he said that.

I got well away from the house. I sat down against a rock in the shadow. The sky was terribly blue and very close to the earth.

I felt I was more alone than anybody had ever been in the world before and I kept thinking, 'No. . . . No. . . . No. . . .' just like that. Then a cloud came in front of my eyes and seemed to blot out half of what I ought to have been able to see. It was always like that when I was going to have a headache.

I thought, 'Well, all right. This time I'll die.' So I took my hat off and went and stood in the sun.

The sun at home can be terrible, like God. This thing here — I can't believe it's the same sun, I simply can't believe it.

I stood there until I felt the pain of the headache begin and then the sky came up close to me. It clanged, it was so hard. The pain was like knives. And then I was cold, and when I had been very sick I went home.

I got fever and I was ill for a long time. I would get better and then it would start again. It went on for several months. I got awfully thin and ugly and yellow as a guinea, my father said.

I asked Hester if I had talked a lot when I was bad and she said, 'Yes, you talked about cats and a great deal about Francine.' It was after that she started disliking Francine so much and saying she ought to be sent away. I had to laugh when I thought that even after all this time she still had to drag Francine in.

I wrote once to Hester but she only sent me a postcard in reply, and after that I didn't write again. And she didn't either.

7

When it was sad was when you woke up at night and thought about being alone and that everybody says the man's bound to get tired. (You make up letters that you never send or even write. 'My darling Walter . . .')

Everybody says, 'Get on.' Of course, some people do get on. Yes, but how many? What about what's-her-name? She got on, didn't she? 'Chorus-Girl Marries Peer's Son.' Well, *what* about her? Get on or get out, they say. Get on or get out.

What I want, Mr Price, is an effective song for a voice trial. *Softly Awakes my Heart as the Flowers Awaken* — that's a very effective one.

Everybody says the man's bound to get tired and you read it in all books. But I never read now, so they can't get at me like that, anyway. ('My darling Walter . . .')

When it was sad was when you lay awake and then it began to get light and the sparrows started — that was when it was sad, a lonely feeling, a hopeless feeling. When the sparrows started to chirp.

But in the daytime it was all right. And when you'd had a drink you knew it was the best way to live in the world, because anything might happen. I don't know how people live when they know exactly what's going to happen to them each day. It seems to me it's better to be dead than to live like that. Dressing to go and meet him and coming out of the restaurant and the lights in the streets and getting into a taxi and when he kissed you in the taxi going there.

A month seemed like a week and I thought, 'It's June already.'

Sometimes it was hot that summer. The day we went to Savernake it was really hot. I had been sitting out on Primrose Hill. There were swarms of children there. Just behind my chair a big boy and a little one were playing with a rope. The little one was being tied up elaborately, so that he couldn't move his arms or legs. When the big one gave him a push he fell flat. He lay on the ground, still laughing for a second. Then his face changed and he started to cry. The big boy kicked him — not hard. He yelled louder. 'Nah then,' the big one said. He got ready to kick again. But then he saw I was watching. He grinned and undid the rope. The little boy stopped crying and got up. They both put out their tongues at me and ran off. The little one's legs were short and dimpled. When he ran he could hardly keep up. However, he didn't forget to turn round and put his tongue out again as far as he could.

There was no sun, but the air was used-up and dead, dirty-warm, as if thousands of other people had breathed it before you. A woman passed, throwing a ball for a dog called Caesar. Her voice was like Hester's:

'See-zah, See-zah . . .'

After a bit I went home and had a cold bath.

When Mrs Dawes came in with Walter's letter I was lying down doing breathing exercises. Price always said that when you were lying down was the time to do them.

'I'll call for you with the car at six o'clock. We're going into the country. Will you bring things for two days and everything else you need — you know?'

As I was going out Mrs Dawes came up from the basement.

'Good-bye,' I said. 'I'll be back on Monday or Tuesday.'

She said, 'Good-bye, Miss Morgan.' She had white hair, a long, placid face and a soft voice — not a cockney voice. She always made her expression blank when she spoke to me.

'I hope you'll enjoy yourself, I'm sure,' she said, and stood at the door watching me get into the car.

I was wondering if I looked all right, because I hadn't had time to dry my hair properly. I was so nervous about how I looked that three-quarters of me was in a prison, wandering round and round in a circle. If he had said that I looked all right or that I was pretty, it would have set me free. But he just looked me up and down and smiled.

'Vincent's coming down by train tomorrow and bringing a girl. I thought it might be fun.'

'Oh, is he?' I said. 'How nice. Is she the girl I met — Eileen?'

'No, not Eileen. Another girl.'

I got happier when it grew darker. A moth flew into my face and I hit at it and killed it.

There were stags' heads stuck up all over the dining-room of the hotel. The one over our table was as big as a cow's. Its enormous glass eyes stared past us. In the bedroom there were prints — 'The Sailor's Farewell', 'The Sailor's Return', 'Reading the Will' and

'Conjugal Affection'. They had a calm, sleepy look, as if they were drawings of stuffed figures — the women very tall and plump and smiling and tidy and the men with long legs and bushy whiskers; but the placid shapes of the trees made you feel that that time must have been a good time.

I woke up very early and couldn't think for a bit where I was. A cool smell, that wasn't the dead smell of London, came in through the window. Then I remembered that I hadn't got to get up and go away and that the next night I'd be there still and he'd be there. I was very happy, happier than I had ever been in my life. I was so happy that I cried, like a fool.

That day it was hot again. After lunch we went to Savernake Forest. The leaves of the beech trees were bright as glass in the sun. In the clearings there were quantities of little flowers in the grass, red, yellow, blue and white, so many that it looked all colours.

Walter said, 'Have you got flowers like these in your island? These little bright things are rather sweet, don't you think?'

I said, 'Not quite like these.' But when I began to talk about the flowers out there I got that feeling of a dream, of two things that I couldn't fit together, and it was as if I were making up the names. Stephanotis, hibiscus, yellowbell, jasmine, frangipani, corolita.

I said, 'Flamboyant trees are lovely when they're flowering.'

There was a lark rising jerkily, as if it went by clock-work, as if someone were winding it up and stopping every now and again.

Walter said, as if he were talking to himself, 'No imagination? That's all rot. I've got a lot of imagination. I've wanted to bring you to Savernake and see you underneath these trees ever since I've known you.'

'I like it here,' I said. 'I didn't know England could be so beautiful.'

But something had happened to it. It was as if the wildness had gone out of it.

We got to where the beech trees grew close together and their branches met, high up. You had the feeling that outside it was a hot, blue day.

We went and sat on a tree that had fallen down, with its roots still partly in the earth. There wasn't enough wind for you to hear the trees. For a long time we didn't say anything. I was thinking how happy I was, and then I didn't think anything — not even how happy I was.

He said, 'You're lovely from this angle.'

'Not from every angle?' I said.

'Certainly not, conceited child. But from this angle you're perfectly satisfactory, and I want very much to make love to you. There are a lot of holes where the deer shelter in winter and where nobody could see us.'

I said, 'Oh no, not here. Just imagine if anybody saw us.' I heard myself giggling.

He said, 'But nobody would. And what if they did? They'd think "these two people are perfectly happy", and be jealous of us and leave us alone.'

I said, 'Well, they might be like that about it, or they mightn't.' I was thinking, 'When we go back to the hotel . . .'

'Shy, Anna,' he said.

'Let's go back to the hotel, anyway,' I said. (You shut the door and you pull the curtains over the windows and then it's as long as a thousand years and yet so soon ended. Laurie saying, 'Some women don't start liking it till they are getting old; that's a bit of bad luck if you like. I'd rather wear myself out while I'm young.')

'My God, yes,' he said. 'That reminds me. Vincent must be there by now. I expect he's waiting for us.'

I had forgotten about Vincent.

'Come on,' Walter said.

We got up. I felt cold, like when you've been asleep and have just woken up.

'You'll like the girl he's bringing with him,' he said. 'Germaine Sullivan, her name is. I'm sure you'll like her. She's an awfully good sort.'

'Is she?' Then I couldn't help saying, 'Vincent isn't.'

'You don't mean to say you don't like Vincent?' he said. 'You're the only girl I've ever heard of who doesn't.'

'Of course I like him. He's certainly very good looking,' I said. 'Is this girl on the stage too?'

'No,' Walter said. 'Vincent met her in Paris. She says she's half-French. God knows what she is; she might be anything. But she really is rather amusing.'

We found the car and went back to the hotel. It was nearly six o'clock. I kept thinking, 'It's unlucky to know you're happy; it's unlucky to say you're happy. Touch wood. Cross my fingers. Spit.'

Vincent said, 'Well, how's the child? How's my infantile Anna?'

He was very good-looking. He had blue eyes with curled-up eyelashes like a girl's, and black hair and a brown face and broad shoulders and slim hips — the whole bag of tricks, in fact. He was a bit like Walter, only younger. And better-looking, I suppose. At least, his face was better-looking. He looked about twenty-five but he was thirty-one really, Walter told me.

'We were wondering what had become of you,' the girl said. 'We've been here nearly two hours. We thought you'd left us in the lurch. I was thinking of finding out if there's a train back.'

She was pretty but she looked as if they had been quarrelling.

'She's in a very bad temper,' Vincent said. 'I don't know what's upset her.'

I went upstairs to change my dress. I put on a dress with a flower-pattern that I had bought at Maud Moore's. The shadows of the leaves on the wall were moving quickly, like the patterns the sun makes on water.

'Look at this thing over the table,' Germaine said. 'This stag or whatever it is. It's exactly like your sister, Vincent, horns and all. D'you remember that time I bumped into her by mistake just outside your flat? Wasn't it funny?'

Vincent didn't answer.

'You think you're perfect, don't you?' Germaine said. 'Well, you're not perfect. Whenever you drink champagne you belch. I was ashamed of you the other night. You go like this.'

She imitated him. The waiter, who was on the other side of the room, heard; and he looked across at us with a shocked expression, pursing his mouth up.

'Did you see that face?' Germaine said. 'Well, that's the way you look sometimes, Vincent. Scorn and loathing of the female — a very common expression in this country. Imitation gold-fish, very difficult.'

'I wouldn't be an Englishwoman,' she said, 'for any money you could give me or anything else.'

'Opportunity's a fine thing,' Vincent said, smiling a little.

She shut up a bit after that, but when we were having more drinks in the lounge she started off again about England. 'It's a very nice place,' she said, 'so long as you don't suffer from claustrophobia.'

'Once,' she said, 'a very clever man said to me . . .'

'A Frenchman, of course,' Vincent said. 'Come on, let's hear what the very clever Frenchman said.'

'Shut up,' Germaine said. 'What he said was quite true. He said that there were pretty girls in England, but very few pretty women. "In fact, hardly any," he said, "I don't believe there are any. Why?

What happens to them? A few pretty girls and then finish, a blank, a desert. What happens to them?" '

'And it's true too,' she said. 'The women here are awful. That beaten, cringing look — or else as cruel and dried-up as they're made! Méchantes, that's what they are. And everybody knows why they're like that. They're like that because most Englishmen don't care a damn about women. They can't make women happy because they don't really like them. I suppose it's the climate or something. Well, thank God, it doesn't matter much to me one way or the other.'

Vincent said, 'Can't they, Germaine? Can't they make women happy?' His face was smooth and smiling.

She got up and looked at herself in the glass. 'I'm going upstairs for a minute,' she said.

'Going to curl your hair?' Vincent said. 'I'm sure you'll find the curl-papers there all right.'

She went out without answering.

Walter said, 'The demoiselle seems annoyed about something. What's the matter with her?'

'Oh, she thinks I ought to have told her before,' Vincent said, 'and she's cut up rough about one thing and another. She started the argument on the way down here. She was all right before that. It'll end in a flood of tears. As usual.'

I hated the way they were looking at each other. I got up.

'Are you also going to curl your hair?' Vincent said.

'No,' I said, 'I'm going to the lavatory.'

'Good for you,' he said.

It seemed a long time since the morning, I was thinking. Last night I was so happy that I cried, like a fool. Last night I was so happy.

I looked out of the bedroom window and there was a thin mist coming up from the ground. It was very still.

Before I came to England I used to try to imagine a night that was quite still. I used to try to imagine it with the crac-cracs going. The verandah long and ghostly — the hammock and three chairs and a table with the telescope on it — and the crac-cracs going all the time. The moon and the darkness and the sound of the trees, and not far away the forest where nobody had ever been — virgin forest. We used to sit on the verandah with the night coming in, huge. And the way it smelt of all flowers. ('This places gives me the creeps at night,' Hester would say.)

•

I was standing in front of the long glass in the bedroom when Walter came in.

He said, 'D'you mind if we go back to London tonight?'

I said, 'I thought the idea was that we were going to stay here tonight and go on to Oxford tomorrow morning.'

'That was the idea,' Walter said. 'But they've had an awful fight and now Germaine says she doesn't want to stay. She says this place gives her the pip.'

'And she's been very rude about Oxford,' he said, starting to laugh. 'I think we'd better take them up tonight. You don't mind, do you?'

'All right,' I said.

'You're sure you don't mind?'

'No,' I said. I began to put my things into the suitcase.

'Oh, leave that,' Walter said. 'The maid will do it. Come downstairs and talk to Germaine. You like her, don't you?'

I said, 'Yes, I like her all right, if she'd only stop going for Vincent all the time.'

'She's very much annoyed with him,' Walter said.

'Yes, I can see she's annoyed. Why? What's the matter with her?'

He put his hands in his pockets and stood rocking backwards and forwards. He said, 'I don't know. Bad temper, I suppose. Vincent's going away next week for some time and she seems to have got into a bad temper over it. The fact is, she wants him to leave her more money than he can afford.'

'Oh, is he going away?' I said. I was still looking in the glass.

He said, 'Yes, I'm going to New York next week and I'm taking him with me.'

I didn't say anything. I put my face nearer the glass. Like when you're a kid and you put your face very near to the glass and make faces at yourself.

'I won't be gone long,' he said. 'I'll be back in a couple of months at the outside.'

'Oh, I see,' I said.

The maid knocked at the door and came in.

We went downstairs and had another drink. 'Drink's pretty nice,' I thought.

Vincent began to talk about books. He said, 'I read a good book the other day — a damned fine book. When I read it I thought, "The man who wrote this should be knighted." *The Rosary*, it was called.'

'A woman wrote that book, you fool,' Walter said.

'Oh?' Vincent said. 'Good Lord! Well, even if a woman wrote it she should be knighted, that's all I can say. That's what I call a fine book.'

'He ought to be put in a glass case, oughtn't he?' Germaine said. 'The perfect specimen.'

Walter said, 'Well, I'd better go and see about the car.'

Germaine was staring at me. 'She looks awfully young, this kid,' she said. 'She looks about sixteen.'

'Yes,' Vincent said. 'Dear old Walter, whom we all know and love, had been doing a bit of baby-snatching, I'm afraid.'

'How old are you?' Germaine said, and I told her, 'Nineteen.'

'She's going to be a great girl one of these days,' Vincent said, putting on his kind expression. 'We're trying to make a start in the autumn, aren't we, Anna? The new show at Daly's. You ought to be able to warble like what's-her-name after all those singing lessons.'

'She's on the stage, is she?' Germaine said.

'Yes, she is or was. You were in a show when you first met Walter, weren't you?' Vincent said.

'Yes,' I said.

They looked at me as if they were expecting me to say something else.

'It was at Southsea,' I said.

'Oh, it was at Southsea, was it?' Vincent said.

They began to laugh. They were still laughing when Walter came in.

'She's been giving you away,' Vincent said. 'She's been telling us how it all started. You dirty dog, Walter. What in God's name were you doing on the pier at Southsea?'

Walter blinked. Then he said, 'You shouldn't let Vincent pump you. He's as inquisitive as an old woman. You wouldn't think it to look at him, but he is.'

He started to laugh too.

'Shut up laughing,' I said.

I thought, 'Shut up laughing,' looking at Walter's hand hanging over the edge of the mantelpiece.

I said, 'Oh, stop laughing at me. I'm sick of it.'

'What's the joke?' I said.

They went on laughing.

I was smoking, and I put the end of my cigarette down on Walter's hand. I jammed it down hard and held it there, and he snatched his hand away and said 'Christ!' But they had stopped laughing.

'Bravo, kid,' Germaine said. 'Bravo.'

'Calm down,' Walter said. 'What's all the excitement about?' He didn't look at me.

'Oh God,' Vincent said. 'Let's get off, shall we?'

We got into the car. Germaine sat next Walter in the front and Vincent and I were at the back.

Vincent started off again about books.

I said, 'I haven't read any of these books you're talking about. I hardly ever read.'

'Well, what do you do with yourself all day?' he said.

'I don't know,' I said.

I said, 'You're going to New York, aren't you?'

He cleared his throat and said, 'Yes, we're going next week.'

I didn't say anything, and he squeezed my hand and said, 'Don't worry. You'll be all right.'

I pulled my hand away. I thought, 'No, I don't like you.'

We stopped at Germaine's flat.

I said, 'Good night, Germaine. Good night, Vincent; thank you very much.' What did I say that for? I thought. I'm always being stupid with this man. I bet he'll make me feel I've said something stupid.

And sure enough he raised his eyebrows, 'Thank me very much? My dear child, why thank me very much?'

'Well,' Walter said, 'where shall we go now? Let's go and have some supper somewhere.'

I said, 'No, let's go back to your house.'

He said, 'Very well. All right.'

We went into a little room on the ground floor and had whiskies-and-sodas and sandwiches. It was stiffly furnished — I didn't like it much. There was a damned bust of Voltaire, stuck up on a shelf, sneering away. There are all sorts of sneers, of course, the high and the low.

I said, 'Germaine's awfully pretty.'

'She's old,' he said.

'I bet she isn't; I bet she isn't any older than Vincent.'

'Well, that is old for a woman. Besides, she'll be blowsy in another year; she's that type.'

'Anyway, she was funny about English people,' I said. 'I liked what she said, rather.'

'I was disappointed in Germaine,' he said. 'I didn't think she could have been such a damned bore. She was simply kicking up a row because Vincent couldn't give her all the money she asked for, and as a matter of fact he's given her far more than he can afford — far more than anybody else would have given her. She thought she had her claws into him. It's a very good thing he's going away.'

'Oh, has he given her far more than he can afford?' I said.

He said, 'By the way, why did you tell Vincent about Southsea? You shouldn't give yourself away like that.'

'But I didn't,' I said.

'But my dear, you must have. Otherwise, how could he have known?'

'Well, I didn't think it mattered. He asked me.'

He said, 'My God, do you consider yourself bound to answer every question anybody asks you? That's a tall order.'

'I don't like this room much,' I said. 'I rather hate it. Let's go upstairs.'

He imitated me. 'Let's go upstairs, let's go upstairs. You really shock me sometimes, Miss Morgan.'

I wanted to pretend it was like the night before, but it wasn't any use. Being afraid is cold like ice, and it's like when you can't breathe. 'Afraid of what?' I thought.

Just before I got up to go I said, 'You don't know how miserable I am about your hand.'

'Oh, that!' he said. 'It doesn't matter.'

There was the clock ticking all the time on a table by the bed.

I said, 'Listen. Don't forget me, don't forget me ever.'

He said, 'No, I won't ever, I tell you,' as if he were afraid I was getting hysterical. I got up and dressed.

My bag was on the table. He took it up and put some money into it. I watched him.

He said, 'I don't know whether we can meet again before I leave London, because I'm going to be most awfully busy. Anyhow, I'll write to you tomorrow. About money. I want you to go away for a change somewhere. Where would you like to go?'

'I don't know,' I said. 'I'll go somewhere.'

He turned round and said, 'Hello, is anything wrong? Don't you feel well?'

'Extraordinary thing,' I was thinking. I felt sick and my forehead was wet.

I said, 'I'm all right. Good-bye for now. Don't bother to come with me.'

'Of course I'm coming with you,' he said.

We went downstairs. When he opened the door there was a taxi passing and he stopped it.

Then he said, 'Come back in here for one minute. Are you sure you're all right?'

I said, 'Yes, quite.'

There was that damned bust smiling away.

'Well, good-bye,' he said. He coughed. 'Take care of yourself.'

'Bless you,' he said and coughed again.

'Oh, yes. Oh, rather,' I said.

I wasn't sleepy. I looked out of the window of the taxi. Men were watering the streets and there was a fresh smell, like an animal just bathed.

When I got home I lay down without undressing. Then it got light and I thought that when Mrs Dawes came in with my breakfast she would think I had gone mad. So I got up and undressed.

'This is no way for a young girl to live,' Mrs Dawes said.

That was because for a week after Walter left I hadn't gone out; I didn't want to. What I liked was lying in bed till very late, because I felt tired all the time, and having something to eat in bed and then in the afternoon staying a long time in the bath. I would put my head under the water and listen to the noise of the tap running. I would pretend it was a waterfall, like the one that falls into the pool where we bathed at Morgan's Rest.

I was always dreaming about that pool, too. It was clear just beyond where the waterfall fell, but the shallow parts were very muddy. Those big white flowers that open at night grew round it. Pop-flowers, we call them. They are shaped like lilies and they smell heavy-sweet, very strong. You can smell them a long way off. Hester couldn't bear the scent, it made her faint. There were crabs under the rocks by the river. I used to splash when I bathed because of them. They have small eyes at the end of long feelers, and when you throw stones at them their shells smash and soft, white stuff bubbles out. I was always dreaming about this pool and seeing the green-brown water in my dream.

'No, this is no way for a young girl to live,' Mrs Dawes said.

People say 'young' as though being young were a crime, and yet they are always scared of getting old. I thought, 'I wish I were old and the whole damned thing were finished; then I shouldn't get this depressed feeling for nothing at all.'

I didn't know what to answer. She was always like that — placid and speaking softly, but a bit as if she were watching me sideways. When I told her that I wanted to get away for a change, she said she had a cousin in Minehead who let rooms, so I went there.

But after three weeks I went back to London because I had a letter from Walter saying that he might be in England again sooner than he had expected. And one day at the beginning of October, when I came in after walking about Primrose Hill in the rain (nothing but the damp trees and the soggy grass and the sad, slow-moving clouds — it's funny how it makes you feel that there's not anything else anywhere, that it's all made up that there is anything else), Mrs Dawes said, 'There's a letter for you. I took it up to your room. I thought you was in.'

I got upstairs. It was lying on the table, and right across the room I thought, 'Who on earth's that from?' because of the handwriting.

8

. . .I was walking along the passage to the long upper verandah which ran the length of the house in town — there were four upstairs bedrooms two on either side of the passage — the boards were not painted and the knots in the wood were like faces — Uncle Bo was on the verandah lying on the sofa his mouth was a bit open — I thought he's asleep and I started to walk on tiptoe — the blinds were down all except one so that you could see the broad leaves of the sandbox tree — I got up to the table where the magazine was and Uncle Bo moved and sighed and long yellow tusks like fangs came out of his mouth and protruded down to his chin — you don't scream when you are frightened because you can't and you don't move either because you can't — after a long time he sighed and opened his eyes and clicked his teeth back into place and said what on earth do you want child — it was the magazine I said — he turned over and went to sleep again — I went out very softly — I had never seen false teeth before not to notice them — I shut the door and went away very softly down the passage . . .

I thought, 'But what's the matter with me? That was years and years ago, ages and ages ago. Twelve years ago or something like that. What's this letter got to do with false teeth?'

I read it again:

My dear Anna,

This is a very difficult letter to write because I am afraid I am going to upset you and I hate upsetting people. We've been back for nearly a week but Walter hasn't been at all well and I have persuaded him to let me write to you and explain matters. I'm quite sure you are a nice girl and that you will be understanding about this. Walter is still very fond of you but he doesn't love you like that any more, and after all you must always have known that the thing could not go on for ever and you must remember too that he is nearly twenty years older than you are. I'm sure that you are a nice girl and that you will think it over calmly and see that there is nothing to be tragic or unhappy or anything like that about. You are young and youth as everybody says is the great thing, the greatest gift of all. The greatest gift, everybody says. And so it is. You've got everything in front of you, lots of happiness. Think of that. Love is not everything – especially that sort of love – and the more people, especially girls, put it right out of their heads and do without it the better. That's my opinion. Life is chock-full of other things, my dear girl, friends and just good times and being jolly together and so on and games and books. Do you remember when we talked about books? I was sorry when you told me that you never read because, believe me, a good book like that book I was talking about can make a lot of difference to your point of view. It makes you see what is real and what is just imaginary. My dear Infant, I am writing this in the country, and I can assure you that when you get into a garden and smell the flowers and all that all this rather beastly sort of love simply doesn't matter. However, you will think I'm preaching at you, so I will shut up. These muddles do happen. They have happened to me, as a matter of fact, worse luck. I can't think why. I can't think why one can't be more sensible. However, I have learnt one thing, that it never helps to let things drag on. Walter has asked me to enclose this cheque for £20 for your immediate expenses because he thinks you may be running short of cash. He will always be your friend and he wants to arrange that you should be provided for and not have to worry about money (for a time at any rate). Write and let him know that you understand. If you really care for him at all you will do this, for believe me he is unhappy about you and he has a lot of other worries as well. Or write me – that would be better still because don't you think it would be just as well for both your sakes if you don't see Walter just now? Then there's that job in the new show. I want to take you along as soon as possible to see my friend. I think I can promise you that something will come of it. I believe that if you will work hard there is no reason why you should not get on. I've always said that and I stick to it.

Yours ever,
Vincent Jeffries.

P.S. Have you kept any of the letters Walter wrote to you? If so you ought to send them back.

I thought, 'What the hell's the matter with me? I must be crazy. This letter has nothing to do with false teeth.'

But I went on thinking about false teeth, and then about piano-keys and about that time the blind man from Martinique came to tune the piano and then he played and we listened to him sitting in the dark with the jalousies shut because it was pouring with rain and my father said, 'You are a real musician.' He had a red moustache, my father. And Hester was always saying, 'Poor Gerald, poor Gerald.' But if you'd seen him walking up Market Street, swinging his arms with his brown shoes flashing in the sun, you wouldn't have been sorry for him. That time when he said, 'The Welsh word for grief is hiraeth.' Hiraeth. And that time when I was crying about nothing and I thought he'd be wild, but he hugged me up and he didn't say anything. I had on a coral brooch and it got crushed. He hugged me up and then he said, 'I believe you're going to be like me, you poor little devil.' And that time when Mr Crowe said, 'You don't mean to say you're backing up that damned French monkey?' meaning the Governor, 'I've met some Englishmen,' he said, 'who were monkeys too.'

When I looked at the clock it was a quarter-past five. I had been sitting there like that for two hours. I thought, 'Go on, get up,' and after a while I went to a post-office and wrote out a telegram to Walter: 'I would like to see you tonight if possible please Anna.'

Then I went back home. My hands were very cold and I kept rubbing them together.

I thought, 'He won't answer, and I don't care, because I don't want to have to move again.' But at half-past seven Mrs Dawes brought up a telegram from him: 'Meet me tonight Central Hotel Marylebone Road 9.30 Walter.'

9

I dressed very carefully. I didn't think of anything while I dressed. I put on my black velvet dress and made up a bit with rather more rouge than usual and when I looked in the glass I thought, 'He won't be able to, he won't be able to.' There was a lump in my throat. I kept swallowing it, but it came back again.

It was pouring with rain. Mrs Dawes was in the hall.

'You'll get wet,' she said. 'I'll send Willie as far as the Tube station to get a taxi for you.'

'Thank you,' I said.

There was a chair in the hall and I sat there and waited.

Willie was gone a long time and Mrs Dawes began to click her tongue and mutter, 'The poor boy — out in the pouring rain. Some people give a lot of trouble.'

I sat there. I had a shrunken feeling just like having fever. I thought, 'When you have fever your feet burn like fire but your hands are clammy.'

Then the taxi came; and the houses on either side of the street were small and dark and then they were big and dark but all exactly alike. And I saw that all my life I had known that this was going to happen, and that I'd been afraid for a long time, I'd been afraid for a long time. There's fear, of course, with everybody. But now it had grown, it had grown gigantic; it filled me and it filled the whole world.

I was thinking, 'I ought to have given Willie a bob. I know Mrs Dawes was annoyed because I didn't give him a bob. It was just that I didn't think of it. Tomorrow some time I must get hold of him and give him a bob.'

Then the taxi got into Marylebone Road and I remembered that once I had been to a flat in Marylebone Road and there were three flights of stairs and then a small room and it smelt musty. The room had smelt musty and through the glass of a window that wouldn't open you saw dark green trees.

The taxi stopped and I got down and paid the man and went into the hotel.

He was waiting for me.

I smiled and said, 'Hullo.'

He had been looking very solemn but when I smiled like that he seemed relieved.

We went and sat in a corner.

I said, 'I'll have coffee.'

I imagined myself saying, very calmly, 'The thing is that you don't understand. You think I want more than I do. I only want to see you sometimes, but if I never see you again I'll die. I'm dying now really, and I'm too young to die.'

... The candles crying wax tears and the smell of stephanotis and I had to go to the funeral in a white dress and white gloves and a wreath round my head and the wreath in my hands made my gloves wet — they said so young to die . . .

The people there were like upholstered ghosts.

I said, 'That letter I had from Vincent —'

'I knew he was writing,' he said, twisting his head a bit.

'You asked him to write?'

'Yes, I asked him to write.'

When he talked his eyes went away from mine and then he forced himself to look straight at me and he began to explain and I knew that he felt very strange with me and that he hated me, and it was funny sitting there and talking like that, knowing he hated me.

I said, 'All right. Listen, will you do something for me?'

'Of course,' he said. 'Anything. Anything you ask.'

I said, 'Well, will you get a taxi, please, and let's go back to your place, because I want to talk to you and I can't here.' I thought, 'I'll hang on to your knees and make you understand and then you won't be able to, you won't be able to.'

He said, 'Why do you ask me the one thing you know perfectly well I won't do?'

I didn't answer. I was thinking, 'You don't know anything about me. I don't care any more.' And I didn't care any more.

It was like letting go and falling back into water and seeing yourself grinning up through the water, your face like a mask, and seeing the bubbles coming up as if you were trying to speak from under the water. And how do you know what it's like to try to speak from under water when you're drowned? 'And I've met a lot of them who were monkeys too,' he said. . . .

Walter was saying, 'I'm horribly worried about you. I want you to let Vincent come and see you and arrange things. I've talked it over with him and we've arranged things.'

I said, 'I don't want to see Vincent.'

'But why?' he said.

'I've talked it over with him,' he said. 'He knows how I feel about you.'

I said, 'I hate Vincent.'

He said, 'But, my dear, you don't imagine, do you, that Vincent's had anything to do with this?'

'He had,' I said, 'he had. D'you think I don't know he's been trying to put you against me ever since he saw me? D'you think I don't know?'

He said, 'It's a damned poor compliment to me if you think I'd let Vincent or anybody else interfere with me.'

'As a matter of fact,' he said, 'Vincent's hardly ever spoken about you. Except that he said once he thought you were very young and didn't quite know your way about and that it was a bit of a shame.'

I said, 'I know the sort of things he says; I can hear him saying them. D'you think I don't know?'

He said, 'I can't stand any more of this.'

'All right,' I said, 'let's go.'

I got up and we went out.

I got a taxi outside the hotel. I felt all right except that I was tired and I couldn't sit up straight. When he said, 'O God, look what I've done,' I wanted to laugh.

'I don't know what you mean,' I said. 'You haven't done anything.'

He said, 'You've got hold of absolutely the wrong end of the stick about Vincent. He's awfully fond of you and he wants to help you.'

I looked through the taxi-window and said, 'Hell to your beloved Vincent. Tell him to keep his bloody help. I don't want it.'

He looked shocked, like that waiter when he said, 'Corked, sir?'

He said, 'I shouldn't wonder if I got ill with all this worry.'

When Mrs Dawes came in with breakfast I was lying on the bed with all my clothes on. I hadn't even taken off my shoes. She didn't say anything, she didn't look surprised, and when she looked at me I knew she was thinking, 'There you are. I always knew this would happen.' I imagined I saw her smile as she turned away.

I said, 'I'm leaving today. I'm sorry. I've had bad news. Will you let me have my bill?'

'Yes, Miss Morgan,' she said, her face long and placid. 'Yes, Miss Morgan.'

'Will you give Willie this five bob?' I said. 'Because he was always getting taxis for me.'

'Yes, Miss Morgan,' she said, 'I will, certainly.'

'I'll come back for my luggage in an hour or two,' I said.

I had fifteen pounds left after I had paid Mrs Dawes. I wrote a letter to Walter and asked her to post it:

Dear Walter,

Don't write here because I'm leaving. I'll let you know my new address.

Yours,
Anna.

I got out into the street. A man passed. I thought he looked at me funnily and I wanted to run, but I stopped myself.

I walked straight ahead. I thought, 'Anywhere will do, so long as it's somewhere that nobody knows.'

PART TWO

1

There were two slices of dark meat on one plate, two potatoes and some cabbage. On the other plate a slice of bread and a lemon-cheese tart.

'I've brought you up the bottle of vermouth and the siphon you asked for,' the landlady said. This one had bulging eyes, dark blobs in a long, pink face, like a prawn. 'Well, you do write a lot of letters, don't you?' 'Yes,' I said. I put my hand over the sheet of paper I was writing on. 'Work quite 'ard, you do.' I didn't answer and she stood there for a bit, looking at me. 'Do you feel better today?' she said. 'You've 'ad influenza, p'raps?' 'Yes,' I said.

She went out. She was exactly like our landlady at Eastbourne. Was it Eastbourne? And the shapes of the slices of meat were the same, and the way the cabbage was heaped was the same, and all the houses outside in the street were the same — all alike, all hideously stuck together — and the streets going north, east, south, west, all exactly the same.

I wasn't hungry but I poured out a glass of vermouth and drank it without soda and went on writing. There were sheets of paper spread all over the bed.

After a while I crossed out everything and began again, writing very quickly, like you do when you write: 'You can't possibly do this you simply don't know what you're doing if I were a dog you wouldn't do this I love you I love you I love you but you're just a god-damned rotter everybody is everybody is everybody is — My dear Walter I've read books about this and I know quite well what you're thinking but you're quite wrong because don't you remember you used to joke because every time you put your hand on my heart it used to jump well you can't pretend that can you you can pretend everything else but not that it's the only thing you can't pretend I do want to ask you one thing I'd like to see you just once more listen it needn't be for very long it need only be for an hour well not an hour then half an hour . . .' And going on like that, and the sheets of paper all over the bed.

The water-jug was broken. I thought, 'I bet she'll say I did that and want me to pay for it.'

The room was at the back of the house, so there were no street noises to listen to, but you could sometimes hear cats fighting or making love, and in the morning voices in the passage outside: 'She says she's ill. . . . What's the matter with 'er? . . . She says she's 'ad flu . . . She says . . .'

I kept the curtains drawn all the time. The window was like a trap. If you wanted to open or shut it you had to call in somebody to help you. The mantelshelf was crowded with china ornaments — several dogs of various breeds, a pig, a swan, a geisha with a kimono and sash in colours and a little naked woman lying on her stomach with a feather in her hair.

After a while I started to sing:

'Blow rings, rings
  Delicate rings in the air;
And drift, drift
  — something — away from despair.'

That was a turn I had seen in a music-hall in Glasgow, where I had got in for a matinée on my card. The singer was a plump girl with very curly pale-gold hair but underneath it she had a long, stupid face. She went down very well.

'And drift, drift
  Legions away from despair.'

It can't be 'legions'. 'Oceans', perhaps. 'Oceans away from despair.' But it's the sea, I thought. The Caribbean Sea. 'The Caribs indigenous to this island were a warlike tribe and their resistance to white domination, though spasmodic, was fierce. As lately as the beginning of the nineteenth century they raided one of the neighbouring islands, under British rule, overpowered the garrison and kidnapped the governor, his wife and three children. They are now practically exterminated. The few hundreds that are left do not intermarry with the negroes. Their reservation, at the northern end of the island, is known as the Carib Quarter.' They had, or used to have, a king. Mopo, his name was. Here's to Mopo, King of the Caribs! But, they are now practically exterminated. 'Oceans away from despair. . . .'

I ate the lemon-cheese tart and began the song all over again. Somebody knocked at the door. I called out, 'Come in.'

It was the woman who had the room on the floor above. She was short and fat. She was wearing a white silk blouse and a dark skirt with stains on it and black stockings and patent-leather shoes and a dirty chemise which showed above her blouse. She had a long face and a long body and short legs, like they say the female should have. (And if she has hell to her because she's a female, and if she hasn't hell to her too, because she's probably not.) She had deep rings under her eyes and her hair looked dusty. She was about forty, but she moved about in a very spry way. She looked just like most other people, which is a big advantage. An ant, just like all the other ants; not the sort of ant that has too long a head or a deformed body or anything like that. She was like all women whom you look at and don't notice except that she had such short legs and that her hair was so dusty.

'Hullo,' she said. 'You don't mind me popping in, do you? Mrs Flower told me there was an ill young lady in this room. Do you feel bad?' she said, looking inquisitive. 'No, I'm all right. I'm better. I've had influenza,' I said. 'Let me put your tray outside. They'll leave it here till midnight. Sloppy, that's what they are. I'm a trained nurse and it gets on my nerves — all this sloppiness.'

She took the tray out and came back.

I said, 'Thank you very much. I'm all right really. I'm just going to get up.'

Then I said, 'No, don't go. Please stay.' Because after all she was a human being.

I got up and dressed, and she sat near the fire with her skirt pulled up and her short, plump, well-shaped legs exposed to the flames, and watched. Her eyes were cleverer than the rest of her. When she half-shut them you saw that she knew she had her own cunning, which would always save her, which was sufficient to her. Feelers grow when feelers are needed and claws when claws are needed and cunning when cunning is needed. . . .

I took all the sheets of paper off the bed and burnt them.

'You know, sometimes you can't get a letter written,' I said. 'I hate letters,' the woman said. 'I hate writing them and I hate getting them. If I don't see people I can't be bothered. My God, that's a lovely fur coat you have there, isn't it? . . . It's an awful day. If you've been ill and are going for a walk, really this isn't the day for it. Come along with me to the cinema in the Camden Town High Street, it's only a couple of minutes' walk. I know one of the girls in the crowd in the film that's on there. I want to see what she looks like.' She was staring at my coat all the time.

'My name's Matthews,' she said. 'Ethel Matthews.'

Just as we went into the cinema the lights went out and the screen flashed, 'Three-Fingered Kate, Episode 5. Lady Chichester's Necklace.'

The piano began to play, sickly-sweet. Never again, never, not ever, never. Through caverns measureless to man down to a sunless sea. . . .

The cinema smelt of poor people, and on the screen ladies and gentlemen in evening dress walked about with strained smiles.

'There!' Ethel said, nudging. 'D'you see that girl — the one with the band round her hair? That's the one I know; that's my friend. Do you see? My God, isn't she terrible? My God, what a scream!'

'Oh, shut up,' somebody said. 'Shut up yourself,' Ethel said.

I opened my eyes. On the screen a pretty girl was pointing a revolver at a group of guests. They backed away with their arms held high above their heads and expressions of terror on their faces. The pretty girl's lips moved. The fat hostess unclasped a necklace of huge pearls and fell, fainting, into the arms of a footman. The pretty girl, holding the revolver so that the audience could see that two of her fingers were missing, walked backwards towards the door. Her lips moved again. You could see what she was saying. 'Keep 'em up. . . .' When the police appeared everybody clapped. When Three-Fingered Kate was caught everybody clapped louder still.

'Damned fools,' I said. 'Aren't they damned fools? Don't you hate them? They always clap in the wrong places and laugh in the wrong places.'

'Three-Fingered Kate, Episode 6,' the screen said. 'Five Years Hard. Next Monday.' Then there was a long Italian film about the Empress Theodora, called 'The Dancer-Empress'. When it was finished I said, 'Let's go out. I don't want to stay any longer, do you?'

It was six o'clock, and when we got into Camden Town High Street it was quite dark. 'Not that there's much difference between the day and the night here, anyway,' I thought. The rain had stopped. The pavement looked as if it was covered with black grease.

Ethel said, 'Did you see that girl — the one who was doing Three-Fingered Kate? Did you notice her hair? I mean, did you notice the curls she had on at the back?'

I was thinking, 'I'm nineteen and I've got to go on living and living and living.'

'Well,' she said, 'that girl who did Three-Fingered Kate was a foreigner. My friend who was working in the crowd told me about it. Couldn't they have got an English girl to do it?' 'Was she?' I said. 'Yes. Couldn't they have got an English girl to do it? It was just because she had this soft, dirty way that foreign girls have. And she stuck red curls on her black hair and she didn't care a scrap. Her own hair was short and black, don't you see? and she simply went and stuck red curls on. An English girl wouldn't have done that. Everybody was laughing at her behind her back, my friend said.' 'I didn't notice,' I said. 'I thought she was very pretty.' 'The thing is that red photographs black, d'you see? All the same, everybody was laughing at her behind her back all the time. Well, an English girl wouldn't have done that. An English girl would have respected herself more than to let people laugh at her like that behind her back.'

She got out her latchkey and said, 'Come on up to my room for a bit.'

Her room was exactly like mine except that the wall-paper was green instead of brown. She put some coal on the fire and sat down and pulled up her skirt. Her feet too were short and fat.

She said, 'Look here, kid, what's the matter with you? Are you in trouble? Are you going to have a baby or something? Because if you are you might as well tell me about it and I might be able to help you. You never know. Well, are you?'

'No,' I said, 'I'm not going to have a baby. What an idea!'

'What's the matter with you then?' Ethel said. 'What do you want to look so miserable about?'

'I'm not miserable,' I said. 'I'm all right, only I'd like a drink.'

Ethel said, 'If that's all you want . . .'

She went to the cupboard and got out a gin-bottle and two glasses and poured out two drinks. I didn't touch mine, because the smell of gin always made me sick and because my eyeballs felt so big inside my head, and turning round like wheels. Who said, 'Oh Lord, let me see?' I would rather say, 'Oh Lord, keep me blind.'

'I hate men,' Ethel said. 'Men are devils, aren't they? But of course I don't really care a damn about them. Why should I? I can earn my own living. I'm a masseuse — I'm a Swedish masseuse. And, mind you, when I say I'm a masseuse I don't mean like some of these dirty foreigners. Don't you hate foreigners?'

'Well,' I said, 'I don't think I do; but, you see, I don't know many.'

'What?' Ethel said, looking surprised and suspicious, 'you don't hate them?'

She drank a little more. 'Well, of course, I know some girls like them. I knew a girl who was crazy about an Italian and she used to rave about him. She said he made her feel important when he made love to her. I ask you! And you should have heard her — it was too damned funny. Is your boy a foreigner?'

'No,' I said. 'Oh no. No.'

'Well,' Ethel said, 'don't go on looking like that — as if, as they say, Gawd 'ates yer and yer eyes don't fit.'

'That's like Maudie,' I said. 'My pal on tour. She used to say, "I feel as if God hates me and my eyes don't fit." '

'Oh, I see,' Ethel said, 'you're on the stage, are you?'

'A long time ago,' I said.

She said, 'Well, anyway, that's a wonderful coat you have.'

She felt my coat. Her little hands, with short, thick fingers, felt it; and he . . . 'Now perhaps you won't shiver so much,' he said.

'I bet you if you took that coat to Attenborough's they'd give you twenty-five quid on it. Well, perhaps they wouldn't give you twenty-five, but I bet they'd give you twenty. And that means it's worth . . .'

She began to giggle. 'People are such damned fools,' she said. 'I can't think why you stay in a room in Camden Town when you've got a coat like that.'

I drank the gin and almost as soon as I'd drunk it everything began to seem rather comical.

'Well, what are you here for then,' I said, 'if you think it's as awful as all that?'

'Oh, I don't need to be here,' she said haughtily. 'I've got a flat. I've got a flat in Bird Street. You know — just off Oxford Street, at the back of Selfridges'. I'm simply here while it's being done up.'

'Well, I don't need to be here either,' I said. 'I can get as much money as I like any time I like.' I stretched, and watched my swollen shadow on the wall stretching too.

She said, 'Well, I should say so — a lovely girl like you. And well under twenty, I should say. I've got a spare bedroom in my flat. Why don't you come along and live with me for a bit? I'm looking for somebody to share with me. As a matter of fact I'd almost fixed it up with a pal of mine. She'll put in twenty-five pounds and do the manicure and we'll start a little business.'

'Oh yes?' I said.

'Well, just between ourselves, I shan't mind if I don't fix it up with her. She's a bit of a Nosey Parker. Why don't you think it over? I've got a lovely spare room.'

'But I haven't got twenty-five pounds,' I said.

She said, 'You could get twenty pounds on that coat any day.'

'I don't want to sell my coat,' I said. 'And I don't know how to manicure.'

'Oh well, that's all right. I don't want to try to persuade you. Only come along and have a look at the room. I'm leaving tomorrow. I'll pop in and give you the address before I go.'

I said, 'I'm feeling a bit sleepy. I think I'll go along to my room. Good night.'

'Good night,' Ethel said. She started rubbing her ankles. 'I'll pop in and see you tomorrow if you don't mind.'

I got down to my room and there was some bread and cheese on a tray and a glass of milk. I felt very tired. I looked at the bed and thought, 'There's one thing — I do sleep. I sleep as if I were dead.'

It's funny when you feel as if you don't want anything more in your life except to sleep, or else to lie without moving. That's when you can hear time sliding past you, like water running.

2

Mrs Flower said, 'Would you mind, miss, coming and sitting downstairs, because we want to turn the room out properly.'

'All right,' I said. 'I'm going out this afternoon.'

I got up and dressed and took the Tube to Tottenham Court Road and went along Oxford Street. As I was passing the Richelieu Hotel a girl in a squirrel coat came out. Two men were with her.

'Hullo,' she said. I looked at her and said, 'Hullo, Laurie?'

'Just bumming around, Anna?' she said in a voice that was as hoarse as a crow's.

She introduced me to the two men. They were Americans. The big one was Carl — Carl Redman — and the other one's name was Adler. Joe, she called him. He was the younger, and very Jewish-looking. You would have known he was a Jew wherever you saw him, but I wasn't sure about Carl.

'Where have you sprung from?' Laurie said. 'Come along up to my flat and have a drink. I live just round the corner in Berners Street.'

'No,' I said, 'I can't today, Laurie.' I didn't want to talk to anybody. I felt too much like a ghost.

'Oh, come on,' she said. She took hold of my arm.

Carl said, 'Well, don't try to kidnap the girl, Laurie. If she doesn't want to come, leave her alone.' He had a calm way of talking, as if he were very sure of himself.

As soon as he said that I changed my mind. 'All right,' I said. 'I wasn't going anywhere in particular. Only I've been ill and I still feel a bit seedy.'

'This kid was with me last year in a show,' Laurie said. She began to laugh. 'My Lord, that was a show, too, wasn't it? I didn't go back with it, you know. There's nothing like that about me. I got a job in town, only the thing didn't run very long.'

Her flat was about half-way along Berners Street, on the second floor. We went upstairs into the sitting-room. There was a table covered with a red cloth in the middle, and a sofa, and flowered wall-paper. The whole place smelt of her scent.

She got whiskies-and-sodas for everybody. Carl and Joe were easy to talk to. You didn't feel they were getting ready to sneer at you behind your back, as you do with some men.

After a bit Carl said, 'At a quarter to nine tonight, then. Will you bring your friend along too?'

'Would you like to come, Anna?' Laurie said.

'Do come along if you'd like to,' Carl said. . . .

'They're both staying at the Carlton,' Laurie told me. 'I met them in Frankfort. And I went to Paris too. My dear, I've been getting about a bit, I can tell you.'

She had hennaed her hair. It was cut short with a thick fringe. It suited her. But she had too much blue on her eyelids. Too much 'Overture and Beginners', I thought. She went on about how lucky she had been and what a lot of men with money she knew and what a good time she was having.

'D'you know,' she said, 'I never pay for a meal for myself — it's the rarest thing. For instance, these two — I said to them quite casually, like that, "When you come over to London, let me know. I'll show you round a bit," and if you please about three weeks ago they turned up. I've been showing them round, I can tell you. . . . I get along with men. I can do what I like with them. Sometimes I'm surprised myself. I expect it's because they feel I really like it and no kidding. But what's the matter with you? You don't look well. Why don't you finish your drink?'

I finished it, and then I found I was crying.

'What's up?' Laurie said. 'Come on, never say die.'

After a bit I said, 'There was a man I was mad about. He got sick of me and chucked me. I wish I were dead.'

'Are you going to have a baby or something?' she said.

'Oh, no.'

'Did he give you any money?'

'Of course he did,' I said, 'and I can get more any time I write to him. I'm going to write to him quite soon about it.' I said that because I didn't want to seem a fool and as if I had been utterly done in.

'Well,' Laurie said, 'I shouldn't wait too long if I were you — not too long. However, if it's like that it's not so bad. It might have been much worse.'

I said, 'It was when I wasn't expecting it to happen, you see — just when I wasn't expecting it. He went away and I worried like anything. But then he wrote to me. About how fond he was of me and so on and how much he wanted to see me, and I thought it was all right. And it wasn't.'

'It's always like that,' she said, looking down at the table. 'They always do it that way. Search me what the whole thing's about. When you start thinking about things the answer's a lemon. A lemon, that's what the answer is. . . . But it's no use worrying. Why worry about a man who's well in bed with somebody else by this time? It's soppy. Think of it like that.'

She had another whisky and went on about being clever and putting money away, and her voice joined in with the smell of the room. 'There are all sorts of lives,' I thought.

'I bank half of everything I get,' she said. 'Even if I have to do without, I still bank half of everything I get, and there's no friend like that. . . . Never mind, you're a good little cow; you'll be all right. Come along and have a look at the flat.'

Her bedroom was small and very tidy. There were no photographs and no pictures. There was a huge bed and a long plait of hair on the dressing-table.

'I kept that,' she said. 'I pin it on sometimes when I wear nightgowns. Of course, in pyjamas I keep my own short hair. Why don't you cut your hair? You ought; it would suit you. Heaps of girls in Paris have their hair cut, and I bet they will here too sooner or later. And false eyelashes, my dear, sticking out yards — you should see them. They know what's what, I tell you. Are you coming tonight? Would you like to? I'm sure you'll go well with Carl because you look awfully young and he likes girls that look young. But he's a funny cuss. He only cares about gambling really. He's found a place in Clarges Street. He took me the other day — I won nearly twenty quid. He's got a business in Buenos Aires. Joe's his secretary.'

I said, 'I can't come in this dress. It's torn under the arm and awfully creased. Haven't you noticed? That's why I kept my coat on. I tore it like that last time I took it off.' It was my black velvet dress that I had on.

'I'll lend you a dress,' she said.

She sat down on the bed and yawned. 'Well, give us a kiss. I'm going to lie down for a bit. There's a gas-fire in the other bedroom if you'd like to go and have a rest.'

'I'd like a bath,' I said. 'Could I?'

'Ma,' she yelled out, 'turn on a bath for Miss Morgan.'

Nobody answered.

'Now, what's she up to?'

We went into the kitchen. And old woman was sitting by the table, asleep, with her head in her arms.

'She's always doing this,' Laurie said. 'She's always going to sleep on me. I'd fire the old sod tomorrow only I know she'd never get another job.' She touched the old woman's shoulder gently. 'Go on, Ma, wake up. Turn a bath on and get some tea. And hurry for once in your life, for God's sake.'

The window of the bathroom was open and the soft, damp air from outside blew in on my face. There was a white bath-wrap on the chair. I put it on afterwards and went and lay down and the old woman brought me in some tea. I felt emptied-out and peaceful — like when you've had toothache and it stops for a bit, and you know quite well it's going to start again but just for a bit it's stopped.

3

We met Carl and Joe at Oddenino's. Melville Gideon was at the piano; he was singing rather well.

Carl talked to the waiter for a long time about what we were going to eat before he ordered it. We had Château Yquem to drink.

By the time we had finished dinner and were having liqueurs Laurie seemed a bit tight.

She said, 'Well, Carl, what do you think of my little pal? Don't you think I've found a nice girl for you?'

'A peach,' Carl said in a polite voice.

'I don't like the way English girls dress,' Joe said. 'American girls dress differently. I like their way of dressing better.'

' 'Ere, 'ere,' Laurie said, 'that'll do. Besides, she's got on one of my dresses if you want to know.'

'Ah,' Carl said, 'that's another story then.'

'Don't you like the dress, Carl, what's wrong with it?'

'Oh, I don't know,' Carl said. 'Anyway it doesn't matter so much.'

He put his hand on mine and smiled. He had very nice teeth. His nose looked as if it had been broken some time.

'Look out, you bloody fool, don't spill it,' Laurie said in a loud voice to the waiter, who was pouring out another liqueur for her.

Joe stopped talking and looked embarrassed.

'And the bill,' Carl said.

'Yes, l'addition, l'addition,' Laurie called out. 'I know a bit of every language in Europe — even Polish. Shall I say my bit of Polish?'

'The woman at the next table's looking at you in a very funny way,' Joe said.

'Well, the woman!' Laurie said. 'She's looking at me. Look, pretty creature, look! And she is a pretty creature too, isn't she? My God, she's got a face like an old hen's. I'll say my bit of Polish to her in a minute.'

'No, don't do that, Laurie,' Carl said.

'Well, why shouldn't I?' Laurie said. 'What right has a woman with a face like a hen's — and like a hen's behind too — to look at me like that?'

Joe started to laugh. He said, 'Oh, women. How you love each other, don't you?'

'Well, that's an original remark,' Carl said. 'We're all being very original.'

'Don't you ever talk at all?' he said to me. 'What do you think about the lady at the next table? She certainly doesn't look as if she loves us.'

I said, 'I think she's terrifying,' and they all laughed.

But I was thinking that it was terrifying — the way they look at you. So that you know that they would see you burnt alive without even turning their heads away; so that you know in yourself that they would watch you burning without even blinking once. Their glassy eyes that don't admit anything so definite as hate. Only just that underground hope that you'll be burnt alive, tortured, where they can have a peep. And slowly, slowly you feel the hate back starting. . . .

'Terrifying?' Laurie said. 'She doesn't terrify me. I'm not so easily terrified. I've got good strong peasant blood in me.'

'That's the first time I've heard an English girl boast about having peasant blood,' Joe said. 'They try to tell you they're descended from William the Conqueror or whatever his name was, as a rule.'

'There's only one Laurie,' Carl said.

'That's right,' Laurie said, 'and when I die there won't be another.'

I kept wondering whether I should be able to walk without staggering when we got up. 'You must seem all right,' I kept telling myself.

We got out of the restaurant.

I said, 'Just a minute.'

'It's through those curtains,' Laurie said.

I stayed a long time in the ladies' room. There was a chair and I sat down. The tune of the Robert E. Lee was going in my head.

After a while the woman said, 'Aren't you feeling well, miss?'

'Oh yes,' I said. 'I'm quite well, thank you.' I put a shilling into the plate on the table and went out.

'We thought you'd got drowned,' Laurie said.

In the taxi I asked, 'Did I seem drunk as we came out?'

'Of course you didn't,' Joe said. He was sitting between Laurie and myself, holding both our hands.

'But where's Carl?' I said.

Laurie said, 'Echo answers Where?'

'Carl asked me to say good night for him to you and to excuse him to you,' Joe said. 'But he had a very urgent telephone message. He's had to go back to the hotel.'

'Back to the hotel my eye,' Laurie said. 'I know where he's gone. He's gone to Clarges Street. I think it's too bad of him to walk off like that. It really is a bit rude.'

'Oh well, you know how Carl is,' Joe said. 'Besides, you've got me. What are you grumbling about?'

4

'Is this right?' Joe said. We got out of the taxi. Laurie put her arm through mine and we went into the hotel. There was a smell of cooking and RITZ-PLAZA in black letters on a dusty doormat.

A fat man came up. Joe spoke to him in German. He said something and then the man said something.

Joe said, 'He won't let us have one room, so I've taken two.'

'This way, please,' the man said.

We followed him upstairs into the big bedroom. It had dark-brown wallpaper and the fire was laid. The man took a box of matches out of his pocket and lit it.

The mantelpiece was very high and painted black. There were two huge dark-blue vases on it and a clock, stopped at ten minutes past three.

'My God,' Joe said, 'this place is kind of gloomy.'

'Lugubrious,' Laurie said. 'That's the word you mean — lugubrious. It's all right. It'll look different when the fire burns up.'

'What a lot of long words she knows, doesn't she?' Joe said.

'Long words is my middle name,' Laurie said.

The man was still standing there, smiling.

'What'll you have to drink, Laurie?' Joe said.

'Just whisky-and-soda for me,' Laurie said. 'I'm going to stick to whisky-and-soda for the rest of the evening and not too much of it either.'

'Let's have a bottle of Black and White,' Joe said, 'and some soda.'

The man went out.

'It's bare,' Joe said. 'You don't go in for frills in this burg, do you?' He went on, talking about barbers' shops in London. He said they weren't comfortable, that they didn't know how to make you comfortable.

The man knocked at the door and brought in the whisky.

'Oh, go on,' Laurie said. 'London's not so bad. It has a certain gloomy charm when you get used to it, as a man I know said.'

'He's right about the gloom,' Joe said.

Laurie began to sing *Moonlight Bay*.

> *'You have stolen my heart,*
> *So don't go away.'*

I said, 'I'll have a whisky-and-soda. Why are you leaving me out?'

I drank half the glass and then I felt very giddy. I said, 'I'm going to lie down. I feel so damned giddy.'

I lay down. As long as I kept my eyes open it wasn't so bad.

Laurie said, 'You ought to take that dress off then. You're creasing it all up.'

'That would be a pity,' I said.

It was a pink dress, with silver bits and pieces dangling here and there.

She came over and helped me to undo it. She seemed very tall and her face enormous. I could see all the lines in it, and the powder, trying to fill up the lines, and just where her lipstick stopped and her lips began. It looked like a clown's face, so that I wanted to laugh at it. She was pretty, but her hands were short and fat with wide, flat, very red nails.

Joe lit a cigarette and crossed his legs and watched us. He was like somebody sitting in the stalls, waiting for the curtain to go up. When it was all over he was ready to clap and say, 'That was well done,' or to hiss and say, 'That was badly done' — as the case might be.

'I feel awfully sick,' I said. 'I must keep still for a bit.'

'Oh, don't go and be sick,' Laurie said. 'Pull yourself to pieces.'

'Well, just a minute,' I said.

I felt very cold. I pulled the eiderdown over my shoulders and shut my eyes. The bed sank under me. I opened them again.

They were sitting near the fire, laughing. Their black shadows on the wall were laughing too.

'How old is she?' Joe said.

'She's only a kid,' Laurie said. She coughed and then she said, 'She's not seventeen.'

'Yes — and the rest,' Joe said.

'Well, she's not a day older than nineteen, anyway,' Laurie said. 'Where do you see the wrinkles? Don't you like her?'

'She's all right,' Joe said, 'but I liked that other kid — the dark one.'

'Who? Renée?' Laurie said. 'I don't know what's happened to her. I haven't seen her since that evening.'

Joe came over to the bed. He took hold of my hand and stroked it.

I said, 'I know what you're going to say. You're going to say it's cold and clammy. Well, it's because I was born in the West Indies and I'm always like that.'

'Oh, were you?' Joe said. He sat on the bed. 'I know, I know. Trinidad, Cuba, Jamaica — why, I've spent years there.' He winked at Laurie.

'No,' I said, 'a little one.'

'But I know the little ones too,' Joe said. 'The little ones, the big ones, the whole lot.'

'Oh, do you?' I said, sitting up.

'Yes, of course I do,' Joe said. He winked at Laurie again. 'Why, I knew your father — a great pal of mine. Old Taffy Morgan. He was a fine old boy, and didn't he lift the elbow too.'

'You're a liar,' I said. 'You didn't know my father. Because my real name isn't Morgan and I'll never tell you my real name and I was born in Manchester and I'll never tell you anything real about myself. Everything that I tell you about myself is a lie, so now then.'

He said, 'Well, wasn't his name Taffy? Was it Patrick, perhaps?'

'Oh, go to hell,' I said. 'And get off this bed. You get on my nerves.'

'Hey,' Laurie said, 'what's the matter with you? Are you tight, or what?'

'I was only joking,' Joe said. 'I didn't mean to hurt your feelings, kid.'

I got out of bed. I was still very giddy.

'Well,' Laurie said, 'what's the matter now?'

'You both get on my nerves, if you want to know,' I said. 'If you could see yourselves when you're laughing you wouldn't laugh so much.'

'You're damned good company, aren't you?' Laurie said. 'What d'you want to ask me to take you out for, if you're going to behave like this?'

I said, 'Well, where's my dress? I'm going home. I'm sick of your damned party.'

'I like that,' Laurie said. 'If you think you're going to walk off with my clothes you've got another guess coming.'

The dress was hanging over the end of the bed. I took hold of it, but she hung on to it. We both pulled. Joe started to laugh.

'If you tear my dress,' Laurie said, 'I'll knock your block off.'

I said, 'Try it. Just try it. And you'll get the surprise of your life.'

'Oh, leave her alone, Laurie. She's drunk,' Joe said. 'You lie down and go to sleep, kid. You'll feel better tomorrow morning. Nobody's going to trouble you.'

'I won't lie down in here,' I said.

'All right,' Joe said, making a movement with his chin. 'There's a room opposite — just opposite. You go in there.'

Laurie didn't say anything. She kept the dress over her arm.

Joe got up and opened the door. He said, 'There you are — the room just opposite, see.'

'And try not to be sick on the floor,' Laurie said. 'There's a lavatory at the end of the passage.'

'Oh, one word to you,' I said.

'And the same to you and many of them,' she said in a mechanical voice. Like the kids at home when they used to answer questions in the catechism. 'Who made you?' 'God made me.' 'Why did God make you?' And so on.

The other room was much smaller. There was no fire. There was no key in the lock. I lay down.

There were only a sheet and a thin counterpane on the bed. It was as cold as being in the street.

I thought, 'Well, what a night! My God, what an idiotic night!'

There was a spot on the ceiling. I looked at it and it became two spots. The two spots moved very rapidly, one away from the other. When they were about six inches apart they remained stationary and grew larger. Two black eyes were staring at me. I stared back at them. Then I had to blink and the whole business began all over again.

There was Joe by the bed, saying, 'Don't be mad with me. I was only teasing you.'

'I'm not,' I said, but when he began to kiss me I said, 'No, don't.'

'Why not?' he said.

'Some other night,' I said. 'Ça sera pour un autre soir.' (A girl in a book said that. Some girl in some book. Ça sera pour un autre soir.)

He didn't say anything for a bit and then he said, 'Why do you go around with Laurie? Don't you know she's a tart?'

'Well,' I said, 'why shouldn't she be a tart? It's just as good as anything else, as far as I can see.'

'I don't get you,' he said. 'You're quaint, as they say over here.'

'Oh God,' I said, 'do leave me alone, do leave me alone.'

Something came out from my heart into my throat and then into my eyes.

Joe said, 'Don't do that, don't cry. D'you know, kid, I like you. I thought I didn't, but I do. I'd better go and get something to put over you. This room's as cold as hell.'

'Is Laurie vexed?' I said.

'She'll get over it,' he said.

I opened my eyes, and he was putting an eiderdown over me, and my coat. I went to sleep again.

Somebody knocked at the door. I got up and there was a can of hot water outside. I poured it into the basin and started washing my face. While I was washing Laurie walked in with the dress over her arm.

She said, 'Come on, let's get out of this.'

I put the dress on. I looked pretty awful, I thought.

'Where's Joe?' I said.

'He's gone,' Laurie said. 'He left half-an-hour ago. What did you imagine — that he'd walk out arm in arm with us? He asked me to say good-bye to you. Come on.'

I was thinking, 'Well, what a night! My God, what a night!'

We got into the street. All the houses seemed to be hotels. The Bellevue, the Welcome, the Cornwall, the Sandringham, the Berkeley, the Waverley. . . . All the way up. And, of course, spiked railings. It was a fine day. The mist was blue instead of grey.

A policeman standing near by stared at us. He was a big man with a small, rosy face. His helmet seemed enormous on the top of his small face.

I said, 'I shall have to come back with you to get my dress. I'm sorry.'

'Well, I didn't say you couldn't, did I?' Laurie said.

She stopped a taxi. When it had started she said, 'Swine!'

'D'you mean me?' I said.

She said, 'Don't be a fool. I meant the bloody bobby.'

'Oh, I thought you meant me.'

'What you do doesn't concern me,' Laurie said. 'I think you're a bit of a fool, that's all. And I think you'll never get on, because you don't know how to take people. After all, to say you'll come out with somebody and then to get tight and start a row about nothing at all isn't a way to behave. And besides, you always look half-asleep and people don't like that. But it's not my business.'

We got to Berners Street and went upstairs. The old woman came to the door to meet us.

'Shall I get breakfast, miss?'

'Yes,' Laurie said, 'and turn a bath on, and hurry up.'

I stood in the passage. She went into the bedroom and brought my dress out.

'Here's your dress,' she said. 'And for God's sake don't look like that. Come on and have something to eat.'

She kissed me all of a sudden.

'Oh, come on,' she said. 'I'm a good old cow really. You know I'm fond of you. To tell you the truth I was a bit screwed last night too. You can pretend to be a virgin for the rest of your life as far as I'm concerned; I don't care. What's it got to do with me?'

'Don't start a speech,' she said, 'I've got a splitting headache. Have a heart.'

It was the first fine day for weeks. The old woman spread a white cloth on the table in the sitting-room and the sun shone in on it. Then she went into the kitchen and started to fry bacon. There was the smell of the bacon and the sound of the water running into the bath. And nothing else. My head felt empty.

5

It was four o'clock when I left the flat. I walked along Oxford Street, thinking about my room in Camden Town and that I didn't want to go back to it. There was a black velvet dress in a shop-window, with the skirt slit up so that you could see the light stocking. A girl could look lovely in that, like a doll or a flower. Another dress, with fur round the neck, reminded me of the one that Laurie had worn. Her neck coming out of the fur was a pale-gold colour, very slim and strong-looking.

The clothes of most of the women who passed were like caricatures of the clothes in the shop-windows, but when they stopped to look you saw that their eyes were fixed on the future. 'If I could buy this, then of course I'd be quite different.' Keep hope alive and you can do anything, and that's the way the world goes round, that's the way they keep the world rolling. So much hope for each person. And damned cleverly done too. But what happens if you don't hope any more, if your back's broken? What happens then?

'I can't stand here staring at these dresses for ever,' I thought. I turned round and there was a taxi going past slowly. The driver looked at me and I stopped him and said, '227, Bird Street.'

There were two bells. I rang the lower one. Nobody came, but when I pushed the door it opened.

There was a passage with a short flight of stairs and a door on the left-hand side. I went outside and rang again. The door on the left opened and an elderly man wearing pince-nez said, 'Well, Miss?'

The room he had come out of was an office. There was a filing-cabinet, and a table with a typewriter and a lot of letters, and two chairs.

I said, 'I wanted to see Miss Ethel Matthews. I thought she lived here.'

'Upstairs,' the man said. 'You rang the wrong bell.'

'I'm sorry.'

'This is the fourth time today,' he said. 'Will you kindly tell Miss Matthews that I object to being disturbed like this?' He stood at the door and talked rather loudly. 'I've got other things to do. I can't be answering her bell all day long.'

I saw Ethel standing at the bend in the staircase. She peered down at me.

'Oh, it's you, is it?' she said.

'Hullo,' I said. I went up.

She was wearing a white overall with the sleeves rolled up. Her hair was tidy. She looked much nicer than I had remembered her.

She said, 'What was Denby gassing about?'

'He was saying that I'd rung the wrong bell.'

'I must have a plate put up,' she said. 'He's such a swine. Come on in; I'm just having tea.'

The sitting-room looked out on Bird Street. There was a gas-stove with a bowl of water in front of it. The two armchairs had glazed chintz covers with a pattern of small rosebuds. There was a very high divan in one corner with a rug over it. And a piano. The wallpaper was white, with stripes.

'I'll get another cup,' she said.

We drank the tea.

'Who's the man downstairs?' I said.

'That's the owner,' she said. 'He's got the office there. Well, he calls it his office; he says he's a stamp-dealer. I believe he just comes and sits there. He's out most of the time. An old devil, he is. . . . I've got this floor and the third floor. There's nothing like glazed chintz for making a room look cheerful, is there? It's small, of course, but the dining-room next door is big and my bedroom's a fair size, too.'

In the dining-room there were the *Cries of London* on the walls and a plate of fruit on the sideboard.

Ethel said, 'You thought I was pretending, didn't you? You didn't believe I had such a nice flat? Come and see the room I told you about.'

We went up to the floor above.

'It's what I call dainty,' Ethel said, 'though I say it myself. And I could have a gas-fire put in.'

The furniture was painted white. It was a big room, but rather dark because the blinds were pulled half-way down. I looked out of the window at a barrel-organ. It was playing *Moonlight Bay*.

'Sit down,' she said, patting the bed. 'You look tired.'

'Yes,' I said, 'I am a bit.'

She said, 'I want somebody to share the flat and help me with my business, as I told you. It's all U.P. with that girl I spoke about. I didn't want her, but I'm sure we'd get on all right. Why don't you make up your mind? Isn't this better than that room in Camden Town?'

I said, 'Yes, the room's fine. It's a very nice room. But you said you wanted somebody to put twenty-five quid into your business. I haven't got twenty-five quid.'

'Oh, twenty-five quid,' she said. 'What about this? We'll say eight quid a month. That'll be for the room and food. And I'll teach you to do manicure and you can get half of what you make out of that. Of course, you'll have to help me out with the house-work and receive the patients and so on. What about it? You don't think eight quid's too much for this lovely room, do you? And the whole flat as bright and clean as anything you'd find anywhere.'

'No,' I said, 'I think it's very cheap.'

'Go on, make up your mind. Sometimes when you do things on the spur of the moment it brings you luck. It changes your luck. Haven't you ever noticed? Can you manage eight quid?'

'Yes, I can manage that.'

'There you are then. That's settled,' Ethel said. 'Only I shall have to ask you to give it to me in advance, because I've had a lot of expenses doing up this place. You can see that, can't you? It cost me pretty nearly six quid to do up this room alone. Well, but it's a lovely room now. And a bathroom next door and everything. You should have seen the state it was in when I came.'

'All right,' I said, 'but it doesn't leave me with much.'

'Don't you worry about that,' Ethel said. 'It's the first few weeks that are going to be difficult in a thing like this. I won't ask you to pay in advance next month. When once I get my business going you'll see it'll be all right about money. You'll be able to make quite a bit.'

We went downstairs. I took two five-pound notes out of my bag and gave her one and three sovereigns and put the other note back.

She said, 'Of course, when I said I'd do it for eight quid I was making it as cheap as possible. God knows if I shall be able to manage. We'll have to see how things go. However, it'll be all right for a couple of weeks anyway with this.'

'I'll have to go to Camden Town and get my things and settle up,' I said.

I got back to Bird Street and told Ethel I wanted to go to bed. My back hurt.

'I'll bring you something to eat,' she said.

I was lying down thinking about money and that I had only three pounds left when she came in with bread and cheese and a bottle of Guinness. She sat by my side while I ate and began to tell me how respectable she was.

'It's all straight and above-board with me,' she said. 'I'm the best masseuse in London. You couldn't learn from anybody better than me. It really is a chance for you. Of course, if you introduce some clients of your own it'll be all the better for both of us.'

'Well,' I said, 'I don't know. I can't think of a soul at present — not a soul.'

'You're a bit tired tonight,' she said. 'I can see that. You'd better have a good rest. I'll put the alarm to eight o'clock. You won't mind getting breakfast, will you? The kitchen's on this floor, so it'll be easy for you. You don't mind?'

'No,' I said. 'All right.'

She went out. And I lay there and thought.

. . . She'll smile and put the tray down and I'll say Francine I've had such an awful dream — it was only a dream she'll say — and on the tray the blue cup and saucer and the silver teapot so I'd know for certain that it had started again my lovely life — like a five-finger exercise playing very slowly on the piano like a garden with a high wall round it — and every now and again thinking I only dreamt it it never happened . . .

PART THREE

1

There were the *Cries of London* in the dining-room. I remember the way they hung, and the bowl of water in front of the gas-fire, and always a plate of oranges in the middle of the table, and two armchairs with chintz cushions — a different pattern from the chintz in the sitting-room — and Ethel talking about how respectable she was. 'If I were to tell you all I know about some of the places that advertise massage. That Madame Fernande, for instance — well, the things I've heard about her and the girls she's got at her place. And how she manages to do it without getting into trouble I don't know. I expect it costs her something.'

The window would be open because it was warm that November, but the blind half-way down at the top. When the bell rang I would go downstairs and bring the man up and say to Ethel, 'He's in the other room.' And after a while she would come back and start again. 'Did I tell you about what happened last week? Well, it just shows you. The day after I'd put in my advertisement there were detectives calling and wanting to see my references and my certificates. I showed them some references, and some certificates too. I was wild. Treating me as if I was a dirty foreigner.'

She used to wear a white overall. Her face was rather red and her nose turned-up with wide nostrils.

She said — that must have been the first day — 'About manicure, the main thing is to have a nice set of manicure things. I'll lend you those. You get them all spread out nicely on the table with a white cloth and a bowl of soapy hot water and you push one of the armchairs forward and smile and say, "Please sit down." And then you say, "Do you mind?" and you put his hand into a bowl of hot water. It's awfully easy. Don't be silly, anybody can do it. You can practise on me if you like. And you can ask five bob. You might even be able to get ten bob. Use your judgment.'

'Of course,' she said, 'you must be a bit nice to them.'

'Why not ten bob?' she said. 'That's all right. Everybody's got their living to earn and if people do things thinking that they're going to get something that they don't get, what's it matter to you or me or anybody else? You let them talk. You can take it from me that when it comes to it they're all so damned afraid of a scene that they're off like a streak of lightning at the slightest . . .'

That's what I can remember best — Ethel talking and the clock ticking. And her voice when she was telling me about Madame Fernande or about her father, who had a chemist's shop, and that she was really a lady. A lady — some words have a long, thin neck that you'd like to strangle. And her different voice when she said, 'A manicure, dear.'

There were never any scenes. There was nothing to make scenes about. But I stopped going out; I stopped wanting to go out. That happens very easily. It's as if you had always done that — lived in a few rooms and gone from one to the other. The light is a different colour every hour and the shadows fall differently and make different patterns. You feel peaceful, but when you try to think it's as if you're face to face with a high, dark wall. Really all you want is night, and to lie in the dark and pull the sheet over your head and sleep, and before you know where you are it is night — that's one good thing. You pull the sheet over your head and think, 'He got sick of me,' and 'Never, not ever, never.' And then you go to sleep. You sleep very quickly when you are like that and you don't dream either. It's as if you were dead.

'Oh, shut up about being tired,' she would say. 'You were born tired. I'm tired too. We're all tired.'

I had been nearly three weeks in Bird Street before I saw Laurie again. She came to lunch.

'Now, that's the sort of girl I should want if I were a man,' Ethel said. 'Look at the way she walks. Look at the way she wears her clothes. My God, that's what I call smart.'

'She's a funny old cow,' Laurie said to me afterwards up in my room. 'But she seems affable — very affable indeed. Is she really teaching you to do manicure? Do you get many people to manicure?'

'I've had four or five,' I said.

'What, to manicure?'

'Yes, to manicure,' I said. 'One of them did ask me to take him upstairs, but when I said No he went off like a shot. He was a bit frightened all the time, you could tell that.'

Laurie laughed. She said, 'I bet the old girl wasn't pleased. I bet you that wasn't her idea at all.'

A car hooted outside and she looked out of the window and made signs. She called out, 'I'll be down in a minute.'

'There they are, my two specimens. Why don't you come out with us for a blow?' she said. 'It'll cheer you up. The old girl won't mind, will she?'

'No, I don't think so. Why should she?'

'Come on then,' Laurie said.

I kept thinking, 'I'm all right. I still like going fast in a car and eating and drinking and hot baths. I'm quite all right.'

'My shoe's undone,' Laurie said. When the man did it up his hands were trembling. ('I can always make people crazy about me.')

The long shadows of the trees, like skeletons, and others like spiders, and others like octopuses. 'I'm quite all right; I'm quite all right. Of course, everything will be all right. I've only got to pull myself together and make a plan.' ('Have you heard the one about . . .')

It was one of those days when you can see the ghosts of all the other lovely days. You drink a bit and watch the ghosts of all the lovely days that have ever been from behind a glass. ('Yes, that's not a bad one, but have you heard the one . . .')

'If you'd let me know you were going to be so late I'd have given you a key,' Ethel said. 'I didn't want to have to sit up half the night to let you in.'

'We went to supper at Romano's,' I said. 'That's why I'm so late.'

'Well, I hope you enjoyed yourself,' she said. But I knew from the way she looked at me that she had started to hate me. I knew she was going to make a row sooner or later.

Nobody came all the next morning.

'I'm fed up,' Ethel said. 'I'm fed up with the whole damned business. There's nobody coming till five.'

She poured herself out another whisky-and-soda. Then she had another and then she said, 'A fourth for luck,' and filled the glass up and took it into the sitting-room.

I heard her talking to herself. She did that sometimes. 'Brutes and idiots, idiots and brutes,' she would say. 'If it's not brutes, it's idiots and if it's not idiots it's brutes.' And 'Oh God, God, God, God, God.'

At about five o'clock somebody rang, and I went down and brought him up. Then she knocked on the wall and called out for hot water. I got the kettle and put it outside the sitting-room door.

The man had been there for about twenty minutes when I heard the crack of wood breaking and he started to swear at the top of his voice. Ethel knocked again.

'Am I to come in?' I said at the door.

'Yes,' she said, 'come in.'

I went in. The massage couch had collapsed at one end and the basin was upset. There was water all over the floor. The man had a blanket wrapped round him. He was hopping around on one leg, holding the other foot, and swearing. He looked very thin and small. He had grey hair; I didn't notice his face.

'There's been an accident,' Ethel said. 'One of the legs of the couch has given way. Get a cloth or the water will drip through on Denby's head. . . . I'm ever so sorry. Does your foot hurt?'

'D'you think I can stand in boiling water and not get hurt, you damned fool?' the man said.

While I was mopping up the water he sat on the piano-stool playing with one finger. But his foot kept jerking up and down, as a thing does when it has been hurt. Long after you have stopped thinking about it, it keeps jerking up and down.

As soon as I got out of the room I began to laugh, and then I couldn't stop. It's like that when you haven't laughed for a long time.

I heard him going downstairs and Ethel came in.

'This is a bit of a change — you laughing,' she said.

'Well,' I said, 'it was damned funny. It was a hymn he was playing, did you hear?'

'One end of the couch gave way,' she said, 'and instead of lying still the silly fool must jump up and put his foot into the basin of hot water. Couldn't he look where he was putting his blasted foot? It's your fault. What did you want to bring scalding water for?'

'Cheer up,' I said. 'It was really rather funny.' I knew she was getting ready to go for me, but I couldn't stop laughing.

'You're a nice one to tell anybody to cheer up,' she said. 'Who are you laughing at? Look here, I'll tell you something. You can clear out. You're no good; I don't want you here.'

'I wanted a smart girl,' she said, 'who'd be a bit nice to people and the way you seemed I thought you were the sort of kid who'd take the trouble to be nice to people and make a few friends and so on and try to make the place go. And as a matter of fact you're enough to drive anybody crazy with that potty look of yours. And then you clear off with your friends and you don't even ask me to come with you. Well, clear out and stay out. I don't want you here, you're no use. I know what you're going to say. You're going to say that you paid for a month, but do you know what it cost me to put in the gas-fire because you said you couldn't stand your bedroom without it, of all the damned nonsense? And always going on about being tired and it's being dark and cold and this, that and the other. What d'you want to stay here for, if you don't like it? Who wants you here anyway? Why don't you clear out?'

'I can't swim well enough, that's one reason,' I said.

'Christ,' she said, 'you're a funny turn, aren't you? Well, anyway, I haven't got any money to give you back, so it's no use expecting any.'

'All right,' I said, 'you can keep the money. There's lots more where that came from. Keep the change.'

'Keep what change?' she said. 'Who are you insulting?'

She was standing with her back to the door so that I couldn't get by.

'The thing about you,' she said, 'is that you're half potty. You're not all there; you're a half-potty bastard. You're not all there; that's what's the matter with you. Anybody's only got to look at you to see that.'

I said, 'All right. Well, get out of the way and let me pass.' But she collapsed on the floor and lay with her head and her back against the door and started to cry. I had never seen anybody cry like that. And all the time she went on talking.

'You went out with your pals and enjoyed yourself and you didn't even ask me. Wasn't I good enough to come?'

'But it's always the same thing. You didn't even ask me,' she said. 'And oh God, what a life I've had. Trying to keep up and everybody else trying to push you down and everybody lying and pretending and you knowing it. And then they down you for doing the same things as they do.'

'D'you know how old I am?' she said. 'If I can't get hold of some money in the next few years, what's going to become of me? Will you tell me that? You wait a bit and you'll see. It'll happen to you too. One day you'll see. You wait, you wait a bit.'

I watched her shoulders shaking. A fly was buzzing round me. I couldn't think of anything, except that it was December and too late for flies, or too soon, or something, and where did it come from?

'I'm always alone,' she said. 'It's awful to be always alone, awful, awful.'

'Never mind, cheer up,' I said.

She started looking for her handkerchief, but she didn't seem to have one. I gave her mine.

'Look here, kid, I didn't mean a word I said. Where are you going? Don't go, for God's sake. I can't stick it any longer. Please don't go. I beg you don't go. I can't stand being alone any longer. If you leave me I swear I'll turn the gas on.'

'I'll come back,' I said. 'I'm only going for a walk.'

'If you're not back in an hour,' she said, 'I'll turn the gas on and you'll have murdered me.'

I walked along imagining that I was going to his house, and the look of the street, and ringing the bell. 'You're late,' perhaps he'd say, 'I expected you before.'

Then I thought, 'If I went to that hotel in Berners Street. I've got just about enough money on me to pay. They'd say, of course, that they hadn't got a room if you went in without any luggage. With the hotel half-empty they'd still say that they hadn't got a room.' I could imagine so well the girl at the desk saying it that I had to begin to laugh again. The damned way they look at you, and their damned voices, like high, smooth, unclimbable walls all round you, closing in on you. And nothing to be done about it, either. The answer's a lemon, as Laurie says. The damned way they look at you and their damned voices and the answer's a lemon as Laurie says.

I had on the jade bracelet that Walter had given me, and I slid it down over my hand. It felt warm and comforting against my hand and I gripped it and looked at it but I couldn't remember the word.

Thinking, 'Everybody says that if you start being afraid of people they see it and you're done for. Besides, it's all imagination.' I argued it out with myself quite solemnly, whether it was imagination or not that people are cruel. And I was holding my bracelet like that, slipped down over my hand. It felt warm and comforting because I knew I could hit somebody pretty hard with it. And I remembered the word. Knuckle-duster.

A man spoke to me out of the side of his mouth, like they do, but he went on quickly, before I could hit him. I went after him meaning to hit him, but he walked too quickly, and a policeman at the corner of the street stared at me like a damned baboon — a fair baboon, too, worse than a dark one every time. (What happened to me then? Something happened to me then?)

I thought, 'You're not going to cry in the middle of the street, are you?' I got into a 'bus and went back to Bird Street.

When I opened the door Ethel called out, 'Oh, there you are, kid. I was awfully worried about you. Come and have some supper.'

She had brushed her hair and put on her black dress with a white collar. She looked quite all right — in fact, better than usual. I found out later that whenever she raved she always looked better than usual afterwards, fresher and younger.

'No, I don't want anything to eat,' I said.

'I'm sorry I went for you like that,' she said. 'I can't say more than that, can I?'

'It's all right,' I said. I only wanted to get upstairs and pull the sheet over my head and sleep.

'Nobody can do any more than say they're sorry,' she said.

The white furniture, and over the bed the picture of the dog sitting up begging — *Loyal Heart.* I got into bed and lay there looking at it and thinking of that picture advertising the Biscuits Like Mother Makes, as Fresh in the Tropics as in the Motherland, Packed in Airtight Tins, which they stuck up on a hoarding at the end of Market Street.

There was a little girl in a pink dress eating a large yellow biscuit studded with currants — what they called a squashed-fly biscuit — and a little boy in a sailor-suit trundling a hoop, looking back over his shoulder at the little girl. There was a tidy green tree and a shiny pale-blue sky, so close that if the little girl had stretched her arm up she could have touched it. (God is always near us. So cosy.) And a high, dark wall behind the little girl.

Underneath the picture was written:

The past is dear,
The future clear,
And, best of all, the present.

But it was the wall that mattered.
And that used to be my idea of what England was like.
'And it is like that, too,' I thought.

2

I didn't get up when the alarm went next morning. Ethel came in to see what was wrong.

I said, 'I want to stay in bed a bit today. I've got a headache.'

'Poor kid,' she said, blinking at me. 'You don't look well and that's a fact. I'll bring you up some breakfast.'

She had two voices — the soft one and the other one.

'Thanks,' I said. 'Just some tea — not anything to eat.'

I had to put the light on to see to pour the tea out.

'It's cold and there's an awful fog,' she said.

When I put the light out again the room was dark, and warm so long as I kept my hands under the blankets. I hadn't got a headache. I was all right really — only damned tired, worse than usual.

I kept telling myself, 'You've got to think of something. You can't stay here. You've got to make a plan.' But instead I started counting all the towns I had been to, the first winter I was on tour — Wigan, Blackburn, Bury, Oldham, Leeds, Halifax, Huddersfield, Southport. . . . I counted up to fifteen and then slid off into thinking of all the bedrooms I had slept in and how exactly alike they were, bedrooms on tour. Always a high, dark wardrobe and something dirty red in the room; and through the window the feeling of a small street would come in. And the breakfast-tray dumped down on the bed, two plates with a bit of curled-up bacon on each. And if the landlady smiled or said 'Good morning' Maudie would say, 'She's very smarmy. What's the matter with her? I bet she puts that down on the bill. For saying Good Morning, half-a-crown.'

And then I tried to remember the road that leads to Constance Estate. It's funny how well you can remember when you lie in the dark with your arm over your forehead. Two eyes open inside your head. The sandbox tree outside the door at home and the horse waiting with his bridle over the hook that was fixed in the tree. And the sweat rolling down Joseph's face when he helped me to mount and the tear in my habit-skirt. And mounting, and then the bridge and the sound of the horse's hoofs on the wooden planks, and then the savannah. And then there is New Town, and just beyond New Town the big mango tree. It was just past there that I fell off the mule when I was a kid and it seemed such a long time before I hit the ground. The road goes along by the sea. The coconut palms lean crookedly down to the water. (Francine says that if you wash your face in fresh coconut-water every day you are always young and unwrinkled, however long you live.) You ride in a sort of dream, the saddle creaks sometimes, and you smell the sea and the good smell of the horse. And then — wait a minute. Then do you turn to the right or the left? To the left, of course. You turn to the left and the sea is at your back, and the road goes zigzag upwards. The feeling of the hills comes to you — cool and hot at the same time. Everything is green, everywhere things are growing. There is never one moment of stillness — always something buzzing. And then dark cliffs and ravines and the smell of rotten leaves and damp. That's how the road to Constance is — green, and the smell of green, and then the smell of water and dark earth and rotting leaves and damp. There's a bird called a Mountain Whistler, that calls out on one note, very high-up and sweet and piercing. You ford little rivers. The noise the horse's hoofs make when he picks them up and puts them down in the water. When you see the sea again it's far below you. It took three hours to get to Constance Estate. It was as long as a life sometimes. I was nearly twelve before I rode it by myself. There were bits in the road that I was afraid of. The turning where you came very suddenly out of the sun into the shadow; and the shadow was always the same shape. And the place where the woman with yaws spoke to me. I suppose she was begging but I couldn't understand because her nose and mouth were eaten away; it seemed as though she were laughing at me. I was frightened; I kept on looking backwards to see if she was following me, but when the horse came to the next ford and I saw clear water I thought I had forgotten about her. And now — there she is.

When Ethel brought me in something to eat at mid-day I pretended to be asleep. Then I did go to sleep.

The next time she came in she said, 'Listen. Two friends of Laurie's are downstairs, a Mr Redman and a Mr Adler. They've asked for you. Go on, go down, it'll cheer you up.'

She put the light on. It was a quarter to six. The tune of *Camptown Racecourse* was going in my head — I suppose I had been dreaming about it. I dressed and went down. Carl and Joe were in the sitting-room, and Ethel wreathed in smiles. I had never seen her look so good-tempered.

'Hullo, Anna,' Joe said, 'how have you been getting on?'

'I've been looking forward to meeting you again, Miss Morgan,' Carl said, in a formal voice.

Ethel smirked and said to Carl, 'Here she is. You wanted a manicure. She's a very good manicurist.'

I took him into the dining-room and got the table and put the armchair close to the fire. I started to file his nails, but my hands were trembling and the file kept slipping.

The third time it happened he began to laugh.

I said, 'I'm sorry, but I've not had a lot of practice at this.'

'I can see that,' he said.

'Ask Ethel to do it,' I said. 'She's really very good. I'll go and call her.'

I got up.

'Oh, don't worry about the manicure,' he said. 'I only wanted to talk to you.'

I sat down again. My mouth smiled at him.

He said, 'I was really sorry the other night about having to go away. I've been meaning to come and see you ever since, especially as I've heard such a lot about you from Laurie.'

He had brown eyes, rather close together. He wasn't nervous or hesitating. He was solid. I kept wanting to ask him, 'Was your nose ever broken?'

He said, 'Laurie's told me all about you.'

'Oh, has she?' I said.

'She likes you. She likes you a lot.'

'D'you think so?' I said.

'Well, she talks as though she does. And this one here — does she like you a lot too?'

'No, this one doesn't like me at all,' I said.

'That's too bad,' he said, 'that's too bad. And so she does the massage and you the manicure? Well, well, well.'

When he kissed me he said, 'You don't take ether, do you?'

'No,' I said, 'that's a face-lotion I use. It has ether in it.'

'Oh, that's it,' he said. 'You know, you mustn't be mad with me, but you look a bit as if you took something. Your eyes look like it.'

'No,' I said, 'I don't take ether. I never thought of it. I must try it sometime.'

He took my hand in both of his and warmed it.

'Cold,' he said, 'cold.' (Cold — cold as truth, cold as life. No, nothing can be as cold as life.)

He said, 'That guy Laurie says you were with — it doesn't look to me as if he was very nice to you.'

'He was. He was very nice,' I said.

He shook his head and said, 'Now, what have they been doing to you?' in that voice which is just part of it. When he touched me I knew that he was quite sure I would. I thought, 'All right then, I will.' I was surprised at myself in a way and in another way I wasn't surprised. I think anything could have happened that day and I wouldn't have been really surprised. 'It's always on foggy days,' I thought.

He said, 'I'll tell you what we'll do. You go and get dressed and we'll go out and have some dinner somewhere. Not Joe — just you and I. Now I'll go and have a talk to Miss What's-her-name.'

All that evening I did everything to the tune of *Camptown Racecourse*. 'I'se gwine to ride all night, I'se gwine to ride all day . . .'

We went to Kettner's, and when we got back Ethel had gone out. There were two bottles of champagne on the table. He said, 'there you are. All done by kindness, as Laurie would say.'

Up in the bedroom I started singing:

> '*Oh, I bet my money on the bob-tailed nag,*
> *Somebody won on the bay,*'

and he said, 'It's "Somebody bet on the bay".'

I said, 'I'll sing it how I like. Somebody won on the bay.'

He said, 'Nobody wins. Don't worry. Nobody wins.'

'Was your nose broken?'

'Yes, I'll tell you about it some time.'

The room still and dark and the lights from cars passing across the ceiling in long rays, and saying, 'Oh please, oh please, oh please. . . .'

I didn't know when he went, because I was sleeping the way I sleep now — like a log.

3

Ethel turned the light on over the bed and woke me up.

'I thought you might like some breakfast. It's late — nearly eleven.'

'Thanks,' I said, 'but would you put the light out? I can see well enough.'

'It's all right between us now, kid, isn't it?'

I said, 'Yes, quite all right,' hoping she'd go out.

She was wearing her purple kimono with the white border and she walked up and down the room with little steps, jabbering.

'Because, I mean to say, I'm a good sport. I don't mind people enjoying themselves, and everybody isn't like that. If you went anywhere else you'd soon find out. But you'll be careful, won't you? Because of that Denby downstairs. He's an awful old cat. You can understand I don't want to give him any chance of turning me out of here after the money I've spent on the place.'

'Of course.'

'Did you have a good time? I bet you did. Redman's a nice man. He knows his way about, you can tell that. Oh, I bet he knows his way about. You know, kid, I've been thinking you'll want to go out more with your friends and not feel you've got to be in all day. I don't mind, but we may have to talk it over a bit about the rent.'

'All right,' I said. Then she did go out.

When she had gone I opened my handbag to get my handkerchief. Carl had put five quid inside. It was still foggy.

It was foggy for days after that and Carl didn't turn up again for a bit, or write or anything.

'I wonder what's happened to Redman,' Ethel said. 'He seems to have vanished.'

'I expect he's left London,' she'd say.

'Yes, probably.'

Then he telephoned and asked me to dine with him; and she cocked her eyes at me, looking surprised, looking suddenly respectful. That was when I started really hating her. I hated the way she smiled, I hated the way she'd say, 'Did you have a good time? Did you enjoy yourself?'

But I didn't see very much of her because I stayed late in bed in the mornings and took a long time dressing. The charwoman came an hour earlier and I didn't have to get up. If I brought Carl back to the flat after dinner she was usually out or in her bedroom. All done by kindness. ('And you do understand, kid, don't you? that under the circumstances two-and-a-half guineas a week isn't too much to ask for this room? And really, you might say, the run of the whole flat. It's a nice flat to bring anybody to. It makes people think something of you when you bring them back to a place like this. People don't give you what you're worth — not in anything they don't. They give you what they think you're used to. That's where a nice flat comes in.')

Sometimes not being able to get over the feeling that it was a dream. The light and the sky and the shadows and the houses and the people — all parts of the dream, all fitting in and all against me. But there were other times when a fine day, or music, or looking in the glass and thinking I was pretty, made me start again imagining that there was nothing I couldn't do, nothing I couldn't become. Imagining God knows what. Imagining Carl would say, 'When I leave London, I'm going to take you with me.' And imagining it although his eyes had that look — this is just for while I'm here, and I hope you get me.

'I picked up a girl in London and she. . . . Last night I slept with a girl who. . . .' That was me.

Not 'girl' perhaps. Some other word, perhaps. Never mind.

'Are you staying much longer in London?'

'Why do you ask?'

'Nothing. It was just that I wondered.'

'Well, I may stay two or three weeks longer, I'm not sure. Joe's leaving next week; he's meeting his wife in Paris.'

'Oh, is Joe married?' I said. 'What a joke! I like Joe.' (He said, one day, 'What's the good of lying about it? We're all crabs in a basket. Have you ever seen crabs in a basket? One trying to get on top of the other. You want to survive, don't you?')

'Yes, he's married, all right. He's got two kids.'

'Are you married?'

'Yes,' he said. He looked vexed.

'Is your wife going to be in Paris too?'

'No.'

'Have you got any kids?'

'Yes,' he said after a while. 'A little girl.'

'Tell me about her,' I said. He didn't answer, so I said, 'Go on, tell me about her. Is she small, big, fair, dark? . . .'

He said, 'Do you want to finish your coffee? Because I thought we might go to a show tonight and it's after nine o'clock.'

'For a change,' he said.

'Oh, I'd love a change, I'm all for that. I think the same thing all the time gets damned monotonous.'

'Oh, yes?' he said.

The streets looked like black oilcloth through the taxi-windows.

'You know, you're sweet when you laugh a lot,' he said. 'I like you best when you laugh a lot.'

'I'm damned nice. Don't you know I'm damned nice really?'

'Sure, I know.'

I said, 'I'll be nicer still when I've had a bit of practice.'

'I wonder,' he said.

He looked as if he were making up his mind not to see me again. But he came back several times after that. And he would say, 'Well, are you having a lot of practice?'

'You bet I am.'

'Well, you're in the right place to have some practice, I should say.'

The last time I went out with him he gave me fifteen quid. For several days after that I kept on planning to leave London. The names of all the places I could go to went round and round in my head. (This isn't the only place in the world; there are other places. You don't get so depressed when you think that.) And then I met Maudie coming out of Selfridge's and we went into a teashop. She didn't ask me many questions because she was full of a long story about an electrical engineer she had met who lived in Brondesbury and who was gone on her. She was sure she could get him to marry her if she could smarten herself up a bit.

She said, 'Isn't it awful losing a chance like that because you haven't got a little money? Because it is a chance. Sometimes you're sure, aren't you? But I'm so damned shabby and, you know, when you're shabby you can't do anything, you don't believe in yourself. And he notices clothes — he notices things like that. Fred, his name is. He said to me the other day, "If there's anything I notice about a girl it's her legs and her shoes." Well, my legs are all right, but look at my shoes. He's always saying things like that and it makes me feel awful. He's a bit strait-laced but that doesn't stop them from being particular. Viv was like that, too. Isn't it rotten when a thing like that falls through just because you haven't got a little cash? Oh God, I wish it could happen. I want it so to happen.'

When I asked her how much she wanted she said, 'I could do a lot with eight pounds ten.' So I lent her eight pounds ten.

It's always like that with money. You never know where it goes to. You change a fiver then it's gone.

4

Going up the stairs it was pretty bad but when we got into the bedroom and had drinks it was better.

'You've got a gramophone,' he said. 'Splendid! Have you got that perfectly lovely record of Bach's? It's a Concerto or something. Played by two violins — Kreisler and Zimbalist. I can't remember the exact name of it.'

He had a little, close-clipped moustache and one wrist was

bandaged. Why was it bandaged? I don't know, I didn't ask. He didn't look as nice as I had thought when he spoke to me. I had gone by his voice. His eyes were a bit bleary.

'No, I haven't got anything of Bach's.'

I put on *Puppchen* and went on turning over the records.

'What's this one? *Connais-tu le Pays?* Do you know the country where the orange-tree flowers? Let's try that.'

'No, it gives me the pip,' I said.

I put on *Just a Little Love, a Little Kiss* and then *Puppchen* again. We started to dance and while we were dancing the dog in the picture over the bed stared down at us smugly. (Do you know the country? Of course, if you know the country it makes all the difference. The country where the orange-tree flowers?)

I said, 'I can't stand that damned dog any longer.'

I stopped dancing and took off my shoe and threw it at the picture. The glass smashed.

'I've wanted to do that for weeks,' I said.

He said, 'Good shot. But we're making rather a row, aren't we?'

I said, 'It's all right. We can make as much noise as we like. It doesn't matter. I should bloody well like to see her come up and say anything if I bloody well want to make a row.'

'Oh, quite,' he said, looking at me sideways.

We went on dancing. It started again.

I said, 'Let me go just a minute.'

'No; why?' he said, grinning at me.

'I feel awfully sick.'

The fool thought I was joking and held on to me.

I said, 'Do let me go,' but still he held on to me. I hit his bandaged wrist to make him let me go. It must have hurt him, because he started cursing me.

'What did you do that for, you little swine? You bitch.' And so on. And I couldn't stop to answer him back, either.

Like seasickness, only worse, and everything heaving up and down. And vomiting. And thinking, 'It can't be that, it can't be that. Oh, it can't be that. Pull yourself together; it can't be that. Didn't I always. . . . And besides it's never happened before. Why should it happen now?'

When I got back to the bedroom he had gone. Like a streak of lightning, as Ethel would have said. There was some glass on the floor. I swept it up into a piece of newspaper and piled the gramophone records one on top of the other. (Don't think of it, don't think of it. Because thinking of it makes it happen.)

I undressed and got into bed. Everything was still heaving up and down.

'Connais-tu le pays où fleurit l'oranger?'

. . . Miss Jackson used to sing that in a thin quavering voice and she used to sing By the Blue Alsatian Mountains I Watch and Wait Alway — Miss Jackson Colonel Jackson's illegitimate daughter — yes illegitimate poor old thing but such a charming woman really and she speaks French so beautifully she really is worth what she charges for her lessons of course her mother was — it was very dark in her sitting-room the shabby palm-leaf fans and yellow photographs of men in uniform and through the window the leaves of the banana tree silken torn (tearing a banana-leaf was like tearing thick green silk but more easily and smoothly than you can tear silk) — Miss Jackson was very thin and straight and she always wore black — her dead-white face and her currant-black eyes glittering — yes you children can come and have your moonlight picnic in the garden but you mustn't throw things at Captain Cameron (Captain Cameron was her cat) — her voice always went so thin and small when she tried to speak loudly — calling out now now children no quarrelling no quarrelling frightening Captain Cameron and everything — the galvanized-iron fence at the end of her garden looked blue in the moonlight — it looked colder than anything I had ever seen or ever will see — and when she sang By the Blue Mountains.

The blue mountains — Morne Grand Bois one was called — and Morne Anglais Morne Collé Anglais Morne Trois Pitons Morne Rest — Morne Rest one was called — and Morne Diablotin its top always covered with clouds it's a high mountain five thousand feet with its top always veiled and Anne Chewett used to say that it's haunted and obeah — she had been in gaol for obeah (obeah-women who dig up dead people and cut their fingers off and go to gaol for it — it's hands that are obeah) — but can't they do damned funny things — Oh if you lived here you wouldn't take them so seriously as all that —

Obeah zombis soucriants — lying in the dark frightened of the dark frightened of souriants that fly in through the window and suck your blood — they fan you to sleep with their wings and then they suck your blood — you know them in the day-time — they look like people but their eyes are red and staring and they're souriants at night — looking in the glass and thinking sometimes my eyes look like a souriant's eyes . . .

The bed was heaving up and down and I lay there thinking, 'It can't be that. Pull yourself together. It can't be that. Didn't I always. . . . And all those things they say you can do. I know when it happened. The lamp over the bed had a blue shade. It was that one I went back with just after Carl left.' Counting back days and dates and thinking, 'No, I don't think it was that time. I think it was when . . .'

Of course, as soon as a thing has happened it isn't fantastic any longer, it's inevitable. The inevitable is what you're doing or have done. The fantastic is simply what you didn't do. That goes for everybody.

The inevitable, the obvious, the expected. . . . They watch you, their faces like masks, set in the eternal grimace of disapproval. I always knew that girl was no good. I always knew that girl was. . . . Why didn't you do this? Why didn't you do that? Why didn't you bloody well make a hole in the water?

I dreamt that I was on a ship. From the deck you could see small islands — dolls of islands — and the ship was sailing in a dolls' sea, transparent as glass.

Somebody said in my ear, 'That's your island that you talk such a lot about.'

And the ship was sailing very close to an island, which was home except that the trees were all wrong. These were English trees, their leaves trailing in the water. I tried to catch hold of a branch and step ashore, but the deck of the ship expanded. Somebody had fallen overboard.

And there was a sailor carrying a child's coffin. He lifted the lid, bowed and said, 'The boy bishop,' and a little dwarf with a bald head sat up in the coffin. He was wearing a priest's robes. He had a large blue ring on his third finger.

'I ought to kiss the ring,' I thought in my dream, 'and then he'll start saying "In nomine Patris, Filii. . . ." '

When he stood up, the boy bishop was like a doll. His large, light eyes in a narrow, cruel face rolled like a doll's as you lean it from one side to the other. He bowed from right to left as the sailor held him up.

But I was thinking, 'What's overboard?' and I had that awful dropping of the heart.

I was still trying to walk up the deck and get ashore. I took huge, climbing, flying strides among confused figures. I was powerless and very tired, but I had to go on. And the dream rose into a climax of meaninglessness, fatigue and powerlessness, and the deck was heaving up and down, and when I woke up everything was still heaving up and down.

It was funny how, after that, I kept on dreaming about the sea.

5

Laurie said, 'I've had a peach of a letter from Ethel. She says you owe her money — two weeks' rent. And she says you've spoilt her eiderdown and a picture and the white paint in the bedroom and — my God, she does go on. I don't see why she wants to tell me about it. Here's the letter, anyway.'

227, Bird Street, W.
March 26th, 1914

My dear Laurie:

I expect by this time you know that Anna left this flat last week. Well, it's true that I had to ask her to go, but I hope you will not take any notice of the things she will tell you about me, because I have my side of the question too. Let me tell you that when I asked Anna to come and live with me I did not know what sort of a girl she was and she is a very deceiving girl. I know what life is and I do not want to be hard on anybody. So when she first started having Mr Redman to see her I did not say anything about it. He was a very nice man and he knew how to behave. But after he left she really overstepped all bounds but not in any way that you could respect because there are ways and ways of doing everything. It is one thing for a girl to have a friend or two but it is quite another for it to be anybody who she picks up in the street and without with your leave or by your leave and never a word to me. And sulky my God. I have never seen a girl like that — never a joke or a pleasant word. And to crown it all last week she came to me and said she was going to have a baby. It appears to me from what she says that she must be nearly three months gone. When I told her she should have spoken to me before if she wanted me to help her — Why did you not do something about it before I said — she said I have been trying everything I ever heard of and thought you might know of something else. With her eyes staring out of her head looking quite silly. You get a desperate feeling it is awful she said. And when I said I think this is a bit much to ask me — won't he help you out — she said I do not know who he is and started laughing quite brazen and that just shows the sort of girl she is because there are ways and ways of doing everything aren't there. And all the time being sick and I said to her I cannot have this sort of thing going on in my flat and you cannot blame me either can you. And if you had only seen the state she left her room and I want to have somebody else there next week. A picture I had — the glass all smashed and there is the picture without a glass and the beautiful silk eiderdown spoilt with wine-stains all over it. That cost me 35/ – and then it was cheap. And burns of cigarettes all over the place on the white paint. I am ashamed of the room now and it was such a beautiful room when she came in — all freshly done up. You can be mistaken about people — that is all I have got to say and have to pay for it. Besides she owes me two weeks money. Five guineas. I know she will come to you sooner or later with a lot of lies and I cannot bear to think that she will come to you like that because you are the sort of girl I think a lot of and I can tell you that I cannot afford to lose money like that either. If you knew the sort of girl she is I do not think you would have anything to do with her. She is not the sort of girl who will ever do anything for herself.

Yours affectionately
Ethel Matthews.

Hoping to see you soon. And my landlord has complained about her too.

'I don't know why she should write all that to you,' I said.

Laurie said, 'I don't know either.'

'You shouldn't give people a handle like you do,' she said. 'If you give people a handle they'll always take it.'

'I don't owe her any money,' I said. 'It's the other way round. She borrowed nearly three quid from me and she never paid it back. I don't know why she should write all that to you.' And all the time thinking round and round in a circle that it is there inside me, and about all the things I had taken so that if I had it, it would be a monster. The Abbé Sebastian's Pills, primrose label, one guinea a box, daffodil label, two guineas, orange label, three guineas. No eyes, perhaps. . . . No arms, perhaps. . . . Pull yourself together.

My hands were getting cold and I knew I was going to be sick again.

'I know of somebody,' Laurie said. 'But whether she'll do it for you now is another question. It's a thing that can happen to anybody, but you really ought to have done something about it before. I could have told you that all that business of taking pills is no good. . . . Those people who sell those things — they must make a pot. . . . I don't know whether she'll do it for you now. Have you got any money?'

'Yes,' I said. 'I sold my fur coat. I could give her ten quid.'

'It's not enough,' Laurie said. 'She won't do it for that. My dear, she'll want about fifty. Don't you know anybody who'll lend it to you? What about that man you talked about who used to give you money? Won't he help you? Or were you kidding about him?'

'No, I wasn't kidding.'

'Well, why don't you write to him?' she said. 'Because I warn you if you go on much longer you won't be able to get it done at all. Why don't you write now? I've got some awfully nice note-paper and you can use it. People go a lot by note-paper. When you're asking for money you don't want to give people the idea that you're down and out, you want to puzzle them a bit.'

'Say you're ill and ask him to come and see you,' she said. 'And give him my address; it's better than asking him to a bed-sitting-room. And for God's sake cheer up. It'll be all right.'

'I don't know what to say,' I said.

'Don't be a fool. Say Dear Flukingirons, or whatever his bloody name is. I'm not very well. I'd like very much to see you. You always promised to help me. Etcetera and so on.'

From a long way off I watched the pen writing: 'My dear Walter . . .'

6

The big tree in the square opposite d'Adhémar's flat was perfectly still, and the forked twigs looked like fingers pointing. Everything was perfectly still, as if it were dead. Then a bird chirped anxiously and they all started — first one, and then another, and then another.

'Listen to that. The poor little devils think it's night,' Laurie said.

'And you can't blame them,' d'Adhémar said.

She had told me, 'He's slightly potty, but an awfully sweet old thing. And he's got a lovely flat and he says he's just bought a marvellous book of dirty pictures.'

I liked him, but he put scent on. I could smell it, and the wine in my glass. The awful thing was that, even when I wasn't feeling sick, I knew it was always just round the corner, waiting to start again.

After lunch he walked up and down the room reciting a poem which began: 'Philistins, épiciers'; and then he talked about Sunday in London; and about the Portobello Road, which was near his flat; and the streets round it, the dead streets, and the blank faces of the houses.

'It's terrible,' he said, waving his hands about. 'The sadness, the hopelessness. The frustration — you breathe it in. You can see it; you can see it as plainly as you see the fog.' He laughed. 'Never mind. Let's look on the bright side of things. Of course, frustration can become something homely, desirable and warm.'

'Go on, Daddy,' Laurie said, 'don't drivel. Show us your book of dirty pictures.'

We looked at a book of drawings by Aubrey Beardsley.

'I'm disappointed,' Laurie said. 'Very disappointed. I don't call that hot stuff. Is that book really worth a lot of money? All I can say is, some people don't know what to do with their money.'

It was a quarter-to-four. I said, 'I must go now.'

'What time's he coming?'

'At half-past four.'

'Have a cognac before you go,' d'Adhémar said. He poured the brandy into three small glasses. 'Here's to the smug snobs and the prancing prigs and the hypocrites and the cowards and the pitiful fools! And then who's left?'

'She'd better not drink; it makes her sick,' Laurie said.

I got a taxi outside.

(Of course it'll be all right. Something will happen when I'm better, and then something else, and then something else. It'll be all right.)

He was late, and while I was waiting I was very nervous. I kept swallowing the lump in my throat and it kept coming back again. Then the bell rang and I went to the door and opened it.

I said, 'Hullo, Vincent,' and he smiled at me and said, 'Hullo.' I took him into the sitting-room.

'Walter wrote and told you I was coming?'

'Yes, he wrote from Paris.'

'Is this your flat?' he said, looking round.

'No, I'm staying here with a friend — Miss Gaynor. It's her flat.'

'I'm awfully sorry to hear you haven't been well,' he said.

'What's the matter?' When I told him he sat forward in his chair and stared at me, looking very fresh and clean and kind, his eyes clear and bright, like blue glass, and his long eyelashes never still for a second. He stared at me — and he might just as well have said it.

'Oh, I don't mean it's Walter's. I don't know whose it is.'

He leaned back in the chair again and didn't speak for a bit. Then he said, 'Of course Walter will help you. Of course he will, my dear. You needn't worry about that. Of course he will. What do you want to do?'

'I want not to have it,' I said.

'I see,' he said. And he went on talking, but I didn't hear a word he was saying. And then his voice stopped.

I said, 'Yes, I know. Laurie's told me of somebody. She wants forty pounds. She says she must have it in gold. She won't take anything else.'

'I see,' he said again. 'All right; you shall have the money. Don't fash yourself; don't be miserable any more.' He took my hand and patted it.

'Poor little Anna,' making his voice very kind. 'I'm so damned sorry you've been having a bad time.' Making his voice very kind, but the look in his eyes was like a high, smooth, unclimbable wall. No communication possible. You have to be three-quarters mad even to attempt it.

'You'll be all right. And then you must pull yourself together and try to forget about the whole business and start fresh. Just make up your mind, and you'll forget all about it.'

'D'you think so?' I said.

'Of course,' he said. 'You'll forget it and it'll be just as though it had never happened.'

'Will you have some tea?' I said.

'No, thanks, I won't have any tea.'

'Then have a whisky-and-soda.'

I had one too — it didn't make me feel sick, for a wonder — and while we were drinking he told me he knew of somebody who had had it done and she had said that it was nothing much, nothing to make a fuss about.

I said, 'It's not that that I make a fuss about. It's that sometimes I want to have it and then I think that if I had it, it would be a . . . It would have something the matter with it. And I think about that all the time, and that's what I mind.'

Vincent said, 'My dear girl, nonsense, nonsense.'

'I can't understand it,' he said. 'I simply can't understand it. Was it money? It can't have been money. You must have known that Walter would look after you. And he'd fixed everything up. He was awfully worried when you went off and didn't let him know where you were. He said several times how worried he was. He'd fixed everything up.'

'So much every Saturday,' I said. 'Receipt-form enclosed.'

'It's no use talking like that. You're going to be pretty glad of it now, aren't you?'

I didn't answer.

'Is this going to be your address? Shall we write here? Are you going to stay on here with your friend?'

'Only for the next four or five days.'

'Then where will you be?'

I said, 'I don't know exactly. Laurie's told me of a flat going in Langham Street.'

'D'you know what the rent is?'

'It's two pounds ten a week.'

'That'll be all right. You'll be able to manage it.' He coughed. 'About the forty pounds — when d'you want it?'

'I'll have to see her first — Mrs Robinson, I mean. I'll have to see her first and find out.'

'Quite,' he coughed again. 'Well, you must let me know. When you write, write to me — not to Walter. He's going to be abroad for some time.'

'Thank you very much,' I said. 'You're awfully kind.'

He looked at Laurie's photograph on the mantelpiece. 'Is this your friend?' he said. 'Is she as pretty as that?'

'Yes, she's pretty,' I said.

'I'm sure I've seen her about somewhere.'

'I daresay you have,' I said. 'She's got a lot of friends; you'd be surprised.'

'She really is pretty. But hard — a bit hard,' as if he were talking to himself. 'They get like that. It's a pity.'

'By the way,' he said, 'there's just one thing. If you have any letters of Walter's I must ask you to give them to me.'

'I'm sorry, I must insist on that,' he said.

I went and got the letters. I didn't look at them, except the one on the top, which was, 'Will you be in a taxi at the corner of Hay Hill and Dover Street at eleven tonight? Just wait there and I'll pick you up. Shy Anna, I love you so much. Always, Walter.'

'Are these all?' Vincent said.

'They're all I kept,' I said. 'I don't keep letters as a rule.'

'There's the one he wrote from Paris, too, saying you were coming — you'd better have it as well.' I took it out of my handbag and gave it to him.

'You're a nice girl, you really are. Now, look, here, don't go getting ideas into your head. You've only got to make up your mind that things are going to be different, and they will be different. . . . Are you sure these are all the letters?'

'I've told you so,' I said.

'Yes, I know.' He pretended to laugh. 'Well, there you are. I'm trusting you.'

'Yes, I see that.'

'Where are you going when you leave here?' I said.

'Who — me? Why?'

'Because I'd just like to know. Because I can't imagine what you're going to do when you leave here and I like to be able to imagine things.'

'I'm going into the country,' he said. 'Till Tuesday morning, thank God.'

'What do you do?'

'I play golf and so on.'

'How nice!' I said. 'How's Germaine?'

'Oh, she's all right. She's gone back to Paris. She doesn't like London.'

'It must be lovely in the country.'

He said, 'It smells good.'

'You told me about it,' I said, 'in your letter.'

'What letter? Oh yes, yes, I remember.'

'It's no use asking me for that one,' I said. 'It wasn't one I kept.'

'Look here, cheer up,' he said. 'It's going to be all right for you. I don't see why it shouldn't be all right for you.'

When Laurie came in I was crying. She said, 'Oh, for God's sake, what's the good of crying? Have you fixed it up all right?'

'Yes,' I said.

'Then what is there to cry about?'

D'Adhémar was with her. He said, 'T'en fais pas, mon petit. C'est une vaste blague.'

7

The bedroom in Mrs Robinson's flat was very tidy, and there was some mimosa in a vase on the table.

She came in, smiling. She was Swiss — French-Swiss.

I said, 'Elles sont jolies, ces fleurs-là.' Simpering, wanting her to know that I could speak French, wanting her to like me.

She said, 'Vous trouvez? On me les a données. Mais moi, j'ai horreur des fleurs dans la maison, surtout de ces fleurs-là.'

She was tall and fair and fat and very fresh-looking. She was dressed in red, close-fitting. Not in very good taste, considering she was so fat. I thought, 'She doesn't look a bit French.' I gave her the money sewn up in a little canvas bag. I didn't know gold was so heavy.

She smiled and nodded and moved her hands, telling me about what I ought to do afterwards. That was the only thing French about her — that she moved her hands a lot.

She brought me a small glass of brandy. I said, 'I thought it was rum they had.'

'Comment?'

I drank it very quickly, but it didn't go to my head at all. I kept telling myself, 'She's awfully clever. Laurie says she's awfully clever.'

She went away and I shut my eyes. I didn't want to see what she was doing. When I felt her standing near me again I said, 'If I can't bear it, if I ask you to stop, will you stop?'

She said, as if she were talking to a child, 'Oh, yes, yes, yes, yes, yes. . . .'

The earth heaving up under me. Very slowly. So slowly.

'Stop,' I said. 'You must stop.'

She didn't answer. I couldn't move. Too late now to move, too late.

She said 'La,' blowing out her breath.

I opened my eyes. I went on crying. She went away from me. I sat up and everything was different. She brought me my handbag. I got out my handkerchief and wiped my face.

I thought, 'It's all over. But is it all over?'

She said, 'That will be all right. In two weeks, three weeks.'

'But it's quite sure?'

'Yes, quite sure.'

She smiled and said politely, 'Vous êtes très courageuse.' She patted me on the shoulder and went out and I got dressed. Then she came back and took me to the door and shook hands with me at the door and said, 'Alors, bonne chance.'

I got outside. I was afraid to cross the street and then I was afraid because the slanting houses might fall on me or the pavement rise up and hit me. But most of all I was afraid of the people passing because I was dying; and, just because I was dying, any one of them, any minute, might stop and approach me and knock me down, or put their tongues out as far as they would go. Like that time at home with Meta, when it was Masquerade and she came to see me and put out her tongue at me through the slit in her mask.

A taxi passed. I put my hand up and the man stopped. I couldn't get the door open and he got down and opened it for me.

Laurie was waiting for me in the flat in Langham Street and when I came in she said, 'Well, has the first part of the programme gone off all right?'

'Yes,' I said. 'She says I've just got to wait and it'll be all right. She says I must walk about as much as I can and wait; and not do anything — just wait, and it'll be all right.'

'Well, I should do just what she says. She's very clever.'

'I'll wait for a bit,' I said. 'But I hope I shan't have to do it for very long. I don't think I'll be able to stand waiting for it to happen for very long. Could you? She said was I alone at night? It would be better not.'

'Well, why not ask that charwoman, Mrs What's-her-name, to stay?'

'Mrs Polo.'

'What a name! Why not ask Mrs Polo to stay?'

'She can't. She's got a baby. Besides, I think I'd better not mix her up in it.'

'That's right,' Laurie said. 'It's just as well not to mix anybody else up in it. You'll be all right. That woman's very clever.'

'Yes, I know. It's only waiting for it to happen that I mind.'

Laurie said, 'Well, anyhow I should go slow on the gin if I were you. You've been taking too much lately.'

The flat was full of furniture and pink curtains and cushions and mats with fringes. Very swanky, as Maudie would say. And the *Cries of London* turned up too, but here in the bedroom.

Everything was always so exactly alike — that was what I could never get used to. And the cold; and the houses all exactly alike, and the streets going north, south, east, west, all exactly alike.

PART FOUR

1

The room was nearly dark but there was a long yellow ray coming in under the door from the light in the passage. I lay and watched it. I thought, 'I'm glad it happened when nobody was here because I hate people.'

I thought, 'Pain . . .' but it was so long ago that I had forgotten what it had been like. I was all right, except that every now and again it was as if I were falling through the bed.

Mrs Polo said, 'It was like this when I come this evening and I didn't know what to do, so I rung you up, miss. And I don't want to be mixed up with a thing like this.'

'But why ring me up? It's nothing to do with me,' Laurie said. 'You ought to have got a doctor.'

Mrs Polo said, 'I thought she wouldn't want a doctor here asking questions. She told me it come on at two o'clock and it's nearly eight now. Supposing anything 'appens and there's a row.'

'Oh, don't be a fool,' Laurie said. 'She'll be all right. It's bound to stop in a minute.'

'Are you all right?' she said.

'I'm a bit giddy,' I said. 'I'm awfully giddy. I'd like a drink. There's some gin in the sideboard.'

'She oughtn't to have anything to drink now,' Mrs Polo said.

Laurie said, 'You don't know anything about it. A drink won't do her any harm. Champagne — that's what they give them; champagne's what she ought to have.'

I drank the gin and listened to them whispering for a long while. Then I shut my eyes and the bed mounted into the air with me. It mounted very high and stayed there suspended — a little slanted to one side, so that I had to clutch the sheets to prevent myself from falling out. And the clock was ticking loud, like that time when I lay looking at the dog in the picture *Loyal Heart* and watching his chest going in and out and I kept saying, 'Stop, stop,' but softly so that Ethel wouldn't hear. 'I'm too old for this sort of thing,' he said;

'it's bad for the heart.' He laughed and it sounded funny. 'Les émotions fortes,' he said. I said, 'Stop, please stop.' 'I knew you'd say that,' he said. His face was white.

A pretty useful mask that white one watch it and the slobbering tongue of an idiot will stick out — a mask Father said with an idiot behind it I believe the whole damned business is like that — Hester said Gerald the child's listening — oh no she isn't Father said she's looking out of the window and quite right too — it ought to be stopped somebody said it's not a decent and respectable way to go on it ought to be stopped - Aunt Jane said I don't see why they should stop the Masquerade they've always had their three days Masquerade ever since I can remember why should they want to stop it some people want to stop everything.

I was watching them from between the slats of the jalousies — they passed under the window singing — it was all colours of the rainbow when you looked down at them and the sky so blue — there were three musicians at the head a man with a concertina and another with a triangle and another with a chak-chak playing There's a Brown Girl in a Ring *and after the musicians a lot of little boys turning and twisting and dancing and others dragging kerosene-tins and beating them with sticks — the masks the men wore were a crude pink with the eyes squinting near together squinting but the masks the women wore were made of close-meshed wire covering the whole face and tied at the back of the head — the handkerchief that went over the back of the head hid the strings and over the slits for the eyes mild blue eyes were painted then there was a small straight nose and a little red heart-shaped mouth and under the mouth another slit so that they could put their tongues out at you — I could hear them banging the kerosene-tins*

'It ought to be stopped,' Mrs Polo said.
'I'm giddy,' I said. 'I'm awfully giddy.'

I was watching them from between the slats of the jalousies dancing along dressed in red and blue and yellow the women with their dark necks and arms covered with white powder — dancing along to concertina-music dressed in all the colours of the rainbow and the sky so blue — you can't expect niggers to behave like white people all the time Uncle Bo said it's asking too much of human nature — look at that fat old woman Hester said just look at her — oh yes she's having a go too Uncle Bo said they all have a go they don't mind — their voices were going up and down — I was looking out of the window and I knew why the masks were laughing and I heard the concertina-music going

'I'm giddy,' I said.

I'm awfully giddy — but we went on dancing forwards and backwards backwards and forwards whirling round and round

The concertina-man was very black — he sat sweating and the concertina went forwards and backwards backwards and forwards one two three one two three pourquoi ne pas aimer bonheur supreme — the triangle-man kept time on his triangle and with his foot tapping and the little man who played the chak-chak smiled with his eyes fixed

Stop stop stop — I thought you'd say that he said

My darling mustn't worry my darling mustn't be sad — I thought say that again say that again but he said it's nearly four o'clock perhaps you ought to be going

You ought to be going he said — I tried to hang back but it was useless and the next moment my feet were groping for the stirrups — there weren't any stirrups — I balanced myself in the saddle trying to grip with my knees

The horse went forward with an exaggerated swaying lilting motion like a rocking-horse — I felt very sick — I heard the concertina-music playing behind me all the time and the noise of the people's feet dancing — the street was in a greenish shadow — I saw the rows of small houses on each side in front of one of them there was a woman cooking fishcakes on an iron stove filled with charcoal — and then the bridge and the sound of the horse's hoofs on the wooden planks — and then the savannah — the road goes along by the sea — do you turn to the right or the left — the left of course — and then that turning where the shadow is always the same shape — shadows are ghosts you look at them and you don't see them — you look at everything and you don't see it only sometimes you see it like now I see — a cold moon looking down on a place where nobody is a place full of stones where nobody is

I thought I'm going to fall nothing can save me now but still I clung desperately with my knees feeling very sick

'I fell,' I said. 'I fell for a hell of a long time then.'

'That's right,' Laurie said. 'When he comes tell him that.'

The bed had gone down to earth again.

'Tell him you had a fall,' she said. 'That's all you've got to say. . . .'

'Oh, so you had a fall, did you?' the doctor said. His hands looked enormous in rubber gloves. He began to ask questions.

'Quinine, quinine,' he said; 'what utter nonsense!'

He moved about the room briskly, like a machine that was working smoothly.

He said, 'You girls are too naïve to live, aren't you?'

Laurie laughed. I listened to them both laughing and their voices going up and down.

'She'll be all right,' he said. 'Ready to start all over again in no time, I've no doubt.'

When their voices stopped the ray of light came in again under the door like the last thrust of remembering before everything is blotted out. I lay and watched it and thought about starting all over again. And about being new and fresh. And about mornings, and misty days, when anything might happen. And about starting all over again, all over again. . . .

Quartet

...Beware
Of good Samaritans—walk to the right
Or hide thee by the roadside out of sight
Or greet them with the smile that villains wear.

—R.C. DUNNING

1

It was about half-past five on an October afternoon when Mar-ya Zelli came out of the Café Lavenue, which is a dignified and comparatively expensive establishment on the Boulevard du Montparnasse. She had been sitting there for nearly an hour and a half, and during that time she had drunk two glasses of black coffee, smoked six caporal cigarettes and read the week's *Candide*.

Marya was a blonde girl, not very tall, slender-waisted. Her face was short, high cheek-boned, full-lipped; her long eyes slanted upwards towards the temples and were gentle and oddly remote in expression. Often on the Boulevards St Michel and Montparnasse shabby youths would glide up to her and address her hopefully in unknown and spitting tongues. When they were very shabby she would smile in a distant manner and answer in English:

'I'm very sorry; I don't understand what you are saying.'

She crossed the boulevard and turned down the Rue de Rennes. As she walked along she was thinking: 'This street is very like the Tottenham Court Road — own sister to the Tottenham Court Road.'

The idea depressed her, and to distract herself she stopped to look at a red felt hat in a shop window. Someone behind her said:

'Hello, Madame Zelli, what are you doing in this part of the world?'

Miss Esther De Solla, tall, gaunt, broad-shouldered, stood looking downwards at her with a protective expression. When Marya answered: 'Hello! Nothing. I was feeling melancholy, to tell you the truth,' she proposed:

'Come along to my studio for a bit.'

Miss De Solla, who was a painter and ascetic to the point of fanaticism, lived in a street at the back of the Lion de Belfort. Her studio was hidden behind a grim building where the housewives of the neighbourhood came to wash their clothes. It was a peaceful place, white-walled, smelling strongly of decayed vegetables. The artist explained that a *marchande des quatre saisons* kept her stock in the courtyard, and that as the woman was the concierge's sister-in-law, complaints were useless.

'Though the smell's pretty awful sometimes. Sit near the stove. It's cold today.'

She opened a massive cupboard and produced a bottle of gin, another of vermouth, two glasses and a cardboard case containing drawings.

'I bought these this morning. What do you think of them?'

Marya, helped by the alcohol, realized that the drawings were beautiful. Groups of women. Masses of flesh arranged to form intricate and absorbing patterns.

'That man's a Hungarian,' explained Miss De Solla. 'He's just over the way in the house where Trotsky used to live. He's a discovery of Heidler's. You know Heidler, the English picture-dealer man, of course.'

Marya answered: 'I don't know any of the English people in Paris.'

'Don't you?' said Miss De Solla, shocked. Then she added hastily: 'How perfectly lovely for you!'

'D'you think so?' asked Marya dubiously.

Miss De Solla assured her that it was.

'I do think that one ought to make an effort to get away from the Anglo-Saxons in Paris, or what on earth is the good of being here at all? And it isn't an easy thing to do, either. Not easy for a woman, anyhow. But, of course, your husband's French, isn't he?'

'No,' said Marya. 'He's a Pole.'

The other looked across at her and thought: 'Is she really married to the Zelli man, I wonder? She's a decorative little person — decorative but strangely pathetic. I must get her to sit to me.'

She began to argue that there was something unreal about most English people.

'They touch life with gloves on. They're pretending about something all the time. Pretending quite nice and decent things, of course. But still . . .'

'Everybody pretends,' Marya was thinking. 'French people pretend every bit as much, only about different things and not so obviously. She'll know that when she's been here as long as I have.'

'As long as I have.' The four years she had spent in Paris seemed to stretch into infinity.

'English people . . .' continued Miss De Solla in a dogmatic voice.

The drone of a concertina sounded from the courtyard of the studio. The man was really trying to play 'Yes, we have no bananas'. But it was an unrecognizable version, and listening to it gave Marya the same feeling of melancholy pleasure as she had when walking along the shadowed side of one of those narrow streets full of shabby *parfumeries*, second-hand book-stalls, cheap hat-shops, bars frequented by gaily-painted ladies and loud-voiced men, midwives' premises . . .

Montparnasse was full of these streets and they were often inordinately long. You could walk for hours. The Rue Vaugirard, for instance. Marya had never yet managed to reach the end of the Rue Vaugirard, which was a very respectable thoroughfare on the whole. But if you went far enough towards Grenelle and then turned down side streets . . .

Only the day before she had discovered, in this way, a most attractive restaurant. There was no *patronne*, but the *patron* was beautifully made up. Crimson was where crimson should be, and rose-colour where rose-colour. He talked with a lisp. The room was full of men in caps who bawled intimacies at each other; a gramophone played without ceasing; a beautiful white dog under the counter, which everybody called Zaza and threw bones to, barked madly.

But Stephan objected with violence to these wanderings in sordid streets. And though Marya considered that he was extremely inconsistent, she generally gave way to his inconsistencies and spent hours alone in the bedroom of the Hôtel de l'Univers. Not that she objected to solitude. Quite the contrary. She had books, thank Heaven, quantities of books. All sorts of books.

Still, there were moments when she realized that her existence, though delightful, was haphazard. It lacked, as it were, solidity; it lacked the necessary fixed background. A bedroom, balcony and *cabinet de toilette* in a cheap Montmartre hotel cannot possibly be called a solid background.

Miss De Solla, who had by this time pretty well exhausted her fascinating subject, stopped talking.

Marya said: 'Yes, but it's pretty lonely, not knowing any English people.'

'Well,' Miss De Solla answered, 'if that's what you're pining for. What are you doing this evening? Come along to Lefranc's and meet the Heidlers. You must have heard of Heidler.'

'Never.'

'Hugh Heidler?' protested Miss De Solla.

She proceeded to explain Mr Heidler, who was a very important person in his way, it seemed. He made discoveries; he helped the young men, he had a flair.

'I believe they intend to settle in France for good now — Provence in the winter and Montparnasse for the rest of the year — you know the sort of thing. He's had a kind of nervous breakdown. Of course, people say—'

Miss De Solla stopped.

'I like Mrs Heidler anyway; she's a very sensible woman; no nonsense there. She's one of the few people in Montparnasse whom I do like. Most of them . . . But abuse isn't any good, and it's better to be clean than kind.'

'Much better!' agreed Marya.

'Not that they are mad on baths or nailbrushes, either,' said the other. 'Never mind.' She got up and lit a cigarette. 'Mrs Heidler paints, too. It's pretty awful to think of the hundreds of women round here painting away, and all that, isn't it?'

She looked round her austere studio, and the Jewess's hunger for the softness and warmth of life was naked in her eyes.

'Well,' said Marya, 'I'd like to come, but I must telephone to Stephan, to my husband. Where can I telephone from?'

'From the Café Buffalo. Wait a minute, I've got to stand on a chair to put my gas out. My shark of a landlady won't put in electric light. Mind you, I'm fond of this place, though the smell is really awful sometimes. That head over there doesn't look so bad in this light, does it?' said Miss De Solla, wistfully.

.   .   .

Lefranc's is a small restaurant half-way up the Boulevard du Montparnasse. It is much frequented by the Anglo-Saxons of the quarter, and by a meagre sprinkling of Scandinavians and Dutch.

The *patron* is provincial and affable. The *patronne*, who sits beaming behind the counter, possesses a mildy robust expression and the figure and coiffure of the nineties; her waist goes in, her hips come out, her long black hair is coiled into a smooth bun on the top of her round head. She is very restful to the tired eye.

The Heidlers were sitting at a table at the end of the room.

'Good evening,' said Mrs Heidler in the voice of a well-educated young male. Her expression was non-committal.

'*Encore deux vermouths-cassis!*' said Mr Heidler to the waitress.

They were fresh, sturdy people. Mr Heidler, indeed, was so very sturdy that it was difficult to imagine him suffering from a nervous breakdown of any kind whatever. He looked as if nothing could break him down. He was a tall, fair man of perhaps forty-five. His shoulders were tremendous, his nose arrogant, his hands short, broad and so plump that the knuckles were dimpled. The wooden expression of his face was carefully striven for. His eyes were light blue and intelligent, but with a curious underlying expression of obtuseness — even of brutality.

'I expect he's awfully fussy,' thought Marya.

Mrs Heidler was a good deal younger than her husband, plump and dark, country with a careful dash of Chelsea, and wore with assurance a drooping felt hat which entirely hid the upper part of her face. She sat in silence for some time listening to Miss De Solla's conversation about the dearth of studios, and then suddenly remarked to Marya:

'H. J. and I have quite made up our minds that eating is the greatest pleasure in life. Well, I mean, it is, isn't it? At any rate, it's one of the few pleasures that never let you down.'

Her eyes were beautiful, clearly brown, the long lashes curving upwards, but there was a suspicious, almost a deadened look in them.

'I'm a well-behaved young woman,' they said, 'and you're not going to catch me out, so don't think it.' Or perhaps, thought Marya, she's just thoroughly enjoying her pilaff.

Miss De Solla, looking more ascetic than ever, agreed that eating was jolly. They discussed eating, cooking, England and, finally, Marya, whom they spoke of in the third person as if she were a strange animal or at any rate a strayed animal — one not quite of the fold.

◆　　◆　　◆

'But you are English — or aren't you?' asked Heidler.

He was walking along the boulevard by her side, his head carefully thrown back.

Marya assured him that she was. 'But I left England four years ago.'

He asked: 'And you've been all the time in Paris?' Then, without waiting for her to answer, he added fussily: 'Where have Lois and Miss De Solla got to? Oh, there they are! I'll just go and see if Guy is in here, Lois.'

He disappeared into the Café du Dôme.

'It's a dreadful place, isn't it?' said Mrs Heidler.

Marya, looking through the door at the mournful and tightly packed assembly, agreed that it was rather dreadful.

Heidler emerged, puffing slightly, and announced in a worried tone:

'He's not here. We'll sit on the terrace and wait for him.'

The terrace was empty and cold, but without argument they all sat down and ordered coffee and liqueur brandies.

Marya, who was beginning to shiver, drank her brandy and found herself staring eagerly and curiously at Mrs Heidler.

A strong, dark woman, her body would be duskily solid like her face. There was something of the earth about her, something of the peasant. Her mouth was large and thick-lipped, but not insensitive, and she had an odd habit of wincing when Heidler spoke to her sharply. A tremor would screw up one side of her face so that for an instant she looked like a hurt animal.

'I bet that man is a bit of a brute sometimes,' thought Marya. And as she thought it, she felt his hand lying heavily on her knee.

He looked kind, peaceful and exceedingly healthy. His light, calm eyes searching the faces of the people passing on the Boulevard Montparnasse, and his huge hand lay possessively, heavy as lead, on her knee.

Ridiculous sort of thing to do. Ridiculous, not frightening. Why frightening?

She made a cautious but decided movement and the hand was withdrawn.

'It's very cold here,' said Heidler in his gentle voice. 'Let's go on to the Select Bar, shall we?'

◆　　◆　　◆

At a little after midnight Marya got back to the Hôtel de l'Univers, Rue Cauchois. She mounted five flights of steep, uncarpeted stairs, felt her way along an unlighted passage, flung her bedroom door open and embraced her husband violently. He looked so thin after the well-fed Heidlers.

'*Tiens, Mado*,' he said. 'You're very late.'

The room was large and low-ceilinged, the striped wallpaper faded to inoffensiveness. A huge dark wardrobe faced a huge dark bed. The rest of the furniture shrank away into corners, battered and apologetic. A narrow door on the left led into a small, very dark dressing-room. There was no carpet on the floor.

I've just this minute got back,' remarked Stephan. Marya said: 'Well, was everything all right?' And when he answered, 'Yes,' she asked no further questions.

Stephan disliked being questioned and, when closely pressed, he lied. He just lied. Not plausibly or craftily, but impatiently and absent-mindedly. So Marya had long ago stopped questioning. For she was reckless, lazy, a vagabond by nature, and for the first time in her life she was very near to being happy.

2

MARYA, YOU MUST understand, had not been suddenly and ruthlessly transplanted from solid comfort to the hazards of Montmartre. Nothing like that. Truth to say, she was used to a lack of solidity and of fixed backgrounds.

Before her marriage she had spent several years as a member of Mr Albert Prance's No.1 touring company. An odd life. Morose landladies, boiled onion suppers. Bottles of gin in the dressing-room. Perpetual manicuring of one's nails in the Sunday train. Perpetual discussions about men. ('Swine, deary, swine.') The chorus knew all about men, judged them with a rapid and terrible accuracy.

Marya had longed to play a glittering part — she was nineteen then — against the sombre and wonderful background of London. She had visited a theatrical agent; she had sung — something — anything — in a quavering voice, and the agent, a stout and weary gentleman, had run his eyes upwards and downwards and remarked in a hopeless voice: 'Well, you're no Tetrazzini, are you, deary? Never mind, do a few steps.'

She had done a few steps. The stout gentleman had glanced at another gentleman standing behind the piano, who was, it seemed, Mr Albert Prance's manager. Both nodded slightly. A contract was produced. The thing was done.

'Miss — I say, what d'you call yourself? — Miss Marya Hughes, hereinafter called the artist.'

Clause 28: no play, no pay.

The next day she attended her first rehearsal and listened to the musical director bawling, with a resigned expression: 'Sopranos on my right, contraltos on my left.'

Mr Albert Prance himself had a curved nose, a large stomach and a long black moustache. He watched the rehearsals and would occasionally make a short speech. Something like this:

'Ladies and gentlemen. This play wants guts!'

He terrified Marya; her knees shook whenever he came anywhere near her.

Sometimes she would reflect that the way she had been left to all this was astonishing, even alarming. When she had pointed out that, without expensive preliminaries, she would be earning her own living, everybody had stopped protesting and had agreed that this was a good argument. A very good argument indeed. For Marya's relatives, though respectable people, presentable people (one might even go so far as to say quite good people), were poverty-stricken and poverty is the cause of many compromises.

There she was and there she stayed. Gradually passivity replaced her early adventurousness. She learned, after long and painstaking effort, to talk like a chorus girl, to dress like a chorus girl and to think like a chorus girl — up to a point. Beyond that point she remained apart, lonely, frightened of her loneliness, resenting it passionately. She grew thin. She began to live her hard and monotonous life very mechanically and listlessly.

A vague procession of towns all exactly alike, a vague procession of men also exactly alike. One can drift like that for a long time, she found, carefully hiding the fact that this wasn't what one had expected of life. Not in the very least.

At twenty-four she imagined with dread that she was growing old. Then during a period of unemployment spent in London, she met Monsieur Stephan Zelli.

He was a short, slim, supple young man of thirty-three or four, with very quick, bright brown eyes and an eager but secretive expression. He spoke English fairly well in a harsh voice and (when he was nervous) with an American accent.

He told Marya that he was of Polish nationality, that he lived in Paris, that he considered her beautiful and wished to marry her. Also that he was a *commissionaire d'objets d'art*.

'Oh, you sell pictures,' she said.

'Pictures and other things.'

•   •   •

Marya, who had painfully learnt a certain amount of caution, told herself that this stranger and alien was probably a bad lot. But she felt strangely peaceful when she was with him, as if life were not such an extraordinary muddle after all, as if he were telling her: 'Now then, look here, I know all about you. I know you far better than you know yourself. I know why you aren't happy. I can make you happy.'

And he was so sure of himself, so definite, with such a clean-cut mind. It was a hard mind, perhaps, disconcertingly and disquietingly sceptical. But at any rate it didn't bulge out in all sorts of unexpected places. Most people hesitated. They fumbled. They were so full of reticences and prejudices and uncertainties and spites and shames, that there was no getting anywhere at all. One felt after a time a blankness and a jar — like trying to walk up a step that wasn't there. But, good or bad, there Monsieur Zelli was. Definite. A person. He criticized her clothes with authority and this enchanted her. He told her that her arms were too thin, that she had a Slav type and a pretty silhouette, that if she were happy and petted she would become charming. Happy, petted, charming — these are magical words. And the man knew what he was talking about, Marya could see that.

As to Monsieur Zelli, he drew his own conclusions from her air of fatigue, disillusion and extreme youth, her shadowed eyes, her pathetic and unconscious lapses into helplessness. But he was without bourgeois prejudices, or he imagined that he was, and he had all his life acted on impulse, though always in a careful and businesslike manner.

It was the end of a luncheon in Soho. Marya finished smoking her cigarette and remarked:

'You know I haven't got any money, not a thing, not a cent.'

She said this because, when he had leaned forward with the lighted match, he had reminded her of China Audley's violinist.

China, also one of Mr Prance's discoveries, was beloved by a tall, fine-looking young man with large income and a charming voice. A chivalrous young man. He had fought the good fight with his mother, who considered that honourable intentions were unnecessary when dealing with chorus girls. There the two were — engaged.

Then China had madly jilted this marvel, this paragon, and had secretly married the short, swarthy violinist of a Manchester café. She had spent the rest of the tour getting telegraphic appeals from her husband; 'Please send five pounds at once Antonio,' or something like that. Which entailed putting her wrist watch into various pawnshops and taking it out again. Constantly. 'Well it serves her right, doesn't it?' said all the other girls.

'No money. Nothing at all,' repeated Marya. 'My father and mother are both dead. My aunt . . .'

'I know; you told me,' interrupted Monsieur Zelli, who had long ago asked adroit questions and found out all there was to find out about Marya's relations. He had reflected that they didn't seem to care in the least what became of her and that English ideas of family life were sometimes exceedingly strange. But he had made no remark.

'It's a pity,' said Monsieur Zelli. 'It's better when a woman has some money, I think. It's much safer for her.'

'I owe for the dress I have on,' Marya informed him, for she was determined to make things perfectly clear.

He told her that they would go next day and pay for it.

'How much do you owe?'

'It's not worth that,' he remarked calmly when she told him. 'Not that it is ugly, but it has no chic. I expect your dressmaker cheats you.'

Marya was annoyed but impressed.

'You know — you'll be happy with me,' he continued in a persuasive voice.

And Marya answered that she dared say she would.

On a June afternoon, heavy with heat, they arrived in Paris.

•   •   •

Stephan had lived in Montmartre for fifteen years, he told her, but he had no intimate friends and very few acquaintances. Sometimes he took her with him to some obscure café where he would meet an odd-looking old man or a very smartly-dressed young one. She would sit in the musty-smelling half-light sipping iced beer and listening to long, rapid jabberings: '*La Vierge au coussin vert – Première version – Authentique – Documents – Collier de l'Impératrice Eugénie . . .*'

'An amethyst necklace, the stones as big as a calf's eye and set in gold. The pendant pear-shaped, the size of a pigeon's egg. The necklace is strung on a fine gold chain and set with pearls of an extraordinary purity.' The whole to be hung as quickly as possible round the neck of Mrs Buckell A. Butcher of something-or-the-other, Pa, or of any lady willing to put up with an old-fashioned piece of jewellery, because *impératrice* is a fine word and even empress isn't so bad.

Stephan seemed to do most of his business in cafés. He explained that he acted as intermediary between Frenchmen who wished to sell and foreigners (invariably foreigners) who wished to buy pictures, fur coats, twelfth-century Madonnas, Madame du Barry's prie-Dieu, anything.

Once he had sold a rocking-horse played with by one of Millet's many children, and that had been a very profitable deal indeed.

One evening she had come home to find Napoleon's sabre lying naked and astonishing on her bed by the side of its cedar-wood case.

('*Oui, parfaitement,*' said Stephan. 'Napoleon's sabre.')

One of his sabres, she supposed. He must have had several of them, of course. A man like Napoleon. Lots. She walked round to the other side of the bed and stared at it, feeling vaguely uneasy. There was a long description of the treasure on the cedar-wood case.

'There are two sheaths, the first of porcelain inlaid with gold, the second of gold set with precious stones. The hilt of the sabre is in gold worked in the Oriental fashion. The blade is of the finest Damascus steel and on it is engraved: "In token of submission, respect and esteem to Napoleon Bonaparte, the hero of Aboukir —Mouhrad Bey".'

That night, long after the cedar-wood case had been packed away in a shabby valise, Marya lay awake thinking.

'Stephan,' she said at last.

'Well?' answer Stephan. He was smoking in front of the open window. 'I thought you were asleep.'

'No,' said Marya. 'Wherever did you get that thing?'

He explained that it belonged to an old French family.

'They're very poor now and they want to sell it. That's all. Why don't they what? The man has to do it on the sly because his mother and his uncle would stop him if they could.'

Marya sat up in bed, put her arms round her knees and said in an unhappy voice:

'He probably has no right to sell it without his mother's consent.'

'His mother has nothing to say,' remarked Stephan sharply. 'But she would bother him if she could.'

Next morning he went out very early, carrying the old valise, and Marya never knew what became of the sabre.

'America,' said Stephan vaguely when she asked. As who should say 'The sea.'

He never explained his doings. He was a secretive person, she considered. Sometimes, without warning or explanation, he would go away for two or three days, and, left alone in the hotel, she dreaded, not desertion, but some vague, dimly-apprehended catastrophe. But nothing happened. It was a fantastic life, but it kept on its legs so to speak. There was no catastrophe. And eventually Marya stopped questioning and was happy.

Stephan was secretive and a liar, but he was a very gentle and expert lover. She was the petted, cherished child, the desired mistress, the worshipped, perfumed goddess. She was all these things to Stephan — or so he made her believe. Marya hadn't known that a man could be as nice as all that to a woman — so gentle in little ways.

And, besides, she liked him. She liked his wild gaieties and his sudden, obstinate silences and the way he sometimes stretched his hands out to her. Groping. Like a little boy, she would think.

Eighteen months later they went to Brussels for a year. By the time they returned to Paris every vestige of suspicion had left her. She felt that her marriage, though risky, had been a success. And that was that. Her life swayed regularly, even monotonously, between two extremes, avoiding the soul-destroying middle. Sometimes they had a good deal of money and immediately spent it. Sometimes they had almost none at all and then they would skip a meal and drink iced white wine on their balcony instead.

From the balcony Marya could see one side of the Place Blanche. Opposite, the Rue Lepic mounted upwards to the rustic heights of Montmartre. It was astonishing how significant, coherent and understandable it all became after a glass of wine on an empty stomach.

The lights winking up at a pallid moon, the slender painted ladies, the wings of the Moulin Rouge, the smell of petrol and perfume and cooking.

The Place Blanche, Paris, Life itself. One realized all sorts of things. The value of an illusion, for instance, and that the shadow can be more important than the substance. All sorts of things.

3

'GOOD EVENING, Madame Zelli,' said the *patronne* of the Hôtel de l'Univers. 'Will you come in here for a moment? I have something to say to you. Edouard, give the lady a chair.'

There was a small sitting-room behind the hotel bureau where Madame Hautchamp and her husband spent more than half their lives, quite happily so far as one could see. It was a dim, airless place crammed with furniture: a large table, a small table, three straight-backed chairs.

Monsieur Hautchamp, a hairy little man with vague and kindly eyes, muttered something and withdrew.

'Of course,' decided Marya, 'they are going to raise the rent.' She waited.

Madame Hautchamp, who was a large, aquiline lady with a detached and inscrutable expression, announced:

'Your husband will not return tonight, Madame.'

'Oh!' said Marya. 'Ah! *Bon*! Did he telephone?'

She looked at a loudly-ticking clock on the mantelshelf. It was just eight.

'Monsieur,' said the *patronne*, 'has been arrested. Yes, Madame, arrested. About an hour ago, about seven o'clock. An inspector and an agent came here. *Enfin* . . .'

She gesticulated with both hands and one eyebrow.

'I understand nothing of all this, nothing. Unhappily, there is no doubt at all that he has been arrested.'

Silence.

Then Marya asked in a careful voice: 'He didn't — say anything before he went?'

'Monsieur asked, I think, if he could leave a letter for you, and the inspector refused.'

'Oh, did he?' said Marya, staring at Madame Hautchamp.

Her heart had stopped; then began to beat so violently that she felt sick. Her hands were damp and cold. Something in her brain was shrieking triumphantly: 'There you are! I knew it! I told you so!'

The *patronne* remarked, after another pause: 'These things are disagreeable, very disagreeable for everybody. Nobody likes to be mixed up with these things.'

The inflection of her voice aroused in Marya some useful instinct of self-defence, and she was able to say that it was evidently a mistake.

'Oh, evidently,' agreed Madame Hautchamp politely. She looked at her client with curiosity and added: 'Well, don't torment yourself too much. The police! Why, the police arrest people for nothing at all! It's perfectly ridiculous. They have some idea — I don't know — they say that there is a bolshevist plot in Paris. They arrest this one, that one. Meanwhile the *voyous* go free. In your place, I should wait for news without tormenting myself, Madame.'

As Marya climbed the stairs to her room her legs were trembling. She was obliged to hold on to the banisters.

'I must go and find De Solla,' she told herself. Her mind clung desperately to the thought of Miss De Solla's calm, her deep and masculine voice.

◆　　◆　　◆

It was raining and the lights of the Moulin Rouge shone redly through a mist: Salle de danse, Revue.

The Grelot was illuminated. The Place Blanche, sometimes so innocently sleepy of an afternoon, was getting ready for the night's work. People hurried along cowering beneath their umbrellas, and the pavements were slippery and glistening, with pools of water here and there, sad little mirrors which the reflections of the lights tinted with a dull point of red. The trees along the Boulevard Clichy stretched ridiculously frail and naked arms to a sky without stars.

Marya emerged from the Métro on to the Place Denfert-Rochereau, thinking: 'In three minutes I'll hear somebody talking English. In two minutes, in a minute.' She ran along the Avénue d'Orléans. But Miss De Solla's studio was in darkness. She knocked, and a woman put her head out of a door on the other side of the courtyard and said that Mademoiselle had gone to London. Mademoiselle might be away for some weeks, but a letter would be forwarded.

'Ah, I didn't know she'd gone,' said Marya.

She stood staring at the dark windows for a minute, then walked very slowly away. As she turned the corner of the Rue Denfert-Rochereau she saw the Heidlers on the other side of the street. They were walking against the wind, both sheltering under a huge umbrella. A gust of wind flapped Heidler's mackintosh like a flag, caught the umbrella and blew it sideways. She saw his annoyed face.

She thought: 'What's it got to do with them, anyway, and what can they do?' She went along up the street. People turned and stared at her because she was walking so slowly in the pouring rain.

．　　．　　．

She spent several hours of the following day in the annexe of the Palais de Justice on the Quai des Orfèvres. Every half-hour she consulted a tall, fat-faced man in a black robe who, she had been told, would be able to tell her why her husband had been arrested.

'What name?' the fat-faced man would ask wearily.

When she told him, he would run his finger down a list and say: 'No information.'

Then a lesser light would enter with a pile of fresh documents, and Marya would go back to her bench and wait. The bench was of an incredible hardness — the room was big and draughty — her back hurt.

On one side of her sat a very respectable lady dressed in black who had brought her *bonne*, for she wore the Breton cap and apron, and, in spite of the whiteness of the linen, she looked very dirty. They both looked dirty, and they whispered interminably ssp . . . ssp . . . ssp.

On the other side sat a young man with new shoes of a bright reddish yellow, his coat and trousers were tight, his hat very small, no overcoat. He seemed gay and carefree, and whistled a little tune as he looked with sympathy at Marya. He asked at last how long she had been there, and when she told him: 'Oh, they don't hurry themselves, *ces messieurs*. We'll take root here in the end,' he prophesied cheerfully.

Everyone else sat as mournfully still as though they were part of the sombre décor of some incredibly dull play. Sometimes a dapper gentleman with an official air would walk quickly through the outer room and smartly into the inner one and then reappear after an interval looking subdued.

Five o'clock.

'What name?' asked the fat-faced man for the sixth time. 'But I tell you I have no information. No, none. I won't know today — it's too late. You'd better go to the Palais de Justice tomorrow morning.'

'Oh, but I must know now,' Marya told him. 'I must know. It's my husband.'

'If it's your husband or your brother, or your father or your uncle, it's just the same,' said the fat-faced man. 'I don't know.'

He added very indignantly: 'No! But!'

The warder who had directed her to the office of the fat-faced man asked, as she passed him, if she had the information she wanted. She shook her head and began to cry. Her back hurt. She was too tired to be able to bear a kind voice.

'Ah, là, là,' said the warder. 'But it's probably nothing. Nothing at all. Reckless driving. Three days. Come, come. Nothing to cry about, *ma petite dame*. Courage!'

A colleague asked him what he knew about the matter and he turned to explain:

'I can't see a woman cry. When I see a woman cry, I am forced to try to comfort her. *C'est plus fort que moi.*'

He began again earnestly: '*Ma petite dame . . .*'

Marya had already walked on.

'Not that way out,' said a vague voice.

She faced round, passed under an archway, and was on the peaceful Quai des Orfèvres. She stayed there for a long time watching the trembling reflections of the lights on the Seine. Yellow lights like jewels, like eyes that winked at her. Red lights like splashes of blood on the stealthy water. Necklaces of lights over the dark, slowly moving water.

She stayed there till a passing youth called: 'Hé, little one. Is it for tonight the suicide?'

Then she hailed a taxi and went back to Montmartre, thinking indifferently as she paid the driver: 'And I haven't much money, either. This is a beautiful muddle I'm in.'

•   •   •

Next day she went to the Palais de Justice.

Shining gates, ascending flights of steps. *Liberté, Egalité, Fraternité* in golden letters; *Tribunal de Police* in black. As it were, a vision of heaven and the Judgment.

She was hurrying along corridors and up staircases after a bright little man in horn-rimmed spectacles, who had informed her that he was a journalist and asked if he could be of any service to her. He knew the Palais very well indeed, he said. He would dart at a door, tap on it, ask a rapid question and set off again in the opposite direction, and Marya, hastening after him, began to feel as though she were playing some intricate game of which she did not understand the rules. As they ran he talked about the bolshevist scare. He said that the arrests had become a scandal, that it was time that they were stopped, that they would be stopped.

'That's what we are here for, we others, we journalists.' Every time she thanked him breathlessly, he would answer: 'I am only too happy to assist a confrère.'

She wondered why he imagined that Stephan was a journalist. 'Now what have I said to make him think that?' she worried.

He rapped at a final door. Two gentlemen wearing long black robes, little white collars and full black beards, looked at them with inquiry.

'The husband of Madame,' explained Marya's friend, 'a Monsieur Stephan Zelli, a confrère,' he smiled and bowed again, 'has been arrested. She is naturally anxious, very anxious indeed to know the reason of his arrest.'

Fluent explanations flowed gently and persuasively from him. Clever little man! And he was going to get what he wanted, too, for one of the lawyers got up, looked through a pile of documents and came back with a dossier. He said:

'Zelli, Stephan. Aha! You wish to know the cause of the arrest? It is an affair of theft, of *escroquerie.*'

The journalist cleared his throat and coughed.

'*Bon soir, Madame, bon soir,*' he said hurriedly. 'I'm most happy to have been of service to you.' He backed towards the door, looking nervous as though he were afraid she would try to keep him with her, drag him by force into her disreputable existence. '*Bon soir, bon soir!*' he kept saying in a bright voice. And vanished.

'Is it a very serious affair?' asked Marya.

She thought of all the corridors and staircases which had led her to this dim, musty-smelling room and felt bewildered and giddy.

Both the lawyers laughed heartily and one of them threw his head back to do it, opening his mouth widely and showing a long pink and white tongue and the beginnings of a palate.

'Theft, Madame,' he said reproachfully, when he had finished laughing, 'is always a serious affair.' He ran hard eyes over her with the look of an expert passing intimate judgments, smiled again and asked her nationality. 'Polish, also?'

'No,' said Marya. She got up.

The less flippant gentleman with the longer beard said that that was all they could tell her.

'Your husband has been arrested on a charge — several charges

— of theft. He is in the Prison de la Santé and you will probably hear from him in a day or two. You can get a permit to see him in the annexe, Quai des Orfèvres.'

'Thank you,' said Marya.

4

A LETTER FROM Stephan arrived next morning.

> *My dear Mado,*
> *I fear that you must be most unquiet. Still I could not write for the reason that I was not allowed to up till yet. When I came in that evening I found two men waiting for me and they showed me the warrant for my arrest. I am accused of selling stolen pictures and other things. This is ridiculous. However, here I am, and I don't think that they will let me go as quickly as all that. Except I can find a very good lawyer. Everything will depend on my lawyer. Come to see me on Thursday, the day of the visits, and I will try to explain things. My dear, I have such a cafard.*
>
> *Stephan*

'It's a pity all the same,' thought the watching Madame Hautchamp, who noticed that the young woman was pale and had a troublesome cough. 'Ah, all these people,' she thought.

Madame Hautchamp meant all of them. All the strange couples who filled her hotel — internationalists who invariably got into trouble sooner or later. She went back into the sitting-room and remarked as much to Monsieur Hautchamp, who was reading the newspaper, and Monsieur Hautchamp shrugged his shoulders; then, with an expression of profound disapproval, he continued his article which, as it happened, began thus:

'*Le mélange des races est à la base de l'évolution humaine vers le type parfait.*'

'I don't think,' thought Monsieur Hautchamp — or something to that effect.

Marya folded her letter, which was written in English on cheap, blue-lined paper, put it carefully into her handbag, and walked out into the Place Blanche. She spent the foggy day in endless, aimless walking, for it seemed to her that if she moved quickly enough she would escape the fear that hunted her. It was a vague and shadowy fear of something cruel and stupid that had caught her and would never let her go. She had always known that it was there — hidden under the more or less pleasant surface of things. Always. Ever since she was a child.

You could argue about hunger or cold or loneliness, but with that fear you couldn't argue. It went too deep. You were too mysteriously sure of its terror. You could only walk very fast and try to leave it behind you.

That evening she sat for a long while in a small bar drinking coffee and after the third glass composed a letter to England asking for some money. Then: 'But they haven't got any to send,' she thought. 'I won't tell them yet anyhow. What's the use?'

She tore the letter up. She told herself: 'I've got to be sensible. I'll get out of this all right if I'm sensible. I've got to have some guts, as Albert Prance would say.'

Opposite her a pale, long-faced girl sat in front of an untouched drink, watching the door. She was waiting for the gentleman with whom she had spent the preceding night to come along and pay for it, and naturally she was waiting in vain. Her mouth drooped, her eyes were desolate and humble.

.   .   .

Marya went back to her bedroom from the misty streets and shut the door with a feeling of relief as if she had shut out a malignant world. Her bedroom was a refuge. She undressed slowly, thinking: 'Funny this room is without Stephan.' Empty it looked and full of shadows. Every now and again she would stop undressing and listen, half expecting to hear him coming along the passage.

When she lay down she put out her hand and touched his pillow gently. . . . Stephan. He was a bad lot. Possibly. Well, obviously. And what if he were? 'I don't care,' thought Marya. 'He's been kind to me. We've been friends. We've had fun together. I don't care what he is.'

She turned several times uneasily; then sighed, put on the light and lit a cigarette with shaking hands. Humbug it all was. The rotten things that people did. The mean things they got away with — sailed away with — smirking. Nobody caring a bit. Didn't she know something about that? Didn't she, though! But, of course, anything to do with money was swooped on and punished ferociously.

'Humbug!' she said aloud.

But as soon as she put the light out the fear was with her again — and now it was like a long street where she walked endlessly. A redly lit street, the houses on either side tall, grey and closely shuttered, the only sound the clip-clop of horses' hoofs behind her, out of sight.

In the morning she went back to the Quai des Orfèvres and was given a permit to visit the Santé prison. Marya Zelli, aged 28 years, British by birth. Polish by marriage. . . . And so on, and so on.

◆   ◆   ◆

The outside wall of the Santé frowns down on the Boulevard Arago. Three hundred blackened yards of it, sombre and hopeless. Also it seemed never-ending and there was no sign of an entrance. Eventually Marya asked a policeman who was pacing up and down outside to direct her, and when he stared, she told him in a low voice that she wished to visit one of the prisoners. He jerked a thumb over his shoulder in the direction of a side-street and turned his back. Inside the entrance a fat, blond warder with a pear-shaped stomach, who sat overlapping a very small chair, waved her onwards with an austere and majestic gesture. She crossed a courtyard paved with grey cobblestones and ascended a flight of stairs into an entrance hall where a bevy of warders were waiting fussily to take the permits. 'It's rather like giving up one's ticket in a Paris theatre,' thought Marya.

She went into the *parloir*, which was a huge room full of the buzz of voices. One of the warders opened the door of a small cubicle, and she sat down on a wooden bench and stared steadily through bars that were like bars of an animal's cage. Her heart began to beat heavily. The buzzing noise deafened and benumbed her. She felt as though an iron band were encircling her head tightly, as though she were sinking slowly down into deep water.

Stephan appeared on the other side suddenly, as if he had somehow been shot out of a trap.

'Hallo, Mado!'

'Hallo,' she said. 'My poor boy, what rotten luck!'

'I think,' said Stephan, glancing round nervously, 'that we are supposed to talk French. Can you hear what I say?' he asked.

'Of course.'

'Well, this hellish noise. One would say that the whole of Paris is in here, yelling. Mado, listen, the worst, the very worst is that this has happened when I have no money. You must write to England at once for money. Have you written yet?'

She answered cautiously: 'Well, I've written, but they haven't much to send, you know. What's the use of worrying them when they can't really help? But I'll be all right,' she added fretfully; 'I'll manage something for myself. Of course, there must be heaps of things I can do, only I've got an awful cold and I can't think properly.'

She felt awkward and ill at ease. It was horrible to see his face peering at her through bars, thin and furtive, scarcely like Stephan at all. She said:

'Tell me what happened exactly. I would rather know.'

He moved his head from side to side awkwardly.

'Well, I told you in my letter, didn't I?'

He doesn't want to tell me, she thought. And, after, all, what does it matter? The iron band round her head was drawn tighter.

He began to talk rapidly, gesticulating, but what he said conveyed nothing at all to her. She had suddenly ceased to be able to understand French. He had become strangely remote.

'And not a sou on me when I was arrested,' continued Stephan. 'That's the stupid thing. That it should have happened just now.' He swore softly: '*Nom de Dieu*! It's you I am worrying about.'

'Oh, I'll be all right,' said Marya.

The warder banged the door open. They grimaced smiles at each other.

At the beginning of the next week she sold her dresses. She lay in bed, for her cold had become feverish. The garments were spread over a chair ready for the inspection of Madame Hautchamp, who, sympathetic without for one moment allowing her sympathy to overflow a certain limit of business-like correctness, explained:

'My sister-in-law is a *teinturière* and I can make an arrangement with her to hang them for sale in her window, otherwise I could not buy them at all. And, as it is, I can't offer you very much. This, for instance, this *robe de soirée* . . .' She pointed out the gem of the collection: 'Who would buy it? Nobody. Except a woman *qui fait la noce*. Fortunately, my sister-in-law has several clients *qui font la noce*.'

'But I don't see why it must be that sort of woman,' argued Marya.

'It's not a practical dress,' said Madame Hautchamp calmly;

'it's a fantasy, one may say. Therefore, if it is bought at all, it will be bought by that kind of woman. Fortunately, as I have told you, my sister-in-law has several clients . . .'

Madame Hautchamp was formidable. One heard the wheels of society clanking as she spoke. No mixing. No ill feeling either. All so inevitable that one could only bow the head and submit.

'I can give you two hundred and fifty francs,' calculated Madame Hautchamp, looking like a well-coiffured eagle with a gift for bargaining.

'All right,' said Marya. She shivered, shut her eyes, moved her head uneasily to find a cool place on the pillow.

'Ah, how stupid I am!' said the lady, gathering up the dresses. 'This pneumatique came for you.'

'Dear Madame Zelli,' wrote Mrs Heidler. 'We had your address from Miss De Solla. Would you care to dine with us tomorrow night and go on to a party given by an American friend of ours whom I'm sure you'll like? Lefranc's at half-past eight. I do hope you will be able to come.'

5

'WELL,' SAID HEIDLER, 'here's hoping.'

Marya smiled and answered: 'Here's hoping.'

She was cold. Her feet were soaked. She imagined that all the people in the restaurant looked sleek, tidy and placid, and envied their well-ordered lives. Then the vermouth warmed her throat and chest and she felt less physically miserable.

'Monsieur Lefranc,' called Heidler.

The patron hurried up to the table; a quick, lively little man, but sparing of word and gesture, recommending this or that with an air as if to say: 'And I wouldn't do this for everybody, mind you.' One saw at once why English people patronized his restaurant. That decent restraint gave them confidence.

Mrs Heidler observed her guest with calm brown eyes.

'But you're wet through, poor child!'

Marya answered that it was nothing, just the sleeve of her coat.

'Then take it off,' advised Mrs Heidler.

She looked past Marya at a girl dressed in red, followed by two young men, who passed the table with coldly averted head.

'Well,' she said, 'did you see Cri-Cri cut me dead, H.J.? Considering that she came to my party last Saturday.'

Cri-Cri, who was a bold spirit and a good sort, sat down with her legs widely apart like some hardy cavalier, seized the menu and began to talk rapidly in a rather cantankerous voice. She was a small, plump girl with an astonishingly accurate make-up, a make-up which never varied, day in and day out, week in and week out. Her round cheeks were painted orange-red, her lips vermilion, her green eyes shadowed with kohl, her pointed nose dead white. There was never too much or too little, or a lock of her sleek black hair out of place. A wonderful performance. She was the famous model of a Japanese painter, also a cabaret singer and a character; and she had ignored the Heidlers because she realized that she could afford to display coldness, and that no good ever comes from being too polite.

Mrs Heidler watched her with a wistful expression, for she was unable to avoid putting a fictitious value on anyone who snubbed her, and she was really anxious to have people like Cri-Cri at her parties. People who got written about. Characters. Types. She began to discuss the famous lady, characters in general, beauty.

'It's an angle of the eyes and mouth,' said Mrs Heidler. She repeated, satisfied: 'That's what it is. I've noticed it over and over again. It's a certain angle of the eyes and mouth.'

Monsieur Lefrane served the fish.

When Marya looked across the table at Heidler, she noticed that he had oddly shaped eyelids, three-cornered eyelids over pale, clever eyes. Not at all an amiable looking person. But nevertheless not without understanding, for every time that her glass was empty he refilled it. She began to feel miraculously reassured, happy and secure. Her thoughts were vague and pleasant, her misery distant as the sound of the rain. She watched through a slight mist a party of people who had just come into the restaurant, the movements of arms taking off overcoats, of legs in light-coloured stockings and feet in low-heeled shoes walking over the wooden floor to hide themselves under the table-cloths. Against a blurred background she saw, with enormous distinctness, a woman's profile, another's back, the row of bottles on the counter, a man's shoulders and his striped tie. Marya sat very upright on the leather bench, talking carefully and coherently. A confused murmur of voices — Mrs Heidler's loud and authoritative, Heidler's gentle and hesitating.

'Oh, Lola,' Heidler was saying, 'Lola is Elizabethan.' They were still discussing types.

The grey-blue room seemed to be growing larger, the walls had receded, the bulbs of the electric lights had expanded mysteriously. Now they looked like small moons.

'Ah, there you are, Anna,' said Mrs Heidler to a small, neat American, with baby-blonde hair, a keen eye and a very firm mouth indeed.

'Lola is in the Select,' remarked this lady. 'She'll be along in a minute.'

Miss Lola Hewitt arrived, accompanied by a fresh-faced youth who wore a *béret basque*, a jersey, and very shabby trousers. Lola was a pretty lady, but she seemed moody. Her long thin fingers twitched on the stem of her glass, and she announced: 'Oh, I am not in my *assiette*, as the dear French say.'

'Darling,' Lois told her, 'don't get depressed. Have another *fine*.'

A gaunt lady wearing a turban was also, it seemed, going to the party; so was a pleasant gentleman who sat down next to Marya and invited her to meet him in the Dôme at half-past ten on the following morning. He added cheerfully: 'I didn't catch your name. Mine's Porson.' And Marya realized from his tone that Mr Porson must be a celebrated person. The turbaned lady was saying jerkily: 'It's a pity about Rolls and the literary gathering, isn't it? Yes, he's got a literary gathering on this evening at the Café Lavenue. Nine o'clock. Rolls and Boyes. Both of them. All the Middle Westerners are going.'

'I say,' persisted Porson, 'couldn't you turn up tomorrow? I wish you would. I feel that I'd like to talk to you. I know that half-past ten is a bit early, but I'm going back to London in the afternoon.' He added, drooping his head mournfully, that he had been getting divorced. 'And it's a miserable business. Oh, wretched! Most depressing.'

It was difficult to listen to the details of Mr Porson's divorce. Marya heard the fresh-faced boy saying: 'I can drink whatever I like, and pull myself together in a minute with the stuff.'

'What is it?' she said, leaning over to him. 'Let me look.'

'Would you like to try one?' asked the boy. He handed her over a small capsule. 'Break it, sniff it up, that's right.'

Marya broke the capsule and inhaled. Her heart stopped with a jerk, then seemed to dilate suddenly and very painfully. The blood rushed over her face and neck. 'I'm going to fall,' she thought with terror, and clutched the edge of the table.

'That got you all right,' said the fresh-faced boy, interested. He appealed to the others: 'I say, do look. She got that all right, didn't she?'

From a great distance Marya heard the voice of the lady with the turban: 'Rolls is, of course, the great stylist, but Boyes — Boyes is the pioneer.'

'I'm so sorry,' she began. Then she explained, speaking carefully, that she was afraid she could not go on to the party, that she was afraid that she must go straight home. 'I've had 'flu and it's pulled me down a bit. I must go home,' she muttered, looking at Heidler with appeal.

'Of course,' he said. 'It's still pouring; you must have a taxi.'

As they walked to the door she felt passionately grateful to him. She was sure that he knew she was ill and near to tears. He was a rock of a man with his big shoulders and his quiet voice.

'Good night,' he said. 'Lois will look you up as soon as we get back from Brunoy. Take care of that cough. Don't worry.'

He shut the taxi door.

6

TEN DAYS LATER Stephan was tried and sentenced to a year's imprisonment to be followed by expulsion from France. Marya went to the Santé to see him, feeling exhausted, listless, drained of all capacity for emotion. But as soon as she entered the dark courtyard of the prison her indifference vanished. In the *parloir* a warder opened the door of a cubicle and signed to her. She waited, breathless, trembling a little.

When Stephan appeared: 'I've been ill,' she began, 'or I'd have come to the Palais de Justice for your trial.'

'But I asked you not to,' answered Stephan. 'Didn't you get my letter? Well . . . no luck.'

He was unshaven and collarless. He sat huddled up on the wooden seat, staring at her with sunken, reddened eyes. 'I'm not going to be able to stand it,' he said in a small voice — a little boy's voice. 'I can't. I can't.'

The loud conversations from the neighbouring cubicles were like the buzzing of gigantic insects. Inexorable, bewildering noise.

'I have such a cafard when I think of you, Mado.'

Marya said: 'Well, I expect I'll be all right. The Heidlers.' She pressed her hands tightly together in her lap. 'I mustn't cry, whatever I do,' she was thinking.

'Heidlers?' questioned Stephan vaguely.

'Mrs Heidler came to see me just after I got your letter and I told her. I'm sorry. I didn't mean to give you away; but I felt, you know — awful.'

'Oh, what's it matter?' said Stephan. '*Je m'en fiche.*' Then he added, curiously: 'What did she say?'

'Nothing very much. I think she's a good sort.' She stopped, remembering Lois's voice when she remarked: 'Of course, something's got to be done about it, my dear.' A masterful voice.

'I'm going to see them tonight,' she went on. 'They will probably be able to help me to a job or something. Besides, I can get a little money from England. I'll be all right.'

They sat in silence for a time, then he told her that he was going to be sent to Fresnes, not to a central prison.

'Fresnes is quite near Paris. Will you come and see me?'

'Of course, of course. . . . Stephan, listen. Don't worry, my dear. You'll be free in September, won't you? It isn't so long. The time will pass quickly.' Not very clever that. But her brain wasn't working properly.

'Quickly! My God, that's funny! Quickly!'

He laughed, but she thought that he looked as though he were begging for help, and she felt desperate with the longing to comfort him.

'I love you,' she said.

'*C'est vrai?*' asked Stephan. 'Well, perhaps. I'll see that.'

She repeated: 'I love you. Don't be too sad, my dear.' But hopelessly, for she felt that he was withdrawn from her, enclosed in the circle of his own pain, unreachable.

A warder behind him flung the door open and he jumped up with an alacrity which she thought dreadful, shocking.

'So long!' he said in English, smiling his grimace of a smile.

The warder bawled something. He started like a nervous horse and disappeared from her view.

◆　　◆　　◆

It was a foggy afternoon, with a cold sharpness in the air. Outside, the street lamps were lit. 'It might be London,' thought Marya. The Boulevard Arago, like everything else, seemed unreal, fantastic, but also extraordinarily familiar, and she was trying to account for this mysterious impression of familiarity.

She felt cold when she reached the Avenue d'Orléans and walked into a bar for some hot coffee. The place was empty save for a big man who was sitting opposite drinking a demi of dark beer. He stared at Marya steadily and heavily as he drank, and when she took Stephan's letter out of her bag and reread it he thought: 'Doubtless a rendezvous.'

'My lawyer didn't know his métier. Instead of defending me he told the court that I knew six languages. A stupid affair at Brussels was referred to. This did me in quite . . .'

A stupid affair at Brussels. But when she tried to think this out her tired brain would only conjure up disconnected remembrances of Brussels: waiters in white jackets bearing aloft tall, slim glasses of beer, the Paris train clanking into the dark station, the sun on the red-striped umbrellas in the flower market, the green trees of the Avenue Louise.

She sat there, smoking cigarette after cigarette, long after the large man had disappeared. Every time that the door of the café swung open to admit a customer she saw the crimson lights of the tobacco shop opposite and the crimson reflection on the asphalt and she began to picture the endless labyrinth of the Paris streets, glistening hardly, crowded with hurrying people. But now she thought of them without fear, rather with a strange excitement.

'What's the use of worrying about things?' she asked herself. 'I don't care. I'm sick of being sad.'

She came out of the café and stood for several minutes looking at the Lion de Belfort fair — the booths, the swings, the crowds of people jostling each other in a white glare of light to the gay, metallic music of the merry-go-rounds.

◆　◆　◆

The Heidlers were waiting at August's Restaurant on the Boulevard St Michel. At a quarter to nine Heidler said:

'I hope nothing's happened to that girl.'

And as Lois was answering that she thought not, she hoped not, Marya entered the restaurant. She was very pale, her eyes were shadowed, her lips hastily and inadequately rouged. She was wearing a black dress under her coat, a sleeveless, shapeless, sack-like garment, and she appeared frail, childish, and extraordinarily shabby.

'Shall I tell her, H.J.?' asked Lois.

'Why not?' answered Heidler, looking majestic but slightly embarrassed.

'Don't look frightened,' said Lois.

Marya glanced rapidly from one to the the other and repeated, 'Frightened—?'

'It's something that you'll like, or at any rate I hope you will. You know, H.J. and I have been thinking a lot about you. And, my dear, you can't be left alone like this. I mean, it's impossible, isn't it?'

She put out her hand caressingly. Marya thought how odd it was that she could never make up her mind whether she liked or intensely disliked Mrs Heidler's touch.

Lois went on: 'Now, look here, we want you to move into the spare room at the studio.' Because she was nervous her voice was even more authoritative than usual. 'It's only a cubby-hole of a place, but you'll be all right there. And you must stay till you've made up your mind what you're going to do. Till you're better. As long as you like, my dear.'

Silence.

Monsieur August placed a large sole on the table, glanced at Heidler with light blue, very ironical eyes, and departed.

'Imposing looking chap, August,' remarked Heidler. He fidgeted. He seemed shy.

Marya said in a low voice: 'I don't know how to thank you. It's so awfully good of you to worry about me. . . .'

Heidler remarked with an air of relief that as it was all decided they needn't talk about it any more. Marya smiled a difficult smile. She told herself: 'These people are wonderfully kind, but I certainly don't want to go and live with them. And so I shan't go. There's nothing to worry about.'

'When can you move?' asked Heidler. 'Tomorrow?'

'But,' said Marya, 'I'm afraid I shall be an awful bother.'

'That's all right!' Heidler assured her. His eyes met hers for a second, then he looked quickly away.

'I'm really afraid,' she persisted, 'that it's quite impossible. You're wonderfully kind, but I couldn't dream of bothering you.'

'Rubbish!' said Lois. 'We'd love to have you and it's all arranged. After dinner you must come round to the studio and we'll talk things over. H.J.'s got to go over the other side to see somebody.'

Marya agreed with relief. 'Yes, we'll talk things over.' She was silent and subdued for the rest of the meal.

When Lois announced: 'I shall certainly want to paint you. In that black dress, I think, and short black gloves. Or shall I have short green gloves? What d'you think, H.J.?' she began to wonder why the idea of living with the Heidlers filled her with such extraordinary dismay. After all, she told herself, it might be fun.

.   .   .

The two women walked along the Boulevard St Michel behind their distorted shadows. They walked in silence, close together, almost touching each other, and as they walked Lois was thinking: 'She can't make her mouth up. The poor little devil has got no harm in her and I shouldn't mind doing her a good turn. She won't be much trouble.'

They passed the deserted entrance of the Bal Bullier and the coloured lights of the Closerie des Lilas, and crossed the street into the dimness of the Avenue de l'Observatoire, where the tops of the trees vanished, ghost-like, in the mist.

The Heidlers lived on the second floor of a high building half-way up the street. The outer door was shut, and, as they waited, Lois began to talk about the concierge. She told Marya that they had a beast of a concierge.

'At one of my Saturday parties,' she explained, 'Swansee Grettle — D'you know her? She's a fine gel. She sculpts. Well, Swansee complained that one of the men had kicked her on purpose. So Swansee's man took the other man out on the landing and fought him.'

The door flew open, and Mrs Heidler led the way up the wooden, uncarpeted, staircase, still talking.

'Well, Swansee's man got a bang on the nose and bled all over the place, and when the concierge saw what she had to mop up next morning she made a dreadful row and has been vile to us ever since. Of course, this place is only a makeshift really till we can find something better. Come in here.'

The studio was a big, high-ceilinged room, sparsely furnished, dimly lit. A doll dressed as an eighteenth-century lady smirked conceitedly on the divan, with satin skirts spread stiffly. There was an elaborate gramophone, several cards were stuck into the looking-glass over the mantelpiece. There was a portrait on the wall above the looking-glass, carefully painted but smug and slightly pretentious, like a coloured photograph. Marya thought: 'It's perfectly extraordinary that Heidler should live in a room like this.'

'I'll go and get some cigarettes for you,' Lois told her. 'Lie down on the divan. You look tired.'

She said when she came back: 'You don't want to come and stay with us, do you? Now, why? What's the fuss about? If you really mean that you're afraid of being a bother, put that right out of your head. I'm used to it. H.J.'s always rescuing some young genius or the other and installing him in the spare bedroom . . . Many's the one we've pulled out of a hole since we've been in Montparnesse, I can tell you.' She added: 'And they invariably hate us bitterly afterwards. Never mind! Perhaps you'll be the brilliant exception.'

Marya answered vaguely: 'Yes, but it's not a question with me of just tiding over a few days or a few weeks. I really haven't got any money at all and I do feel I ought to do something about it.'

'Well,' said Lois, 'what will you do?' She looked at Marya with a dubious but intelligent expression as if to say: 'Go on. Explain yourself. I'm listening. I'm making an effort to get at your point of view.'

Marya began with difficulty: 'You see, I'm afraid the trouble with me is that I'm not hard enough. I'm a soft, thin-skinned sort of person and I've been frightened to death these last days. I don't at all mean physically frightened . . .' She stopped.

Mrs Heidler still gazed at her with sensible and inquiring brown eyes.

'I've realized, you see, that life is cruel and horrible to unprotected people. I think life is cruel. I think people are cruel.' All the time she spoke she was thinking: 'Why should I tell her all this?' But she felt impelled to go on. 'I may be completely wrong, of course, but that's how I feel. Well, I've got used to the idea of facing cruelty. One can, you know. The moment comes when even the softest person doesn't care a damn any more; and that's a precious moment. One oughtn't to waste it. You're wonderfully kind, but if I come to stay with you it'll only make me soft and timid and I'll have to start getting hard all over again afterwards. I don't suppose,' she added hopelessly, 'that you understand what I mean a bit.'

Lois argued: 'I don't see why you should have to start getting hard all over again afterwards. People aren't such ogres as all that. People can be quite kind if you don't rub them up the wrong way.'

'Can they?' said Marya.

Lois coughed: 'That's all very well, but, getting down to brass tacks, what exactly do you think of doing? I feel a certain responsibility for you. I don't see why I should. I suppose you're the sort of person one does feel responsible for. You were on the stage, weren't you? Well, I hope you're not thinking of trying for a job as a *femme nue* in a music hall. They don't get paid anything at all, poor dears.'

'I know they don't,' answered Marya. 'No, I won't try to be a *femme nue*. I don't know what I shall do...I don't care, and that's a big advantage, anyway.'

She leaned her head back against the cushions and half shut her eyes. Suddenly she felt horribly tired, giddy with fatigue.

'Of course,' Lois remarked in a reflective voice, 'men . . . a man would possibly . . . yes, in a way . . . But the sort of thing must be done carefully, my girl, or it's the most ghastly fiasco. I mean, even if you make up your mind that it's your best way out, you must plan it very carefully, and however carefully you plan it's often a fiasco, it seems to me.'

'I don't think I'd ever plan anything out carefully,' said Marya, 'and certainly not that. If I went to the devil it would be because I wanted to, or because it's a good drug, or because I don't give a damn for my idiotic body of a woman, anyway. And all the people who yap.' She spoke very quickly, flushed, then burst into tears. 'Now I'm a gone coon,' she thought. 'I've begun to cry and I'll never stop.'

Lois said: 'You see how right I was to tell you that you must come and stay with us, that you mustn't be left alone.' Her voice trembled. Marya was amazed to see tears in her eyes. . . . 'You know,' Lois added, 'H.J., I love him so terribly . . . and he isn't always awfully nice to me.'

They sat side by side on the divan and wept together. Marya wondered how she could ever had thought Lois hard. This soft creature, this fellow-woman, hurt and bewildered by life even as she was. 'She simply is more plucky than I am,' she thought. 'She puts a better face on it.'

Lois was saying: 'When you told me that your husband was in jail — d'you remember? — I felt as if you'd stretched out a hand for help. Well — and I caught hold of your hand. I want to help you. I'll be awfully disappointed and hurt if you don't allow me to.'

'I didn't mean that, really, really,' answered Marya shakily.

Lois blew her nose. Then she remarked with earnestness: 'You mustn't think that I don't see the — the angle you look at life from. Because I do. If I were you I'd hate, loathe, detest everybody safe, everybody with money in the bank.'

'But I wasn't thinking of money so much,' interrupted Marya.

'It's appalling, perfectly appalling,' continued the other in a complacent voice, 'to think of the difference that money makes to a woman's life. I've always said so.'

'Yes, doesn't it?' said Marya.

'Come up and see your room,' Lois suggested, and Marya followed her up a narrow staircase to a little room which smelt clean and cold. Striped grey and green curtains hung straightly over the long windows.

'Now, when do you think you can move?' said Lois briskly. 'Better do it as soon as you can, won't you?'

'You're a darling to worry about me,' answered Marya. 'A darling.'

But as soon as the cold air touched her face outside she felt sobered and melancholy. She hailed a taxi and climbed into it wearily.

'*Ah, ma pauvre vieille!*' she told herself.

7

WHEN THE PARIS tram to Fresnes stopped outside the café called the Cadran Bleu, Marya got down. She walked up a wide road bordered with magnificent trees to the prison, a high, grey building standing in large grounds.

The usual formalities. The usual questioning warders whom she found herself regarding with a mixture of fear and hatred. Then she crossed a cobblestoned courtyard and a dark, dank corridor like the open mouth of a monster swallowed her up. At the extreme end of this corridor a queue of people, mostly women, stood waiting, and as she took her place in the queue she felt a sudden, devastating realization of the essential craziness of existence. She

thought again: people are very rum. With all their little arrange-
ments, prisons and drains and things, tucked away where nobody
can see.

She waited with cold hands and a beating heart, full of an
unreasoning shame at being there at all. Every time the warder
approached her she moved her shoulders nervously, and when he
laid a fat, lingering hand on the arm of one of the women to push
her into place, she thought: if he touches me I shall have to hit him,
and then what will happen to me? I'll be locked up, too, as sure as
God made Moses.

Eventually she was conducted to the inevitable small, roofless
cubicle. A warder paced up and down a wooden platform
overhead, stopping every now and again to listen to the conversations. Stephan appeared with a piece of coarse sacking over his
head. He was like some bright-eyed animal, staring at her, and she
sat in an embarrassed silence, wondering how she could ever have
thought that he would be able to talk things over with her or give
her advice. At last, spurred by the knowledge that soon the warder
would bang on the door and the interview be over, she began to
murmur: 'My poor darling, my poor darling, my poor dear.'

'*Oh, ça!*' said Stephan. He shrugged, leaned forward and asked:
'What's that scarf you've got on? I don't know that scarf, do I?'

They talked about the scarf for a time and then she told him that
the Heidlers had asked her to go and stay with them.

'Look here, Stephan, I don't want to go a bit,' she added.

'Why not?'

'I don't know.'

'Then, for God's sake, why not?' asked Stephan nervously.
'They're your country-people, aren't they? You understand them
and they understand you.'

'I'm not so sure of that,' Marya answered in an obstinate voice.

He went on fretfully:

'Do you want to drive me mad? I wonder if you know what it's
like for me shut up here, thinking of you without a sou. Is Mrs
Heidler nice?'

'Very nice!'

'A good sort? *Bonne camarade?*'

'Oh, yes. . . . Oh, very, I should think.' She added: 'If they
weren't awfully kind people they wouldn't ask me to stay with
them under the circumstances, would they?'

'No, naturally not,' Stephan answered with bitterness. 'Well, if she's as kind as that, why don't you want to stay with her? You must go, Mado; it seems to me so much the best thing for you to do. Look here, you must go.'

'All right!' she said. She would have agreed to anything to quieten him and make him happier, and she was still full of the sense of the utter futility of all things.

As she walked back to the tram she wondered why she had ever thought the matter important at all. There was a merry-go-round at the Porte d'Orléans where the tram stopped. Children were being hoisted on to the backs of the gaily painted wooden horses. Then the music started to clank: '*Je vous aime.*' And the horses pranced around, pawing the air in a mettlesome way.

Marya stayed there for a long time watching a little frail, blonde girl, who careered past, holding tightly on to the neck of her steed, her face tense and strained with delight. The merry-go-round made her feel more normal, less like a grey ghost walking in a vague, shadowy world.

The day before Marya left the Hôtel de l'Univers she received a money order for five pounds from her aunt and namesake enclosed in a letter:

My dear Marya,

Your letter distressed me. You are rather vague — you always are a little vague, dear child. But I gather that all is not well with you. It is difficult for me to offer my advice, since you write so seldom and say so little when you do write. I feel that we live, and have lived for a long time, in different worlds. However, I send the money you ask for. I only wish it were at all possible to send more.

Is your husband well? You don't mention him. You have not quarrelled with him, I hope, or he with you. As I say, your letter distressed me and I feel so powerless to offer help of any sort.

Do write soon and tell me that things are going better with you.

> *Your affectionate aunt,*
> *Maria Hughes.*

P.S. Have you thought of visiting the British clergyman resident in Paris? He might be able to help you. There are, I believe, several. You could easily find out the address of one of them, or I could find out and send it to you.

8

AT NINE O'CLOCK every morning the *femme de ménage* tapped at the door of the little room where the grey and green striped curtains hung straightly over long windows, to announce that coffee was ready.

When Marya went down to the studio she would find Lois lying on the divan. Heidler sat in a big armchair near the stove opening his letters, and when the last letter was read he unfolded the *Matin* and asked for more coffee. Marya always brought the cup and the sugar, for he was very majestic and paternal in a dressing-gown, and it seemed natural that she should wait on him. He would thank her without looking at her and disappear behind the newspaper. He had abruptly become the remote impersonal male of the establishment.

The trio would lunch at Lefranc's, and as Lois had decided that she wished to begin her portrait of the sleeveless dress and the short black gloves at once, Marya spent long, calm afternoons staring through the windows at the tops of the leafless trees and listening to stories about Montparnasse. Lois wore a flowered overall and stood very straight as she worked, her chest well out, her round, brown eyes travelling rapidly from the sitter to the canvas and back again. The movement of her head was oddly like that of a bird picking up crumbs. She talked volubly. She would often stop painting to talk, and it was evident that she took Montparnasse very seriously indeed. She thought of it as a possible stepping-stone to higher things and she liked explaining, classifying, fitting the inhabitants (that is to say, of course, the Anglo-Saxon inhabitants) into their proper places in the scheme of things. The Beautiful Young Men, the Dazzlers, the Middle Westerners, the Down-and-Outs, the Freaks who never would do anything, the Freaks who just possibly might.

Sometimes she would ask questions, and Marya, longing to assert her point of view, would try to describe the charm of her life with Stephan. The vagabond nights, the fresh mornings, the long sleepy afternoons spent behind drawn curtains.

'Stephan's a — a vivid sort of person, you see. What a stupid word! I mean natural. Natural as an animal. He made me come alive; he taught me everything. I was happy. Sometimes just the way the light fell would make me unutterably happy.'

'Yes, of course,' Lois would say intelligently. 'I can quite see how he got hold of you. Quite.'

Lois was extremely intelligent. She held her head up. She looked at people with clear, honest eyes. She expressed well-read opinions about every subject under the sun in a healthy voice, and was so perfectly sure of all she said that it would have been a waste of time to contradict her. And, in spite of all this, or because of it, she gave a definite impression of being insensitive to the point of stupidity —or was it insensitive to the point of cruelty? Which? That was the question. But that, of course, always is the question.

Marya admired her benefactress, but the moment of soft intimacy had come and gone. She felt remote and lonely perched up on the model-stand, listening. Besides, after a time she began to feel that she knew all there was to be known about the various couples of Beautiful Young Men or the charm and chic of Plump Polly. The Beautiful Young Men undulated — they wore jerseys and *bérets basques*; they were spiteful and attractive and talented, and could be little English gentlemen when they liked.

'And that,' said Lois, 'is a very useful quality. In fact — call me a snob if you like — it's my favourite quality. That and good dancing. And, after all, you've got to be careful, haven't you? There's no knowing what you mightn't be let in for. There're some funny ones round here, I can tell you. Some of H.J.'s discoveries I wouldn't trust a yard.'

As for Plump Polly, a former Ziegfeld Folly, she, it seemed, had started a riot in the Dôme on the 14th of July.

'She got up on a bench and sang the Marseillaise. Oh, she was very serious, tears in her eyes and all that. All the Americans were delighted, but the French people thought that she was singing an English parody — well, you know what French people are sometimes. And it was the 14th of July. They broke a lot of glasses and things, and Plump Polly had to be hustled out of the back door by the *patron*.'

Lois also discussed Love, Childbirth (especially childbirth, for the subject fascinated her), Complexes, Paris, Men, Prostitution, and Sensitiveness, which she thought an unmitigated nuisance.

'Clergymen's daughters without any money. Long slim fingers and all the rest. What's the use of it? Those sort of people don't do any good in the world.'

'Well, don't worry,' answered Marya. 'They're getting killed off slowly.'

'Lois is as hard as nails,' she would find herself thinking. A sentence she had read somewhere floated fantastically into her mind: ' "It's so nice to think that the little thing enjoys it too," said the lady, watching her cat playing with a mouse.'

   . . .

Every Thursday Lois gave a party, and Marya felt strangely at a loss during these gatherings where everyone seemed so efficient, so up and doing, so full of That Important Feeling and everything —even sin — was an affair of principle and uplift if you were an American, and of proving conclusively that you belonged to the upper classes, but were nevertheless an anarchist, if you were English. The women were long-necked and very intelligent and they would get into corners and say simple, truthful things about each other. Sometimes they were both intelligent and wealthy and would come to Montparnasse seeking cheap but effective protégés.

'Does that nice-looking young man write? Because if he does I might be able to help him. You know my Ting-a-Ling, Lois? Sweet thing! Well, the little woman who used to look after Ting-a-Ling writes. She writes poems. I got something of hers into our club magazine. Oh, well, then she got very careless and absent-minded and I found a flea on Ting. So I sent her off.'

Marya liked the parties best when, about midnight, everybody was a little drunk. She would watch Heidler, who could not dance, walking masterfully up and down the room to the strains of 'If you knew Susie as I know Susie' played on the gramophone, and wonder almost resentfully why his eyes were always so vague when he looked at her. His sidelong, cautious glances slid over her as it were.

'He looks very German,' she decided. But when they danced she felt a definite sensation of warmth and pleasure.

   . . .

Every Saturday Marya went to Fresnes and waited in the queue of poor and patient people till she saw Stephan, who, craning forward, would talk to her in a voice that seemed to be growing rusty. She thought of him jumping about to the orders of the fat red warder and felt repugnance, a pity which seemed as if it would break her heart, a dreadful, cold loneliness. She would go back to the studio and sit very silent with haunted eyes.

'D'you intend to go on doing this?' asked Lois one day.

Marya told her that she did.

'Well,' remarked Lois, 'I don't approve. The whole atmosphere of a place like that is awfully bad for you. Prisons . . .'

'Please,' said Marya, 'don't talk about it.'

She felt that it would be really unbearable to hear Lois talking common sense about prison and the punished in her young man's voice. Lois said that she intended to talk about it.

'Because I do feel so strongly — we both feel so strongly — that your only chance is to put the whole thing behind you and start again.'

'Start what?' asked Marya.

'You're a very tiresome child,' answered Lois. 'Very. You know that I'm pulling every string I can, and so's H.J. We're certain to fix you up. For instance, I'm almost sure I could get you a mannequin job in about a month or six weeks at What's-his-name in the Rue Royale. You'll be all right,' she continued. 'You'll row your little boat along. You've got your own little charm, and so on.'

Marya looked up suddenly. There was something very like a menace in her long eyes. . . .

'Your own little charm and so on,' repeated Lois. 'But if you try to help your husband, you're done.'

Marya got up and walked to the window. She was crying, and Lois watched her with a puzzled expression, strangely without pity. She said:

'Lots of gels make extraordinary marriages, for all sorts of reasons. When a gel is really lonely and hasn't got a bean it's no use asking why she does things. But the time comes when, if you want to save yourself, you must cut loose. Can't you see that?'

'No, I can't,' said Marya. She repeated with violence: 'I can't. I don't think about things in that way.' Words that she longed to shout, to scream, crowded into her mind: 'You talk and you talk and you don't understand. Not anything. It's all false, all second-hand. You say what you've read and what other people tell you. You think you're very brave and sensible, but one flick of pain to yourself and you'd crumple up.'

She muttered: 'You don't understand.'

'Well, all right,' said Lois, 'let's talk about something else. Will you make me up for the Russian ball at the Bullier tomorrow? I'm going to wear a purple wig. . . . You know I hate myself made up. I don't think it's my genre, as they say here. But H.J. likes it. And I always give way to H.J. I give him what he wants until his mood changes. I found out long ago that that was the only way to manage him.' She suddenly looked complacent, smug, and very female and added: 'H.J.'s an autocrat, I can tell you.'

'Oh, is he?' said Marya vaguely. 'Yes, he is, I think.' She thought with horror: 'I do hope she isn't going to start talking about love and the pangs of childbirth.'

But Lois said: 'D'you mind going to the coiffeur's shop tomorrow to fetch the wig? I want to be quite sure to have it in time. It's a place in the Rue St Honoré.'

Marya answered that of course she would go.

She dined that night by herself in a little crêmerie in the Rue St Jacques. After the meal, which she paid for with her last carefully hoarded hundred-franc note, she walked very quickly along the winding street, between two rows of gas-lamps, past the low doors of little buvettes, where a gramophone played gaily and workmen in caps stood drinking at the counters. It was a beautiful street. The street of homeless cats, she often thought. She never came into it without seeing several of them, prowling, thin vagabonds, furtive, aloof, but strangely proud. Sympathetic creatures, after all.

There was a smell of spring in the air. She felt unhappy, excited, strangely expectant. She tried — and failed — to imagine herself as a mannequin and she thought a great deal with deliberate gratitude about Lois. Lois in her most charming aspect, lying on the divan in the morning pouring out coffee, soft and lazy in a fragile dressing-gown, her beautiful strong arms bare to the shoulder. The next night she waited eagerly on Lois dressing for the dance and spent half an hour carefully making her up. Ochre powder, a little rouge, the tips of the ears, just under the eyes. Huge, sombre eyes and a red mouth — that's what she was getting at. Lois sat before the mirror in the studio. The light was so much better there.

'You ought always to do it,' said Heidler, looking at his wife with interest.

'Do you think so?' answered Lois. She pulled on the purple wig carefully. Her reddened mouth looked extraordinarily hard, Marya thought. When she was following Lois into the bedroom: 'No, sit down for a minute,' Heidler said. 'What a fidget you are!'

He wore spectacles. She thought that he looked kinder, older, less German.

'Don't rush off,' he said. And then, 'Oh, God, I am so utterly sick of myself sometimes. D'you ever get sick of yourself? No, not yet, of course. Wait a bit, you will one of these days.'

'No,' answered Marya reflectively. 'I'm not sick of myself. I'm rather sick of my sort of life.'

'Well, I'm sick of myself,' Heidler said gloomily. 'And yet it goes on. One knows that the whole damn thing's idiotic, futile, not even pleasant, but one goes on. One's caught in a sort of trap, I suppose.'

He stared at the ground between his big knees.

9

THE SPRING came early that year and very suddenly. So that one day the branches of the trees in the Luxembourg Gardens were bare and grim and the next they waved cool leaves in a kind wind. Or so it seemed. Then the chestnuts flowered and the girls walking along with linked arms began to discuss their new clothes endlessly. '*Ma robe verte . . . mon costume gris. . . .*' And on the Boulevard St Michel bevies of young men of every nationality under the sun strolled along smiling at every woman they passed. The Latins were gay and insolent, the Northerns lustful, shamefaced and condescending, the Easterns shy, curious and contemptuous.

Nearly every week-end the Heidlers went down to a country cottage they had found near Brunoy on the way to Fontainebleau. Twice Marya went with them.

Left alone at the flat in the Avenue de l'Observatoire she would dine in the Rue St Jacques and go for solitary walks when the meal was over. But she vaguely disliked the Boulevard St Michel with its rows of glaring cafés, and always felt relieved when she turned into the Boulevard Montparnasse, softer, more dimly lit, more kindly. There she could plunge herself into her dream.

Fancy being shut up in a little dark dirty cell when the spring was coming. Perhaps one morning you'd smell it through the window and then your heart would nearly burst with the longing for liberty.

One evening, just outside the Café de la Rotonde, she met Miss De Solla. That lady had been ill, and seemed discontented with Montparnasse. She was going to Florence for some months, she said, and would not be back in Paris before June.

When Marya informed her that she was living with the Heidlers:

'Yes,' said Miss De Solla, with an uneasy expression, 'as a matter of fact, I heard that you were.'

She added: 'I must be getting along.'

10

THE BAL DU PRINTEMPS is a small, dingy café in the Rue Mouffetard. There is a long zinc bar where the clients can drink a peaceful apéritif after the day's work. There are painted wooden tables, long wooden benches and a small gallery where the band sits – a concertina, a flute and a violin. The couples dance in a cleared space at the end of the room. Men in caps and hatless girls cling together, shake themselves and turn with abandon and a certain amount of genuine enjoyment.

Two policemen at the door supervise the proceedings, and there is a large placard on the wall:

'*Une tenue correcte est rigoureusement exigée.*'

The Bal du Printemps is a family ball. If you want something *louche* you walk further on and turn twice to the left. Mr Rolls, the author, always hired this place for his weekly parties. Sometimes in the midst of the proceedings the surprised head of one of the usual clients would be thrust into the doorway. The landlord would shrug, wink, gesticulate, explain, and the pale youth would disappear, muttering something like: '*Mince de poules de luxe!*' But the quality of the brandy left a great deal to be desired. Imagining that it was very weak, people drank a good deal of it, and it generally had a very bad effect on their tempers.

Midnight. The band struck up *Valencia* for the sixth time.

Somebody said to somebody else: 'It's all very well to talk about Jew noses, but have you ever tried to paint your own mouth?'

The artist addressed burst into tears.

'He's only trying to be modern and brutal and all that, poor dear,' said her friend. . . . 'Don't mind him.'

'*Fine à l'eau,*' bawled a tall dark gentleman immediately in Mr Rolls's ear.

'Don't shout in my ear,' said Mr Rolls irritably.

'Well, get out of the way,' said the tall dark gentleman. 'Always blocking up the bar.'

'It's my bar,' remarked Mr Rolls with majesty.

'Then you ought to give your clients a chance,' said the other.

Mr Rolls wandered about, asking: 'Who brought that chap? How did that chap get in here? Who on earth is that chap?' Nobody knew. It did not matter.

An unknown lady seated herself at the end of one of the benches and remarked to Marya:

'Doesn't Swansee Grettle look awful tonight?'

'She looks,' said the unknown lady, smiling slowly, 'like a hundred gone bad, don't you think?' She was very healthy looking, was the unknown lady, with long, very sharp teeth.

How terrifying human beings were, Marya thought. But she had drunk two fines and a half-bottle of something which the *patron* of the Bal du Printemps called champagne, and after all it was a lovely party. Then she saw Lois standing near the doorway with her coat on. She beckoned and Marya got up with reluctance. It was only just half-past twelve.

'H.J.'s had enough of this,' said Lois. 'He wants to be taken home. D'you mind walking?'

'Not a bit,' answered Marya.

They went arm in arm through the lovely, crooked, silent streets. As they passed a little café on the Boulevard St Michel: 'This place is still open,' remarked Heidler. 'Let's have a bock.'

Lois said that she was tired.

'I'm going home. Don't be too long, you two.'

She disengaged herself, and walked on so abruptly that Marya stood looking after her with some astonishment.

'Come along,' said Heidler.

It was warm as a night in summer — a wonderfully still and brooding night. A sleepy waiter appeared with two glasses of beer and placed them on the only table left on the terrace.

'Do you know why Lois has gone off?' asked Heidler.

'No,' said Marya. 'Why?'

He spoke slowly, without looking at her:

'She's gone away to leave us together — to give me a chance to talk to you, d'you see? She knows that I'm dying with love for you, burnt up with it, tortured with it. That's why she's gone off.'

He had tilted his hat to the back of his head and was looking fixedly across the deserted street. He looked much younger, she thought, and extraordinarily hard.

'You think I'm drunk, don't you?' he said.

'Yes,' she told him. 'Of course.' She repeated: 'Of course. And I'm tired, so let's go home.'

'Do you know why your door is open every morning?' asked Heidler. 'Have you noticed that it's open? No? Stay where you are and listen to what I've got to say. I've had enough. Now you've got to listen. Your door is open because I come up every night and open it. Then I look at you and go away again. One does meaningless things like that when one is tortured by desire. Don't you know that I wanted you the first time I saw you?' He nodded. 'Yes, dare say that you didn't know.'

She stared at him, silent.

'Lois knows it now, anyway. . . . Well, I kept off you, didn't I? I knew that I could have you by putting my hand out, and I kept off you. I thought it wouldn't be playing the game. But there comes a limit, you see. There comes a limit to everything. I've been watching you; I watched you tonight and now I know that somebody else will get you if I don't. You're that sort.'

She said: 'You're abominably rude and unkind and unfair. And you're stupid in a lot of ways. Too stupid to realize how unfair you are.'

'Don't be silly,' he told her calmly. 'You've every right to be like that if you want to be like that, and I've every right to take advantage of it if I want to. That's truth, and all the rest is sob stuff.'

She thought: 'Sob stuff, sex stuff. That's the way men talk. And they look at you with hard, greedy eyes. I hate them with their greedy eyes.' She felt despair and a sort of hard rage. 'It's all wrong,' she thought. 'Everything's wrong.'

'Talk!' she said rudely. 'Talk. I'm going.'

She got up. He left money on the table, followed her and took her arm in his. When he touched her she felt warm and secure, then weak and so desolate that tears came into her eyes.

'It's all right, it's all right!' said Heidler soothingly.

The street was quite empty, a long street glistening with light like a sheet of water. Their footsteps echoed mournfully.

When they reached the studio:

'So you think I'm drunk,' said Heidler. 'So I am. So are you. But I'll talk to you tomorrow when I'm not drunk.'

Marya bolted the door of her room, collapsed on the bed and undressed dizzily and with difficulty. The nasal music of the concertina of the *bal musette* was still in her ears. 'I love you' they played, and *Valencia* and *Mon Paris*. The sound was still in her ears.

And the voice of the little funny man. What was his name? The little sculptor. 'You're a victim. There's no endurance in your face. Victims are necessary so that the strong may exercise their will and become more strong.'

'I shall have to go away,' she decided. 'Of course. Naturally.'

Sleep was like falling into a black hole.

• ◆ •

Next morning she woke early and lay watching the wind blow the striped curtain outwards. It was like the sail of a ship, she thought. Voices, steps, a knock on the door. She held her breath.

Lois called: 'Still asleep, Mado?'

'No, but I'm tired. I don't want any coffee. I've promised to lunch with Cairn.'

'Oh, all right, then,' said Lois.

Marya did not get up till after she heard the sound of the front-door being shut.

It was a cloudless, intoxicating day. The light pale gold, sky silvery blue, the breeze sweet and fresh as if it blew up from the sea.

A tram-car lumbered past her, and she began to think of the women who stood in the queue at the prison of Fresnes and of the way they would edge forward mechanically and uselessly, pushing her as they edged. So that she was always forced to stand touching their musty clothes and their unwashed bodies. She remembered her tears and her submissions and the long hours she had spent walking between two rows of street lamps, solitary, possessed by pity as by a devil. 'I've been wasting my life,' she thought. 'How have I stood it for so long?'

And her longing for joy, for any joy, for any pleasure was a mad thing in her heart. It was sharp like pain and she clenched her teeth. It was like some splendid caged animal roused and fighting to get out. It was an unborn child jumping, leaping, kicking at her side.

• ◆ •

'You're very late,' said Cairn, who was waiting for her in a restaurant in the Place Pigalle. 'I thought you weren't coming.'

He looked solemnly through his horn spectacles at her as she explained that she had walked part of the way, agreed that it was a lovely day and invited her to have a cocktail.

'Olives?'

He was an American, a writer of short stories; ugly, broad-shouldered, long-legged, slim-hipped.

'I thought you weren't coming,' said Cairn, and added astonishingly: 'I thought Heidler would stop you.'

Marya asked why he should stop her.

'Because he is a . . . oh, well, doesn't matter.'

'But he's very kind,' said Marya.

There was a question in her voice, for she felt a great longing to hear Heidler spoken of. She would have discussed Heidler with pleasure throughout the entire meal.

'Kind?' said Cairn. 'Heidler kind? My God!'

'Don't you think he's kind?' she persisted childishly.

'Don't let's talk about him,' said Cairn impatiently. 'What's he matter, anyway?'

'No,' said Marya, with regret, 'don't let's talk about him.' She added: 'They've been nice to me, you know, wonderfully nice.'

'Have they?'

He flashed a quick, curious look from under the spectacles, hesitated, then said:

'Ah, Marya mia . . . Well, that's all right, then.'

They talked about Cairn's new hat — whether it was or was not too small for him, and about a story that he wished to write and about money.

'Haven't any,' said Cairn gloomily.

Then they talked about Life.

'It frightens me,' said Marya. But as they drank their coffee, she said to him: 'Cairn, isn't not caring a damn a nice feeling?'

'Of course it is,' said Cairn cheerfully. 'You've got to be an *arriviste* or a *je m'en fichiste* in this life.' He added: 'Only, of course, if you are going to be a *je m'en fichiste*, you must have the nerve to stand the racket afterwards, because there always is a racket, you know.'

'Yes, I know,' said Marya. 'I've found that out already.'

    • • •

It was late when she got back to the Avenue de l'Observatoire. When she looked up from the street the windows were in darkness, but as soon as she opened the door Heidler called out from the studio:

'Hullo! There you are! You're late. Did you enjoy yourself?'

'Yes, very much,' said Marya.

He got up and turned on one of the lights, but the room was still full of shadows. He looked tired.

'After all, he's quite old,' she thought and faced him, feeling ironical and defiant.

'I love you,' said Heidler. 'I love you, my dear, I love you. And I wish I were dead. For God's sake, be a little kind to me. Oh, you cold and inhuman devil!'

'I'm not cold,' answered Marya

Suddenly she was full of a great longing to explain herself.

'H.J., I want to be happy. Oh, I want it so badly. You don't know how badly. I don't want to be hurt. I don't want anything black or miserable or complicated any more. I want to be happy, I want to play around and have good times like — like other people do. . . . Oh, do leave me alone. I'm so scared of being unhappy.'

'You've got a fear complex,' remarked Heidler, 'that's what's the matter with you.'

'I don't want to be hurt any more,' she told him in a low voice. 'If I'm hurt again I shall go mad. You don't know. . . . How can you know? I can't stand any more, I won't stand it.'

'Rubbish!' said Heidler tenderly. 'Rubbish!'

'You don't know anything about me,' she went on fiercely. 'Nothing! You can't lay down the law about me because you don't know anything.'

'But I want to make you happy,' he exclaimed loudly. 'It's my justification that I want to. And that I will, d'you hear? In spite of you, I'll do it!'

'Yes?' said Marya. 'And what about Lois?'

Heidler leaned back in his chair, crossed his legs, cleared his throat.

'My dear,' he remarked, 'you don't understand Lois.'

'Don't I?' asked Marya.

'Not a bit. Lois,' he went on, speaking carefully and persuasively, 'is not an excitable person.'

'I've gathered that much,' remarked Marya dryly.

'You are so excitable yourself,' declared Heidler. 'You tear yourself to pieces over everything and, of course, your fantastic existence has made you worse. You simply don't realize that most people take things calmly. Most people don't tear themselves to bits. They have a sense of proportion and so on. Lois and I each go our own way and that's been the arrangement for some time, if you want to know. Why, look here; do you know what she said about you a few days ago? I tell you because I want you to realize that Lois simply doesn't come into this at all between you and me. . . . She said: "The matter with Mado is that she's too virtuous".' He nodded. 'Yes, that's what she said; that's what she thinks about the situation.'

'Oh, is that so?' Marya spoke thoughtfully.

He asked her if she couldn't understand that all that didn't matter.

'I want to comfort you. I want to hold you tight — and safe — d'you see. Safe?'

'H.J., don't.' She put her hand up to her mouth as if to hide her lips. 'Oh, well! Give me a cigarette, will you, please?'

'You smoke too much,' he told her irritably. 'I'm never alone with you, never. And if I'm alone with you for five minutes, you smoke or you paint your mouth or you perform some other monkey trick of the sort — instead of listening to me. Lois will come in, in a minute.'

'She is in,' said Marya; 'I heard her some time ago.'

'Oh, is she?' He hesitated, looked at Marya, went out of the room.

She drew her feet up on to the sofa, clasped her hands around her knees and stared fixedly in front of her.

II

LOIS CAME INTO the room carrying a small flowered paper bag. 'Hello, Mado, why are you sitting in this half-darkness?' She put on the light near the door. 'I've been running round the shops all the afternoon. I've brought you this to cheer your black dress up.'

She opened the paper bag and took out a lace collar, touching it with careful fingers.

'Thank you,' said Marya in a low voice.

Lois went on: 'I'm going to dine with Maurice and Anna. And I'm late. I must fly.' Her eyes, which were swollen as if she had been crying, travelled restlessly round the room. 'Get H.J. to take you somewhere. He'll be here in a minute; he's gone for some cigarettes.' She turned to walk out of the room.

'Lois!' said Marya. And stopped breathless.

'Well, what is it?'

'I want to talk to you.'

'Won't tomorrow do?' Lois asked coldly. 'I'm really in an awful hurry. I don't want to keep Anna waiting.'

'Well, it needn't be a long conversation,' Marya told her. 'I want to go, and the sooner the better, don't you think so? I must ask you to lend me a hundred francs because I haven't any money left at all. I'll go at once, and you can tell H.J. that I insisted on it.'

All the time that she spoke she was thinking: 'This is perfectly useless. She doesn't believe a word I'm saying. She hates me. She's going to try to down me. Whatever I do, she'll hate me and try to down me.'

'Don't be silly, Mado,' said Lois uncertainly. She looked at Marya with the painfully intent expression of a slowbrained person who is trying to think quickly.

'What's her game? What's she up to? I must be clever and try to find out what she's up to.'

'Of course, you can't go.'

'And why not?'

'Well,' asked Lois, 'where would you go to?' Her brown eyes were suspicious, troubled like pools when the mud beneath has been stirred up.

'When I say: go off,' said Marya, 'I mean, go right off.'

They watched each other cautiously and steadily for some moments. Then Lois sat down in the chair facing the divan and remarked with calmness:

'All this, of course, is because H.J.'s been making love to you, I know. I was listening just now, if it comes to that. Well,' she added defiantly, 'in my place you'd have done the same thing.'

'No,' said Marya.

'No?' echoed Lois unbelievingly.

'I might come into the room and make a hell of a scene, but I'd never listen at the door, because I've not got patience enough. We're different people, Lois.'

'Yes,' agreed Lois reluctantly. 'I suppose we are. But that's no reason why we should quarrel, is it?'

She began to fidget nervously with the fastening of her handbag.

'I don't see what good it will do if you go off. It seems such a pity to smash up all our plans for you, just because H.J. imagines that he's in love with you — for the minute.' She went on in a reflective voice: 'Of course, mind you, he wants things badly when he does want them. He's a whole hogger.'

'So am I,' Marya told her. 'That's just why I must go off.'

The other made an impatient and expressive gesture, as if to say: 'D'you suppose that I care what you are, or think or feel? I'm talking about the man, the male, the important person, the only person who matters.'

'He's a whole hogger,' Lois repeated, 'and if you go away now he'll go after you. That's what he'll do.'

'It's fatal making a fuss,' she muttered. 'The more fuss one makes . . . I don't believe in making scenes about things, forcing things. I believe in letting things alone. I hate scenes.'

She stopped. All day she had tormented herself and now she was on the brink of an abyss of sincerity. She twisted her hands in her lap, thinking: Oh, no, my girl, you won't go away. You'll stay here where I can keep an eye on you. It won't last long . . . It can't last long. I've always let him alone and given him what he wanted and it's never failed me. It won't fail me now. He'll get tired of her as soon as she gives in. Pretty! She's revolting. You can see when you look at her that she's been chewed up. God! what have I done to be worried like this? Didn't I try to do a decent thing? This is the result; this is what I get for it.

She said bitterly: 'Of course, I was a fool to have you here, only a fool like me would have done a thing like that, but I don't see what good your going away now will do.'

Her eyes, when she looked at Marya, were hard, false, questioning. It was as if she were observing some strange animal that might be dangerous, debating the best method of dealing with it.

'I tell you that I'll go off,' said Marya. 'Tonight, if you like. Right off. What more can I do? I won't see H.J. again.'

('Come, come,' answered Lois's eyes. 'As woman to woman, do you suppose I believe that?')

'Well, it's very dramatic and generous of you and all that,' she remarked. 'Why don't you talk it over with him? I should if I were you. As far as I'm concerned, I don't see any reason why you should go. I don't want to send you away and then have it on my conscience that you've gone to the devil and all that. Well, that's what you said, that you didn't care what happened to you. I thought that a dreadful thing.'

Her voice was so prim that Marya began to laugh, suddenly and loudly. Lois stared at her, got up, went to the looking-glass, arranged her side-locks carefully, and continued in a calm voice:

'We're making a great fuss about nothing at all, aren't we?

Drama is catching, I find. In any case, you can't go tonight.'

Marya asked abruptly: 'Tell me, did you really say that what is the matter with me is that I am too virtuous?'

'Well, all this looks rather like it, doesn't it?' Lois answered. 'You must be rather worried about your virtue if you want to rush off at a minute's notice. Look here, I must be off; I'm horribly late.'

At the door she turned suddenly: 'What? What did you say?' she asked.

'Nothing.' Marya lay back and shut her eyes.

Lois was a shadow, less than a shadow. Lois had simply ceased to exist.

The front door banged.

Marya lay very still listening to the hooting of the cars outside. She felt sharply alive but very tired, so languid as to be almost incapable of movement. A profound conviction of the unreality of everything possessed her. She thought: 'I wonder if taking opium is like this?'

.   .   .

'Hullo, H.J.,' she said, and sat up quickly. He was too formidable standing over her. 'Listen. I've been telling Lois that I want to go — I think I'd better.'

'Oh, I think I'd better. I think I'd better,' she kept on saying in a little, pitiful voice; but when he took her in his arms she thought: 'How gentle he is. I was lost before I knew him. All my life before I knew him was like being lost on a cold, dark night.'

She shivered. Then she smiled and shut her eyes again.

He whispered: 'I love you, I love you. What did you say?'

'That you don't understand.'

'Oh, yes, I do, my dear,' said Heidler. 'Oh, yes, I do.'

12

THE THREE DINED together at Lefranc's the next evening. They sat, as usual, at a table in a little alcove at the end of the room, and Monsieur Lefranc (also as usual) hovered about them attentively.

Monsieur Lefranc admired Lois Heidler. He considered her a good-looking woman, a sensible, tidy, well-dressed woman who knew how to appreciate food. Marya he distrusted, and he had told his wife so more than once. 'And who is she, that one?' he would say. On this particular evening, then, he served first the soup and then the fish with his own hands and asked:

'Ça vous plaît, Madame Heidler?'

'Oh, very nice, very nice,' answered Lois.

Then Monsieur Lefranc cast one astute glance at her deeply circled eyes, another at Marya's reflection in the glass and told himself: 'Ça y est. I knew it! Ah, the grue!' So he waited on Lois with sympathy and gentleness; he waited on Marya grimly, and when he looked at Heidler, his expression said: 'Come, come, my dear sir. As man to man, what a mistake you're making!'

Madame Lefranc, from behind her bar, was also watching the trio with interest and curiosity. But she beamed on Marya every bit as kindly as she beamed on Lois, for she was a plump and placid woman who never took sides, and when her husband (a very moral man) judged a female client with severity, she would often say: 'Life is very droll. One never knows, Josef, one never knows.'

Marya was unconscious of Monsieur Lefranc's hostility. She was absorbed, happy, without thought for perhaps the first time in her life. No past. No future. Nothing but the present: the flowers on the table, the taste of wine in her mouth. She glanced at the rough texture of Heidler's coat-sleeve and longed to lay her face against it.

Lois, however, instantly reacting to the atmosphere of sympathy and encouragement, sat very straight, dominating the situation and talking steadily in a cool voice.

'We must get Mado another hat, H.J.'

Heidler looked sideways at Marya cautiously and critically.

'She must be chic,' his wife went on. 'She must do us credit.' She might have been discussing the dressing of a doll.

'Let's go to Luna-park after dinner,' she said. 'We'll put Mado on the joy wheel, and watch her being banged about a bit. Well, she ought to amuse us sometimes; she ought to sing for her supper; that's what she's here for, isn't it?'

Heidler's face was expressionless. It was impossible to tell whether this badinage amused or annoyed him.

'Well, shall we go to Luna-park?' persisted Lois.

'No,' answered Heidler reflectively. 'No, I don't think so.'

Lois said in a high, excited voice that she was bored to death with Montparnasse.

'I'm bored, bored, bored! Look here. Let's go to a music-hall, the *promenoir* of a music-hall, that's what I feel like. Something *canaille,* what?'

◆   ◆   ◆

Two naked girls were dancing before a background of blue and mauve which was like a picture by Marie Laurencin.

'If they'd only keep still,' Marya thought. 'They would be awfully nice if they were perfectly still.'

But the girls hopped with persistence. She looked away from the stage at an enormously stout lady promenading in a black and salmon georgette dress. The lady was worth watching. She had the head of a Roman emperor and she paced up and down with great dignity, glancing at various men with a good-natured but relentless expression.

The two girls having pranced smilingly off the stage, the curtain fell and rose again on the Spanish singer who was the star of the evening: a slim creature in a black crinoline gown, who wore her hair swept away from her face and ears. She was charming. She was like some frail and passionate child, and she sang her songs simply in a sweet, small voice.

'Oh, what a darling!' said Marya after the first song. But Lois ejaculated at intervals:

'Oh, very disappointing. Most!' and finally announced that she wanted to go to the Select bar (the Montparnasse one) and eat a Welsh rarebit.

That night the place seemed to be full of red-haired ladies in *robes de style*. Mr Blinks, the brilliant American, was balancing himself on a stool at one end of the bar. Guy Lester was at the other end, very drunk. All the dear old familiar faces, as Lois said.

'But a bit pink-eyed. Or are they not? Perhaps I just think they are because I'm in a bad temper.' She began to disparage the Spaniard at length: 'Not half fine gel enough, was she?'

'Did you like her, Mado?' asked Heidler.

'Yes, I did, very much.'

'Oh, charming!' said Lois. Her voice went up a semi-tone. 'But small, small. I liked the dancers rather.'

Marya remarked in a cold, hostile way that she thought the dancers were bouncers.

'Hate bouncers!'

'I don't see,' went on Lois, 'what the girl was driving at, myself.

She tries to get an atmosphere of fate and terror. The weak creature doomed and all that — such nonsense. And, besides, she doesn't do it. That song where she stabbed her lover, for instance. You don't stab a man with a little feeble gesture and a sweet and simple smile.'

Heidler said: 'Lois doesn't believe in fate, and she doesn't approve of weakness.'

'Oh, it's a damn convenient excuse sometimes,' answered Lois. The two women stared coldly at each other.

'After all,' remarked Marya suddenly, 'weak, weak, how does anybody really know who's weak and who isn't? You don't need to be a fine bouncing girl to stab anybody, either. The will to stab would be the chief thing, I should think.'

Heidler coughed.

'Have some more stout,' he said: 'have another Welsh rarebit,' He added with relief: 'Come along over here, Guy.'

Guy, who was a tall and beautiful and willowy young man, came along. He fixed a severe, slightly bleared blue eye on Marya and declared that he thought she was a hussy. He was very drunk.

'I'm young and innocent,' said Guy, 'but I know a hussy when I see one.'

'Darling Marya,' said Lois, laughing on a high note. 'You don't know her, you don't. She's as harmless as they're made, Guy. A sweet young thing on the sentimental side.'

'And one word to you both,' thought Marya. The music-hall had excited her. She felt pugnacious. She sat silent with a sullen, resentful expression on her face. From time to time Heidler looked at her under his eyebrows with clever, cautious eyes.

Lois began: 'There was a young woman called Marya. Who thought, "But I must have a caree — er." ' And so on and so on....

They walked home along the street which runs close to the Luxembourg Gardens, empty, silent and enchanted in the darkness.

'Good night, you two,' said Lois when they got to the studio. She went to her room and locked the door.

•   ◆   •

'H.J.,' said Marya. 'It's no use. I can't go on with this. I can't stick it. It isn't my line at all.'

'But that's not playing the game, is it?' remarked Heidler, in an impersonal voice. 'Not any sort of game.'

'What game?' answered Marya fiercely. 'Your game? Lois's game? Why should I play Lois's game? Yes, that is just it, it's all a game I can't play, that I don't know how to play.'

He said: 'You're making a stupid mistake, a really tragic mistake about Lois. I tell you that you misunderstand her utterly. You will persist in judging us by the standards of the awful life you've lived. Can't you understand that you are in a different world now? People breed differently after a while, you know. You won't be let down. There's no trick, no trap. You're with friends. And look here, my dear, what's the use of starting this conversation at this time of night? We'll talk about it tomorrow. Lois doesn't want to be given away; she doesn't want anybody to know, and I assure you that that's all she cares about. Of course, she'll be furious if anybody knows, and that's why if you go off in a hurry you will make things difficult for me. I beg you not to make things so difficult for me.'

She felt hypnotized as she listened to him, impotent.

As she lay in bed she longed for her life with Stephan as one longs for vanished youth. A gay life, a carefree life just wiped off the slate as it were. Gone! A horrible nostalgia, an ache for the past seized her.

> *Nous n'irons plus au bois;*
> *Les lauriers sont coupés. . . .*

Gone, and she was caught in this appalling muddle. Life was like that. Here you are, it said, and then immediately afterwards. Where are you? Her life, at any rate, had always been like that.

'Of course,' she told herself, 'I ought to clear out.'

But when she thought of an existence without Heidler her heart turned over in her side and she felt sick.

A board creaked outside.

She watched the handle of the door turning very gently, very slowly. And during the few moments that passed from the time she heard the board creak to the time she saw Heidler and said, 'Oh, it's you then, it's you,' she was in a frenzy of senseless fright. Fright of a child shut up in a dark room. Fright of an animal caught in a trap.

'What is it? What is it, then?' whispered Heidler. 'My darling! There, there, there!'

13

ONE AFTERNOON AT the end of April, whilst sitting in the Café du Dôme, drinking a gin and vermouth, Cairn, that imaginative and slightly sentimental young man, wrote the following pneumatique to Marya.

Mon vieux,
   I haven't met you for an age. Can you come to August's for lunch tomorrow — Saturday, one o'clock? Do. I'll be tickled to death to see you.
                                                          Yours,
                                                          Cairn

Then, full of imaginative and slightly sentimental resolution, he went out and posted the pneumatique. 'For,' thought he, 'that girl's not getting a fair deal.'

However, throughout luncheon with Marya, he felt doubtful, cautious and somewhat embarrassed. That day she was not so pretty as he remembered her. 'After all,' he told himself, 'I've got no money. I can't do anything for her. She probably knows perfectly well what she's up to, and can bargain while the bargaining's good.'

'Shall we drink Burgundy?'

'Yes, let's,' said Marya.

He wondered if she knew the sort of thing people were saying about her, and decided she probably did because her mouth was so hard and her eyes were so sad. Lost she looked. L'Enfant Perdu or The Babe in the Wood. Something like that. And she was the type he liked, too. Not a beautiful specimen of the type, of course.

After the meal was over: 'Let's go and have coffee at the Closerie des Lilas.'

'Yes, do let's,' said Marya.

It was a sunny day and they sat on the terrace. Cairn sneezed and she started so violently that half her coffee was spilt over into the saucer.

'Nerves, nerves,' said Cairn. 'Now then, what's the matter? Something's the matter; you're not looking well.'

She told him irritably: 'Don't poor-little-thing me. I can't stand it this morning.'

'You ought to be talked to sensibly,' said Cairn. 'Why have you got to look so peaky all of a sudden?'

'Because I hate trailing about with the Heidlers.'

'He said 'Oh!' and looked taken aback.

'I don't care,' said Marya, 'what it sounds like. There's the truth.'

Cairn's little twinkling eyes behind his spectacles were suddenly very wary. Of course he was a clever young man, but how clever, that was the question. Clever enough to recognize the truth when he heard it? Hardly anybody was clever enough for that. People went ludicrously wrong. You told the truth, the stárk truth — or perhaps you gave it a fig-leaf so as not to harrow too much — and everybody said: 'Come, come,' and 'Don't tell me,' and: 'Do you think I was born yesterday?' You told lies and they said: 'Ah, the *cri du cœur*!' Supposing that she said: 'Very well then, I will tell you. Listen. Heidler thinks he loves me and I love him. Terribly. I don't like him or trust him. I love him. D'you get me? And Lois says that she doesn't mind a bit and gives us her blessing — the importance of sex being vastly exaggerated and any little thing like that. But she says that I mustn't give her away. So does Heidler. They call that playing the game. So I have to trail around with them. And she takes it out on me all the time in all sorts of ways. I can just keep my end up now, but soon I won't be able to. And then, you see, I'm conscience-stricken about her. I'm horribly sorry for her. But I know that she hasn't a spark of pity for me. She's just out to down me — and she will.'

Supposing that she said all that to this calm, clever young man? No, his eyes were too cautious. He wouldn't be clever enough, she decided. Besides, one didn't say that sort of thing.

He was asking her reasonably why she didn't go off if she was not happy.

'Because I haven't anywhere else to go. Oh, don't let's talk about it. I realize what a feeble excuse that is. Besides, it isn't the real excuse.'

Cairn said slowly that it wasn't so feeble as all that.

'Not for a woman, anyway.'

'For a woman — for a woman. Why this sudden tenderness for the female sex? But, my poor dear,' she mocked, 'you're positively rococo, as what's-her-name would say.'

'Oh, it's a sad world!' grumbled Cairn. 'Sometimes it's so difficult to know what the hell to say.'

'Don't say anything,' she told him firmly.

'Look here,' he said, 'I'll say this much anyhow. I haven't got any money myself, as you know, but I'll borrow five hundred francs for you. It's not much, but, after all, you can live in the Dôme on coffee and croissants for quite a long time on that. Besides, when I get back to America I'll probably be able to send you some more. Heidler is a humbug,' he added violently, 'and God help you if you don't see it.'

'You think so?' asked Marya.

'I don't think; I know, and as for Mrs Heidler . . .'

'She hates me,' said Marya in a low voice.

'Of course she hates you,' Cairn replied impatiently. 'What do you expect? She'd be a very unnatural woman if she didn't hate you.'

'But I don't mind her hating me,' continued Marya. 'What I mind is that she pretends she doesn't.'

'That,' said Cairn, 'is what is known here as a *moyen classique.*'

'So it's as obvious as all that?' asked Marya after a silence.

'Oh, yes, it's fairly obvious.'

Cairn looked away with an embarrassed, even alarmed expression, fidgeted and cleared his throat.

'I must go,' she told him. 'I'm going to meet Heidler.'

'Oh, are you?' said Cairn, looking grim.

'Yes, at St Julien le Pauvre. He wants to show it to me.'

'He would,' muttered Cairn; 'he would choose a church for a background. Oh, my God!'

But Marya had decided that Cairn couldn't help her. He only added a sharp edge to her obsession.

'You'll come on Tuesday?' said Cairn, still with that air of being exceedingly embarrassed.

'Yes,' she said absently.

There he was, incapable of helping.

Before she had walked three steps from the Closerie des Lilas she had forgotten all about him.

•   ♦   •

The church was very cool and dark-shadowed, when they came in out of the sun. It smelled of candles and incense and ancient prayers. Marya stood for a long time staring at the tall Virgin and wondered why she suggested not holiness but rather a large and peaceful tolerance of sin. We are all miserable sinners and the dust of the earth. A little more or a little less, a dirty glass or a very dirty glass, as Heidler would say . . .

'And you don't suppose that it matters to me,' said the tall

Virgin smiling so calmly above her candles and flowers.

Marya turned to watch Heidler go down on one knee and cross himself as he passed the altar. He glanced quickly sideways at her as he did it, and she thought: 'I'll never be able to pray again now that I've seen him do that. Never! However sad I am.' And she felt very desolate.

•   •   •

'Hep!' shouted Heidler to a passing taxi. 'Get in. Look here,' he said, 'I don't want you to see Cairn again.'

'All right,' answered Marya.

His hand was over hers. Peace had descended on her and to that peace she was ready to sacrifice Cairn or anybody or anything.

'But I promised to lunch with him on Tuesday.'

'Well, write and say that you can't come. You must cut Cairn right out, you see.'

'Very well. I'm sorry, because I think he's kind; I like him.'

'He's hysterical,' said Heidler contemptuously.

The taxi jolted onwards.

'We want you to come down to Brunoy with us this afternoon.'

'Oh, no,' she told him hastily, 'I don't want to come.'

'But you must come. You're not looking well. We both think you need a change. What's the matter?'

'Nothing.'

'Why did you stiffen all over like that? Can't you come just to please me? Can't you not go to Fresnes for once?'

'Yes,' she said. And stopped herself from saying: 'I'll do anything to please you — anything.'

'What were you praying about just now?' she asked him suddenly.

'You!' he said.

'God's quite a pal of yours?'

'Yes,' said Heidler.

14

THEY SAT FACING her in the railway carriage and she looked at them with calmness, clear-sightedly, freed for one moment from her obsessions of love and hatred. They were so obviously husband and wife, so suited to each other, they were even in some strange way a little alike. 'Every pot has its lid,' says the French proverb, or perhaps Belgian — but French or Belgian, it's a good proverb.

Lois sat sturdily, with her knees, as usual, a little apart; her ungloved hands were folded over a huge leather handbag; on her dark face was the expression of the woman who is wondering how she is going to manage about the extra person to dinner. She probably was wondering just that. Her adequately becoming and expensive hat was well pulled down over her eyes. Her beige coat was well cut. Obviously of the species wife.

There she was: formidable, very formidable, an instrument made, exactly sharpened for one purpose. She didn't analyse; she didn't react violently; she didn't go in for absurd generosities or pities. Her motto was: 'I don't think women ought to make nuisances of themselves. I don't make a nuisance of myself; I grin and bear it, and I think that other women ought to grin and bear it, too.'

And there he was, like the same chord repeated in a lower key, sitting with his hands clasped in exactly the same posture as hers. Only his eyes were different. He could dream, that one. But his dreams would not be many-coloured, or dark shot with flame like Marya's. No, they'd be cold, she thought, or gross at moments. Almost certainly gross with those pale blue, secretive eyes. It seemed to her that, staring at the couple, she had hypnotized herself into thinking, as they did, that her mind was part of their minds and that she understood why they both so often said in exactly the same tone of puzzled bewilderment: 'I don't see what you're making such a fuss about.' Of course! And then they wanted to be excessively modern, and then they'd think: 'After all, we're in Paris.'

There they were. And there Marya was; haggard, tortured by jealousy, burnt up by longing.

They reached Brunoy. The cab was there and Lois said, exactly as Marya had known she would say: 'I must stop on the way because there's not much to eat in the house.'

The old horse set off at jog-trot up the street and stopped outside the grocer's shop with its display of piles of dried fruit, packets of coffee and a jovial advertisement for Pâtés de la Lune. Next door, in the hairdresser's window, was the bust of a pink and white lady in a provocative attitude and a huge bottle of bright green liquid; then came a shoemaker's necklaces of hobnailed boots.

It was all very peaceful.

Lois came out, accompanied by a boy carrying parcels; the cabman flicked up his horse; they passed the last houses and the road stretched long and grey in front of them. Marya sat squeezed between the Heidlers, listening to the melancholy sound of the hoofs and the rattling of the old cab. In the dusk the trunks of the trees gleamed as though they were made of some dull metal, but when they had been driving for half an hour it had grown dark and she could only see the shadows of the branches running along in front of the cab. There were lights in the windows of a straggling row of small houses.

The cab stopped. They got out, walked along a muddy path, and Lois pushed a door open and led the way into a room with gay check curtains, straw armchairs, and a divan with coloured cushions. The table was laid ready for a meal.

'D'you want to go up?' asked Lois. 'Here's a candle for you. You know where your room is?'

Marya said that she remembered. She went through the kitchen, up a narrow staircase into a room which smelt sweet and cool. Rabbits chased each other over the wallpaper. The window was wide open and the stillness outside seemed wonderful after the shriek of Paris. Soft, like velvet.

'Hurry up,' called Lois from the foot of the stairs. 'H.J.'s mixing the cocktails.'

Marya thought: 'Oh, Lord! what a fool I am.' Her heart felt as if it were being pinched between somebody's fingers. Cocktails, the ridiculous rabbits on the wallpaper. All the fun and sweetness of life hurt so abominably when it was always just out of your reach.

Dinner was a silent, solemn meal. A dog howled with melancholy persistency. Lois sat with an invulnerable expression on her dark face. It was as if she were saying: 'You can't down me. My roots go very deep.' She ate heartily and rather noisily, drank a good deal more than usual, and then announced that she was going to bed.

'Goodnight, you two.'

The door shut sharply behind her.

.   .   .

'You're not going,' said Heidler to Marya. He came over to take her in his arms.

'You must be mad,' she told him fiercely. 'D'you think I am a *bonne* or something to be made love to every time the mistress's back is turned? Can't you see? You must be the cruellest devil in the world.' She burst into miserable tears.

'I'm as unhappy as you are,' muttered Heidler. His face looked white and lined. He began to argue: 'I don't show it as much as you do, because I've trained myself not to show things, but I'm so miserable that I wish I were dead. You don't help at all, Mado. You make things worse. I love you; I can't help it. It's not your fault; it's not my fault. I love you; I'm burnt up with it. It's a fact. There it is, nobody's fault. Why can't you just accept it instead of straining against it all the time? You make things so difficult for me and for yourself.'

She asked him if he really imagined she could live there between them. And as she asked it, she thought: 'I wonder how many times I've said that. A vain repetition, that's what it is. A vain repetition.'

'I don't see why not,' he said slowly. 'After all, you're supreme here; you've only to say what you want and it will be done.'

There was a loud bump from upstairs. Heidler remarked indifferently:

'There's Lois falling about.'

'Oh, you must go up,' said Marya in a very low voice. 'She may be ill—'

'I'm going,' he answered wearily, taking one of the lamps.

He was away for quite a long time, and she waited with her head in her hands, listening.

Steps, more bumps, the dog in the garden of the next cottage still howling. Then Heidler tramped down the creaking stairs again, the lamp with the green and yellow check shade in his hand.

'Poor Lois is quite seedy,' he remarked, putting the lamp down on the table with an expressionless face. 'She's been awfully sick, nearly fainted.'

Marya asked, without lifting her eyes: 'What's the matter?'

'Well,' said Heidler, 'she thinks it's the cassoulet. So do I. I don't trust this tinned stuff.'

Of course, there they were: inscrutable people, invulnerable people, and she simply hadn't a chance against them, naïve sinner that she was.

•   •   •

The night before they were to return to Paris she woke about midnight to a feeling of solitude and desolation. She had gone with Lois down to the village to buy plants, and they had walked almost all the way in dead silence. It was comical, of course, and degrading. They were like two members of a harem who didn't get on. When Lois did speak to her it was with a strained politeness which at moments was cringing — as if she said: I must keep her in a good temper. Marya was brooding, nervous, waiting and hoping for the violent reaction that might free her from an impossible situation.

The room was full of night noises. 'After all,' she thought, 'I can't lie here for ever listening to these cracks and tappings.' She got up, lit the lamp and went downstairs for a bottle of Vittel and a book. There was a light under the sitting-room door. Voices. A vague murmur from Heidler. And then Lois, very clear and loud:

'And she's so rude sometimes — surly. It gets on my nerves. Her whole attitude gets on my nerves. I don't trust her, let me tell you that. She isn't to be trusted.'

Another murmur from Heidler.

'They're talking about me,' Marya told herself. 'They're sitting there talking about me. Those two. I can't stick this,' she thought. 'Not a minute longer. It's got to finish, quick.'

Then she realized that she was holding the lamp at a dangerous angle and put it down on the kitchen table. But her breath had gone. One moment to fill her lungs — she didn't want to stammer stupidly — then she opened the door as noisily as she could.

'Hullo!' said Heidler, looking round.

Lois made a wincing movement with her mouth and pulled her dressing-gown together at the throat, looking frightened.

Marya told them: 'I heard what you said just now.'

'Well, why not?' said Heidler with an expression of good-natured sarcasm.

'You were talking about me.'

'Well,' he asked again, 'and why shouldn't we?'

'You mustn't think. . . .' Her breath had gone again and her voice trembled. 'You mustn't think that I don't realize . . . that I haven't realized for a long time the arrangement that you and Lois have made about me.'

'You're mad,' said Lois with indignation.

'You have made an arrangement!' said Marya loudly. 'Not in so many words, perhaps, a tacit arrangement. If he wants the woman let him have her. Yes. D'you think I don't know?'

Heidler got up and said nervously: 'Don't shout. You can hear every single word that's said at Madame Guyot's next door!'

'*Tant mieux!*' screamed Marya. '*Tant mieux, tant mieux!*'

Lois made a nervous movement.

'No, let me talk to her,' said Heidler. 'You don't understand how to deal with this sort of woman; I do.'

It was horrible, the power he had to hurt her.

'Look out, Heidler,' she said.

'Don't be hysterical,' he told her with contempt, 'talk calmly. What do you want? What's it all about?'

But every vestige of coherence, of reason had fled from her brain. Besides, however reasonably or coherently she talked, they wouldn't understand, either of them. If she said: 'You're torturing me, you're mocking me, you're driving me mad,' they wouldn't understand.

She muttered: 'I'm not going to live with Lois and you any longer. I — am — not! And you must arrange . . .'

'Ah!' said Heidler, 'it's a question of money. I rather thought that was what you were getting at.'

She jumped forward and hit him as hard as she could.

'Horrible German!' she said absurdly. 'Damned German! *Crapule!*' She stood panting, waiting for him to drop his arm that she might hit again.

'You're quite right,' he muttered, and put his head in his hands. 'You're quite right. Oh God! Oh God!'

Lois went up to him and he lifted his head and looked at her with hatred.

'Leave me alone,' he said. 'I've done with you.'

She began to talk in a caressing voice.

'Damn you, leave me alone!' he shouted, and pushed her so that she staggered back against the wall. Then he buried his face in his arms again and began to sob.

Marya's calm came back to her as theirs disappeared. She began to think how ridiculous it all was, that it was chilly, that she wanted to go upstairs, that she had only imagined the love and hate she felt for these two, that she had only imagined that such emotions as love and hate existed at all. She stood looking at the floor, feeling undecided and self-conscious. Then:

'I'm awfully drunk,' said Heidler suddenly, in a calm and as it were explanatory way. 'I'm going to bed. I shan't remember a thing about all this tomorrow morning.'

'He always does that,' Lois remarked in a sisterly manner when he had gone. The contempt had left her voice. It was as if she respected the outburst which seemed to Marya more and more ridiculous and inexcusable.

'When there's been a scene he always says, next morning, that he was drunk and that he doesn't remember anything that happened. It's his way of getting out of things. . . . Why did you come downstairs?'

'I was thirsty.'

'Oh, were you?' Lois said. 'I'll bring you up a bottle of Vittel.'

Marya stared at her, answered with the uttermost politeness: 'No, please don't bother,' and left her anxiously picking up the chair that had fallen down.

♦　　♦　　♦

When she woke next morning the whole thing seemed very unreal and impossible. But even while it was going on it had seemed unreal. She had felt like a marionette, as though something outside her were jerking strings that forced her to scream and strike. Heidler, weeping, was a marionette, too. And Lois, anxious-eyed, in her purple dressing-gown. 'Anyhow,' thought Marya, 'I'm going away. I'll stick to that.'

Peace, the normal, reigned downstairs. Madame Guillot was in the kitchen, bustling about and singing.

'*Bonjour, mademoiselle,*' said Madame Guillot, smiling. '*Pardon. Madame.*'

Twenty years ago Madame Guillot's husband had killed her lover — or the other way round. In any case there had been a tragedy and a scandal, and things had apparently been made pretty hot for Madame Guillot by the village in general. But now here she was singing away among her pots and pans, and her fat back seemed to say: 'Life has got to be lived, mademoiselle or madame. One might as well be cheerful about it.' It was a lovely blue day, too.

'Good morning, my dear,' said Heidler. 'The fly will be here at eleven. I'm coming with you to Paris to help you to find an hotel.'

He looked so calm that their dispute seemed more incredible than ever.

'Lois has gone to the village to shop. She wants to stay on here for a few days and I shall probably come straight back. About money. Well, we'll talk that over at lunch.'

She flushed and turned her head away.

'Look here, H.J. . . .'

'I'm not going to discuss last night,' interrupted Heidler. 'If you're not happy here we must find you an hotel, that's all. But I don't intend to let you go. Don't you make any mistake about that. Of course, if you force me to break with Lois I will. Is that what you're trying to do?'

'No,' she said. 'No. You don't understand me. I'm not trying to force you to do anything.'

He repeated: 'I'll break with her and take you away somewhere. Is that what you want?'

'No, not for anything,' said Marya again. 'No, I can't do that.' She added in a very low voice: 'Be kind to Lois, H.J.'

'Ah?' remarked Heidler. 'H-m!'

He looked half contemptuous, half pitiful, as if he were thinking: 'No, she can't play this game.'

Marya went on sullenly: 'But I couldn't help last night. I couldn't stick it any longer.'

'I'm not saying,' he told her, with a judicial expression, 'that I don't see your point of view.'

She said: 'Why did you say such a damnable thing to me last night? About money.'

'I don't remember saying anything about it,' he answered. 'I remember that you were rather damnable.'

He was still looking steadily at her. His eyes were clear, cool and hard, but something in the depths of them flickered and shifted. She thought: 'He'd take any advantage he could — fair or unfair. Caddish he is.' Then as she stared back at him she felt a great longing to put her head on his knees and shut her eyes. To stop thinking. Stop the little wheels in her head that worked incessantly. To give in and have a little peace. The unutterably sweet peace of giving in.

She pressed her lips together and said: 'Well, you did. And I hit you. And I'm jolly glad I hit you, too. Look here, I must go and pack.'

'Lois will come up and help you,' said Heidler. 'Yes. I remember your hitting me — quite well.'

When Lois appeared she said, in an oddly apologetic manner: 'You know, Mado, you can't think how sorry I am about all this. What an awful pity I think it is.'

'It doesn't matter,' answered Marya coldly. She hated Lois. She hated her air of guilt. She hated her eyes of a well-trained domestic animal.

Lois continued, with suspicion: 'You are not going to talk to anybody in Paris about all this, are you?'

'Who could I talk to?' asked Marya in an aggressive voice.

But in the cab she said to Heidler over and over again: 'Oh, Heidler, be good to Lois, be good to Lois, you must be good to Lois.'

'I shouldn't worry too much about Lois if I were you,' Heidler answered.

15

CROWDS OF PEOPLE were waiting at the Porte d'Orléans for the trams to Fresnes. They stood with phlegmatic patience, craning their necks, and each tram was immediately packed when it did come with parties going to spend Sunday in the country. With each party was a jocular young man and two girls who giggled, or that was what it seemed like to Marya. The neat little houses slipped past and the endless row of sycamore trees. At the Café of the Cadran Bleu she got down.

The warder who took the permits knew her. His '*Qui êtes-vous?*' was mechanical.

'*Sa femme.*'

'*Passez,*' said the warder. And she passed into the cobblestoned courtyard. She had begun to have a dreadful feeling of familiarity with the place: the whitewashed corridor that smelt of damp and rot, the stone staircase, the queue of women awaiting their turn in the cubicles. That day it was all arm-in-arm as it were. The drably terrible life of the under-dog.

The prison was familiar, but it seemed to her that Stephan was a stranger: dark-bearded, shaven-headed, very thin, very bright-eyed. He wore — as usual — a piece of sacking over his head and he gripped the bars and leaned forward, talking slowly in his rusty voice.

He asked her why she had left the Heidlers.

'Because you weren't free there? *Mais, tu es folle, Mado.* What do you want to be free for? Have you got a job? What are you going to do now? Really you must be mad to do a thing like that.'

She reminded him, feeling nervous and awkward, that he would be at liberty in four months.

'Only four months! Only four months! My God, it's so easy to talk, isn't it?' He went on irritably, but always with those imploring eyes of a small boy. 'How do I know what will happen when I am free? I've no money. I'll have to leave France. You have friends and you lose them. You're not clever. But I don't mean to quarrel. I'm going off my head here. You're not vexed?'

'No,' she said. 'No, no, no.'

'Last Sunday,' he said, 'when you didn't come I felt awful. Of course, I didn't get your letter in time and I was waiting for them to call out my number when visiting-time came. Every number that was called out I thought was mine. And it never was. And then I thought, "She's late today." And then I thought, "She's never as late as this. She must be ill. She's not coming." But still I couldn't help listening for my number each time they called. I was glad when the time was up, I can tell you. It sounds nothing, but it was awful. One goes mad shut up here.'

She smiled. 'I never will not turn up again, Stephan. Never. So don't worry.'

The warder banged open the door and snarled. Stephan disappeared.

As she walked away she knew why the prison had seemed closer and more terrible than ever before. It was because the thought of Heidler had always stood between her and the horror of it. He was big and calm and comforting. He said: 'Don't worry. I love you, d'you see?' And one hadn't worried. At least, not so much.

She sat in the corner of the tram watching the sycamore trees speed past.

Heidler, Heidler, Heidler.

Supposing she asked him, next time she saw him: 'Heidler, save me. I'm afraid. Save me.' Just like that. Then he'd think her a coward. 'I wonder if I am a coward,' reflected Marya. And then: 'And how many of them could stick it — all the people who'd call me coward? Not many — with their well-fed eyes and their long upper lips.' Something hard and dry in her chest was hurting her.

When she got back to her hotel, which was near the Gard de Montparnasse, she took all Heidler's letters and re-read them. Five letters. She had left Brunoy four days before. Very good letters they were, too. Very convincing. She had answered once — shortly and coldly. The fifth and last letter told her that he was coming to the

Hôtel du Bosphore to see her next afternoon. It began: 'Dearest. Dearest in all the world,' and ended with an effect as of a sudden attack of caution — 'So I'll be with you about four. Yours H.'

•   •   •

The Hôtel du Bosphore looked down on Montparnasse station, where all day a succession of shabby trains, each trailing its long scarf of smoke, clanked slowly backwards and forwards.

Behind the trains a background of huge advertisements: a scarlet-haired baby Cadum: a horrible little boy in a sailor suit: *Exigez toujours du Lion Noir.* A horrible little girl with a pigtail: *Evitez le contrefaçons.*

An atmosphere of departed and ephemeral loves hung about the bedroom like stale scent, for the hotel was one of unlimited hospitality, though quietly, discreetly and not more so than most of its neighbours. The wallpaper was vaguely erotic — huge and fantastically shaped mauve, green and yellow flowers sprawling on a black ground. There was one chair and a huge bed covered with a pink counterpane. It was impossible, when one looked at that bed, not to think of the succession of *petites femmes* who had extended themselves upon it, clad in carefully thought out pink or mauve chemises, full of tact and savoir faire and savoir vivre and all the rest of it.

On the morning after her visit to Fresnes, Marya woke early and dressed slowly, listening for the man with the flock of goats who passed under her window every morning at about half-past ten, playing a frail little tune on a pipe. He was a sturdy man who looked as if he were out in all weathers. He wore country clothes and a *béret basque*, and he carried on his back a black bag marked in white letters: *Fromage de chèvre.*

But it was the little tune he played which enchanted her. Not a gay blast on a trumpet like the glazier. He also passed, but earlier. This was thin, high, sweet music like water running in the sun, and the man played, not to attract customers, but to keep his flock in order. They were wonderful goats, five of them, all black and white, and they crossed the street calmly, avoiding trams with dignity and skill. One behind the other and no jostling, like the perfect ladies that they were.

Marya listened to the music of the pipe, dwindling away in the distance, persistent as the hope of happiness. Then she lunched at Boots' Bar (once A la Savoyard, renamed by the proprietor, an anglophile), and after lunch went back to her melancholy bedroom and slept, for she had lain awake all night, tormented by doubts and fears. When she awoke, bewildered, Heidler was there looking down on her.

She had meant to tell him: 'I love you. You aren't making any mistake about that, are you?' But all she said was: 'Please will you draw the curtains?'

'H.J. . . .'

'What is it, my darling?'

'You aren't sad?'

'My dear, no, of course not.'

She said: 'Listen. I feel as if I'd fallen down a precipice.'

'You funny thing,' said Heidler.

But that was how she felt. Because she knew that she would never be able even to pretend to fight him again, and because, when she looked anxiously into his eyes, she had imagined that they were sad and cold like ashes.

'Well, look here, my dear one, I must go. I've got to—' He stopped.

Of course he'd been going to say, 'I've got to go back to Lois.'

She thought: 'I must get used to this. No use making a fuss,' and fixed a mechanical smile on her lips.

'Don't get up,' said Heidler. 'I'll send you in dinner and some wine. And a book. Have you got any books? It's horrible outside.'

When he went he left the door open. The gramophone belonging to the South American gentleman next door was playing 'I want to be happy.' Naturally.

◆　　◆　　◆

He was very different next morning. A new Heidler, one she had never seen before. To begin with, he wore a bowler hat. When they were seated in the Restaurant de Versailles she was still thinking uneasily about the hat, because it seemed symbolical of a new attitude. He looked self-possessed, respectable, yet not without a certain hard rakishness. There is something impressive, something which touches the imagination about the sight of an English bowler hat in the Rue de Rennes. . . . In the middle of the meal he announced:

'Lois is expecting you to tea this afternoon.'

'But I don't want to go.'

'My darling child,' said Heidler with calmness, 'your whole point of view and your whole attitude to life is impossible and wrong and you've got to change it for everybody's sake.'

He went on to explain that one had to keep up appearances. That everybody had to. Everybody had for everybody's sake to keep up appearances. It was everybody's duty, it was in fact what they were there for.

'You've got to play the game.'

Marya said: 'Lois simply wants me around so that she can tear me to bits and get her friends to help her to tear me to bits.' She added slowly: 'They'll tear me up and show you the bits. That's what will happen. And you won't see it. A Frenchman would see the game at once, but you won't see it, or you pretend not to.'

'Rubbish!' said Heidler, looking vexed. 'Lois is very fond of you. One's got to take certain things into account which may not seem to you very important. But which. . . .' His nose seemed to lengthen oddly as he spoke.

Marya thought: 'He looks exactly like a picture of Queen Victoria.'

But he was convincing, impressive and full of authority. He overwhelmed her. She made one last effort.

'H.J., Lois doesn't like me,' she said. 'She can't possibly want to see me.'

'I tell you that she's extremely fond of you,' asserted Heidler. 'She's always saying so. She's very sorry for you, for the dreadful life you've had and all that.'

'Ah,' said Marya, helplessly.

'I hate explaining these things,' Heidler went on fretfully. 'I hate talking about things, but you surely must see that you can't let Lois down. Everybody knows that you were staying with us and if there's a definite split it will give the whole show away. I can't let Lois down,' he kept saying, 'we must keep up appearances, we must play the game.'

Marya told him at last miserably: 'Oh, all right, of course.'

'Savage,' he said, watching her, 'Bolshevist! You'll end up in red Russia, that's what will happen to you.'

'I thought that you understood that in me.'

'Oh, theoretically,' answered Heidler. 'Theoretically, of course I do. My darling, have a chartreuse and don't look so miserable.'

'But he really is like Queen Victoria sometimes,' thought Marya.

He took his bowler hat and they departed. They bought cakes on the way.

Lois greeted Marya in a high voice and with a gleam of triumph in her eyes. She wore a gown of purple georgette, silk stockings and high-heeled shoes. She had changed the colour of her face-powder and looked younger. Below the décolleté of her dress was a glimpse of a rose-coloured chemise.

Marya thought: 'How ridiculous we both are,' and sat on the divan feeling like a captive attached to somebody's chariot wheels.

Miss Nicholson arrived, and Mrs O'Mara, and the Satterbys and Guy and partner, and several young men of various nationalities.

Lois handed cups of tea and ordered Heidler about and called Marya 'Darling Mado' when he was there, and was spiteful when he was out of earshot. They talked about a new dance club they were starting, and whether the countess Stadkioff ought to be barred.

'Bar a countess?' Marya expected to hear Lois say. 'No certainly not.' She turned politely in her direction. But, to her surprise, Lois nodded.

Everybody said: 'Yes, we'll bar the countess this time.' Then they all looked relieved, as though they had sacrificed to some tribal god.

Miss Anna Nicholson, who painted landscapes and was a very bright talker indeed, was witty about the colour of the countess's hair.

She was Lois's friend and confidante and, as she talked, she watched Marya with amused and virginal eyes. She was thinking:

'The idea of a woman making such an utter fool of herself. It's hardly to be believed. Her hand is trembling. No poise. . . . Lois needn't be afraid of her. But then, Lois is a bit of a fool herself. Englishwomen very often are.'

16

THE LITTLE CLOCK on the table by the bed was ticking so loudly that Marya got up and shut it away in a drawer. But she could still hear it, fussy and persistent. Then a train gave a long piercing shriek and she sighed, turned on the light and lay contemplating the flowers which crawled like spiders over the black walls of her bedroom. The mechanism of her brain got to work with a painful jerk and began to tick in time with the clock.

She made a great effort to stop it and was able to keep her mind a blank for, say, ten seconds. Then her obsession gripped her, arid, torturing, gigantic, possessing her as utterly as the longing for water possesses someone who is dying of thirst. She had made an utter mess of her love affair, and that was that. She had made an utter mess of her existence. And that was that, too.

But of course it wasn't a love affair. It was a fight. A ruthless, merciless, three-cornered fight. And from the first Marya, as was right and proper, had no chance of victory. For she fought wildly, with tears, with futile rages, with extravagant abandon — all bad weapons.

'What's the matter with you?' she would ask herself. 'Why are you like this? Why can't you be clever? Pull yourself together!' Uselessly.

'No self-control,' thought Marya. 'That's what's the matter with me. No training.'

But of course he was very clever. And Lois, just sitting tight and smiling, was very clever. Oh, very clever! And she, Marya, was a fool who could do nothing but cry behind a locked door.

She shut her eyes and at once his face was close to hers, hard and self-contained. 'All that!' his cool eyes said. 'Oh, yes, very nice. But all that grows on every blackberry bush, my dear.' His cool eyes that confused and hurt her.

He wasn't a good lover, of course. He didn't really like women. She had known that as soon as he touched her. His hands were inexpert, clumsy at caresses; his mouth was hard when he kissed. No, not a lover of women, he could say what he liked.

He despised love. He thought of it grossly, to amuse himself, and then with ferocious contempt. Not that that mattered. He might be right. On the other hand, he might just possibly be wrong. But it didn't really matter much.

What mattered was that, despising, almost disliking, love, he was forcing her to be nothing but the little woman who lived in the Hôtel du Bosphore for the express purpose of being made love to. A *petite femme*. It was, of course, part of his mania for classification. But he did it with such conviction that she, miserable weakling that she was, found herself trying to live up to his idea of her.

She lived up to it. And she had her reward.

'. . . You pretty thing — you pretty, pretty thing. Oh, you

darling. I say, did you notice what I did with my wrist watch? Lois has got hold of two Czecho-Slovakians and that young American chap — you know — what's-his-name? — the sculptor — for tonight and I promised I'd turn up. Are you all right for money? I'd better leave some money, hadn't I?'

The endless repetition of that sort of thing became a torture. She would wait for him to say, 'Look here, I must go now. Because Lois . . .'

As he dressed she would lie with one arm over her eyes and think: 'A bedroom in hell might look rather like this one. Yellow-green and dullish mauve flowers crawling over black walls.'

Her lips were dry. Her body ached. He was so heavy. He crushed her. He bore her down.

The dim room smelt of stale scent. She began to imagine all the women who had lain where she was lying. Laughing. Or crying if they were drunk enough. She felt giddy and curiously light, as if she were floating about bodiless in the scented dimness.

'It's frightfully hot in here,' Heidler was saying. 'D'you mind if I pull the curtains and open the window? Where's your handbag? Look here — do go and dine somewhere decent, for God's sake.'

He always hurried the end of his dressing, as if getting out of her bedroom would be an escape.

'Yes,' said Marya dully. 'All right. I will.'

'It oughtn't to be like this. I oughtn't to let it be like this. It's ugly like this.'

All very well to think that. But he crushed her. He bore her down.

Besides, she hadn't a leg to stand on, really. He had everything on his side — right down to the expression on the waiter's face when he brought up her breakfast. Everything. Including Logic and Common Sense. For he could so easily say — he often did say — 'Why did you leave the Avenue de l'Observatoire?'

Or, 'Why don't you come along with me and see Lois? Come to Lefranc's tomorrow for lunch. Lois is very fond of you. And you must turn up occasionally, my dear; you really must.'

They would be sitting in the Café de Versailles, a peaceful place at three o'clock in the afternoon, given up to middle-aged gentlemen drinking bocks and young men writing letters. The vague smell of lunch still hung on the air. Outside, the Rue de Rennes stewed drearily in the sun.

'I don't want people to know anything. It isn't anybody's

business. We can't let Lois down, surely you must see that. She's been awfully generous and we can't let her down.'

'But everybody knows already,' said Marya. 'If you think they don't, your crest ought to be an ostrich.'

'Nonsense!'

She persisted. 'Everybody cuts me dead all along the Boulevard Montparnasse, anyway. Even De Solla cuts me. I'm the villain of the piece, and they do know. They say that Lois picked me up when I was starving and that the moment I got into her house I tried to get hold of you. And that there are limits. Or they say — shall I tell you what else they say, the ones who have lived here long enough?'

'Oh, I know the sort of thing,' said Heidler. 'But what if they do? They can't be sure. You must live it down. My dear child, you can live everything down, believe me, if you keep your head and don't give yourself away.'

'And if you have a good little income. Don't forget that.'

'Why should I be a butt for Lois and her friends?' Marya went on excitedly. 'She wants me there so that she can talk at me. She wants me there so that she can watch out for the right moment to put her enormous foot down.'

She began to laugh loudly. There was a coarse sound in her laughter. Heidler looked at her sideways. He disliked her when she laughed like that.

He told her coldly: 'You talk the most awful nonsense sometimes, don't you?'

'What?' said Marya. 'Aren't Lois's feet enormous? Well, I think they are. You didn't exactly look for *fines attaches* when you married, did you?'

His eyes were very hostile. When she saw his hostile eyes she stopped laughing and her lips trembled.

'All right. Very well. Just as you like,' said Marya. 'What's it matter, anyway?'

•   •   •

It was no good arguing, there she was, the villain of the piece; and it hurt, of course. When the lonely night came it started hurting like hell. Then she would drink a couple of Pernods at Boots's Bar to deaden the hurt and, carefully avoiding the Boulevard du Montparnasse, she would walk to a side-street off the Boulevard St Michel and dine in a students' restaurant, not frequented by the Montparnos.

'A Pernod fils, please.'

'Pernod is very bad for the stomach, mademoiselle,' the *patronne* said disapprovingly. 'If mademoiselle had a Dubonnet instead?'

The *patronne* was really a wonderfully good sort. Fancy caring what happened to the stomach of a stray client. On the other hand, fancy facing life — that is to say, facing Heidler and Lois — on a Dubonnet! Marya could have cackled with laughter.

'No, a Pernod,' she insisted.

And a minute afterwards the merciful stuff clouded her brain. Then, dazed, she watched the lady who was sitting opposite dining slowly and copiously. Soup; a beefsteak; a salad; cheese. She was a lady with a pale face, crimson lips, a close-fitting black hat, and eyebrows like half moons. She was indeed exactly like Pierrot and every now and then she would turn and look at herself in the glass approvingly. Eventually, gathering up her belongings, she moved out with stately and provocative undulations of the hips.

But the students at the next table were *camelots du roi*. They were talking politics and the lady passed out unnoticed. Then Marya, imitating her, turned round and looked at herself in the mirror at the back, powdered her face and reddened her lips. But hopelessly, thinking, 'Good God, how ugly I've grown!' Loving had done that to her — among other things — made her ugly. If this was love — this perpetual aching longing, this wound that bled persistently and very slowly. And the devouring hope. And the fear. That was the worst. The fear she lived with — that the little she had would be taken from her.

Love was a terrible thing. You poisoned it and stabbed at it and knocked it down into the mud — well down — and it got up and staggered on, bleeding and muddy and awful. Like — like Rasputin. Marya began to laugh.

As she walked back to the hotel after her meal Marya would have the strange sensation that she was walking under water. The people passing were like the wavering reflections seen in water, the sound of water was in her ears. Or sometimes she would feel sure that her life was a dream — that all life was a dream. 'It's a dream,' she would think; 'it isn't real' — and be strangely comforted.

A dream. A dream. '*La vie toute faite des morceaux. Sans suite comme des rêves.*' Who wrote that? Gauguin. '*Sans suite comme des rêves.*' A dream. Long shining empty streets and tall dark houses looking down at her.

Often during these walks she passed under the windows of the studio in the Avenue de l'Observatoire. Once it was on a Thursday night. Lois's party, of course. She stood outside in the dark street imagining that she heard the sound of the gramophone playing, 'If you knew Suzie like I know Suzie.'

Then she thought, 'No, this is too stupid. I'm going home.' But still she stood there listening, looking up at the lit windows.

Well, there she was. In a bad way. Hard hit. All in. And a drunkard into the bargain. And she had to stuff herself with veronal before she could sleep.

But when she tried to argue reasonably with herself it seemed to her that she had forgotten the beginnings of the affair, when she had still reacted and he had reconquered her painstakingly. She never reacted now. She was a thing. Quite dead. Not a kick left in her.

When Lois sneered she sat with bent head and never answered.

'Oh, I know I've got a terrible tongue,' Lois would say complacently. And Marya, watching her, silent, would think: 'One of these days just when she's thought of something clever to say about me for her friends to snigger at, just when she's opening her mouth to say it, I'll smash a wine-bottle in her face.'

Sitting there silent, her hands cold and a little fixed smile on her face, she would imagine the sound of the glass breaking, the sight of the blood streaming. As she lay awake she imagined it, breathing quickly, and then she would tell herself, horrified: 'My God, I'm going mad!'

Little wheels in her head that turned perpetually. I love him. I want him. I hate her. And he's a swine. He's out to hurt me. What shall I do? I love him. I want him. I hate her.

So she would lie for hours, tortured by love and hate, till the morning came and the coloured tepid water which they called coffee in the Hôtel du Bosphore. Then she would get up and look at herself in the glass, thinking: 'Good Lord! can that be me? No wonder people think I'm a bad lot.'

Her eyelids were swollen and flaccid over unnaturally large, bright eyes. Her head seemed to have sunk between her shoulders, giving her a tormented and deformed look. Her mouth drooped, her skin was greyish, and when she made up her face the powder and rouge stood out in clownish patches.

She would stare at herself, feeling a horrible despair. A feeling of sickness would come over her as she stared at herself. She would get back into bed and lie huddled with her arm over her eyes.

This was Marya's life for six days of the week. On the seventh she went to Fresnes and returned soothed, comforted, and, because she reacted physically so quickly, once more desirable.

'My dear, how much better you look!' Heidler would never fail to remark the next day. 'Not half so peaky. My darling child. You pretty thing.'

Marya thought of her husband with a passion of tenderness and protection. He represented her vanished youth — her youth, her gaiety, her joy in life. She would tell herself: 'He was kind to me. He was awfully chic with me.'

Soon, for her sentimental mechanism was very simple, she extended this passion to all the inmates of the prison, to the women who waited with her under the eye of the fat warder, to all unsuccessful and humbled prostitutes, to everybody who wasn't plump, sleek, satisfied, smiling and hard-eyed. To all the people who never went to tea-parties or gave them. To everybody, in fact, who was utterly unlike the Heidlers.

She went to the prison gaily, as if she were going to visit a friend, and all the way there she would revolve her plans for Stephan.

．　　．　　．

It was the beginning of August. Stephan was to be released on the second Sunday in September.

'I'll have to find a coiffeur,' he said anxiously. 'I don't want to go around Paris with my hair on my shoulders and a long beard. . . .'

The warder who shaved the prisoners' heads was, it seemed, a good sort. A few weeks before they were released he let them start to grow their hair.

'Not a bad type,' said Stephan. 'Many of them are not bad. They do their work, what do you wish? I daresay they'd prefer to do something else.'

'Oh, you'll find a coiffeur,' said Marya. 'I'll get a room for you in the Quartier Latin somewhere, will that do?'

'Look in the Rue Tollman,' he advised.

'Well, you can go straight there from Fresnes and in the afternoon I'll turn up with the money.'

'It's all very well,' said Stephan, 'but what about you? How will you manage about money?'

She answered: 'I've told you, the Heidlers have lent me some money.'

'They're chic,' remarked Stephan.

17

AUGUST WAS A HOT, oppressive month, the sun beating down on sleepy streets, the cafés and restaurants nearly empty, the staircase and passages of the Hôtel du Bosphore and its fellows pervaded by an extraordinary mixture of smells. Drains, face powder, scent, garlic, drains. Above all, drains, Heidler decided. He reached the second floor and knocked at Marya's door.

'I'm not late,' he said when she opened it. 'Your clock's fast.' He sat down, with a sigh, thinking: 'Oh, God, what depressing places hotel bedrooms can be.' He looked at the bed, averted his eyes instantly and lit a cigarette. When he had smoked it, he suggested:

'Why shouldn't you go into the country for a bit? Somewhere not too far from Brunoy. Paris is hateful in August. And you really aren't looking well.'

'I can't go away just now,' she told him. 'What's the good? I must be here when my husband comes out of jail.'

'Oh! Of course,' said Heidler. He coughed and added: 'But look here, my dear, you surely don't intend. . . .'

'Intend what?'

There was an edge to her voice.

'If you go back to your husband,' he declared, 'I can't see you again, you understand that?' He leaned back, looking impenetrable and alert, like a chess-player who has just made a good move.

It was a greyish day and she was sitting with her back to the light. He couldn't see her face well. She answered sharply:

'I'm certainly going to see Stephan and do what I can for him. It won't be much. Are you thinking of trying to stop me, you and your damned Lois?'

She was astonished at herself. 'After all,' she thought, 'I've still got a kick left in me.'

Heidler began to argue patiently, talking as it were from the other side of a gulf between them.

'You don't seem to realize that I'm merely trying to save you from a very dreadful existence, an unthinkable existence. Your husband is going to be expelled from France. And he's in trouble with the Belgian police, you say. Have you imagined what your life will be? You'll career about Europe without any money or any friends in a perpetual and horrible insecurity. And sooner or later he'll probably try to get back to Paris. That's what they all do, it seems. They come back to Paris and hide till they're arrested again. I mean, I'm not going to be mixed up with all that sort of thing. I can't be. I can't afford to be. You simply don't know what you're letting yourself in for, my dear. I'm trying to stop you from having anything to do with him for your own sake.'

'I shall never live with him again. That's finished,' said Marya.

'Oh!' answered Heidler. 'That's all right then.'

She went on: 'But d'you think I could possibly be more miserable than I have been during the last few months? How could I? Don't you understand that I'm unbearably miserable?'

'No,' he answered, still patiently. 'I'm afraid that I don't understand — I do my best.'

'Oh, don't you? Don't you?' She was excited and bitter. 'Don't you understand that I hate this *louche* hotel and the bedroom and the wallpaper and the whole situation, and my whole life?'

'Why don't you change your hotel?'

'All these sort of hotels are the same,' she said drearily. 'It's the whole situation, I tell you. It's my own fault. I've been a fool. I've let Lois—'

'Why not leave Lois out of the question? She has nothing to do with it. She had nothing to do with it.'

'Oh, one word to that,' said Marya rudely. 'She had a lot to do with it, and you know it. You drink in every word she says about me.'

'You imagine that.' He looked at his watch and sighed.

'You've smashed me up, you two,' she was saying.

That was pitiful because it was so obviously true. It was also in an obscure way rather flattering.

She put her hands up to her face and began to cry. Long-fingered hands she had with beautifully shaped nails. She cried quietly, all soft and quivering, her little breasts heaving up and down in painful, regular jerks.

'I'm still fond of her,' he told himself. 'If only she'd leave it at that.'

But no. She took her hands away from her face and started to talk again. What a bore! Now, of course, she was quite incoherent.

'The most utter nonsense,' thought Heidler. Utter nonsense about (of all things) the visiting cards stuck into the looking-glass over Lois's damned mantelpiece, about Lois's damned smug pictures and Lois's damned smug voice. She said that Lois and he pretended to be fair and were hard as hell underneath. She said they couldn't feel anything and pretended that nobody else could. She said that she hated their friends.

'Imagining they know a thing when they know its name,' said Marya. 'And guzzling and yapping at Lefranc's.'

Heidler was stung and interrupted coldly:

'It's extraordinary that you don't see how unintelligent it is of you to abuse Lois.'

But she didn't take the slightest notice. She just went on talking. She drank so much that she was getting as hoarse as a crow. He tried not to listen. He wouldn't listen to this torrent of nonsense. Then he heard her say in a cold hard voice:

'Didn't you say that sex was a ferocious thing?'

He answered: 'Oh yes. So it is. A terrible thing. I ought to know that.'

He was still watching the shape of her breasts under the thin silk dress she wore — a dark-coloured, closely fitting dress that suited her.

'Terrible as an army set in array. Terrible and pitiful and futile,' he thought. 'All that. And a nuisance, too.'

She mocked: 'So it is. So it is. But you don't really believe it, do you? Well, one day I'll walk into your studio and strangle your cad of a Lois — kill her, d'you see? Get my hands round her thick throat and squeeze. Then, perhaps, you'll believe it.'

He said calmly: 'I know. As a matter of fact, I've thought several times that you might try some nonsense of that sort. So has she. So I'll simply give the concierge orders not to let you up in future if you do come. I'm not going to have Lois threatened, don't you make any mistake.'

'Oh, H.J.,' she said. 'Oh, H.J.,' in a little voice like a child.

In the shadow he saw her face crimson and then go white. He got up then because she was so white and trembling and took her in his arms and said pityingly:

'There! There! There!'

When he kissed her her lips were cold.

He said again: 'There! There! There!' And took two clumsy steps forwards, still holding her. She collapsed on to the bed and lay there breathing loudly and quickly as if she had been running. He stood looking down on her, feeling helpless and rather alarmed. He knelt down and stared at her. Her head had dropped backwards over the edge of the bed and from that angle her face seemed strange to him: the cheek-bones looked higher and more prominent, the nostrils wider, the lips thicker. A strange little Kalmuck face.

He whispered: 'Open your eyes, savage. Open your eyes, savage.'

She opened her eyes and said: 'I love you, I love you, I love you. Oh, please be nice to me. Oh, please, say something nice to me. I love you.'

She was quivering and abject in his arms, like some unfortunate dog abasing itself before its master.

They dined at a restaurant on the other side of the river, and he felt tender towards her and very anxious to see her smile and be happy. He began to talk about the studio he was going to take on the Boulevard Raspail and the way they were planning to decorate it.

Then: 'I suppose that will get on her nerves, too,' he thought. And stopped abruptly.

She was tired, unable to respond to his gentleness as eagerly as usual.

While they were drinking coffee she said suddenly: 'I'm going to see Stephan, you know.'

'Of course,' agreed Heidler. 'I quite understand that you want to help him. I meant that your going back to live with him would make an impossible situation.'

The next time he saw her he suggested a meeting with Stephan in the Taverne du Panthéon, and Marya lost herself in wonder at this suggestion. Was it his idea of playing the game? Or was Lois curious? Probably it was that, she decided.

18

'MONSIEUR HAS ARRIVED,' announced the landlady of the hotel in the Rue Tollman. 'Yes. Number 19, Madame, the room you booked.' When Marya opened the door of Room 19 Stephan was sitting at the table writing a letter. He looked like some frail and shrunken apostle, his beard and hair flowed.

When he took her in his arms she felt his thin body tremble. It was as if a stranger were touching her.

She said: 'Hello, my dear. Well, couldn't you find a coiffeur's shop open after all?'

He explained that he had been kept at the Palais de Justice for several hours. 'And I wanted to be here when you came. Oh, I know that I look awful.'

She smiled at him and answered: 'You look a regular Montparno.' — 'I didn't know how thin he was,' she was thinking.

'There's a place open just round the corner. I'll go there now,' said Stephan.

She walked restlessly up and down the room till he came back shaved and carrying a cardboard box of cream cakes. As he opened the box, she watched his hands: thin, brown, quickly moving. Clever hands he had.

'A savarin, an éclair, two meringues — the ones you like, and I've ordered tea downstairs. I looked for flowers but I didn't see any.'

'But I can't eat all those cakes,' she told him.

'Well, you must. You don't look well, Mado. You look — I don't know; you're changed. Oh, zut!' He lit a cigarette. 'Don't let's be sad.'

'No, don't let's be sad,' she said and thought again: 'He's simply dreadfully thin.' Every bone in his face showed. His clothes hung on him.

The tea arrived.

'Arrange yourself on the bed, Mado. It's more comfortable.' He piled pillows behind her back, poured the tea out and brought the cup, waiting on her with anxious gentleness.

She ate and drank quickly and then lay back, relaxed. Gradually an irrational feeling of security and happiness took possession of her. She sighed deeply like a child when a fit of crying is over, lit a cigarette and smoked it slowly, luxuriously. It was extraordinary, but there it was. This was the only human being with whom she had ever felt safe or happy.

His old grey felt hat was lying at the foot of the bed.

She said: 'About your clothes — I packed them all away in your trunk. They're at the Hôtel de l'Univers.'

'Oh, I'll sell the lot,' answered Stephan. 'The less I have with me the better.'

A shaft of sunlight made patterns through the lace curtains on the carpet. It was oppressively hot and airless in the little bedroom. From some distant — probably subterranean — region came the sound of a laboriously played piano.

She opened her handbag and looked at herself in the little glass, and was astounded because her mouth was so smiling and peaceful.

Stephan, seated in the one armchair near the window, was saying: 'I'll be able to stay four days in Paris. A type who left Fresnes with me this morning is going to lend me some money tomorrow. And with what you've brought . . . You know, I took care of the books at the end — the library — oh, my dear, *what* a selection of books! I'll tell you that one day. Well, this man, a Russian Jew, Schlamovitz is his name, was there, too. We talked sometimes — it was a funny life — well, if you knew.' He was silent, as if he were remembering the bizarre and cynical conversations of the Santé and Fresnes. 'He lives with a girl in Montmartre and she was there to meet him this morning.'

'What sort of girl?' asked Marya, interested.

'Oh, well, a *grue*, it seems. But she's a good girl. She was awfully happy when she saw him.'

'Was she?'

'Yes. She cried. Oh, they're fond of their men, these girls, I tell you.'

Marya looked away. But there had been no reproach in his voice, and he went on speaking very quickly and excitedly about the man Schlamovitz who, it seemed, spent an extraordinary existence, being petted by women in Montmartre ('My dear, what a beautiful boy!') and at regular intervals being arrested and taken to jail. He had been expelled from Paris two years before.

'Well,' said Stephan. 'What can you expect? When he was fourteen a rich old woman adopted him. And she made love to him very soon because he was so beautiful. Then she died without leaving him a penny.'

There was also another individual released two days before, known as Michel the nigger, a former soldier of the Foreign Legion, who would put a knife in anybody's back as soon as look at him. 'But a *bon camarade*.' Michel was apparently contemplating reform and turning an honest sou or two. He had a soap-making apparatus in his little two-roomed flat.

'Yes. That transparent soap, you know. And he makes cold cream and the stuff women put on their faces at night.'

'Skin food? Good Lord! All that in his two rooms?'

'Yes,' said Stephan. 'Of course, his wife helps him. And he sells it to the big Paris stores very cheap. But it seems that it's awfully cheap to make. The pots are the most expensive part of it.'

Marya considered him all the while he was talking, and thought: 'He's changed, he's awfully changed.'

She said suddenly, 'If anybody tried to catch me and lock me up I'd fight like a wild animal; I'd fight till they let me out or till I died.'

Stephan laughed. 'Oh, no, you wouldn't, not for long, believe me. You'd do as the others do — you'd wait and be a wild animal when you came out.' He put his hand to his eyes and added: 'When you come out — but you don't come out. Nobody ever comes out.'

She stared at him, impressed by this phrase.

'Let's not talk of it. Later on, Marya, one day I'll tell you everything, everything from the beginning, but let it go now for a while, let it . . .' He began to walk up and down the room. 'Imagine. In a few more days, no more Paris for me. I can't believe it.'

'Don't think about it,' she said, 'don't let's think.'

Then he told her that he had determined to go to Amsterdam, that he knew a man there who might help him, a Jew, a friend of his father's.

'People abuse Jews, but sometimes they help you when nobody else will.'

'Yes,' said Marya, 'I think so, too. They often understand better than other people.'

But now peace had left her again. She was too restless to lie still. She got up and, sitting on the edge of the bed, watched him gesticulate. His optimism seemed pitiful to her, and strange. She remembered Stephan calm, silent and self-contained; now it was as if prison had broken him up.

He assured her that in six weeks' time he would have arranged something and that he would send for her.

'Can you manage for another six weeks?'

'Of course,' muttered Marya. 'I must tell him,' she thought, and then: 'Oh, I can't now — I must wait a bit. It would be too horribly cruel.' She lit a cigarette, let it go out and then tore it to pieces.

'Don't strew tobacco on my bed, Marya,' said Stephan. 'And, look here, I want to be able to thank your friends, the Heidlers. I suppose they can't want to meet me, but all the same I would like to thank them. It was *chic* what they did, to take you into their house when I was in jail and to be your friends; yes, it was *chic*.'

'Wasn't it?' said Marya in a hard voice.

She asked for another cigarette and went on: 'They'll be in the Taverne this evening at half-past nine, if you want to see them. The Panthéon, you know. But why should you want to? Don't let's go.' She thought of Lois's brown eyes raking Stephan, shabby and shrunken, and she repeated: 'Don't let's go.'

'Are you ashamed of me?' he asked. 'Am I such a scarecrow, so *moche* as all that?'

'Good God, no!' she said. 'You really want to see them? All right.'

'Is Madame Heidler pretty?' inquired Stephan.

'No,' answered Marya. Then she added at once: 'I don't know. She has lovely eyes; she dances well. . . .'

'Good!' said Stephan, '*à la bonheur*! And now, how about two Mominettes in the little bar on the corner?'

•   •   •

Almost immediately after they reached the café Marya, who had her eyes fixed on the door, saw Lois come in and look round with an expression of defiance. Heidler followed her. They came up to the table and sat down. The horrible moment of meeting was over.

Lois began a smooth and tactful monologue. As she talked she fidgeted with her long necklace of huge, brownish yellow beads and watched the ex-convict with antagonism and curiosity.

'Oh, is that so, Madame?' from Stephan.

Heidler had carefully arranged his face to look perfectly expressionless, but when he lit a cigarette his hand trembled. He cut Stephan's thanks short with nervousness. Silence. And then more desperate conversation about the café — how old it was, how famous it was, how ugly it was.

Marya gazed intently at a woman behind the counter and wondered whether she wore a wig or whether her hair had by some extraordinary freak of nature remained blonde, supple, and vital above her rather terrible mask of an avaricious and sensual old woman.

'If it's a wig,' thought Marya, 'it's the most marvellous one I've ever seen. It's darker at the roots. Can't be a wig.'

She stared at the woman, who was arranging a huge green bow round the neck of a minute and hairy dog that stood on the counter, shivering violently. Then she listened again to the careful and nervous conversation of her three companions, and every time she heard Lois's sharply patronizing accents a feeling of such intense irritation shot through her that she clenched her hands under the table.

'For God's sake,' she said suddenly, 'ask the waiter for a *fine*; I'm so thirsty.'

Stephan began to protest. 'Don't have brandy, Mado. She oughtn't to drink brandy, you know . . .' Heidler gave him a furious glance; Lois lifted her eyebrows.

'*Garçon, une fine pour Madame.*'

Another silence.

The violin wailed with pathos: 'Laugh, Pagliacci, for your love is ended.'

Three girls passed the table, disappeared into a door marked telephone and emerged shortly afterwards, relieved, powdered and smiling, their lips very red. The woman behind the counter kissed her dog passionately, calling it the *fille de sa mémère*.

Lois looked round her in an undecided fashion, fixed her eyes on a wall painting and murmured: 'Well, I'm afraid. . . .'

'You're coming back with us, aren't you?' said Heidler to Marya with authority. 'We'll drop you at your hotel.'

She looked at Stephan. He made a quick movement: 'You're very kind, Monsieur,' he said; 'I'll take her home.'

'Oh, I think she'd better come with us,' answered Heidler, staring over Stephan's head. 'It's all on the way.'

'And it's pouring with rain,' added Lois.

'I'll meet you at the little restaurant near the Panthéon tomorrow, Stephan,' said Marya without looking at him.

The three got up. The violin was still wailing. Stephan bowed. Heidler muttered something, looking rather awkward. At the door, she looked back and saw her husband leaning forward staring after them.

•   •   •

'Well, he looks all right,' said Lois in the taxi. She spoke with cool contempt. 'And his hair's not short, that's one good thing for him, isn't it?'

'No, on the contrary, it was too long,' Marya told her.

'I think he seems quite all right,' continued Lois. 'I shouldn't worry about him at all, if I were you.'

Marya stared at her without answering.

As they passed Montparnasse station: 'Stop here, will you,' she said. 'I want to get a taxi.'

'What d'you want another taxi for?' asked Heidler. His mouth opened a little as it always did when he was surprised.

Marya said: 'I'm only going home to get some things. I'm going back to the Rue Tollman; I'm going to stay with my husband while he's in Paris, naturally.'

'Naturally!' she repeated, staring hardly at Lois.

She rapped on the glass in front. The driver looked round. She rapped again and he stopped. She opened the door for herself and got down.

'Good night,' she said and shut the door on them. She ran up to the nearest taxi. 'First to the Hôtel Bosphore, then to the Rue Tollman, number — I'll stop you.'

As she spoke, she was thinking with agony: Heidler! Heidler!

'Extraordinary thing to do,' remarked Heidler. He was very pale.

Lois said: 'Yes. Monsieur Zelli is a funny little man, isn't he? But she's obviously very fond of him.'

He was silent.

She went on in a low voice: 'My poor H.J. Oh, my poor, poor H.J. All this is so abominably sordid.'

She looked sharply at him as she spoke, then out of the window at the wet streets.

'That's that,' she thought. And suddenly she felt weak, exhausted like someone at the end of a long and terrible effort. Tears came into her eyes. She blinked, pressed her lips together, and told herself: 'Yes, that's that.'

◆　　◆　　◆

It was very quiet in the room at the hotel in the Rue Tollman. Only the gentle sound of falling rain came up from the dark street outside.

'You don't love me any more,' said Stephan. 'I feel it. I know it. You stiffen when I touch you. Well, I don't blame you. A year in jail doesn't make a man appetizing.'

'I'm awfully tired,' said Marya, 'and awfully sad. Will you just be kind to me for a little? And don't let's think about love at all. You know, sometimes I'm so sad! Life is so hard and puzzling, awful, it seems to me. If I could rest just for a bit. I'm longing to rest for a bit.'

He said gently: 'Don't worry. *T'en fais pas!*' He put his arms round her. 'Can't you sleep like that? Are you well like that?'

'Oh, yes,' she sighed. And slept at once, rocked by the sound of the rain.

The next few days passed like a dream. Lovely days, fresh, and washed and clean. And the knowledge that this was the irrevocable end of their life in Paris made every moment vivid, clearly cut and very sweet. Those were strange days, detached from everything that had gone before or would follow after.

On their last evening they dined recklessly in the Restaurant Chinois of the Rue de l'Ecole de Médécine.

As they began the meal Stephan remarked: 'I've just enough money left for my fare to Amsterdam and a hundred francs for when I get there.' Marya was silent. Then he said: 'Your friends the Heidlers don't like me.'

'Oh yes, they do,' Marya answered feebly. She was taken aback. It was the first time he had mentioned the Heidlers since their meeting.

'And to tell you the truth. . . . What wine shall we drink? Here's a good Sauternes. I suppose you still like Sauternes? To tell you the truth I care as little as I care what's happened to my first shirt whether they like me or not.'

'Stephan,' she asked, 'tell me what you think about Lois.' She waited for his answer nervously as if a great deal depended on it.

'Madame Heidler? I think she is absolutely primitive.'

'You think she's primitive?' Marya repeated slowly. 'You don't think that she might be — very clever?'

'Look here, Mado,' said Stephan, shrugging, 'I've only met Madame Heidler once for a short time, I can't tell you all that. Primitive people follow their instinct and sometimes that's the cleverest thing one can do. Why do you ask me? Madame Heidler is a woman who could be cruel, I think, and very hypocritical, but I saw her squeeze your hand under the table, so I can only suppose that she likes you very much.'

'Oh, she often does that,' said Marya.

Silence.

Then she added, with an effort: 'Don't let's talk about them, don't let's spoil our last evening.'

'No, don't let's spoil it,' said Stephan.

After they had dined they went upstairs to the red-lit bar where several Chinese students were dancing with very blonde women long past their first youth. The students strutted past in a stiffly correct way, melancholy for the sake of dignity, but obviously highly pleased with themselves. At intervals the lights were lowered and a good-looking young violinist played sentimental music on muted strings, and occasionally the something-or-other girls, four of them, pranced in and did a few acrobatics in strict time.

'Wait a moment,' said Stephan. 'I'm going to talk to that boy, I know him.'

'What boy?'

'The violinist.'

He crossed the room and began a long conversation. At the next table a little fat-faced Japanese was drawing on the tablecloth and she longed to see what he was doing. The problem of her existence had got beyond her, her brain had given up grappling with it. She stared curiously, absorbed, at her neighbour's thin beautiful hands.

The violinist, finishing his smiling conversation with Stephan, placed his violin under his chin with affection and began to play. It seemed to Marya that the music he played had fate in it. And what was there to catch on to in life but that same idea of fate? A dark river that swept you on you didn't know where — nobody knew where. What was the use of worrying, anyway? *Nitchevo!* 'And have another *fine*, for the Lord's sake.' It was Stephan asking her to have another *fine*.

The Japanese at the next table got up and left. She could lean over and and look at his drawings, which were of elongated and gracefully perverse little women.

'It's a funny thing,' said Stephan, 'that Russian song that the violinist is playing, I had it on the brain when I was in Fresnes. Oh, it's called in French *Par Pitié*. I asked him to play it. I absolutely had it on the brain; I made up words to it.' He looked at the clock above the buffet. 'It's eleven o'clock. If I want to get a seat in the third-class carriage we must go. And I must call at the hotel for my bag.'

In the taxi she turned to him to say: 'Stephan, don't leave me here. For God's sake, take me with you.' But before she could speak, he was talking to her: 'Yes, only just the money for the fare and a very little over.' He spoke as if he had half forgotten her, as if his mind had leaped forward and was already in Amsterdam. 'Oh, I expect I'll be able to manage something,' he said.

'I expect you will,' answered Marya mechanically.

The Gare du Nord was dimly lit, gigantic in the half light. . . .

'I'm not going to wait to see your train out,' she said when he had found a seat. 'It's unlucky and I do so want good luck for you, my dear. Good-bye.'

She kissed him and walked away, turning round several times to wave her hand.

She stood for a moment outside the station looking about her with a bewildered, undecided expression. Then she walked up to a taxi stand. 'Hôtel du Bosphore, Place du Maine, please.'

She rang the night bell and was let in. She looked in the letter-rack. There were no letters.

Then she mounted the stairs to her room, where green-yellow and dullish mauve flowers crawled over the black walls.

She undressed, and all the time she was undressing it was as if Heidler were sitting there watching her with his cool eyes that confused and hurt her.

She lay down. For perhaps thirty seconds she was able to keep her mind a blank; then her obsession gripped her, arid, torturing, gigantic, possessing her as utterly as the longing for water possesses someone who is dying of thirst.

19

MARYA ASKED: 'Any letters for me?'

'Nothing, Madame,' answered the patron, smiling. Smiling? No, grinning was the word. Hateful man. He always grinned when he looked at her. She kept her mouth steady with an effort and stood in the hall putting on her gloves deliberately.

Four days of this. Four days can be a long time.

Across the street was a tobacco shop where they sold pneumatiques. She went there, bought a card and wrote to Heidler, standing at the counter.

> My dear,
>   I want to see you as soon as possible. Please.

When she had posted the pneumatique she felt relieved, but numb and grey, like a soul in limbo. Four days can be interminable.

She lunched, sat for a long while over her coffee, walked for an hour.

When she got back to the hotel, he had answered: 'Can you come to the Versailles about nine this evening? I'll be waiting for you.'

'I must pull myself together,' thought Marya. She was trembling all over. Even her legs were trembling.

As she was dressing, a letter from Stephan arrived. Things weren't going well, he wrote. He might have to leave Amsterdam and go farther on. An evasive letter, which she read indifferently, almost impatiently, finding in it an echo of her own indifference. She put it away in a drawer and went on with her careful preparations.

'Sit here,' said Heidler, 'and have a *café fine.*' He gave her a cold sidelong look. 'Did you see your husband off?'

'Yes.'

'He's gone to Amsterdam, hasn't he?'

She nodded.

A waiter with a benevolent eye brought the coffee and brandies. From the farther side of the café, where Jimmie's Jazz performed nightly, the sound of music reached them faintly, as it were with regret.

'Are you vexed with me?' asked Marya.

'Not at all,' answered Heidler. He cleared his throat. 'My dear Mado . . .' He began to talk dispassionately and deliberately. He spoke with dignity and with a certain relief, as though he were saying something which he had often longed to say. Towards the end of his explanation he became definite, even brutal, though not to excess. All the time that he was speaking she was looking into his eyes. Then she said slowly:

'You're horribly treacherous, Heidler. I suppose you can't help it. I don't suppose you even know it. But you are.'

'I'm not being treacherous; I'm being cruel perhaps,' he added, not without complacency. 'But I'm not being treacherous. I've never shared a woman in my life, not knowingly anyhow, and I'm not going to start now.'

He folded his arms over his chest and looked across into one of the mirrors.

'You forced me to share you,' said Marya, 'for months. Openly and ridiculously. You used your wife to torture me with.'

He answered coldly: 'I don't know what you mean.'

And she saw that it was true.

Then she said: 'But, H.J., I — I love you.'

'You haven't behaved as though you did,' answered Heidler. 'And it's too late now.' He began to talk again — more emphatically, as if her persistence irritated him.

'How cold it is in here,' said Marya when he stopped.

The odd thing was that sitting on a café bench opposite was a little man whom she had met when she first came to Paris five years before, a little, yellow, wizened man and his name was — she couldn't remember — something like Monferrat, Monlisson, Mon.

It seemed to her enormously important that she should remember the name of the little man who, staring at her, was obviously also thinking: 'Who is she, where have I met her?'

She couldn't see his face clearly. There was a mist round it. Her hands were so cold that she felt them through the thin stuff of her dress. Mon. Monvoisin, that was it.

Heidler was saying in a low voice: 'I have a horror of you. When I think of you I feel sick.'

He was large, invulnerable, perfectly respectable. Funny to think that she had lain in his arms and shut her eyes because she dared no longer look into his so terribly and wonderfully close. She began to laugh. After all, what did you do when the man you loved said a thing like that? You laughed, obviously.

She said, still laughing: 'So this is the *café fine* of rupture.'

'It is,' said Heidler; 'don't get hysterical about it.'

'Why hysterical?' asked Marya. 'I can laugh if I want to, I suppose. You're funny enough to make anybody laugh sometimes.'

'Of course, laugh. Laugh, but don't cry at the same time.'

'Oh, am I crying?' she said, surprised. She put her hand up to her face.

Monsieur Monvoisin was gazing at her with an expression of avid curiosity. She began to remember all about Monsieur Monvoisin. He was one of Stephan's friends. They had been out together one night, the four of them; Monsieur Monvoisin had brought a girl called Lisette and they had wandered from bar to bar till four o'clock in the morning. A very tall young man had joined the party, who had hummed '*Si j'étais roi*' all the time. The jingling tune began to run in her head.

'Awfully funny,' she remarked to Heidler; 'do you see that man opposite? Well, I know him and he knows me. And he knows, I'm sure, that you are *plaquéing* me. And so does the waiter. Isn't *plaquer* a good word?'

'Very,' he said. 'Now pull yourself together, because we've got several things to talk about.' He looked away from her and added uncomfortably: 'You haven't got to worry, you know.'

'What?' said Marya. 'Oh, yes. Well, you can write to me about that. Let's go now, shall we?'

He seemed surprised and taken aback and made a feeble detaining gesture.

'Wait a minute, wait a minute.'

She turned and looked at him, and when he saw her eyes he put his hand up to his tie, fidgeted with it and said: 'Oh God! Oh God!'

She passed her tongue over her dry lips, put her handkerchief into her bag and shut it carefully.

He began talking again, hurriedly and uncertainly.

'Look here, Marya, don't suppose . . . I want you to go down South to get well, to forget everything and get well. It's the only thing, believe me. Will you?'

'No,' said Marya.

'Well, I beg you to.'

'No.'

'Why not?'

'I'm very tired,' Marya said, 'I want to go.'

Outside the café he told her: 'Get your things packed,' then he turned and left her.

◆　　◆　　◆

Marya walked straight ahead, her face stiff and set, across the boulevard which looked to her as if it were blazing with lights, across the Place du Maine and up the avenue.

When she passed under the railway bridge where the cobblestones are always black and glistening, and the walls ooze with damp, she felt for the first time a definite sensation of loss and pain, and tears came into her eyes. She walked on with the fixed idea that if she went far enough she would reach some obscure, dark cavern away from the lights and the passers-by. Surely at the end of this long and glaring row of lamps she would find it, the friendly dark where she could lie and let her heart burst. And as she walked she was certain that every woman she passed was mocking her gleefully and every man she passed was mocking her contemptuously. After a time she felt tired and went into a café, a vast echoing place, nearly empty. The electric lights were arranged in a square pattern overhead and for some reason this made the place look like a casino. The orchestra was seated on a raised platform in the middle of the room; it had just finished playing *The Huguenots*, and the pianist, in spectacles, leaned forward arranging the music of *The Barber of Seville* with a fussy, conscientious look on her face. Jazz was far from her well-ordered mind.

As Marya was drinking the brandy she had ordered, the music blared forth. It echoed lugubriously in that barn of a place, and a young man who was writing letters at the next table looked up with a pained expression, sighed and pushed away his blotter; then he proceeded to stare with interest at Marya.

She paid the waiter, got up and went out, and he followed her, leaving money on the table. When he spoke to her she looked up at him with vacant eyes. He repeated his question:

'Why are you sad?'

'I'm not sad,' answered Marya mechanically; 'I'm tired.'

But now she walked to the rhythm of the words.

'Why are you sad? *Pourquoi êtes-vous triste? Pourquoi? Pourquoi?*'

The young man by her side began to talk. He told her all sorts of things. That he had been born in Tonkin, that his nurse had had a name which meant spouse. That most of the Annamite women seemed to have a name which meant spouse. That his family had returned to France when he was nine years of age. To Toulon. That was ten years ago. That he, also, was sad as his mistress had betrayed him.

'I ought to know better by this time. Nevertheless, I'm sad. I know what it is to love.' As he talked he observed her carefully, glancing sideways. 'If you're tired,' he said at last, 'won't you come to my room and rest?' He took her firmly by the arm. 'I live not so far away — in the Rue Racine. You must come up to my room and rest.'

'Why not?' said Marya. 'What's it matter?'

She laughed suddenly, and when she laughed the young man looked surprised, even shocked. Then he gripped her arm more firmly and led her across the road to a taxi. She went with him silently — like a sleep-walker.

When they got to his room she said: 'Oh, but I don't like the light. Light hurts me.'

'Well,' answered the young man, 'don't worry about that. I'll soon arrange that.'

He went to a drawer and produced two enormous blue silk handkerchiefs, which he proceeded to tie round the electric light.

'I've often noticed,' he continued, 'that women, for one reason or another. . . . *Enfin.*'

20

HEIDLER SAID: 'Well, are your things packed?' He walked across to the window and flung it wider open. 'Much too hot in here.'

'I'm not going,' said Marya stubbornly. She was lying huddled on the bed and he sat on a chair near her and took her hand in his.

'How cold you are.'

His eyes were very cautious. He was thinking that it wouldn't do to leave the girl trailing round Montparnasse looking as ill as that. She was lying huddled. As if there were a spring broken somewhere. He felt at once flattered, impatient and pitiful.

He said, speaking very gently, that he had arranged everything. The train next day at twelve, the night at Lyons. 'And you'll be in Cannes the following morning.'

'I'm not going,' repeated Marya.

'You'll like Cannes,' said Heidler persuasively. 'Sure to. Everybody likes Cannes. Well, I mean everybody wants to be there. And you can stay some days at Cannes and look round for somewhere else.'

'I won't go,' Marya said in a high voice. 'I won't go. Leave me alone.'

She jumped up. Her felt hat was lying on the floor and she gave it a violent kick.

'Leave me alone!'

Heidler looked at her sharply, then picked the hat up, smoothed it and put it on the table. He said:

'Don't worry about your things. I'll tell the maid here to pack for you. She'll do it all right. Come out and have something to eat. We'll ring for her before we go.'

He walked up to her and put his hands on her shoulders. When he touched her, she flushed scarlet and her mouth twitched.

'There, there, there!' said Heidler soothingly. 'It's all right. It's all right. Come along. Put your hat on. . . .'

21

THE BEACH WAS strewn with old sardine tins and fishing nets spread to dry in the sun. A little white boat, called *Je m'en fous*, heaved very slowly up and down at the end of its rope. Beyond the pebbles and the sardine tins the sea was the colour of a field of blue hyacinths.

Marya lay in the sun hour after hour and her thoughts were vague and pale, like ghosts. At the back of the beach a sparse line of eucalyptus trees danced gaily in the wind. Sometimes a brown, sturdy fisherwoman or a thin yellow dog would pass and look down on her, lying motionless with one arm over her eyes.

'But you ought to go to Nice, Madame,' said the landlady of the Hôtel des Palmiers. She was pretty, dark and fat, and she enjoyed relating the complicated history of her inside. '*Hélas!* What it is to be a woman,' she would say at the finish.

'I don't like Nice,' answered Marya.

'The tram stops outside the door every twenty minutes,' continued the landlady, ignoring, as was proper, her client's last foolish remark.

'Well,' said Marya suddenly, 'I'll go this afternoon; why not?'

In Nice the sun blazed down on the white houses along the sea front and the strong-winged gulls swooped and dived gracefully, and the stone ladies smiled complacently from the front of the Hôtel Negresco, as if to say: 'Think what you like, curves are charming.' There was a sort of sweet reasonableness in the very air; everything logical, arranged, purposeful, under a surface of grace, lightness and gaiety. Life as it should be lived.

Marya sat in an empty café out of the sun and looked for a long time at the blank sheet of writing paper in front of her, imagining it covered with words, black marks on the white paper. Words. To make somebody understand.

'I must make him understand,' she thought. Then wrote slowly:

Dear Heidler,

I am horribly unhappy. I'm simply going mad down here. When I think of you and Lois together I really feel as if I were going mad. You don't believe me. I can see you smiling. But it's true. It's as if all the blood in my body is being drained, very slowly, all the time, all the blood in my heart. What can I say to make you believe me? I can't think properly any more. I'm fichue.

Please be patient with me. But I want to go back to Paris; I shouldn't have come down here. Surely you must see that. I mean, will you send enough money for me to go back to Paris and live there for a week or two? That's all I want of you. It was like drinking something very bitter to the last drop when I wrote that. And now I know that I'm nothing at all. Nothing. Nothing. But I did love you. If I were dying, that would be the last thing I would say, that I loved you. That's one of the things that torments me that I don't believe you ever knew how much I loved you. Well, and I can see you smiling at all this. My dear, my dear, for God's sake, send me the money at once and let me go. I'm being tormented here. Please.

'That's a rotten letter,' thought Marya. She sighed and asked the waiter for more paper. And, seeing that he looked sulky: 'And another *café crème*, take this one away.'

The waiter looked at the first glass of coffee, cold and untouched, raised his eyebrows, shrugged his shoulders and departed, dragging his feet. As she waited for him, Marya watched a fierce-eyed, beak-nosed girl opposite who was also writing rapidly. As she wrote, tears came to her eyes. Probably a letter of rupture. When the waiter came back with the coffee and the paper Marya had addressed her letter.

'I can't write it again,' she thought.

She paid him and went out, leaving him staring after her and smiling. But as soon as she posted her incoherent epistle she felt relieved and even peaceful. She went back to the Hôtel des Palmiers and lay in her bedroom with her eyes shut, thinking: 'I ought to have an answer in four or five days. I must have an answer.'

It was a large bedroom with a stone-flagged floor, and the palm trees leant in a friendly fashion almost through the windows of the room. Outside in the passage the little *bonne*, Marya's namesake, sang as she mopped the floor. She was sixteen years of age, and pretty with a soft, warm, broad-browed prettiness. She sang, she mopped, she minded the *patronne*'s baby, who on its unformed legs wobbled about in an extraordinary wooden contraption on wheels.

•   •   •

A few mornings later the *patronne* knocked at Marya's door to say:

'A lady to see you, Madame. She's in the garden.'

'Good morning,' said Miss Nicolson with an efficient smile. 'Lois asked me to look you up.'

Marya greeted her, then threw a desperate glance backwards into the hotel with a wild idea of escaping this reincarnation of her torment.

Miss Nicolson stood sturdily in the sun, long-bodied, short-legged, neat, full of common sense, grit, pep and all the rest. She was dressed in grey; she wore a green scarf and a becoming hat. Her small feet were shod with crocodile-skin shoes. It was oddly shocking to catch glimpses of very hairy legs through her thin silk stockings.

'I'm staying at Antibes,' said Miss Nicolson. 'I had Lois's letter about you this morning.'

Her eyes travelled rapidly upwards and downwards gathering information, searching hopefully for the inevitable weak point. Marya muttered an invitation to luncheon and the other looked doubtfully into the dark dining-room of the hotel.

'We can go to the zoo,' suggested Marya, 'it's quite close by. Some Russian people have a restaurant there.'

As they walked down the sunny road, Miss Nicolson chattered gaily about Lois Heidler, about Heidler, ('Dreadful man!' said Miss Nicolson), about Lois's extraordinary affection for Marya.

They lunched in the sun on heavy Russian food. It was very hot. There was a pungent smell of animals in the air.

Miss Nicolson still discoursed, gradually approaching her climax: Montparnasse, her darling Lois, the husband of her darling Lois, men in general, men who get sick of their mistresses and send them away into the country to get rid of them.

Marya listened with a curiously helpless feeling. It was as if bandages were being torn from an unhealed wound.

'Lois thought, when she read your last letter to them, that you must be seedy.'

'To them?'

'Yes,' said Miss Nicolson innocently, but with a shrewd sidelong look. 'You did write to them saying you were ill or something, didn't you?' She added after a pause: 'Lois told me to tell you that H.J.'s very busy just now, but that she'll see that he answers your letter in a day or two.'

Marya paid for the meal in silence with the last hundred francs in her purse.

Miss Nicolson, looking away into the blue distance, remarked: 'Women are pitiful, I do think.' Then, because she was light of touch and by no means hard-hearted, she stopped talking about Montparnasse. She said that she despised women from the

Southern states because they weren't efficient. She said that her mother had divorced her father and that 'all we children sympathized with mother, all of us.' Father, it seemed, was from South Carolina and shiftless. She said that that marvellous blue made her feel peaceful, that she adored Beauty, that she lived for Beauty.

Marya looked at her curiously. It was strange to think that Miss Nicolson adored beauty and yearned and all the rest. Because she looked such a tightly packed, shrewd-eyed little person. But obviously she did yearn, for here she was saying so.

'I don't leap to it any more, though,' said Miss Nicolson sadly. 'I used to leap to beauty, but not now.'

'Let's go and look at the animals,' suggested Marya.

There was a young fox in a cage at the end of the zoo — a cage perhaps three yards long. Up and down it ran, up and down, and Marya imagined that each time it turned it did so with a certain hopefulness, as if it thought that escape was possible. Then, of course, there were the bars. It would strike its nose, turn and run again. Up and down, up and down, ceaselessly. A horrible sight, really.

'Sweet thing,' said Miss Nicolson.

'You know, one sometimes takes great dislikes to people who aren't at all what one imagines they are,' said Miss Nicolson. 'People often aren't, are they?'

'Yes,' agreed Marya. 'I mean, no, they aren't. Will you come back to the hotel for some coffee? They'll know the trains to Antibes. Or there's a 'bus from Cagnes every half-hour.'

She was thinking: 'I must get drunk tonight. I must get so drunk that I can't walk, so drunk that I can't see.'

Miss Nicolson decided on a train about six.

'Good-bye,' she said, as she leapt lightly up the high carriage-step with her scarf fluttering bravely behind her. 'Will you come and lunch with me at Antibes next week — say Tuesday?'

'Yes,' said Marya. 'Of course. Good-bye.'

After the fifth Pernod drunk at the little café on the beach Marya thought: 'It's as if I were drinking water. Never mind.'

At the hotel she made a pretence of dining, then went up to her room and took several cachets of veronal. As soon as she lay down she slept. It was still light.

At about two o'clock in the morning she awoke moaning. She lay very still for a moment, then sat up in bed with tightly pressed lips. Every muscle in her body was taut.

'Hold on! Don't be a fool,' she said to herself.

She lay back and shut her eyes and saw Heidler kneeling down to pray in the little church and looking sideways at her to see if she were impressed. He got up and walked out of the church into the room. 'God's a pal of mine,' he said. 'He probably looks rather like me, with cold eyes and fattish hands. I'm in His image or He's in mine. It's all one. I prayed to Him to get you and I got you. Shall I give you a letter of introduction? Yes, I might do that if you remind me. No trouble at all. Now then, don't be hysterical. Besides, Lois was there first. Lois is a good woman and you are a bad one; it's quite simple. These things are. That's what is meant by having principles. Nobody owes a fair deal to a prostitute. It isn't done. My dear girl, what would become of things if it were? Come, come to think it over. Intact or not intact, that's the first question. An income or not an income, that's the second.'

Then she found herself thinking with lucidity: 'He gave her my letter to read, of course. It's like being stripped and laughed at.'

She put the light on and looked at the red marks on her arm, where her teeth had nearly met. 'And I haven't got a dress with long sleeves, either.'

She worried about that for a while, then got up and arranged the bedclothes carefully. Her nightgown was soaked with sweat. She took a fresh one from the cupboard and lay down again with relief. The room had swayed with her when she stood up.

The croaking of frogs came in through the open window and, very faintly, the sound of the sea. Then it was not the sound of the sea, but of trees in a gale. Dark trees growing close together with thick creepers which hung down from the branches like snakes. Virgin forest. Intact. Never been touched.

She sighed because the pillow was so hot, moved uneasily and opened her eyes. She thought: 'What a row the sea is making tonight.' But there was a noise in her head, too, a roaring noise, and the bed kept sinking under her in a sickening fashion. 'I've doped myself properly,' she thought. 'Perhaps if I leaned out of the window.' But she was too giddy to get up. She was too giddy to keep her eyes open. She shut them and again the bed plunged downwards with her — sickeningly — into blackness.

She was trying to climb out of the blackness up an interminable ladder. She was very small, as small as a fly, yet so heavy, so weighted down that it was impossible to hoist herself to the next rung. The weight on her was terrible, the vastness of space round her was terrible. She was going to fall. She was falling. The breath left her body.

'Yes I heard you being sick this morning, Madame,' said Madame Moreau with an inquisitive look.

'I'll just stay in bed today,' explained Marya, 'and then I'll be all right tomorrow. I was— ' She stopped, because she realized in time that if she said, 'I was drunk,' Madame Moreau would be disgusted and shocked to the core. 'I had an awful headache yesterday,' she said. 'I still have.'

'You look ill,' said the *patronne*.

A couple of hours afterwards she came back, had another look at Marya and then remarked: 'If I telephone to Nice for a doctor?' She went away to do it.

The doctor was small and brown and he asked a great many questions in a staccato voice. Then he tapped and pinched and probed with hands that hurt rather.

'I want,' said Marya, 'something to make me sleep. Something rather strong, please. I've been taking veronal, but it makes me sick.'

'Ah?' said the doctor. He wrote out two prescriptions, told her to wear a hat in the sun and went away looking wise.

In two days Heidler replied:

Dear Mado,

I've had your letter. I cannot for many reasons send you a large sum of money. I certainly do not intend to help you to join your husband and I don't consider that you are well enough to get back to Paris yet. I'm glad Miss Nicolson came to see you. Lois thought she might cheer you up. Here is a cheque for three hundred francs for your hotel this week. Do try to get well.

Yours, H.

She read this letter indifferently. Nothing mattered just then. It was extraordinary that anything had ever mattered at all. Extraordinary and unbelievable that anything had ever mattered.

The days were hot and very lovely. Loveliest in the morning, because then there were grey and silver in the blue dream and cool shadows on the water that was so hot and sticky at midday. Rather like bathing in warmish oil. But sticky or not, it was a caressing sea.

If you had any guts; if you were anything else but a tired-out coward, you'd swim out into the blue and never come back. A good way to finish if you'd make a mess of your life.

When she had bathed she would lie and think of little things, stupid things like a yellow dress that Stephan had bought her once at Ostend. He always chose beautiful clothes. He had a flair for that sort of thing. It had been fun to wear beautiful clothes and to feel fresh and young and like a flower. The greatest fun in the world.

One day, quite suddenly, the weather changed and that morning she had a letter from Stephan to say that he was coming back to Paris.

I can't get any work here, he wrote, *I won't tell you how I've been existing for I don't want to depress you, but I've made up my mind that to get right away is my only chance, and I'm going to try for the Argentine. But I want to see you again before I go and that's why I'm coming to Paris. Don't be afraid; there is no risk. I know a man with whom I can stay quite safely and as long as nobody actually denounces me to the police, I am all right. I've managed to borrow eight hundred francs. I am sending four hundred to help you to pay your journey. Come as quickly as you can. I'll let you know an address to write to.*

Stephan

She meditated over this letter, seated in the dark dining-room of the Hôtel des Palmiers. The grey sky and the cold were a relief and the mistral galvanized her into some sort of activity. She sat with her chin on her hand, a glass of black coffee before her, and felt a faint stirring of hope.

22

'I'VE GOT A room for you in a hotel near the Gare du Nord,' said Stephan. He took her arm protectingly. 'You're awfully tired, aren't you? Stay here for a moment; give me the *fiche* of your baggage.' It was a grey morning. The sky was the colour of train smoke. 'My friend Jacques Bernadet lives in that quarter,' he explained in the taxi, 'in the Rue Bleue. But I'll tell you afterwards; you must have breakfast and a rest first.'

'Is that where you can hide?' inquired Marya.

'Hide, well, hide,' said Stephan, shrugging. 'As long as I haven't to register, the police won't bother about me.'

'D'you think so?' asked Marya doubtfully.

He was leaning back smoking a cigarette and smiling, his felt hat at the back of his head. When she looked at him she felt reassured. Stephan was like that. He was always able to make his doings appear reasonable. A comforting quality that.

'Well, here we are,' he said. 'You remember that little café just round the corner, don't you? We often used to go there.'

The hotel, which was called the Hôtel de Havane, was brand new. It smelt of paint and there were ladders and pails of whitewash on the staircase. Marya had often wandered about that part of Paris with Stephan when they lived in Montmartre, and she remembered the dingy streets, the vegetable shops kept by sleek-haired women, the bars haunted by gaily dressed little prostitutes who seemed to be perpetually making the gesture of opening their bags to powder their noses. Over the whole of the quarter the sinister and rakish atmosphere of the Faubourg Montmartre spread like some perfume.

Stephan came in to announce that the bath would be ready in half an hour, and that the bathroom was at the end of the corridor. He added that he had not much money left.

'How much have you got?'

'I don't know,' said Marya; 'look in my bag.'

'You have fifty-five francs,' he told her. 'Well, we'll talk about that afterwards.'

He came towards her with open arms and a mouth that looked greedy.

'What did you say?'

'Nothing.'

(She had said: 'Heidler! Heidler!')

'Nothing,' she muttered. 'I'm awfully tired. It was a ghastly journey. The carriage was packed. I couldn't lie down at all.'

'You'll be able to sleep after we've eaten,' he said.

Then he told her that he had promised to meet his benefactor, Monsieur Bernadet, and Monsieur Bernadet's girl, that evening at half-past six.

Monsieur Jacques Bernadet was a plump young man of middle

height. His face was round, smooth and carefully powdered. He had large-pupilled, long-lashed, blue eyes which he used in a practised and effective manner, a very small pursed mouth and a high tenor voice.

'Madame,' he said, 'I am enchanted to meet you.'

'What a dreadful man!' thought Marya.

But the girl with him (her name, it seemed, was Mademoiselle Simone Chardin) was certainly attractive. Astoundingly pretty indeed. She was young, swarthy, and wore a red dress tightly fitting and long sleeved, buttoning closely up to the throat. She spoke very little.

'I'm here,' her eyes seemed to say, 'because for the moment I can't find anything better to do. But don't try to mix me up too much in your affairs.'

The party sat in a very small café in the Rue Lamartine. There was a bar upstairs and a coal shop in the cellar, an unexpected but usual combination. Through the open door they could see the Place Cadet and its kiosk of flowers, the red back of a newspaper stall, and the open mouth of the Metro station.

Stephan ordered four Pernods.

'We always come here for apéritifs,' he explained to Marya, 'because the man who owns the place is a good type.'

'*Très délicat, cet homme là,*' affirmed Monsieur Bernadet.

He began a long, involved story illustrating the extraordinary delicacy of the *patron*, a heavily moustached individual who sat behind his bar with an immovable face, pouring out the drinks at intervals with a steady hand. The mirror at his back reflected his head, round as a bullet, covered with a coarse mane of hair, and the multi-coloured row of bottles. A hatless woman came in, drank a glass of white wine at the bar counter and inquired after a certain *beau blond*.

'Tell him from me that I'm still waiting for him,' she said and drifted out, laughing.

'I know a type,' said Bernadet, gloomily finishing his Pernod, 'who makes a fortune every three years in the Argentine, and then he comes to Paris to spend it, the fool. Let me once be out of this misery and I wouldn't be back in a hurry, I tell you! My God, Paris. Paris. Well, and then? Without money Paris is as rotten as anywhere else and worse.'

'It's nice all the same, Paris,' murmured the girl.

She had taken off her hat. Her hair, which was curly and worn cut to the neck, fell very beautifully about her face and smelt of some warm perfume. Her mouth was like a child's.

'Paris is the most beautiful place in the world,' she said seriously. 'Everybody knows that.'

Monsieur Bernadet chanted with sarcasm:

> '*Oh!*
> *Que c'est beau,*
> *Mon village-e,*
> *Mon Paris . . .*'

'*Air connu.*'

'What scent do you use?' asked Marya suddenly, speaking to Mademoiselle Chardin. 'Chypre?'

'I? L'Heure Bleue of Guerlain.'

'Guerlain! Listen to that,' said Bernadet. 'I ask you.' He gave a short laugh like a bark. 'Guerlain!'

'You get on my nerves,' answered the girl with calm dignity.

Stephan suggested more Pernod and, as Mademoiselle Chardin refused, three more apéritifs were ordered and the two men discussed the Argentine with gravity.

You could make your way there, it seemed, provided that you turned your back on the towns. The country was the thing. Ranches. Cattle.

'But you can't ride,' said Mademoiselle Chardin to her friend. 'You're talking about ranches and you've never been on the back of a horse in your life.'

'One learns that quickly,' answered Monsieur Bernadet hopefully. 'Besides, there are other jobs to be had on ranches, aren't there? They want cashiers, for instance.'

He spoke without smiling. Marya had a swift vision of Monsieur Bernadet clad in the becoming costume of a cowboy, escaping with the cash box of some confiding ranch owner under his arm. Rolling down to Rio as it were. But it would have to be a very confiding ranch owner indeed, she thought.

After the third round of apéritifs, Monsieur Bernadet rose and, bowing politely, remarked that Stephan doubtless wished to conduct his lady to dine somewhere.

'The *prix fixe* place round the corner is not bad,' he advised. 'Three francs fifty, wine included. *A tout à l'heure, mon vieux.*'

'I don't like that man,' said Marya at once. 'Where ever did you get hold of him?'

Stephen twirled his empty glass in his fingers with a moody expression.

'I knew him at the Santé. He was my left-hand neighbour, and when we went out to take exercise in the courtyard I spoke one or two words to him. Then we telephoned to each other. You don't know that there is a telephone system in the prison, naturally. Well, I'd forgotten all about him, when we met by chance in Rotterdam, and he told me that if I wanted to come to Paris I could stay at his place quietly without anyone knowing it. I understand quite well,' he added with bitterness, 'that these are not the sort of people you like, but *voilà*. I don't think any respectable gentleman would risk lending me his flat, and I have to take what I can get in the way of friends.'

'You're quite wrong,' answered Marya, 'about the sort of people I like, only I wouldn't trust this particular man very far, if I were you.'

Stephan remarked scornfully: 'Trust! You're funny with your trust. No, of course, I don't trust him, any more than I trust anybody else. I make use of him and that's all. Let's go and eat.'

After dinner, in the evil-smelling little restaurant, Stephan said suddenly:

'You understand, don't you, that I must get away? I've lost my luck. I care too much. I did my best but it was no good. I've lost my luck.'

His mouth drooped at the corners. There was something wolf-like about his sharpened features. He went on:

'I can't any more. You don't know what it is. I can't. I've cried myself to sleep like a little boy night after night. Well, and what's the use of that? One stays and cries, that's all. And there's so much that I want to forget and so much that I don't dare to think of. I'm not myself any more. Life is pressing on me all the time. Constantly. To doubt everything. My God, it's horrible, I must get away. If I could get away, I might be myself again. There's an emigration bureau at Genoa. I'm going there. . . . *Partir. Partir.* To get away,' he muttered.

She said: 'Stephan, look here. Don't leave me. All the way to Paris I was thinking that I'd tell you this. Don't leave me, please. Take me with you. We needn't go to the Argentine, need we? Because that would be horribly expensive. But there are lots of other places. It isn't impossible if you really want it. Nothing is.'

He told her: 'You don't know what it is, *la misère*. Nobody knows what it is till it's got them.'

Marya looked away and answered slowly: 'No. That's true. Nobody knows what it is till it's got them. But suppose that I could borrow some money. I might be able to.'

He gave her a sidelong look. 'Bernadet says that he may be able to lend me some in a week.'

'Oh, Bernadet,' said Marya impatiently. 'I don't believe a word of that.'

'Neither do I,' confessed Stephan.

Silence.

'I must be somewhere where I can work,' he muttered. 'People talk, but let them be in my situation and they would see. My God! to go smash, to go right under for want of a little money.'

She looked at him, and said in a very low voice: 'I'll write to . . . I'll write . . . or perhaps there's a letter for me at the Hôtel du Bosphore.'

After that they talked again about Monsieur Bernadet. His business, it seemed, was the enlargement of photographs. Marya said that she didn't know that anybody ever wanted their photographs enlarged these days.

'Well, they don't,' said Stephan. 'Hardly anybody. But that's supposed to be his business. Well, shall we go along to see them now?'

•   •   •

The three rooms where Bernadet and Mademoiselle Chardin lived were on the third floor of a dark and dilapidated house in the Rue Bleue. Stephan remarked as they went upstairs: 'The concierge hates Bernadet, I shall have to be careful of her. She sympathizes with his wife. You know, Bernadet chased his wife, sent her off.'

'What? When he met this girl?' asked Marya innocently.

'This girl? Oh, no, another one; this one is nothing. Bernadet met her at the Moulin Rouge the other night and she had nowhere to go, nowhere to sleep. So he asked her to come back with him.'

'She's awfully pretty,' said Marya.

Stephan answered indifferently: 'Oh, she's a good girl. My coat was torn and she mended it very nicely. She's fed up with Bernadet. But I mean, I must be careful of the concierge.'

Mademoiselle Chardin opened the door and led the way into a high-ceiling room where a great many gigantic photographs — mostly family groups — stared down from the walls. There was a dusty counter down the middle of it and piles of cardboard boxes in the corner. It was crowded with odds and ends of furniture. A place like a bric-à-brac shop, smelling of dust and of Mademoiselle Chardin's perfume.

23

'YOU THINK TOO much,' said Monsieur Bernadet kindly. 'That's what's the matter with you. When I saw you last night I said to myself: "That's a pretty girl, but a girl who thinks too much." For instance, just now when I passed, what were you thinking of?'

Marya said: 'The newspaper kiosk.'

'Ah?' He lifted supple eyebrows.

She explained: 'I like sitting on the terrace of a café near a kiosk and looking at the names of the newspapers. Can you see? *Magyar Hirlap, Svenska, Poochi, Pesti Hirlap.* I like looking at them ranged one under the other because— ' She stopped and shrugged a little.

'Evidently,' remarked Monsieur Bernadet, 'it's an amusement like another.'

('My God, what a neurasthenic!' he was thinking. 'But she has beautiful eyes.')

'To tell you the truth,' he continued, 'I have no curiosity at all about other countries. None. After all, what can I find in other countries that I can't find better in France? Of course, if one went to make money it would be different.'

'Evidently,' answered Marya in her turn. 'A Pernod fils, please. One pretends that one will find something different. It's only a game.'

Bernadet said, after a silence: 'Stephan is waiting for you at the Rue Bleue. You know that he'll be alone there for a few days. Do you drink that without water?'

'Yes,' answered Marya. And, 'Yes, Stephan told me that you were going away this evening. You've been kind to him, Monsieur Bernadet. Thank you.'

'It's nothing at all,' muttered the other. 'One does what one can for a comrade.'

He fidgeted, then drew his chair closer and went on in a mysterious voice.

'And if I tell you that Stephan ought to leave Paris as quickly as possible, I say it for his sake. Yes. And the less he goes out while he is here the better. A man thinks, "I'm quite safe. Nobody is bothering about me." He goes out; someone who knows him sees him on the boulevard and — there you are. Next day the police. People are *vache*, people play dirty tricks for no reason at all. That's life.'

'Perhaps it makes them feel warm and comfortable,' suggested Marya.

Monsieur Bernadet said: 'What? Well, it's no use making philosophy about these things. Nearly everybody will be *vache* if you give them a chance; the best way is not to give them a chance. That's life.'

'You understand,' he went on after a pause, 'that it's not my business. I'm going away and if anything happens, it will not be seen, not known as far as I'm concerned.'

'I bet it will,' thought Marya. But she liked him better than she had done.

He finished his apéritif.

'Well, Madame, I hope to see you when I come back. Don't worry too much. Stephan is a clever boy and energetic. Anybody who looks at him can see that. He won't stay long in *la misère*. But, of course, if he can have a little money to help him so much the better. People may talk,' said Monsieur Bernadet, 'but without money — without any money at all — well.'

He pressed his lips together and shook his head several times. Then he rapped for the waiter, paid and got up.

She watched him walking up the street. He wore a very tight brown overcoat cut in at the waist. He sidled past people who got in his way with peculiar eel-like motions of his shoulders.

'Perhaps when I've sat here for a while,' Marya told herself, 'I'll be able to think better. Can't think now. So damn tired.'

Her brain was working slowly and confusedly; it seemed at moments to stop working altogether.

'But I've lots of time,' she assured herself again. 'Lots. Hours and hours.'

She stared at the newspaper kiosk and again began to imagine herself in the train, thudding across the great plain of Europe. With Stephan. Hundreds of miles of plain for the wind to sweep over.

Stephan. He looked so thin and his eyes were horribly sad. She remembered him saying, 'I cried like a little boy,' and her heart twisted with pity.

The tears came into her eyes and she told herself: 'That's this damned apéritif. I must pull myself together; I must think properly.' She pushed the glass, which was still half full, away from her.

After a time she took Heidler's letter out of her bag and looked at it. He had written: 'I'm sending this to the Hôtel du Bosphore and hope you'll get it. I'm worried about you. Why have you come back to Paris so suddenly? Will you let me know where and when we can meet? I am only too anxious to do all I can to help you. Please believe that.'

When and where? In some café, of course. The unvarying background. Knowing waiters, clouds of smoke, the smell of drink. She would sit there trembling, and he would be cool, a little impatient, perhaps a little nervous. Then she would try to explain and he would listen with a calm expression. Top dog.

'Of course you want money,' he would be thinking. 'Naturally. How much? I'm willing to give the traditional sum, the sum which is right and proper under the circumstances, and no more. Well, talk. I'm listening.'

She'd talk and all the time her eyes would be saying, 'I loved you. I loved you. D'you remember?'

But he wouldn't look at her eyes, or if he did he'd look away again very quickly. He'd be feeling healthy-minded, outrageously so. He'd long for cold baths and fresh air. Can't she explain and get it over?

'Didn't I tell her that she made me feel sick? The extraordinary persistence of this type of woman.'

Explain? But she couldn't explain. She'd have to be clever and cunning, or she wouldn't get any money at all.

'I've got to be clever,' she thought, 'clever.' Then again something in her head clicked and jarred like a rundown machine. It was cold on the café terrace. She began to shiver.

'Must be pretty late. I've been here a long time.'

She opened her bag, put away Heidler's letter, paid the waiter and walked away, moving stiffly.

'I can't any more — I can't. I must be comforted. I can't any more. I can't any more. Can't go on. Can't . . .'

•   •   •

Stephan had spread the table with cold sausage cut into slices, potato salad, a bottle of wine and a half-emptied bottle of rum. The huge photographs stared down at them with glassy eyes.

They ate in silence. She noticed that the cardboard boxes had disappeared and that he must have spent a long time trying to make the room look tidy. He had a mania for order, had Stephan.

When the meal was over Marya cleared away the plates and piled them in the kitchen.

She said to him when she came back: 'Stephan, listen. I've something to tell you.'

'Well?'

'I've something to tell you,' she repeated and, turning her eyes away from him, fixed them on a big spider motionless on the dirty white wall.

'What is it, Mado?'

'It's that. . . . D'you love me?' she asked.

'Yes.'

'Really, really?'

'Yes.'

'I'm terribly unhappy,' said Marya.

She knelt down by his chair and put her head on his knees. Then she thought it would be ridiculous to talk to him like that.

'Nothing to kneel about. How perfectly ridiculous!'

She got up, sat in one of the hard, straight-backed chairs, gripped the sides of it and fixed her eyes on the spider.

She said: 'I'm unhappy. Help me, Stephan, do help me.'

'I see that you're unhappy,' he told her gently. 'I want to help you.'

'I found a letter from Heidler at the hotel,' she said. 'I . . . I want to tell you about him . . . and Lois.'

She flushed as she pronounced the name of her enemy. Then she went on in the voice of someone talking aloud in an empty room.

'Yes. There was a letter from him at the hotel today. But first . . . I must tell you. When I'd been there with them . . . a little time, Heidler started making love to me. And so I went to her, to Lois, and I told her what was happening and I asked her to let me have the money to go away. And she said . . . that what was the matter with me was that I was too virtuous and that she didn't mind. And that I was a fool not to trust Heidler. And that night she went out somewhere and left me alone with him.'

She was silent for a while. Then she repeated:

'Lois said: "What's the matter with you is that you are too virtuous." And she went out and left me alone with him. . . .'

He leaned forward, and looking at her with an expression of curiosity, said:

'Mado — did you let Heidler make love to you?'

She answered impatiently: 'Wait and let me tell you. When she said that, I knew she was lying, but I despised her, hated her for lying, and I made up my mind not to think about her any more. And I was awfully tired. You don't know. . . . I was tired. He kept saying, "I love you." Over and over again. Just "I love you, I love you, my dear." And I loved him too,' she whispered.

'I loved him too — quite suddenly.'

Then she was silent for a moment.

'Listening outside the door,' she went on. 'Putting on carpet slippers and creeping up outside the door to listen.'

'Who did, Heidler?'

'No, she did. She used to put on carpet slippers and come and listen at the door. She said "What's the matter with you is that you're too virtuous." I swear to God she said that. And she sneered. She was always sneering. She has that sort of mouth. You don't know how often I've lain awake and longed . . . to smash her mouth so that she could never sneer again.'

He listened to this incoherent speech without moving, but when she was silent:

'When did all this happen?' he asked.

Marya thought how ugly his voice sounded. 'What am I doing here with this man?' she thought. 'This foreigner with his ugly voice?'

'It happened,' she said vaguely, 'oh, quite soon. And they wanted me to go on staying with them, but I wouldn't because I heard them whispering together one night about me. That was why I went to the hotel.'

'You mean to say,' said Stephan, 'that all the time you used to come and see me in jail you were Heidler's mistress? You used to come and laugh at me, well put away behind the bars so that I couldn't interfere?'

'I didn't come to laugh at you. Oh, no! But I wish you'd listen,' she exclaimed fretfully. 'You keep stopping me. And I want to tell you.'

'I'm listening,' said Stephan. 'I'm listening. You can go on.'

'She said to me: "What's the matter with you is that you're too virtuous." ' Then again she was silent. An expression of hatred convulsed her face.

'But what's the use,' interrupted Stephan, 'of going on about what Heidler's wife told you? She did the best for herself and I don't blame her. D'you think she's the only woman who shuts her eyes? More than shuts eyes if necessary. Come! Don't be a fool. If you were so naïve you have only yourself to blame. When you went to the hotel, Heidler came to see you? When did he come? Often?'

'No, I don't remember,' said Marya vaguely. 'It doesn't matter.'

'Oh, it doesn't matter!' Stephan laughed loudly. 'You are funny, you! You have a special way of looking at things. Well, and then? Go on, go on!'

'He told me,' said Marya, 'that I mustn't have anything more to do with you, or see you when you came out of jail. But I longed to see you. Because I thought it would help me. I was awfully unhappy. Oh, awfully. But when you'd gone to Amsterdam, you know, and I met him he . . .'

She stopped, passed her tongue over her dry lips, swallowed.

'He chucked you, hein?'

'Yes,' said Marya. 'He said he was disgusted with me. And that he had a horror of me and that when he thought of me he felt sick.' She stared unseeingly with the eyes of a fanatic at a little pulse that was throbbing in Stephan's cheek just above the jawbone.

He passed his hand over his mouth.

'*Quelle saleté!*' he said, '*quelle saleté!*'

Then he laughed and said:

'*C'est bien boche, ça.*'

She went on: 'It wasn't that that I wanted to tell you. Because really, you see, it doesn't matter. I wanted to beg you to be good to me, to be kind to me. Because I'm so unhappy that I think I'm going to die of it. My heart is broken. Something in me is broken. I feel. . . . I don't know. . . . Help me!'

'You must think I'm Jesus Christ,' said Stephan, laughing again. 'How can I help you? What fools women are! It isn't only that they're beasts and traitors, but they're above all such fools. Of course, that's how they get caught. Unhappy! Of course you're unhappy.'

He began to walk up and down the room.

'My poor Mado!' he said, and again, 'My poor Mado!'

'Help me,' she said.

But when he tried to take her in his arms she shrank away.

'No, don't touch me, she said. 'Don't kiss me. That isn't what I want.'

He looked at her in silence, then shrugged his shoulders, poured himself out a half-glass of rum and said:

'Wait a bit. Where is the letter you told me you had from Heidler?'

He took it from her bag.

'So, now . . . Wait a bit . . . He seems to have forgotten that you make him sick. Well, that sort of feeling, it comes and it goes. Everyone knows that. He wants to see you? Well, now you have a place for him to come to. It's not very chic, but still. So you will write to Heidler that he comes here tomorrow afternoon. Go on, write now! And I'll post the letter. He's made a fool of you — but he forgot me when he did that. Wait a bit. I'll be waiting for him when he comes. You want me to help you. All right!'

'You must be mad,' said Marya. And to gain time she added: 'And do you suppose, if you have a row up here with Heidler, that the concierge won't call in the police at once?'

'She won't,' answered Stephan, 'before I have had time to break his back.'

'You won't break his back as easily as all that,' said Marya.

'No? Well, we'll see. I think I'll have a little advantage because he won't expect me. I'll jump on him from behind the door. He won't even have time to make a row.'

'You must be mad,' said Marya again.

'Write the letter,' he told her. 'Write it now and I'll go and post it.'

'No, I won't.'

'You poor thing!' he mocked. 'You poor thing! You have no blood, you. You were born to be made a fool of.'

'Leave me alone,' she said. 'I might have known that you'd only hurt me worse. I was crazy to tell you.' She began to cry. 'Oh, God, why did I tell you?'

'Well,' said Stephan with contempt, 'stay here and cry. It's all you're good for. I'll go and find Heidler myself. After all, it'll be better like that. Look here, d'you see this? A revolver, yes. You didn't know that I had it, did you?'

He put the revolver back in his pocket, muttering:

'He thought I was well put away behind the bars. Wait a bit!'

'No!' said Marya.

She was standing near the door; she spread out her hands to prevent him passing.

'You shan't!' she said again. And then: 'You think I'd let you touch him? I love him.' A delicious relief flooded her as she said the words and she screamed again louder: 'I love him! I love him!'

He muttered something, collapsed on the broken armchair, and sat staring at her with miserable eyes. He looked small, shrunken, much older.

'You left me all alone without any money,' she said. 'And you didn't care a bit what happened to me. Not really, not deep down, you didn't. And now you say beastly things to me. I hate you.'

She began to laugh insultingly. Suddenly he had become the symbol of everything that all her life had baffled and tortured her. Her only idea was to find words that would hurt him — vile words to scream at him.

'So,' he said when she stopped breathless, 'now I know. Very well. As you like. Now will you get away from in front of that door?'

'No!'

He gave an impatient click of the tongue and caught her wrist to swing her aside. She fought him wildly, with frenzy.

Now, added to all her other terrors, was the terror of being left alone in that sinister, dusty-smelling room with the enlarged photographs of young men in their Sunday best smirking down at her.

'You shan't go, you shan't! I'll call for the police. If you go out of this room I'll go straight to the police-station and give you up.'

She saw the expression in his eyes and was afraid.

'No,' she said piteously, backing away from him. 'I didn't mean. . . .'

He caught her by the shoulders and swung her sideways with all his force. As she fell, she struck her forehead against the edge of the table, crumpled up and lay still.

'*Voilà pour toi*,' said Stephan.

He straightened his tie carefully, put on his hat and went out of the room without looking behind him. He felt dazed and at the same time extraordinarily relieved. As he went down the stairs he was thinking: 'The concierge; I must be careful of the concierge.' But the concierge's *loge*, when he passed it, was in darkness.

Outside in the cool street he found himself face to face with Mademoiselle Chardin.

'*Tiens*,' she said, 'good evening you . . . I left my bottle of scent upstairs; have you seen it? Is your wife there?'

'No,' said Stephan, 'there's nobody there.'

She looked sharply at him, took his arm and asked what was the matter.

'Why, nothing,' said Stephan, beginning to laugh. 'Nothing at all. I am looking for a taxi. I'm going off.'

'Take me with you,' said Mademoiselle Chardin suddenly.

She had a very pretty voice. She thrust her hand into his arm and walked along with him.

She repeated: 'Take me with you, Stephan.'

'But I tell you I am going off,' said Stephan. 'Off, off! I'm staying one night in some hotel near the Gare de Lyon. Tomorrow morning I'm off.'

'Exactly,' said Mademoiselle Chardin. 'As it happens, I know a very good little hotel around there. Comfortable, not expensive. We'll talk.'

A taxi crawled past them. Stephan signalled to the driver.

'I'll take you there,' said Mademoiselle Chardin.

She climbed into the taxi and, leaning forward, gave the driver an address in an authoritative voice. Stephan hesitated, climbed in after her.

'*Encore une grue*,' he was thinking.

At that moment women seemed to him loathsome, horrible —soft and disgusting weights suspended round the necks of men, dragging them downwards. At the same time he longed to lay his head on Mademoiselle Chardin's shoulder and weep his life away.

She put her warm hand over his firmly and said:

'My little Stephan, don't worry.'

The taxi rattled on towards the Gare de Lyon.

PART ONE

1

THE HOTEL ON THE QUAY

After she had parted from Mr Mackenzie, Julia Martin went to live in a cheap hotel on the Quai des Grands Augustins. It looked a lowdown sort of place and the staircase smelt of the land-lady's cats, but the rooms were cleaner than you would have expected. There were three cats — white Angoras — and they seemed usually to be sleeping in the hotel bureau.

The landlady was a thin, fair woman with red eyelids. She had a low, whispering voice and a hesitating manner, so that you thought: 'She can't possibly be a Frenchwoman.' Not that you lost yourself in conjectures as to what she was because you didn't care a damn anyway.

If you went in to inquire for a room she was not loquacious. She would tell you the prices and hand you a card:

> ### HOTEL ST. RAPHAEL
> QUAI DES GRANDS AUGUSTINS
> #### PARIS, 6ME
> CHAUFFAGE CENTRAL. EAU COURANTE
> CHAMBRES AU MOIS ET À LA JOURNÉE

Julia paid sixteen francs a night. Her room on the second floor was large and high-ceilinged, but it had a sombre and one-eyed aspect because the solitary window was very much to one side.

The room had individuality. Its gloom was touched with a fantasy accentuated by the pattern of the wallpaper. A large bird, sitting on the branch of a tree, faced, with open beak, a strange, wingless creature, half-bird, half-lizard, which also had its beak open and its neck stretched in a belligerent attitude. The branch on

---

2 3 7

which they were perched sprouted fungus and queerly shaped leaves and fruit.

The effect of all this was, oddly enough, not sinister but cheerful and rather stimulating. Besides, Julia was tired of striped papers. She had discovered that they made her head ache worse when she awoke after she had been drinking.

The bed was large and comfortable, covered with an imitation satin quilt of faded pink. There was a wardrobe without a looking-glass, a red plush sofa and — opposite the bed and reflecting it — a very spotted mirror in a gilt frame.

The ledge under the mirror was strewn with Julia's toilet things — an untidy assortment of boxes of rouge, powder, and make-up for the eyes. At the farther end of it stood an unframed oil-painting of a half empty bottle of red wine, a knife, and a piece of Gruyère cheese, signed 'J. Grykho, 1923'. It had probably been left in payment of a debt.

Every object in the picture was slightly distorted and full of obscure meaning. Lying in bed, where she was unable to avoid looking at it, Julia would sometimes think: 'I wonder if that picture's any good. It might be; it might be very good for all I know. . . . I bet it is very good too.'

But really she hated the picture. It shared, with the colour of the plush sofa, a certain depressing quality. The picture and the sofa were linked in her mind. The picture was the more alarming in its perversion and the sofa the more dismal. The picture stood for the idea, the spirit, and the sofa stood for the act.

•   •   •

Julia had come across this hotel six months before — on the fifth of October. She had told the landlady she would want the room for a week or perhaps a fortnight. And she had told herself that it was a good sort of place to hide in. She had also told herself that she would stay there until the sore and cringing feeling, which was the legacy of Mr Mackenzie, had departed.

At first the landlady had been suspicious and inclined to be hostile because she disapproved of Julia's habit of coming home at night accompanied by a bottle. A man, yes; a bottle, no. That was the landlady's point of view.

But Julia was quiet and very inoffensive. And she was not a bad-looking woman, either.

The landlady thought to herself that it was extraordinary a life like that, not to be believed. 'Always alone in her bedroom. But it's the life of a dog.' Then she had decided that Julia was mad, slightly pricked. Then, having become accustomed to her lodger, she had ceased to speculate and had gradually forgotten all about her.

Julia was not altogether unhappy. Locked in her room — especially when she was locked in her room — she felt safe. She read most of the time.

But on some days her monotonous life was made confused and frightening by her thoughts. Then she could not stay still. She was obliged to walk up and down the room consumed with hatred of the world and everybody in it — and especially of Mr Mackenzie. Often she would talk to herself as she walked up and down.

Then she would feel horribly fatigued and would lie on the bed for a long time without moving. The rumble of the life outside was like the sound of the sea which was rising gradually around her.

She found pleasure in memories, as an old woman might have done. Her mind was a confusion of memory and imagination. It was always places that she thought of, not people. She would lie thinking of the dark shadows of houses in a street white with sunshine; or of trees with slender black branches and young green leaves, like the trees of a London square in spring; or of a dark-purple sea, the sea of a chromo or of some tropical country that she had never seen.

Nowadays something had happened to her; she was tired. She hardly ever thought of men, or of love.

◆   ◆   ◆

On Tuesday morning at half-past nine, Liliane, the chambermaid, would bring up the letter from Mr Mackenzie's solicitor on the tray with coffee and a croissant.

She was a big, fair girl, sullen and rather malicious because she worked without stopping from six in the morning until eleven or twelve at night, and because she knew that, being plain, she would probably have to work like that until she died. Her eyes were small and hard in her broad face, and there were little pin-points of inquisitiveness in them like the pin-points of light in the pupils of a cat's eyes.

She would wish Julia good morning and then go out, banging the door, and on the tray would be the letter, typewritten in English:

Madame,
Enclosed please find our cheque for three hundred francs (fcs. 300), receipt
of which kindly acknowledge and oblige

Yours faithfully
Henri Legros
per N.E.

• • •

When Liliane had gone Julia opened her eyes unwillingly, bracing herself up. And this morning the letter was not there. Sometimes it did not come until a later post.

She drank her coffee. The curtains were still drawn. She turned on the electric light and began to read.

As she read a strained, anxious expression never left her face, which was round and pale with deep, bluish circles under the eyes. Her eyebrows were thin, finely marked; her very thick dark hair was lit by too red lights and stood out rather wildly round her head. Her hands were slender, narrow-palmed with very long fingers, like the hands of an oriental.

Her career of ups and downs had rubbed most of the hall-marks off her, so that it was not easy to guess at her age, her nationality, or the social background to which she properly belonged.

At twelve o'clock the maid knocked at the door and asked in a sullen voice when she could do the room.

'All right, all right,' Julia called. 'In half an hour.'

The central heating was not working properly and she felt cold. She dressed herself and then went and stood by the window to make up her face and to put kohl on her eyes, which were beautiful — long and dark, very candid, almost childish in expression.

Her eyes gave her away. By her eyes and the deep circles under them you saw that she was a dreamer, that she was vulnerable — too vulnerable ever to make a success of a career of chance.

She made herself up elaborately and carefully; yet it was clear that what she was doing had long ceased to be a labour of love and had become partly a mechanical process, partly a substitute for the mask she would have liked to wear.

To stop making up would have been a confession of age and weariness. It would have meant that Mr Mackenzie had finished her. It would have been the first step on the road that ended in looking like that woman on the floor above — a woman always dressed in black, who had a white face and black nails and dyed hair which she no longer dyed, and which had grown out for two inches into a hideous pepper-and-salt grey.

The woman had a humble, cringing manner. Of course, she had discovered that, having neither money nor virtue, she had better be humble if she knew what was good for her. But her eyes were malevolent — the horribly malevolent eyes of an old, forsaken woman. She was a shadow, kept alive by a flame of hatred for somebody who had long ago forgotten all about her.

Julia looked out of the window at the bookstalls on the quay. And beyond the bookstalls was the Seine, brown-green and sullen. When a river-boat passed, it would foam and churn up for a while. Then, almost at once, it was again calm and sluggish.

When she looked at the river she shivered. She felt certain that the water made her room much colder. It was only at night that she loved it. Then it seemed mysteriously to increase in width and the current to flow more strongly. When you were drunk you could imagine that it was the sea.

•   •   •

At one o'clock the maid knocked again.

'Yes, yes, yes,' said Julia fretfully.

Her coat was very old. She had grown fatter in the last few months and it was now too tight and too short for her. She imagined that it gave her a ridiculous appearance, especially behind. Indeed, her rare impulses towards activity vanished when she thought of her coat.

'I'm going out now,' she called.

It was drizzling. Julia walked quickly past the bookstalls and turned the corner by the big café on the Place St Michel. She stopped at the kiosk opposite and bought a newspaper.

She always lunched at a German restaurant in the Rue Huchette. When she came in the proprietor of the place wished her good morning from his strategic position on the stairs leading down to the kitchen. From there he could survey the waiters, the serving-up, and the legs of the women customers.

Julia took a seat at her usual table, propped her newspaper up in front of her and read it while she ate.

2

MR MACKENZIE

WHEN SHE had finished her meal Julia went for a walk. She did this every day whatever the weather. She was so anxious not to meet anybody she knew that she always kept to the back streets as much as possible.

When she passed the café terraces her face would assume a hard forbidding expression, but she loitered by the shop-windows. Books and books, and again books. And then there would be windows exhibiting casts of deformed feet, stuffed dogs and foxes, or photographs of the moon.

That afternoon she stood for a long time in the Rue de Seine looking at a picture representing a male figure encircled by what appeared to be a huge mauve corkscrew. At the end of the picture was written, '*La vie est un spiral, flottant dans l'espace, que les hommes grimpent et redescendent très, très, très sérieusement.*'

She walked on towards the quay, feeling serene and peaceful. Her limbs moved smoothly; the damp, soft air was pleasant against her face. She felt complete in herself, detached, independent of the rest of humanity.

It was half-past four when she got back to her hotel and found Maître Legros' letter in the rack.

When she got up to her room she put the letter on the table. She was reluctant to open it. She wanted to retain her sense of well-being.

She lay down on the bed, lit a cigarette and watched the lights coming out in the Palais de Justice across the river like cold, accusing, jaundiced eyes.

The gramophone in the next room started. The young man who lodged there sometimes had a girl to see him, and then they would play the same record over and over again. Once, when Julia had passed the room, the door had been open. She had seen them together, the girl sitting by the young man's side and stroking his thigh upwards from the knee with a smooth, regular gesture; while he stared over her shoulder into vacancy, with an expression at once sensual and bored.

Julia got up and switched on the light. She read her letter:

Madame,

    Enclosed please find our cheque for one thousand five hundred francs (fcs. 1,500). Our client has instructed us to make this final payment and to inform you that, from this date, the weekly allowance will be discontinued.

    Kindly acknowledge receipt and oblige

Yours faithfully,
Henri Legros.

•   •   •

Julia unfolded the cheque. The words '*Quinze cents francs*' were written in a round, clear hand.

She had always expected that one day they would do something like this. Yet, now that it had happened, she felt bewildered, as a prisoner might feel who has resigned herself to solitary confinement for an indefinite period in a not uncomfortable cell and who is told one morning, 'Now, then, you're going to be let off today. Here's a little money for you. Clear out.'

Then she started to walk up and down the room with the palms of her hands pressed tightly together. She was planning her future in an excited and confused manner, for at that moment all sense of the exact value of the money had left her.

As she put on her hat she stared at herself in the looking-glass. She told herself, 'I must get some new clothes. That's the first thing to do.' And she longed for someone to whom she might say: 'I don't look so bad, do I? I've still got something to fight the world with, haven't I?'

The room already had a different aspect. It was strange — as a place becomes strange and indifferent when you are leaving it.

Now the gramophone next door began to play again. . . . People were laughing, talking, pushing. Crowds of people were elbowing each other along a street, going to a fair. They pushed and laughed. And you heard the tramp of feet and the noise of the fair coming nearer; and the people calling. Then at last the noise of the crowd died away and you only heard the fair-music, vulgar, and yet lovely and strange.

When Julia got out into the street a certain caution awoke in her. She thought: 'I must go and sit somewhere and really make up my mind what I'd better do.'

She went into the café on the corner of the street; it was nearly empty. She sat down and ordered a drink. While she waited for it she looked at herself in the mirror opposite, still thinking of the new clothes she would buy.

She thought of new clothes with passion, with voluptuousness. She imagined the feeling of a new dress on her body and the scent of it, and her hands emerging from long black sleeves.

The waiter brought the Pernod she had ordered and she drank half the glass without adding any water. Warmth ran to her face and her heart began to beat more quickly.

She finished the drink. It seemed to her that it had left a bitter taste in her mouth. A heat, which was like the heat of rage, filled her whole body.

There was a blotter and pen-and-ink on the table before her. She opened the blotter and began to draw little flags on the paper. As she drew she was watching the face of Mr Mackenzie, which floated, wearing a cool and derisory smile, between her eyes and the blotter.

Suddenly a sensation of such dreary and abject humiliation overcame her that she would have liked to put her arms on the table and her head on her arms and to sob aloud, regardless of the people who might be looking at her or of what anybody might think.

She began to write a letter:

I got the cheque this afternoon. Why didn't you give me enough to go away when first I asked you? I am so horribly down now that I am absolutely good for nothing. And what do you think I can do with fifteen hundred francs, anyway?

At this point she stopped, realizing that she did not even know whether or not Mr Mackenzie were still in Paris. The last time she had seen him he was on the point of going away — for an indefinite time, he had said. . . . Besides, she was old enough to know that that sort of letter was never a bit of use, anyhow.

It was seven o'clock and the café was beginning to fill up. Julia went into the street and turned in the direction of the Boulevard Montparnasse.

•   •   •

The Boulevard St Michel was very crowded. Walking along blindly, Julia would bump every now and again into somebody coming in the opposite direction. When the people glared at her and muttered it seemed as if shadows were gesticulating.

The lights of the cafés were hard and cold, like ice.

When she had been walking for about twenty minutes she turned into a side-street, a narrow, rather deserted street of tall, quiet houses. Opposite number 72 she hesitated; then, instead of ringing the bell of the concierge, she crossed to the other side of the street and looked up at a window which she knew to be the window of Mr Mackenzie's bedroom. There was a light there. When she saw it she pressed her lips together with rather a grim expression.

She walked a few paces up and down the street, went back to a doorway opposite Mr Mackenzie's flat and stood there. Something in her brain that still remained calm told her that she was doing a very foolish thing indeed, and that the whole affair was certain to end badly for her. Nevertheless, she felt that she must see Mr Mackenzie. Six months of resignation were blotted out. She knew that she intended to wait until the occupant of the flat, whoever it was, left it.

She had been standing there for perhaps half an hour when the light went out. Then, after an interval, the gate opposite opened and Mr Mackenzie came out into the street. He turned towards the Boulevard Montparnasse.

At the sight of him Julia's heart began to beat furiously and her legs trembled. She was excited to an almost unbearable degree, for, added to her other emotions, was the fact that she was very much afraid both of him and of his lawyer. When she thought of the combination of Mr Mackenzie and Maître Legros, all sense of reality deserted her and it seemed to her that there were no limits at all to their joint powers of defeating and hurting her. Together, the two perfectly represented organized society, in which she had no place and against which she had not a dog's chance.

She thought stubbornly, 'I don't care. I'm going to have it out with him. I don't care.'

When Mr Mackenzie was about twenty yards off she crossed over and followed him.

He made his way into the Boulevard Montparnasse and Julia saw him go into the Restaurant Albert.

*   *   *

Mr Mackenzie was a man of medium height and colouring. He was of the type which proprietors of restaurants and waiters respect. He had enough nose to look important, enough stomach to look benevolent. His tips were not always in proportion with the benevolence of his stomach, but this mattered less than one might think.

Monsieur Albert asked if Monsieur were alone; and Mr Mackenzie answered, with a smile that he had trained not to be bashful, that he was quite alone that evening. Then he ordered veau Clamart, which Monsieur Albert said was very good, and a carafe of red wine.

Mr Mackenzie was comfortably off, but no millionaire. Helped by his father, who had owned a line of coastal steamers, and by a certain good luck which had always attended him, he had made his pile fairly early in life. He was not one of those people who regard the making of money as an adventure and cannot stop and do something else. He had made a fair sufficiency and then retired. He was forty-eight years old.

Paris had attracted him as a magnet does a needle. When in England he would always say, 'I like Paris, but I loathe the French.' When in Paris he disliked to be recognized as English, but at the same time, when he heard Frenchmen being funny about England, he would become hot and aggressive and would feel a righteous sense of betrayal.

He hid behind a rather deliberately absentminded expression. Once, in his youth, he had published a small book of poems. But when it came to actualities his mind was a tight and very tidy mind. He had discovered that people who allow themselves to be blown about by the winds of emotion and impulse are always unhappy people, and in self-defence he had adopted a certain mental attitude, a certain code of morals and manners, from which he seldom departed. He did depart from it, but only when he was practically certain that nobody would know that he had done so.

His code was perfectly adapted to the social system and in any argument he could have defended it against any attack whatsoever. However, he never argued about it, because that was part of the code. You didn't argue about these things. Simply, under certain circumstances you did this, and under other circumstances you did that.

Mr Mackenzie's code, philosophy or habit of mind would have been a complete protection to him had it not been for some kink in his nature — that volume of youthful poems perhaps still influencing him — which morbidly attracted him to strangeness, to recklessness, even unhappiness. He had more than once allowed himself to be drawn into affairs which he had regretted bitterly afterwards, though when it came to getting out of these affairs his business instinct came to his help, and he got out undamaged.

•   •   •

Mr Mackenzie began to think about Julia Martin. He did this as seldom as possible, but the last time he had seen her had been in that restaurant. Now he remembered her unwillingly. That affair had ended very unpleasantly.

An insanity! Looking back on it, he thought, 'My God, why did I do it? Why did I want to sleep with her?' Yet there was no getting away from it; for a time she had obsessed him. He had lied, he had made her promises which he never intended to keep; and so on, and so on. All part of the insanity, for which he was not responsible.

Not that many lies had been necessary. After seeing him two or three times she had spent the night with him at a tawdry hotel. Perhaps that was the reason why, when he came to think of it, he had never really liked her.

'I hate hypocrites.' She had said that once. Quite casually.

He agreed. 'So do I,' he had said.

But he disliked the word 'hypocrite'. It was a word which he himself never used — which he avoided as if it had been an indecency. Too many senseless things were said by idiotic people about hypocrisy and hypocrites.

Yet she wasn't the hard-bitten sort. She was the soft sort. Anybody could tell that. Afraid of life. Had to screw herself up to it all the time. He had liked that at first. Then it had become a bit of a bore.

Julia had told him that she had married and had left England immediately after the armistice. She had had a child. The child had died — in Central Europe, somewhere — and then she had separated from her husband and had divorced him or been divorced by him, Mr Mackenzie could not gather which. Or perhaps she had never really been married at all. In any case she had come to Paris alone.

She had been an artist's model. At one time she had been a mannequin. But it was obvious that she had been principally living on the money given to her by various men. Going from man to man had become a habit. One day she had said to him, 'It's a very easy habit to acquire.'

On another occasion she had said, 'You see, a time comes in your life when, if you have any money, you can go one way. But if you have nothing at all — absolutely nothing at all — and nowhere to get anything, then you go another.'

He had thought that there was something in what she said, and yet he had not quite agreed with her. There would have been no end to the consequences of whole-hearted agreement.

He soon stopped asking intimate questions, because he knew that it was a mistake to be too curious about people who drift into your life and must soon inevitably drift out again. That wasn't the way to live.

The secret of life was never to go too far or too deep. And so you let these people alone. They would be pretty certain to tell you lies, anyhow. And they had their own ways of getting along, don't you worry.

He merely asked himself, as a man of the world, 'Does she, or does she not, get away with it?' And the answer was in the negative. She was at once too obvious and too obscure. The really incredible thing was that she did not seem to want to get away with it, that she did not seem to understand the urge and the push to get away with it at all costs. He knew, for instance, that she had not a penny of her own. After all that time she had not saved a penny.

Almost he was forced to believe that she was a female without the instinct of self-preservation. And it was against Mr Mackenzie's code to believe that any female existed without a sense of self-preservation.

She was irresponsible. She had fits of melancholy when she would lose the self-control necessary to keep up appearances. He foresaw that the final stage of her descent in the social scale was inevitable, and not far off. She began to depress him.

Certainly, she could be very sweet sometimes. But that's part of these people's stock-in-trade. You don't take any account of that.

He had always intended their parting to be a final one — these things had to come to an end. When he told her that he was going away, and that he proposed to present her with a certain sum of money weekly to give her time to rest, to give her time to look about her, etc, etc, she had answered that she did not want either to rest or to look about her. She had asked him to help her to get right away. But something which rose from the bottom of Mr Mackenzie's soul objected to giving her a lump sum of money, which of course she would immediately spend. Then, however much she might now protest to the contrary, she would come back for more.

He had abruptly refused, adding some scathing but truthful remarks.

Julia had wept; she had become hysterical. She had made a scene, sitting in that very restaurant, under the shocked and disapproving eyes of Monsieur Albert. She had made him look a fool.

A feeling of caution and suspicion which almost amounted to hatred had entirely overcome him. He had definitely suspected her of hoarding some rather foolish letters which he had written and which she had insisted that she had torn up. One of the letters had begun, 'I would like to put my throat under your feet.' He wriggled when he thought of it. Insanity! Forget it; forget it.

Caution was native to him — and that same afternoon he had placed the whole affair in the capable hands of Maître Legros — and he had not seen Julia since.

She haunted him, as an ungenerous action does haunt one, though Mr Mackenzie persisted in telling himself that he had not been ungenerous. Ungenerous! That was all nonsense.

Then he lifted his eyes from the veal — and there she was, coming in at the door.

* * *

She walked in — pale as a ghost. She went straight up to Mr Mackenzie's table, and sat down opposite to him. He opened his mouth to speak, but no words came. So he shut it again. He was thinking, 'O God, oh Lord, she's come here to make a scene. . . . Oh God, oh Lord, she's come here to make a scene.'

He looked to the right and the left of him with a helpless expression. He felt a sensation of great relief when he saw that Monsieur Albert was standing near his table and looking at him with significance.

'That's the first time I've ever seen that chap look straight at anybody,' Mr Mackenzie thought.

Monsieur Albert was a small, fair man, an Alsatian. His eyes telegraphed, 'I understand; I remember this woman. Do you want to have her put out?'

Mr Mackenzie's face instinctively assumed a haughty expression, as if to say, 'What the devil do you mean?' He raised his eyebrows a little, just to put the fellow in his place.

Monsieur Albert moved away. When he had gone a little distance, he turned. This time Mr Mackenzie tried to telegraph back, 'Not yet, anyhow. But stand by.'

Then he looked at Julia for the first time. She said, 'Well you didn't expect to see me here, did you?'

She coughed and cleared her throat.

Mr Mackenzie's nervousness left him. When she had walked in silent and ghost-like, he had been really afraid of her. Now he only felt that he disliked her intensely. He said in rather a high-pitched voice, 'I'd forgotten that I had invited you, certainly. However, as you are here, won't you have something to eat?'

Julia shook her head.

There was a second place laid on the table. She took up the carafe of wine and poured out a glass. Mr Mackenzie watched her with a sardonic expression. He wondered why the first sight of her had frightened him so much. He was now sure that she could not make much of a scene. He knew her; the effort of walking into the restaurant and seating herself at his table would have left her in a state of collapse.

'But why do it?' thought Mr Mackenzie. 'Why in the name of common sense do a thing like that?'

Then he felt a sudden wish to justify himself, to let her know that he had not been lying when he had told her that he was going away.

He said, 'I only got back a couple of weeks ago.'

Julia said, 'Tell me, do you really like life? Do you think it's fair? Honestly now, do you?'

He did not answer this question. What a question, anyway! He took up his knife and fork and began to eat. He wanted to establish a sane and normal atmosphere.

As he put small pieces of veal and vegetable into his mouth, he was telling himself that he might just let her talk on, finish his meal, pay the bill, and walk out. Or he might accompany her out of the restaurant at once, under pretext of finding a quieter place to discuss things. Or he might hint that if she did not go he would ask Monsieur Albert to put her out. Though, of course, it was rather late to do that now.

At the same time he was thinking, 'No. Of course life isn't fair. It's damned unfair, really. Everybody knows that, but what does she expect me to do about it? I'm not God Almighty.'

She asked, 'How's your pal, Maître Legros?'

'Very well indeed, I think,' he said stiffly.

She began to talk volubly, in a low, rather monotonous voice. It was like a flood which has been long dammed up suddenly pouring forth.

He listened, half-smiling. Surely even she must see that she was trying to make a tragedy out of a situation that was fundamentally comical. The discarded mistress — the faithful lawyer defending the honour of the client. . . . A situation consecrated as comical by ten thousand farces and a thousand comedies.

As far as he could make out she had a fixed idea that her affair with him and her encounter with Maître Legros had been the turning-point in her life. They had destroyed some necessary illusions about herself which had enabled her to live her curious existence with a certain amount of courage and audacity.

At the mention of Maître Legros Mr Mackenzie pricked up his ears, for he had only received three very businesslike communications from that gentleman, and he was rather curious to know how French lawyers manage these affairs.

She said that Maître Legros had bullied her about letters that she had destroyed and possible unpleasantness that she never intended to make.

Well, he probably had. For to put the fear of God into her was what he was paid for. On the other hand, if she had any sense she must have realized that three-quarters of it was a bluff.

She said that the lawyer had told his clerk to lock the door and send for an *agent*.

He wondered whether to believe this, for he had a vague idea that locking doors is one of the things that is not legal.

She said that he had threatened to have her deported, and he talked a great deal about the *police des mœurs*. She said that there had been a lot of clerks and typists in the room who had stared at her and laughed all the time.

'A lot?' he thought. 'Well, three or four at the outside.'

She said that she had begun to cry.

Well, in all careers one must be prepared to take the rough with the smooth.

She said that she had been determined never to accept the money offered.

'Well, well,' thought Mr Mackenzie. '*Tiens, tiens.*'

She said that she had fallen ill, and then she hadn't cared about anything except to lie in peace and be ill. And then she had written to the lawyer and asked for the allowance to be sent to her. And after that something had gone *kaput* in her, and she would never be any good any more — never, any more.

She raised her voice. 'Why did you pay a lawyer to bully me?' she said.

Mr Mackenzie pushed away his plate. This was intolerable. He could not go on pretending to eat — not if she were going to say that sort of thing at the top of her voice.

Besides, while she was talking, a chap whom he knew, a journalist called Moon, had come in with a friend, and was sitting two or three tables away. Moon was a gossip. He was talking volubly, and the friend, a thin, dark, youngish man, was glancing round the restaurant with rather a bored expression. At any moment the attention of these two might be attracted. Who knew to what wild lengths Julia would go?

Mr Mackenzie thought, 'Never again — never, never again — will I get mixed up with this sort of woman.'

His collar felt too tight for him. He thrust his chin out in an instinctive effort to relieve the constriction. The movement was exactly like that of a horse shying.

He looked at Julia and a helpless, imploring expression came into his eyes. His hand was lying on the table. She put her hand on his, and said, in a very low voice, 'You know, I've been pretty unhappy.'

At this change of attitude, Mr Mackenzie felt both relieved and annoyed. 'She's trying to get hold of me again,' he thought. 'But what a way to do it! My God, what a way to do it!'

He drew his hand away slowly, ostentatiously. Keeping his eyes fixed on hers, he deliberately assumed an expression of disgust. Then he cleared his throat and asked, 'Well, what exactly did you want when you came in here?'

Julia grew paler. The hollows under her eyes were deeper. She looked much older. But Mr Mackenzie had no pity for her; she was a dangerous person. A person who would walk in and make an uncalled-for scene like this was a dangerous person.

She said, 'Oh, yes, look here, this cheque . . . This cheque I got today. I don't want it.'

'Good,' said Mr Mackenzie. 'Just as you like, of course. You're the best judge of that.'

But he felt surprised and not at all pleased. He knew that hysteria ruled these people's lives, but he would never have thought that it would be carried to the extremity of giving up money.

'Wait a minute,' she said. 'That isn't what I came here for.'

Mr Mackenzie was afraid of the expression in her eyes. He thought, 'My God, she's going to attack me. I ought to stop her.'

But, as it might have been in a nightmare, he could not do anything to stop her.

Assault! Premeditation could be proved. She wouldn't get away with it — not even here in Paris.

A cunning expression came into Julia's face. She picked up her glove and hit his cheek with it, but so lightly that he did not even blink.

'I despise you,' she said.

'Quite,' said Mr Mackenzie. He sat very straight, staring at her.

Her eyes did not drop, but a mournful and beaten expression came into them.

'Oh, well,' she said, 'all right. Have it your own way.'

Then, to Mr Mackenzie's unutterable relief, she gathered up her gloves and walked out of the restaurant.

♦   ♦   ♦

Mr Mackenzie ate a few more mouthfuls of veal. By this time it was quite cold. But he wanted to gain time to compose himself.

Then he drank a little wine.

Then he looked round the room.

As he did so he was convinced that nobody had noticed anything. Not even Monsieur Albert, who had gone to the other side of the restaurant and was attending to a couple who had just come in.

Nobody had noticed anything.

Julia had not been in the restaurant for more than twelve minutes at the outside. His table was in a corner and she had sat with her back to the room. The last ghastly incident had happened so quickly that it was long odds against anybody having seen it.

Gradually Mr Mackenzie became calm. He felt he wanted some hot food.

He looked across the room, trying attract Monsieur Albert's attention, and saw that the dark young man at the neighbouring table was staring at him with curiosity.

The dark young man instantly averted his eyes and his face assumed a completely blank expression — too blank.

'Hell!' thought Mr Mackenzie, 'that chap saw.'

But when Monsieur Albert had brought the hot food and another carafe of wine he began to eat again, though without much appetite.

Then he began to pity Julia.

'Poor devil,' he thought. 'She's got damn all.'

3

MR HORSFIELD

THE NAME of the dark young man was George Horsfield. Half an hour afterwards he came out of the Restaurant Albert, thinking that he had spent a disproportionately large part of the last six months in getting away from people who bored him. (The last six months had been his kick of the heels.) The habit of wanting to be alone had grown upon him rather alarmingly.

He wondered whether it had been worth while to spend the only legacy he ever had, or was ever likely to have, in travelling about Spain and the south of France, because he had a vague idea that the sight of the sun would cure all his ills and would develop the love of life and humanity in which he felt that he was lamentably deficient.

Then he told himself that after all it had done him good; it had been worth while. He felt particularly well that evening; he felt in the mood to enjoy himself. He walked along slowly.

There was a tourist-car between the Dôme and the Rotonde. The small, black, pathetic figure of the guide stood mouthing and gesticulating.

Two women passed flaunting themselves; they flaunted their legs and breasts as if they were glad to be alive. There was zest in the air and a sweet sadness like a hovering ghost.

'Not sad,' Mr Horsfield thought. And then, 'Yes, but lots of these things are sad.'

He crossed the street and went into the Select-Bar for ten minutes. While he was sitting there, he remembered the quarrel he had seen in the Restaurant Albert and smiled to himself. The idea came to him, 'That woman's probably in one of these cafés having a drink.' He looked round; somehow he was pretty sure he would know her again.

There had been something fantastic, almost dream-like, about seeing a thing like that reflected in a looking-glass. A bad looking-glass, too. So that the actors had been slightly distorted, as in an unstill pool of water.

He had been sitting in such a way that, every time he looked up, he was bound to see the reflection of the back of Mr Mackenzie's head, round and pugnacious — somehow in decided contrast with his deliberately picturesque appearance from the front — and the face of the young woman, who looked rather under the weather. He had not stared at them, but he had seen the young woman slapping the man's face. He had gathered from her expression that it was not a caress, or a joke, or anything of that sort.

He had said, 'Good Lord.'

'What is it?' Moon had asked.

But the woman in the looking-glass seemed to be about to cry. Mr Horsfield felt uncomfortable. He averted his eyes, and replied, 'Oh, nothing, nothing.'

As she walked out of the restaurant he had turned to look after her, and asked, 'Do you know that woman?'

He said this because his companion claimed to know almost everybody in that quarter of Paris. He knew who lived with whom, and he could be illuminating on the subject of the Arts. He would say, 'D'you see that girl in the cocked hat and the top-boots? She's writing a novel about Napoleon.' Or, 'That man fiddling with his glass and muttering — he's really rather a genius. He's a sculptor; he reduces everybody's ego to an egg.'

However, Moon had been decidedly sniffy about the young woman. When he said. 'Oh, yes. I think I've seen her about at one time and another,' his tone put the strange creature so much in her place that Mr Horsfield felt rather ashamed of having expressed any kind of interest in her.

'A stolid sort of chap, Moon,' he thought, as he walked back down the boulevard, 'though jumpy on the surface. A bit of a bore, too.'

◆　　◆　　◆

A little farther on Mr Horsfield went into another large and glaring café where a great many people were talking at the tops of their voices, mostly in German. He had a drink at the bar and then walked among the tables, found a vacant place, and sat down.

He looked about him, and saw the woman he had been thinking of sitting in a corner.

He recognized her hat — a dark-blue turban with a little veil hanging from the brim, but not low enough altogether to hide her eyes. He watched her, warming his glass of brandy in his hands. He felt detached and ironical.

She was sitting wedged against a very fat man with a bald head. A lengthy tube, with a cigarette stuck in the end of it, protruded from the fat man's mouth. His expression was eager. He was obviously waiting for a friend. Every now and then he would get up and crane his neck in an attempt to keep his eye on all three entrances to the café.

Mr Horsfield thought that the young woman looked pretty lonely. He decided that, as soon as he could, he would go and sit at her table and try to talk to her.

The fat man got up and waved his hand violently at the door. Then he sat down again with a disappointed expression. Mr Horsfield finished his drink, and got the money to pay for it ready to leave on the table. He did not want any complications with the waiters.

An old chap at the next table was holding forth about Anglo-Saxons, and the phrase, '*cette hypocrisie froide*' came back and back into what he was saying. The word 'froide' sounded vicious and contemptuous. Mr Horsfield wanted to join in the argument, and say, 'Look here, you're quite wrong. Anyhow, you're not altogether right. What you take to be hypocrisy is sometimes a certain caution, sometimes genuine — though ponderous — childishness, sometimes a mixture of both.'

'*Ça vous écoeure à la fin,*' jabbered the old chap. Rather a nice-looking old chap, too. All the more a pity.

The fat man at the young woman's table waved his arm again violently. He took the cigarette out of his mouth, smiled largely, and at last got up and hurried to meet his friend.

'D'you mind if I sit here?' Mr Horsfield asked.

'Of course, why not?' she said in an indifferent voice.

Mr Horsfield looked sideways at her. She was not so young as he had thought.

'I saw you in the restaurant where I was dining,' he said.

'You know Mackenzie, then?' she asked sharply.

'Not from Adam,' said Mr Horsfield. Then, because something in the place had momentarily freed him from self-consciousness, he added, 'I've been watching you. I thought you looked frightfully lonely.'

As he said this it occurred to him that as a rule he fought shy of lonely people; they reminded him too painfully of certain aspects of himself, their loneliness, of course, being a mere caricature of his own.

She said, 'Oh . . . Yes.'

Then she gulped at her drink and began to talk quite calmly and conversationally. Mr Horsfield rather admired the way she seemed to have been able to pull herself together.

She powdered her face. He thought that, for a moment, a furtive and calculating expression came into it.

She was telling him that she had not been to London for a very long time. 'I went back three years ago, but only for a fortnight.'

As she talked she looked at him unwinkingly, like a baby. Her eyes were very sad; they seemed to be asking a perpetual question. 'What?' thought Mr Horsfield. A deep black shadow painted on the outside of the corners accentuated their length.

She talked about a night-club in London which he knew had been going strong just before the war broke out. Mr Horsfield thought, 'She must be thirty-four or thirty-five if she's a day — probably older.' Of course, that explained a lot of things.

He interrupted something she was saying and, though he was not aware that he had done this with any accent of suspicion or scepticism, a sulky expression came over her face. She shrugged one shoulder a little and, without answering him, again relapsed into silence and indifference.

'But why should she be annoyed?' thought Mr Horsfield. 'Supposing I were to say to somebody, "I'm a hop factor; I own a small and decaying business," and he were to look incredulous. Should I be insulted? Not a bit of it. I shouldn't care a hoot.'

He wanted to laugh and say aloud, 'I'm a decaying hop factor, damn you! My father did the growth and I'm doing the decay.'

After a time he suggested that they should go on to some dancing place.

'Oh, no,' she said. 'I can't. I don't want to.'

'Why not? Come on.'

'No,' she said obstinately, 'I'm not going to any of the Montparnasse places.'

Mr Horsfield said that they could go anywhere she liked. He would not care.

To his own ears his voice sounded slightly thickened. Yet he was not in the least drunk. He simply felt that he understood life better than he understood it as a general rule.

They went out and found a taxi. She gave the driver an address. 'Good,' said Mr Horsfield. 'Splendid.'

But he was not altogether happy. He missed in her the response to his own unusually reckless mood.

The taxi went a short distance up one street and down another, and then stopped. He thought, 'This place looks as if it had seen its best days.' Indeed it was unpretentious — even mediocre.

He was rather disappointed. However, he paid the driver and looked round for his companion.

'Well, good night,' she said. 'It isn't up to much here, but don't worry. You'll soon find a girl who'll show you something better.'

She was already walking along the street, which was dark, narrow, and inclined steeply up a little hill. He went after her and took her by the arm, feeling defrauded and extremely annoyed.

'But look here . . .'

'My clothes are too shabby.' She spoke in a passionate and incoherent way. 'I don't feel well. I don't feel up to it. My clothes are too shabby. . . . Besides, I hate people. I'm afraid of people. I never used to be like this, but now I'm going dippy, I suppose.'

'You were all right in the café just now,' he argued.

She pulled her arm away without answering. A young man passing by looked curiously at them and it flashed into Mr Horsfield's mind that they must seem like some sordidly disputing couple. If all this had happened in the daylight he would have been shamefaced and would have left her as soon as he decently could. But this deserted street, with its shabby, red-lit hotels, cheap refuges for lovers, was the right background for what she was saying.

'She's had a rum existence, this woman,' he thought, staring at her.

However, they could not stand there for ever. He felt very much at a loss.

He kept his arm in hers and they walked along together. They came to a cross-street, and he saw in the distance the Jewish twin-triangles illuminated as a sign over a cinema. He proposed with relief that they should go in.

'You won't mind sitting in a cinema, surely?'

'Oh, that cinema,' she said. 'It's rather a funny sort of place. I don't think you'd like it.'

'Never mind,' he said. 'Come along.'

◆　　◆　　◆

An old woman peeped out of a little window and sold Mr Horsfield two tickets at three francs fifty each. Then they went into a large, bare hall where perhaps twenty people were scattered about, sitting on wooden seats.

They had come in during the interval, and a second old woman in a black dress was walking about the hall and occasionally

upstairs into the balcony, calling out in a gentle voice: '*Cacahuètes.
. . . Pastilles de menthe. . . .*'

'It's always empty like this,' said Julia. 'I think those two old girls
— the one outside and the one here — own it. I don't know, but I
expect it will have to shut up soon.'

A loud clicking noise filled the emptiness. The lights went out
and a strange, old-fashioned film flickered on the white screen.
Someone began to play on a cracked piano. 'Valse Bleue',
'Myosotis', 'Püppchen'. . . . Mr Horsfield shut his eyes and listened
to the pathetic voice of the old piano.

On the screen a strange, slim youth with a long, white face and
mad eyes wooed a beautiful lady the width of whose hips gave an
archaic but magnificent air to the whole proceeding.

After a while a woman behind them told the world at large that
everybody in the film seemed to be *dingo*, and that she did not like
films like that and so she was going out.

Mr Horsfield disliked her. He felt that in that bare place and to
the accompaniment of that frail music the illusion of art was almost
complete. He got a kick out of the place for some reason.

The film was German and rather good.

The noise of Julia blowing her nose jarred him like a light turned
on suddenly in a room in which one is trying to sleep. Then, a sharp
intake of her breath.

Of course, he might have known that that was what she would
do.

But he felt that her sorrows were nothing whatever to do with
him. On the contrary, he was the injured party. Ever since they
had left the café she had been embarrassing and annoying him
when all he wanted to do was to have a good time and not think.
And God knew that he did not often feel like that.

He decided that when they left the cinema he would find out
where she lived, get a taxi, take her home — and there would be the
end of it. Once you started letting the instinct of pity degenerate
from the general to the particular, life became completely
impossible.

She caught her breath again. He put his hand out and felt for
hers.

'Look here,' he said, 'please don't cry.'

She did not answer him.

'Will you come back to my hotel?' he asked. 'We can talk much
better there.'

Then he got up and went out, knowing that she would follow.

•

Outside she walked along with her head bent. Her face was quite calm, and he wondered if indeed she had been crying or whether he had imagined it or whether she had meant him to imagine it.

They passed a little wine-shop where some men were having drinks at the bar. And then a dingy hotel. They reached the angle of the street where they had stood arguing.

A taxi passed. Mr Horsfield stopped it and told the man to drive to his hotel. The driver seemed rather sulky when he heard the address, probably because it was too near. However, Mr Horsfield settled the matter by getting firmly in, shutting the door and calling out in a loud voice, 'All right, go ahead.'

The driver started with a series of violent jerks. Then in an effort to relieve his bad temper, he shot off like an arrow from a bow.

She sighed deeply. Then she took from her bag a small gilt powder-box and began to powder her face carefully.

Mr Horsfield's mouth and throat were dry. He felt he wanted a long cool drink, and he remembered with relief the bottle of whisky and the syphon in his room.

•   •   •

There in his room was the tray with a syphon and glasses — two glasses, luckily. Mr Horsfield had locked the whisky away. He got it out and poured the drinks. Then he said: 'Perhaps you'd prefer some wine. Shall I get some wine up?'

She shook her head and began to sip mechanically.

'Well, here's luck,' said Mr Horsfield, sighing.

'Chin-chin,' said Julia. Over the rim of her glass her eyes looked cloudy and dazed.

'My God, it's hot in here,' he said. He opened the long windows, which looked out on to the courtyard of the hotel. In one of the rooms opposite the light was on and he saw a young man and a girl embracing each other passionately.

He felt impatient. You couldn't get away from that sort of thing for a moment in this place.

He turned from the window and said: 'Tell me, are you stuck for money? Is that it?'

She opened her bag and took out two ten-franc notes and some small change.

'This is all I've got. I had a cheque for fifteen hundred francs but I went and gave it back.'

'I see. Quite,' said Mr Horsfield.

Then he thought that after all there was only one end to all this, and as well first as last. He opened his pocket-book. In it there were two notes for a thousand francs, one for five hundred, and some smaller money. He took out the five hundred and one of the thousand notes. They were creased carefully into four.

He put them into her hand and shut her fingers on them gently. When he had done this he felt powerful and dominant. Happy. He smiled at Julia rather foolishly.

'Will that do you for a bit?' he asked. 'Will you be able to manage?'

'Yes,' she said. 'Thank you. You're very kind. You're kind and a dear.'

But he noticed that she took the money without protest and apparently without surprise, and this rather jarred upon him.

'Oh, that's all right,' he said.

The silence between them was an anti-climax.

Then it occurred to him that she might think that he had brought her to his room in order to make love to her. And he did not want to make love to her. That had all gone when she had started to cry and sniff in the cinema.

He felt embarrassed. You gave way to an impulse. You did something you wanted to do — and then you were enmeshed in all sorts of complications.

He went and stood by the window again, tapping on the glass. His fingers were stained with cigarette smoking. Then he looked round and saw that Julia had taken off her hat. But she did not look in the glass and made no effort to arrange her hair.

She was certainly rather drunk. Her eyes were fixed as if upon some far-off point. She seemed to be contemplating a future at once monotonous and insecure with an indifference which was after all a sort of hard-won courage.

For want of anything better to say, Mr Horsfield made a remark about Paris being a difficult place for Anglo-Saxons to be sober in.

She said: 'Oh, no place is a place to be sober in. That's what I think.'

This struck Mr Horsfield as being an extremely pathetic remark.

She began: 'After all . . .' and then stopped. She had the look in her eyes of someone who is longing to explain herself, to say: 'This is how I am. This is how I feel.'

He suddenly remembered: 'Pa was a colonel. I was seduced by a clergyman at a garden-party. Pa shot him. Heavens, how the blighter bled!' He wanted to laugh.

He sat down by her side. 'Tell me,' he said gently.

'Well, I told you. I left London after the armistice. What year was that?'

'Nineteen-eighteen.'

'Yes. I left February the year after. Then I wandered about a good deal with — with the man I left London with. Most places, but not Spain or Italy. And then I came to Paris.'

'I see,' said Mr Horsfield encouragingly.

She said in a low voice, which was suddenly full of hatred: 'I was all right till I met that swine Mackenzie. But he sort of — I don't know — he sort of smashed me up. Before that I'd always been pretty sure that things would turn out all right for me, but afterwards I didn't believe in myself any more. I only wanted to go away and hide. Perhaps I was getting tired; perhaps I'd have smashed up anyway.'

Mr Horsfield thought: 'Well, nobody can go on for ever.'

But because he was rather drunk what she was saying seemed to him very intimate and close. He began to apply it to himself and he thought with anger, 'It's always like that. When you are tottering, somebody peculiarly well qualified to do it comes along and shoves you down. And stamps on you.'

'Well,' said Julia, 'that's that. And it's no use talking. And here's to a good life and a quick death. . . . When I'm drunk it's all right. Then I can think back and I know just why I did everything. It all falls into place, and I know that I couldn't have done anything else and that it's no use worrying.'

She sighed. 'But you can't be drunk the whole time.'

'You shouldn't sit and think too much,' Mr Horsfield said. 'You ought to get out and about and talk to people, not stay by yourself and brood.'

'Yes,' she said, 'of course.'

She stared at him, thinking: 'What's the use of trying to explain? It's all gone on too long.' Her mind went off at a tangent. She said: 'Well, it doesn't always help to talk to people. For instance. When I first came to Paris I used to sit to a woman, a sculptor — '

'You mean, when you first left England?'

'No, no,' she said in an impatient voice. 'I left England ages ago.'

Then her face assumed such a vague expression that Mr Horsfield thought: 'Well, go on, get on with it. If it's going to be the story of your life, get on with it.'

After a moment he prompted, 'Well, what about this woman you sat to?'

'I'd come from Ostend,' Julia explained. She spoke as if she were trying to recall a book she had read or a story she had heard and Mr Horsfield felt irritated by her vagueness, 'because,' he thought, 'your life is your life, and you must be pretty definite about it. Or if it's a story you are making up, you ought at least to have it pat.'

Then she brightened up, and added: 'I like Ostend. I like it very much. I was happy there, and I always remember places I was happy in. I mean, I remember them so that I can shut my eyes and be there. . . . We stayed at a little place called Coq-sur-Mer, near Ostend. And the water was cold and lovely. Yet not grey. And then I came along to Paris by myself. And then after a while I met this woman, and I started sitting for her. She gave me so much a week, and I used to go there nearly every day for as long as she wanted me.'

'Did you like her?' asked Mr Horsfield.

'I don't know if I liked her. I suppose so. She was all right in her way. Sometimes I liked her. Only she was all shut up. . . . And she thought that everything outside was stupid and that annoyed me. She was a bit fanatical, you know. She had something of an artist in her — I mean really. So, of course she was fanatical. And then she was a woman. About thirty-five years old. And so she simply wouldn't believe that anything was true which was outside herself or anything but what she herself thought and felt. She just thought I was stupid because it was outside her scheme of things that anybody like me should not be stupid. She thought me stupid and would say little things to hurt me. Like somebody flicking at you with a whip.

'Well, one day when we were having tea, because when it got too dark to work we would have tea and bread-and-butter and sometimes cake . . . I wish I could tell you how much I liked it, just having tea with her like that. . . .

'And so one day, when we were sitting smoking, and having tea, I started to tell her about myself. I was just going to tell her why I left England. . . . One or two things had happened, and I wanted to go away. Because I was fed up, fed up, fed up.

'I wanted to go away with just the same feeling a boy has when he wants to run away to sea — at least, that I imagine a boy has. Only, in my adventure, men were mixed up, because of course they had to be. You understand, don't you? Do you understand that a girl might have that feeling?

'I wanted to get away. I wanted it like — like iron. Besides, I wasn't frightened of anything. So I did get away. I married to get away.

'Well, I told her all about that. And then, before I knew where I was, I was telling her everything else too. Everything that had happened to me, as far as I could.

'And all the time I talked I was looking at a rum picture she had on the wall — a reproduction of a picture by a man called Modigliani. Have you ever heard of him? This picture is of a woman lying on a couch, a woman with a lovely, lovely body. Oh, utterly lovely. Anyhow, I thought so. A sort of proud body, like an utterly lovely proud animal. And a face like a mask, a long, dark face, and very big eyes. The eyes were blank, like a mask, but when you had looked at it a bit it was as if you were looking at a real woman, a live woman. At least, that's how it was with me.

'Well, all the time I was talking I had the feeling I was explaining things not only to Ruth — that was her name — but I was explaining them to myself too, and to the woman in the picture. It was if I were before a judge, and I were explaining that everything I had done had always been the only possible thing to do. And of course I forgot that it's always so with everybody, isn't it?'

Mr Horsfield said after a silence: 'Well, I think there's a good deal of tosh talked about free will myself.'

'I wanted her to understand. I felt that it was awfully important that some human being should know what I had done and why I had done it. I told everything. I went on and on.

'And when I had finished I looked at her. She said: "You seem to have had a hectic time." But I knew when she spoke that she didn't believe a word.'

There was another long pause. Then Mr Horsfield said: 'Didn't she? . . . Good Lord.'

Feeling this was inadequate, he added: 'She must have been rather an ass.'

'Yes,' said Julia. 'But it wasn't like that. Because I might have known she would be like that. It was a beastly feeling I got.'

She wrinkled up her forehead. She looked as if she were in pain.

Well, don't worry about it now,' said Mr Horsfield. 'Have another whisky.'

'It was a beastly feeling I got — that I didn't quite believe myself, either. I thought: "After all, is this true? Did I ever do this?" I felt as if the woman in the picture were laughing at me and saying: "I am more real than you. But at the same time I *am* you. I am all that matters of you."

'And I felt as if all my life and all myself were floating away from me like smoke and there was nothing to lay hold of — nothing.

'And it was a beastly feeling, a foul feeling, like looking over the edge of the world. It was more frightening than I can ever tell you. It made me feel sick in my stomach.

'I wanted to say to Ruth: "Yes, of course you're right. I never did all that. But who am I then? Will you tell me that? Who am I, and how did I get here?" Then I had just sense enough to pull myself together and not say anything so dotty.

'Then we went out to dinner. When I got home I pulled out all the photographs I had, and letters and things. And my marriage-book and my passport. And the papers about my baby who died and was buried in Hamburg.

'But it had all gone, as if it had never been. And I was there, like a ghost. And then I was frightened, and yet I knew that if I could get to the end of what I was feeling it would be the truth about myself and about the world and about everything that one puzzles and pains about all the time.'

She was swaying very slightly backwards and forwards, holding her knees, her eyes fixed.

Mr Horsfield was filled with a glow of warm humanity. He thought: 'Hang it all, one can't leave this unfortunate creature alone to go and drink herself dotty.'

He said: 'Now look here, I'm going to talk sense to you. Why don't you come back to London?'

She looked at him steadily with her large, unwinking eyes. She said: 'I don't know. I might go back to London. There's nothing to stop me.'

Then he thought: 'Good God, why in the world have I suggested that?' and added cautiously, 'I mean, you've surely got people there, haven't you?'

'Yes,' she said. 'Of course. My mother and my sister. But my mother's pretty sick. She's been ill for a long time.'

He felt that he could imagine what her mother and her sister were like. No money. No bloody money. Bloody money! You might well say 'Bloody money'. They would be members of the vast crowd that bears on its back the label, 'No money' from the cradle to the grave . . . And this one had rebelled. Not intelligently, but violently and instinctively. He saw the whole thing.

'I'm tired,' she said. And she was — very tired. Her excitement and the relief of having got some money were both swallowed up. She wanted to sleep. She felt very cold — the cold of drunkenness

— as if something huge, made of ice, were breathing on her. She felt it most in her chest. But in spite of this her brain kept on working and planning in a worried fashion.

She said: 'You know, I've often thought of going back to London. Because I've got a friend there. I saw him again when I was in London three years ago. He'd help me. And goodness knows I want not to have to worry for a bit.' In a voice that was pathetically like a boast she added: 'He's a very rich man. He is...' And then stopped.

'Good,' he said. 'Go ahead, then. Take a chance.'

'Nobody's ever said that I can't take a chance. That's the last thing anybody can say of me.'

He suddenly felt sorry for her.

'If you do come to London,' he said, 'ring me up or write or something, will you? Here's my address.'

She took the card and said: 'Yes. All right.' And he thought, rather grimly: 'I bet you will. . . .'

He saw her into a taxi.

It seemed to him that for a festive evening it had not been very festive.

The last thing in his mind before he went to sleep was:

> Roll me over on my right side,
> Roll me over slow;
> Roll me over on my right side,
> 'Cause my left side hurts me so.

He did not know where or when he had heard this. For some reason it seemed to him peculiarly applicable to Julia.

4

THE FIRST UNKNOWN

LILIANE PUT the breakfast tray down on the end of the bed, and on going out, banged the door loudly.

Julia opened her eyes, remembering everything. She still felt fatigued and very anxious, and she opened her handbag to reassure herself by the sight of the money. She turned her head over on the pillow, shut her eyes, and saw herself slapping Mr Mackenzie's face. That seemed to have happened a long time ago. She knew that she would always remember it as if it were yesterday — and always it would seem to have happened a long time ago.

She thought: 'I must go away. That was a good idea. That's the only thing to be done.'

The difficulty was that she felt so tired. How to do all that must be done while she was feeling so tired?

She thought: 'If a taxi hoots before I count three, I'll go to London. If not, I won't.'

She counted, 'One . . . Two . . .' slowly. A car shrieked a loud blast.

She drank her coffee and began to plan out how she would spend her fifteen hundred francs. So much was the least she must have on arrival in London, so much for her ticket, so much then was left for new clothes.

The idea of buying new clothes comforted her, and she got out of bed and dressed.

At three o'clock she was back at her hotel, carrying the boxes containing the clothes she had bought at a second-hand shop in the Rue Rocher — a dark grey coat and hat, and a very cheap dress, too short for the prevailing fashion.

She at once dressed herself in the new clothes, but the effect was not so pleasing as she had hoped. She fidgeted before the glass for a while, viewing herself from different angles. She began to reckon up the money she still had, and came to the conclusion that, on arriving in London, there would be about thirty shillings left.

Suddenly she began to doubt the wisdom of going there with so little money. She had no illusions as to the way in which her sister would receive her. It was pretty awful being in London without any money. Drabness swallowed you up, very quickly.

Then she told herself that she had made up her mind to go, and what was the use of all this chopping and changing?

My dear Norah,
I am in London. I don't know how long I'll stay, but I should like to see you. I have come over in a hurry or I would have let you know before. Will you telephone me or come to see me?

After she had finished her letter, which she intended to post in London, she began to pack her clothes. All the time she packed she was thinking: 'After all, I haven't taken my ticket yet. I needn't go if I don't want to.'

A feeling of foreboding, of anxiety, as if her heart were being squeezed, never left her.

•　•　•

That night, coming back from her meal, a man followed her. When she had turned from the Place St Michel to the darkness of the quay he came up to her, muttering proposals in a low, slithery voice. She told him sharply to go away. But he caught hold of her arm, and squeezed it as hard as he could by way of answer.

She stopped. She wanted to hit him. She was possessed with one of the fits of rage which were becoming part of her character. She wanted to fly at him and strike him, but she thought that he would probably hit her back.

She faced him and said: 'Let me tell you, you are — you are . . .' The word came to her. 'You are *ignoble*.'

'Not at all,' answered the man in an aggrieved voice. 'I have some money and I am willing to give it to you. Why do you say that I am *ignoble*?'

They were now arrived at Julia's hotel. She went in, and pushed the swing-door as hard as she could into his face.

She could not have explained why, when she got to her room, her forebodings about the future were changed into a feeling of exultation.

She looked at herself in the glass and thought: 'After all, I'm not finished. It's all nonsense that I am. I'm not finished at all.'

•　•　•

Julia left Paris the next day by the midday boat train for Calais. She had bought an English illustrated paper at the Gare du Nord. In the train she read steadily down the glossy pages, which chattered about a world as remote and inaccessible as if it existed in another dimension.

The people sitting opposite to her — obviously a married couple — were also English and they were reading the English papers. To all intents and purposes she was already in England. She felt strange and subdued.

In the wagon restaurant they were shown to the seats opposite to her, and they began to talk to the tall, fat man who was sitting next to Julia. He was a German. He seemed to be some sort of commercial traveller.

The couple had travelled from Marseilles on their return from somewhere in the Far East. They spoke in calm voices — cautiously. 'I think' or 'I believe' came into every sentence.

'Life out there has its disadvantages,' said the woman. 'But then, of course, it has its advantages, too.'

They were friendly people. They talked — or, rather, they answered the commerical traveller's questions — with volubility. But they always preserved a curious air of pale aloofness or perhaps of uncertainty.

The train swayed and the red wine jiggled about gaily in the glasses.

'Bombay?' said the man. 'Oh, yes, I remember Bombay. We managed to get a double-bedded room there.'

When the meal was over and they were all three back in the compartment the couple relapsed into silence. You could look for ever into their sunburnt faces and never be quite sure whether they were very kind or very hard, naïvely frank or very sly.

An hour from Calais the woman opposite took out a box of Mothersill's remedy for sea-sickness and swallowed differently coloured pills in accordance with the directions.

Julia planned that, on arriving at Victoria, she would get a taxi and ask the man to drive her to a cheap hotel in Bloomsbury. She hoped that she would get in somewhere quickly. The thought of driving from hotel to hotel alarmed her.

Then the throbbing of the train made her calm and sleepy, resigned as if she had taken some irrevocable step. She began to read her paper again. England. . . . English. . . . Our doggy page. . . .

PART TWO

/

RETURN TO LONDON

The taxi stopped at 33 Arkwright Gardens, WC. The street was dark and deserted as if it had been midnight instead of eight o'clock.

Julia said to the driver: 'Just wait a minute.' He did not answer or turn his head. He sat like a broad-shouldered image.

She went into the hotel.

'Will you show the lady number nine?' said the man at the bureau.

A young man, who had been sitting listlessly by the telephone, led the way upstairs and along a passage.

Number nine was small and very cold. There were an iron bedstead, an old-fashioned washstand with a tin slop-pail standing by the side of it, and a dressing-table with a wad of newspaper stuck into the frame to keep the glass at the required angle. The lace curtains were torn and very dirty. Behind the curtains was a green and optimistic sun-blind, faintly irritating, like a stupid joke.

The young man said: 'This room is eight-and-six a night, madam.'

'My God,' said Julia, 'what a place!'

The young man stared at her.

'All right. Very well.'

She opened her bag and took out a ten-shilling note with a slow and calculating gesture. She asked the young man to pay her taxi and bring up her luggage. He seemed surprised and looked at her, from the feet up. Then a knowing expression came into his face.

'Certainly, madam.'

In the passage he began to whistle shrilly: 'I Can't Give You Anything But Love, Baby.'

When he returned with her trunk Julia was standing at the looking-glass. He stared at her back inquisitively. She turned round and smiled at him.

'Your change, madam,' he said with austerity, averting his eyes.

She said she was very cold and she wanted to know how the gas-fire worked. The young man explained that it was a penny-in-the-slot meter, volunteered to let her have a shilling's worth, accepted an extra shilling for himself, smiled for the first time and departed.

She turned and looked into the glass again, sighed, and put her hand to her forehead with a worried gesture. Then she opened her trunk, found writing materials and began:

My dear Neil,

Would you write to this address and let me know when I can see you? Or would you telephone? I'll be very anxious until I hear from you. I hope you don't mind my writing to you. I hope you won't think of me as an importunate ghost.

She signed her name, wrote 'W. Neil James, Esq' on an envelope, hesitated a moment, and then added the address of a club.

A church clock chimed the hour. At once all feeling of strangeness left her. She felt that her life had moved in a circle. Predestined, she had returned to her starting-point, in this little Bloomsbury bedroom that was so exactly like the little Bloomsbury bedroom she had left nearly ten years before. And even the clock which struck each quarter in that aggressive and melancholy way was the same clock that she used to hear.

Perhaps the last ten years had been a dream; perhaps life, moving on for the rest of the world, had miraculously stood still for her.

◆   ◆   ◆

The little old man in the bowler-hat who sold violets was at the corner of Woburn Square when she passed the next morning. While she was still some way off the idea that he might recognize her half pleased and half embarrassed her. She stopped and bought some flowers. He was just the same — shrunken, perhaps, under his many layers of dirty clothes. His light-blue eyes, which were like bits of glass, looked at her coldly. He turned his head away and went on calling: 'Violets, lady, violets,' in a thin, feeble voice.

She walked on through the fog into Tottenham Court Road. The houses and the people passing were withdrawn, nebulous. There was only a grey fog shot with yellow lights, and its cold breath on her face, and the ghost of herself coming out of the fog to meet her.

The ghost was thin and eager. It wore a long, very tight check skirt, a short dark-blue coat, and a bunch of violets bought from the old man in Woburn Square. It drifted up to her and passed her in the fog. And she had the feeling that, like the old man, it looked at her coldly, without recognizing her.

That cinema on the right-hand side. . . . She remembered going in there with a little Belgian when they had shown some town in Belgium being bombarded. And the little Belgian had wept.

During the war . . . My God, that was a funny time! The mad things one did — and everybody else was doing them, too. A funny time. A mad reckless time.

An exultant and youthful feeling took possession of her.

She crossed Oxford Street into Charing Cross Road. But in Soho she missed her way and her exultation suddenly vanished. She began to think that she must look idiotic, walking about aimlessly. She found her way back into Oxford Street and went into Lyons'.

A band filled the vast room with military music, played at the top of its voice. Grandiose. . . .

At the table where she sat down two rather battered-looking women with the naïve eyes of children were eating steak-and-kidney pudding. One said to the other: 'This place is on a big scale, you can't deny that.'

Her companion agreed, and said that she thought the ladies' room very fine — all in black-and-white marble.

The two women left quickly. They melted away, as it were, and their place was taken by a little man who, in the midst of his meal, uttered an exclamation, seized his bill, and rushed off.

'Your gentleman friend has left his hat behind,' said the waitress amiably.

'Oh, has he?' said Julia. She began to put on her gloves.

When she looked up the little man was once more seated opposite her. He said excitedly: 'A most extraordinary thing! I've just seen a man I thought was dead. Well, that's an extraordinary thing. A thing like that doesn't happen every day to anybody, does it? A man I thought was killed in the Japanese earthquake.'

'Were you pleased to see him?' asked Julia.

'Pleased to see him?' echoed the little man cautiously. 'Well, I don't know. But it gave me a bit of a turn, I can tell you.'

Julia left him talking to the waitress, who was making clicking, assenting noises with her tongue.

It was three o'clock, and before each of the cinemas a tall commissionaire was calling: 'Plenty of seats. Seats at one-and-two. Plenty of seats.'

Vague-looking people hesitated for a moment, and then drifted in, to sit in the dark and see *Hot Stuff from Paris*. The girls were perky and pretty, but it was strange how many of the older women looked drab and hopeless, with timid, hunted expressions. They looked ashamed of themselves, as if they were begging the world in general not to notice that they were women or to hold it against them.

The porter told her when she got back to the hotel that Miss Griffiths was waiting for her upstairs.

'She's been there nearly half an hour,' he said.

2

NORAH

NORAH GRIFFITHS was a tall, dark girl, strongly built and straight-backed.

'Hullo, Norah, my dear,' said Julia.

'Hullo, Julia.'

They both hesitated, then both at the same moment bent forward to kiss each other. Norah gave her sister one rapid, curious glance. Then she sat down again, looking calm and as though she were waiting for explanations. Her head and arms drooped as she sat. She was pale, her colourless lips pressed tightly together into an expression of endurance. She seemed tired.

Her eyes were like Julia's, long and soft. Fine wrinkles were already forming in the corners. She wore a pale-green dress with a red flower fixed in the lapel of the collar. But the dress had lost its freshness, so that the flower looked pathetic.

'Well, I got your letter this morning, and I thought I'd come along at once,' she said.

She had a sweet voice, a voice with a warm and tender quality. This was strange, because her face was cold, as though warmth and tenderness were dead in her.

Julia, who felt very nervous, fidgeted about the room. She took off her hat, powdered her face, rouged her lips. Norah followed her every movement with an expression of curiosity.

Julia sat down on the bed and began: 'I decided to come over very suddenly.'

Then she stopped. 'If a car hoots before I count three, I'll do this. If it doesn't, I'll do that. . . .' To know that this was the only reasonable way to live was one thing; to explain and justify it to somebody else — especially to Norah — was quite another.

Norah asked: 'Are you going to stay for long?'

'I don't know.'

Then there was a silence, like that between travellers in a railway carriage who have started a conversation which dies from lack of subjects of mutual interest.

Julia asked how their mother was, and Norah answered that she was much the same. 'The doctor says she's getting weaker, but I don't see any difference myself.'

'When may I come to see her?'

'She won't know you,' Norah said. 'You realize that, don't you? She doesn't know anybody. However, come whenever you like. Come tomorrow afternoon.'

'It doesn't bear thinking of,' Julia said miserably.

She had been accustomed for years to the idea that her mother was an invalid, paralysed, dead to all intents and purposes. Yet, when Norah said in that inexorable, matter-of-fact voice: 'She doesn't know anybody,' a cold weight descended on her heart, crushing it.

Norah agreed. 'The way people die doesn't bear thinking of.'

Julia said: 'That chair's awfully uncomfortable. Won't you sit on the bed near me, and let's talk?'

She made an awkward gesture. Her eagerness made her awkward. She had been longing for some show of affection, or at any rate of interest, but Norah kept looking at her as if she were something out of the zoo. She felt an answering indifference, and at the same time pain and a tightness of the throat.

She wanted to say: 'Do you remember the day I took off my shoes and stockings when we were paddling and carried you because the pebbles hurt your feet? Well, I've never forgotten that day.'

'I can't stay for very long,' said Norah without moving, 'because I'm going to see Uncle Griffiths. He's in London now, and he always asks me to tea when he comes.'

'Oh, does he?' said Julia. 'Kind man!'

Norah said calmly: 'Yes, I think he is kind.'

When she had read Julia's letter she had said: 'You'll never guess who's turned up again. . . . Well, I suppose I'd better go along and see her.' She was feeling curious, even pleased. Because something fresh was always something fresh — a little excitement to break the monotony.

But now all her curiosity had departed and she only wanted to get away. Her first sight of Julia had shocked her, for it seemed to her that in the last three years her sister had indisputably changed for the worse.

She thought: 'She doesn't even look like a lady now. What can she have been doing with herself?'

Norah herself was labelled for all to see. She was labelled 'Middle class, no money.' Hardly enough to keep herself in clean linen. And yet scrupulously, fiercely clean, but with all the daintiness and prettiness perforce cut out. Everything about her betrayed the woman who had been brought up to certain tastes, then left without the money to gratify them; trained to certain opinions which forbid her even the relief of rebellion against her lot; yet holding desperately to both her tastes and her opinions.

Her expression was not suppressed or timid, as with so many of her kind. Her face was dark and still, with something fierce underlying the stillness.

She said: 'D'you know, I'm afraid I must go now. What time will you come round tomorrow?'

'Look here, Norah,' said Julia, 'it isn't that I want to bother you, but I came over without much money. I've only got a little over a pound left. I won't be able to stay in this place much longer.'

Norah opened her eyes widely, and said in a cold voice: 'I've got eight pounds, and that's got to last for a month, and the doctor comes nearly every day. Count up for yourself.'

'I know,' said Julia eagerly, 'I know. I don't want you to lend me money. I know perfectly well that you can't. I simply thought you might let me stay at the flat for a few days, till I get an answer from a man I've written to.'

Norah's expression confused her, and she went on, raising her voice: 'I'll be quite all right in a week or so. Only he may be away. He may not be able to answer at once.'

'I'm awfully sorry,' Norah replied coldly, 'but I've got a friend staying with me — Miss Wyatt, she's a trained nurse. I can't turn her out at a moment's notice, can I? And there's not a scrap more room in the place.'

'Oh, I see,' said Julia. She sighed. She stretched her legs out and put her head on the pillow. 'Well, all right. There's a light outside. Mind you put it on as you go out, or you may fall down those stairs.'

'Yes, but look here, this is perfectly absurd,' said Norah fretfully. 'You've had practically nothing to do with us for years — and you don't seem to have starved.'

Julia did not answer.

'And who's better dressed — you or I?' said Norah. A fierce expression came into her eyes.

Julia said, bursting into a loud laugh: 'Yes, d'you know why that is? Just before I came over here I spent six hundred francs on clothes, because I thought that if I was too shabby you'd all be ashamed of me and would give me the cold shoulder. Of course, I didn't want to risk that happening, did I?'

'You're an extraordinary creature,' said Norah.

Something in her voice enraged Julia, who began to argue rather incoherently: 'Why should you be like this? What do you blame me for — exactly?'

'But I don't blame you,' said Norah. 'I don't consider that what you do is any business of mine. Besides, I'm far past blaming anybody for anything. Oh, yes, I've got far past that stage, believe me. . . . I simply said I thought it very very odd of you to turn up here at a moment's notice and to send for me and expect that I can produce money for you.'

'Oh, God!' said Julia loudly. 'But it wasn't money I wanted.'

She went on in a totally different voice: 'Well, it doesn't matter, anyway.'

Standing at the door, a feeling of compunction touched Norah. She looked round the room and said: 'This really is an awful place. Why on earth do you come to a place like this?'

'Yes, look at it,' said Julia, suddenly bitter. 'Look at those filthy curtains. My God, foreigners must have a fine idea of London — coming to hotels like this. No wonder they avoid it like the plague.'

Norah did not answer this, because the opinion which foreigners might have of London was a matter of complete indifference to her. She said: 'Why don't you go to a boarding-house?'

Then she added, for the sake of something to say: 'Uncle Griffiths' place is awfully comfortable. He's at a boarding-house at Bayswater. A private hotel place.'

'Oh, is he?' said Julia. 'What's his address?'

Norah told her. Then the thought came to her: 'I hope to God she won't go and ask him for money.' And she added suspiciously: 'Why do you want to know?'

'Oh, nothing,' said Julia. 'Well . . . I'll come along tomorrow.'
'All right. Good-bye,' said Norah.
'Good-bye.'

◆　　◆　　◆

'Well, I suppose I've changed too,' thought Julia. 'I suppose I look much older, too.'

She began to imagine herself old, quite old, and forsaken. And was filled with melancholy and a terror which was like a douche of cold water, first numbing and then stimulating. She lit a cigarette and began to walk up and down the room.

She had lost the feeling of indifference to her fate, which in Paris had sustained her for so long. She knew herself ready to struggle and twist and turn, to be unscrupulous and cunning as are all weak creatures fighting for their lives against the strong.

Of course, say what you like, London was a cold and terrifying place to return to like this after ten years. She told herself that after all the idea of going to a boarding-house was a good idea. There she would have bed and food for a week without any need to bother.

She made anxious calculations and decided that with about another couple of pounds she would be all right.

The thing was to keep calm and try everything possible.

She found Mr Horsfield's card in her bag.

At the telephone she became very nervous. Mr Horsfield was not able to hear what she was saying, and this made her still more nervous. The man at the bureau was looking at her. Julia fixed him with a cold and defiant stare.

'Oh, yes,' said Mr Horsfield. 'Yes, yes. . . . Of course. . . .'

Then there was a long pause while he was making up his mind. He was thinking: 'That woman! I suppose I did give her my address. Well, she hasn't been long about turning up.' He wished he could remember more clearly what she looked like. Then, as invariably happened, he gave way to his impulse.

'Hullo,' he said. 'Are you there?'

'Yes,' said Julia.

When he asked her if she would dine with him that night she answered: 'Yes,' smiling at the telephone.

'Where are you staying?' he said. 'I'll call for you about eight o'clock if I may.'

She told him her address and rang off. It was just after four o'clock.

3

UNCLE GRIFFITHS

JULIA'S UNCLE GRIFFITHS was dressing for dinner when the page-boy knocked and told him that there was a lady downstairs who wished to see him. The page's face was serious, but something about his intonation suggested a grin.

'A lady?' said Mr Griffiths, in a voice which sounded alarmed and annoyed, as he might have said: 'A zebra? A giraffe?'

He was about sixty-five years of age, looking a good ten years younger. His face was short, broad, almost unwrinkled, red — but not unhealthily so. His hair was white. His eyes were pale-blue and cold as stones.

The page-boy said: 'I told the lady I wasn't quite sure if you were in, sir.'

Mr Griffiths turned to his wife and said in a resigned voice: 'That must be Julia.'

'Ask her if she'd mind waiting a few minutes,' he told the boy.

Julia waited in a large, lofty room, crowded with fat, chintz-covered arm-chairs. Two middle-aged women were sitting by the fire talking. They looked comfortable and somnolent. But Julia sat outside the sacred circle of warmth. She was cold, and held her coat together at the throat. The coat looked all right but it was much too thin. She had hesitated about buying it for that reason, but the woman in the second-hand shop had talked her over.

She thought: 'Of all the idiotic things I ever did, the most idiotic was selling my fur coat.' She began bitterly to remember the coat she had once possessed, the sort that lasts for ever, astrakhan, with a huge skunk collar. She had sold it at the time of her duel with Maître Legros.

She told herself that if only she had had the sense to keep a few things, this return need not have been quite so ignominious, quite so desolate. People thought twice before they were rude to anybody wearing a good fur coat; it was protective colouring, as it were.

She began to regret having come. And yet why should she not have come? Uncle Griffiths had always seemed to like her. Once when she was a child he had said that she was pretty, and this had thrilled her. At that time he had represented to the family the large and powerful male. She did not remember her father well; he had died when she was six and Norah a baby of one.

Uncle Griffiths came in and she got up eagerly. He said: 'Well, Julia,' and put out a stiff and warning hand. 'Come along upstairs to my room, will you?'

On the staircase he said: 'No use talking in there, with people listening to every word you say.'

He gripped the upper part of her arm to guide her along the passage.

'Oh, yes, very well — very well indeed,' she replied to his questions, still smiling mechanically.

In the bedroom he introduced Julia to his wife, who said in a placid voice that she had better leave them to talk, hadn't she?

She was his second wife. He had met her at a small hotel at Burnham-on-Crouch and had married her without knowing anything about her. It was the one impulsive action of his life, and he had never regretted it.

'Sit down,' said Uncle Griffiths.

Julia sat down. Uncle Griffiths stood with his back to the fire, sucking at his white moustache and staring at her. He looked inquisitive but cautious — slightly amused, too, as if he were thinking: 'Now, then, what have you been up to? Of course, I know what you've been up to.'

To Julia he appeared solid and powerful, and she felt a great desire to please him, to make him look kindly at her.

Uncle Griffiths cleared his throat and said: 'I was very much surprised to hear from Norah that you were in London, Julia. I thought that you were quite settled in — where was it?'

Julia said that she had been in Paris.

'Dear me,' said Uncle Griffiths. 'Was it Paris?'

All the furniture in the room was dark, with a restful and inevitable darkness; and sombre curtains hung over the windows. The long, thin flames of the fire sprang from an almost solid mass of coal.

She said: 'I left on Thursday. It's funny, for it seems much longer ago than that.'

'I see,' said Uncle Griffiths. 'So you made up your mind to come over and pay us a flying visit, did you?'

But this was merely rhetoric. He had summed her up. He knew, both from what Norah had told him and from his own observation, that she had made a mess of things and was trying to get hold of some money.

She said: 'I don't know why I came. A sort of impulse, I suppose.'

'Good God,' said Uncle Griffiths. His voice always sounded as if he were speaking between closed teeth. 'If I were you,' he went on, 'I should go back again. Things are very difficult over here, you know. Hard. Yes, yes — hard times.'

She said: 'I daresay, but you see, I haven't any money to go back with.'

Uncle Griffiths considered her for some seconds without speaking, and then said: 'Do you know where your husband is?'

Julia said in a low voice: 'You know. . . . I thought you knew. . . . I left him. I don't know where he is now. He went absolutely smash, you know.'

'He was a damned bad lot,' said Uncle Griffiths.

'He wasn't,' said Julia sullenly.

She felt as though her real self had taken cover, as though she had retired somewhere far off and was crouching warily, like an animal, watching her body in the arm-chair arguing with Uncle Griffiths about the man she had loved.

'What?' said Uncle Griffiths loudly. 'He married you and left you stranded, and then you tell me that he wasn't a bad lot?'

'He didn't leave me,' argued Julia. 'I left him.'

'Nonsense,' said Uncle Griffiths.

He thought: 'Why should I have to bother about this woman?' But some vague sense of responsibility made him go on asking questions.

He said: 'I thought he was supposed to have some money. He must have had some money, gallivanting about as you did. Why didn't you make him settle something on you?'

'When he had money, he gave me a lot,' said Julia. She added in a low voice: 'He gave me lovely things — but really lovely things.'

'I never heard such nonsense in my life,' said Uncle Griffiths sturdily.

Suddenly, because of the way he said that, Julia felt contemptuous of him. She thought: 'I know you. I bet you've never bought lovely things for anybody. I bet you've never given anybody a lovely thing in your life. You wouldn't know a lovely thing if you saw it.'

Because she felt such contempt her nervousness left her.

Her uncle said he wasn't going to argue with her, and that he couldn't imagine what good she thought she would do by coming over to England, and that he was astounded when he heard that she had come — astounded, because he had understood that she had some sort of job in Paris, or wherever it was, and jobs were not easy to get in London. He said that he had not got any money and that if he had he would not give it to Julia, certainly not, but to her sister Norah, and that he would like to help Norah, because she was a fine girl, and she deserved it.

'But the truth is that I haven't got any money to give to anybody,' he said. 'In fact, if things go on as they are going now, goodness knows what'll become of me.'

An anxious expression spread over his face as he thought to himself that the time was coming when he would have to give up this comfort, and then that comfort, until God knew what would be the end of it all. In his way he was an imaginative man, and when these fits of foreboding overcame him he genuinely forgot that only a succession of highly improbable catastrophes could reduce him to the penury he so feared.

Julia was thinking that she might try to pawn something and that she had forgotten where the pawnshops were. There was one in a side-street near Leicester Square — Rupert Street, wasn't it? Silver things in the window. But anyhow what had she to pawn that would fetch even a few shillings?

Uncle Griffiths was still talking: 'You always insisted on going your own way. Nobody interfered with you or expressed any opinion on what you did. You deserted your family. And now you can't expect to walk back and be received with open arms.'

'Yes,' she said, 'it was idiotic of me to come. It was childish, really. It's childish to imagine that anybody cares what happens to anybody else.'

He chuckled, and said with an air of letting her into a secret and an expression that was suddenly open and honest: 'Of course, everybody has to sit on their own bottoms. I've found that out all my life. You mustn't grumble if you find it out too.'

Then he said: 'I tell you what I'll do. I'll give you a pound to help you pay your fare back to Paris.'

He brought out a pocket-book, and handed her a note. She took it, put it into her bag, immediately got up, and said: 'Good night.'

Uncle Griffiths, looking more cheerful now that the interview was over, answered: 'Good night,' and put his hand out kindly. Julia walked past him without taking it, and he put it back into his pocket, and said: 'Take my advice. You get along back as quickly as you can.'

•   •   •

Julia felt bewildered when she got into the street. She turned and walked without any clear idea of the direction she was taking. Each house she passed was exactly like the last. Each house bulged forward a little. And before each a flight of four or five steps led up to a portico supported by two fat pillars.

Down at the far end of the street a voice quavered into a melancholy tune. The voice dragged and broke — failed. Then suddenly there would be a startlingly powerful bellow. The bellow was not fierce or threatening, as it might have been; it was complaining and mindless, like an animal in pain.

Julia thought: 'They might light the streets a bit better here.'

It was the darkness that got you. It was heavy darkness, greasy and compelling. It made walls round you, and shut you in so that you felt you could not breathe. You wanted to beat at the darkness and shriek to be let out. And after a while you got used to it. Of course. And then you stopped believing that there was anything else anywhere.

The singer — a drably vague figure standing as near as he dared to the entrance to a public bar — had started *The Pagan Love Song* for the second time.

The buses would stop near the pub.

She got on the next one that was going in the direction of Oxford Circus, mounted to the top, and sat there with her eyes shut.

4

CAFÉ MONICO

MR HORSFIELD was waiting for her. Julia went up to him and said: 'I'm afraid I'm late.'

'Not at all.'

He shook hands without smiling, then looked away from her instantly, his face assuming an expression of detached politeness.

As they waited in the street for a taxi he looked sideways at her, coldly. A sensation of loneliness overcame her. She thought that there was something in the expression of the eyes of a human being regarding a stranger that was somehow a dreadful give-away.

They got into the taxi.

'My God,' she muttered, 'what a life! What a life!'

'I expect London's depressing you,' said Mr Horsfield.

'It's a bit dark, when one comes back to it.'

There was a pause. Then he asked: 'Do you like sherry? I hope you do, because the sherry at this place we're going to is rather good.'

•   •   •

He looked very tidy and very precise. He looked the sort that never gives itself away and that despises people who do, that despises them and perhaps takes advantage of them. He would think: 'Poor devil.' Yes, he might go so far as to think like that, but the poor devil would remain a poor devil whom you theorized about but never tried to understand.

Julia thought: 'He's been taught never to give himself away. Perhaps he's had a bad time learning it, but he's learnt it now all right.'

He was hollow-cheeked. His mouth drooped at the corners — not bad-temperedly, but sadly. He looked rather subdued, till you saw in his eyes that he was not quite subdued yet, after all.

He said: 'Well, do you like the sherry?'

'No, not terribly.'

'Then we'll try something else.'

They sat at a table near the window, and were waited on by a tall, fat, pale Frenchman with a Bourbon nose who was pompous and superior to the verge of bursting. His fat white face and his little scornful eyes irritated Julia. She thought that she would like to turn round and say something rude to him. Just one word — one little word — to see the expression on his face when she said it.

Then food and the rosy lights comforted her. She began to feel aloof and she forgot the waiter.

Mr Horsfield talked politely. He was trying to find out what was expected of him, but she answered him vaguely and absent-mindedly in monosyllables.

She wanted to attract and charm him. She still realized that it might be extremely important that she should attract and charm him. But she was unable to resist the dream-like feeling that had fallen upon her which made what he was saying seem unreal and rather ludicrously unimportant.

When they were drinking coffee, she said. 'My hotel's a dreadful place. I hate it.'

'I don't wonder,' said Mr Horsfield. 'Why did you go there?'

Julia explained: 'The taxi-man took me. I said to him: "Take me to a quiet hotel, not expensive, in Bloomsbury." Because, you see, I was afraid of having to go from one place to another and I didn't remember where I could go. He sort of eyed me, and then he took me there.'

Mr Horsfield said: 'I'll find you a better place than that.' He asked: 'I suppose you've made up your mind to stay for some time?'

'I don't know,' said Julia. 'I've no idea. I don't really know at all.' And then she once more remembered that, when she had rung him up, she had intended to explain her situation and ask him to help her.

She realized with a shock that the meal was nearly over. She thought: 'If I'm going to do it at all I must do it now.'

She felt nervous and shivered.

'I'm awfully cold,' she said.

It was stupid that, when you had done this sort of thing a hundred times, you still felt nervous and shivered as you were doing it.

Mr Horsfield stared at her and said: 'What's the matter? Are things going badly?' He thought: 'After all, fifteen hundred francs isn't much. Fancy having to rely for good and all on fifteen hundred francs!' And then he thought: 'Oh, God, I hope she's not going to cry.'

He said: 'Look here, let's go somewhere else and talk. Don't tell me about things here. We'll go somewhere else to talk.'

She said, speaking quickly: 'You surprised me, because people nearly always force you to ask, don't they?'

'They do,' said Mr Horsfield.

Her face was red. She went on talking in an angry voice: 'They force you to say — and then they refuse you. And then they tell you all about why they refuse you. I suppose they get a subtle pleasure out of it, or something.'

Mr Horsfield said: 'Subtle pleasure? Not at all. A very simple and primitive pleasure.'

'It's so easy to make a person who hasn't got anything seem wrong.'

'Yes,' he said. 'I know. That's dawned on me once or twice, extraordinary as it may seem. It's always so damned easy to despise hard-up people when in one way and another you're as safe as houses. . . . Have another liqueur.'

But he was relieved when she declined, because he was afraid she

284

looked rather drunk. He watched her anxiously, feeling all at once very intimate with her. And he hated the feeling of intimacy. It made something in him shrink back and long to escape.

She made her inevitable, absent-minded gesture of powdering her face. She looked happier, and relieved. That, of course, was because she imagined that she was now going to cast all her woes on his shoulders. Which was all very well, he thought, but he had his own troubles.

•   •   •

When he took her arm to pilot her across Regent Street he touched her as lightly as possible. They turned to the right and walked along aimlessly.

Julia thought: 'This place tells you all the time, "Get money, get money, get money, or be for ever damned." Just as Paris tells you to forget, forget, let yourself go.'

Mr Horsfield said, in an aimless voice: 'Now, let me see, where shall we go?'

'This will do as well as anywhere, won't it?'

They were passing the Café Monico. She walked in, and he followed her. When they had sat down she said: 'I hate drifting about streets. Do you mind? It makes me awfully miserable.'

Then she said that she would have a *fine*. And Mr Horsfield ordered a *fine* and a whisky and watched her drinking.

She looked older and less pretty than she had done in Paris. Her mouth and the lids of her eyes drooped wearily. A small blue vein under her right eye was swollen. There was something in a background, say what you like.

The suggestion of age and weariness in her face fascinated Mr Horsfield. It was curious to speculate about the life of a woman like that and to wonder what she appeared to herself to be — when she looked in the glass, for instance. Because, of course, she must have some pathetic illusions about herself or she would not be able to go on living. Did she still see herself young and slim, capable of anything, believing that, though every one around her grew older, she — by some miracle — remained the same? Or perhaps she was just heavily indifferent. . . .

His thoughts went off at a tangent and became suddenly tinged with irritation. People ought not to look obvious; people ought to take the trouble to look and behave like all other people. And if they didn't it was their own funeral.

He said in a formal voice: 'What I meant to say was that if there is anything I can do to help you . . .'

She took out her little powder-box, opened it and looked at herself in the mirror. He went on impatiently: 'If only you'd stop worrying about how you look and tell me what's the matter.'

She said: 'I thought from the way you were staring at me that I must be looking pretty ugly.'

He felt rather ashamed, but he did not really see why he should feel ashamed.

'I didn't mean that at all,' he said.

She said: 'Oh, I know, you're one of those kind blokes England is so famous for, aren't you?'

'Is England famous for kind blokes?'

'Well,' she said thoughtfully, 'that's just what England isn't famous for, really. However, kid yourself that it is. What's it got to do with me?'

'I'm all right, really,' she added, in a voice that was suddenly aloof. 'I've enough to get along with for a bit. It's simply that I wasn't able to sleep last night. The bed had a ridge right down the middle.'

Then she began to boast — boast was the only word — about some man to whom she said she written. Apparently he had been her lover. He remembered that she had talked of the fellow when he saw her in Paris.

Mr Horsfield became rather bored. He thought that her vanity anyhow was still alive and kicking. He could not resist saying: 'I expect you have several friends in London you can write to?'

'Not me,' she said with conviction. 'I wouldn't waste three-halfpenny stamps on anybody but this man.'

Then she took a box of matches from her bag and amused herself by lighting them one after another and watching them burn down to the end. In the midst of this proceeding, she said: 'It's funny how you say one thing when you're thinking of quite another, isn't it?'

Mr Horsfield agreed.

'I must go back now,' she said. 'Truly . . . I'm pretty tired. You'll see, I shan't be like this when I've had a decent night's sleep.'

Mr Horsfield hesitated. She seemed to be waiting for something anxiously. He said: 'Well, will you dine with me next Friday?'

'Yes, I'll be very glad. I'm going to leave my hotel in a day or two, but I'll write you my new address.'

They went out and got into a taxi. He thought that she was

leaning very close to him. Her breath smelt of the brandy she had been drinking. He drew away.

Then he took her hand, squeezed it, and said: 'Well, on Friday then.'

A sudden stop of the taxi in a block threw her against him. Her body felt soft and yielding.

'Sorry,' he said stiffly.

. . .

Mr Horsfield got out of the taxi with some relief. When he looked at Julia as he was saying good night he suddenly knew intimately and surely that she was perfectly indifferent to him, that the moment he had gone she would have forgotten all about him.

He said: 'Till Friday then. Good night . . . And here! Have this to go on with.'

He had a pound-note ready folded, which he pushed into her hand.

Then he drove back to his house, which was in a small dark street in the neighbourhood of Holland Park. Five rooms over a stable, which had been converted into a garage.

Just outside his gate a black-and-white cat sat huddled. When it saw him it opened and shut its mouth in a soundless mew.

Mr Horsfield said caressingly: 'Come along, Jones. Pretty Jones.' The cat got up, stretched slowly and, with uplifted tail, followed its master into the house.

ACTON

THE NEXT afternoon Julia went down to the flat at Acton to see her mother.

A square of paper on which was written: OUT OF ORDER — PLEASE KNOCK, was pinned under the bell. When she had rapped twice the door opened and a boy of about sixteen stood in the dark hall staring at her.

'Is Miss Griffiths in?'

'Second floor,' said the boy. 'Oh, yes, they're in; there's always somebody there.'

.

The door on the second floor was opened by a middle-aged woman. Her brown hair was cut very short, drawn away from a high, narrow forehead, and brushed to lie close to her very small skull. Her nose was thin and arched. She had small, pale-brown eyes and a determined expression. She wore a coat and skirt of grey flannel, a shirt blouse, and a tie.

She said, without smiling: 'Good afternoon, Julia. Come along in.'

Julia followed her into the sitting-room.

'My name's Wyatt,' she said. 'I expect Norah's spoken about me. She'll be back in a minute or two. Have some tea.'

Her voice was casual and very agreeable.

Julia refused tea, sat down, crossed her legs, and stared downwards. She felt too nervous to talk. The meeting with her mother was very near; yet she was still unable to imagine or realize it. Supposing that her mother knew her or recognized her and with one word or glance put her outside the pale, as everybody else had done.

She felt a sort of superstitious and irrational certainty that if that happened it would finish her; it would be an ultimate and final judgement. Yet she felt cold even about this. She could not realize that it would matter.

'Can I go right in?' she said.

'She's asleep,' said Miss Wyatt. 'Just dropped off. Better not go in just yet. Norah will be back here in a minute.'

An open tin of Navy Cut tobacco and a book of cigarette-papers lay on the table near Miss Wyatt. She rolled herself a cigarette very quickly and neatly. Her gestures were like the gestures of a man. Her hands were small and thin but short-fingered and without delicacy. She said: 'Have a cigarette, Julia? There's a box of Marcovitches on the table behind you. I got them for Norah — not that she smokes much.'

Julia wanted to say: 'Please make one for me. I'd like that.' But when she met Miss Wyatt's eyes she turned without speaking, took a cigarette from the box behind her, and lit it.

'I always make my own,' Miss Wyatt said. 'I have to; it's cheaper. I started doing it a long time ago — when I was in Paris. I remember I never could stand French tobacco.'

Julia said: 'Couldn't you?'

There was a long pause.

Then Miss Wyatt began: 'In my time everybody smoked those Algerian things.' She lifted her head with an alert expression, like that of a terrier. 'There's Norah.'

Norah came in and stood by the fire, taking off her hat and coat. Her face was reddened with the cold. She seemed nervous, as though she too realized that this was a solemn and dramatic occasion. She said: 'Just a minute. I'll go in and see.'

Miss Wyatt looked at the fire without speaking. Her face had assumed a very severe expression.

Then Norah called: 'Come along in now.'

*   *   *

Julia stared at the bed and saw her mother's body — a huge, shapeless mass under the sheets and blankets — and her mother's face against the white-frilled pillow. Dark-skinned, with high cheek-bones and an aquiline nose. Her white hair, which was still long and thick, was combed into two plaits which lay outside the sheet. One side of her face was dragged downwards. Her eyes were shut. She was breathing noisily, puffing out one corner of her mouth with each breath.

And yet the strange thing was that she was still beautiful, as an animal would be in old age.

Julia said: 'She's so much more beautiful than either of us.'

'Everybody who sees her says how nice she looks,' said Norah with pride and satisfaction in her voice. 'Would you like to sit in here for a bit? I'll go and talk to Wyatt.'

The bedroom was white-papered and comfortable. It smelt of disinfectants and eau-de-Cologne and rottenness.

Julia touched her mother's hand, which was lying outside the bedclothes. Then she whispered very softly: 'Darling.' She said 'darling' with her lips, but her heart was dead.

She only knew that the room was very quiet — quiet and shut away from everything.

Curtains of thick green stuff were drawn over the windows, and the fire leaped up with small, crooked flames. A dog barked outside, far off, and somehow that made her feel happy and rested.

The things one did. Life was perfectly mad, really. And here was silence — the best thing in the world.

It seemed as if she had been sitting there for many years and that if she could go on sitting there she would learn many deep things that she had only guessed at before.

She began to whisper soundlessly: 'Oh, darling, there's something I want to explain to you. You must listen.'

Her mother's eyes opened suddenly and stared upwards. Julia put her face closer and said in a frightened, hopeful voice: 'I'm Julia, do you know? It's Julia.'

The sick woman looked steadily at her daughter. Then it was like seeing a spark go out and the eyes were again bloodshot, animal eyes. Nothing was there. She mumbled something in a thick voice, then turned her head away and began to cry, loudly and disconsolately, like a child.

Julia heard the door of the sitting-room open and Norah running along the passage.

'What is it? What is it? Is she awake?'

'She woke up suddenly. I thought she knew me just for a moment.'

'Oh, no, I shouldn't think so,' muttered Norah. 'She often cries like this.'

She took a handkerchief from under the pillow, wiped her mother's eyes, and said in a crooning and mechanical voice: 'What is it, my darling? Tell me. Do you want anything? Press my hand if you want anything. . . . . I expect she wants to be moved, really.'

When Julia offered to help her she answered: 'No, it's all right. The doctor showed me how to manage.'

She hauled at the inert mass, contrived to raise the head and arranged the pillows. The paralysed woman stopped crying, gave a little snort, and shut her eyes.

'She's gone to sleep again,' whispered Norah. She was breathing quickly. 'You know,' she said, 'she's a dead weight.'

They stood together at the foot of the bed.

'But I think she did know me,' persisted Julia in a whisper. 'She said something.'

'Oh, did she?'

'Yes, It sounded like "orange-trees". She must have been thinking of when she was in Brazil.'

'Oh, I daresay,' said Norah. 'You know, she called me Dobbin the other day. And I was feeling so exactly like some poor old cart-horse when she said it, too, that I simply had to laugh.'

She laughed in a high-pitched, hysterical way. Julia echoed her nervously. But when once she had begun to laugh she found it was impossible to stop herself and she went on laughing, holding on to the foot of the bed and staring at her mother.

Then she saw her mother's black eyes open again and stare back into hers with recognition and surprise and anger. They said: 'Is this why you have come back? Have you come back to laugh at me?'

Julia's heart gave a horrible leap into her throat.

She said: 'Norah, she does know me. I'm sure she does.'

The whimpering began again. Now it was louder. It was almost like a dog howling.

'Look here,' said Norah, 'you'd better go and wait in the other room for a bit.'

'Do you think I upset her?'

'Sometimes anybody strange seems to upset her. Go on; you'd better go.'

Julia went out of the room listening to Norah's crooning and authoritative voice. 'Don't cry, my darling. Don't cry, my sweet. Now, what is it? What is it you want?'

It was getting dark. . . .

·   ◆   ·

Miss Wyatt was obviously on the point of going out. She wore a macintosh. She said: 'Will you tell Norah that I'll be back before nine?'

'Yes,' said Julia. Then she said: 'Do you think my mother suffers much?'

'The doctor says she hardly suffers at all,' Miss Wyatt answered in a non-committal voice. 'Of course, she's got worse lately. She's undoubtedly worse. Norah had to sit up with her every night last week. I haven't liked the look of her at all this last day or two.

'Norah's a good kid,' added Miss Wyatt. 'She's had a long time of this and I've never heard her grouse, never once. She's a good kid. And she'll be all right. She'll be all right. She's young yet.'

When Miss Wyatt had gone Julia put her hands over her ears to shut out the cries from the next room, which had grown louder and more pitiful. Then they stopped abruptly. Julia took a deep breath, got a handkerchief out of her bag, and wiped her hands.

Norah came in almost at once. She said: 'Where's Wyatt?'

'Gone out. She said she'd be back before nine. Has she gone to sleep?'

Norah nodded.

'But it's horrible,' muttered Julia. 'Horrible.'

'Yes,' answered Norah. 'It is. . . . Let's make some more tea, shall we? Or, wait a minute, will you have some vermouth? Wyatt brought me a bottle the other day.'

She found the bottle, filled two glasses, and drank her own quickly. Then she said in a voice that sounded defiant: 'I expect you find all this very sordid and ugly, don't you?'

Julia said: 'No, no.' But she stopped because she was unable to put her emotion into words. At the moment her sister seemed to her like a character in a tremendous tragedy moving, dark, tranquil, and beautiful, across a background of yellowish snow.

'Not a bit,' she said.

They did not speak for some seconds; then Norah said with a half-laugh; 'Well, we've neither of us done very well for ourselves, have we?'

Julia lifted her shoulders, as if to say: 'Well, don't ask me.'

'The fact is,' said Norah, 'that there's something wrong with our family. We're soft, or lazy, or something.'

'I don't think you are lazy,' said Julia. 'And I shouldn't say that you were too soft, either.'

She spoke gently, but Norah felt suddenly breathless, as if they were on the verge of a quarrel. She muttered: 'No, I don't think I'm soft now. . . . Perhaps I'm not very soft now.'

She felt a tightness of the throat, and her eyes stung. She opened them widely, and leaned her head back, because she knew that if she did that the tears would not fall; they would go back to wherever they came from. She did not want to give herself away before Julia — Julia with her hateful, blackened eyelids. What was the use of telling Julia what she thought of her? It was ridiculous to make a scene. You ignored people like that.

And yet every time she looked at Julia she felt a fierce desire to hurt her or to see her hurt and humiliated. She thought in a confused way, 'It's because I'm so tired.' All day she had felt like that, as if she could not bear another instant. When she had held a spoon of medicine to her mother's lips her hands had shaken so violently that it had all been spilled. And all last night she had lain awake thinking, instead of sleeping, now that Wyatt was there, and she had a chance to sleep. She had lain awake thinking and crying — and to cry was a thing she hardly ever did.

It was as if meeting Julia had aroused some spirit of rebellion to tear her to bits. She thought over and over again, 'It isn't fair, it isn't fair.'

She picked up the book lying on her bed-table — *Almayer's Folly* — and had begun to read:

The slave had no hope, and knew of no change. She knew of no other sky, no other water, no other forest, no other world, no other life. She had no wish, no hope, no love. . . . The absence of pain and hunger was her happiness, and when she felt unhappy she was tired, more than usual, after the day's labour.

Then she had got up and looked at herself in the glass. She had let her nightgown slip down off her shoulders, and had a look at herself. She was tall and straight and slim and young — well, fairly young. She had taken up a strand of her hair and put her face against it and thought how she liked the smell and the feel of it. She had laughed at herself in the glass and her teeth were white and sound and even. Yes, she had laughed at herself in the glass. Like an idiot.

Then in the midst of her laughing she had noticed how pale her lips were; and she had thought: 'My life's like death. It's like being buried alive. It isn't fair, it isn't fair.'

She could not stop crying. It had been as if something terribly strong were struggling within her, and tearing her in its struggles. And then she had thought: 'If this goes on for another year I'm finished. I'll be old and finished, and that's that.'

Of course, she had thought that sort of thing before. But always vaguely — and there had not been anything vague about the way she had thought last night.

Everybody always said to her: 'You're wonderful, Norah, you're wonderful. I don't know how you do it.' It was a sort of drug, that universal, that unvarying admiration — the feeling that one was doing what one ought to do, the approval of God and man. It made you feel protected and safe, as if something very powerful were fighting on your side.

Besides, she wasn't a squeamish sort. She could bear disgusting sights and sounds and smells. And so she had slaved. And she had gradually given up going out because she was too tired to try to amuse herself. Besides, there wasn't any money.

That had gone on for six years. Three years ago her mother had had a second stroke, and since then her life had been slavery.

Everybody had said: 'You're wonderful, Norah.' But they did not help. They just stood around watching her youth die, and her beauty die, and her soft heart grow hard and bitter. They sat there and said: 'You're wonderful, Norah.' Beasts. . . . Devils. . . .

For a long time she had just lain on her bed, thinking: 'Beasts and devils.' And then gradually she had begun to think: 'No that isn't fair.' They were not beasts. They approved, and were willing to back their approval, but not in any spectacular fashion. And then she had begun to think — in a dull, sore sort of manner

— about Aunt Sophie's will, and the will her mother had made. And that at long last she would have some money of her own and be able to do what she liked.

And then she had felt very cold, and had pulled the bedclothes over her. And then she had felt so tired that after all nothing mattered except sleep. And then she must have slept.

Julia moved; she uncrossed her legs. She had been thinking of the words 'Orange-trees', remembering the time when she had woven innumerable romances about her mother's childhood in South America, when she had asked innumerable questions, which her mother had answered inadequately or not at all, for she was an inarticulate woman. Natural, accepting transplantation as a plant might have done. But sometimes you could tell that she was sickening for the sun. Julia remembered her saying: 'This is a cold, grey country. This isn't a country to be really happy in.' Had she then been unhappy? No, Julia did not remember her as an unhappy woman. Austere, unconsciously thwarted perhaps, but not unhappy.

She said, in a different voice: 'Can I come again tomorrow?'

'Of course,' Nora said. And then: 'Have something to eat before you go. Bread and cheese, or an egg, or something.'

'No, thank you,' said Julia. 'No, thank you. Don't bother.'

'I'll come to the door with you,' said Norah. She now felt that she did not want to let Julia go. She hated her, but she felt more alive when her sister was with her.

Outside, the sky was clear and pale blue. There was a thin young moon, red-gold.

'Look,' said Julia. 'New moon.'

Norah suddenly began to shiver violently. Julia could see her teeth chattering. She said: 'Till tomorrow, then,' and went in and shut the door.

•   •   •

On the next day, which was a Sunday, Julia went down to Acton and sat for an hour in her mother's room.

This time the sick woman lay like a log, without moving, without opening her eyes.

Julia sat there remembering that when she was a very young child she had loved her mother. Her mother had been the warm centre of the world. You loved to watch her brushing her long hair; and when you missed the caresses and the warmth you groped for them. . . . And then her mother — entirely wrapped up in the new baby — had said things like, 'Don't be a cry-baby. You're too old to go on like that. You're a great big girl of six.' And from being the warm centre of the world her mother had gradually become a dark, austere, rather plump woman, who, because she was worried, slapped you for no reason that you knew. So that there were times when you were afraid of her; other times when you disliked her.

Then you stopped being afraid or disliking. You simply became indifferent and tolerant and rather sentimental, because after all she was your mother.

It was strange sitting there, and remembering the time when she was the sweet, warm centre of the world, remembering it so vividly that mysteriously it was all there again.

When it began to grow dark she went back into the sitting-room.

Miss Wyatt asked: 'Are you going?'

'Is there nothing I can do?' said Julia.

'No,' said Miss Wyatt. 'Norah will be back very soon.'

Then she began to read again, because she did not like, approve of, or even trust the creature and she made no bones about showing it.

Julia felt herself dismissed. After fidgeting about a little, she said: 'Well, good night.'

'Good night,' said Miss Wyatt, without looking up. 'Are you coming here tomorrow?'

'I don't know,' said Julia in a low voice. 'Yes, I think I will. . . . But I don't know, because I'm changing my room. Here's my new address. Will you give it to Norah?'

On her return to the hotel the young man at the reception desk presented her with a bit of paper.

'A telephone message for you, madam.'

Julia read:

'Mr James says he will be pleased to see Madame Martin either tonight or tomorrow night between nine and ten if she will call round at his house.'

6

MR JAMES

THIS WAS the affair which had ended quietly and decently, without fuss or scenes or hysteria. When you were nineteen, and it was the first time you had been let down, you did not make scenes. You felt as if your back was broken, as if you would never move again. But you did not make a scene. That started later on, when the same thing had happened five or six times over, and you were supposed to be getting used to it.

Nineteen — that was a hell of a long time ago. Well, you had your reward, because there was a man who had become your friend for life. Always at the back of your mind had been the thought: 'If the worst absolutely comes to the worst he'll help.'

He had said: 'I am your friend for life. I am eternally grateful to you — for your sweetness and your generosity.' And so on and so on.

He was *chic*, too. He had lent her a good deal of money, first and last. And she had always said: 'This money I have borrowed. I will pay you back one day.'

And then he would reply: 'Of course you will. Don't you worry about that.'

And after all this time he had answered almost at once. That was *chic*.

•   •   •

The servant who opened the door had a nice face — not the sort that sneered at you after your back was turned. There was a big wood fire burning in the hall, and a lot of comfortable chairs.

Then the servant showed her upstairs and opened the door of a room, and there he was.

Another person. Nothing to be nervous about or sentimental about. This was simply another person — just as she was another person. That was strange and rather sad.

Then she began thinking that it must be strange to be very rich and absolutely secure, and not stupid. Because so many very rich people were stupid; only half their brains worked. 'But after all, perhaps he is stupid,' she thought. 'I don't really know.'

'My dear, I'm awfully glad to see you. You were a dear to write.'

He was thinking: 'These resurrections of the past are tactless, really — not amusing. But what is one to do?'

He had the beginnings of a headache — the faint throbbings in the temples.

Julia said, with a coquettish expression: 'Well, d'you think I've changed?'

He reassured her. 'You've never looked prettier. Never prettier.'

'Not too fat?' she said anxiously.

He said: 'Just exactly right,' and smiled at her.

But she felt a little as though she were sitting in an office waiting for an important person who might do something for her — or might not. And when she looked round the room it seemed to her a very beautiful room, and she felt that she had no right to sit there and intrude her sordid wish somehow to keep alive into that beautiful room.

Then he said, trying to be kind: 'Look here, you can tell me all about it, because I've got loads of time — heaps of time. Nearly three-quarters of an hour.'

She thought that she must start the explanation she had prepared. She said, as one would say something off by heart: 'I tried, you know, to make things a success after I married, but I didn't pull it off. It fell through.'

'Yes, I gathered that when I saw you last. I'm sorry for it.'

'And then, you see, when he didn't really care any more it seemed natural to leave him.'

'And there was somebody else who did care, or said he did? Was that it?'

'Oh, not particularly,' she said. 'After a time there was somebody, but that was never the real reason. It was just that everything had gone wrong and he seemed fed up and I felt it was natural to go away if he was like that.'

'I see,' said Mr James.

She was thinking: 'It was just my luck, wasn't it, that when we needed it most we should have lost everything? When you've just had a baby, and it dies for the simple reason that you haven't enough money to keep it alive, it leaves you with a sort of hunger. Not sentimental — oh, no. Just a funny feeling, like hunger. And then, of course, you're indifferent — because the whole damned thing is too stupid to be anything else but indifferent about. . . . He's so little. And he dies and is put under the earth.'

She looked at Mr James, his slightly puckered forehead and the carefully kind expression on his face.

'And then you rush round to raise money enough to bury him. You don't want to leave him lying in the hospital with a card tied round his wrist. And the tart downstairs lends money and buys flowers and comes to see you and cries because you are crying. "Look here, I don't believe that; you're making it up." All right, don't believe it then.'

And there was Neil James puckering his forehead, trying to be so kind. So kind, so cautious, so perfectly certain that all is for the best and that no mistakes are ever made.

'How rum if after all these years I hated him — not for any reason except that he's so damned respectable and secure. Sitting there so smugly.'

Mr James looked at her, rather uneasy at her long silence, and said: 'Look here, have a whisky-and-soda.'

He rang the bell and, when the servant arrived, said: 'Bring whisky and glasses.'

'Well,' she said slowly, 'I've been all right really, as a matter of fact.'

Mr James glanced sideways at the clock.

'But you want to go out,' she said. 'I'm keeping you.'

'For God's sake sit still, there's heaps of time.'

So many threads. To try to disentangle them — no use. Because he has money he's a kind of God. Because I have none I'm a kind of worm. A worm because I've failed and I have no money. A worm because I'm not even sure if I hate you.

She said, rather sullenly: 'I got fed up. I felt I needed a rest. I thought perhaps you'd help me to have a rest.'

At last she has come to the point — relief of Mr James! And yet he felt harder, now that he was sure she had come to ask for money. Everybody tried to get money out of him. By God, he was sick of it. 'If I don't look out this is never going to stop; it's going to be an unending business.'

A suspicion came into his mind. He asked, even as Uncle Griffiths had done: 'And you don't know where your husband is?'

She looked at him with a bewildered expression and shook her head.

'Of course, my dear,' he said, 'I'll do something for you. Look here. I'll write you tomorrow and send you something. Don't worry, I won't forget. I promise. You'll be able to have a rest. . . . Now let's talk about something else for God's sake.'

She said, rather stubbornly: 'But I always meant, when I saw you, to explain. . . .'

Mr James said: 'My dear, don't harrow me. I don't want to hear. Let's talk about something else.'

Then, when the man had brought the whisky and retired, he said: 'There's your whisky. Go on, drink it up.'

For the first time she looked straight into his eyes. She said: 'My dear, I wouldn't harrow you for the world. "No harrowing" is my motto.'

She drank the whisky. Gaiety spread through her. Why care a damn?

She said: 'Look here, why talk about harrowing? Harrowing doesn't come into it. I've had good times — lots of good times.'

She thought: 'I had a shot at the life I wanted. And I failed. . . . All right! I might have succeeded, and if I had people would have licked my boots for me. There wouldn't have been any of this cold-shouldering. Don't tell me; leave me alone. If I hate, I've a right to hate. And if I think people are swine, let me think it. . . .'

She said: 'Anyhow, I don't know how I could have done differently. I wish I'd been cleverer about it, that's all. Do you think I could have done differently?'

He looked away from her, and said: 'Don't ask me. I'm not the person to ask that sort of thing, am I? I don't know. Probably you couldn't. You know, Julietta, the war taught me a lot.'

'Did it?' she said, surprised. 'Did it though?'

'Yes. Before the war I'd always thought that I rather despised people who didn't get on.'

'Despised,' thought Julia. 'Why despised?'

'I despised a man who didn't get on. I didn't believe much in bad luck. But after the war I felt differently. I've got a lot of mad friends now. I call them my mad friends.'

'People who haven't got on?' Julia asked.

'Yes. People who've come croppers.'

'Men?'

'Oh, no, some women too. Though mind you, women are a different thing altogether. Because it's all nonsense; the life of a man and the life of a woman can't be compared. They're up against entirely different things the whole time. What's the use of talking nonsense about it? Look at cocks and hens; it's the same sort of thing,' said Mr James.

Then he said: 'Look here, Julietta, before you go you must come and look at my pictures.'

◆   ◆   ◆

When they looked at the pictures he became a different man. Because he loved them he became in their presence modest, hesitating, unsure of his own opinion.

'Do you like that?'

'Yes, I like it.'

'I wish I could get somebody who knows to tell me whether it's any good or not,' he said, talking to himself.

He was anxious because he did not want to love the wrong thing. Fancy wanting to be told what you must love!

'Well, look here, Julietta, good-bye. Don't worry. I'll write at once; you shall have your rest. And let me know your address when you go back to Paris.'

'Yes,' she said, 'I will. And I'm at another place here. I'll write it down for you.' She got an envelope and a stump of pencil out of her bag, wrote on it and gave it to him.

'All right, all right,' said Mr James, putting it into his pocket without looking at it. 'I won't forget.'

She wanted to cry as he went down the stairs with her. There was a lump in her throat. She thought: 'That wasn't what I wanted.' She had hoped that he would say something or look something that would make her feel less lonely.

There was a vase of flame-coloured tulips in the hall — surely the most graceful of flowers. Some thrust their heads forward like snakes, and some were very erect, stiff, virginal, rather prim. Some were dying, with curved grace in their death.

7

CHANGE OF ADDRESS

THE NEXT day Julia did not go down to Acton. She walked all the afternoon in a pale sunlight — sunlight without warmth. She did not think, because a spell was on her that forbade her to think. She walked with her eyes on the ground, and a puff of wind blew capriciously before her a little piece of greasy brown paper, omnibus-tickets, a torn newspaper poster, coal dust, and dried horse dung.

These streets near her boarding-house on Notting Hill seemed strangely empty, like the streets of a grey dream — a labyrinth of streets, all exactly alike.

She would think: 'Surely I passed down here several minutes ago.' Then she would see the name Chepstow Crescent or Pembridge Villas, and reassure herself. 'That's all right; I'm not walking in a circle.'

At last she got on a bus and went to a cinema in the Edgware Road. A comic film was going on, and a woman behind her laughed, 'Heh, heh, heh.' A fat, comfortable laugh, pleasant to listen to, so that without looking round she could tell what the woman was like.

After the comedy she saw young men running races and some of them collapsing exhausted. And then — strange anti-climax — young women ran races and also collapsed exhausted, at which the audience rocked with laughter.

She came out of the cinema at nine o'clock, ate something at a Lyons' tea-shop, went back to her bedroom, and slept.

•   •   •

Somebody was knocking at the door.

Julia called out sleepily: '*Entrez*. . . . Come in.'

The knocking went on and she shrieked, sitting up in bed: 'Come in, I said.'

A yellow-haired maid advanced one pace into the room and said in a detached manner: 'You're wanted on the telephone, miss.'

'What? . . . Yes, I'm coming, I'm coming.'

Her slippers were by the bedside. She could not see her dressing-gown. She could not remember where she had put it. It didn't matter.

Outside on the landing a gust from the open window cut through her thin pyjamas. She put up her hand to shield her chest and rushed past the maid. Her hair stood wildly up around her head. Her eyes were dark with last night's make-up, which she had been too tired to take off.

The maid thought: 'Tart.'

'Is that Mrs Martin? Miss Griffiths says, will you come as quickly as possible. Mrs Griffiths is very bad. As quickly as possible.'

'Yes,' said Julia to the telephone. 'Yes. At once. In three-quarters of an hour, say.'

As she mounted the stairs she was filled with a sort of helpless terror at the thought of the time that must elapse before she reached Acton and of the innumerable details that must fill up that time. She was thinking as she ran up the stairs: 'I'll never do it, never. Oh God, all the things I'll have to do before I'm there!'

Her legs were weak.

In seven minutes she was ready, but when she looked in the glass she thought that she had never seen herself looking quite so ugly. It would be a kind of disrespect to go like that. She took her hat off and sponged her face with cold water, powdered it, brushed her hair flat and pulled out her side-locks carefully from under her hat.

All the time she was doing this, something in her brain was saying coldly and clearly: 'Hurry, monkey, hurry. This is death. Death doesn't wait. Hurry, monkey, hurry.'

She walked along the street wondering whether she should take a taxi and ask Norah to pay for it. She was still arguing the matter to herself when she reached the Tube station. She had imagined that it was very early in the morning, but when she looked at the clock she found that it was a quarter to ten.

The girl standing next to her in the lift stared at her persistently. She grew angry and thought: 'Well, I can stare too, if it comes to that.' She narrowed her eyes and glared. The girl was short and slim. She had a round face, round brown eyes, a small nose, and a small round hat. She wore a tight-waisted coat trimmed with fur and her gloveless hands, protruding thick and red from her coat sleeves, grasped a patent-leather bag. Some fool probably thought her pretty. Some male fool-counterpart with round eyes and a little button mouth.

When she realized that Julia was staring at her she coughed, drew her lips down, and turned her back. 'Bad luck to you then,' thought Julia. 'Bad luck to you.'

The lift gates slid open. . . .

When Julia was sitting in the train she stopped thinking of the people around. She became calm.

8

DEATH

NORAH OPENED the door. She wore her green dress with the red rose sewn on the shoulder. They went along the dark passage. Julia was frightened. She was also intensely curious.

But when she saw her mother she forgot herself and began to cry from pity.

Her mother's face was white and sunken in and covered with sweat. She was fighting hard for every breath, and every breath seemed to be torture. 'She can't breathe again,' Julia thought. 'That must be the last time.'

But still she fought. A strong woman.

Norah sat on a wicker chair near the bedside. Beyond her tears and fright she was thinking: 'I did all I could. I did all I could.' She had a handkerchief in her hand and every now and then she leant forward and wiped her mother's face with a grave gesture, as if she were accomplishing a rite. Something in the poise of her body and in her serene face was old, old, old.

The blinds were half-lowered in the room. A nurse sat at the back. She was a fat blonde. Norah whispered: 'Yesterday afternoon, when nurse came, she thought it was only a matter of a few hours. And when the doctor came this morning, he said: "An hour or so."'

The nurse leaned forward and whispered rather fussily to Julia: 'You mustn't be too distressed, my dear, because your mother is not suffering. She isn't conscious. She isn't suffering at all.'

'Oh, isn't she?' said Julia. She thought: 'I must pray. It's probably no good, but somebody must try. It might be some good.'

She shut her eyes on the twilight of the room and began to mutter:

> *Eternal rest give unto her, O Lord.*
> *Let perpetual light shine upon her.*
> *May she rest in peace.*

Her lips were dry. She moistened them and went on praying. Norah was whispering: 'Would you like something to eat?'

'No.'

'Some tea? Jane's in the kitchen; she'll make you some.'

'No,' Julia whispered. 'I'm not hungry. Really.'

Norah got up and went and spoke in a low voice to the nurse. She was saying: 'Go and have something to eat — or some tea,' and the nurse was answering: 'No, my dear, no.'

That again was as if she were following a ritual, because death and eating were connected.

But after that Julia stopped praying. She could think no more than 'If she could only die. . . . If she could only die. She must be suffering.'

•   •   •

It was nearly two o'clock when the sick woman gave a groan. The nurse got up. 'Call Miss Wyatt,' she said.

And then Miss Wyatt was standing there too. Standing as if she were waiting for something to happen. Everyone stood waiting for something to happen.

The dying woman breathed three times gently, without any effort Her head dropped sideways.

'She's gone,' said the nurse. She stopped crying and her expression became professional.

'Gone.' That was the word. Norah bent down, weeping, and kissed her mother's forehead. Then she drew aside and looked at her sister. In her turn Julia bent for the ritual kiss — rather awkwardly. She thought that they were all looking at her, expecting perhaps some violent and hysterical outburst.

Miss Wyatt had her hand on Norah's shoulder. Julia trailed after them into the sitting-room, which looked very bright and cheerful. Through the glass door one could see the thin branches of a solitary tree against the cold grey sky. Her mother had said: 'I can't rest in this country. This is such a cold, grey country.'

Suddenly Julia thought: 'All the same, we have left her just when she wants us.' She got up to go back into the bedroom, but her legs felt weak.

Miss Wyatt was patting her on the shoulder. 'Cheer up, Julia,' she said.

The pretty little maid came in with tea and bread-and-butter. She also was crying, but one could see that the excitement was not altogether unpleasant to her.

The tea tasted good. Suddenly there was a feeling of rest and relaxation in the room. 'That's over. Life is sweet.'

'Just a minute,' muttered Julia. The feeling that her mother needed her urgently was too strong. It forced her out of the room.

When she turned the handle of the bedroom door the nurse's fussy voice called: 'What is it?'

'Can I came in, nurse, just for a minute?'

'No, not now. I'll call you when you can come. Not now.'

Julia went back into the sitting-room and drank some more tea. Nobody spoke. Every now and then Norah would begin to cry gently; and then she would wipe her face and blow her nose and sit motionless again, her head bent.

At about five o'clock the nurse knocked at the door and called Norah. There was a lot of whispering in the passage and then, after a while, the nurse put her head in again and called Julia. She followed the other woman into the bedroom. Contrary to what she imagined, it felt empty, and she was bewildered, as though some comfort that she had thought she would find there had failed her.

'Doesn't she look lovely?' said the nurse.

But Julia thought that her mother's sunken face, bound with white linen, looked frightening — horribly frightening, like a mask. Always masks had frightened and fascinated her.

She forced herself to stoop and kiss the dead woman.

Norah put her hand out and squeezed her sister's arm. Norah was very tired and sad, but behind her sadness was a rested feeling which made her feel gentle and pitiful to everyone, even for the moment to Julia. It was as if the hard core of her heart was melted.

When they got out of the bedroom she said very gently: 'Sure you're all right, Julia?'

'Oh, yes,' said Julia. She was all right. She was only very sleepy, horribly sleepy, as a child would be after a very exciting day.

•   •   •

Out in the street Julia thought suddenly, 'I must look ghastly.'

She stood under a lamp-post and powdered her face, and pulled her hat over her eyes. 'It seems a year since last night,' she thought.

There was a barrel-organ playing at the corner of the street, and that made her want to cry again. To its jerky tune she tried to set words:

> *Go rolling down to Rio*
> *(Roll down – roll down to Rio!)*
> *And I'd like to roll to Rio*
> *Some day before I'm old!*

All the way home she was thinking: 'If I have any luck, I oughtn't to meet anybody on the stairs. They all ought to be eating just now.'

She opened the door of her boarding-house very gently and

cautiously. On the fifth landing the door opposite her bedroom opened, and her neighbour, who was a small thin woman, with dark hair, put her head out.

'Good evening,' she said.

'Good evening,' said Julia.

'Aren't you going down to dinner?'

Julia shook her head. She was suddenly unable to speak.

'Well, won't you have some tea?' said the woman, staring at her with curiosity. 'I'm just making myself a cup.'

'No,' answered Julia. 'No, thank you.' She went quickly into her bedroom, and locked the door.

As soon as she was alone the desire to cry left her again, and she was filled with only one wish — a longing for sleep. The stupid thing was that the barrel-organ tune was still ringing in her head, and she could not quite fit the words to it:

> *Yes, weekly from Southampton,*
> *Great steamers, white and gold,*
> *Go rolling down to Rio*
> *(Roll down – roll down to Rio!)*
> *And I'd like to roll to Rio*
> *Some day before I'm old.*

9

GOLDERS GREEN

JULIA SAID: 'How much are these roses?'

'Six shillings the bunch, madam. Roses are expensive at this time of the year,' said the florist.

They were red roses, but frail and drooping, with very long, thin stalks. They would not last long.

Julia thought: 'Poor devils, poor devils, what a fate for them!' But she remembered that she had determined the day before to buy roses for her mother.

'Give me that bunch,' she said. She took her last ten-shilling note from her bag.

When she arrived in the afternoon carrying the roses, Norah was fussing about the death certificate, which she thought she had lost.

'Where is it? I know I put it down somewhere.'

'Oh, it'll turn up. Don't get in a state,' said Miss Wyatt.

Julia sat silently by the fire. She looked ill. Norah thought she had a lost expression, but Norah was too busy to think about that. She came in to ask: 'Look here, Julia, do you think we ought to have the choir?'

'No,' said Julia. 'Why?'

Norah said: 'I think she'd have liked it.'

'Oh, well, have it then, have it.'

'It's that I have so little ready money,' said Norah unhappily. 'I'm so afraid of running short.'

It was decided at last they should have the organist, but no choir. The choir was a luxury they could not afford. And then they decided that Chopin was preferable to the *Dead March In Saul*. And then Julia said she must go, that she was horribly tired, that she had not slept, that she must go home.

'Are you coming tomorrow?'

'No,' said Julia. 'At least, I'm not sure.'

'Well, you'll be here on Friday,' persisted Norah. 'Friday at nine o'clock.'

'Oh, yes, rather,' said Julia. 'Of course.'

She turned at the door to say: 'Those roses. Put them in water, will you? Not — not inside.'

•   •   •

On the Friday morning at nine o'clock, everybody was thinking: 'Why don't we start?'

'We are waiting for Julia,' Norah whispered to Uncle Griffiths at last.

'Well, I shouldn't wait an indefinite time if I were you,' he whispered back. 'Not an indefinite time.'

Norah thought miserably: 'I knew there'd be a hitch.'

Her heart was beating with nervousness. She felt that her sister's absence would be an unbearable calamity, a disgrace, the last straw. When the bell rang, she was so relieved that she forgot to be annoyed.

Julia said: 'I'm sorry; I couldn't help it.'

They went together into the sitting-room, where there were two women whom Julia did not know.

A fussy voice called: 'Ladies for the first carriage, please.' And then: 'Ladies for the second carriage.'

With solemn faces everyone trooped out of the front door to the two waiting cars.

In the first car Norah and Julia sat side by side. Miss Wyatt and Uncle Griffiths faced them. Julia sat sideways, so that her knees should not touch her uncle's knees. He gave her one disapproving, almost furtive look, then turned his head away and looked out of the window. He was spick and span, solemn and decorous, but he felt old and very melancholy that morning.

He thought how he disliked that woman and her expression, and her eyes, which said: 'Oh, for God's sake, leave me alone. I'm not troubling you; you've no right to trouble me. I've as much right as you to live, haven't I?' But you were sure that, underneath that expression, people like her were preparing the filthy abuse they would use, the dirty tricks they would try to play, if they imagined you were not leaving them alone.

◆　◆　◆

It was a mild day. The sky was the rare, hazy, and tender blue of the London sky in spring. There was such sweetness in the air that it benumbed you. It woke up in you a hope that was a stealthy pain.

Julia watched the shadows as they passed — the angular shadows of houses and the dark, slender shadows of the leafless branches, like an uneven row of dancers in the position 'Arabesque.'

She heard Uncle Griffiths saying: 'Oh, yes, these people must have the best of everything nowadays. The best meat, the best butter. . . .'

Norah was silent, looking down at her hands clasped together in her lap.

◆　◆　◆

The car stopped. Everybody walked in a short procession up to the chapel of the Crematorium, where a clergyman with very bright blue eyes was waiting. That was a dream, too, but a painful dream, because she was obsessed with the feeling that she was so close to seeing the thing that was behind all this talking and posturing, and that the talking and the posturing were there to prevent her from seeing it. Now it's time to get up; now it's time to kneel down; now it's time to stand up.

But all the time she stood, knelt, and listened she was tortured because her brain was making a huge effort to grapple with nothingness. And the effort hurt; yet it was almost successful. In another minute she would know. And then a dam inside her head burst, and she leant her head on her arms and sobbed.

The coffin slid forward in a slow and very stealthy manner. Norah watched it with eyes wide open. Her hands were clutching at the back of the pew in front of her. She glanced sideways at Uncle Griffiths. He looked frightened. Yes, there was a look of fear in his eyes. She thought: 'Poor old boy.'

The thing was going so slowly. She shut her eyes and tried to pray, but she could not. They managed it all very well, very well indeed. The word slick came into her mind. Slick.

Julia had abandoned herself. She was kneeling and sobbing and wishing she had brought another handkerchief. She was crying now because she remembered that her life had been a long succession of humiliations and mistakes and pains and ridiculous efforts. Everybody's life was like that. At the same time, in a miraculous manner, some essence of her was shooting upwards like a flame. She was great. She was a defiant flame shooting upwards not to plead but to threaten. Then the flame sank down again, useless, having reached nothing.

She sat up and blinked. Her arm had been pressed over her eyes so tightly that she could not see. Norah was not there; she had followed the parson somewhere. Uncle Griffiths had retired to the farthest end of the pew.

They were all standing on a wide portico at the back of the chapel. A wide portico. A lot of flowers. And then an open space spotted with sunlight.

When you cried like that it made you feel childish. You could be comforted quite childishly. 'Of course,' she thought, 'Heaven. Naturally. I daresay all this is a lot of fuss about nothing.'

Miss Wyatt came up and took her arm. She said: 'Come along now, Julia, come along.'

They were seated in the car. It was all over. Life was sweet and truly a pleasant thing.

Norah said: 'Are you coming back to lunch, Uncle Griffiths?'

And Uncle Griffiths answered that he didn't mind if he did.

•   •   •

During luncheon Uncle Griffiths talked about pickpockets. He told them that he had discovered, or had been informed, that the best pickpockets wore false arms which they kept ostentatiously folded over their chests while the real ones did the job. He told a long story about a pickpocket with false arms whom he had met in a lift. 'But I spotted the chap at once.'

Somebody said: 'And did he pick your pocket?'

Uncle Griffiths said: 'I didn't give him the chance.'

'Poor man!' murmured Miss Wyatt. 'After taking all that trouble. Let's hope he managed to pick somebody's.'

Everybody laughed.

The french window into the little garden was open. The room was full of sunlight subdued to a grey glare and then suddenly of shadows. 'Life is sweet and truly a pleasant thing.'

Norah sat with her shoulders bowed a little, as though both the effort and the relief were over and she faced a certain blankness.

When luncheon was over, Uncle Griffiths sat in the arm-chair and went on talking, eagerly, as if the sound of his own voice laying down the law to his audience of females reassured him. He talked and talked. He talked about life, about literature, about Dostoievsky.

He said: 'Why see the world through the eyes of an epileptic?'

Julia spoke mechanically, as one's foot shoots out when a certain nerve in the knee is struck: 'But he might see things very clearly, mightn't he? At moments.'

'Clearly?' said Uncle Griffiths. 'Why clearly? How d'you mean clearly?'

Nobody answered.

Norah said: 'Julia, will you come out here for a minute? I want to talk to you.'

.   .   .

The blinds were still drawn in the bedroom where their mother had lain, and the room was dark and cold and very empty. It smelt, faintly, of roses, and another smell, musty and rotten.

Norah said: 'I wanted to give you this.' She handed her sister a thin gold ring with a red stone in it. 'She'd have liked you to have something.'

'Oh, thank you,' said Julia. Her eyes were fixed on the bed.

Norah said in a confidential voice, averting her eyes: 'I've decided to leave London at once. I'm going to shut this place up. You know, I feel rather awful now it's all over. Wyatt's coming with me. I hope to get away the day after tomorrow. Write and tell me how you get on, won't you?'

Julia made an assenting noise. She sat huddled up. Her nose shone brightly through an inadequate coating of powder. She looked ugly and dazed.

Norah said: 'And look here; don't ever pawn that ring. If you're on the verge of pawning it, send it back to me and I'll always give you a pound for it.'

'Oh, I won't do that,' said Julia in a hostile voice.

Then she said: 'I've managed to borrow something from that man I told you about. And that's pretty lucky for me, isn't it?'

She stopped. There was nothing more to be said, but neither of them made any movement to go. Norah stood near the door. When she looked at her sister her eyes were inquisitive. They were inquisitive, and there was a yellow flicker in them.

She said: 'I'm sorry that you were so upset today, but I can understand that you feel miserable. Sorry for everything.'

Julia said: 'Sorry? But it was rage. Didn't you understand that? Don't you know the difference between sorrow and rage?'

'Rage? Why rage?' said Norah sharply.

'Oh, it doesn't matter,' muttered Julia. 'This isn't the time to talk about it, anyway.'

Her hands were very cold and she rubbed them together in her lap.

'But I think it is the time to talk about it,' persisted Norah. Then the thought came to her: 'Now then, that's enough. Stop it. Leave her alone.'

Yet she went on in a cold voice: 'How do you mean rage?'

Julia said: 'Animals are better than we are, aren't they? They're not all the time pretending and lying and sneering, like loathsome human beings.'

'You're an extraordinary creature,' said Norah. She enjoyed seeing her sister grow red and angry, and begin to talk in an incoherent voice.

Julia talked on and on, answering the yellow gleam of cruelty in Norah's eyes.

'People are such beasts, such mean beasts,' she said. 'They'll let you die for want of a decent word, and then they'll lick the feet of anybody they can get anything out of. And do you think I'm going to cringe to a lot of mean, stupid animals? If all good, respectable people had one face, I'd spit in it. I wish they all had one face so that I could spit in it.'

'You mean all that for me, I suppose,' said Norah. She spoke calmly, but she felt very giddy. Now the blood ran up to her own face. There was tingling in her finger-tips. She thought: 'She's disgusting, that's what she is. She's my sister, and she's disgusting.'

Julia said in a sullen voice: 'Mean it for you? I don't know. Perhaps I do.' She saw before her a huge, stupid face. 'Spit in it,' she thought. 'Spit in it once before I die.' She clutched her hands, and made a grimace.

Norah said: 'Perhaps if I were to start telling you my opinion of you, I'd have something to say too. After the way you've gone on.' She thought: 'Now then, hold on. Shut up.'

'You don't know anything about the way I've gone on,' said Julia. 'Not a thing. What do you know about me, or care? Not a damn thing. Listen! When I saw that you'd changed and that you looked older, as if you'd had a rotten time, I cried, d'you see? I cried about you. Have you ever cried one tear for me? You've never once looked at me as if you cared whether I lived or died. And you think I don't know why? It's because you're jealous. That's the bedrock. All you people who've knuckled under — you're jealous. D'you think I don't know? You're jealous of me, jealous, jealous. Eaten up with it.'

Norah's face went dusky-red, then white. She lifted her hand threateningly.

'Jealous,' screamed Julia. Then a horrible spasm of pity shot through her because her sister's face was so white — white, with bluish lips.

Norah opened the door, and ran along the passage, sobbing loudly. She went into the sitting-room and shut the door after her. Julia, following her, heard her talking and making sobbing explanations, and she began to shout some incoherent defence of herself through the door. 'I didn't start it. I didn't start it.'

The door of the sitting-room opened, and Uncle Griffiths appeared. He said: 'Will you stop making that noise? It's disgraceful; it's unheard of. Today of all days. You've forgotten how to behave yourself among respectable people. This,' said Uncle Griffiths with emphasis, 'is not a bad house.'

'You're an abominable old man,' said Julia.

Uncle Griffiths made a rapid and dignified movement backwards, and shut the door in her face.

She stood for a second or two outside it, listening to Norah sobbing and talking at the same time. Then she went back into the bedroom. And suddenly she was immensely calm and indifferent to anything that had ever happened or could possibly happen to her. It was like that. Just when in another moment your brain would burst, it was always like that. She sat placidly with her knees rather wide apart, and her eyes fixed calm.

She felt nothing, except that she was tired and that she wished to be left alone to rest there, quietly, in the darkened room. It seemed to her that she had been there for ever and that she always would be there, and that getting up, moving, would be impossible. But they must leave her alone, leave her alone. Then even that thought left her. She floated . . . floated. . . . And shut her eyes.

She heard someone go along the passage. The front door shut. Then, almost immediately, Miss Wyatt came in.

Miss Wyatt said in a detached voice, nodding towards the sitting-room: 'You've done a good deal of harm in there.'

Julia opened her eyes, and looked up with a stupid expression.

Miss Wyatt said: 'I don't think you'd better stay here any longer, do you? Come along now, here's your hat. You'd better go home and try to rest.'

Julia took the hat, looked at it with a surprised expression, then put it on awkwardly. She took out her powder and then returned it to her bag, obviously under the impression that she had used it. Miss Wyatt watched her with raised eyebrows. Then, as Julia still made no movement to get up, she put her hand on the other's shoulder and repeated firmly: 'Come along now, you must go. I can't have Norah upset any more. She's been through enough.'

'But I've been through something too,' said Julia in a sad, quiet voice. 'Don't you believe otherwise.'

'I daresay,' agreed Miss Wyatt. 'You can write to Norah if you've anything more to say, but you really must not stay here now.'

Julia got up. 'Oh, you needn't worry,' she said. 'I shall never bother any of you any more after this. Really.'

She walked towards the front door with a rather grotesque attempt at dignity. Then she stopped again.

'Come along now,' said Miss Wyatt soothingly but with finality. She put her hand on Julia's shoulder, gave her a very slight push, and shut the door on her gently.

◆　◆　◆

Norah was sitting up on the sofa. She said, 'Where's Julia?'

'She's gone home,' answered Miss Wyatt. 'Much better for her.'

'Oh, no,' said Norah in a hysterical voice. 'We can't send her away like that. I don't believe she's got any money.'

'My dear,' said Miss Wyatt, 'just you lie down and keep yourself still. Your sister's going to write.'

'Oh,' said Norah.

'Of course,' said Miss Wyatt with contempt. 'She'll write.'

Norah lay back, with her eyes shut. She thought: 'My God, how hard I've got!' Her lips trembled. 'What's happened to me?' For a moment she was afraid of herself.

Presently she heard from the kitchen the rattling noise of teacups in saucers. A feeling of rest crept from her knees upwards to her eyes. The clock ticked: 'You're young yet — young yet — young yet.'

Coming out of the chemist's shop at the end of the street Uncle Griffiths saw Julia approaching. As she walked she jerked herself from side to side, in the manner of a woman who is tired and no longer young walking on very high heels. People turned round to look at her.

Uncle Griffiths thought: 'Now what'll become of her, I wonder?' And, with decision, he crossed over to the other side of the street.

10

NOTTING HILL

AS SHE walked, Julia felt peaceful and purified, as though she were a child. Because she could not imagine a future, time stood still. And, as if she were a child, everything that she saw was of profound interest and had the power to distract and please her. She looked into the faces of the people passing, not suspiciously or timidly, as was usual with her, but with a gentle and confident expression.

She went into the Tube station at the end of the road and took a ticket to Notting Hill Gate. As she sat waiting, a man hurried on to the platform, looked to the right and the left for a train, and then sat down heavily by her side. He was short and fat, dressed neatly in a grey suit, a dark overcoat, and a grey felt hat. He said, leaning towards Julia: 'Can you tell me, madam, if this platform is right for Oxford Circus?'

'Yes,' said Julia, 'I think so.'

'I'm a stranger here,' said the man. 'I don't know my way about very well.'

When the train came in he followed her into a carriage which was nearly empty. There were two men with their eyes fixed upon their newspapers, and a woman with a large attaché case who, when she saw that Julia was looking at her, drew down her lips with a prim and furtive expression.

The fat man, who had seated himself next to Julia, was saying: 'It's a bit lonely here for a stranger.'

He glanced at her sideways as he spoke.

'Are you a Londoner?'

'No,' said Julia.

'Ah,' he said, 'I thought not. I thought you looked a bit as if you were a stranger too.'

He went on talking. He said he was from South Africa, that he had spent most of his holiday in Berlin, but that he had thought he wanted to have a look at London too before he went back. Then, as if intoxicated by this long monologue about himself, he ended with, 'Would you care to have dinner with me tonight?'

'No,' Julia said. 'I can't.'

'Tomorrow, then?'

She shook her head.

The man said, 'Will you write or telephone me at this address? I shall be here for another couple of weeks.'

He gave her a card, on which were his name and the address of a club. Without looking at it, Julia let it drop into her lap, and said, 'Yes,' smiling mechanically, and: 'Yes, of course. Yes.'

When the train stopped at Notting Hill Gate station she got up quickly, and the card fell from her lap on to the floor. The man stared after her, and reddened. Then he looked hastily about him. No one was watching. He picked the card up, brushed it, and put it back into his pocket, crossed his legs, and composed his countenance.

◆　　◆　　◆

Julia turned the key in her door and sat down on the bed with her hands on her knees, staring in front of her with a rather puzzled expression. Then she sighed, took off her hat, and lay down, smoothing the hair away from her forehead with a regular and mechanical gesture. She was horribly tired, and it was good to lie down. But her finger-tips tingled and the muscles at the back of her neck were tight. Her thoughts were confused and blurred. She was certain that if a stranger were suddenly to appear before her and ask in a sharp voice: 'What's your name?' she would not know what to answer.

At about seven o'clock the yellow-haired maid brought up a letter:

Dear Madam Martin,
I am so sorry, but I must postpone our dinner tonight. I have a very urgent business appointment which simply has to be kept. Please forgive me. And I do hope we shall meet again before you go back to Paris.
With kindest regards,
Yours sincerely,
George Horsfield.

When Julia opened her eyes again it was dark. The idea of staying alone in the dark room was horrible to her, and as she dressed she twice looked suddenly and fearfully over her shoulder.

•   •   •

The street was a dark tunnel between the high walls of the houses. Down at the far end she saw a man walking very quickly, moving his arms as he walked like a tall, thin bird flapping its wings. They drew level under a lamp-post.

'I'm awfully glad I caught you,' said Mr Horsfield in a rather embarrassed voice. 'You see, I managed to scratch my appointment after all.'

Then he said: 'I felt I had to come. I wanted to see you.'

'I'm glad,' said Julia, but without surprise. 'I didn't want to be alone this evening.'

'Good,' said Mr Horsfield heartily. 'And you can dine with me?'

She looked surprised at the question and nodded.

As they walked along side by side, Mr Horsfield felt that her simplicity was touching.

He said: 'D'you like the place we went to the other night? Shall we go back there?'

She muttered: 'I'm tired, too tired to go far. It must be somewhere quite near.'

'I don't know a decent place round here,' said Mr Horsfield.

'It doesn't matter,' she answered. 'Anywhere will do — anywhere near.'

'What is it? Is anything the matter?' Mr Horsfield inquired.

She wanted to laugh and say: 'You don't suppose I'm mad, do you? To tell you what's the matter. You'd simply make some excuse to go off and leave me if I told you what was really the matter.' As if at this time of day she did not know that when you were in trouble the only possible thing to do was to hide it as long as you could.

She said: 'Why, no. Nothing's the matter.'

'Well, there's an Italian place not far off. Shall we try it?'

.   .   .

The restaurant was long and narrow. Red-shaded lamps stood on the tables, and the walls were decorated with paintings of dead lobsters and birds served up on plates ready to be eaten, with flowers and piles of fruit in gilt baskets.

When Julia and Mr Horsfield came in the atmosphere in the restaurant was tense. A row was going on. One of the customers was bawling at the waiter that the soup was muck, and the other diners were listening with shocked but rather smirking expressions, like good little boys who were going to hear the bad little boy told off. The complainant, who must have been sensitive and have felt the universal disapproval, put up his hand to shield a face that grew redder and redder. However, he bawled again: 'Take it away. I won't eat it. It's not mulligatawny, it's muck.'

Mr Horsfield said: 'Let's have a gin-and-vermouth and go somewhere else.'

'No,' said Julia. 'Why? It's quite all right here.'

The rebellious gentleman was handed a bill and walked out, his face crimson, but still stubborn. The waiter said loudly to his back: 'Some people don't know how to behave themselves in a good-class restaurant.' And a very thin woman, dressed in black, who was sitting at the cash desk, echoed him in a thin, mincing voice: 'Some people aren't used to a good-class restaurant.'

The door swung violently behind the back of the rebellious gentleman and immediately an atmosphere of restraint, decorum, and perfect gentility reigned in the restaurant. Even the fat Italian seated opposite to Mr Horsfield was affected by it. He began to pick his teeth with a worried expression, shielding the toothpick with one hand.

All through the meal Mr Horsfield talked without thinking of what he was saying. He was full of an absurd feeling of expectancy.

He noticed that Julia appeared fatigued, as if she had been crying. Yet he thought, too, that her face was thinner and somehow more youthful than when he had last seen her. Her eyes had a vague expression when she looked at him, as though she did not see him.

.

Outside a fine rain was falling. The darkness was greasy in spite of the rain. A woman in a long macintosh passed them, muttering to herself and looking mournful and lost, like a dog without a master.

Julia said: 'What's that over there? That red light with "Dancing"? Let's go there.'

．　　　．　　　．

They went up a narrow flight of stairs into a large room where about a dozen people were sitting at small tables and drinking lemonade or coffee. A gramophone was playing *Hallelujah*, and two couples were dancing in a square space in the middle of the room. The girls were young and pretty. Of the two men, one was young, with sleek hair and a self-satisfied expression. The other male dancer was elderly, nearer seventy than sixty, thin, dressed in a very loosely fitting grey suit. His face was cadaverous, his nose long and drooping. He smiled continually as he danced, displaying very yellow teeth.

Mr Horsfield looked round at this scene and sighed. He felt a slight astonishment. He had never before encountered a place like this in London. It was more to be expected in the provinces or in a very distant suburb.

He said to the hovering waiter: 'Two coffees, please.'

Julia was looking at the old man dancing with an absorbed expression. Mr Horsfield said: 'Will you have coffee?'

Julie shook her head and answered, without moving her eyes: 'No, thanks, a *fine* — a brandy.'

'I'm afraid it's too late,' he explained. 'But, you know, I think we'd be in time for a drink at the Café Royal.'

'But it's all right here, isn't it?'

The gramophone stopped. A woman appeared from a room at the back, and put another record on. The old gentleman and another man in plus fours began to dance again with different partners. Mr Horsfield perceived that the feeling of mellowness and good-nature induced by the Chianti at dinner was deserting him.

After a time he said to Julia: 'Don't you think it's a bit lugubrious here?'

He felt that he disliked the place and he was irritated by the monosyllabic answers Julia made whenever he spoke to her. It was as if she were hardly listening to what he was saying. He thought that she looked at the dancers as if she had never seen anybody dancing before.

．

When they had been sitting for about half an hour and he was about to say: 'Look here, do you mind going and trying somewhere else?' he saw that the old gentleman was approaching their table. He walked mincingly, on the tips of his toes.

'May I have the pleasure?' he said to Julia.

As he leaned over the table his face was all bones and hollows in the light of the lamp striking upwards, like a skeleton's face.

'Wonderful old chap!' thought Mr Horsfield. He looked across at Julia. Her eyes had a surprised, even horror-stricken expression.

'Yes, I'd like to,' she said in a breathless voice.

She got up. Her manner was constrained, full of an unnecessary bravado.

'She really is a bit odd,' thought Mr Horsfield. But he felt irritated and depressed. He would not let himself look at the dancers for a time.

When he did so, Julia was being hugged very tightly by her partner, who hung a little over her shoulder, pervading her, as it were, and smiling. How idiotic all this dancing was, idiotic and rather sinister!

Her body looked abandoned when she danced, but not voluptuously so. It was the abandonment of fatigue.

Mr Horsfield lowered his eyes moodily, so that as Julia and her partner passed his table he saw only her legs, appearing rather too plump in flesh-coloured stockings. She seemed to him to be moving stiffly and rather jerkily. It was like watching a clockwork toy that has nearly run down.

'I congratulate you on your partner, sir. I congratulate you on your partner,' the old fool was saying. Then he hung about talking, obviously waiting for the gramophone to start again.

Mr Horsfield smiled unwillingly, and said something polite. then he said he wanted to get some cigarettes and left the room as they began to dance again. It took him some time to find an automatic machine.

When he got back to the place the red light outside the door was out. He looked at his watch. It was five minutes to twelve. He mounted the stairs very quickly.

Julia was sitting alone at the table. He raised his eyebrows and said in an ironical way: 'Well?'

She laughed so hysterically that he was taken aback, and glanced round rather nervously. The man in plus fours, who was staring at them, said something with a sneering expression on his face. 'The tick!' thought Mr Horsfield, staring coldly back. He signalled to the waiter.

'Come along, this place will be shutting now, I expect,' he said to Julia.

•   •   •

In the taxi she leaned her head back, and shut her eyes. He thought that he had never seen anyone stay so perfectly still.

When they stopped at her boarding-house, he put his hand on hers and said: 'Here we are.'

They got out, and he paid the driver.

'Good night,' said Mr Horsfield mechanically.

'No,' she whispered.

He stared at her.

She said: 'You mustn't leave me. Don't leave me. You must stay with me. Please.'

He thought: 'I knew she'd do this.'

Then he said in a slow voice: 'Of course I will, if you want me to.'

//

IT MIGHT
HAVE BEEN ANYWHERE

SHE MOUNTED the steps without a word, and put her latch-key into the door.

'But if anybody sees you?' she asked.

Her voice sounded as if she were shivering. He thought: 'Well, you'll get turned out, my girl, that's a sure thing.' He said: 'It looks to me as if everybody in here has gone to bed long ago. I can walk without making any noise. Nobody will hear me, I promise you. Do the stairs creak?'

'The top flight does a little,' she said. 'Not the others. My room's right at the top.'

'All right,' he said. 'I'll be careful. I can walk pretty quietly.'

He put his hand on her arm, and felt that she was shivering. This added to his sensation of excitement and triumph.

'Come along,' he said.

He turned the key and walked first into the house.

When the door shut behind them they were in darkness and silence.

They reached the staircase. He put his hand on the banisters, and mounted noiselessly after her. She was invisible in the darkness, but he followed the sound of her footsteps, placing his feet very carefully, so that they made no sound.

The stairs were solid; there was not a creak.

They mounted silently, like people in a dream. And as in a dream he knew that the whole house was solid, with huge rooms — dark, square rooms, crammed with unwieldy furniture covered with chintz; darkish curtains would hang over the long windows. He knew even the look of the street outside when the curtains were drawn apart — a grey street, with high, dark houses opposite.

On the landing of the fourth floor Julia stopped for a moment and listened. Then they went together up the last flight of wooden stairs.

There were three doors on the landing. She opened one of them very cautiously, switched on a light, and turned the key on the inside when he had passed her.

It was a large room, sparsely furnished. Mr Horsfield walked over to the window, which looked out on to the common garden at the back shared by all the houses on that side of the street. A square of blackness. He saw the bare branches of a tree, like fine lace, against the blackness. He heard the throb and far-off, calling whistle of a train. He thought: 'That must be the Great Western.'

A little playful wind lifted the curtains.

'Do shut the window,' she said. 'It's cold.'

He shut the window and pulled the curtains across it, then turned back into the room. He tried to do this without making any noise at all.

'I've only got one neighbour,' she said. 'She's asleep. Listen. . . . And there's a bathroom. That's all.'

She sighed very deeply, bent down, and lighted the gas fire.

'Sit there, I'll have this cushion.'

She leaned her head back, and said: 'I'm so tired, so tired.'

He stretched out his hand to touch her hair, and then drew it back because something sensitive in him was puzzled and vaguely unhappy.

He said: 'Well, your partner was a good show, don't you think?'

'No,' she said. 'No, I thought him horrible, horrible.'

'Then why did you dance with him?'

'Sometimes one has to do things, haven't you ever felt that?

You're very lucky, then. But if you haven't felt it, it's no use talking. Because you won't believe.'

'Don't you be so sure,' he said, 'about what I've felt and what I haven't felt.'

She said: 'D'you know what I think? I think people do what they have to do, and then the time comes when they can't any more, and they crack up. And that's that.'

'Yes,' he said, 'and perhaps I know something about cracking up too. I went through the war, you know.'

'I was twenty when the war started,' she told him. 'I rather liked the air raids.'

He began to stroke her hair mechanically. He pushed it upwards from the nape of her neck. He had imagined that her hair would be harsh to the touch, because he was certain that she dyed it, and dyed hair was always harsh to the touch. But in pushing it upwards it felt soft and warm, like the feathers of a very small bird. He stroked it first with the palm of his hand, and then with the back, and felt an extraordinary pleasure.

She said: 'You're awfully good to me.'

'You mustn't say that,' said Mr Horsfield, pulling his hand away abruptly. 'I absolutely forbid you to say that. I mean, it's the most fearful rot to say it.'

She said: 'No, you're good and kind and dear to me.'

He leaned forward and stared at her, and she looked back to him in a heavy, bewildered, sleepy way.

'She asked me up here,' he thought. 'She asked me.'

When he kissed her, her body was soft and unresisting.

There was a subdued rumble of trains in the distance. He thought again: 'The Great Western.'

You are thirsty, dried up with thirst, and yet you don't know it until somebody holds up water to your mouth and says: 'You're thirsty, drink.' It's like that. You are thirsty, and you drink.

And then you wonder all sorts of things, discontentedly and disconnectedly.

'But the worst of it is,' he thought, 'that one can never know what the woman is really feeling.'

．　　　．　　　．

He moved cautiously, and at once she opened her eyes.

'What is it?' she asked. 'You aren't going? You promised to stay with me.'

He was astonished at the sharpness in her voice. He said: 'My dear, of course. I'll lie on these two cushions by the side of your bed. I just thought you'd sleep better like that.'

He got the cushions and lay down, wondering what the time was. He thought: 'I wonder if they get up early here.'

Her arm was hanging down by the side of the bed. It looked pathetic, like a child's arm. He said: 'Julia, your hand is so lovely it makes me want to cry.'

'Oh,' she said, 'I was awfully pretty when I was a kid. Really I was, *sans blague*.'

'Don't talk like that,' said Mr Horsfield in a gruff voice. 'Of course you're pretty now.'

She sighed and turned over. Neither of them spoke again, and the next time he looked at her she seemed to be sleeping. He lit a cigarette and smoked it very slowly. Then he looked at her again with a rather stealthy expression, got up, and tiptoed to the window and pulled the curtains aside.

He looked out. A freshness came up from the garden. It was light enough to see the leaning trees and the bare brown patches of earth trodden by the feet of children playing. He thought: 'It's getting light. I must clear out.'

He looked at his watch. It was five o'clock. Again he gave a cautious glance at the bed. Then he tore a leaf out of his note-book and wrote:

Dear,

It's morning. So I'm going, or I'll risk meeting somebody on the stairs. I don't want to wake you. You might not get off to sleep again, and you look tired. I kiss your lovely hands and your lovely dark eyelids (what is the stuff you put on them?).

He stopped, frowned, pressed his lips together and tapped the pencil against his finger-nail. Then he went on writing:

I'll be here about six tomorrow evening or earlier if I can manage it. You are adorable.

> *Good-bye,*
> *G.H.*

He folded the sheet, addressed it, and put the note on the mantelpiece in a prominent position.

Every moment his desire to get out of the room was growing

stronger. He tiptoed to the door, carrying his shoes in his hand, opened and shut it with infinite precaution, and crept down the still-dark stairs as silently as he could.

In the dimness of the hall a white face glimmered at him. He started, and braced himself for an encounter. Then, relieved, he saw a bust of the Duke of Wellington. He put his shoes on hastily and fumbled his way to the front-door.

• • •

When the door closed behind him he felt an extraordinary relief. At once the whole affair took on a normal and slightly humorous aspect. He smiled as he bent down to tie his shoelaces.

When he lifted his head he saw a policeman, who was standing on the pavement a few paces away, staring disapprovingly at him. The policeman stood with his legs very wide apart and his mouth pursed, looking extremely suspicious.

'This is grotesque,' muttered Mr Horsfield. He did not know whether he meant the policeman, or his excess of caution, or the Duke of Wellington, or the night he had just spent.

The two men stared at each other for a few seconds. Then Mr Horsfield said: 'Good morning, constable.'

'Perhaps I ought to have said sergeant,' flashed across his mind, for at the moment he was in dread of the policeman.

The policeman did not answer, but he slowly turned his head as Mr Horsfield passed and watched him as he walked quickly along the street in the direction of Ladbroke Grove.

CHILDHOOD

EVERY DAY is a new day. Every day you are a new person.

Julia felt well and rested, not unhappy, but her mind was strangely empty. It was an empty room, through which vague memories stalked like giants.

She read Mr Horsfield's note, and it was as if she were reading something written by a stranger to someone she had never seen.

She lay down stiff and straight on her back, with her arms close to her side. Every day is a new day; every day you are a new person. What have you to do with the day before?

There was a sharp rap at the door and she started violently. Her heart jumped in her side and hurt her.

The maid came in without waiting for an answer to her knock and asked: 'Have you finished with the breakfast tray?'

Keeping her eyes shut, Julia said: 'Yes, I've quite finished.'

'I'm supposed to get the bedrooms done by twelve,' said the girl.

'Will you leave mine this morning?' said Julia. 'I'll do it myself.' She would have liked to put her head under the sheets to escape from the girl's cold, pale blue stare. Or to get up and push her out of the room and curse her and bang the door after her.

'Well, I'm supposed to get the rooms done in the morning,' the girl repeated in a monotonous voice as she went out.

Julia leant over, took a small glass from the dressing-table and looked at herself. She looked at her hand, too, with the unaccustomed ring on it. It was rather tight, because her mother's hand had been so small and slim.

She wondered why the maid had looked at her with such unfriendly eyes. But hadn't she always suspected, ever since she knew anything, that human beings were — for no reason or for any reason — unfriendly?

When you were a child, you put your hand on the trunk of a tree and you were comforted, because you knew that the tree was alive — you felt its life when you touched it — and you knew that it was friendly to you, or, at least, not hostile. But of people you were always a little afraid.

When you are a child you are yourself and you know and see everything prophetically. And then suddenly something happens and you stop being yourself; you become what others force you to be. You lose your wisdom and your soul.

How far back could you remember?

The last time you were really happy — happy about nothing? When you were happy about nothing you had to jump up and down. 'Can't you keep still, child, for one moment?' No, of course you couldn't keep still. You were too happy, bursting with happiness. You ran as if you were flying, without feeling your feet. And all the time you ran, you were thinking, with a tight feeling in your throat: 'I'm happy — happy — happy. . . .'

That was the last time you were really happy about nothing, and you remembered it perfectly well. How old were you? Ten?

Eleven? Younger . . . yes, probably younger.

And you could remember the first time you were afraid.

You were walking along a long path, shadowed for some distance by trees. But at the end of the path was an open space and the glare of white sunlight. You were catching butterflies. You caught them by waiting until they settled, and then creeping up silently on tiptoe and squatting near them. Then, when they closed their wings, looking like a one-petalled flower, you grabbed them quickly, taking hold low down or the wings would break in your hand.

When you had caught the butterfly you put it away in an empty tobacco tin, which you had ready. And then you walked along, holding the tin to your ear and listening to the sound of the beating of wings against it. It was a very fascinating sound. You wouldn't have thought a butterfly could make such a row.

Besides, it was a fine thing to get your hand on something that a minute before had been flying around in the sun. Of course, what always happened was that it broke its wings; or else it would fray them so badly that by the time you had got it home and opened the box and hauled it out as carefully as you could it was so battered that you lost all interest in it. Sometimes it was too badly hurt to be able to fly properly.

'You're a cruel, horrid child, and I'm surprised at you.'

And, of course, you simply did not answer this. Because you knew that what you had hoped had been to keep the butterfly in a comfortable cardboard-box and to give it the things it liked to eat. And if the idiot broke its own wings, that wasn't your fault, and the only thing to do was to chuck it away and try again. If people didn't understand that, you couldn't help it.

That was the first time you were afraid of nothing — that day when you were catching butterflies — when you had reached the patch of sunlight. You were not afraid in the shadow, but you were afraid in the sun.

The sunlight was still, desolate, and arid. And you knew that something huge was just behind you. You ran. You fell and cut your knee. You got up and ran again, panting, your heart thumping, much too frightened to cry.

But when you got home you cried. You cried for a long time; and you never told anybody why.

The last time you were happy about nothing; the first time you were afraid about nothing. Which came first?

• • •

'What have you done all day?' said Mr Horsfield at dinner.

'Nothing. I just stayed in my room.'

Mr Horsfield said, shocked: 'What? Didn't you have anything to eat? Well, eat now, for goodness' sake.'

'At about four o'clock,' she said, 'I went in next door and the woman there gave me a cup of tea.'

'Do you mean the one that was snoring?'

'Yes.'

'Why ever did you go in there?'

'I don't know. I didn't want to be alone, I suppose.'

'Haven't you been doing anything? Have you been just lying there and thinking?'

She made no answer.

He asked, with a certain curiosity: 'What do you think about, Julia?'

She said: 'All the time about when I was a kid.'

'It's the easiest thing in the world to imagine you a kid.' Mr Horsfield felt sentimental about her. And then he wanted to laugh at himself because he was feeling sentimental.

She said she wanted to go to a cinema. She did not like plays; she had got out of the way of plays. They seemed unreal.

• • •

In the taxi he said to her: 'Do you know what you've done for me, Julia? You've given me back my youth. That's a big thing to do for anybody, isn't it?'

He went on: 'Look here, I can't take you back to my house tonight, because I've got a friend staying there. And a hotel would be perfectly foul. Do you mind if I come up to your room again?'

'Oh, no, I don't mind,' she said. 'I don't mind at all. Why should I mind?'

13

THE STAIRCASE

'YOU GO first, and I'll follow you, like last night.'

He heard a rustling sound, the noise of Julia's dress, which was of stiff silk.

On the third landing she stopped. He knew it, because he could not hear the sound of her dress any longer. He heard her breathing loudly, as though she were exhausted. After a few seconds he whispered: 'Julia.'

She did not answer.

'Oh Lord,' he thought, 'What's the matter now?'

He waited a little longer, wondering whether he ought to strike a match, then walked carefully forwards, and passed her, groping for the banisters. His foot struck the first stair of the next flight, and he was convinced that he made a very loud noise; yet somehow he did not wish to strike a match or speak again.

He groped and touched her hand, then her arm, and the fur collar of her coat. Then he ran his fingers downwards again, as a blind man might have done. He felt a strange pleasure in touching her like that — wordlessly, in the dark.

She said in a loud voice: 'Oh God, who touched me?'

He was too much astonished to answer.

'Who touched me?' she screamed. 'Who's that? Who touched my hand? What's that?'

'Julia!' he said.

But she went on screaming loudly: 'Who's that? Who's that? Who touched my hand?'

'Well,' thought Mr Horsfield, 'that's torn it.' He wondered if he would have time to bolt; dismissed the idea. There must be an electric switch somewhere.

He got his hand on to the wall, and began to feel for it. Matches. . . .

He said: 'Julia, my dear . . .'

Then the lights on the landing went on, and two bedroom doors opened simultaneously. Out of one appeared a dark young man with tousled hair, wearing striped pyjamas. He gave one look; then, without a word or a change of expression, he went back into his room and slammed the door. Out of the second door emerged a lady in a pink dressing-gown, with her hair hidden by a slumber-net. She was a young and good-looking woman, and she advanced upon Mr Horsfield with an air of authority. She was certainly the lady of the house.

'I'm frightfully sorry,' he said. His lips stretched themselves of their own accord into a conventional and very apologetic smile. 'Madame Martin isn't very well.'

The lady stared at Julia. In spite of himself, Mr Horsfield also turned and stared at Julia as though he had never seen her before. She made a movement of her mouth which was like a grimace. Then she said: 'I'm sorry. I'm not well. The stairs are so dark. I thought somebody touched me and I was frightened. I'm sorry if I disturbed you.'

The lady advanced two steps. Something in the way she walked and the poise of her head reminded Mr Horsfield of a cat advancing upon a mouse. She said in a soft, smooth voice: 'Well, I'm sorry you're ill, Mrs Martin. But you need not be frightened, you know. There are no dark corners in my house. I don't allow dark corners in my house.'

'Oh, nonsense,' said Mr Horsfield. 'Your stairs are dark enough, anyhow.' He added, in rather a high voice: 'After all, it's only just after twelve.'

Someone called up from the floor below: 'What's the matter, Mrs Atherton?'

'Nothing,' said the lady, peering over the banisters, 'nothing at all.'

A feeling which was a reaction against her pleasant voice, her pink dressing-gown, and the net over her hair swept over Mr Horsfield. He put his arm round Julia, and said: 'Come along, my dear.'

He knew that he looked a fool, but he did not care.

'Who was it touched me?' said Julia. Her eyes were very wide open, the pupils dwindled to pin-points.

'But, my dear,' he said, 'I touched you.'

She shook her head.

'You were behind me.'

'Yes, but I passed you on the landing.'

'I thought it was — someone dead,' she muttered, 'catching hold of my hand.'

'Oh, Julia, my dear, look here, you're sick. Let me help you.'

The strangest understandings, the wildest plans, lit up his brain — together with an overwhelming contempt for the organization of society. Someone knocked at the door. Mrs Atherton, still wearing her pink dressing-gown but without the slumber-net, was there. She said: 'I came to see if there is anything I can do.'

'No, thank you,' said Julia. 'Nothing.'

'Ah,' said Mrs Atherton. She gazed at some point beyond both Julia and Mr Horsfield, looking utterly sure of herself.

'Are you all right?' said Mr Horsfield in an undecided voice.

Mrs Atherton waited.

'Damn and blast this landlady,' thought Mr Horsfield. He was opening his mouth to say: 'Look here, get out,' when Julia said; 'Good night.'

He looked at her.

'I'm all right,' she said.

Her eyes were cold and hostile. 'As if she hates me,' he thought.

He knew that she wanted nothing but to be left alone and to sleep.

She was very tired, her muscles were relaxed, her eyes half shut. She was thinking: 'Nothing matters. Nothing can be worse than how I feel now, nothing.' It was like a clock ticking in her head, 'Nothing matters, nothing matters. . . .'

'Good night,' she said again, in a cold withdrawn voice.

Mr Horsfield still hesitated.

'I'll call at ten o'clock tomorrow morning,' he said.

Mrs Atherton was still waiting. When he went out she followed him, without having once looked directly at Julia.

*　　*　　*

Mr Horsfield decided that he would walk home. He would try to walk off this feeling of rage and disappointment.

As he walked he began to plan what he would do the next morning. He imagined himself going into Julia's bedroom and talking, telling everything that was in his heart. He would hold her two hands and take her close to the window and say: 'Don't look at me like that. That was how you looked at me last night. Why should you look at me suspiciously, as if I were one of the others: I'm not one of the others; I'm on your side. Can't you see that? I'm for you and for people like you, and I'm against the others. Can't you see that?' he would say.

'I hate things as much as you do,' he would say. 'I'm just as fed up as you are. You hate hotly like a child because you've been hurt. But I hate coldly, and that's worse. I'm ready to chuck up everything and clear out. Lots of us are like that. Just the touch is wanted — something to set us off. You, and what happened last night, have done that for me.'

He stopped elaborating his speech to Julia. He thought: 'Anyhow I must clear out — get away. A succession of uncongenial tasks — that's what my life is. I'll chuck everything — sell the business for what it will fetch, get something out of life before I'm too old to feel. Get a bit of sun anyway.'

The sun. Oh, God, this stuffy, snuffy life! A white house with green blinds. . . .

He turned into the narrow street in which he lived. It was cobble-stoned and silent. There was a wall at the end, overhung by four stark trees.

His cat, waiting in his gateway, galloped to meet him as a dog might have done. It gave a soft, purring cry. Mr Horsfield bent down to stroke it, saying, 'Pretty Jones.'

The cat arched its back and purred again. In the light of the street-lamps its eyes shone, yellow-green, rather malevolent.

'Well, come on in then,' said Mr Horsfield. 'Come on in. And do get out of my way.'

There was nobody in the sitting-room. He got himself a whisky and soda and sat down. He realized that he was very tired.

Two walls of the room were covered with books almost from the ceiling to the floor. It was a low-pitched room, and there was only one small window. Nevertheless, it had a pleasant and peaceful, even spacious, appearance.

He thought: 'I don't see how I can bring her here exactly. . . . I can't possibly bring her here.'

Suddenly he saw Julia not as a representative of the insulted and injured, but as a solid human being. She must be taken somewhere — not later than the next morning. She must have a bed to sleep in, food, clothes, companionship — or she would be lonely; under-standing of her own peculiar point of view — or she would be aggrieved.

He saw all this with great clarity, and felt appalled.

But he must find a room for her. He would have to. In Paddington or obscurer Bloomsbury.

Undertaking a fresh responsibility was not the way to escape when you came to think of it. . . .

He suddenly remembered that, after all, he was not in love with Julia; and he thought, 'I am not going to be rushed into anything.'

14

DEPARTURE

JULIA WAS packing her trunk when Mr Horsfield arrived the next morning. He asked whether the landlady had told her to go.

'She told me that a woman who always stays here had written to ask when the room would be vacant. Would I prefer to leave this morning or this afternoon? So I said this morning.'

'Don't worry,' he said. 'Don't worry. I'll find a place for you.'

But he was shocked to see how old she looked. She had made herself up badly; that must be it. A faint revulsion mingled with his feeling of disappointment. He could not help thinking: 'Oh Lord, where is this going to lead me? Where is this going to stop?'

Then she said: 'I'm going back to Paris.' And he felt relieved. He said in a perfunctory voice: 'But why? Why not stay here?'

She looked at him, and then looked away again quickly.

'I'll be able to manage better there, I think.'

'I see.' He was suddenly light-hearted, irresponsible, almost happy.

He began to think about money, and that he must raise something. He must give her all he could. He wondered how his balance stood at the bank.

He said: 'Look here, I'll come over soon and see you.'

'Yes, of course.' She stared at him, not sadly, but with a heavy, dead indifference.

She knelt down by her trunk and locked it. Then, still kneeling, she looked up and said: 'All right. Everything's ready.'

He felt a pain, deep down. Like the pain of a loss.

'Your bill?' he said.

'I've paid it. Everything's ready; everything's done. If you'll just call a taxi.'

She stood at the glass straightening her hat. Her face looked hard and sullen. She made an involuntary little grimace at herself and again Mr Horsfield felt that tugging pain, as of a disappointed child.

'Come on,' she said impatiently. 'You'll have to help with the trunk, for I don't believe the servants here will do it.'

She looked at him with an air of bravado, raising her shoulders slightly, and he said, without meaning to say it: 'You've got some pluck.'

As he went downstairs to find the taxi, he thought: 'It isn't the first time she's been turned out of a room, that's clear.'

.   .   .

Everything that he had imagined the night before seemed fantastic — fantastic as a fairy tale. Yet he still kept on thinking out plans, worrying over details. 'How would I do it if I were going to do it?'

He said: 'What about letters? Would you like to have letters forwarded to my address?'

Julia answered that the letter she was expecting had been sent to her that morning by messenger and that she did not think there would be any more.

He said, hesitatingly: 'About money. . . .'

She took an envelope out of her bag and handed it to him. 'Read that.'

The letter was written in a large, clear handwriting, rather like a boy's.

Dear Julietta,

I ought to have sent this before. I didn't forget, but I mislaid that address you gave me. I've thought a good deal over what you said to me and I am very sorry that things haven't gone well with you. I am sending you some money because I want you to have a rest and a holiday, but I am afraid that after this I can do no more.

Mr Horsfield did not know what to say; he wondered what he could say. So much depended on the amount Julia's friend had sent.

'He sent twenty quid,' she said in a matter-of-fact voice. 'So, you see, I'm quite all right. I don't want any more money.'

'Well, twenty quid won't last for ever.'

'He collects pictures, this man. I suppose he must have been always fond of pictures, but I didn't know that. I didn't know anything about him, really. You see, he never used to talk to me much. I was for sleeping with — not for talking to. And quite right, too, I suppose. My God, isn't life funny, though?'

She began to laugh.

'Of course, I didn't think about it like that at the time. It never dawned on me. He was a sort of god to me and everything he did was right. Isn't one a fool when one's a kid? But sometimes I used to pray that he'd lose all his money, because I imagined that if that happened I'd see him oftener. And then I'd imagine myself working for him, or somehow getting money to give him. He'd have thanked me if he'd known what I was praying for, wouldn't he?'

'Oh, I daresay he'd have felt flattered,' said Mr Horsfield.

The bottle of wine was empty; Julia had drunk most of it. He called the waiter and ordered another.

She said: 'Oh, but that was nothing to a girl I knew, who used to pray that the man she loved might go blind.'

'Good God, that was surely a bit excessive, wasn't it?'

'Yes; so that he might be entirely dependent on her, d'you see? She loved him awfully and he made her jealous. But I didn't pray that. Oh, no, I couldn't have prayed that. . . . But I did pray about the money. It's pretty funny, isn't it?' "After this I can do no more." "Good-bye-ee. Don't cry-ee." Do you remember that?' she said.

'Yes, I remember.'

He was thinking: 'It's so easy, isn't it, to be as bloody to you as everybody else has been?'

He said: 'Look here, in a week or ten days I'll come over to see you. Or, if I can't manage that, I'll send you some money.'

His voice was cold, but he could not help it. He could not put any warmth into it.

Her face grew very red. He averted his eyes.

'I don't care whether you send me any money or not,' she said. 'And I don't care whether you come or not. Now then!'

A muscle under her left eye was twitching.

'If you think,' she said, 'that I care. . . . I can always get somebody, you see. I've known that ever since I've known anything.'

'I daresay,' said Mr Horsfield. He felt horrified by the loudness of her voice. He was sure that the people in the restaurant were beginning to stare at them.

'Yes,' she went on, even more loudly, 'I can. Don't you worry.'

Then her lips trembled, tears came into her eyes. She said: 'Hell to all of you! Hell to the lot of you. . . .'

Something in Mr Horsfield's expression penetrated to her consciousness and she began to make grimaces in an effort to restrain herself.

He looked away from her.

She said sullenly: 'I'm sorry. You see, that's how I am.'

'Oh, that's all right.'

For the life of him he was unable to think of anything more sympathetic; yet he could imagine everything she had left unsaid. he understood her, but in a cold and theoretical way.

He looked at his watch and saw with relief that it was nearly time to go.

•   •   •

On his way home Mr Horsfield tried to put Julia entirely out of his mind.

As he was opening the door of his house he thought: 'Well, that's all over, anyway.' And then he wondered how he should send money to her if she did not write. 'But, of course, she will write,' he told himself.

He shut the door and sighed. It was as if he had altogether shut out the thought of Julia. The atmosphere of his house enveloped him — quiet and not without dignity, part of a world of lowered voices, and of passions, like Japanese dwarf trees, suppressed for many generations. A familiar world.

PART THREE

1

ÎLE DE LA CITÉ

The visit to London had lasted ten days, and already it was a
little blurred in Julia's memory. It had become a disconnected
episode to be placed with all the other disconnected episodes
which made up her life.

Her hotel looked out on a square in the Île de la Cité, where the
trees were formally shaped, much like the trees of a box of toys you
can buy at Woolworth's. The houses opposite had long rows of
windows, and it seemed to Julia that at each window a woman sat
staring mournfully, like a prisoner, straight into her bedroom.

At night she slept heavily, without dreaming. When she awoke
she was still weighed down with fatigue, so that she could dress only
very slowly, and with great effort.

She thought: 'I've been back a week and three days — a week
and four days today. Well, I can't go on like this.'

She got up and shut the window, so as not to be overlooked.

She wrote:

*Jeune dame (36), connaissant anglais, français, allemand, cherche situation
dame de compagnie ou gouvernante. Hautes références.* . . .

As she wrote *références*, she thought: 'Now, where did I put that
letter?' It had been given her three years before by a Frenchwoman.

A feeling of panic seized her. She was sure she had lost it. And if
she had, where was she to get anything else that would serve as a
reference? Her hands trembled with fright as she searched.

'Anything puts me in a state now,' she thought.

She found it at last, in an envelope with a card on which was
written: '*Wien, le* 24 *août,* 1920. *Menu*' At the back of it were a
number of signatures.

She looked at the menu for a long time. 'I can't believe that was
me.' And then she thought: 'No, I can't believe that this is me,
now.'

She had worn a white crêpe de Chine dress, and red slippers. 'Of course, you clung on because you were obstinate. You clung on because people tried to shove you off, despised you, and were rude to you. So you clung on. Left quite alone, you would have let go of your own accord. The *Figaro* for the advertisement, of course.'

There was a knock at the door, and a postman came in with a registered letter. It was from Mr Horsfield.

My dear Julia,

I was awfully glad to get your card. I wish I could send you something more than the enclosed but, as you may have gathered times are a bit hard with me.

I'm afraid I shan't be able to turn up quite so soon as I had hoped, but if and when I can manage it I do hope you'll let me come to see you. You were a dear to me, and I feel most awfully grateful.

Wishing you the very best of luck,

Yrs.,
G.H.

Enclosed were two five-pound notes.

.   .   .

As soon as she got out-of-doors she felt calmer and happier. She told herself that, of course, it was the room which depressed her because it was so narrow, and because it was so horrible not to be able to open the window without having several pairs of eyes glued upon you. She thought: 'We're like mites in a cheese in that damned hotel.'

It was a very sunny day. The sun was as strong as if it were already summer.

She sat on one of the stone seats near the statue of Henri IV on the Pont Neuf.

An old woman mounted the steps leading from the *quais*. She had a white face, white frizzy hair, and a very pale blue apron. In the sun she looked transparent, like a ghost.

As Julia walked along the Quai des Orfèvres the light was silver and the wind was soft. The river was brown and green — olive-green under the bridges — and a rainbow coloured scum floated at the sides. Anything might happen. Happiness. A course of face massage.

She began to imagine herself in a new black dress and a little black hat with a veil that just shadowed her eyes. After all, why

give up hope when so many people had loved her? . . . 'My darling.
. . . My lovely girl. . . . *Mon amour*. . . . *Mon petit amour*. . . .'

But when the men who passed glanced at her, she looked away
with a contracted face. Something in her was cringing and broken,
but she would not acknowledge it.

In her mind she was repeating over and over again, like a charm:
'I'll have a black dress and hat and very dark grey stockings.'

Then she thought: 'I'll get a pair of new shoes from that place in
the Avenue de l'Opéra. The last ones I got there brought me luck.
I'll spend the whole lot I had this morning. It seems a mad thing to
do, but I don't care. . . . Besides, getting that job is all bluff. What
chance have I really?'

A ring with a green stone for the forefinger of her right hand.

At lunch she drank a half-bottle of Burgundy and felt very hopeful.
She spent the whole afternoon in the Galeries Lafayette choosing a
dress and a hat. Then she went back to her hotel, dressed herself in
her new clothes, and walked up and down her room, smoking. She
decided that after dinner she would go to Montparnasse. She
would go latish — between ten and eleven.

At seven o'clock a gramophone started in a little café near by.
Simultaneously, a smell of sulphur which had been perceptible for
the last hour suddenly grew so strong that is was almost impossible to
breathe. Curls of acrid smoke came in under the bottom of the door.

There was a knock, and the landlady came in to explain that the
gentleman who had occupied the next room had left a few lice
behind him and, as they were clean people, they had been obliged
to take precautions. She said: 'I thought there wasn't anybody in
on this floor. Would you like to come down and sit in the bureau?'

Julia said no, that she was going out.

.   ◆   ◆

When she had finished dinner it was nearly nine o'clock. She
walked in the direction of the river. It fascinated her, because every
hundred yards or so it was different. Sometimes it was sluggish and
oily, then, after you had walked a little farther, the current flowed
strongly.

She watched the shadows of the branches trembling in the
water. In mid-stream there was a pool of silver light where the
shadows danced and beckoned. She thought: 'It can't be the trees
right out there.'

A cloud of smoke was coming from the funnel of a flat boat. Shadows of smoke in the water.

She leaned against the wall, and watched the shadows as they danced, but without joy. They danced, they twisted, they thrust out long, curved, snake-like arms and beckoned.

Someone behind her said: 'There's something that doesn't go, madame?'

She turned and saw a policeman just behind her. She answered in a cold voice: 'I haven't the slightest intention of committing suicide, I assure you.'

'Oh, that wasn't my idea either,' said the policeman politely. '*Seulement* . . .'

She looked again at the river, and then said: 'What are those shadows, do you see? There, right in the middle of the water.'

'It's a tree, the branch of a tree.'

Julia thought: 'That's what *you* say.'

'Of course,' said the policeman, who was an affable and rather good-looking young man. 'That big branch, do you see?'

The shadows seemed not to be on the surface, but to be struggling, wriggling upwards from the depths of the water.

She said to the policeman: 'I was only looking.'

She walked off along the quay, went into a café, and had a *fine*. It was a low-down place. She sat and stared at the woman behind the counter.

The woman behind the counter was beautiful. When she spoke to the customers, her voice was very soft and her eyes were big and dark. She was a slim woman with full, soft breasts.

Julia had a great longing to go up to the woman and talk to her. It was rum; some people did look like that — not cruel, but kind and soft. One in a million looked like that.

She sat thinking: 'If I could talk to her, if only I could go up and tell her all about myself and why I am unhappy, everything would be different afterwards.'

When she came out of the café she walked towards the Place St Michel, and as she reached it, it began to rain. Everybody rushed to the cafés for shelter.

'I mustn't get my clothes wet,' she thought.

Just opposite was a Pathéphone Salon. She went in, sat down on one of the swivel-chairs, bought several discs, and, without changing the register before her, set the thing in motion. A woman's voice, harsh and rather shrewish, began to sing in her ear.

All the time she listened she was thinking: 'After all, what have I done? I haven't done anything.'

She felt the hardness of the receiver pressed up against her ear. The voice sang the chorus of a sentimental and popular song. *'Pars, sans te retourner, pars.'* An unlucky song. Songs about parting were always unlucky. That was a sure thing.

She put the receiver down hastily and looked up something else.

2

THE SECOND UNKNOWN

THE RAIN had nearly stopped when Julia came out of the Pathéphone Salon, but she thought she felt a few drops still falling. The air was very sweet. It smelt of trees and grass.

She crossed the street and went into the big café opposite. It was very full of talking and gesticulating men. The few women who were there were unpretentious and rather subdued.

She ordered a brandy and a blotter. After what seemed an interminable time the waiter brought the brandy.

'And the blotter, please,' she said.

After another long interval the blotter appeared.

She felt that her nerves were exposed and raw.

'Thank you,' she said in a sarcastic voice. 'That's quickly done, isn't it?'

The waiter was a fat, dark, good-looking young man with a mop of frizzy black hair. He stared at her, shrugged, made with his arms a large gesture which expressed to perfection a not ill-natured indifference.

'And another brandy,' she called after him with a black look.

She had meant to write to Mr Horsfield, but when she took up the pen she made meaningless strokes on the paper. And then she began to draw faces — the sort of faces a child would draw, made up of four circles and a straight line.

'Well,' she thought suddenly, 'no use getting into a state.'

She wrote on the paper: *'Doucement, doucement.'*

When she had finished the second brandy her plan of spending the evening in Montparnasse had retreated into the background of her mind. She only wanted to walk somewhere straight ahead.

She turned her back on the Place St Michel and began to walk towards the Châtelet. Then she realized that a man was walking just behind her. He kept step with her; he cleared his throat; he was getting ready to speak.

The man drew level with her and they walked on side by side. She turned her head away and pressed her lips together. She wanted to say: 'Go away, you're annoying me,' but a ridiculous bashfulness kept her from doing so.

They walked on side by side — tense, like two animals.

Julia thought: 'I can't stand this. When we pass the next lamp-post I'm going to tell him to go off.'

When they reached the next lamp she turned and looked at him. He was young — a boy — wearing a cap, very pale and with very small, dark eyes set deeply in his head. He gave her a rapid glance.

'*Oh, la la,*' he said. '*Ah, non, alors.*'

He turned about and walked away.

'Well,' said Julia aloud, 'that's funny. The joke's on me this time.'

She began to laugh, and on the surface of her consciousness she was really amused. But as she walked on her knees felt suddenly weak, as if she had been struck a blow over the heart. The weakness crept upwards.

As she walked she saw nothing but the young man's little eyes, which had looked at her with such deadly and impartial criticism.

She thought again: 'That was really funny. The joke was on me that time.'

.   .   .

The Place du Châtelet was a nightmare. A pale moon, like a claw, looked down through the claw-like branches of dead trees.

She turned to the left and walked into a part of the city which was unknown to her. 'Somewhere near the Halles,' she thought. 'Of course, at the back of the Halles.'

She saw a thin man, so thin that he was like a clothed skeleton, drooping in a doorway. And the horses, standing like statues of patient misery. She felt no pity at all.

It used to be as if someone had put out a hand and touched her heart when she saw things like that, but now she felt nothing. Now she felt indifferent and cold, like a stone.

'I've gone too far,' she thought. She sat down on the terrace of a little café and had another brandy.

And it was funny to end like that — where most sensible people start, indifferent and without any pity at all. Just saying: 'It's nothing to do with me. I've got my own troubles. It's nothing to do with me.'

3

LAST

'THAT'S THE worst of the hot weather.' Mr Mackenzie was thinking. 'Somehow it always brings these accursed nuisances out of their shells.'

He had been having a row with a dirty old man who had insisted on playing a mandolin into his ear; and the waiter whom he had called to his assistance had seemed very unwilling to do anything definite about it. But, by a display of firmness, Mr Mackenzie had won. The dirty man was shambling away, down-at-heel and dejected.

It was a little café in the Rue Dauphine. He had never been there before and was never likely to return to it. But he had felt tired and had thought that a drink would refresh him. He sipped at it and stretched his legs and felt gladly conscious of the beginnings of a sensation of restfulness.

He glanced about him. The mandolin-player had disappeared, but Julia Martin was advancing towards him.

Mr Mackenzie checked an impulse to put a hand up to shield his face. It was too late; she had seen him. She met his eyes and looked away. She passed within a yard of him, still looking away.

'Well,' thought Mr Mackenzie. A blank expression came over his face. Then he thought suddenly: 'Good God, what is the use of all this bad blood?'

She walked on slowly, aimlessly, holding her head down.

The romantic side of his nature asserted itself. He got up and followed her. She was standing on the edge of the pavement, waiting for an opportunity to cross the street. He touched her arm.

'Hullo, Julia.'

'Hullo,' she said, looking round.

'Well, how are things?'

'All right,' she said.

Mr Mackenzie smiled, displaying all his teeth. He wavered for a moment. Then he said: 'Come along and have a drink.'

'All right,' she said.

They sat down — inside the little café this time. 'I'm not a bad sort,' he was thinking. 'Who says that I'm a bad sort? I wish all the swine who do could see me now. How many of them would give a drink to a woman who had smacked them in the face in public?'

'I'll have a Pernod, please,' said Julia.

She drank, and then cleared her throat. 'I've gone back to that hotel. You know — the one on the Quai Grands Augustins.'

'Oh, yes?' He did not know what she was talking about. 'Is it a good place?'

'Not bad. Only there's a woman upstairs who gives me a *cafard* — you know, who depresses me.'

'That's a bore for you,' said Mr Mackenzie.

She looked untidy. There were black specks in the corners of her eyes. Women go phut quite suddenly, he thought. A feeling of melancholy crept over him.

He said: 'It's getting pretty hot. You ought to get away for a change. I'm off tomorrow.'

She made no answer, but she finished her Pernod quickly.

'Lend me a hundred francs, will you?' she said. 'Please.'

This shocked Mr Mackenzie. He flushed. He said: 'Good Lord, yes.'

He stripped two ten-franc notes off a bundle of small change and pushed the rest over to her. 'Have this, will you?' he said. 'There's a bit more than a hundred there, I think.'

Julia put the money into her bag without counting it.

Mr Mackenzie fidgeted. 'I'm afraid I must be getting along now. Will you have another drink before I go?'

'Yes, another Pernod, please,' she said. And then: 'So long.'

'Good-bye,' said Mr Mackenzie.

The street was cool and full of grey shadows. Lights were beginning to come out in the cafés. It was the hour between dog and wolf, as they say.

Good Morning, Midnight

Good morning, Midnight!
I'm coming home,
Day got tired of me—
How could I of him?

Sunshine was a sweet place,
I liked to stay—
But Morn didn't want me—now—
So good night, Day!

—EMILY DICKINSON

PART ONE

1

'Quite like old times,' the room says. 'Yes? No?'

There are two beds, a big one for madame and a smaller one on the opposite side for monsieur. The wash-basin is shut off by a curtain. It is a large room, the smell of cheap hotels faint, almost imperceptible. The street outside is narrow, cobble-stoned, going sharply uphill and ending in a flight of steps. What they call an impasse.

I have been here five days. I have decided on a place to eat in at midday, a place to eat in at night, a place to have my drink in after dinner. I have arranged my little life.

The place to have my drink in after dinner. . . . Wait, I must be careful about that. These things are very important.

Last night, for instance. Last night was a catastrophe. . . . The woman at the next table started talking to me — a dark, thin woman of about forty, very well made-up. She had the score of a song with her and she had been humming it under her breath, tapping the accompaniment with her fingers.

'I like that song.'

'Ah, yes, but it's a sad song. *Gloomy Sunday.*' She giggled. 'A little sad.'

She was waiting for her friend, she told me.

The friend arrived — an American. He stood me another brandy-and-soda and while I was drinking it I started to cry.

I said: 'It was something I remembered.'

The dark woman sat up very straight and threw her chest out.

'I understand,' she said, 'I understand. All the same. . . . Sometimes I'm just as unhappy as you are. But that's not to say that I let everybody see it.'

Unable to stop crying, I went down into the lavabo. A familiar lavabo, and luckily empty. The old dame was outside near the telephone, talking to a girl.

I stayed there, staring at myself in the glass. What do I want to cry about? . . . On the contrary, it's when I am quite sane like this, when I have had a couple of extra drinks and am quite sane, that I realize how lucky I am. Saved, rescued, fished-up, half-drowned, out of the deep, dark river, dry clothes, hair shampooed and set. Nobody would know I had ever been in it. Except, of course, that there always remains something. Yes, there always remains something. . . . Never mind, here I am, sane and dry, with my place to hide in. What more do I want? . . . I'm a bit of an automaton, but sane, surely — dry, cold and sane. Now I have forgotten about dark streets, dark rivers, the pain, the struggle and the drowning. . . . Mind you, I'm not talking about the struggle when you are strong and a good swimmer and there are willing and eager friends on the bank waiting to pull you out at the first sign of distress. I mean the real thing. You jump in with no willing and eager friends around, and when you sink you sink to the accompaniment of loud laughter.

Lavabos. . . . What about that monograph on lavabos — toilets — ladies? . . . A London lavabo in black and white marble, fifteen women in a queue, each clutching her penny, not one bold spirit daring to dash out of her turn past the stern-faced attendant. That's what I call discipline. . . . The lavabo in Florence and the very pretty, fantastically-dressed girl who rushed in, hugged and kissed the old dame tenderly and fed her with cakes out of a paper bag. The dancer-daughter? . . . That cosy little Paris lavabo, where the attendant peddled drugs — something to heal a wounded heart.

When I got upstairs the American and his friend had gone. 'It was something I remembered,' I told the waiter, and he looked at me blankly, not even bothering to laugh at me. His face was unsurprised, blank.

That was last night.

I lie awake, thinking about it, and about the money Sidonie lent me and the way she said: 'I can't bear to see you like this.' Half-shutting her eyes and smiling the smile which means: 'She's getting to look old. She drinks.'

'We've known each other too long, Sasha,' she said, 'to stand on ceremony with each other.'

I had just come in from my little health-stroll round Mecklen-burgh Square and along the Gray's Inn Road. I had looked at this, I had looked at that, I had looked at the people passing in the street and at a shop-window full of artificial limbs. I came in to somebody who said: 'I can't bear to see you looking like this.'

'Like what?' I said.

'I think you need a change. Why don't you go back to Paris for a bit? . . . You could get yourself some new clothes — you certainly need them. . . . I'll lend you the money,' she said. 'I'll be over there next week and I could find a room for you if you like.' Etcetera, etcetera.

I had not seen this woman for months and then she swooped down on me. . . . Well, here I am. When you've been made very cold and very sane you've also been made very passive. (Why worry, why worry?)

I can't sleep. Rolling from side to side. . . .

Was it in 1923 or 1924 that we lived round the corner, in the Rue Victor-Cousin, and Enno bought me that Cossack cap and the imitation astrakhan coat? It was then that I started calling myself Sasha. I thought it might change my luck if I changed my name. Did it bring me any luck, I wonder — calling myself Sasha?

Was it in 1926 or 1927?

I put the light on. The bottle of Evian on the bedtable, the tube of luminal, the two books, the clock ticking on the ledge, the red curtains. . . .

I can see Sidonie carefully looking round for an hotel just like this one. She imagines that it's my atmosphere. God, it's an insult when you come to think about it! More dark rooms, more red curtains. . . .

But one mustn't put everything on the same plane. That's her great phrase. And one mustn't put everybody on the same plane, either. Of course not. And this is my plane. . . . Quatrième à gauche, and mind you don't trip over the hole in the carpet. That's me.

There are some black specks on the wall. I stare at them, certain they are moving. Well, I ought to be able to ignore a few bugs by this time. 'Il ne faut pas mettre tout sur le même plan. . . .'

I get up and look closely. Only splashes of dirt. It's not the time of year for bugs, anyway.

I take some more luminal, put the light out and sleep at once.

I am in the passage of a tube station in London. Many people are in front of me; many people are behind me. Everywhere there are placards printed in red letters: This Way to the Exhibition, This Way to the Exhibition. But I don't want the way to the exhibition — I want the way out. There are passages to the right and passages to the left, but no exit sign. Everywhere the fingers point and the placards read: This Way to the Exhibition . . . I touch the shoulder of the man walking in front of me. I say: 'I want the way out.' But he points to the placards and his hand is made of steel. I walk along with my head bent, very ashamed, thinking: 'Just like me — always wanting to be different from other people.' The steel finger points along a long stone passage. This Way — This Way — This Way to the Exhibition. . . .

Now a little man, bearded, with a snub nose, dressed in a long white night-shirt, is talking earnestly to me. 'I am your father,' he says. 'Remember that I am your father.' But blood is streaming from a wound in his forehead. 'Murder,' he shouts, 'murder, murder.' Helplessly I watch the blood streaming. At last my voice tears itself loose from my chest. I too shout: 'Murder, murder, help, help,' and the sound fills the room. I wake up and a man in the street outside is singing the waltz from *Les Saltimbanques*. 'C'est l'amour qui flotte dans l'air à la ronde,' he sings.

I believe it's a fine day, but the light in this room is so bad that you can't be sure. Outside on the landing you can't see at all unless the electric light is on. It's a large landing, cluttered up from morning to night with brooms, pails, piles of dirty sheets and so forth — the wreckage of the spectacular floors below.

The man who has the room next to mine is parading about as usual in his white dressing-gown. Hanging around. He is like the ghost of the landing. I am always running into him.

He is as thin as a skeleton. He has a bird-like face and sunken, dark eyes with a peculiar expression, cringing, ingratiating, knowing. What's he want to look at me like that for? . . . He is always wearing a dressing-gown — a blue one with black spots or the famous white one. I can't imagine him in street clothes.

'Bonjour.'

'Bonjour,' I mutter. I don't like this damned man. . . .

When I get downstairs the patron tells me that he wants to see my passport. I haven't put the number of the passport on the fiche, he says.

This patron is exactly like one of the assistants who used to be in the pawnshop in the Rue de Rennes — the one who scowled at you and took your stuff away to be valued. A fish, lording it in his own particular tank, staring at the world outside with a glassy and unbelieving eye.

What's wrong with the fiche? I've filled it up all right, haven't I? Name So-and-so, nationality So-and-so. . . . Nationality — that's what has puzzled him. I ought to have put nationality by marriage.

I tell him I will let him have the passport in the afternoon and he gives my hat a gloomy, disapproving look. I don't blame him. It shouts 'Anglaise', my hat. And my dress extinguishes me. And then this damned old fur coat slung on top of everything else — the last idiocy, the last incongruity.

Never mind, I have some money now. I may be able to do something about it. Twelve o'clock on a fine autumn day, and nothing to worry about. Some money to spend and nothing to worry about.

But careful, careful! Don't get excited. You know what happens when you get excited and exalted, don't you? . . . Yes . . . And then, you know how you collapse like a pricked balloon, don't you? Having no staying power. . . . Yes, exactly. . . . So, no excitement. This is going to be a quiet, sane fortnight. Not too much drinking, avoidance of certain cafés, of certain streets, of certain spots, and everything will go off beautifully.

The thing is to have a programme, not to leave anything to chance — no gaps. No trailing around aimlessly with cheap gramophone records starting up in your head, no 'Here this happened, here that happened'. Above all, no crying in public, no crying at all if I can help it.

Thinking all this, I pass the exact place for my after-dinner drink. It's a café on the Avenue de l'Observatoire, which always seems to be empty. I remember it like this before.

I'll go in and have a Pernod. Just one, just once, for luck. . . . Here's to the Miracle, I'll say, to the Miracle. . . .

A man who looks like an Arab comes in, accompanied by a melancholy girl wearing spectacles.

'Life is difficult,' the Arab says.

'Yes, life isn't easy,' the girl says.

Long pause.

'One needs a lot of courage, to live,' the Arab says.

'Ah, I believe you,' the girl says, shaking her head and clicking her tongue.

They finish their vermouth and go out and I sit alone in a large, clean, empty room and watch myself in the long glass opposite, turning over the pages of an old number of *l'Illustration*, thinking that I haven't got a care in the world, except that tomorrow's Sunday — a difficult day anywhere. Sombre dimanche. . . .

Planning it all out. Eating. A movie. Eating again. One drink. A long walk back to the hotel. Bed. Luminal. Sleep. Just sleep — no dreams.

•

At four o'clock next afternoon I am in a cinema on the Champs Elysées, according to programme. Laughing heartily in the right places.

It's a very good show and I see it through twice. When I come out of the cinema it's night and the street lamps are lit. I'm glad of that. If you've got to walk around by yourself, it's easier when the lamps are lit.

Paris is looking very nice tonight. . . . You are looking very nice tonight, my beautiful, my darling, and oh what a bitch you can be! But you didn't kill me after all, did you? And they couldn't kill me either. . . .

Just about here we waited for a couple of hours to see Anatole France's funeral pass, because, Enno said, we mustn't let such a great literary figure disappear without paying him the tribute of a last salute.

There we were, chatting away affably, paying Anatole France the tribute of a last salute, and most of the people who passed in the procession were chatting away affably too, looking as if they were making dates for lunches and dinners, and we were all paying Anatole France the tribute of a last salute.

I walk along, remembering this, remembering that, trying to find a cheap place to eat — not so easy round here. The gramophone record is going strong in my head: 'Here this happened, here that happened. . . .'

I used to work in a shop just off this street.

I can see myself coming out of the Métro station at the Rond-Point every morning at half-past eight, walking along the Avenue Marigny, turning to the left and then to the right, putting my coat and hat into the cloak-room, going along a passage and starting in with: 'Good morning, madame. Has madame a vendeuse?'

2

. . . It was a large white-and-gold room with a dark-polished floor. Imitation Louis Quinze chairs, painted screens, three or four elongated dolls, beautifully dressed, with charming and malicious oval faces.

Every time a customer arrived, the commissionaire touched a bell which rang just over my head. I would advance towards the three steps leading down to the street-door and stand there, smiling a small, discreet smile. I would say 'Good afternoon, madame. . . . Certainly, madame,' or 'Good afternoon, madame. Mademoiselle Mercédès has had your telephone message and everything is ready,' or 'Certainly, madame. . . . Has madame a vendeuse?'

Then I would conduct the customer to the floor above, where the real activities of the shop were carried on, and call for Mademoiselle Mercédès or Mademoiselle Henriette or Madame Perron, as the case might be. If I forgot a face or allotted a new customer to a saleswoman out of her turn, there was a row.

There was no lift in this shop. That's why I was there. It was one of those dress-houses still with a certain prestige — anyhow among the French — but its customers were getting fewer and fewer.

I had had the job for three weeks. It was dreary. You couldn't read: they didn't like it. I would feel as if I were drugged, sitting there, watching those damned dolls, thinking what a success they would have made of their lives if they had been women. Satin skin, silk hair, velvet eyes, sawdust heart — all complete. I used to envy the commissionaire, because at least he could watch the people passing in the street. On the other hand, he had to stand up all the time. Yes, perhaps I had rather be myself than the commissionaire.

There was always a very strong smell of scent. I would pretend that I could recognize the various scents. Today it's L'Heure Bleue; yesterday it was Nuits de Chine. . . . The place also smelt of the polish on the floor, the old furniture, the dolls' clothes.

The shop had a branch in London, and the boss of the London branch had bought up the whole show. Every three months or so he came over to the French place and it was rumoured that he was due to arrive on a certain day. What's he like? Oh, he's the real English type. Very nice, very, very chic, the real English type, le businessman. . . . I thought: 'Oh, my God, I know what these people mean when they say the real English type.'

. . . He arrives. Bowler-hat, majestic trousers, oh-my-God expression, ha-ha eyes — I know him at once. He comes up the steps with Salvatini behind him, looking very worried. (Salvatini is the boss of our shop.) Don't let him notice me, don't let him look at me. Isn't there something you can do so that nobody looks at you or sees you? Of course, you must make your mind vacant, neutral, then your face also becomes vacant, neutral — you are invisible.

No use. He comes up to my table.

'Good morning, good morning, Miss—'
'Mrs Jansen,' Salvatini says.
Shall I stand up or not stand up? Stand up, of course. I stand up.
'Good morning.'
I smile at him.
'And how many languages do you speak?'
He seems quite pleased. He smiles back at me. Affable, that's the word. I suppose that's why I think it's a joke.
'One,' I say, and go on smiling.
Now, what's happened? . . . Oh, of course. . . .
'I understand French quite well.'
He fidgets with the buttons on his coat.
'I was told that the receptionist spoke French and German fluently,' he says to Salvatini.
'She speaks French,' Salvatini says. 'Assez bien, assez bien.'
Mr Blank looks at me with lifted eyebrows.
'Sometimes,' I say idiotically.
Of course, sometimes, when I am a bit drunk and am talking to somebody I like and know, I speak French very fluently indeed. At other times I just speak it. And as to that, my dear sir, you've got everything all wrong. I'm here because I have a friend who knows Mr Salvatini's mistress, and Mr Salvatini's mistress spoke to Mr Salvatini about me, and the day that he saw me I wasn't looking too bad and he was in a good mood. Nothing at all to do with fluent French and German, dear sir, nothing at all. I'm here because I'm here because I'm here. And just to prove to you that I speak French, I'll sing you a little song about it: 'Si vous saviez, si vous saviez, si vous saviez comment ça se fait.'
For God's sake, I think, pull yourself together.
I say: 'I speak French fairly well. I've been living in Paris for eight years.'
No, he's suspicious now. Questions short and sharp.
'How long have you been working here?'
'About three weeks.'
'What was your last job?'
'I worked at the Maison Chose in the Place Vendôme.'
'Oh, really, you worked for Chose, did you? You worked for Chose.' His voice is more respectful. 'Were you receptionist there?'
'No,' I say. 'I worked as a mannequin.'
'You worked as a mannequin?' Down and up his eyes go, up and down. 'How long ago was this?' he says.
How long ago was it? Now, everything is a blank in my head —

years, days, hours, everything is a blank in my head. How long ago
was it? I don't know.

'Four, nearly five, years ago.'

'How long did you stay there?'

'About three months,' I say.

He seems to be waiting for further information.

'And then I left,' I say in a high voice. (Decidedly this is one of
my good days. This is one of the days when I say everything right.)

'Oh, you left?'

'Yes, I left.'

Yes, my dear sir, I left. I got bored and I walked out on them. But
that was four, nearly five, years ago and a lot can happen in five
years. I haven't the slightest intention of walking out on you, I can
assure you of that. And I hope you haven't the slightest intention of
— And just the thought that you may have the slightest intention
of — makes my hands go cold and my heart beat.

'Have you worked anywhere else since then?'

'Well, no. No, I haven't.'

'I see,' he says. He waves backwards and forwards like a tall tree
that is going to fall on me. Then he makes a sound like 'Hah', and
goes off into a room at the back, followed by Salvatini.

Well, this has gone badly, there's no disguising it. It has gone as
badly as possible. It couldn't have gone worse. But it's over. Now
he'll never notice me again; he'll forget about me.

An old Englishwoman and her daughter come into the shop. I
escort them upstairs and then fidget about arranging the showcases
at the back of the room. In an hour or so they come down again.
They walk up to the showcases, the old lady eager, the daughter
very reluctant.

'Can you show me some of these pretty things?' the old lady says.
'I want something to wear in my hair in the evening.'

She takes off her hat and she is perfectly bald on top — a white,
bald skull with a fringe of grey hair. The daughter stays in the
background. She is past shame, detached, grim.

'Come along, mother, do let's go. Don't be silly, mother. You
won't find anything here.'

There is a long glass between the two windows. The old lady
complacently tries things on her bald head.

The daughter's eyes meet mine in the mirror. Damned old hag,
isn't she funny? . . . I stare back at her coldly.

I will say for the old lady that she doesn't care a damn about all this. She points to various things and says: 'Show me that — show me that.' A sturdy old lady with gay, bold eyes.

She tried on a hair-band, a Spanish comb, a flower. A green feather waves over her bald head. She is calm and completely unconcerned. She was like a Roman emperor in that last thing she tried on.

'Mother, please come away. Do let's go.'

The old lady doesn't take the slightest notice, and she has everything out of both of the cases before she goes. Then: 'Well,' she says, 'I'm so sorry to have given you so much trouble.'

'It's no trouble at all, madame.'

As they go towards the door the daughter bursts out. A loud, fierce hiss: 'Well, you made a perfect fool of yourself, as usual. You've had everybody in the shop sniggering. If you want to do this again, you'll have to do it by yourself. I refuse, I refuse.'

The old lady does not answer. I can see her face reflected in a mirror, her eyes still undaunted but something about her mouth and chin collapsing. . . . Oh, but why not buy her a wig, several decent dresses, as much champagne as she can drink, all the things she likes to eat and oughtn't to, a gigolo if she wants one? One last flare-up, and she'll be dead in six months at the outside. That's all you're waiting for, isn't it? But no, you must have the slow death, the bloodless killing that leaves no stain on your conscience. . . .

I put the ornaments back in the cases slowly, carefully, just as they were.

That brings me up to déjeuner. I go upstairs. One long table here, the mannequins and saleswomen all mixed up.

There is, of course, an English mannequin. 'Kind, kind and gentle is she' — and that's another damned lie. But she is very beautiful — 'belle comme une fleur de verre'. And the other one, the little French one whom I like so much, she is 'belle comme une fleur de terre. . . .'

I still can't get over the meal at this place. I have been living for some time on bread and coffee, and it blows my stomach out every time. Hors d'oeuvres, plat du jour, vegetables, dessert. Coffee and a quarter of wine are extra, but so little extra that everybody has them.

Nobody talks about the English manager — a wary silence.

I go downstairs, feeling dazed and happy. Gradually the happiness goes; I am just dazed.

Salvatini puts his head out of the door behind me and says: 'Mr Blank wants to see you.'

I at once make up my mind that he wants to find out if I can speak German. All the little German I know flies out of my head. Jesus, help me! Ja, ja, nein, was kostet es, Wien ist eine sehr schöne Stadt, Buda-Pest auch ist sehr schön, ist schön, mein Herr, ich habe meinen Blumen vergessen, aus meinen grossen Schmerzen, homo homini lupus, aus meinen grossen Schmerzen mach ich die kleinen Lieder, homo homini lupus (I've got that one, anyway), aus meinen grossen Schmerzen homo homini doh ré mi fah soh la ti doh. . . .

He is sitting at the desk, writing a letter. I stand there. He is sure to notice how shabby my shoes are.

Salvatini looks up, gives me a furtive smile and then looks away again.

Come on, stand straight, keep your head up, smile. . . . No, don't smile. If you smile, he'll think you're trying to get off with him. I know this type. He won't give me the benefit of a shadow of a doubt. Don't smile then, but look eager, alert, attentive. . . . Run out of the door and get away. . . . You fool, stand straight, look eager, alert, attentive. . . . No, look here, he's doing this on purpose. . . . Of course he isn't doing it on purpose. He's just writing a letter. . . . He is, he is. He's doing it on purpose. I know it, I feel it. I've been standing here for five minutes. This is impossible.

'Did you wish to see me, Mr Blank?'

He looks up and says sharply: 'Yes, yes, what is it? What do you want? Wait a minute, wait a minute.'

At once I know. He doesn't want me to talk German, he's going to give me the sack. All right then, hurry up, get it over. . . .

Nothing. I just stand there. Now panic has come on me. My hands are shaking, my heart is thumping, my hands are cold. Fly, fly, run from these atrocious voices, these abominable eyes. . . .

He finishes his letter, writes a line or two on another piece of paper and puts it into an envelope.

'Will you please take this to the kise?'

Take this to the kise. . . . I look at Salvatini. He smiles encouragingly.

Mr Blank rattles out: 'Be as quick as you can, Mrs — er — please. Thank you very much.'

I turn and walk blindly through a door. It is a lavatory. They look sarcastic as they watch me going out by the right door.

I walk a little way along the passage, then stand with my back against the wall.

This is a very old house — two old houses. The first floor, the shop proper, is modernized. The showrooms, the fitting-rooms, the mannequins' room. . . . But on the ground floor are the workrooms and offices and dozens of small rooms, passages that don't lead anywhere, steps going up and steps going down.

Kise — kise. . . . It doesn't mean a thing to me. He's got me into such a state that I can't imagine what it can mean.

Now, no panic. This envelope must have a name on it. . . . Monsieur L. Grousset.

Somewhere in this building is a Monsieur L. Grousset. I have got to take this letter to him. Easy. Somebody will tell me where his room is. Grousset, Grousset. . . .

I turn to the right, walk along another passage, down a flight of stairs. The workrooms. . . . No, I can't ask here. All the girls will stare at me. I shall seem such a fool.

I try another passage. It ends in a lavatory. The number of lavatories in this place, c'est inoui. . . . I turn the corner, find myself back in the original passage and collide with a strange young man. He gives me a nasty look.

'Could you tell me, please, where I can find Monsieur Grousset?'

'Connais pas,' the young man says.

After this it becomes a nightmare. I walk up stairs, past doors, along passages — all different, all exactly alike. There is something very urgent that I must do. But I don't meet a soul and all the doors are shut.

This can't go on. Shall I throw the damned thing away and forget all about it?

'What you must do is this,' I tell myself: 'You must go back and say — quite calmly — "I'm very sorry, but I didn't understand where you wanted me to take this note." '

I knock. He calls out: 'Come in.' I go in.

He takes the note from my hand. He looks at me as if I were a dog which had presented him with a very, very old bone. (Say something, say something. . . .)

'I couldn't find him.'

'But how do you mean you couldn't find him? He must be there.'

'I'm very sorry. I didn't know where to find him.'

'You don't know where to find the cashier — the counting-house?'

'La caisse,' Salvatini says — helpfully, but too late.

But if I tell him that it was the way he pronounced it that confused me, it will seem rude. Better not say anything. . . .

'Well, don't you know?'

'Yes, I do. Oh yes, I do know.'

That is to say, I knew this morning where the cashier's office is. It isn't so far from the place where we put our hats and coats. But I don't know a damned thing now. . . . Run, run away from their eyes, run from their voices, run. . . .

We stare at each other. I breathe in deeply and breathe out again.

'Extraordinary,' he says, very slowly, 'quite extraordinary. God knows I'm used to fools, but this complete imbecility. . . . This woman is the biggest fool I've ever met in my life. She seems to be half-witted. She's hopeless. . . . Well, isn't she?' he says to Salvatini.

Salvatini makes a rolling movement of his head, shoulders and eyes, which means: 'I quite agree with you. Deplorable, deplorable.' Also: 'She's not so bad as you think.' Also: 'Oh, my God, what's all this about? What a day, what a day! When will it be over?' Anything you like, Salvatini's shrug means.

Not to cry in front of this man. Tout, mais pas ça. Say something. . . . No, don't say anything. Just walk out of the room.

'No, wait a minute,' he says. 'You'd better take that note along. You do know who to take it to now, don't you? The cashier.'

'Yes.'

He stares at me. Something else has come into his eyes. He knows how I am feeling — yes, he knows.

'Just a hopeless, helpless little fool, aren't you?' he says. Jovial? Bantering? On the surface, yes. Underneath? No, I don't think so.

'Well, aren't you?'

'Yes, yes, yes, yes. Oh, yes.'

I burst into tears. I haven't even got a handkerchief.

'Dear me,' Mr Blank says.

'Allons, allons,' Salvatini says. 'Voyons. . . .'

I rush away from them into a fitting-room. It is hardly ever used. It is only used when the rooms upstairs are full. I shut the door and lock it.

I cry for a long time — for myself, for the old woman with the bald head, for all the sadness of this damned world, for all the fools and all the defeated. . . .

In this fitting-room there is a dress in one of the cupboards which has been worn a lot by the mannequins and is going to be sold off for four hundred francs. The saleswoman has promised to keep it for me. I have tried it on; I have seen myself in it. It is a black dress with wide sleeves embroidered in vivid colours — red, green, blue, purple. It is my dress. If I had been wearing it I should never have stammered or been stupid.

Now I have stopped crying. Now I shall never have that dress. Today, this day, this hour, this minute I am utterly defeated. I have had enough.

Now the circle is complete. Now, strangely enough, I am no longer afraid of Mr Blank. He is one thing and I am another. He knew me right away, as soon as he came in at the door. And I knew him. . . .

I go into the other room, this time without knocking. Salvatini has gone. Mr Blank is still writing letters. Is he making dates with all the girls he knows in Paris? I bet that's what he is doing.

He looks at me with distaste. Plat du jour — boiled eyes, served cold. . . .

Well, let's argue this out, Mr Blank. You, who represent Society, have the right to pay me four hundred francs a month. That's my market value, for I am an inefficient member of Society, slow in the uptake, uncertain, slightly damaged in the fray, there's no denying it. So you have the right to pay me four hundred francs a month, to lodge me in a small, dark room, to clothe me shabbily, to harass me with worry and monotony and unsatisfied longings till you get me to the point when I blush at a look, cry at a word. We can't all be happy, we can't all be rich, we can't all be lucky — and it would be so much less fun if we were. Isn't it so, Mr Blank? There must be the dark background to show up the bright colours. Some must cry so that the others may be able to laugh the more heartily. Sacrifices are necessary. . . . Let's say that you have this mystical right to cut my legs off. But the right to ridicule me afterwards because I am a cripple — no, that I think you haven't got. And that's the right you hold most dearly, isn't it? You must be able to despise the people you exploit. But I wish you a lot of trouble, Mr Blank, and just to start off with, your damned shop's going bust. Alleluia! Did I say all this? Of course I didn't. I didn't even think it.

I say that I'm ill and want to go. (Get it in first.) And he says he quite agrees that it would be the best thing. 'No regrets,' he says, 'no regrets.'

And there I am, out in the Avenue Marigny, with my month's pay — four hundred francs. And the air so sweet, as it can only be in Paris. It is autumn and the dry leaves are blowing along. Swing high, swing low, swing to and fro. . .

•

Thinking of my jobs. . . .

There was that one I had in the shop called Young Britain. X plus ZBW. That meant fcs. 68.60. Then another hieroglyphic —XQ15tn — meant something else, fcs. 112.75. Little boys' sailor suits were there, and young gentlemen's Norfolk suits were there. . . . Well, I got the sack from that in a week, and very pleased I was too.

Then there was that other job — as a guide. Standing in the middle of the Place de l'Opéra, losing my head and not knowing the way to the Rue de la Paix. North, south, east, west — they have no meaning for me. . . . They want to saunter, this plump, placid lady and her slightly less placid daughter. They want to saunter in the beautiful Paris sunlight, to the Rue de la Paix.

I pull myself together and we get to the Rue de la Paix. We go to the French-English dress-shops and we go to the French-French dress-shops. And then they say they want to have lunch. I take them to a restaurant in the Place de la Madeleine. They are enormously rich, these two, the mother and the daughter. Both are very rich and very sad. Neither can imagine what it is like to be happy or even to be gay, neither the mother nor the daughter.

In the restaurant the waiter suggests pancakes with rum sauce for dessert. They are strict teetotallers, but they lap up the rum sauce. I've never seen anybody's mood change so quickly as the mother's did, after they had had two helpings of it.

'What delicious sauce!' They have a third helping. Their eyes are swimming. The daughter's eyes say 'Certainly, certainly'; the mother's eyes say 'Perhaps, perhaps. . . .'

'It is strange how sad it can be — sunlight in the afternoon, don't you think?'

'Yes,' I say, 'it can be sad.'

But the softened mood doesn't last.

She has coffee and a glass of water and is herself again.

Now she wants to be taken to the exhibition of Loie Fuller materials, and she wants to be taken to the place where they sell that German camera which can't be got anywhere else outside Germany, and she wants to be taken to a place where she can buy a hat which will épater everybody she knows and yet be easy to wear, and on top of all this she wants to be taken to a certain exhibition of pictures. But she doesn't remember the man's name and she isn't sure where the exhibition is. However, she knows that she will recognize the name when she hears it.

I try. I question waiters, old ladies in lavabos, girls in shops.

They all respond. There is a freemasonry among those who prey upon the rich. I manage everything, except perhaps the hat.

But she saw through me. She only gave me twenty francs for a tip and I never got another job as guide from the American Express. That was my first and last.

I try, but they always see through me. The passages will never lead anywhere, the doors will always be shut. I know. . . .

Then I start thinking about the black dress, longing for it, madly, furiously. If I could get it everything would be different. Supposing I ask So-and-so to ask So-and-so to ask Madame Perron to keep it for me? . . . I'll get the money. I'll get it. . . .

Walking in the night with the dark houses over you, like monsters. If you have money and friends, houses are just houses with steps and a front-door — friendly houses where the door opens and somebody meets you, smiling. If you are quite secure and your roots are well struck in, they know. They stand back respectfully, waiting for the poor devil without any friends and without any money. Then they step forward, the waiting houses, to frown and crush. No hospitable doors, no lit windows, just frowning darkness. Frowning and leering and sneering, the houses, one after another. Tall cubes of darkness, with two lighted eyes at the top to sneer. And they know who to frown at. They know as well as the policeman on the corner, and don't you worry. . . .

Walking in the night. Back to the hotel. Always the same hotel. You press the button. The door opens. You go up the stairs. Always the same stairs, always the same room. . . .

The landing is empty and deserted. At this time of night there are no pails, no brooms, no piles of dirty sheets. The man next door has put his shoes outside — long, pointed, patent-leather shoes, very cracked. He does get dressed, then. . . . I wonder about this man. Perhaps he is a commercial traveller out of a job for the moment. Yes, that's what he might be — a commis voyageur. Perhaps he's a traveller in dressing-gowns.

Now, quiet, quiet. . . . This is going to be a nice sane fortnight. 'Quiet, quiet,' I say to the clock when I am winding it up, and it makes a noise between a belch and a giggle.

3

The bathroom here is on the ground floor. I lie in the bath, listening to the patronne talking to a client. He says he wants a room for a young lady-friend of his. Not at once, he is just looking around.

'A room? A nice room?'

I watch cockroaches crawling from underneath the carpet and crawling back again. There is a flowered carpet in this bathroom, two old arm-chairs and a huge wardrobe with a spotted mirror.

'A nice room?' Of course, une belle chambre, the client wants. The patronne says she has a very beautiful room on the second floor, which will be vacant in about a month's time.

That's the way it is, that's the way it goes, that was the way it went. . . . A room. A nice room. A beautiful room. A beautiful room with bath. A very beautiful room with bath. A bedroom and sitting-room with bath. Up to the dizzy heights of the suite. Two bedrooms, sitting-room, bath and vestibule. (The small bedroom is in case you don't feel like me, or in case you meet somebody you like better and come in late.) Anything you want brought up on the dinner-wagon. (But, alas! the waiter has a louse on his collar. What is that on his collar? . . . Bitte schön, mein Herr, bitte schön. . . .) Swing high. . . . Now, slowly, down. A beautiful room with bath. A room with bath. A nice room. A room. . . .

Now, what are they saying? 'Marthe, montrez le numéro douze.' And the price? Four hundred francs a month. I am paying three times as much as that for my room on the fourth floor. It shows that I have ended as a successful woman, anyway, however I may have started. One look at me and the prices go up. And when the Exhibition is pulled down and the tourists have departed, where shall I be? In the other room, of course — the one just off the Gray's Inn Road, as usual trying to drink myself to death. . . .

When I get upstairs the man next door is out on the landing, also yelling for Marthe. His flannel night-shirt scarcely reaches his knees. When he sees me he grins, comes to the head of the stairs and stands there, blocking the way.

'Bonjour. Ça va?'

I walk past him without answering and slam the door of my room. I expect all this is a joke. I expect he tells his friend on the floor below: 'An English tourist has taken the room next to mine. I have a lot of fun with that woman.'

A girl is making-up at an open window immediately opposite. The street is so narrow that we are face to face, so to speak. I can see socks, stockings and underclothes drying on a line in her room. She averts her eyes, her expression hardens. I realize that if I watch her making-up she will retaliate by staring at me when I do the same thing. I half-shut my window and move away from it. A terrible hotel, this — an awful place. I must get out of it. Only I would have landed here, only I would stay here. . . .

I have just finished dressing when there is a knock on the door. It's the commis, in his beautiful dressing-gown, immaculately white, with long, wide, hanging sleeves. I wonder how he got hold of it. Some woman must have given it to him. He stands there smiling his silly smile. I stare at him. He looks like a priest, the priest of some obscene, half-understood religion.

At last I manage: 'Well, what is it? What do you want?'

'Nothing,' he says, 'nothing.'

'Oh, go away.'

He doesn't answer or move. He stands in the doorway, smiling. (Now then, you and I understand each other, don't we? Let's stop pretending.)

I put my hand on his chest, push him backwards and bang the door. It's quite easy. It's like pushing a paper man, a ghost, something that doesn't exist.

And there I am in this dim room with the bed for madame and the bed for monsieur and the narrow street outside (what they call an impasse), thinking of that white dressing-gown, like a priest's robes. Frightened as hell. A nightmare feeling. . . .

This morning the hall smells like a very cheap Turkish bath in London — the sort of place that is got up to look respectable and clean outside, the passage very antiseptic and the woman who meets you a cross between a prison-wardress and a deaconess, and everybody speaking in whispering voices with lowered eyes: 'Foam or Turkish, madam?' And then you go down into the Turkish bath itself and into a fog of stale sweat — ten, twenty years old.

The patron, the patronne and the two maids are having their meal in a room behind the bureau. They have some friends with them. Loud talking and laughing. . . . ' "Tu n'oses pas," qu'elle m'a dit. "Ballot!" qu'elle m'a dit. Comment, je n'ose pas? Vous allez voir ce que je lui ai dit: "Attends, attends, ma fille. Tu vas voir si je n'ose pas." Alors, vous savez ce que j'ai fait? J'ai. . . .'

His voice pursues me out into the street. 'Attends, ma fille, attends. . . .'

I've got to find another hotel. I feel ill and giddy, I'd better take a taxi. Where to? I remember that I have an address in my handbag, a brochure with pictures. Le hall, le restaurant, le lounge, a bedroom with bath, a bedroom without bath, etcetera. Everything of the most respectable — that's the place for me. . . .

There is a porter at the door and at the reception-desk a grey-haired woman and a sleek young man.

'I want a room for tonight.'

'A room? A room with bath?'

I am still feeling ill and giddy. I say confidentially, leaning forward: 'I want a light room.'

The young man lifts his eyebrows and stares at me.

I try again. 'I don't want a room looking on the courtyard. I want a light room.'

'A light room?' the lady says pensively. She turns over the pages of her books, looking for a light room.

'We have number 219,' she says. 'A beautiful room with bath. Seventy-five francs a night.' (God, I can't afford that.) 'It's a very beautiful room with bath. Two windows. Very light,' she says persuasively.

A girl is called to show me the room. As we are about to start for the lift, the young man says, speaking out of the side of his mouth, 'Of course you know that number 219 is occupied.'

'Oh no. Number 219 had his bill the day before yesterday,' the receptionist says. 'I remember. I gave it to him myself.'

I listen anxiously to this conversation. Suddenly I feel that I must have number 219, with bath — number 219, with rose-coloured curtains, carpet and bath. I shall exist on a different plane at once if I can get this room, if only for a couple of nights. It will be an omen. Who says you can't escape from your fate? I'll escape from mine, into room number 219. Just try me, just give me a chance.

'He asked for his bill,' the young man says, in a voice which is a triumph of scorn and cynicism. 'He asked for his bill but that doesn't mean that he has gone.'

The receptionist starts arguing. 'When people ask for their bills, it's because they are going, isn't it?'

'Yes,' he says, '*French* people. The others ask for their bills to see if we're going to cheat them.'

'My God,' says the receptionist, 'foreigners, foreigners, my God. . . .'

The young man turns his back, entirely dissociating himself from what is going on.

Number 219 — well, now I know all about him. All the time they are talking I am seeing him — his trousers, his shoes, the way he brushes his hair, the sort of girls he likes. His hand-luggage is light yellow and he has a paunch. But I can't see his face. He wears a mask, number 219. . . .

'Show the lady number 334.'

The lady-like girl — we are all ladies here, all ladies — takes me up in the lift and shows me a comfortably furnished room which looks on to a high, blank wall.

'But I don't want a room looking on the courtyard. I want a light room.'

'This is a very light room,' the girl says, turning on the lamp by the bed.

'No,' I say. 'I mean a light room. A *light* one. Not a dark one.' She stares at me. I suppose I sound a bit crazy. I say: 'Yes. . . . Thank you very much — but no.'

The receptionist downstairs tries to stop me and argue about other rooms she has — beautiful rooms. I say: 'Yes, yes, I'll telephone,' and rush out.

A beautiful room with bath? A room with bath? A nice room? A room? . . . But never tell the truth about this business of rooms, because it would bust the roof off everything and undermine the whole social system. All rooms are the same. All rooms have four walls, a door, a window or two, a bed, a chair and perhaps a bidet. A room is a place where you hide from the wolves outside and that's all any room is. Why should I worry about changing my room?

When I get back to the hotel after I have had something to eat, it looks all right and smells as respectable as you please. I imagined it all, I imagined everything. . . . Somebody's *Times Literary Supplement* peeps coyly from the letter-rack. A white-haired American lady and a girl who looks like her daughter are talking in the hall.

'Look here, look at this. Here's a portrait of Rimbaud. Rimbaud lived here, it says.'

'And here's Verlaine. . . . Did he live here too?'

'Yes, he lived here too. They both lived here. They lived here together. Well now, isn't that interesting?'

The commis is on the landing. He scowls at me and at once goes into his bedroom and shuts the door. Well, that's all right, that's all right. If we both try hard to avoid each other, we ought to be able to manage it.

The room welcomes me back.

'There you are,' it says. 'You didn't go off, then?'

'No, no. I thought better of it. Here I belong and here I'll stay.'

4

He always called that bar the Pig and Lily, because the proprietor's name was Pecanelli. It is in one of those streets at the back of the Montparnasse station. Got up to look like an olde English tavern. I don't see why I shouldn't revisit it. I have never made scenes there, collapsed, cried — so far as I know I have a perfectly clean slate. We used to go there, have a couple of drinks, eat hot dogs and talk about the next war or something like that. Nothing to cry about, I mean. . . .

'We?' Well, he was one of those people with very long, thin faces and very pale blue eyes. After working in a Manchester shipping-office until he was twenty-five, he had broken away and come to Paris, and was reading for his medical degree at the University. A loving relative supplied him with the money — that was one story. But another was that he really kept going on money he won at cards. That might have been true, for he was the sort that plays cards very well.

He loved popular fairs, this boy — the Neuilly fair, the Montmartre fair, even the merry-go-rounds at the Lion de Belfort — and he had painfully taught himself to like music. Bach, of course, was his favourite composer. The others, he said, he preferred to read, not to listen to. 'Heard melodies are sweet, but those unheard are sweeter' — that sort of thing. He was a bit of a fish, really. Sometimes he made my blood run cold. And in spite of his long, thin face, he wasn't sensitive.

One day he said: 'I'll take you to see something rather interesting.' And, wandering along the streets at the back of the Halles, we came to a café where the clients paid for the right, not to have a drink, but to sleep. They sat close-pressed against each other with their arms on the tables, their heads in their arms. Every place in the room was filled; others lay along the floor. We squinted in at them through the windows. 'Would you like to go in and have a look at them?' he said, as if he were exhibiting a lot of monkeys. 'It's all right, we can go in — the chap here knows me. There's one fellow who is usually here. If you stand him a few drinks and get him really going he tries to eat his glass. It's very curious. You ought to see that.'

When I said: 'Not for anything on earth,' he thought I had gone shy or sentimental. 'Well,' I said, 'all right. I'll watch you eating a glass with pleasure.' He didn't like that at all.

I arrive thinking of this boy, and screw myself up to go into a room full of people. But the place is empty — dead as a door-nail. There is a new proprietor — a fat, bald man with a Dutch nose. He has only been here for two years, he tells me.

The speciality now is Javanese food, and the English hunting-scenes on the walls look very exotic. . . . Tally-ho, tally-ho, tally-ho, a-hunting we will go. . . . The cold, clear voices, the cold, light eyes. . . . Tally-ho, tally-ho, tally-ho. . . .

A party of three comes in — two men and a girl. One of the men stares at me. He says to the girl: 'Tu la connais, la vieille?'

Now, who is he talking about? Me? Impossible. Me — la vieille?

The girl says: 'The Englishwoman? No, I don't know her. Why should you imagine I know her?'

This is as I thought and worse than I thought. . . . A mad old Englishwoman, wandering around Montparnasse. 'A Paris il y a des Anglaises, Oah, yes, oah, yes, Aussi plat's comm' des punaises, Oah, yes, oah, yes. . . .' This is indeed worse than I thought.

I stare at the young man. He looks embarrassed and turns his eyes away. Not French. . . .

This is indeed worse than I thought. That's what I was told when I came back to London that famous winter five years ago. 'Why didn't you drown yourself', the old devil said, 'in the Seine?' In the Seine, I ask you — but that was just what he said. A very proper sentiment — but what a way to put it! Talk about being melodramatic! 'We consider you as dead. Why didn't you make a hole in the water? Why didn't you drown yourself in the Seine?' These phrases run trippingly off the tongues of the extremely respectable. They think in terms of a sentimental ballad. And that's what terrifies you about them. It isn't their cruelty, it isn't even their shrewdness — it's their extraordinary naïveté. Everything in their whole bloody world is a cliché. Everything is born out of a cliché, rests on a cliché, survives by a cliché. And they believe in the clichés — there's no hope.

Then the jam after the medicine. I shall receive a solicitor's letter every Tuesday containing £2 10s 0d. A legacy, the capital not to be touched. . . . 'Who?' When I heard I was very surprised — I shouldn't have thought she liked me at all. 'You may consider yourself very fortunate,' he said, and when I saw the expression in his eyes I knew exactly why she did it. She did it to annoy the rest of the family. . . . And of course it was impossible to tell me of this before, because they didn't know my address. There was nothing to say to that except: 'Good-bye, dear sir, and mind you don't trip over the hole in the carpet.'

It's so like him, I thought, that he refuses to call me Sasha, or even Sophie. No, it's Sophia, full and grand. Why didn't you drown yourself in the Seine, Sophia? . . . 'Sophia went down where the river flowed — Wild, wild, Sophia. . . .'

Well, that was the end of me, the real end. Two-pound-ten every Tuesday and a room off the Gray's Inn Road. Saved, rescued and with my place to hide in — what more did I want? I crept in and hid. The lid of the coffin shut down with a bang. Now I no longer wish to be loved, beautiful, happy or successful. I want one thing and one thing only — to be left alone. No more pawings, no more pryings — *leave me alone*. . . . (They'll do that all right, my dear.)

'At first I was afraid they would let gates bang on my hindquarters, and I used to be nervous of unknown people and places.' Quotation from *The Autobiography of a Mare* — one of my favourite books. . . . We English are so animal-conscious. We know so instinctively what the creatures feel and why they feel it. . . .

It was then that I had the bright idea of drinking myself to death. Thirty-five pounds of the legacy had accumulated, it seemed. That ought to do the trick.

I did try it, too. I've had enough of these streets that sweat a cold, yellow slime, of hostile people, of crying myself to sleep every night. I've had enough of thinking, enough of remembering. Now whisky, rum, gin, sherry, vermouth, wine with the bottles labelled 'Dum vivimus, vivamus. . . .' Drink, drink, drink. . . . As soon as I sober up I start again. I have to force it down sometimes. You'd think I'd get delirium tremens or something.

Nothing. I must be solid as an oak. Except when I cry.

I watch my face gradually breaking up — cheeks puffing out, eyes getting smaller. Never mind. 'While we live, let us live,' say the bottles of wine. When we give, let us give. Besides, it isn't my face, this tortured and tormented mask. I can take it off whenever I like and hang it up on a nail. Or shall I place on it a tall hat with a green feather, hang a veil over the lot, and walk about the dark streets so merrily? Singing defiantly 'You don't like me, but I don't like you either. "Don't like jam, ham or lamb, and I *don't* like roly-poly. . . ." ' Singing 'One more river to cross, that's Jordan, Jordan. . . .'

I have no pride — no pride, no name, no face, no country. I don't belong anywhere. Too sad, too sad. . . . It doesn't matter, there I am, like one of those straws which floats round the edge of a whirlpool and is gradually sucked into the centre, the dead centre, where everything is stagnant, everything is calm. Two-pound-ten a week and a room just off the Gray's Inn Road. . . .

All this time I am reading the menu over and over again. This used to be a place where you could only get hot dogs, choucroute, Vienna steak, Welsh rabbit and things like that. Now, it's more ambitious. 'Spécialités Javanaises (par personne, indivisibles): Rystafel complet (16 plats), 25.00, Rystafel petit (10 plats), 17.50, Nassi Goreng, 12.50. . . .' The back of the menu is covered with sketches of little women and 'Send more money, send more money' is written over and over again. This amuses me. I think of all the telegraph-wires buzzing 'Send more money'. In spite of everything, the wires from Paris always buzzing 'Send more money'.

The three people at the next table are talking about horse-racing. The two men are Dutch.

I get a pencil out of my bag. I write in a corner of the menu 'As-tu compris? Si, j'ai compris. I hope you got that. Yes, I got it.' I fold the menu up and put it in my bag. A little souvenir. . . .

The door opens. Five Chinese come in. They walk down to the end of the room in single file and stand there, talking. Then they all file solemnly out again, smiling politely. The proprietor mutters for a bit. Then he pretends to arrange the forks and knives on a table near by, and tells us that before they ordered drinks they wanted to see the fire lighted in the open grate, which is part of the olde English atmosphere. They wanted to see the flames dance. For a long time, he says, he has known that everybody in Montparnasse is mad, but this is the last straw. 'Tous piqués,' he says, with such an accent of despair, 'tous dingo, tous, tous, tous. . . .'

I am not at all sad as I walk back to the hotel. When I remember how one well-directed 'Oh, my God,' lays me out flat in London, I can only marvel at the effect this place has on me. I expect it is because the drink is so much better.

No, I am not sad, but by the time I get to the Boulevard St Michel I am feeling tired. I have walked along here so often, feeling tired. . . . Here is the fountain with the beautiful prancing horses. There is a tabac where I can have a drink near the next statue, the quinine statue.

Just then two men come up from behind and walk along on either side of me. One of them says: 'Pourquoi êtes-vous si triste?'

Yes, I am sad, sad as a circus-lioness, sad as an eagle without wings, sad as a violin with only one string and that one broken, sad as a woman who is growing old. Sad, sad, sad. . . . Or perhaps if I just said 'merde' it would do as well.

I don't speak and we walk along in silence. Then I say: 'But I'm not sad. Why should you think I'm sad?' Is it a ritual? Am I bound to answer the same question in the same words?

We stop under a lamp-post to guess nationalities. So they say, though I expect it is because they want to have a closer look at me. They tactfully don't guess mine. Are they Germans? No. Scandinavians, perhaps? No, the shorter one says they are Russians. When I hear that I at once accept their offer to go and have a drink. Les Russes — that'll wind up the evening nicely. . . .

There are two cafés opposite each other in this street near my hotel — the one where the proprietor is hostile, the one where the proprietor is neutral. I must be a bit drunk, because I lead them into the wrong one.

My life, which seems so simple and monotonous, is really a complicated affair of cafés where they like me and cafés where they don't, streets that are friendly, streets that aren't, rooms where I might be happy, rooms where I never shall be, looking-glasses I look nice in, looking-glasses I don't, dresses that will be lucky, dresses that won't, and so on.

However, being a bit tight, here I am on the wrong side of the street in the hostile café. Not that it matters, as I am not alone.

One of the Russians, the younger, is good-looking in a gentle, melancholy way. He is vaguely like the man who always took the spy-parts in German films some years ago. It's the shape of his head. The other is short and fair, with very blue eyes. He wears pince-nez. He must be the more alive of the two, because I find myself looking at him and talking to him all the time.

The usual conversation. . . . I say that I am not sad. I tell them that I am very happy, very comfortable, quite rich enough, and that I am over here for two weeks to buy a lot of clothes to startle my friends — my many friends. The shorter man, who it seems is a doctor, is willing to believe that I am happy but not that I am rich. He has often noticed, he says, that Englishwomen have melancholy expressions. It doesn't mean anything. The other one is impressed by my fur coat, I can see. He is willing to believe that I am rich but he says again that he doesn't think I am happy. The short man must be the more worldly-wise; the other one is like me — he has his feelings and sticks to them. He is the one who accosted me.

'I feel a great sadness in you,' he says.

Tristesse, what a nice word! Tristesse, lointaine, langsam, forlorn, forlorn. . . .

Now, for goodness' sake, listen to this conversation, which, after the second drink, seems to be about gods and goddesses.

'Madame Vénus se fâchera,' the short one is saying, wagging his finger at me.

'Oh, her!' I say. 'I don't like her any more. She's played me too many dirty tricks.'

'She does that to everyone. All the same, be careful. . . . What god do they worship in England, what goddess?'

'I don't know, but it certainly isn't Venus. Somebody wrote once that they worship a bitch-goddess. It certainly isn't Venus.'

Then we talk about cruelty. I look into the distance with a blank expression and say: 'Human beings are cruel — horribly cruel.'

'Not at all,' the older one answers irritably, 'not at all. That's a very short-sighted view. Human beings are struggling, and so they are egotists. But it's wrong to say that they are wholly cruel — it's a deformed view.'

That goes on for a bit and then peters out. Now we have discussed love, we have discussed cruelty, and they sheer off politics. It's rather strange — the way they sheer off politics. Nothing more to be discussed.

Well, we'll meet again, shan't we? . . . Of course we shall. It would be a pity not to meet again, wouldn't it? Will I meet them at the Pékin tomorrow for lunch? I have an idea that I shan't be feeling much like Chinese food at half-past twelve tomorrow. We arrange to meet at the Dôme at four o'clock.

They conduct me to the door of my hotel. The younger one remembers that I have left my menu behind — I had been showing it to them, the sketches of the little women and the 'Send more money, send more money' — and goes back to get it.

'Don't trouble. I don't really want it.'

But he has gone before I can stop him. I must keep this thing. It's fate.

Again I lie awake, trying to resist a great wish to go to a hairdresser in the morning to have my hair dyed.

5

When I come out of the hotel next morning a little old woman stops me and asks for money. I give her two francs. When she thanks me she looks straight into my eyes with an ironical expression.

As I go past the baker's shop at the corner of the street she comes out, with a long loaf of bread, smiles at me and waves gaily, I wave back. For a moment I escape from myself. But she disappears along a side-street, eating the loaf, and again I start thinking about dyeing my hair.

I pass the Italian restaurant. I pass Théodore's. It's a long way to the place I usually eat at. I hesitate, turn back, go in. I had meant to avoid Théodore's, because he might recognize me, because he might think I am changed, because he might say so.

I sit down in a corner, feeling uneasy.

He hasn't changed at all. He looks across the room at me from behind the bar and half-smiles. He has recognized me. . . . Very unlikely. Besides, what if he has, what's it matter? They can't kill you, can they? Oh, can't they, though, can't they?

Today I must be very careful, today I have left my armour at home.

Théodore's is more expensive than most of the restaurants round here and it is not very full. I watch the girl opposite cutting up the meat on her plate. She prongs a bit with her fork and puts it into her companion's mouth. He eats, registers pleasure as hard as he can, prods round for the best bit on his plate and feeds her with it. At any moment you expect these two to start flapping wings and chirping.

Then there's a middle-aged couple with their napkins tucked under their chins and a pretty woman accompanied by her husband — husband, I think, not lover.

These people all fling themselves at me. Because I am uneasy and sad they all fling themselves at me larger than life. But I can put my arm up to avoid the impact and they slide gently to the ground. Individualists, completely wrapped up in themselves, thank God. It's the extrovert, prancing around, dying for a bit of fun — that's the person you've got to be wary of.

I order sole and white wine. I eat with my eyes glued on my plate, the feeling of panic growing worse. (I told you not to come in here, I told you not to.)

At last, coffee. I wish I wasn't sitting so far from the door. However, it's nearly over. Soon I shall be out in the street again. I feel better.

I light a cigarette and drink the coffee slowly. As I am doing this two girls walk in — a tall, red-haired one and a little, plump, dark one. Sports clothes, no hats, English.

Théodore waddles up to their table and talks to them. The tall girl speaks French very well. I can't hear what Théodore is saying, but I watch his mouth moving and the huge moon-face under the tall chef's cap.

The girls turn and stare at me.

'Oh, my God!' the tall one says.

Théodore goes on talking. Then he too turns and looks at me. 'Ah, those were the days,' he says.

'Et qu'est-ce qu'elle fout ici, maintenant?' the tall girl says, loudly.

Now everybody in the room is staring at me; all the eyes in the room are fixed on me. It has happened.

I am calm, but my hand starts shaking so violently that I have to put the coffee-cup down.

'Everybody', Théodore says, 'comes back to Paris. Always.' He retires behind the bar.

I make a great effort and look at the tall girl. She immediately turns her eyes away and starts talking about food — different ways of cooking chicken. The little one hangs on every word.

Her red hair is arranged so carefully over her tiny skull. Her voice is hard and clear. Those voices like uniforms — tinny, meaningless. . . . Those voices that they brandish like weapons.

But what language! Considering the general get-up what you should have said was: 'Qu'est-ce qu'elle fiche ici?' Considering the general get-up, surely that's what you should have said. What language, what language! What would Debenham & Freebody say, and what Harvey Nichols?

Well, everybody has had a good stare at me and a short, disapproving stare at the two girls, and everybody starts eating again.

'Ah! quelle plaie, quelle plaie, les Anglais,' as the old gentleman in the Cros de Cagnes bus said. But a plague that pays, my dear, a plague that pays. And merrily, merrily, life goes on. . . . 'Quelle plaie, quelle plaie, les Anglais,' he said, sighing so deeply.

The waitress passes by my table and I ask for the bill.

'There is still some coffee left, madame. Will you have some more?' She smiles at me. Without waiting for me to answer, she pours what remains in the pot into my cup. She is sorry for me, she is trying to be kind.

My throat shuts up, my eyes sting. This is awful. Now I am going to cry. This is the worst. . . . If I do that I shall really have to walk under a bus when I get outside.

I try to decide what colour I shall have my hair dyed, and hang on to that thought as you hang on to something when you are drowning. Shall I have it red? Shall I have it black? Now, black — that would be startling. Shall I have it blond cendré? But blond cendré, madame, is the most difficult of colours. It is very, very rarely, madame, that hair can be successfully dyed blond cendré. It's even harder on the hair than dyeing it platinum blonde. First it must be bleached, that is to say, its own colour must be taken out of it — and then it must be dyed, that is to say, another colour must be imposed on it. (Educated hair. . . . And then, what?)

I finish the coffee, pay the bill and walk out. I would give all that's left of my life to be able to put out my tongue and say: 'One word to you,' as I pass that girl's table. I would give all the rest of my life to be able even to stare coldly at her. As it is, I can't speak to her, I can't even look at her. I just walk out.

Never mind. . . . One day, quite suddenly, when you're not expecting it, I'll take a hammer from the folds of my dark cloak and crack your little skull like an egg-shell. Crack it will go, the egg-shell; out they will stream, the blood, the brains. One day, one day. . . . One day the fierce wolf that walks by my side will spring on you and rip your abominable guts out. One day, one day. . . . Now, now, gently, quietly, quietly. . . .

Théodore comes out from behind the bar and opens the door for me. He smiles, his pig-eyes twinkle. I can't make out whether his smile is malicious (that goes for me, too) or apologetic (he meant well), or only professional.

•

What about the programme for this afternoon? That's the thing
—to have a plan and stick to it. First one thing and then another,
and it'll all be over before you know where you are.

But my legs feel weak. What, defeated already? Surely not. . . .
No, not at all. But I think I'll cross the road and sit quietly in the
Luxembourg Gardens for a while.

Piecing it together, arguing it out. . . .

All that happened was this: Théodore probably said to the girl:
'I think there's a compatriot of yours over there,' and the girl said:
'Oh, my God!' And then Théodore probably said: 'I remember
her. She used to come here a good deal some years ago. Ah, those
were the days. . . .' And this and that. And then the girl said:
'Qu'est-ce qu'elle fout ici?' partly because she didn't like the look of
me and partly because she wanted to show how well she spoke
French and partly because she thought that Théodore's was her
own particular discovery. (But, my dear good lady, Théodore's
had been crawling with kindly Anglo-Saxons for the last fifteen
years to my certain knowledge, and probably much longer than
that.) And that's everything that happened, and why get in a state
about it? . . . But I'm not, I'm not. Can I help it if my heart beats, if
my hands go cold?

I turn my chair round with its back to the pond where the
children sail their boats. Now I can see nothing but the slender,
straight trunks of trees. They look young, these trees. This is a
gentle place — a gentle, formal place. It isn't sad here, it isn't even
melancholy.

The attendant comes up and sells me a ticket. Now everything is
legal. If anyone says: 'Qu'est-ce qu'elle fout ici?' I can show the
ticket. This is legal. . . . I feel safe clutching it. I can stay here as long
as I like, putting two and two together, quite calmly, with nobody
to interfere with me.

Last night and today — it makes a pretty good sentence. . . .
Qu'est-ce qu'elle fout ici, la vieille? What the devil (translating it
politely) is she doing here, that old woman? What is she doing here,
the stranger, the alien, the old one? . . . I quite agree too, quite. I
have seen that in people's eyes all my life. I am asking myself all the
time what the devil I am doing here. All the time.

Old people pass and shabby women, and every now and again a
gay-looking one, painted, in a big fur coat. A man goes by,
strutting like a cock, wheeling a big pram. He is buttoned very
tightly into a black overcoat, his scarf carefully arranged under a

blue chin. Then another man, who looks almost exactly like him, playing with a little girl who can only just walk. He is shouting at her: 'You have a drop on your nose.' The little girl runs away from him shrieking in delighted fright, and he runs after her, taking small, fussy steps. They disappear into the trees and I hear him still calling out: 'Come here, you have a drop on your nose, you have a drop on your nose. . . .'

It's all right. I'm not unhappy. But I start thinking about that kitten.

This happened in London, and the kitten belonged to the couple in the flat above — a German hairdresser and his English wife. The kitten had an inferiority complex and persecution mania and nostalgie de la boue and all the rest. You could see it in her eyes, her terrible eyes, that knew her fate. She was very thin, scraggy and hunted, with those eyes that knew her fate. Well, all the male cats in the neigbourhood were on to her like one o'clock. She got a sore on her neck, and the sore on her neck got worse. 'Disgusting,' said the German hairdresser's English wife. 'She ought to be put away, that cat.' Then the kitten, feeling what was in the wind, came down into my room. She crouched against the wall, staring at me with those terrible eyes and with that big sore on the back of her neck. She wouldn't eat, she snarled at caresses. She just crouched in the corner of the room, staring at me. After a bit of this I couldn't stand it any longer and I shooed her out. Very reluctantly she went at first, with those eyes still staring at me. And then like an arrow through the door and down the stairs. I thought about her all the rest of that day and in the evening I said: 'I chased that unfortunate kitten out of my room. I'm worried about her. Is she all right?' 'Oh, haven't you heard?' they said. 'She got run over. Mrs Greiner was going to take her to the chemist's to be put away, and she ran right out into the street.' Right out into the street she shot and a merciful taxi went over her. . . .

I look at myself in the glass of my handbag. I said I would meet the Russian at four o'clock at the Dôme. He is one of those people with bright blue eyes and what they call a firm tread. He is sure to be an optimist.

We'll sit in the Dôme and talk sanity and normal human intercourse. He'll say: 'No, no, not cruelty — just egotism. They don't mean it.' He will explain just where I'm wrong, just where the reasoning has tripped up. Perhaps. . . .

There are hollows under my eyes. Sitting on the terrace of the Dôme, drinking Pernods and talking about sanity with enormous hollows under my eyes?

I hear a clock striking and count the strokes. It's four o'clock.

'No, thank you,' I think, 'I'm not going wandering into the Dôme looking like this — no, thank you.'

At once I feel a great regret. He might have said something to comfort me. . . .

I am empty of everything. I am empty of everything but the thin, frail trunks of the trees and the thin, frail ghosts in my room. 'La tristesse vaut mieux que la joie.'

In the glass just now my eyes were like that kitten's eyes.

I sit without moving, not unhappy.

Now it's getting dark. Now the gates are shutting. (Qu'est-ce qu'elle fout ici, la vieille?)

Get up, get up. Eat, drink, walk, march. . . . Pourquoi êtes-vous triste?

Tomorrow I must certainly go and have my hair dyed. I know exactly the man I'll go to. His name is Félix, but I'm not sure of the street. However, if I go to the Galeries Lafayette I can find my way from there.

When you go into the room Félix is seated at a desk. He has curly hair, a sensitive face, very nice hands. He wears a black velvet jacket. The complete artist — Antoine's only rival. In the window of his shop a large photograph with an inscription: 'To Monsieur Félix, who has kept my hair beautiful for so long — Adrienne.' There's no hope of getting Félix to attend to me, of course, but I may have a good assistant.

It's all right. Tomorrow I'll be pretty again, tomorrow I'll be happy again, tomorrow, tomorrow. . . .

I get up into the room. I bolt the door. I lie down on the bed with my face in the pillow. Now I can rest before I go out again. What do I care about anything when I can lie on the bed and pull the past over me like a blanket? Back, back, back. . . .

•

... I had just come up the stairs and I had to go down them again.
'No, no, your room's not ready. You must come back, come back. Come back between five and six.' 'What time is it now?' 'It's half-past ten.'

'Courage, courage, ma petite dame,' she says. 'Everything will go well.'

I go down the stairs again, clutching the banisters, step by step.

I stop a taxi. The man looks at me and hesitates. Perhaps he is afraid I may have my baby in his nice new taxi. What a thing to happen!

No danger at all, I want to say. Hours and hours and hours yet, she says.

I get back to the hotel and climb upstairs to my room. This is a hard thing to do. Has anybody ever had to do this before? Of course, lots of people — poor people. Oh, I see, of course, poor people. . . . Still, it is a hard thing to do, walking around when you're like this. And half-past five is a long time off — centuries of time.

When I climb the stairs again I am not seeing so well.

'Courage, my little lady. Your room is ready now.'

A room, a bed where I can lie down. Now the worst is surely over. But the long night, the interminable night. . . .

'Courage, courage,' she says. 'All will be well. All is going beautifully.'

This is a funny house. There are people having babies all over the place. Anyhow, at least two are having babies.

'Jesus, Jesus,' says one woman. 'Mother, Mother,' says another.
I do not speak. How long is it before I speak?

'Chloroform, chloroform,' I say when I speak. Of course I would. What nonsense! There is no doctor to give chloroform here. This is a place for poor people. Besides, she doesn't approve of chloroform. No Jesus, no Mother, and no chloroform either. . . .

What, then?
This.
Always?
Yes, always.

She comes and wipes my forehead. She speaks to me in a language that is no language. But I understand it.

Back, back, back. . . . This has happened many times.

What are you? I am an instrument, something to be made use of. . . .

She darts from one room to another, encouraging, soothing,

reproaching. 'Now, you're not trying. Courage, courage.' Speaking her old, old language of words that are not words.

A rum life, when you come to think of it. I'd hate to live it. However, to her it is just life. . . .

Afterwards I couldn't sleep. I would sleep for an hour or two, and then wake up and think about money, money, money for my son; money, money. . . .

Do I love him? Poor little devil, I don't know if I love him.

But the thought that they will crush him because we have no money — that is torture.

Money, money for my son, my beautiful son. . . .

I can't sleep. My breasts dry up; my mouth is dry. I can't sleep. Money, money. . . .

'Why!' she says. 'Can't you sleep? This will never do, never do.'

She probably knows why I can't sleep. I bet some of the others here can't either. Worrying about the same thing. (This is not *a* child; this is *my* child. Money, money. . . .)

'Well, why can't you sleep?' she says. 'Does he cry, this young man?'

'No, he hardly cries at all. Is it a bad sign, that he doesn't cry?'

'Why no, not at all. A beautiful, beautiful baby. . . . But why can't you sleep?'

She has slanting eyes, very clear. I like people with clear, slanting eyes. I can still give myself up to people I like. (Tell me what to do. Have you a solution? Tell me what to do.)

She pats me on the shoulder and says: 'You're worrying about nothing at all. Everything will come right for you. I'll send you in a tisane of orange-flower water, and tonight you must sleep, sleep. . . .'

I can't feed this unfortunate baby. He is taken out and given Nestlé's milk. So, I can sleep. . . .

The next day she comes in and says: 'Now I am going to arrange that you will be just like what you were before. There will be no trace, no mark, nothing.'

That, it seems, is her solution.

She swathes me up in very tight, very uncomfortable bandages. Intricately she rolls them and ties them. She gives me to understand that this is usually an extra. She charges a great deal for this as a rule.

'I do this better than anyone in the whole of Paris,' she says. 'Better than any doctor, better than any of these people who advertise, better than anyone in the whole of Paris.'

And there I lie in these damned bandages for a week. And there he lies, swathed up too, like a little mummy. And never crying.

But now I like taking him in my arms and looking at him. A lovely forehead, incredibly white, the eyebrows drawn very faintly in gold dust. . . .

Well, this was a funny time. (The big bowl of coffee in the morning with a pattern of red and blue flowers. I was always so thirsty.) But uneasy, uneasy. . . . Ought a baby to be as pretty as this, as pale as this, as silent as this? The other babies yell from morning to night. Uneasy. . . .

When I complain about the bandages she says: 'I promise you that when you take them off you'll be just as you were before.' And it is true. When she takes them off there is not one line, not one wrinkle, not one crease.

And five weeks afterwards there I am, with not one line, not one wrinkle, not one crease.

And there he is, lying with a ticket tied round his wrist because he died in a hospital. And there I am looking down at him, without one line, without one wrinkle, without one crease. . . .

7

The hair-dresser also ends by calling me 'Ma petite dame'.

He reflects for some time about my hair, feels it between his fingers. Then: 'In your place, madame, I shouldn't hesitate. But not for a moment. A nice blond cendré,' he says.

That was just the right way to put it. 'If I were in your place, madame, I shouldn't hesitate.'

He touches my hair gently. The smell of soap, scent, hair lotion, the sound of the dryer in the next cubicle, his fingers touching my hair — I could go to sleep.

'Very well,' I say in a sulky voice. (At it again, dearie, at it again!)

Of course I can't look on at this operation. I read magazines —

Féminas, Illustrations, Eves. Then I start in on the *Hairdresser*, the *Art of Hairdressing*, the *Hairdresser's Weekly* and a curious journal, with a large section called 'the Hive' — answers to correspondents.

'*Pierrette Clair de la Lune* — No, mademoiselle, your letter is nonsensical. You will never get thin that way — never. Life is not so easy. Life, mademoiselle, is difficult. At your age it will be very difficult to get thin. But. . . .

'*Petite Maman* — No, Petite Maman, you are not reasonable. Love is one thing; marriage — alas! — is quite another. If you haven't found that out yet you soon will, I assure you. Nevertheless. . . .'

No, mademoiselle, no, madame, life is not easy. Do not delude yourselves. Nothing is easy. But there is hope (turn to page 5), and yet more hope (turn to page 9). . . .

I am in the middle of a long article by a lady who has had her breasts lifted when he takes the dryer off my head.

'Voilà,' he says. . . .

'Yes,' he says, 'a very good blond cendré. A success.'

I had expected to think about this damned hair of mine without any let-up for days. (Is it all right? Is it not all right?) But before the taxi has got back to Montparnasse I have forgotten all about it.

I don't want to eat. I decide to go into the Luxembourg Gardens and sit there as I did yesterday. It's curious how peaceful I feel — as if I were possessed by something. Not that way — this way. Not up that street — this street. Just dance, and leave the music to me. . . . Like that.

There are some fish in the pool of the Médicis fountain. Three are red and one gold. The four fish look so forlorn that I wonder whether they are just starting them, or whether they have had a lot, and they have died off.

I stand for a long time, watching the fish. And several people who pass stop and also watch them. We stand in a row, watching the fish.

8

I must go and buy a hat this afternoon, I think, and tomorrow a dress. I must get on with the transformation act. But there I sit, watching the same procession of shabby women wheeling prams, of men tightly buttoned up into black overcoats.

One of the figures detaches itself from the procession and comes towards me. It is only when he is close to me and puts his hand out that I recognize him. The younger Russian, the melancholy one.

He also is tightly buttoned into a black overcoat. His scarf is carefully tied. He is wearing a black felt hat. Just like all the fathers attending the prams. Very correct, very respectable. He bows and shakes hands.

'You allow me?' He brings a chair close up to mine.

'You didn't go to meet my friend yesterday afternoon,' he says. 'No, I'm sorry, but I wasn't feeling well.' 'He was angry. He thought it wasn't at all nice of you. He said — ' He starts to laugh. 'Well, what did he say?' 'Oh, he was in a bad temper. He had an annoying letter this morning.' 'I was vexed with myself,' I say, 'but I couldn't go.'

He says, not taking his eyes from mine: 'When I make an appointment I always keep it, even though I think the other person won't be there.' 'Do you? That's not my idea of a Russian at all.' 'Oh, Russians, Russians — why do you think they are so different from other people?'

He comes from the Ukraine, he tells me, and it's very hot there, and very cold in the winter. But again he slides away from the subject of Russia and everything Russian, though in other ways he is communicative about himself. He is a naturalized Frenchman and he has done his military service in France. He says his name is Nicolas Delmar, which doesn't sound very Russian to me. Anyway, that's what he calls himself, and he writes it on a bit of *Le Journal*, with his address, and gives it to me. He lives in Montrouge. He has some female relative — sister, mother, aunt, I can't make out — who is ill, which makes him very sad.

'But I can forget it,' he says. 'Every day I come up to the Quartier Latin, or I walk in the Luxembourg Gardens. I can forget it.'

He speaks French slowly and ponderously. This gives me confidence. Off we go into a full blast of philosophical discussion. He says: 'For me, you see, I look at life like this: If someone had come to me and asked me if I wished to be born I think I should have answered No. I'm sure I should have answered No. But no one asked me. I am here not through my will. Most things that happen to me — they are not my will either. And so that's what I say to myself all the time: "You didn't ask to be born, you didn't make the world as it is, you didn't make yourself as you are. Why torment yourself? Why not take life just as it comes? You have the right to: you are not one of the guilty ones." When you aren't rich or strong or powerful, you are not a guilty one. And you have the right to take life just as it comes and to be as happy as you can.'

While he is talking I have a strange idea that perhaps it is like that. . . . Now then, you, X — you must go down and be born. Oh, not me, please, not me. Well then, you, Y, you go along and be born — somebody's got to be. Where's Y? Y is hiding. Well, come on Z, you've got to go and be born. Come on, hurry up, hurry up. . . . There's one every minute. Or is it every second?

'But don't you ever wish to be rich or strong or powerful?'

'No longer,' he says, 'no longer. I prefer to be as I am. As things are now, I wouldn't wish to be rich or strong or powerful. I wouldn't wish to be one of the guilty ones. I know I am not guilty, so I have the right to be just as happy as I can make myself.'

We go on in this strain for some time. I wonder what on earth he does, what he is. He looks like a person who is living on a very small fixed income. As I am thinking this he tells me that he loves this part of Paris, the Quartier Latin, because he loves youth. I look very hard at him when he says this. But he just means that he loves youth.

'Yes,' I say. 'I love youth too. Who doesn't? And this is just the place, full of prams, babies and so forth.'

'I very seldom go to Montmartre,' he says. 'I very seldom go anywhere else. This is the part of Paris that I like — the Quartier Latin and Montparnasse.'

'Side by side and oh, so different.'

'Have you ever noticed,' he says, 'that when you go from one part of Paris to another, it's just like going from one town to another — even from one country to another? The people are different, the atmosphere is different, even the women dress differently.'

I don't know why I don't quite like him. This gentle, resigned melancholy — it seems unnatural in a man who can't be much over thirty, if so much as that. Or perhaps it is because he seems more the echo of a thing than the thing itself. One moment I feel this, and another I like him very much, as if he were the brother I never had.

I say: 'Montparnasse is very changed since I knew it first, I can tell you. That was just after the war,' I say recklessly. (As you love youth so much, that'll give you something to think about.)

'You came here just after the war?'

'Yes, and I lived here up to five years ago. Then I went back to England.'

'Yes, it must be very changed, very changed,' he says, pursing his lips and nodding his head.

'Oh, terrible,' I say. 'But I don't believe things change much really; you only think they do. It seems to me that things repeat themselves over and over again.'

He says: 'I think you are getting cold, madame. You are shivering. Would you like to go to a pâtisserie and have a cup of chocolate? There is a nice one near here.'

I say: 'I'd much rather go to a café and have a drink.'

I have an idea that he disapproves of this, but he says: 'Yes, certainly. Let's go.'

I make no mistake this time. We go to the neutral café.

When we are in a corner with a coffee and a *fine* each he says: 'Do you know what I feel about you? I think you are very lonely. I know, because for a long time I was lonely myself. I hated people, I didn't want to see anyone. And then one day I thought: "No, this isn't the way." And now I go about a lot. I force myself to. I have a lot of friends; I'm never alone. Now I'm much happier.'

That sounds pretty simple. I must try it when I get back to London. . . .

I say: 'I liked your friend the other night.'

'Ah, yes,' he says, shaking his head. 'But he was vexed, and he's had bad news. . . .' (The optimist hasn't any more use for me, I can see that.) 'But I have many friends. I'll introduce you to all of them if you wish. Will you allow me? Then you will never be alone and you'll be much happier, you'll see.'

'But do you think they'd like me, your friends?'

'But certainly. Absolutely yes.'

This young man is very comforting — almost as comforting as the hairdresser.

'Will you come along now and see a friend of mine? He's a painter. I think he is a man you'd like. He's always gay and he knows how to talk to everybody. . . . Yes, Serge understands everybody — it's extraordinary.' (And, whether prince or prostitute, he always did his best. . . .) 'Mais au fond, vous savez, il s'en fiche de tout, il s'en fiche de tout le monde.'

He sounds fine.

'Yes, I'd like to,' I say. 'But I can't this afternoon. I have to go and buy a hat.'

'Well, would you like to come tomorrow?' he says, and we arrange to meet at four o'clock the next day.

There used to be a good hat-shop in the Rue Vavin.

It doesn't exist any longer. I wander aimlessly along a lot of back streets where there aren't any hat-shops at all. And then a street that is alive with them — Virginie, Josette, Claudine. . . . I look at the window of the first shop. There is a customer inside. Her hair, half-dyed, half-grey, is very dishevelled. As I watch she puts on a hat, makes a face at herself in the glass, and takes it off very quickly. She tries another — then another. Her expression is terrible — hungry, despairing, hopeful, quite crazy. At any moment you expect her to start laughing the laugh of the mad.

I stand outside, watching. I can't move. Hat after hat she puts on, makes that face at herself in the glass and throws it off again. Watching her, am I watching myself as I shall become? In five years' time, in six years' time, shall I be like that?

But she is better than the other one, the smug, white, fat, black-haired one who is offering the hats with a calm, mocking expression. You can almost see her tongue rolling round and round inside her cheek. It's like watching the devil with a damned soul. If I must end like one or the other, may I end like the hag.

I realize that I can't stay gaping in on them any longer and move off, very much shaken. Then I remember the Russian saying: 'I didn't ask to be born; I didn't make the world as it is; I didn't make myself as I am; I am not one of the guilty ones. And so I have a right to. . . .' Etcetera.

There are at least ten milliners' shops in this street. I decide to go into the last but one on the left-hand side and hope to strike lucky.

The girl in the shop says: 'The hats now are very difficult, very difficult. All my clients say that the hats now are very difficult to wear.'

This is a much larger shop than the other one. There is a cruel, crude light over the two mirrors and behind a long room stretching into dimness.

She disappears into the dimness and comes back with hat after hat, hat after hat, murmuring: 'All my clients are complaining that the hats now are very difficult to wear, but I think — I am sure — I shall manage to suit you.'

In the glass it seems to me that I have the same demented expression as the woman up the street.

'My God, not that one.'

I stare suspiciously at her in the glass. Is she laughing at me? No, I think not. I think she has the expression of someone whose pride is engaged. She is determined that before I go out of the shop I shall admit that she can make hats. As soon as I see this expression in her eyes I decide to trust her. I too become quite calm.

'You know, I'm bewildered. Please tell me which one I ought to have.'

'The first one I showed you,' she says at once.

'Oh, my God, not that one.'

'Or perhaps the third one.'

When I put on the third one she says: 'I don't want to insist, but yes — that is your hat.'

I look at it doubtfully and she watches me — not mockingly, but anxiously.

She says: 'Walk up and down the room in it. See whether you feel happy in it. See whether you'll get accustomed to it.'

There is no one else in the shop. It is quite dark outside. We are alone, celebrating this extraordinary ritual.

She says: 'I very seldom insist, but I am sure that when you have got accustomed to that hat you won't regret it. You will realize that it's your hat.'

I have made up my mind to trust this girl, and I must trust her.

'I don't like it much, but it seems to be the only one,' I say in a surly voice.

I have been nearly two hours in the shop, but her eyes are still quite friendly.

I pay for the hat. I put it on. I have a great desire to ask her to come and dine with me, but I daren't do it. All my spontaneity has gone. (Did I ever have any? Yes, I think sometimes I had — in flashes. Anyway, it's gone now. If I asked her to dine with me, it would only be a failure.)

She adjusts the hat very carefully. 'Remember, it must be worn forward and very much on one side. Comme ça.'

She sees me out, still smiling. A strange client, l'étrangère. . . . The last thing she says is: 'All the hats now are very difficult. All my clients are complaining.'

I feel saner and happier after this. I go to a restaurant near by and eat a large meal, at the same time carefully watching the effect of the hat on the other people in the room, comme ça. Nobody stares at me, which I think is a good sign.

A man sitting near by asks if he may look at my evening paper, as he wants to go to the cinema tonight. Then he tries to start a conversation with me. I think: 'That's all right. . . .'

9

When I go out into the Place de l'Odéon I am feeling happy, what with my new hair and my new hat and the good meal and the wine and the *fine* and the coffee and the smell of night in Paris. I'm not going to any beastly little bar tonight. No, tonight I'm going somewhere where there's music; somewhere where I can be with a lot of people; somewhere where there's dancing. But where? By myself, where can I go? I'll have one more drink first and then think it out.

Not the Dôme. I'll avoid the damned Dôme. And, of course, it's the Dôme I go to.

The terrace is crowded, but there are not many people inside. What on earth have I come in here for? I have always disliked the place, except right at the start, when the plush wasn't so resplendent and everybody spat on the floor. It was rather nice then.

I pay for my drink and go out. I am waiting to cross the street. Someone says: 'Excuse me, but can I speak to you? I think you speak English.'

I don't answer. We cross side by side.

He says: 'Please allow me to speak to you. I wish to so much.'

He speaks English with a very slight accent. I can't place it. I look at him and recognize him. He was sitting at a table in the corner opposite to mine at the Dôme.

'Please. Couldn't we go to a café and talk?'

'Of course,' I say. 'Why not?'

'Well, where shall we go?' he says in a fussy voice. 'You see, I don't know Paris well. I only arrived last night.'

'Oh?' I say.

As we walk along, I look sideways at him and can't make him

out. He isn't trying to size me up, as they usually do — he is exhibiting himself, his own person. He is very good-looking, I noticed that in the Dôme. But the nervousness, the slightly affected laugh. . . .

Of course. I've got it. Oh Lord, is that what I look like? Do I really look like a wealthy dame trotting round Montparnasse in the hope of — ? After all the trouble I've gone to, is that what I look like? I suppose I do.

Shall I tell him to go to hell? But after all, I think, this is where I might be able to get some of my own back. You talk to them, you pretend to sympathize; then, just at the moment when they are not expecting it, you say: 'Go to hell.'

We are passing the Closerie des Lilas. He says: 'This looks a nice café. Couldn't we go in here?'

'All right. But it's very full. Let's sit on the terrace.'

The terrace is cold and dark and there is not another soul there. 'What about a drink?'

'You'll have to get hold of the waiter. He won't come out here.'

'I'll get him.'

He goes into the café and comes back with the waiter and two brandies.

He says: 'Have you ever felt like this — as if you can't bear any more, as if you must speak to someone, as if you must tell someone everything or otherwise you'll die?'

'I can imagine it.'

He is not looking at me — he hasn't looked at me once. He is looking straight ahead, gathering himself up for some effort. He is going to say his piece. I have done this so often myself that it is amusing to watch somebody else doing it.

'But why do you want to talk to me?'

He is going to say: 'Because you look so kind.' or 'Because you look so beautiful and kind,' or subtly, 'Because you look as if you'll understand. . . .'

He says: 'Because I think you won't betray me.'

I had meant to get this man to talk to me and tell me all about it, and then be so devastatingly English that perhaps I should manage to hurt him a little in return for all the many times I've been hurt. . . . 'Because I think you won't betray me, because I think you won't betray me. . . .' Now it won't be so easy.

'Of course I won't betray you. Why should I betray you?'

'No,' he says. 'Why?'

He throws back his head and laughs. That's the gesture for showing off the teeth. Also, I suppose he is laughing at the idea of my being able to betray him.

'Very nice, very nice indeed. Beautiful teeth,' I say in an insolent voice.

'Yes, I know,' he answers simply.

But I have jarred him a bit. He finishes his drink and starts again. 'I am what they call in French a mauvais garçon.'

'But I like them. I like les mauvais garçons.'

For the first time he looks straight at me. He doesn't look away again, but goes on in the same nervous voice: 'I got into bad trouble at home. I ran away.'

'I am a Canadian, a French-Canadian,' he says.

'French-Canadian? I see.'

'Shall we have another drink?'

Again he has to go inside the café to fetch the waiter and the drinks. Now it's creeping into me, the brandy, creeping into my arms, my legs, making me feel hazy.

I listen to his story, which is that he joined the Foreign Legion, was in Morocco for three years, found it impossible to bear any longer, and escaped through Spain — Franco Spain. Just escaped from the Foreign Legion. . . . La Légion, La Légion Etrangère. . . .

'I had enormous luck, or I couldn't have done it. I got to Paris last night. I'm at a hotel near the Gare d'Orsay.'

'Is it as bad as they say, the Legion?'

'Oh, they tell a lot of lies about it. But I'd had enough. . . . You don't believe me, do you? You don't believe anything I'm telling you. But it's always when a thing sounds not true that it is true,' he says.

Of course. I know that. . . . You imagine the carefully-pruned, shaped thing that is presented to you is truth. That is just what it isn't. The truth is improbable, the truth is fantastic; it's in what you think is a distorting mirror that you see the truth.

'I'll tell you one thing I don't believe. I don't believe you're a French-Canadian.'

'Then what do you think I am?'

'Spanish? Spanish-American?'

He blinks and says to himself: 'Elle n'est pas si bête que ça.' Well, that might mean anything.

'It's awfully cold here,' I say, 'too cold to stay any longer.'

'No, please. Please don't go, you mustn't go. Or, if you wish, let's go somewhere else. But I must talk to you.'

His voice is so urgent that I begin to feel exasperated.

'But, my dear friend, I don't know what you think I can do. People who are in trouble want someone with money to help them. Isn't it so? Well, I haven't got any money.'

The corners of his mouth go down. They all say that.

I want to shout at him 'I haven't got any money, I tell you. I know what you're judging by. You're judging by my coat. You oughtn't to judge by my coat. You ought to judge by what I have on under my coat, by my handbag, by my expression, by anything you like. Not by this damned coat, which was a present — and the only reason I haven't sold it long ago is because I don't want to offend the person who gave it to me, and because if you knew what you really get when you try to sell things it would give you a shock, and because — '

Well, there you are — no use arguing. I can see he has it firmly fixed in his head that I'm a rich bitch and that if he goes on long enough I can be persuaded to part.

'But it isn't money I want,' he says. 'Really it isn't money. What I hoped was that we could go somewhere where we could be quite alone. I want to put my head on your breast and put my arms round you and tell you everything. You know, it's strange, but that's how I feel tonight. I could die for that — a woman who would put her arms round me and to whom I could tell everything. Couldn't we go somewhere like that?'

'No, we can't,' I say. 'Impossible.'

'Well,' he says, accepting this calmly, 'if you won't do that, I thought perhaps you could help me about my papers. You see, I have no papers, no passport. That's just why I'm in trouble. The slightest accident and I'm finished. I have no papers. But if I could get a passport, I would go to London. I'd be safe there. I could get in touch with friends.

I say: 'And you think I can help you to get a passport? I? Me? But who do you think I am? This must be one of my good nights.'

At this moment I find everything so funny that I start laughing loudly. He laughs too.

'I can't stay on this damned terrace any longer. It's too cold.'

He raps on the window and, when the waiter comes, pays for the drinks.

'Now, where shall we go?' He puts his arm through mine and says, in French: 'Now, where?'

Well, what harm can he do to me? He is out for money and I haven't got any. I am invulnerable.

There we are, arm in arm, outside the Closerie des Lilas and when I think of my life it seems to me so comical that I have to laugh. It has taken me a long time to see how comical it has been, but I see it now, I do.

'You must tell me where to go,' he says, 'because I don't know Paris.'

I take him to the café where I go most nights — the place that is always empty. This is the first time that I have seen him in a bright light, close by. It is also the first time that, on these occasions, I haven't cared in the least what the man thinks of me, and am only curious to see what he looks like.

He doesn't look like a gigolo — not my idea of a gigolo at all. For instance, his hair is rather untidy. But, nice hair.

Another brandy-and-soda. I suppose all this money that he is spending on me is the sprat to catch a whale.

The waiter, giving him change, brings out of his pocket the most extraordinary collection of small money. Pieces of twenty-five centimes, of ten, of five — the table is covered with them. When he has slowly collected it all once more, he goes into the corner of the room, takes off his shoes and starts cleaning them.

I say: 'This is my sort of place — this chic, gay place. Do you like it?'

'No, I don't like it, but I understand why you come here. I'm not always so fond of human beings, either.'

Well, here's another who isn't as stupid as all that.

He says: 'You know, that waiter — he was quite sure we loved each other and were going to be very happy tonight. He was envying us.'

'Yes, I expect he'll stay awake all night thinking of it. Like hell he will.'

He looks disconsolate, tired, as if he were thinking: 'No good. Everything's got to be started all over again.' Poor gigolo!

I say: 'About your papers — there are people here who sell false passports. It can be done.'

'I know. I'm in touch with somebody already.'

'What, and you only got here last night! You haven't wasted much time.'

'No, and I'd better not, either.'

He is in some sort of trouble. I know that look. I want very much to comfort him — to say something to cheer him up.

'I like les mauvais garçons,' I say. He smiles. 'I know exactly what you want,' I say. 'You want somebody very rich and very chic.'

'Yes,' he says, 'yes, that's what would just suit me. And beautiful.'

'But, my dear, you're not going to find that at the Dôme.'

'Where shall I go, then? Where shall I find all that?'

'Ritz Bar,' I say vaguely.

After this I start my piece. I tell him my name, my address, everything. He says his name is René, and leaves it at that. I say I am sick of my hotel and want to leave it and find a flat or a studio.

He is on the alert at once. 'A studio? I think I could get you exactly the place you want.'

I am not so drunk as all that.

'I thought you said you'd just escaped from the Foreign Legion and only got to Paris last night and were going away again as soon as you could.'

'Why should that prevent me from trying to get you a studio if you want one?'

(Let it pass, dearie, let it pass. What's it matter?)

'Can I take you back to your hotel?'

'Yes, but it's too far to walk. I want a taxi.'

We sit in the taxi in silence. At the corner of the street we get out. I let him pay. (So much the worse for you. That will teach you to size up your types a bit better.)

'Let's have one more drink,' he says.

We walk up the street, trying to find a place that is open. Everything seems to be shut; it is past twelve. We go along the Rue St Jacques hand in hand. I am no longer self-conscious. Hand in hand we walk along, swinging our arms. Suddenly he stops, pulls me under a lamp-post and stares at me. The street is empty, the lights in the bars are out.

'Hey, isn't it a bit late in the day to do this?'

He says: 'Mais c'est complètement fou. It's hallucinating. Walking along here with you, I have the feeling that I'm with a — '

'With a *beau*-tiful young girl?'

'No,' he says. 'With a child.'

Now I have had enough to drink, now the moment of tears is very near. I say: 'Well, nothing's open. Everything's shut. I'm going home.'

He looks up at the door of my hotel.

'Can I come up to your room?'

'No, you can't.'

'Well, can I come back in a little while and get a room here myself and then come to see you?'

(The patronne saying: 'L'Anglaise has picked up someone. Have you seen?')

'No, don't come here. I shall be awfully vexed if you come here. Please don't.'

'Of course I won't if you ask me not to,' he says. Tactful. 'What about the hotel next door? Perhaps I could get a room there.'

The hotel next door? No, the hotel five or six doors off. That's the one. In that hotel there is a room with the biggest bed I have ever known — the biggest bed in the world, the bed of beds. . . . Everything in the room is red. And there is nothing in it but this huge bed and a wash-stand and a bidet. Shall I go and lie on it again tonight, when everything is a caricature, a grimace?

I say: 'Well, I shouldn't if I were you. The hotels in this street —they look all right by this light, but they're not so comfortable. Try something more modern.'

'Rien à faire?'

'Rien à faire.'

He shrugs his shoulders. 'I'm sorry,' he says. . . . 'What's this street? How can I get to the Boulevard St Michel?'

I don't believe in this pose of being a stranger to Paris, but he is certainly keeping it up pretty well.

Somebody is hammering at the door. I have bolted it — unnecessarily, as it can't be opened from the outside without a key.

Marthe says: 'You're wanted on the telephone. It's not very convenient when you bolt the door.'

I expect she has been trying to get in for some time.

I have a headache and feel very bad-tempered. I think: 'It's that man, of course. He's made up his mind that he's going to get some money out of me and "Vénus toute entière à sa proie attachée," isn't it in it.'

While I am thinking this I am putting on my dressing-gown. I comb my hair without daring to look at myself in the glass.

I get downstairs to the telephone. There is nobody on the line.

'There was a monsieur,' the patronne says.

There was a monsieur, but the monsieur has gone.

I feel ill today. This would be an awful place to be ill in. They wouldn't even get me another bottle of Evian when the first was finished — they wouldn't do a thing.

I expect if I rang the bell and said that they must change the sheets they would do it. That's my idea of luxury — to have the sheets changed every day and twice on Sundays. That's my idea of the power of money.

Yes, I'll have the sheets changed. I'll lie in bed all day, pull the curtains and shut the damned world out. . . . There was a monsieur, but the monsieur has gone. There was more than one monsieur, but they have all gone. What an assortment! One of every kind. . . .

I'll lie in bed all day, pull the curtains and shut the damned world out.

PART TWO

1

A ll the same, at three o'clock I am dressing to meet the Russian.

He is waiting. He says his friend Serge is expecting us. 'Le peintre,' he calls him.

I suggest taking a taxi but he seems horrified at the idea.

'No, no. We'll go by bus. It's quite near. It's only a few minutes away.' 'Couldn't we walk then?' 'Oh yes, we could walk. It's just off the Avenue d'Orléans, about five minutes' walk.' 'It's more than five minutes,' I argue. 'It's more like half an hour.'

Soon now it will be winter. There are hardly any leaves on the trees and the man outside the Luxembourg Gardens is selling roast chestnuts.

We stand at the end of a long queue. No bus.

'Do let's take a taxi.' 'Very well. If you like,' he says unwillingly. 'But the man will be very vexed at having to go such a short distance. — Place Denfert-Rochereau, the Métro,' he says to the driver. — 'It won't be far to walk from there.' 'But couldn't we go straight to the place where your friend lives?' 'No, I don't know the name of the street.' 'You don't know the name of the street?' 'No, I've never noticed it.'

When I see how anxiously he is watching the meter I am sorry I insisted on taking the taxi. All the same, I should have dropped dead if I had tried to walk this distance.

'Do let me pay, because it was I who insisted.'

But he has got the money in his hand already and is counting it out.

He takes my arm and we walk along. 'It's just a minute, it's just a minute,' he keeps saying.

Walking to the music of *L'Arlésienne*, remembering the coat I wore then — a black-and-white check with big pockets. We have just passed the hotel I lived in. That was the high spot — when I had

---

nothing to eat for three weeks, except coffee and a croissant in the morning.

I slept most of the time. Probably that was why it was so easy. If I had had to go about a lot I might have felt worse. I got so that I could sleep fifteen hours out of the twenty-four.

Twice I said I was ill, and they sent me up soup with meat in it from downstairs, and I could get an occasional bottle of wine on tick from the shop round the corner. It wasn't starvation at all when you come to think of it. Still, I'm not saying that there weren't some curious moments.

After the first week I made up my mind to kill myself — the usual whiff of chloroform. Next week, or next month, or next year I'll kill myself. But I might as well last out my month's rent, which has been paid up, and my credit for breakfasts in the morning.

'My child, don't hurry. You have eternity in front of you.' She used to say that sarcastically, Sister Marie-Augustine, because I was so slow. But the phrase stayed with me. I have eternity in front of me. Soon I'll be able to do it, but there's no hurry. Eternity is in front of me. . . .

Usually, in the interval between my afternoon sleep and my night sleep I went for a walk, turned up the Boulevard Arago, walked to a certain spot and turned back. And one evening I was walking along with my hands in the pockets of my coat and my head down. This was the time when I got in the habit of walking with my head down. . . . I was walking along in a dream, a haze, when a man came up and spoke to me.

This is unhoped-for. It's also quite unwanted. What I really want to do is to go for my usual walk, get a bottle of wine on tick and go back to the hotel to sleep. However, it has happened, and there you are. Life is curious when it is reduced to its essentials.

Well, we go into the Café Buffalo. Will I have a little apéritif? I certainly will. Two Pernods arrive.

I start thinking about food. Choucroute, for instance — you ought to be able to get choucroute garnie here. Lovely sausage, lovely potato, lovely, lovely cabbage. . . . My mouth starts watering violently. I drink half the glass of Pernod in order to swallow convenablement. And then I feel like a goddess. It might have made me sick, but it has done the other thing.

The orchestra was playing *L'Arlésienne*, I remember so well. I've just got to hear that music now, any time, and I'm back in the Café Buffalo, sitting by that man. And the music going heavily. And he's talking away about a friend who is so rich that he has his photograph on the bands of his cigars. A mad conversation.

'One day', he says, 'I too will be so rich that I shall have my photo on the bands of the cigars I offer to my friends. That is my ambition.'

Will I have another little Pernod? I certainly will have another little Pernod. (Food? I don't want any food now. I want more of this feeling — fire and wings.)

There we are, jabbering away as if we had known each other for years. He reads me a letter that he has just had from a girl.

What's the matter with it? It seems to me a letter any man ought to be proud to have. All about frissons and spasms and unquestionable réussites. (Chéri, chéri, rappelles-tu que. . . .) A testimonial, that letter is.

But the snag is at the end, as usual. The girl wants a new pair of shoes and she is asking for three hundred francs to buy them. Chéri, you will remember the unforgettable hours we passed together and not refuse me when I tell you that my shoes are quite worn out. I am ashamed to go into the street. The valet de chambre knows that there are large holes in both my shoes. Really, I am ashamed to be so poor. I stay all the time in my room. And so, chéri, etcetera, etcetera, etcetera. . . .

He is chewing and chewing over this letter. 'I don't believe it,' he says. 'It's all a lie, it's a snare, it's a trap. This girl, you understand, is a liar. What she wants is three hundred francs to give to her maquereau. Will I give her three hundred francs for her maquereau? No, I won't. I will not. . . . All the same,' he says, 'I can't bear to think of that poor little one with holes in her shoes. That can't be amusing, walking about with your feet on the ground.'

'No, it isn't amusing,' I say. 'Especially on a rainy day.'

'Well, what do you think? Do you think this letter can be genuine? What do you think?'

Every word has been chewed over by the time we have finished our second drink.

'Besides,' he says, 'even if it is genuine, I mustn't send the money at once. That would never do. If she thought she had only to ask, to have — that would never do. No, no, I must keep her waiting.'

Chew, chew, chew. . . .

'No. I think she's lying.'

All the time he is staring at me, sizing me up. He has his hand on my knee under the table.

He is not a Parisian. He lives in Lille. He is staying at a friend's flat, he says, and it's a very nice flat. Will I come along there and have a little porto? . . . Well, why not?

What does this man look like? I don't remember. I don't think I ever looked at him. I remember that he had very small hands and that he wore a ring with a blue stone in it.

We get out into the street. And, of course, vlung — first breath of fresh air and I'm so drunk I can't walk.

'Hé là,' he says. 'What's the matter? Have you been dancing too much?'

'All you young women,' he says, 'dance too much. Mad for pleasure, all the young people. . . . Ah, what will happen to this after-war generation? I ask myself. What will happen? Mad for pleasure. . . . But we'll take a taxi.'

We cross the road unsteadily and stand under a sickly town-tree waiting to signal a taxi. I start to giggle. He runs his hand up and down my arm.

I say: 'Do you know what's really the matter with me? I'm hungry. I've had hardly anything to eat for three weeks.'

'Comment?' he says, snatching his hand away. 'What's this you're relating?'

'C'est vrai,' I say, giggling still more loudly. 'It's quite true. I've had nothing to eat for three weeks.' (Exaggerating, as usual.)

At this moment a taxi draws up. Without a word he gets into it, bangs the door and drives off, leaving me standing there on the pavement.

And did I mind? Not at all, not at all. If you think I minded, then you've never lived like that, plunged in a dream, when all the faces are masks and only the trees are alive and you can almost see the strings that are pulling the puppets. Close-up of human nature — isn't it worth something?

I expect that man thought Fate was conspiring against him — what with his girl's shoes and me wanting food. But there you are, if you're determined to get people on the cheap, you shouldn't be so surprised when they pitch you their own little story of misery sometimes.

In the middle of the night you wake up. You start to cry. What's happening to me? Oh, my life, oh, my youth. . . .

There's some wine left in the bottle. You drink it. The clock ticks. Sleep. . . . People talk about the happy life, but that's the happy life when you don't care any longer if you live or die. You only get there after a long time and many misfortunes. And do you think you are left there? Never.

As soon as you have reached this heaven of indifference, you are pulled out of it. From your heaven you have to go back to hell. When you are dead to the world, the world often rescues you, if only to make a figure of fun out of you.

Walking to the music of *L'Arlésienne*. . . . I feel for the pockets of the check coat, and I am surprised when I touch the fur of the one I am wearing. . . . Pull yourself together, dearie. This is late October, 1937, and that old coat had its last outing a long time ago.

We go up the stairs of a block of studios into a large, empty, cold room, with masks on the walls, two old arm-chairs and a straight-backed wooden chair on which is written 'Merde'. The answer, the final answer, to everything?

The friend is a Jew of about forty. He has that mocking look of the Jew, the look that can be so hateful, that can be so attractive, that can be so sad.

He keeps putting bits of screwed-up newspaper into the stove.

'It won't burn. It's in a bad mood today. I'll get tea,' he says. 'The water will be boiling soon.'

'West African masks?'

'Yes, straight from the Congo. . . . I made them. This one isn't bad.'

He takes it down and shows it to me. The close-set eye-holes stare into mine. I know that face very well; I've seen lots like it, complete with legs and body.

That's the way they look when they are saying: 'Why didn't you drown yourself in the Seine?' That's the way they look when they are saying: 'Qu'est-ce que'elle fout ici, la vieille?' That's the way they look when they are saying: 'What's this story?' Peering at you. Who are you, anyway? Who's your father and have you got any money, and if not, why not? Are you one of us? Will you think what you're told to think and say what you ought to say? Are you red, white or blue — jelly, suet pudding or ersatz caviare?

Serge puts some béguine music, Martinique music, on an old gramophone in the corner and asks whether I'd like to dance.

'No, I'd rather watch you.'

He holds the mask over his face and dances. 'To make you laugh,' he says. He dances very well. His thin, nervous body looks strange, surmounted by the hideous mask. Delmar, very serious and correct, claps his hands in time to the music.

(*Have you been dancing too much?*) 'Don't stop.'

(*Mad for pleasure, all the young people.*) 'Please don't stop.'

The gramophone is grinding out 'Maladie d'amour, maladie de la jeunesse. . . .'

I am lying in a hammock looking up into the branches of a tree. The sound of the sea advances and retreats as if a door were being opened and shut. All day there has been a fierce wind blowing, but at sunset it drops. The hills look like clouds and the clouds like fantastic hills.

> *Pain of love,*
> *Pain of youth,*
> *Walk away from me,*
> *Keep away from me,*
> *Don't want to see you*
> *No more, no more. . . .*

Then we talk about negro music and about various boîtes in Montparnasse. The Highball? No, the Highball isn't nice any more. It's a dirty place now. Oh, is it? Yes, it is. Nobody goes there now. But the Cuban Cabin in Montmartre, that's quite good. You might like that. They play very well there. It's gay.

I am talking away, quite calmly and sedately, when there it is again — tears in my eyes, tears rolling down my face. (Saved, rescued, but not quite so good as new. . . .)

'I'm so sorry. I'm such a fool. I don't know what's the matter with me.'

'Oh, madame, oh, madame,' Delmar says, 'why do you cry?'

'I'm such a fool. Please don't take any notice of me. Just don't take any notice and I'll be all right.'

'But cry,' le peintre says. 'Cry if you want to. Why shouldn't you cry? You're with friends.'

'If I could have a drink. . . .'

'A drink. I have some porto somewhere.'

He bustles around. He produces three very small cups — the things you drink saké from.

'Japanese,' I say, intelligently.

He doesn't answer. He is searching for the bottle of port.

He pours out what is left of it. It just fills one saké cup. That, a drink!

I have an irresistible longing for a long, strong drink to make me forget that once again I have given damnable human beings the right to pity me and laugh at me.

I say in a loud, aggressive voice: 'Go out and get a bottle of brandy,' take money out of my bag and offer it to him.

This is where he starts getting hold of me, Serge. He doesn't accept the money or refuse it — he ignores it. He blots out what I have said and the way I said it. He ignores it as if it had never been, and I know that, for him, it has never been. He is thinking of something else.

'Don't drink just now,' he says. 'Later, I'll get some, if you like. I'll make you some tea now.'

He comes back with the tea and puts lemon into it. It tastes good to me.

'I often want to cry. That is the only advantage women have over men — at least they can cry.'

We seriously discuss the subject of weeping.

Delmar doesn't cry easily, he says. No, not so easily as all that. Le peintre, it seems, cries about Van Gogh. He speechifies about 'the terrible effort, the sustained effort — something beyond the human brain, what he did.' Etcetera, etcetera. . . .

When he gives me a cigarette his hand is shaking. He isn't lying. I think he has really cried over Van Gogh.

We drink more tea. The stove has quite gone out and it is very cold, but they don't seem to notice it. I am glad of my coat. I think I ought to ask to see his pictures, but he is in a flow of talk which I can't interrupt. He is relating an experience he had in London.

'Oh, you've lived in London?'

'Yes, I was there for a time, but I didn't stay long — no. But I got a fine suit,' he says. 'I looked quite an Englishman from the neck down. I was very proud. . . . I had a room near Notting Hill Gate. Do you know it?'

'Oh yes, I know it.'

'A very comfortable room. But one night this happened. Talking about weeping — I still think of it. . . . I was sitting by the fire, when I heard a noise as if someone had fallen down outside. I opened the door and there was a woman lying full-length in the passage, crying. I said to her: "What's the matter?" She only went on crying. "Well," I thought, "it's nothing to do with me." I shut the door firmly. But still I could hear her. I opened the door again and I asked her: "What is it? Can I do anything for you?" She said: "I want a drink." '

'Exactly like me,' I say. 'I cried, and I asked for a drink.' He certainly likes speechifying, this peintre. Is he getting at me?

'No, no,' he says. 'Not like you at all.'

He goes on: 'I said to her "Come in if you wish. I have some whisky." She wasn't a white woman. She was half-negro — a mulatto. She had been crying so much that it was impossible to tell whether she was pretty or ugly or young or old. She was drunk too, but that wasn't why she was crying. She was crying because she was at the end of everything. There was that sound in her sobbing which is quite unmistakable — like certain music. . . . I put my arm round her, but it wasn't like putting your arm round a woman. She was like something that has been turned into stone. She asked again for whisky. I gave it to her, and she started a long story, speaking sometimes in French, sometimes in English, when of course I couldn't understand her very well. She came from Martinique, she said, and she had met this monsieur in Paris, the monsieur she was with on the top floor. Everybody in the house knew she wasn't married to him, but it was even worse that she wasn't white. She said that every time they looked at her she could see how they hated her, and the people in the streets looked at her in the same way. At first she didn't mind — she thought it comical. But now she had got so that she would do anything not to see people. She told me she hadn't been out, except after dark, for two years. When she said this I had an extraordinary sensation, as if I were looking down into a pit. It was the expression in her eyes. I said: "But this monsieur you are living with, what about him?" "Oh, he is very Angliche, he says I imagine everything." I asked if he didn't find it strange that she never went out. But she said No, he thought it quite natural. She talked for a long time about this monsieur. It seemed that she stayed with him because she didn't know where else to go, and he stayed with her because he liked the way she cooked. All this sounds a little ridiculous, but if you had seen this woman you'd understand why it is I have never been able to forget her. I said to her: "Don't let yourself get hysterical, because if you do that it's the end." But it was difficult to speak to her reasonably, because I had all the time this feeling that I was talking to something that was no longer quite human, no longer quite alive.'

'It's a very sad story,' I say. 'I'm sure you were kind to her.'

'But that's just it. I wasn't. She told me that that afternoon she'd felt better and wanted to go out for a walk. "Even though it wasn't quite dark," she said. On the way out she had met the little girl of one of the other tenants. This house was one of those that are let off in floors. There were several families living in it. She said to the little girl: "Good afternoon. . . ." It was a long story, and of course, as I said, I couldn't understand everything she said to me. But it seemed that the child had told her that she was a dirty woman, that she smelt bad, that she hadn't any right in the house. "I hate you and I wish you were dead," the child said. And after that she had drunk a whole bottle of whisky and there she was, outside my door. Well, what can you say to a story like that? I knew all the time that what she wanted was that I should make love to her and that it was the only thing that would do her any good. But alas, I couldn't. I just gave her what whisky I had and she went off, hardly able to walk. . . . There were two other women in the house. There was one with a shut, thin mouth and a fat one with a bordel laugh. I must say I never heard them speaking to the Martiniquaise, but they had cruel eyes, both of them. . . . I didn't much like the way they looked at me, either. . . . But perhaps all women have cruel eyes. What do you think?'

I say: 'I think most human beings have cruel eyes.' That rosy, wooden, innocent cruelty. I know.

'When I passed her on the stairs next day I said good morning, but she didn't answer me. . . . Once I saw the child putting her tongue out at the poor creature. Only seven or eight, and yet she knew so exactly how to be cruel and who it was safe to be cruel to. One must admire Nature. . . . I got an astonishing hatred of the house after that. Every time I went in it was as if I were walking into a wall — one of those walls where people are built in, still alive. I've never forgotten this. Seriously, all the time I was in London, I felt as if I were being suffocated, as if a large derrière was sitting on me.'

'Well, some people feel that way and other people, of course, don't. It all depends.'

'But it's six o'clock,' he says. 'I have someone I must see at six o'clock. Would you mind if I leave you here with my friend, and he will show you everything. Please stay. I'll be back in an hour. But I must go now. I promised, and I shall be already half an hour late. Vous êtes chez vous.'

A dialogue with Delmar as to the best way to get to this place, which seems to be in the Rue du Bac. He turns at the door and, with the mocking expression very apparent, says something in Russian. At least, I suppose it's Russian.

Delmar puts on a feeble light in the middle of the room, then comes up to me and, in a hesitating way, takes my hand and kisses it. Then he kisses my cheek.

'When you cried I was so sad.'

I kiss him. Two loud, meaningless kisses, like a French general when he gives a decoration. Nice boy. . . .

'What did he say before he went out?'

'He said that if you didn't want to buy a picture you needn't buy
one. Nobody expects you to.'

'Oh, but I do. I absolutely want one.'

'Wait, I know how we can arrange it, so that you can really see
the pictures.'

There are a lot of empty frames stacked up against the wall.
Delmar arranges them round the room and puts the canvases one
by one into them. The canvases resist. They curl up; they don't
want to go into the frames. He pushes and prods them so that they
go in and stay in, in some sort of fashion.

'Ought we to do this? What will he say when he comes back?'

'Oh, it doesn't matter. It's all right. I want you to be able to see
them.'

When he has finished pictures are propped up on the floor round
three sides of the room.

'Now you can see them,' he says.

'Yes, now I can see them.'

I am surrounded by the pictures. It is astonishing how vivid they
are in this dim light. . . . Now the room expands and the iron band
round my heart loosens. The miracle has happened. I am happy.

Looking at the pictures, I go off into a vague dream. Perhaps one
day I'll live again round the corner in a room as empty as this.
Nothing in it but a bed and a looking-glass. Getting the stove lit at
about two in the afternoon — the cold and the stove fighting each
other. Lying near the stove in complete peace, having some bread
with pâté spread on it, and then having a drink and lying all the
afternoon in that empty room — nothing in it but the bed, the stove
and the looking-glass and outside Paris. And the dreams that you
have, alone in an empty room, waiting for the door that will open,
the thing that is bound to happen. . . .

It is after seven when Serge comes back. He rushes in, panting: 'I'm
sorry I'm late.' He talks to Delmar in Russian. Is he saying: 'Well,
was she any good?' or is he saying: 'Will she buy a picture and is she
going to pay up?' The last, I think — the tone was businesslike.

'I want very much to buy one of your pictures — this one.'

It is an old Jew with a red nose, playing the banjo.

'The price of that is six hundred francs,' he says. 'If you think it's
too much we'll arrange some other price.'

All his charm and ease of manner have gone. He looks anxious
and surly. I say awkwardly: 'I don't think it at all too much. But I
haven't got the money. . . .'

Before I can get any further he bursts into a shout of laughter. 'What did I tell you?' he says to Delmar.

'But have it, take it, all the same. I like you. I'll give it you as a present.'

'No, no. All I meant was that I can't pay you now.'

'Oh, that's all right. You can send me the money from London. I'll tell you what you can do for me — you can find some other idiots who'll buy my pictures.'

When he says this, he smiles at me so gently, so disarmingly. The touch of the human hand. . . . I'd forgotten what it was like, the touch of the human hand.

'I'm serious. I mean that. Take the picture and send me the money when you can.'

'I can let you have it tonight.'

We argue for some time as to where we shall meet.

'I can't stand Montparnasse now,' he says. 'Those faces, those gueules! They make me sick. Somewhere in the Quartier Latin.'

We decide on the Capoulade at half-past ten. He rolls up the picture in tissue-paper, ties it round with a bit of string and I take it under my arm. Then he gives my hand a long, hard shake and says 'Amis'.

When he shakes my hand like that and says 'Amis' I feel very happy. . . .

We get out into the courtyard, Delmar and I. It is a very cold, clear night. The outer door is shut. Business with the concierge.

Now I am not thinking of the past at all. I am well in the present.

'Capoulade — half-past ten. . . .'

The pictures walk along with me. The misshapen dwarfs juggle with huge coloured balloons, the four-breasted woman is exhibited, the old prostitute waits hopelessly outside the urinoir, the young one under the bec de gaz. . . .

At ten-twenty-five — still fairly exalted — I am in the Capoulade. I wait for a quarter of an hour, twenty minutes. Nobody turns up. . . . Bon, bien, that's what you get for being exalted, my girl. But the protective armour is functioning all right — I don't mind at all.

I am just worrying about the way I am going to give this man his money. I can't write, because I don't remember the number of the house. Shall I push it under the door of his studio and trust to luck?

As I am thinking this Delmar comes in. Correct, gloves in his left hand.

'Oh, I'm so sorry, so sorry. I waited at the studio for le peintre for half an hour and he never turned up. I didn't know what to do. I thought it was better to come here. I've been so worried about it.'

'That's all right. It doesn't matter at all.'

I give him the envelope with the money.

Is there a closing of the eyes, a slightly relieved expression on his face? Yes, I think so. And why not? Have a heart. Why not?

However, he does seem annoyed — so far as he can be annoyed, which isn't very far. Here is someone who firmly believes in his own creed: 'I didn't ask to be born, I didn't ask to be put into the world, I didn't make myself, I didn't make the world as it is, I am a guiltless one. So I have the right,' etcetera, etcetera, etcetera. . . .

'Le peintre!' he says. 'Il est fou, le peintre. . . . Did you like him?'

'Yes, I liked him very much.'

He lays his gloves carefully down on the table.

'Will you have a coffee, madame?'

'No, I'll have a brandy, please.'

He looks anxious, orders the brandy and a coffee for himself. God, this is awful!

'Le peintre,' he says, 'he's mad. I don't know why he has been so impolite, but it's just what he would do. Because he's mad. You know, two years ago, this man, he was living. . . . Terrible. . . . La crasse, madame. . . . I said to him: "You can't go on living like this." "Je m'en fous," he said. . . . However, I talked to him and in the end he managed to get the money to give his exhibition. And his pictures were bought. Yes, they were bought. . . . Eighteen thousand francs. C'est inouï, une somme pareille. . . . And then he did move. He went to this beautiful, respectable room where you saw him. . . . All the same he is mad.'

He goes on talking about le peintre. I gather that he is impressed but jealous. He can't see the attraction. Why, why?

'So you liked him?'

'Yes, I did. Very much.'

'Ah,' he says, gloomily, 'voilà. All the same, I've had enough of these people of the extreme Left. They have bad manners. Moi, je suis monarchiste. . . . And, mind you, when he says he is of the extreme Left, it's all nonsense. He doesn't really care.'

'Of course he doesn't.'

'Yes, yes. . . . Moi, je suis monarchiste. A queen, for instance, a princess — that must be something.'

If he feels like that, what's the use of arguing with him? . . . I agree with everything. A queen, a princess — that's something.

When he asks if I can meet him again: 'Well, I'll try,' I say. 'But I'm very much occupied.'

I can't stand this business of not being able to have what I want to drink, because he won't allow me to pay and certainly doesn't want to pay himself. It's too wearing.

'I'm leaving Paris next week. Sooner than I thought.'

Will I let him know when I am going, so that he can come to the Gare du Nord to see me off?

'Yes, please do. It would be so nice if you would. It's sad to go away from a place with nobody to tell you good-bye.'

When I am back in my room I start worrying about him and the money he has spent on me. And then I think: 'I bet he'll get his percentage on that six hundred francs. Or perhaps he won't hand the money over at all.'

This idea makes me laugh all the time I am undressing.

2

Wandering about the narrow streets near the Panthéon. It starts to rain.

I go into a tabac. The woman at the bar gives me one of those looks: What do you want here, you? We don't cater for tourists here, not our clientèle. . . . Well, dear madame, to tell you the truth, what I want here is a drink — I rather think two, perhaps three.

It is cold and dark outside, and everything has gone out of me except misery.

'A Pernod,' I say to the waiter.

He looks at me in a sly, amused way when he brings it.

God, it's funny, being a woman! And the other one — the one behind the bar — is she going to giggle or to say something about me in a voice loud enough for me to hear? That's the way she's feeling.

No, she says nothing. . . . But she says it all.

Well, that's O.K., chère madame, and very nicely done too.

You've said nothing but you've said it all. Never mind, here I am and here I'm going to stay.

Behind my table there is a door. Toilette — they needn't have said so. And then another, smaller door. Service. I hear noises of washing-up going on behind this door.

After a while a girl comes out, with a tray piled with clean glasses. She leaves the door open. Inside, a sink, a tap and more dirty glasses and plates, waiting to be washed. There is just room for the girl to stand. An unbelievable smell comes from the sink.

She passes me without looking at me. Bare, sturdy legs, felt slippers, a black dress, a filthy apron, thick, curly, untidy hair. I know her. This is the girl who does all the dirty work and gets paid very little for it. Salut!

She goes into the room behind the bar, puts the glasses down, walks back to the cupboard and shuts herself in again. How does she manage not to knock her elbows every time she moves? How can she stay in that coffin for five minutes without fainting? . . . Sorry for her? Why should I be sorry for her? Hasn't she got sturdy legs and curly hair? And don't her strong hands sing the Marseillaise? And when the revolution comes, won't those be the hands to be kissed? Well, so Monsieur Rimbaud says, doesn't he? I hope he's right. I wonder, though, I wonder, I wonder. . . .

I call the waiter, to pay. I give him a large tip. He looks at it, says 'Merci', and then 'Merci beaucoup'. I ask him to tell me the way to the nearest cinema. This, of course, arises from a cringing desire to explain my presence in the place. I only came in here to inquire the way to the nearest cinema. I am a respectable woman, une femme convenable, on her way to the nearest cinema. Faites comme les autres — that's been my motto all my life. Faites comme les autres, damn you.

And a lot he cares — I could have spared myself the trouble. But this is my attitude to life. Please, please, monsieur et madame, mister, missis and miss, I am trying so hard to be like you. I know I don't succeed, but look how hard I try. Three hours to choose a hat; every morning an hour and a half trying to make myself look like everybody else. Every word I say has chains round its ankles; every thought I think is weighted with heavy weights. Since I was born, hasn't every word I've said, every thought I've thought, everything I've done, been tied up, weighted, chained? And, mind you, I know that with all this I don't succeed. Or I succeed in flashes only too damned well. . . . But think how hard I try and how seldom I dare. Think — and have a bit of pity. That is, if you ever think, you apes, which I doubt.

Now the waiter has finished telling me how to get to the nearest cinema.

'Another Pernod,' I say.

He brings it. He fills my glass almost to the brim, perhaps in anticipation of another tip, perhaps because he wants to see me drunk as soon as possible, or perhaps because the bottle slipped.

The girl comes out with the last lot of glasses. I'm glad. It has just occurred to me that if I weren't here the door of her coffin might be kept open. *Might* be. Not that I would have gone away if it had occurred to me before. Why should I? The hands that sing the Marseillaise, the world that could be so different — what's all that to me? What can I do about it? Nothing. I don't deceive myself.

That's settled. I can start on the second Pernod.

Now the feeling of the room is different. They all know what I am. I'm a woman come in here to get drunk. That happens sometimes. They have a drink, these women, and then they have another and then they start crying silently. And then they go into the lavabo and then they come out — powdered, but with hollow eyes — and, head down, slink into the street.

'Poor woman, she has tears in her eyes.'

'What do you expect? Elle a bu.'

That's it, chère madame, I'm drunk. I have drunk. There's nothing to be done about it now. I have drunk. But otherwise quiet, fearful, tamed, prepared to give big tips. (I'll give a big tip if you'll leave me alone.) Bon, bien, bien, bon. . . .

Sometimes somebody comes in for stamps, or a man for a drink. Then you can see outside into the street. And the street walks in. It is one of those streets — dark, powerful, magical. . . .

'Oh, there you are,' it says, walking in at the door, 'there you are. Where have you been all this long time?'

Nobody else knows me, but the street knows me.

'And there you are,' I say, finishing my Pernod and rather drunk. 'Salut, salut!'

(But sometimes it was sunny. . . . Walking along in the sun in a gay dress, striped red and blue. . . . I won't walk along that street again.)

The Cinéma Danton. Watching a good young man trying to rescue his employer from a mercenary mistress. The employer is a gay, bad old boy who manufactures toilet articles. The good young man has the awkwardness, the smugness, the shyness, the pathos of good young men. He interrupts intimate conversations, knocking loudly, bringing in letters and parcels, etcetera, etcetera. At last the lady, annoyed, gets up and sweeps away. She turns at the door to say: 'Alors, bien, je te laisse à tes suppositoires.' Everybody laughs loudly at this, and so do I. She said that well.

The film goes on and on. After many vicissitudes, the good young man is triumphant. He has permission to propose to his employer's daugher. He is waiting on the bank of a large pond, with a ring that he is going to offer her ready in his waistcoat pocket. He takes it out to make sure that he has it. Mad with happiness, he strides up and down the shores of the pond, gesticulating. He makes too wild a gesture. The ring flies from his hand into the middle of the pond. He takes off his trousers; he wades out. He has to get the ring back; he must get it back.

Exactly the sort of thing that happens to me. I laugh till the tears come into my eyes. However, the film shows no signs of stopping, so I get up and go out.

Another Pernod in the bar next door to the cinema. I sit at a corner table and sip it respectably, with lowered eyes. Je suis une femme convenable, just come out of the nearest cinema. . . . Now I really am O.K., chère madame. If I have a bottle of Bordeaux at dinner I'll be almost as drunk as I'd hoped to be.

There is a letter from le peintre at the hotel. He says he is very sorry he didn't turn up the other evening — il faut m'excuser. He says Delmar has handed over the six hundred francs, and he thanks me. He says that if I don't like the bonhomme, if I find him too sad, he will change him for one of the landscapes or for anything else I want and that he will try to get to the Gare du Nord to say au revoir to me (I bet he won't), and he is my friend, Serge Rubin.

Well, I'll have a whisky on that.

I unroll the picture and the man standing in the gutter, playing his banjo, stares at me. He is gentle, humble, resigned, mocking, a little mad. He stares at me. He is double-headed, double-faced. He is singing 'It has been', singing 'It will be'. Double-headed and with four arms. . . . I stare back at him and think about being hungry, being cold, being hurt, being ridiculed, as if it were in another life than this.

This damned room — it's saturated with the past. . . . It's all the rooms I've ever slept in, all the streets I've ever walked in. Now the whole thing moves in an ordered, undulating procession past my eyes. Rooms, streets, streets, rooms. . . .

PART THREE

1

...*The room at the Steens'.*

It was crowded with red plush furniture, the wood shining brightly. There were several vases of tulips and two cages with canaries, and there were two clocks, each trying to tick louder than the other. The windows were nearly always shut, but the room wasn't musty. When the door into the shop was open you could smell drugs and eau-de-Cologne. On a table at the back there was a big pot of tea over a spirit-lamp. The little blue light made it look like an altar.

In that room you couldn't think, you couldn't make plans. Just the way the clocks ticked, and outside the clean, narrow streets, and the others talking Dutch and I listening, not understanding. It was like being a child again, listening and thinking of something else and hearing the voices — endless, inevitable and restful. Like Sunday afternoon.

Well, London. . . . It has a fine sound, but what was London to me? It was a little room, smelling stuffy, with my stockings hanging to dry in front of a gas-fire. Nothing in that room was ever clean; nothing was ever dirty, either. Things were always half-and-half. They changed one sheet at a time, so that the bed was never quite clean and never quite dirty.

Thinking: 'I've got away from all that, anyhow. Not to go back, not to go back. . . .'

I liked Tonny; she was gentle. But I hated Hans Steen. He had a blustering look. He didn't bluster, he was very polite. But his pale blue eyes had that look, and his hands.

Narrow streets, with the people walking up one way and down another. So tidily. In the park, the Haagsche Bosch, the trees upside-down in the ice green water.

We go every day to the Centraal for an apéritif. We eat at a little place where the violinist plays sentimental tunes very well. ('Will you play *Le Binyou* for madame? . . .')

I haven't any money. He hasn't any either. We both thought the other had money. But people are doing crazy things all over the place. The war is over. No more war — never, never, never. Après la guerre, there'll be a good time everywhere. . . . And not to go back to London. It isn't so fine, what I have to go back to in London.

But no money? Nix? . . . And the letter in my hand-bag: 'I think you must be mad. If you insist on doing this. . . .'

A tall vase of sprawling tulips on the table. How they give themselves! 'Perhaps it's because they know they have nothing to give,' Enno says.

Talking about Paris, where he has lived since he was eighteen. He was a chansonnier, it seems, before he became a journalist. He enlisted during the first week of the war. From 1917 onwards a gap. He seemed very prosperous when I met him in London, but now no money — nix. What happened? He doesn't tell me.

But when we get to Paris the good life will start again. Besides, we have money. Between us we have fifteen pounds.

All the same, I never thought we should really get married. One day I'll make a plan, I'll know what to do. . . .

Then I wake up and it's my wedding-day, cold and rainy. I put on the grey suit that a tailor in Delft has made for me on tick. I don't like it much. Enno comes in with a bunch of lilies-of-the-valley, pins it in my coat and kisses me. We get a taxi and drive through the rain to the town-hall and we are married with a lot of other couples, all standing round in a circle. We come out of the town-hall and have one drink with Tonny and Hans. They they go home to look after the shop. We go on to another place. Nobody else is there — it's too early. We have two glasses of port and then another two.

'How idiotic all that business was!' Enno says.

We have more port. It's the first time that day that I have felt warm or happy.

I say: 'You won't ever leave me, will you?'

'Allons, allons, a little gaiety,' Enno says.

He has a friend called Dickson, a Frenchman, who sings at the Scala. He calls himself Dickson because English singers are popular at the moment. We go to his flat that afternoon and drink champagne. Everybody gets very gay. Louis and Louise, tango dancers, also at the cabaret, do their show for us. Dickson sings *In These Hard Times*:

That funny kind of dress you wear
Leaves all your back and your shoulders bare,
But you're lucky to be dressed up to there
In these hard times.

Enno sings:

Quand on n'a pas de chaussures
On fait comme les rentiers,
On prend une voiture,
On ne vous voit pas les pieds!

Parlons donc de chaussettes:
Faut pas les nettoyer,
On les retourne, c'est pas bête,
Puis on les change de pied!

I sing: 'For tonight, for tonight, Let me dream out my dream of delight, Tra-la-la. . . . And purchase from sorrow a moment's respite, Tra-la-la. . . .'

Mrs Dickson reads aloud excitedly from a theatrical paper. Two girls they know are mixed up in a murder case. She reads about Riri and Cricri, rolling her 'r's'. Rrrirrri, Crrricrrri. . . .

I am a bit drunk when we take the train to Amsterdam.

2

. . . The room in the hotel in Amsterdam that night.

It was very clean, with a rose-patterned wallpaper.

'Now, you mustn't worry about money,' Enno says. 'Money's a stupid thing to worry about. You let me do. I can always get some. When we get to Paris it'll be all right.'

(*When — we — get — to — Paris. . . .*)

There's another bottle of champagne on the table by the bed.

'Love,' Enno says, 'you mustn't talk about love. Don't talk. . . .'

You mustn't talk, you mustn't think, you must stop thinking. Of course, it is like that. You must let go of everything else, stop thinking. . . .

•

Next morning we eat an enormous breakfast of sausages, cold meat, cheese and milk. We walk about Amsterdam. We look at pictures in the Rijksmuseum. 'Would you like to see your double?' Enno says.

I am turned up to top pitch. Everything is smooth, soft and tender. Making love. The colours of the pictures. The sunsets. Tender, north colours when the sun sets — pink, mauve, green and blue. And the wind very fresh and cold and the lights in the canals like gold caterpillars and the seagulls swooping over the water. Tuned up to top pitch. Everything tender and melancholy — as life is sometimes, just for one moment. . . . And when we get to Paris; *When — we — get — to — Paris. . . .*

'I want very much to go back to Paris,' Enno would say. 'It has no reason, no sense. But all the same I want to go back there. Certain houses, certain streets. . . . No sense, no reason. Just this nostalgia. . . . And, mind you, some of my songs have made money. . . .'

Suddenly I am in a fever of anxiety to get there. Let's be on our way, let's be on our way. . . . Why shouldn't we get as far as Brussels? All right, we'll get as far as Brussels; might be something doing in Brussels.

But the fifteen pounds have gone. We raise every penny we can. We sell most of our clothes.

My beautiful life in front of me, opening out like a fan in my hand. . . .

3

What happened then? . . . Well, what happens?

The room in the Brussels hotel — very hot. The bell of the cinema next door ringing. A long, narrow room with a long, narrow window and the bell of the cinema next door, sharp and meaningless.

Things haven't gone. Enno saying: 'We've only got thirty francs left.' (My Lord, is that all?) 'Yes, only thirty francs. We'll have to do something about it tomorrow.'

The bell of the cinema kept on ringing and every time it rang I could feel him start.

When he went out next morning he said: 'I think I'll be able to raise some money. Wait in here for me.'

'Will you be a long time?'

'No. . . . Anyhow, don't go out.'

Sitting on the bed, waiting. Walking up and down the room, waiting. I can't stand it, this waiting.

Then, as if somebody had spoken it aloud in my head — Mr Lawson. Of course, Mr Lawson. . . .

I hadn't remembered how glassy his eyes were, Mr Lawson's.

'Yes?' he says. 'You asked to see me?' Raising his eyebrows a little, he says: 'Ye-es?'

He doesn't recognize me. I must look rather awful.

I say: 'I'm afraid you don't remember me. I was staying in those rooms in the Temple that you came to look over, and you took me to dinner. We had oysters and we talked about Ireland. Don't you remember? Then we were on the boat going over to Holland and you gave me your address in Brussels. You said if I got here, would I look you up? Don't you remember?'

'Of course. Little Miss—'

'Not little,' I say, 'not little.' Because I can't have a man like that calling me little.

I talk away, saying, as if it were a joke: 'We're not exactly stranded. We shall be quite all right as soon as we get to Paris. In fact, we shall be quite all right in a day or two. Only, stupidly, just for the moment, we're a bit stranded.'

Mr Lawson talks back and in the end he gives me a hundred francs. 'If this is any good to you. And now, I'm very sorry, but I've got to rush.'

I am standing there with the note in my hand, when he comes up to me and kisses me. I am hating him more than I have ever hated anyone in my life, yet I feel my mouth go soft under his, and my arms go limp. 'Good-bye,' he says in imitation American, and grins.

'Did you have any luck?'

'Not much,' Enno says.

I say: 'I've managed to borrow a hundred francs.'

'Who did you borrow it from?'

'Well, it's a woman I used to know very well in London. I knew she lived here and I found her address in the directory. She knew Miss Cavell. Yes, a friend of Miss Cavell's. She lives in the Avenue Louise, and I went and saw her.

'She's not exactly a friend,' I say. 'As a matter of fact, she was horribly rude, the old bitch. She as good as told me she wouldn't see me if ever I went there again. Mademoiselle regrette, mais mademoiselle ne reçoit pas aujourd'hui. . . .'

'Avenue Louise? What number Avenue Louise?'

'Oh, shut up about it.' I lie down on the bed and begin to cry.

'Don't cry. If you cry I shall go mad.'

'Shut up, then, and don't talk about the damned hundred francs.' (With a hundred francs they buy the unlimited right to scorn you. It's cheap.)

'What are you crying about?' he says.

'It's my dress. I feel so awful. I feel so dirty. I want to have a bath. I want another dress. I want clean underclothes. I feel so awful. I feel so dirty.'

'I'll get you another dress as soon as we get to Paris. I know somewhere where we can get credit. . . . You'll see, when we get to Paris it'll be all right.'

He goes out to buy something to eat. I lie there and I am happy, forgetting everything, happy and cool, not caring if I live or die. I think of the way Mr Lawson looked at me when I first went in — his long, narrow, surprised face. I laugh and I can't stop laughing.

4

The lavatory at the station — that was the next time I cried. I had just been sick. I was so afraid I might be going to have a baby. . . .

Although I have been so sick, I don't feel any better. I lean up against the wall, icy cold and sweating. Someone tries the door, and I pull myself together, stop crying and powder my face.

We are going to Calais. Enno has made pals with a waiter who lives there and who has promised to lend us some money.

He is very good at salad-dressing, this waiter. We eat with him and his wife next day. There he is, with his fat back and thick neck, mixing the dressing. He uses sugar in the German way. His wife watches him, looking spiteful and frightened. She is thin and ugly and not young.

The waiter mixes the dressing for the salad very slowly at the sideboard. I can see myself in the mirror. I look thin — too thin — and dirty and haggard, with that expression that you get in your eyes when you are very tired and everything is like a dream and you are starting to know what things are like underneath what people say they are.

I hadn't bargained for this. I didn't think it would be like this —shabby clothes, worn-out shoes, circles under your eyes, your hair getting straight and lanky, the way people look at you. . . . I didn't think it would be like this.

Walking about the streets of Calais with the waiter's wife. We went to see that statue by Rodin. All the time she was complaining in a thin voice that he never let her have any money for clothes, and that it was her money after all; he hadn't a sou when she married him.

She didn't seem at all curious about us, or to want to know where he picked us up. She just went on and on about his unkindness and the clothes she wanted.

It was a grey day. It was like walking in London, like walking in a dream. My God, how awful I looked in that mirror! If I'm going to look like that, there's not a hope. Fancy having to go to Paris looking like that. . . .

When we got back we drank absinthe. The waiter prepared it for us elaborately. It took a long time. I didn't like the taste, but I was cold and it warmed me. We sat there sipping and Enno and the waiter talked in a corner. The wife didn't say anything and after a while I didn't either. But the absinthe made me feel quarrelsome and I began to wish I could shout 'Shut up' at them and to dislike the waiter because I knew he wasn't thinking much of my looks. ('She's not much. I thought she was better-looking than that the first time I saw her.')

I stopped listening to them, but when the absinthe went really to my head I thought I was shouting to them to shut up. I even heard my voice saying: 'Shut up; I hate you.' But really I didn't say anything and when Enno looked at me I smiled.

Well, Gustave — the waiter — lent us the money he had promised and we left Calais.

Enno had taken a dislike to Gustave's wife. 'That to call itself a woman!' he said.

'But it was her money,' I said.

'Oh well,' Enno said, 'he makes very good use of it, doesn't he? He makes much better use of it than she would.'

It was a slow train and we were tightly packed in the compartment. Lying in the luggage-rack, trying to sleep, propped up by Enno's stick, and the wheels of the train saying: 'Paris, Paris, Paris, Paris. . . .'

5

A girl came into the café and sat down at the next table. She was wearing a grey suit, the skirt short and tight and the blouse very fresh and clean. And a cocky black hat like a Scots soldier's glengarry. Her handbag was lying on the table near her — patent leather to match her shoes. (Handbag. . . . What a lot of things I've got to get! Would a suit like that be a good thing to get? No, I think I had better get. . . .) And she walked so straight and quick on her high-heeled shoes. Tap, tap, tap, her heels. . . .

'I'll take you somewhere to wait,' Enno said. 'I must see one or two people.'

Drinking coffee very early in the morning, everything like a dream. I was so tired.

We got out of the Métro into the Boulevard Montparnasse.

'In here,' Enno said. He took me by the arm.

The Rotonde was full of men reading newspapers on long sticks. Shabby men, not sneering, not taking any notice. Pictures on the walls.

The hands of the clock moving quickly. One hour, two hours, three hours. . . .

How long will they let me sit here? Not a drop of coffee left. The last drop was very cold and very bitter — very cold and bitter, the last drop. I have five francs, but I daren't order another coffee. I mustn't spend it on that.

The colours of the pictures melting into each other, my head back against the bench. If I go to sleep they'll certainly turn me out. Perhaps they won't, but better not risk it.

Three hours and a half. . . .

•

As soon as I see him I know from his face that he's got some money. A tall man is with him, a man with a gentle face and long, thin hands.

We go next door to a place called La Napolitaine and eat ravioli. Warming me. Eat slowly, make it last a long time. . . .

I've never been so happy in my life. I'm alive, eating ravioli and drinking wine. I've escaped. A door has opened and let me out into the sun. What more do I want? Anything might happen.

'I've got a room,' Enno says. 'Rue Lamartine.'

'I had a chase,' he says. 'Paulette wasn't in. I left a note. I ran into Alfred just outside her apartment.'

Alfred smiles, bows, twists his hands nervously and departs.

'He's nice,' I say.

'Yes, he's a nice boy. He's a Turk.'

'Oh, I thought he was French.'

'No, he's a Turk.'

How much money has he got? No, don't ask. I don't want to know. Tell me later on, tell me tomorrow. Let me be happy just for now. . . .

An old man comes up, selling red roses. Enno buys some. He must have enough money for a bit.

The old boy shuffles off. Then he turns round, comes back and puts two extra roses on the table near my plate. 'Vous permettez, monsieur?' he says to Enno, bowing like a prince.

Paris. . . . I am in Paris. . . .

6

The room we got in the hotel in the Rue Lamartine looked all right. It was on the fourth floor, the top floor. There was a big bed, covered with a red eiderdown, and outside a little balcony. You could stand and lean your arms on the cool iron and look down at the street.

We took it and paid a month's rent in advance — and that night we woke up scratching, and the wall was covered with bugs, crawling slowly.

I didn't mind the bugs much. I didn't mind anything then. . . .

'Impossible, monsieur. Mais qu'est-ce que vous me dites là? Ce n'est pas possible. Voyons. . . .' Etcetera, etcetera.

She didn't want to give the money back, and after a while it was arranged that she should have the place fumigated and give us another room while it was being done. I was glad we didn't have to leave.

I am lying on a long chair in the middle of the room, which still smells of sulphur. I have opened the door and stuck a piece of paper in it so that it shall stay open. I have shut the shutters to keep the sun out. The room is dim and the ceiling seems to be pressing on my head. I have been going through the advertisements in the *Figaro*, marking those of people who want English lessons.

Enno sits by the table, smoking his pipe, Monsieur Alfred on the bed. I watch the beads of sweat trickling down his face from his temples to his chin. I have never seen anybody sweat like that — it's extraordinary. Every now and again he blows through closed lips, takes out his handkerchief and wipes his face. Then, in a minute, it is wet and shining again.

I like Alfred. Once he said to me: 'It's very warm today. I'll make you feel cool and happy.' He took my wrist and blew on it, very gently, very regularly. I tried to take it away, didn't because he had lent us five hundred francs, then I began to feel cool, peaceful.

And Alfred recites. 'Answer with a cold silence the eternal silence of the divinity,' he says. Sweating like hell.

'Do you mind if I shut the door, madame? There's a terrible draught in this room.'

'Ah, non, mon vieux, non,' Enno says. 'Leave the door open.'

'Just as you like,' says Alfred, fingering his moustache with his long, beautiful hands. He looks shy and pained. 'I thought it wasn't good for madame to sit in a draught like this.'

'I'm not in a draught,' I say. 'I'm all right.'

Alfred goes on stroking his moustache. His eyes look malicious, in the same way that a woman's eyes look suddenly malicious.

He says, looking malicious: 'I think it's a good idea, madame, this giving lessons.' Then, speaking to Enno: 'Not a bad idea, not at all a bad idea. You get two or three good bourgeois to pay up, and afterwards — ça va. Talk, say what you like, but you can't do without the bourgeoisie.'

Enno doesn't answer.

'If I were married,' Alfred says, 'I wouldn't let my wife work for another man. No, no. I should think it a terrible disgrace to let my wife work for any other man but me. I wouldn't do it. Nothing would make me do it.'

'Tu m'emmerdes!' Enno yells, jumping up, 'tu m'emmerdes, je te dis. What are you trying to say, then?'

'Bon, bon, I'm going,' Alfred says, getting up. 'I see you are in a bad temper. I'm going. You needn't shout at me.'

'Oh, don't go,' I say.

'You shut up,' Enno says.

'Madame,' says Alfred from the door, bowing.

I laugh when he bows. I keep on saying: 'Isn't this funny, isn't this funny?' I remember Alfred blowing on my wrists to cool them and I can't stop laughing. I get so tired that I put my head into my hands.

Enno says: 'I'm going out to buy something to eat.'

'Already? It's too early.'

He goes out without answering, slamming the door.

7

'You don't know how to make love,' he said. That was about a month after we got to Paris. 'You're too passive, you're lazy, you bore me. I've had enough of this. Good-bye.'

He walked out and left me alone — that night and the next day, and the next night and the next day. With twenty francs on the table. And I'm sure now that I'm going to have a baby, though I haven't said a word about it.

I have to go out to get myself something to eat. The patron knows, the patronne knows, everybody knows. . . . Waking up at night, listening, waiting. . . .

The third day I make up my mind that he isn't coming back. A blue day. This is the first time that I look at the patronne instead of sliding past her with my eyes down. She inquires about monsieur. Monsieur may be away for some time.

Blue sky over the streets, the houses, the bars, the cafés, the vegetable shops and the Faubourg Montmartre. . . .

I buy milk, a loaf of bread, four oranges, and go back to the hotel.

Squeezing the rind of an orange and smelling the oil. A lot of oil

— they must be pretty fresh. . . . I think: 'What's going to happen?'
After all, I don't much care what happens. And just as I am
thinking this Enno walks in with a bottle of wine under his arm.
'Hello,' he says.
'I've got some money,' he says. 'My god, isn't it hot? Peel me an
orange.'
'I'm very thirsty,' he says. 'Peel me an orange.'
Now is the time to say 'Peel it yourself', now is the time to say 'Go
to hell', now is the time to say 'I won't be treated like this'. But
much too strong — the room, the street, the thing in myself, oh,
much too strong. . . . I peel the orange, put it on a plate and give it
to him.
He says: 'I've got some money.'
He brings out a mille note, a second mille note. I don't ask where
he has got them. Why ask? Money circulates; it circulates — and
how! Why, you wouldn't believe it sometimes.
He pours me out a glass of wine. 'It's fresh. I've kept it away from
the sun.'
'But your hands are so cold,' he says. 'My girl. . . .'
He draws the curtains to keep the sun out.
When he kissed my eyelids to wake me it was dark.

But it wasn't all that that mattered. It wasn't that he knew so
exactly when to be cruel, so exactly how to be kind. The day I was
sure I loved him was quite different.
He had gone out to buy something to eat. I was behind the
curtain and I saw him in the street below, standing by a lamp-post,
looking up at our window, looking for me. He seemed very thin and
small and I saw the expression on his face quite plainly. Anxious, he
was. . . .
The bottle of wine was under one arm, and his coat was sticking
out, because the loaf of bread was hidden under it. The patronne
didn't like us to eat in our room. Just once in a while she didn't
mind, but when people eat in their room every night, it means they
really have no money at all.
When I saw him looking up like that I knew that I loved
him, and that it was for always. It was as if my heart turned
over, and I knew that it was for always. It's a strange feeling
—when you know quite certainly in yourself that something is for
always. It's like what death must be. All the insouciance, all
the gaiety is a bluff. Because I wanted to escape from London
I fastened myself on him, and I am dragging him down. All the

gaiety is going and now he is thin and anxious. . . .

I didn't wave to him. I stayed by the curtain and watched him, and after a while he crossed the street and went into the hotel.

'I can't sleep,' he said. 'Let me lie with my head on your silver breast.'

8

The curtains are thin, and when they are drawn the light comes through softly. There are flowers on the window-sill and I can see their shadows on the curtains. The child downstairs is screaming.

There is a wind, and the flowers on the window-sill, and their shadows on the curtains, are waving. Like swans dipping their beaks in water. Like the incalculable raising its head, uselessly and wildly, for one moment before it sinks down, beaten, into the darkness. Like skulls on long, thin necks. Plunging wildly when the wind blows, to the end of the curtain, which is their nothingness. Distorting themselves as they plunge.

The musty smell, the bugs, the loneliness, this room, which is part of the street outside — this is all I want from life.

Things are going well. We have settled down. Enno has sold two articles. He has been to see the old boy at the Lapin Agile, and now sings there every night. And there is a real job in prospect. A publicity campaign, to popularize tea in France — Timmins' Tea. He is very excited about this, and he has designed a poster, which he says will appeal to the French: 'Tea is the most economical drink in the world. It costs less then one sou a cup.' I give English lessons. Ten francs an hour. I have three pupils — a girl who works in a scent-shop, a man who advertised in the *Figaro*, and a young Russian whom Enno met at the Lapin Agile. He speaks English just as well as I do.

I have bought a Berlitz book and follow it blindly. Farcical, these lessons, except the Russian's. He is determined to get value for his ten francs, and he does.

'Would you tell me, please, if I have the "th" correctly?' The, this, that, these, those — all correct.

He brings along a collected edition of Oscar Wilde's works and says he wants to read them through. 'Will you stop me, please, if I mispronounce a word? . . . I think Oscar Wilde is the greatest of English writers. Do you agree?'

'Well. . . .'

'Ah, you do not agree.'

'But I do like him. I think he is very — sympathique.'

He makes a little speech about English hypocrisy. Preaching to the converted.

The streets, blazing hot, and eating peaches. The long, lovely, blue days that lasted for ever, that still are. . . .

At the corner of the street, the chemist's shop with the advertisement of the Abbé Something's Elixir — it cures this, it cures that, it cures the sickness of pregnant women. Would it cure mine? I wonder.

My face is pretty, my stomach is huge. Last time we ate at the Algerian restaurant I had to rush away and be sick. . . . People are very kind to me. They get up and give me their seats in buses. Passe, femme sacrée. . . . Not exactly like that, but still — it seemed to me that they were kind. All the same, I'm not so mad now about going out, and I spend long hours by myself.

There is a bookshop next door, which advertises second-hand English novels. The assistant is a Hindu. I want a long, calm book about people with large incomes — a book like a flat green meadow and the sheep feeding in it. But he insists upon selling me lurid stories of the white-slave traffic. 'This is a very good book, very beautiful, most true.'

But gradually I get some books that I do like. I read most of the time and I am happy.

9

In and out of the room — Lise, Paulette, Jean, Alfred the Turk. I watch them, and I never quite know them, but I love Lise.

She is a brodeuse — or she has been a brodeuse. Now she sings English songs in a cheap cabaret in the Rue Cujas — *Roses of Picardy* and *Here Is My Heart*. She can't speak English at all. She is twenty-two years old, three years younger than I am.

Everything about Lise surprises me — her gentleness, her extreme sentimentality, so different from what I had been led to expect in a French girl. Airs from *Manon*, pink garters with little silk roses on them, Gyraldose. . . . 'Is it true that Englishwomen never use a douche? Myself, I use one twice a day. . . . And all my underclothes made by hand. Yes, every stitch.'

She has black, curly hair, a very pretty face and — unfortunately — thick ankles. . . . 'I love Gounod's *Ave Maria*. The music is like a prayer, don't you think?. . . .' She often comes in and eats with us.

One night I am in the room with Lise. We have just had a fine meal — spaghetti cooked on the flamme bleue and a bottle of Asti spumante. I am feeling rather good.

She says: 'I wish there'd be another war.'

'Oh, Lise, don't say that.'

'Yes, I do. I might have a bit of luck. I might get killed. I don't want to live any more, me.'

Then she's off. She has nobody. She doesn't think anybody likes her. The engagement in the Rue Cujas is finished. She can't get another. She will once more have to try for a job as a brodeuse. 'And the light in the workrooms isn't so good. Sometimes your eyes hurt so much that you can hardly open them.' She is going to have to go back to live with her mother, who keeps a grocer's shop at Clamart. She is afraid of her mother. When she was a little girl her mother beat her. 'For anything, for nothing. You don't know. And all the time she says bad things to me. She likes to make me cry. She hates me, my mother. I have no one. Soon I shall have to wear spectacles. Soon I shall be old.'

'My God, Lise, you've got a few more years, surely. Cheer up.'

'Non, j'en ai assez,' she says. 'Already. I've had enough.'

'Lise, don't cry.'

'Non, non, j'en ai assez.'

I also start to cry. No, life is too sad; it's quite impossible.

Sitting in front of the flamme bleue, arms round each other's waists, crying. No, life is too sad. . . . My tears fall on her thick hair, which always smells so nice.

Enno, coming in with another bottle of Asti spumante, says: 'Oh, my God, this is gay,' and laughs loudly. Lise and I look at each other and start laughing too. Soon we are all rolling, helpless with laughter. It's too much, I can't any more, it's too much. . . .

'Poor little Lise,' Enno says, 'she's a nice little girl, but too sentimental.'

Paulette is a very different matter. She is a gay, saucy wench, a great friend of Enno's. I admire and try to copy her and am jealous of her.

She reads extracts from letters written to her by a lover in the provinces. ' "Tu es belle et tu sens bon." Well, what about it? And listen to this: "Your breasts fulfil the promise of your eyes." He's original, isn't he? And the two thousand francs I asked you for — where are they, vieux con? Never mind, he'll part before I've done with him. Wait a bit. Attends, mon salaud.'

One day they came back, Enno and Paulette, with a steak for me. They had had dinner out. I hadn't gone with them because I felt so sick, but that was over and I was hungry. Paulette cooked the steak over the flamme bleue and I ate it all up. 'Did you like it?' she said. 'Yes, I did.' 'You didn't notice anything about it?' 'I noticed it was a bit tough,' I said. 'Otherwise I liked it all right.' 'It was horse-steak,' she said. 'Oh, was it?' They were both watching me with narrowed eyes, expecting me to do the Anglaise stuff. But after I said: 'Oh, was it?' their mouths, that were wide open to laugh, went small again. After that I think Paulette knew I wasn't one of the comfortable ones, and never had been, and hadn't had such a grand time as all that. Afterwards she liked me better.

In the romantic tradition, Paulette. Long, yellow hair, soft, brown eyes, a bowl of violets in her room. When she looks at herself in the glass, naked, she's as proud as Lucifer. In the romantic tradition, and very generous. She brings me presents of silk stockings. She turns up with several pairs of socks for Enno. 'I've snaffled them,' she says. 'He won't know — he has too many.'

She tells us that one of her lovers, the Count of so-and-so, wants to marry her, but his family is shocked and horrified. 'Voilà,' says Paulette, 'je ne joue pas du piano, moi.' She is not bitter — she is regretful, fatalistic.

Besides, she has such bad luck — it's Fate. For instance, the other day the mother was actually persuaded to lunch with her. And what happened as they were walking out of the restaurant? Paulette's drawers fell off.

Do I believe this? Well, I believe that bit anyway, because exactly the same thing has happened to me.

Chuckling madly, on the bed in the hotel in the Rue Lamartine, and thinking of when that man said to me: 'Can you resist it?' 'Yes, I can,' I said, very coldly. I can resist it, just plain and Nordic like that, I certainly can. 'You must be mad,' he said, 'mad.' (Where is this happening? In Kensington.) The next thing he says is that he will see me to my bus. 'Stupid, stupid girl,' he says, doing up buttons, and he takes me to the bus stop. We are standing by a lamp-post, in dead silence, waiting for the bus, and what happens? My drawers fall off. I look down at them, step out of them neatly, pick them up, roll them into a little parcel and put them into my handbag. What else is there to do? He stares into vacancy, shocked beyond measure. The bus comes up. He lifts his hat with a flourish and walks away.

Next morning I realize that it is I who have lost ground. Decidedly. I feel awful about everything. I go to the nearest telephone and ring him up. 'Are you vexed with me about last night?' He answers: 'Yes, I am vexed, I am very vexed. . . . I'll send you a box of Turkish Delight,' he says, and rings off.

Well now, what is it, this Turkish Delight? Is it a comment, is it irony, is it compensation, is it apology, or what? I'll throw it out of the window, whatever it is.

10

Now snow is falling. There is the reflection of snow in the room. The light makes everything seem strange. The mound of my stomach is hidden under the bedclothes. So calm I feel, watching myself in the glass opposite. My hair hangs down on my shoulders. It is curly again and the corners of my mouth turn up. I like myself today. I am never sick now. I am very well and very happy. I never think of what it will be like to have this baby or, if I think, it's as if a door shuts in my head. Awful, terrible! And then a door shuts in your head.

I hardly ever think about money either, or that when it happens I may be alone. If the tea job comes off it won't do to risk losing it. So I may be in Paris alone.

But it's all arranged. As soon as it starts I am to get into a taxi and go off to the sage femme. My room is booked — it's all arranged.

It's nothing to make a fuss about, everybody says.

We are friendly with the patronne. She will keep an eye on me while Enno is away. I'll be all right.

The Russian for his lesson. I gave Enno a note putting him off — he must have forgotten to post it.

He looks surprised to find me in bed, the Russian — surprised, then cynical. Does he think it's all arranged, this being in bed? Does he think I want him to make love to me? But surely he can't think that. I believe he does, though.

The corners of his mouth go down when he says 'femme'. (Hatred or fear?) Les femmes — he doesn't trust them, they are capable of anything.

So calm I feel, amused as God, with the huge mound of my stomach safe under the bedclothes. . . . It's no use arguing. As he's here, let's get on with it.

'I'm afraid this will have to be the last lesson,' I say.

The light makes everything seem strange. He kisses my hand, and I watch my hand as he kisses it — white, with red, varnished nails.

We are reading *Lady Windermere's Fan*.

' "The laughter, the horrible laughter of the world — a thing more tragic than all the tears the world has ever shed. . . ." Will you stop me, please, if I mispronounce a word?'

The English conversation. . . . He tells me about the Russian princess who was shut up in the prison of Peter and Paul to be eaten by rats, because she was a revolutionary. 'She screamed for ten days, and then there was silence. And then they let one day pass, and went into the cell. And there was nothing left of her but her hair. She had long and beautiful black hair.'

His conversation is nearly always about pain and torture.

He is going to join his family in London and then he is going up to Oxford. They have been very lucky. They have escaped with a good deal of money. The, this, that, these, and those are all correct.

'Do you think English people will like me?'

'Yes, I'm certain they will.' (I've only got to look at you to know that they'll like you in England.)

'And my English?'

'But you speak English perfectly.'

He is pleased at this. He smirks. 'I try to keep in constant practice,' he says. He gives me the ten francs, kisses my hand again, bows from the waist and goes. Good-bye, dear sir, good-bye. . . .

I put the ten francs under the pillow. I put the light out. While I can sleep, let me sleep. A boat rocking on a river, a smooth, green river. Outside, the secret streets. The man who sings 'J'ai perdu la lumière. . . .'

//

. . . The house in the Boulevard Magenta.

The sage femme has very white hands and clear, slanting eyes and when she looks at you the world stops rocking about. The clouds are clouds, trees are trees, people are people, and that's that. Don't mix them up again. No, I won't.

And there's always the tisane of orange-flower water.

But my heart, heavy as lead, heavy as a stone.

He has a ticket tied round his wrist because he died. Lying so cold and still with a ticket round his wrist because he died.

Not to think. Only to watch the branches of that tree and the pattern they make standing out against a cold sky. Above all, not to think. . . .

When we got back to the hotel I felt very tired. I sat on the bed and looked down at the carpet. Except that I was tired I felt all right. But I kept thinking of the dress he had on — so pretty. It'll get all spoiled, I thought. Everything all spoiled.

'God is very cruel,' I said, 'very cruel. A devil, of course. That accounts for everything — the only possible explanation.'

'I'm going out,' Enno said. 'I can't stay in here. I must go out.'

I stayed there, looking down at the dark red, dirty carpet and seeing a dark wall in the hot sun — the wall so hot it burned your hand when you touched it — and the red and yellow flowers and the time of day when everything stands still.

12

Now the lights are red, dusky red, haggard red, cruel red. Strings plucked softly by a man with a long, thin nose and sharp, blue eyes.

Our luck has changed and the lights are red.

There we all are — Lise, Alfred, Jean. . . . A fat man is shouting: 'La brune et la blonde, la brune et la blonde.' The cork of a champagne bottle pops. Why worry? Our luck has changed.

The fat man and I are in a corner by ourselves.

He says: 'Life is too awful. Do you know that story about the man who loved a woman who was married to somebody else, and she fell ill? And he didn't dare go and ask about her because the husband suspected her and hated him. So he just hung about the house and watched. And all the time he couldn't make up his mind whether he'd be a coward if he went and asked to see her or whether he'd be a coward if he didn't. And then one day he went and asked, and she was dead. Doesn't that make you laugh? She was dead, you see, and he had never sent one word. And he loved her and she was dying and he knew she was dying and he never sent one word. That's an old story, but doesn't it make you laugh? It might be true, that story, mightn't it?'

(Pourquoi êtes-vous triste, madame? Il ne faut pas être triste, madame. You mustn't be sad; you must laugh, you must dance. . . .)

The fat man is still talking away.

'My partner has a very pretty wife and for some reason she was unhappy and so she went into the Bois de Boulogne and she walked a long way and got under a big tree. And there she put a revolver to her breast and pulled the trigger. Did she die? Of course not. Not a bit of it. If you really want to die you must put it into your mouth — up to the roof of your mouth. Well, she's still in the hospital. . . . And just at first this made a great impression on my partner. He was in an awful state, thinking how unhappy she must have been to try to kill herself. But that was a week ago, and now he's just made up his mind that it's all a nuisance and that she made a fool of herself, and he's stopped being sorry for her. Isn't life droll?'

Well, there you are. It's not that these things happen or even that one survives them, but what makes life strange is that they are forgotten. Even the one moment that you thought was your eternity fades out and is forgotten and dies. This is what makes life so droll — the way you forget, and every day is a new day,

and there's hope for everybody, hooray. . . .
Now our luck has changed and the lights are red.

13

A room? A nice room? A beautiful room? A beautiful room with bath? Swing high, swing low, swing to and fro. . . . This happened and that happened. . . .

And then the days came when I was alone.

14

'I'll write,' he said. 'I'll try to send you some money.'

But I knew it was finished. From the start I had known that one day this would happen — that we would say good-bye.

He leant out of the carriage window. I looked up at him and wondered if it were tears that made his eyes so bright. He wasn't one of those men who cry easily, Enno.

When the train had gone I had coffee in a bar near the Gare du Nord and looked through the window at the dark world and wide.

It's only for a time. We'll be together again when things go better. Knowing in myself that it was finished. . . .

Did I love Enno at the end? Did he ever love me? I don't know. Only, it was after that that I began to go to pieces. Not all at once, of course. First this happened, and then that happened. . . .

15

. . . I go to an hotel near the Place de la Madeleine. There are a lot of flies in this room. They torment me. I kill one. I didn't know flies have blood just like you or me. Well, there it lies, with its wings still and its legs turned up. You won't dance again. . . .

I write to England, to try and borrow some money. They keep

me waiting a long time for an answer and I start eating at a convent near by, where the nuns supply very cheap meals for destitute girls. She is kind, the old nun in charge, or she seems to me not unkind. The room where we eat looks on to a large stone courtyard. You can get a quarter of wine for a few sous.

But there's an English valet de chambre at the hotel who tells the patron that whatever I call myself now he had known me very well in London and that I had come to Paris with a great friend of his, a jockey, and that I had treated his friend very badly and that I was the dirtiest bitch he had ever struck, which was saying something. Useless to deny all this — quite useless. . . . Was it hysteria, or a case of hate at first sight, or did he really mistake me for this other girl? I shall never know.

But he makes life hell for me, this valet de chambre.

At last the money comes from England. 'We can't go on doing this,' they say. 'You insisted on it against everybody's advice.' And so on. . . . All right, I won't ask you again. A Spartan lot, they are.

I leave the hotel, I leave the quarter. For the last time I have washed my knife, fork and spoon and put them away in the locker. No more meals with the destitute girls.

But, after all, those were still the days when I went into a café to drink coffee, when I could feel gay on half a bottle of wine, when this happened and that happened.

But they never last, the golden days. And it can be sad, the sun in the afternoon, can't it? Yes, it can be sad, the afternoon sun, sad and frightening.

Now, money, for the night is coming. Money for my hair, money for my teeth, money for shoes that won't deform my feet (it's not so easy now to walk around in cheap shoes with very high heels), money for good clothes, money, money. The night is coming.

That's always when there isn't any. Just when you need it there's no money. *No money*. It gets you down.

Is it true that I am moche? God, no. I bet it was a woman said that. No, it wasn't. It was a man said it. Am I moche? No, no, you're young, you're beautiful.

Sometimes it's quite all right, sometimes it works. Often it works. And days. And nights. . . .

Eat. Drink. Walk. March. Back to the hotel. To the Hotel of Arrival, the Hotel of Departure, the Hotel of the Future, the Hotel of Martinique and the Universe. . . . Back to the hotel without a name in the street without a name. You press the button and the door opens. This is the Hotel Without-a-Name in the Street Without-a-Name, and the clients have no names, no faces. You go up the stairs. Always the same stairs, always the same room.

The room says: 'Quite like old times. Yes? . . . No? . . . Yes.'

16

After all this, what happened?

What happened was that, as soon as I had the slightest chance of a place to hide in, I crept into it and hid.

Well, sometimes it's a fine day, isn't it? Sometimes the skies are blue. Sometimes the air is light, easy to breathe. And there is always tomorrow. . . .

Tomorrow I'll go to the Galeries Lafayette, choose a dress, go along to the Printemps, buy gloves, buy scent, buy lipstick, buy things costing fcs. 6.25 and fcs. 19.50, buy anything cheap. Just the sensation of spending, that's the point. I'll look at bracelets studded with artificial jewels, red, green and blue, necklaces of imitation pearls, cigarette-cases, jewelled tortoises. . . . And when I have had a couple of drinks I shan't know whether it's yesterday, today or tomorrow.

PART FOUR

1

When I go into the bureau for my key the patronne tells me that an English monsieur has left a note for me. An English monsieur? . . . Yes, that's what she understood — a monsieur from London.

Allo! just dropped in to see you. Everything goes well with me. I have had enormous luck. I am leaving Paris tomorrow or the day after. So sorry I missed you.

RENÉ

As I get up to the fourth-floor landing the commis opens his door and puts his head out. 'Vache! Sale vache,' he says when he sees me. His head disappears and the door is slammed, but he goes on talking in a high, thin voice.

I take off my coat and hat and put away the scent and stockings I have just bought. All the time I am listening, straining my ears to hear what he is saying.

The voice stops. A loud knock. Now, this is too much, now I'm going to say a few things. If you think I'm afraid of you, you're mistaken. Wait a bit. . . .

I march to the door and fling it open.

The gigolo is outside, looking excited and pleased with himself. He takes my hand in both of his.

'I came before. Did they tell you? . . . But what's the matter? Why are you looking so frightened?'

'I'm not. I'm looking vexed.'

'Oh, no, you're looking frightened. Who are you frightened of? Me? But how flattering!'

'I thought it was the man next door. He's been shouting at me. He gets on my nerves.'

'He was rude to you? Voulez-vous que je lui casse la gueule?' he says.

'Certainly not. Not on any account.'

'I will if you wish. I can be useful in more ways than one.'

'Good God, no! Don't do anything of the sort.'

'Well, perhaps better not. I'd better not get into a row before I have my papers. But I shall have them. That's going to be all right tomorrow. . . . I like this room,' he says. 'A nice room, a charming room. Nothing but beds. Can I sit down?'

'There are only two beds.'

'Ah, yes, so I see — only two. But somehow it gives the impression that it's full of beds. . . . I waited up here for you nearly an hour this afternoon. I told your landlady I was a friend of yours from London. I spoke English to her. And she asked me if I'd like to wait in your room.'

I suppose this explains the 'Vache! Sale vache!'

'It's all very fine, but I asked you not to come up here and you said you wouldn't.'

'But why? The woman downstairs is so nice. . . . I don't understand you. She doesn't mind in the least. You could have someone up here every hour and she wouldn't mind. It's a shame to waste this hotel, and this room. Very, very good to make love in, this room. Have you really been wasting it? I don't believe you have.' He laughs loudly. 'Those eyes, those deep shadows under your sad eyes — what about them?'

'Not what you think at all. I don't sleep well, and I take a lot of luminal to make me sleep.'

'Poor girl, poor girl,' he says, touching my eyes. 'And you won't let me even try to do anything about it?'

Now I am sick of being laughed at — sick, sick, sick of being laughed at. Allez-vous-en, salaud. I'm sick of being laughed at.

He feels that I am vexed. He says in a polite, formal voice: 'I came to ask you if you'd have an apéritif with me this evening. Please do. I shall be very disappointed if you can't.'

Very quick, very easy, that change of attitude, like a fish gliding with a flick of its tail. now here, now there.

'All right. I'll be at the Closerie des Lilas at half-past seven. I'm glad you've been lucky.'

'I've met an American,' he says mysteriously. 'Beautiful. And very, very rich. How do you say — bursting with it?'

'Lousy with it.'

'Yes, lousy with it.'

'Did you go to the Ritz bar?'

'No.'

'Don't tell me you met her at the Dôme?'

'Not the Dôme. That Danish place — you know. Well, we were talking and she said she wanted to go on somewhere else to dance. I said, quite frankly — Quite frank, you know. . . .'

'I bet you were.'

'I said: "There's nothing I'd like better, nothing. But unfortunately at the moment I'm penniless — at least almost penniless." After that it was all right. She's staying at the Meurice. It's been a great success.'

'Well, it's nice of you to come all the way over here to tell me about it.'

'That's just it. That's something you wouldn't understand. But when you're living like I do, you get very superstitious, and I think you bring me luck. Remember — that evening I met you. I was discouraged, very discouraged. You brought me luck.'

The luck-bringer. . . . Well, I've never thought of myself in that way before.

He takes my hand in his and looks at my ring, his eyes narrowing.

'No good,' I say. 'Only worth about fifty francs — if that.'

'What, your hand?'

'You weren't looking at my hand, you were looking at my ring.'

'Oh, how suspicious she is, this woman! It's extraordinary. . . . But you will come this evening, won't you?'

'Yes, I'll be there. Where we talked the other night. I'll be there at half-past seven.'

He goes off, still looking triumphant.

I start walking up and down the room. I feel excited. I go to the glass, look at myself, stare at myself, make a grimace, look at my teeth. Damn this light — how can I see to make-up properly in this light?

Well, there I am, prancing about and smirking, and suddenly telling myself: 'No, I won't do a thing, not a thing. A little pride, a little dignity at the end, in the name of God. I won't even put on the stockings I bought this afternoon. I won't do a thing — not a thing. I will not grimace and posture before these people any longer.'

And, after all, the agitation is only on the surface. Underneath I'm indifferent. Underneath there is always stagnant water, calm, indifferent — the bitter peace that is very near to death, to hate. . . .

I have sixteen hundred francs left. Enough to pay for the dress I chose today, enough to pay my hotel bill and the journey back to London. How much over? Say four hundred francs. I take two hundred and fifty. Two hundred francs for the meal, if there is a meal; fifty francs behind the mirror at the back of my handbag, for a taxi home in case we quarrel, in case he turns nasty. 'Hey, taxi' — and you're out of everything.

I time myself to be ten minutes late and arrive at the Closerie des Lilas at twenty minutes to eight. I look round the terrace. Nobody there. I won't go round the corner and look on the other side. He is sure to be indoors on such a cold night.

A very pretty girl is sitting on one of the stools at the bar, having a drink. No sign of the gigolo.

I order a Cinzano, feeling my pulse, as it were, all the time. Am I disappointed, am I vexed? No, I am quite calm, also quite confident. He's somewhere around, I think.

I say to a waiter: 'Is there anybody on the terrace?'

'Oh, no, I don't think so. It's too cold tonight.'

'Would you go and have a look,' I say, quite calm, quite confident. 'And if there's anyone waiting, will you please tell him that I'm inside here.'

In a minute he comes back, followed by the gigolo.

'So here you are. I thought you'd stood me up.'

'I bet you thought the world had come to an end. I bet you couldn't believe it.'

'Well, no, I couldn't,' he says. 'But I was just beginning to believe it when the waiter came. I've been cursing you. You said where we talked the other night, and that's where I've been waiting. . . . I'm cold. I've had two Pernods to keep me warm, but still I'm cold. Feel my hands. I'm going to have another Pernod.'

He looks a bit drunk, but drunk in the Latin way — very vivid, keyed-up.

The girl at the bar gets off her stool and walks out, passing slowly in front of us.

'Oh, what a beautiful girl! Look. Look at the way she walks — that movement of the hips. Oh, isn't she beautiful? What a lovely body that girl must have!'

'Wouldn't you like to go after her and find out?' I say. 'I rather think that was the idea.'

'No, no, it's you I want to talk to.'

'That's what I'm here for. Go ahead.'

'While we're having dinner,' he says. . . . Pause of half a second for me to speak.

I ask him to have dinner with me.

'Thank you,' he says. 'To be frank, when I've paid for this lot of drinks I shan't have much money left.'

'What, haven't you got any money out of your American?'

'Oh no, not yet, not yet. When I ask her for something it'll be something. But one mustn't do that too quickly, of course. She must be ready. . . . She's nearly ready. I think perhaps tomorrow she'll be ready.'

He looks straight into my eyes all the time he is talking, with that air of someone defying you.

'Would you give me the money to pay for dinner now instead of in the restaurant?' he says, in the taxi. 'I'd prefer that.'

'Of course. I was going to.'

I give him the two hundred francs and the corners of his mouth go down.

'When you've settled up — dinner, drink, taxi,' I say, 'there'll be about two francs left. I planned it out.'

'Oh, ce qu'elle est rosse, cette femme!'

I don't know what it is about this man that seems to me so natural, so gay — that also makes me feel natural and happy, just as if I were young — but really young. I've never been young. When I was young I was strained-up, anxious. I've never been really young. I've never played. . . .

'I'm hungry,' he says. 'I'm so hungry that I can't think of anything but eating. To eat, to eat, and afterwards what's it matter?'

'This is another of my gay, chic places,' I say. 'You'll see, we'll have it all to ourselves.'

However, as it happens, there are several other people there, all eating seriously.

I want to see myself in a good light and I go upstairs to the lavabo, one of the attractions of the Pig and Lily. So clean and so resplendent, so well lit, with plenty of looking-glasses and not a soul there to watch you. Am I looking all right? Not so bad. Surely, not so bad. . . .

'At last,' he says when I come down. 'At last we are going to eat.'

I am not hungry. I expect he notices that the food isn't at all good, in this damned boîte that isn't at all gay. However, he doesn't seem to notice. He eats a lot. He talks.

I don't believe in his American — he's probably invented her. And yet something must have happened to make him feel so pleased with himself and so sure of himself. Also he seems certain that he will be in London in a few days.

He tries to get useful information from me. Night clubs, for instance, restaurants. Which are the ones to go to? Everything is clubs in London, isn't it? Clubs, clubs. . . . Yes, everything is clubs, clubs, clubs, clubs, clubs in London. . . . How can he find a really chic tailor? Do the good ones advertise?

'I don't know. I'm the wrong person to ask all this.'

'Couldn't you give a party and introduce me to your friends?' Half-mocking, half-wheedling.

'I haven't any friends.'

'Ah, too bad, too bad.'

He has never been to London, it seems, but he knows all about it. He has been told this and he has been told that.

By the time we have started on the second bottle of wine I have heard all about the gold-mine just across the Channel.

A curious situation — according to his friends. At least fifty per cent of the men homosexual and most of the others not liking it so much as all that. And the poor Englishwomen just gasping for it, oh, boy! And aren't they prepared to pay, if you go about it the right way, oh, boy! A curious situation.

The untapped gold-mine just across the Channel. . . .

I am eating very little, so the wine has an effect, and I begin to argue with this optimistic idiot.

But at the end of my arguments he says calmly: 'You talk like that because you're a woman, and everybody knows England isn't a woman's country. You know the proverb — "Unhappy as a dog in Turkey or a woman in England"? But for me it will be different.'

That's his idea. But he'll find out that he will be up against racial, not sexual, characteristics. Love is a stern virtue in England. (Usually a matter of hygiene, my dear. The indecent necessity — and who would spend money or thought or time on the indecent necessity? . . . We have our ration of rose-leaves, but only because rose-leaves are a gentle laxative.)

'You take care. You'll probably get a cigarette case en toc with your initials on it after a lot of hard work.'

He's so sure that everything is going to be all right, you have to be sorry for him. And he's so good-looking, this poor devil, so alive, gay, healthy, so as if he didn't drink much, so as if. . . . Talking away about the technique of the métier — it sounds quite meaningless. It probably is meaningless. He's just trying to shock me or excite me or something. . . .

It's half-past nine. There we still sit, jabbering.

'Is it true that Englishmen make love with all their clothes on, because they think it's more respectable that way?'

'Yes, certainly. Fully dressed. They add, of course, a macintosh.'

After this we are properly off.

'Now I'll show you something really funny,' he says. 'Look at this in the spoon. . . .'

'Yes. It is rather funny, isn't it?'

'I can do better than that,' he says.

I watch very carefully. If I learn this trick, it ought to raise my amusement-value.

Do you like this? Do you like that? What do you really like worse than anything else? I'll tell you something very curious I heard of the other day. Etcetera, etcetera. . . .

He is very good at this — calm, indifferent, without a glint in his eye. But his voice gets louder. Happily there is only one lot of people left in the room, and I don't think they understand English.

But the proprietor certainly understands. When he comes up with the coffee he looks at me in a half-pitying, half-severe way, as if to say: 'Really, really, really. . . . I should have thought you'd have more sense than this. Really, really. . . .' He certainly does understand English.

I stare back at him. Well, and what about it, you damned old goop? Are you as blameless as all that? Are you? I shouldn't think so. I don't criticize you, so don't you criticize me. See?

He walks away in a dignified manner. 'Tous piqués,' he is thinking, 'tous dingo, tous, tous, tous. . . .'

All the same, this conversation is becoming a bit of a strain. What is it leading up to? . . . Ah! here it comes.

'I've arranged everything. While I was waiting for you on the terrace I asked the waiter to tell me a place I could take you to as you said you didn't want to go back to your hotel with me. He told me of a very good place in the Boulevard Raspail.'

'My God!' I say. 'You asked the waiter?'

'Yes, of course. Waiters always know about that sort of thing.'

'Well, that's somewhere else I'll never be able to show my face in again.'

'And then you say you're not a bourgeoise!'

'I didn't say that. You said it.'

All the same, he's quite right. Tomorrow I must walk into that café and go to that same table on the terrace and have a drink. But when I think 'tomorrow' there is a gap in my head, a blank — as if I were falling through emptiness. Tomorrow never comes.

I say: 'Tomorrow never comes.'

'I don't understand.'

'Listen. I've told you this from the start — nothing doing. Why do you go on about it? It's stupid.'

'A pity,' he says, indifferently, 'a pity. It would have been so nice. You wouldn't have been disappointed in me.'

(But supposing you were disappointed in me.)

He's clever, this man, he feels what I am thinking. He says: 'You know, you needn't be afraid of me. I'd never say cruel things to you, nor about you either. I'm not cruel to women — not in that way. You see, I like them. I don't like boys; I tried in Morocco, but it was no use. I like women.'

'Then you ought to be worth your weight in gold. I only hope you get it.'

'Do you like girls?' he says, looking inquisitive.

'No, I don't.'

'What, have you never in your life seen a girl you could have loved?'

'No, never. . . . Yes, once I did. I saw a girl in a bordel I could have loved.'

'Oh, how convenient!'

He laughs. The proprietor starts, looks towards us, shrugs his shoulders and turns his back.

'Why did you love her?'

'Well,' I say, 'what a question, anyway!'

How on earth can you say why you love people? You might as well say you know where the lightning is going to strike. At least, that's how it has always seemed to me.

'Tell me about this girl.'

'There isn't anything to tell, except that I liked her. She looked awfully sad and very gentle. That doesn't happen often.'

He seems much amused.

'Did she make love to you?'

'No, of course not,' I say. 'Certainly not.'

'What happened? Do tell me.'

'Well, while I was thinking these sentimental thoughts a fresh client came in and she rushed off to join the crowd that was twittering round him. You know how they do. . . . I loathe bordels, anyway.'

(Now, why has this girl suddenly come up out of the past? She wasn't beautiful, not a star at all. I expect she didn't have a very good time. But I wanted to put my arms round her, kiss her eyes and comfort her — and if that's not love, what is?)

'Oh, all women hate bordels,' he says.

'Oh, yeah? Well, you wouldn't think so to hear some of them talk. Besides, don't tell me that I'm like other women — I'm not.'

'Yes, but all women say that too,' he says.

Now it seems to me that there is antagonism in the air. It would be a pity if we ended with a quarrel.

'I'm no use to anybody,' I say. 'I'm a cérébrale, can't you see that?'

Thinking how funny a book would be, called 'Just a Cérébrale or You Can't Stop Me From Dreaming'. Only, of course, to be accepted as authentic, to carry any conviction, it would have to be written by a man. What a pity, what a pity!

'Is that your idea of yourself?' he says.

'It is, certainly.'

'It's not mine at all. I should have thought you were rather stupid.'

This pulls me up short. If he thinks me stupid now I wonder what he would say to my usual conversation, which goes like this: 'I believe it's going to be fine today — yes, I hope it is — yes — yes — yes — '

'You think me stupid?' I say.

'No, no. Don't be vexed. I don't mean stupid. I mean that you feel better than you think.'

Do I? I wonder. . . . Oh well, stupid. . . . An extremely funny monologue is going on in my head — or it seems to me extremely funny. I want to stop myself from laughing out loud, so I say: 'We're getting very high-toned. What is a cérébrale, anyway? I don't know. Do you?'

'A cérébrale,' he says, seriously, 'is a woman who doesn't like men or need them.'

'Oh, is that it? I've often wondered. Well, there are quite a lot of those, and the ranks are daily increasing.'

'Ah, but a cérébrale doesn't like women either. Oh, no. The true cérébrale is a woman who likes nothing and nobody except herself and her own damned brain or what she thinks is her brain.'

So pleased with herself, like a little black boy in a top-hat. . . .

'In fact, a monster.'

'Yes, a monster.'

'Well, after all that it's very comforting to know that you think I'm stupid. . . . Let's ask for the bill, shall we? Let's go.'

'I rang you up the other morning,' he says.

'Yes, I know. I was asleep. I got down to the telephone too late.'

'You knew who it was?'

'Oh, I thought it might be you. I wasn't sure.'

'You have friends in Paris, then?'

'I don't know a soul here, except two Russians I met the other day. I like them very much.'

'Russians,' he says in a spiteful voice, 'Russians in Paris! Everybody knows what they are — Jews and poor whites. The most boring people in the world. Terrible people.'

For some reason I am very vexed at this. I start wondering why I am there at all, what I am doing in this box of a restaurant, swapping dirty stories with a damned gigolo. I want to get away. I want to be out of the place.

'I'm going to the Exhibition,' I say. 'I want to see it again at night before I go.'

'The Exhibition?'

'Haven't you been to it?'

'No, I haven't. What should I do at the Exhibition?'

'Well, I'm going. You needn't come if you don't want to. I'll go by myself.'

I want to go by myself, to get into a taxi and drive along the streets, to stand by myself and look down at the fountains in the cold light.

'But of course,' he says. 'If you want to go to the Exhibition, we'll go. Naturally.'

2

We go in by the Trocadéro entrance. There aren't many people about. Cold, empty, beautiful — this is what I imagined, this is what I wanted.

'What's that light up there?' he says.

'That's the Star of Peace. Don't you recognize it?'

He stares back at it.

'How mesquin! It's vulgar, that Star of Peace.'

'The building is very fine,' I say, in a schoolmistress's voice.

We stand on the promenade above the fountains, looking down on them. This is what I wanted — the cold fountains, the cold, rainbow lights on the water. . . .

He says again: 'It's mesquin, your Star of Peace.'

We stand for some time, leaning over the balustrade. He puts his arm through mine. I can feel him shivering. When I tell him so he answers: 'Well, it's cold here after Morocco.'

'Oh yes, of course. Morocco.'

'You don't believe I've just come from Morocco, do you?'

Whatever else is a lie about him, it's certainly true that he isn't dressed for this weather.

The lights shimmering on the water, the leaping fountains, cold and beautiful. . . .

'Why don't you borrow some money from your American and buy yourself an overcoat?'

'No, I'm going to wait. I want to get my clothes in London.'

For God's sake — he's going to start up again about the addresses of London tailors. . . .

'Let's go and have a drink somewhere. That'll make us warm.'

'A drink?' he says. 'Oh yes, of course. But supposing I don't want to walk a long way in the cold just to get a cheap drink.'

He begins to whistle, like a little boy whistles when he is trying to keep his courage up — loud, clear and pure.

'What's that tune? I like it.'

'That's the march of the Legion,' he says, 'the real one. Or that's what I think it is. But how should I know.'

'Tell me about Morocco.'

'No I don't want to talk about it. . . . I don't want to think about it,' he says loudly. 'Come on, let's go and have our drink.'

'The goodbye one,' I say.

'All right — the goodbye one. But not in here. Let's get out of here. . . .'

We sit side by side in the taxi, not touching each other. He is whistling softly all the time. I watch the streets through the window. Well, there you are, Paris, and this is the goodbye drink. . . .

'Where are we going?' he says.

We are passing the Deux Magots.

'This is all right. Let's go in here.'

The café is not very full. I choose a table as far away from everyone else as possible. We order two brandies.

He has told me that he is twenty-six, but I think he is older than that — he's about thirty. And he doesn't look like a gigolo, not at all like a gigolo.

Suddenly I feel shy and self-conscious. (How ridiculous! Don't let him see it, for God's sake.) I drink half my brandy-and-soda and start talking about the last time I was in the Deux Magots and how I had been staying at Antibes and how I came back very brown and on top of the world and with some money too, and all the rest.

'Money I had earned. Sans blague. It was too funny. I wrote up fairy stories for a very rich woman. She came to Montparnasse looking for somebody and of course there was a rush. She chose me because I was the cheapest. The night I got back to Montparnasse — very rich — we celebrated. We started up in this café because I was staying at a hotel near here.'

What with the brandy-and-soda and going back to the Deux Magots, the whole thing is whirling nicely round in my head. She would come into my room very early in the morning in her dressing-gown, her hair hanging down in two plaits, looking rather sweet, I must say. 'Are you awake, Mrs Jansen? I've just thought of a story. You can take it down in shorthand, can't you?' 'No, I'm afraid I can't.' (Cheated! For what I'm paying she ought to know shorthand.) 'But if you'll tell me what you want to say I think I can get it down.' Off she'd go. 'Once upon a time there was a cactus — ' Or a white rose or a yellow rose or a red rose, as the case might be. All this, mind you, at six-thirty in the morning. . . . 'This story', she would say, looking anxious, 'is an allegory. You understand that, don't you?' 'Yes, I understand.' But she was never very specific about the allegory.' 'Could you make it a Persian garden?' 'I don't see why not.' 'Oh, and there's something I want to speak to you about, Mrs Jansen. I'm afraid Samuel didn't like the last story you wrote.' Oh God, this awful sinking of the heart — like going down in a lift. I knew this job was too good to be true. 'Didn't he? I'm sorry. What didn't he like about it?' Well, I'm afraid he doesn't like the way you write. What he actually said was that, considering the cost of these stories, he thinks it strange that you should write them in words of one syllable. He says it gets monotonous, and don't you know any long words, and if you do, would you please use them? . . . Madame Holmberg is most anxious to collaborate with me. And she's a real writer — she's just finished the third volume of her Life of Napoleon.' After this delicate hint she adds: 'Samuel wished to speak to you himself, but I told him that I preferred to do it, because I didn't want to hurt your feelings. I said I was sure, if I told you his opinion, you'd try to do better. I should hate to hurt your feelings because in a strange way I feel that we are very much alike. Don't you think so?' (No, I certainly don't think so, you pampered chow.) 'I'm awfully sorry you didn't like the story,' I say.

Sitting at a large desk, a white sheet of paper in front of me and outside the sun and the blue Mediterranean. Monte Carlo, Monte Carlo, by the Med-it-er-rany-an sea-ee, Monte Carlo, Monte Carlo, where the boy of my heart waits for me-ee. . . . Persian garden. Long words. Chiaroscuro? Translucent?. . . . I bet he'd like cataclysmal action and centrifugal flux, but the point is how can I get them into a Persian garden?. . . . Well, I might. Stranger things have happened. . . . A blank sheet of paper. . . . Once upon a time, once upon a time there lived a lass who tended swine. . . . Persian gardens. Satraps — surely they were called satraps. . . . It's so lovely outside, and music has started somewhere. . . . Grinding it out, oh God, with all the long words possible. And the music outside playing *Valencia.* . . . 'Are you still there, Mrs Jansen? You haven't gone out? I've just thought of a new story. Once upon a time there lived. . . .'

Shrewd as they're born, this woman, hard as a nail, and with what a sense of property! She'd raise hell if a spot of wine fell on one of her Louis Quinze chairs. Authentic Louis Quinze, of course they were.

They explain people like that by saying that their minds are in watertight compartments, but it never seemed so to me. It's all washing about, like the bilge in the hold of a ship, all washing around in the same hold — no watertight compartments. . . . Fairies, red roses, the sense of property — Of course they don't feel things like we do — Lilies in the moonlight — I believe in survival after death. I've had personal proof of it. And we'll find our dear, familiar bodies on the other side — Samuel has forgotten to buy his suppositoires — Pity would be out of place in this instance — I never take people like that to expensive restaurants. Quite unnecessary and puts ideas into their heads. It's not *kind*, really — Nevertheless, all the little birdies sing — Psycho-analysis might help. Adler is more wholesome than Freud, don't you think? —English judges never make a mistake — The piano is quite Egyptian in feeling. . . .

All washing around in the same hold. No watertight compartments. . . .

Well, I am trying to tell René about all this and giggling a good deal, when he stops me.

'But I know that woman. I know her very well. . . . Again you don't believe me. This time you shall believe me. Listen, she was like this — ' He describes her exactly. 'And the house was like this — ' He draws a little plan on the back of an envelope. 'Here are the palm trees. Here are the entrance steps. That terrible English butler they had — do you remember? The two cabinets here with jade, the other two cabinets with a collection of china. The double circular staircase — do you remember how they used to come down it at night?'

'Yes,' I say. ' "I know how to walk down a staircase, me." '

'Which bedroom did you have? Did you have the one on the second floor with the green satin divan in the ante-chamber to the bathroom?'

'No. I had a quite ordinary one on the third floor. But what an array of scent-bottles! I dream of them sometimes.'

'It was a ridiculous house, wasn't it?'

'I was very much impressed,' I say. 'It's the only millionaire's house I've ever stayed in in my life.'

'I've stayed in much richer ones than that. I've stayed in one so rich that when you pulled the lavatory-plug it played a tune. . . . Rich people — you have to be sorry for them. They haven't the slightest idea how to spend their money; they haven't the slightest idea how to enjoy themselves. Either they have no taste at all, or, if they have any taste, it's like a mausoleum and they're shut up in it.'

'Well you're going to alter all that, aren't you?'

Of course, there's no doubt that this man has stayed in this house and does know these people. One would think that that would give us more confidence in each other. Not at all, it makes us suspicious. There's no doubt that a strict anonymity is a help on these occasions.

When did all this happen, and what is his story? Did he stay in France for a time, get into trouble over here and then join the Legion? Is that the story? Well, anyway, what's it matter to me what his story is? I expect he has a different one every day.

I say: 'Excuse me a minute,' primly, and go down to the lavatory.

This is another lavatory that I know very well, another of the well-known mirrors.

'Well, well,' it says, 'last time you looked in here you were a bit different, weren't you? Would you believe me that, of all the faces I see, I remember each one, that I keep a ghost to throw back at each one — lightly, like an echo — when it looks into me again?' All glasses in all lavabos do this.

But it's not as bad as it might be. This is just the interval when drink makes you look nice, before it makes you look awful.

He says: 'You're always disappearing into the lavabo, you. C'est agaçant.'

'What do you expect?' I say, staring at him. 'I'm getting old.'

He frowns. 'No, don't say that. Don't talk like that. You're not old. But you've got to where you're afraid to be young. I know. They've frightened you, haven't they? Why do you let them frighten you? They always try to do that, if it isn't in one way it's in another.'

'Thanks for the good advice. I'll try to remember it. Now I'm all ready for another *fine*.'

'But you said that if you drink too much you cry. And I have a horror of people who cry when they're drunk.'

'I don't feel a bit like that. Never happier in my life.'

He looks at me and says: 'No, I don't think you are going to cry. All right.'

And here's another brandy. I squirt the soda in and watch the bubbles rising up from the bottom of the glass. I'll drink it slowly, this one.

'Well, don't be too long. Finish that, and then we'll go.'

'Where to?'

'Well, to your hotel or to the Boulevard Raspail. Just as you like. . . . You're such a stupid woman,' he says, 'such a stupid woman. Why do you go on pretending? Now, look me straight in the eyes and say you don't want to.'

'Of course I do.'

'Then why won't you? At least tell me why you won't. Something that you would like and that I would like — '

'Something so unimportant.'

'Oh, important!' he says. 'But it would be nice. At least tell me why you won't, or is that too much to ask?'

'Oh no, it's not too much to ask. I'll tell you. It's because I'm afraid.'

'Afraid,' he says, 'afraid! But what are you afraid of? . . . You think I'll strangle you, or cut your throat for the sake of that beautiful ring of yours. Is that it?'

'No, I'm sure you wouldn't kill me to get my ring.'

'Then perhaps you are afraid I'll kill you, not because I want money, but because I like to do bad things. But that's where you're so stupid. With you, I don't want to do bad things.'

'There's always the one that you don't want to do bad things with, isn't there?'

'Yes, there's always the one,' he says. 'I want to lie close to you and feel your arms round me.'

— And tell me everything, everything. . . . He has said that bit before.

'Oh, stop talking about it.'

'Of course,' he says. 'But first, just as a matter of curiosity, I'd like to know what you are so afraid of. Finish your drink and tell me. Just as a matter of curiosity.'

I drink. Something in his voice has hurt me. I can't say anything. My throat hurts and I can't say anything.

'You are afraid of me. You think I'm méchant. You do think I might kill you.'

If I thought you'd kill me, I'd come away with you right now and no questions asked. And what's more, you could have any money I've got with my blessing. . . .

'I don't think you're any more méchant than anybody else. Less, probably.'

'Then what are you afraid of? Tell me. I'm interested. Of men, of love? . . . What, still? . . . Impossible.'

You are walking along a road peacefully. You trip. You fall into blackness. That's the past — or perhaps the future. And you know that there is no past, no future, there is only this blackness, changing faintly, slowly, but always the same.

'You want to know what I'm afraid of? All right, I'll tell you. . . . I'm afraid of men — yes, I'm very much afraid of men. And I'm even more afraid of women. And I'm very much afraid of the whole bloody human race. . . . Afraid of them?' I say. 'Of course I'm afraid of them. Who wouldn't be afraid of a pack of damned hyenas?'

Thinking: 'Oh, shut up. Stop it. What's the use?' But I can't stop. I go on raving.

'And when I say afraid — that's just a word I use. What I really mean is that I hate them. I hate their voices, I hate their eyes, I hate the way they laugh. . . . I hate the whole bloody business. It's cruel, it's idiotic, it's unspeakably horrible. I never had the guts to kill myself or I'd have got out of it long ago. So much the worse for me. Let's leave it at that.'

. . . I know all about myself now, I know. You've told me so often. You haven't left me one rag of illusion to clothe myself in. But by

God, I know what you are too, and I wouldn't change places. . . .
Everything spoiled, all spoiled. Well, don't cry about it. No, I won't cry about it. . . . But may you tear each other to bits, you damned hyenas, and the quicker the better. . . . Let it be destroyed. Let it happen. Let it end, this cold insanity. Let it happen.

Only five minutes ago I was in the Deux Magots, dressed in that damned cheap black dress of mine, giggling and talking about Antibes, and now I am lying in a misery of utter darkness. Quite alone. No voice, no touch, no hand. . . . How long must I lie here? For ever? No, only for a couple of hundred years this time, miss. . . .

I heave myself out of the darkness slowly, painfully. And there I am, and there he is, the poor gigolo.

He looks sad. He says, speaking in a low voice and for the first time with a very strong accent: 'I have wounds,' pronouncing 'wounds' so oddly that I don't understand what he means.

'You have what?'

I look round. Have I screamed, shouted, cursed, cried, made a scene? Is anyone looking at us, is anyone noticing us? No, nobody. . . . The woman at the desk is sitting with her eyes cast down. I notice the exact shade of the blue eye-shadow on her lids. They must see the start of some funny things, these women perched up in cafés, perched up like idols. Especially the ones at the Dôme.

'You have what?'

'Look,' he says, still speaking in a whisper. He throws his head up. There is a long scar, going across his throat. Now I understand what it means — from ear to ear. A long, thick, white scar. It's strange that I haven't noticed it before.

He says: 'That is one. There are other ones. I have been wounded.'

It isn't boastful, the way he says this, nor complaining. It's puzzled, puzzled in an impersonal way, as if he is asking me — me, of all people — why, why, why?

Pity you? Why should I pity you? Nobody has ever pitied me. They are without mercy.

'I have too,' I say in a surly voice. 'Moi aussi.'

'I know. I can see that. I believe you.'

'Well,' I say, 'if we're going to start believing each other, it's getting serious, isn't it?'

I want to get out of this dream.

'But why shouldn't we believe each other? Why shouldn't we

believe each other just for tonight? Will you believe something I'm going to say to you now? I want absolutely to make love to you.'

'I told you from the start you were wasting your time.'

'What happened to you, what happened?' he says. 'Something bad must have happened to make you like this.'

'One thing? It wasn't one thing. It took years. It was a slow process.'

He says: 'It doesn't matter. What I know is that I could do this with you' — he makes a movement with his hands like a baker kneading a loaf of bread — 'and afterwards you'd be different. I know. Believe me.'

I watch the little grimacing devil in my head. He wears a top-hat and a cache-sexe and he sings a sentimental song — 'The roses all are faded and the lilies in the dust.'

I say: 'Now who's trying to make an unimportant thing sound important?'

'Oh, important, unimportant — that's just words. If we can be happy for a little, forget everything for a little, isn't that important enough? . . . Now we'll go. We'll go back to your hotel.'

'No.'

Leave me alone. I'm tired. . . .

'Still rien à faire?' He starts to laugh.

'Still rien à faire. Absolutely rien à faire.'

But everything is so changed, I can't look at him.

'I must go. Please. I'm so tired.'

In the taxi I say: 'Whistle that tune, will you? The one you said is the march of the Legion.'

He whistles it very softly. And I watch the streets through the window. A l'Hôtel de l'Espérance. . . .

3

I am in a little whitewashed room. The sun is hot outside. A man is standing with his back to me, whistling that tune and cleaning his shoes. I am wearing a black dress, very short, and heel-less slippers. My legs are bare. I am watching for the expression on the man's face when he turns round. Now he ill-treats me, now he betrays me. He often brings home other women and I have to wait on them, and I don't like that. But as long as he is alive and near me I am not unhappy. If he were to die I should kill myself.

My film-mind. . . . ('for God's sake watch out for your film-mind. . . .')

'What are you laughing at now?' he says.

'Nothing, nothing. . . . I do like that tune. Do you think I could get a gramophone record of it?'

'I don't know.'

We are at the door of the hotel.

'Good night,' he says. 'Sleep well. Take a big dose of luminal.'

'I will. And the same to you.'

I am not sad as I go upstairs, not sad, not happy, not regretful, not thinking of anything much. Except that I see very clearly in my head the tube of luminal and the bottle of whisky. In case. . . .

Just as I have got to my door there is a click and everything is in darkness. Impossible to get the key in. I must cross the pitch-black landing to the head of the stairs and put the time-switch on again.

I am feeling for the knob when I see the light of a cigarette a yard or two from my face. I stand for what seems a long while watching it. Then I call out: 'Who is it? Who's there? Qui est là?'

But before he answers I know. I take a step forward and put my arms round him.

I have my arms round him and I begin to laugh, because I am so happy. I stand there hugging him, so terribly happy. Now everything is in my arms on this dark landing — love, youth, spring, happiness, everything I thought I had lost. I was a fool, wasn't I? to think all that was finished for me. How could it be finished?

I put up my hand and touch his hair. I've wanted to do that ever since I first saw him.

'Did I frighten you at first?'

He has put the light on. He looks pleased, but surprised.

'No, no,' I say. 'Yes, a bit. . . . No.'

But I whisper and look round fearfully. What do I expect to see? There is nobody on the landing — nothing. Nothing but the commis' shoes by his door, the toes carefully pointed outwards as usual.

He takes the key from my hand, opens the door and shuts it after us. We kiss each other fervently, but already something has gone wrong. I am uneasy, half of myself somewhere else. Did anybody hear me, was anybody listening just now?

'It's dark in here. . . . Just a minute, I'll fix it.'

The switch in my room works either the light near the bed or the one over the curtained wash-basin — it depends on how far the knob is pushed. But it is always going wrong and doing one thing when you expect it to do another. I fumble with it for some time before I can get the lamp near the bed going.

Now the room springs out at me, laughing, triumphant. The big bed, the little bed, the table with the tube of luminal, the glass and the bottle of Evian, the two books, the clock ticking on the ledge, the menu — 'T'as compris? Si, j'ai compris. . . .' Four walls, a roof and a bed. *Les Hommes en Cage.* . . . Exactly.

Here we are. Nothing to stop us. Four walls, a roof, a bed, a bidet, a spotlight that goes on first over the bidet and then over the bed — nothing to stop us. Anything you like; anything I like. . . . No past to make us sentimental, no future to embarrass us. . . . A difficult moment when you are out of practice — a moment that makes you go cold, cold and wary.

'Would you like some whisky?' I say. 'I've got some.'

(That's original. I bet nobody's ever thought of that way of bridging the gap before.)

I take my coat and hat off, get the bottle of whisky. I rinse the tooth-glass out, mix myself a drink and mix one for him in the Evian glass, which is clean. I do all this as slowly as possible. Time, time, give me time — wait a minute, wait a minute, not yet. . . .

We sit on the small bed. He takes one sip of whisky and puts the glass away.

'Isn't it right? Don't you like it?'

'Yes, it's all right. I don't want to drink.'

'Mine tastes awful. It tastes of mouthwash.'

'Then why do you drink it? Don't drink it.'

All the same, I go on sipping away. Small sips. Not yet, not yet. . . . Wait a minute. . . . You won't be unkind, will you? For God's sake, say something kind to me. . . . But his eyes are ironical as he watches me. I don't think he is going to say anything kind. On the contrary. But that's natural. I've got to expect that. Technique.

I say: 'It's funny how some men try to get you to swill as much as you can hold, and others try to stop you. Automatically. Some profound instinct seems to get going. Something racial — yes, I'm sure it's racial.'

He says: 'Just now on the landing — you knew it was me?'

'Yes of course.'

'But how could you have known before I said anything?'

'I did know,' I say obstinately.

'Then you knew that I was coming up after you. You expected me to?'

'Oh no, I didn't. I didn't a bit.'

He laughs and puts his hand on my knee under my dress. I hate that. It reminds me of — Never mind. . . .

'You love playing a comedy, don't you?'

'How do you mean — a comedy?'

I shouldn't have taken whisky on top of brandy. It's making me feel quarrelsome. Sparks of anger, of resentment, shooting all over me. . . . A comedy, what comedy? A comedy, my God!

The damned room grinning at me. The clock ticking. Qu'est-ce qu'elle fout ici, la vieille?

'I'm going to have another whisky.'

'No, don't drink any more.'

Oh, go to hell. . . . I push his hand away and get up.

'Tell me something. You think that I meant you all the time to come up here, and that everything else I said this evening was what you call a comedy?'

'I knew you really wanted me to come up — yes. That was easy to see,' he says.

I could kill him for the way he said that, and for the way he is looking at me. . . . Easy, easy, free and easy. Easy to fool, easy to torture, easy to laugh at. But not again. Oh no, not again. . . . You've been unkind too soon. Bad technique.

'Hooray,' I say, 'here's to you. It was sweet of you to come up and I was very pleased to see you. Now you've got to go.'

'Of course I'm not going. Why are you like this? Don't be like this.'

'No, it's no use. I'd rather you went.'

'Well, I'm not going,' he says. 'I want to see this comedy. You'll have to call for someone to put me out. . . . Au secours, au secours,' he shouts in a high falsetto voice. 'Like that. . . . If you want to make yourself ridiculous.'

'I've been so ridiculous all my life that a little bit more or a little bit less hardly matters now.'

'Call out, then. Go on. Or why don't you rap on the wall and ask your friend next door to help you?'

As soon as he says this I am very quiet. If there is one thing on earth I want to avoid, it is a scene in this hotel.

'I don't want to have a row here,' I say. 'Only you've got to go.'

'Why?'

'Well, because I tell you to go. And you'll go.'

'Just like that?'

'Yes, just like that.'

'But what do you think I am — a little dog? You think you can first kiss me and then say to me "Get out"? You haven't looked well at me. . . . I don't like it,' he says, 'that voice that gives orders.'

Well, I haven't always liked it, either — the voice that gives orders.

'Very well, I ask you to go.'

'Oh, you annoy me,' he says. 'You annoy me, you annoy me.'

And there we are — struggling on the small bed. My idea is not so much to struggle as to make it a silent struggle. Nobody must hear us. At the end, he is lying on me, holding down my two spread arms. I can't move. My dress is torn open at the neck. But I have my knees firmly clamped together. This is a game — a game played in the snow for a worthless prize. . . .

He is breathing quickly and I can feel his heart beating. I am quite calm. 'This is really a bit comic,' I keep thinking. Also I think: 'He looks méchant, he could be méchant, this man.'

I shut my eyes because I want to stay calm, I want to be able to keep thinking: 'This is really damned comic.'

'We're on the wrong bed,' I say. 'And with all our clothes on, too. Just like English people.'

'Oh, we have a lot of time. We have all night. We have till tomorrow.'

A long time till tomorrow. A hundred years, perhaps, till tomorrow. . . .

'There's a very good truc', he says, 'for women like you, who pretend and lie and play an idiotic comedy all the time.'

He tells me about it.

'Very good, very good. Where did you learn that? In Morocco?'

'Oh, no,' he says, 'in Morocco it's much easier. You get four comrades to help you, and then it's very easy. They each take their turn. It's nice like that.' He laughs loudly.

'For goodness' sake,' I say — 'you can describe your charming methods without shouting at the top of your voice, surely.'

'You think you're very strong, don't you? he says.

'Yes, I'm very strong.'

I'm strong as the dead, my dear, and that's how strong I am.

'If you're so strong, why do you keep your eyes shut?'

Because dead people must have their eyes shut.

I lie very still, I don't move. Not open my eyes. . . .

'Je te ferai mal,' he says. 'It's your fault.'

When I open my eyes I feel the tears trickling down from the outside corners.

'That's better, that's better. Now say "I tell you to go, and you'll go".'

I can't speak.

'That's better, that's better.'

I feel his hard knee between my knees. My mouth hurts, my breasts hurt, because it hurts, when you have been dead, to come alive. . . .

'Now everything's going to be all right,' he says.

'T'as compris?' he says.

Of course, the ritual answer is 'Si, j'ai compris. . . .'

I lie there, thinking 'Yes, I understand'. Thinking 'For the last time'. Thinking nothing. Listening to a high, clear, cold voice. My voice.

'Of course I understand. Naturally I understand. I should be an awful fool if I didn't. If you look in the right-hand pocket of the dressing-case over on that table you'll find the money you want.'

He lets go of my wrists. I feel him go very still.

'It isn't locked. Take the thousand-franc note. But for God's sake leave me the others, or I'll be in an awful jam.'

But how heavy he is, how much heavier than one would have thought. . . .

'You mustn't think,' I say, 'that I'm vexed about anything, because I'm not. Everybody's got their living to earn, haven't they? I'm just trying to save you a lot of trouble.'

Don't listen, that's not me speaking. Don't listen. Nothing to do with me — I swear it. . . .

'And I thought you were awfully sweet to me,' I say. 'I loved all the various stories you told me about yourself. Especially that one about your wounds and your scars — that amused me very much.'

I put my arm up over my face, because I have a feeling that he is going to hit me.

'I'm just trying to save you a whole lot of trouble,' I say, 'a whole lot of waste of time. You can have the money right away, so it would be a waste of time, wouldn't it?'

His weight is not on me any longer. He is standing up. He has moved so quickly that I haven't had time to put my arms round him, or to say 'Stay', to say 'Don't do this, don't leave me like this, don't.'

'Yes, you're right,' he says. 'It would be a waste of time.'

'You and your wounds — don't you see how funny you are? You did make me laugh. Other people's wounds — how funny they are! I shall laugh every time I think about you. . . .'

I keep my arm over my eyes. He is walking over to the glass, looking at himself, putting his tie straight. Now he is opening the dressing-case. I keep my arm over my eyes because I don't want to see him take the money; I don't want to see him go. . . .

He might say something. He might say good night, or goodbye, or good luck or something.

The door shuts.

When he has gone I turn over on my side and huddle up, making myself as small as possible, my knees almost touching my chin. I cry in the way that hurts right down, that hurts your heart and your stomach. Who is this crying? The same one who laughed on the landing, kissed him and was happy. This is me, this is myself, who is crying. The other — how do I know who the other is? She isn't me.

Her voice in my head: 'Well, well, well, just think of that now. What an amusing ten days! Positively packed with thrills. The last performance of What's-her-name And Her Boys or It Was All Due To An Old Fur Coat. Positively the last performance. . . . Go on, cry, allez-y. Encore. Tirez, as they say here. . . . Now, calm, calm, say it all out calmly. You've had dinner with a beautiful young man and he kissed you and you've paid a thousand francs for it. Dirt cheap at the price, especially with the exchange the way it is. Don't forget the exchange, dearie — but of course you wouldn't would you? And you've picked up one or two people in the street and you've bought a picture. Don't forget the picture, to remind you of — what was it to remind you of? Oh, I know — of human misery. . . .'

He'll stare at me, gentle, humble, resigned, mocking, a little mad. Standing in the gutter playing his banjo. And I'll look back at him because I shan't be able to help it, remembering about being young, and about being made love to and making love, about pain and dancing and not being afraid of death, about all the music I've ever loved, and every time I've been happy. I'll look back at him and I'll say: 'I know the words to the tune you're playing. I know the words to every tune you've ever played on your bloody banjo. Well, I mustn't sing any more — there you are. Finie la chanson. The song is ended. Finished.'

Then I shall think of this hotel, the exact shape of the bed and the comic papers in the lavatory. There was that quite ordinary joke that made me laugh so much because it was signed God. Just like that — G-O-D, God. Joke, by God. And what a sense of humour! Even the English aren't in it.

She says: 'I hate to stop you crying. I know it's your favourite pastime, but I must remind you that the man next door has probably heard every damned thing that's happened and is now listening-in to the sequel. Not exactly what one would have expected, perhaps. But still — quite amusing.'

I stop crying. I stretch my legs out. I feel very tired.

'And another thing,' she says. 'If he's taken all the money — which he almost certainly has — that'll be a lovely business, won't it?'

I get up and blow my nose. There is blood on the handkerchief. I look in the glass and see that my mouth is swollen, and it is still bleeding where he bit it. I go over to the dressing-case.

'Go on, look. You might as well know.'

I feel in the right-hand pocket, take the money out and look at it. Two hundred-franc notes, a mille note.

'Well! *What* a compliment! Who'd have thought it?'

'I knew,' I say, 'I knew. That's why I cried.'

I get the tooth-glass and half-fill it with whisky. Here's to you, gigolo, chic gigolo. . . . I bow deeply. Have another. . . .

I have another.

I appreciate this, sweet gigolo, from the depths of my heart. I'm not used to these courtesies. So here's to you. And here's to you. . . .

4

I am very drunk. I see the Russian's face and his mouth moving, saying: 'Madame Vénus se fâchera.' 'Oh, her!' I say. 'What do I care about her? She's never done anything for me except play me a lot of dirty tricks.' 'She does that to everybody,' he says. 'All the same, be careful of her. Take care, take care. . . .'

A hum of voices talking, but all you can hear is 'Femmes, femmes, femmes, femmes. . . .' And the noise of a train saying:

'Paris, Paris, Paris, Paris. . . .' Madame Vénus is angry and Phoebus Apollo is walking away from me down the boulevard to hide himself in la crasse. Only address: Mons P. Apollo, La Crasse. . . . But I know quite well that all this is hallucination, imagination: Venus is dead; Apollo is dead; even Jesus is dead.

All that is left in the world is an enormous machine, made of white steel. It has innumerable flexible arms, made of steel. Long, thin arms. At the end of each arm is an eye, the eyelashes stiff with mascara. When I look more closely I see that only some of the arms have these eyes — others have lights. The arms that carry the eyes and the arms that carry the lights are all extraordinarily flexible and very beautiful. But the grey sky, which is the background, terrifies me. . . . And the arms wave to an accompaniment of music and of song. Like this: 'Hotcha — hotcha — hotcha. . . .' And I know the music; I can sing the song. . . .

I have another drink. Damned voice in my head, I'll stop you talking. . . .

I am walking up and down the room. She has gone. I am alone.

It isn't such a long time since he left.

Put your coat on and go after him. It isn't too late, it isn't too late. For the last time, for the last time. . . .

Well, I can't, my dear. Not because I'm too proud or anything like that, but because my legs feel funny.

'Come back, come back,' I say. Like that. Over and over again. 'You must come back, you shall come back. I'll force you to come back. No, that's wrong. . . . I mean, please come back, I beg you to come back.'

I press my hands over my eyes and I see him. He is walking along the Boulevard St Michel towards Montparnasse, thinking: 'Sale femme. Ridiculous woman.'

'Come back, come back, come back,' I say.

He doesn't hear.

He is walking along as quickly as he can. He is cold and vexed.

'You don't like men, and you don't like women either. You like nothing, nobody. Sauf ton sale cerveau. Alors, je te laisse avec ton sale cerveau. . . .'

(A monster. . . . The monster that can only crawl, or fly. . . . Ah! but fly. . . .)

'But why the gesture of not taking the money?' I argue. 'It was simply ridiculous. You know you're regretting it already. Go back and get it. You could walk in, you could say "I forgot something", take it and walk out again.'

Come back, come back, come back. . . .

This is the effort, the enormous effort, under which the human brain cracks. But not before the thing is done, not before the mountain moves.

He hesitates. He stops. I have him.

'Listen. You hear me now, don't you? It's quite early — not twelve yet. The door will still be open. All you've got to do is walk upstairs. If anybody speaks to you, say: "The woman in number forty-one, she expects me; she's waiting for me." Say that.'

I see him, very clearly, in my head. I daren't let him go for a moment.

Come back, come back, come back. . . .

He mustn't have to knock, I think. He must be able to walk straight in.

I get up and try to put the key on the outside of the door. I drop it. I leave the door a little open.

'I've got all my clothes on,' I think. 'How stupid!'

I undress very quickly. I am watching every step he takes.

Now he is turning into the end of the street. Very clear he is in my head. He is turning into the end of my street. I see the houses. . . .

I get into bed. I lie there trembling. I am very tired.

Not me, no. Don't worry, it's my sale cerveau that's so tired. Don't worry about that — no more sale cerveau.

I think: 'How awful I must look! I must put the light out.'

But it doesn't matter. Now I am simple and not afraid; now I am myself. He can look at me if he wants to. I'll only say: 'You see, I cried like that because you went away.'

(Or did I cry like that because I'll never sing again, because the light in my sale cerveau has gone out?)

He presses the button and the door opens.

He is coming up the stairs.

Now the door is moving, the door is opening wide. I put my arm over my eyes.

He comes in. He shuts the door after him.

I lie very still, with my arm over my eyes. As still as if I were dead. . . .

I don't need to look. I know.

I think: 'Is it the blue dressing-gown, or the white one? That's very important. I must find that out — it's very important.'

I take my arm away from my eyes. It is the white dressing-gown.

He stands there, looking down at me. Not sure of himself, his mean eyes flickering.

He doesn't say anything. Thank God, he doesn't say anything. I look straight into his eyes and despise another poor devil of a human being for the last time. For the last time. . . .

Then I put my arms round him and pull him down on to the bed, saying: 'Yes — yes — yes. . . .'

Wide
Sargasso Sea

PART ONE

THEY say when trouble comes close ranks, and so the white people did. But we were not in their ranks. The Jamaican ladies had never approved of my mother, 'because she pretty like pretty self' Christophine said.

She was my father's second wife, far too young for him they thought, and, worse still a Martinique girl. When I asked her why so few people came to see us, she told me that the road from Spanish Town to Coulibri Estate where we lived was very bad and that road repairing was now a thing of the past. (My father, visitors, horses, feeling safe in bed — all belonged to the past.)

Another day I heard her talking to Mr Luttrell, our neighbour and her only friend. 'Of course they have their own misfortunes. Still waiting for this compensation the English promised when the Emancipation Act was passed. Some will wait for a long time.'

How could she know that Mr Luttrell would be the first who grew tired of waiting? One calm evening he shot his dog, swam out to sea and was gone for always. No agent came from England to look after his property — Nelson's Rest it was called — and strangers from Spanish Town rode up to gossip and discuss the tragedy.

'Live at Nelson's Rest? Not for love or money. An unlucky place.'

Mr Luttrell's house was left empty, shutters banging in the wind. Soon the black people said it was haunted, they wouldn't go near it. And no one came near us.

I got used to a solitary life, but my mother still planned and hoped — perhaps she had to hope every time she passed a looking glass.

She still rode about every morning not caring that the black people stood about in groups to jeer at her, especially after her riding clothes grew shabby (they notice clothes, they know about money).

Then one day, very early, I saw her horse lying down under

the frangipani tree. I went up to him but he was not sick, he was dead and his eyes were black with flies. I ran away and did not speak of it for I thought if I told no one it might not be true. But later that day, Godfrey found him, he had been poisoned. 'Now we are marooned,' my mother said, 'now what will become of us?'

Godfrey said, 'I can't watch the horse night and day. I too old now. When the old time go, let it go. No use to grab at it. The Lord make no distinction between black and white, black and white the same for Him. Rest yourself in peace for the righteous are not forsaken.' But she couldn't. She was young. How could she not try for all the things that had gone so suddenly, so without warning. 'You're blind when you want to be blind,' she said ferociously, 'and you're deaf when you want to be deaf. The old hypocrite,' she kept saying. 'He knew what they were going to do.' 'The devil prince of this world,' Godfrey said, 'but this world don't last so long for mortal man.'

She persuaded a Spanish Town doctor to visit my younger brother Pierre who staggered when he walked and couldn't speak distinctly. I don't know what the doctor told her or what she said to him but he never came again and after that she changed. Suddenly, not gradually. She grew thin and silent, and at last she refused to leave the house at all.

Our garden was large and beautiful as that garden in the Bible — the tree of life grew there. But it had gone wild. The paths were overgrown and a smell of dead flowers mixed with the fresh living smell. Underneath the tree ferns, tall as forest tree ferns, the light was green. Orchids flourished out of reach or for some reason not to be touched. One was snaky looking, another like an octopus with long thin brown tentacles bare of leaves hanging from a twisted root. Twice a year the octopus orchid flowered — then not an inch of tentacle showed. It was a bell-shaped mass of white, mauve, deep purples, wonderful to see. The scent was very sweet and strong. I never went near it.

All Coulibri Estate had gone wild like the garden, gone to bush. No more slavery — why should *anybody* work? This never saddened me. I did not remember the place when it was prosperous.

My mother usually walked up and down the *glacis,* a paved roofed-in terrace which ran the length of the house and sloped upwards to a clump of bamboos. Standing by the bamboos she had a clear view of the sea, but anyone passing could stare at her. They stared, sometimes they laughed. Long after the sound was far away and faint she kept her eyes shut and her hands clenched. A frown came between her black eyebrows, deep — it might have been cut with a knife. I hated this frown and once I touched her forehead trying to smooth it. But she pushed me away, not roughly but calmly, coldly, without a word, as if she had decided once and for all that I was useless to her. She wanted to sit with Pierre or walk where she pleased without being pestered, she wanted peace and quiet. I was old enough to look after myself. 'Oh, let me alone,' she would say, 'let me alone,' and after I knew that she talked aloud to herself I was a little afraid of her.

So I spent most of my time in the kitchen which was in an outbuilding some way off. Christophine slept in the little room next to it.

When evening came she sang to me if she was in the mood. I couldn't always understand her patois songs — she also came from Martinique — but she taught me the one that meant 'The little one grows old, the children leave us, will they come back?' and the one about the cedar tree flowers which only last for a day.

The music was gay but the words were sad and her voice often quavered and broke on the high note. 'Adieu.' Not adieu as we said it, but à dieu, which made more sense after all. The loving man was lonely, the girl was deserted, the children never came back. Adieu.

Her songs were not like Jamaican songs, and she was not like the other women.

She was much blacker — blue-black with a thin face and straight features. She wore a black dress, heavy gold earrings and a yellow handkerchief — carefully tied with the two high points in front. No other negro woman wore black, or tied her handkerchief Martinique fashion. She had a quiet voice and a quiet laugh (when she did laugh), and though she could speak good English if she wanted to, and French as well as patois, she took care to talk as they talked. But they would have nothing to do with her and she never saw her son who worked in Spanish Town. She had only one friend — a woman called Maillotte. and Maillotte was not a Jamaican.

The girls from the bayside who sometimes helped with the washing and cleaning were terrified of her. That, I soon discovered, was why they came at all — for she never paid them. Yet they brought presents of fruit and vegetables and after dark I often heard low voices from the kitchen.

So I asked about Christophine. Was she very old? Had she always been with us?

'She was your father's wedding present to me — one of his presents. He thought I would be pleased with a Martinique girl. I don't know how old she was when they brought her to Jamaica, quite young. I don't know how old she is now. Does it matter? Why do you pester and bother me about all these things that happened long ago? Christophine stayed with me because she wanted to stay. She had her own very good reasons you may be sure. I dare say we would have died if she'd turned against us and that would have been a better fate. To die and be forgotten and at peace. Not to know that one is abandoned, lied about, helpless. All the ones who died — who says a good word for them now?'

'Godfrey stayed too,' I said. 'And Sass.'

'They stayed,' she said angrily, 'because they wanted somewhere to sleep and something to eat. That boy Sass! When his mother pranced off and left him here — a great deal *she* cared — why he was a little skeleton. Now he's growing into a big strong boy and away he goes. We shan't see him again. Godfrey is a rascal. These new ones aren't too kind to old people and he knows it. That's why he stays. Doesn't do a thing, but eat enough for a couple of horses. Pretends he's deaf. He isn't deaf — he doesn't want to hear. What a devil he is!'

'Why don't you tell him to find somewhere else to live?' I said and she laughed.

'He wouldn't go. He'd probably try to force us out. I've learned to let sleeping curs lie,' she said.

'Would Christophine go if you told her to?' I thought. But I didn't say it. I was afraid to say it.

It was too hot that afternoon. I could see the beads of perspiration on her upper lip and the dark circles under her eyes. I started to fan her, but she turned her head away. She might rest if I left her alone, she said.

Once I would have gone back quietly to watch her asleep on the blue sofa — once I made excuses to be near her when she brushed her hair, a soft black cloak to cover me, hide me, keep me safe.

But not any longer. Not any more.

•

These were all the people in my life — my mother and Pierre, Christophine, Godfrey, and Sass who had left us.

I never looked at any strange negro. They hated us. They called us white cockroaches. Let sleeping dogs lie. One day a little girl followed me singing, 'Go away white cockroach, go away, go away.' I walked fast, but she walked faster. 'White cockroach, go away, go away. Nobody want you. Go away.'

When I was safely home I sat close to the old wall at the end of the garden. It was covered with green moss soft as velvet and I never wanted to move again. Everything would be worse if I moved. Christophine found me there when it was nearly dark, and I was so stiff she had to help me to get up. She said nothing, but next morning Tia was in the kitchen with her mother Maillotte, Christophine's friend. Soon Tia was my friend and I met her nearly every morning at the turn of the road to the river.

Sometimes we left the bathing pool at midday, sometimes we stayed till late afternoon. Then Tia would light a fire (fires always lit for her, sharp stones did not hurt her bare feet, I never saw her cry). We boiled green bananas in an old iron pot and ate them with our fingers out of a calabash and after we had eaten she slept at once. I could not sleep, but I wasn't quite awake as I lay in the shade looking at the pool — deep and dark green under the trees, brown-green if it had rained, but a bright sparkling green in the sun. The water was so clear that you could see the pebbles at the bottom of the shallow part. Blue and white and striped red. Very pretty. Late or early we parted at the turn of the road. My mother never asked me where I had been or what I had done.

Christophine had given me some new pennies which I kept in the pocket of my dress. They dropped out one morning so I put them on a stone. They shone like gold in the sun and Tia stared. She had small eyes, very black, set deep in her head.

Then she bet me three of the pennies that I couldn't turn a somersault under water 'like you say you can'.

'Of course I can.'

'I never see you do it,' she said. 'Only talk.'

'Bet you all the money I can,' I said.

But after one somersault I still turned and came up choking. Tia laughed and told me that it certainly look like I drown dead that time. Then she picked up the money.

'I did do it,' I said when I could speak, but she shook her head. I hadn't done it good and besides pennies didn't buy much. Why did I look at her like that?

'Keep them then, you cheating nigger,' I said, for I was tired, and the water I had swallowed made me feel sick. 'I can get more if I want to.'

That's not what she hear, she said. She hear all we poor like beggar. We ate salt fish — no money for fresh fish. That old house so leaky, you run with calabash to catch water when it rain. Plenty white people in Jamaica. Real white people, they got gold money. They didn't look at us, nobody see them come near us. Old time white people nothing but white nigger now, and black nigger better than white nigger.

I wrapped myself in my torn towel and sat on a stone with my back to her, shivering cold. But the sun couldn't warm me. I wanted to go home. I looked round and Tia had gone. I searched for a long time before I could believe that she had taken my dress — not my underclothes, she never wore any — but my dress, starched, ironed, clean that morning. She had left me hers and I put it on at last and walked home in the blazing sun feeling sick, hating her. I planned to get round the back of the house to the kitchen, but passing the stables I stopped to stare at three strange horses and my mother saw me and called. She was on the *glacis* with two young ladies and a gentleman. Visitors! I dragged up the steps unwillingly — I had longed for visitors once, but that was years ago.

They were very beautiful I thought and they wore such beautiful clothes that I looked away down at the flagstones and when they laughed — the gentleman laughed the loudest — I ran into the house, into my bedroom. There I stood with my back against the door and I could feel my heart all through me. I heard them talking and I heard them leave. I came out of my room and my mother was sitting on the blue sofa. She looked at me for some time before she said that I had behaved very oddly. My dress was even dirtier than usual.

'It's Tia's dress.'

'But why are you wearing Tia's dress? Tia? Which one of them is Tia?'

Christophine, who had been in the pantry listening, came at once and was told to find a clean dress for me. 'Throw away that thing. Burn it.'

Then they quarrelled.

Christophine said I had no clean dress. 'She got two dresses, wash and wear. You want clean dress to drop from heaven? Some people crazy in truth.'

'She must have another dress,' said my mother. 'Somewhere.' But Christophine told her loudly that it shameful. She run wild, she grow up worthless. And nobody care.

My mother walked over to the window. ('Marooned,' said her straight narrow back, her carefully coiled hair. 'Marooned.')

'She has an old muslin dress. Find that.'

While Christophine scrubbed my face and tied my plaits with a fresh piece of string, she told me that those were the new people at Nelson's Rest. They called themselves Luttrell, but English or not English they were not like old Mr Luttrell. "Old Mr Luttrell spit in their face if he see how they look at you. Trouble walk into the house this day. Trouble walk in.'

The old muslin dress was found and it tore as I forced it on. She didn't notice.

No more slavery! She had to laugh! 'These new ones have Letter of the Law. Same thing. They got magistrate. They got fine. They got jail house and chain gang. They got tread machine to mash up people's feet. New ones worse than old ones — more cunning, that's all.'

All that evening my mother didn't speak to me or look at me and I thought, 'She is ashamed of me, what Tia said is true.'

I went to bed early and slept at once. I dreamed that I was walking in the forest. Not alone. Someone who hated me was with me, out of sight. I could hear heavy footsteps coming closer and though I struggled and screamed I could not move. I woke crying. The covering sheet was on the floor and my mother was looking down at me.

'Did you have a nightmare?'

'Yes, a bad dream.'

She sighed and covered me up. 'You were making such a noise. I must go to Pierre, you've frightened him.'

I lay thinking, 'I am safe. There is the corner of the bedroom door and the friendly furniture. There is the tree of life in the garden and the wall green with moss. The barrier of the cliffs and the high mountains. And the barrier of the sea. I am safe. I am safe from strangers.'

The light of the candle in Pierre's room was still there when I slept again. I woke next morning knowing that nothing would be the same. It would change and go on changing.

I don't know how she got money to buy the white muslin and the pink. Yards of muslin. She may have sold her last ring, for there was one left. I saw it in her jewel box — that, and a locket with a shamrock inside. They were mending and sewing first thing in the morning and still sewing when I went to bed. In a week she had a new dress and so had I.

The Luttrells lent her a horse, and she would ride off very early and not come back till late next day — tired out because she had been to a dance or a moonlight picnic. She was gay and laughing — younger than I had ever seen her and the house was sad when she had gone.

So I too left it and stayed away till dark. I was never long at the bathing pool, I never met Tia.

I took another road, past the old sugar works and the water wheel that had not turned for years. I went to parts of Coulibri that I had not seen, where there was no road, no path, no track. And if the razor grass cut my legs and arms I would think 'It's better than people.' Black ants or red ones, tall nests swarming with white ants, rain that soaked me to the skin — once I saw a snake. All better than people.

Better. Better, better than people.

Watching the red and yellow flowers in the sun thinking of nothing, it was as if a door opened and I was somewhere else, something else. Not myself any longer.

I knew the time of day when though it is hot and blue and there are no clouds, the sky can have a very black look.

I was bridesmaid when my mother married Mr Mason in Spanish Town. Christophine curled my hair. I carried a bouquet and everything I wore was new — even my beautiful slippers. But their eyes slid away from my hating face. I had heard what all these smooth smiling people said about her when she was not listening and they did not guess I was. Hiding from them in the garden when they visited Coulibri, I listened.

'A fantastic marriage and he will regret it. Why should a very wealthy man who could take his pick of all the girls in the West Indies, and many in England too probably?' 'Why *probably?*' the other voice said. '*Certainly.*' 'Then why should he marry a widow without a penny to her name and Coulibri a wreck of a place? Emancipation troubles killed old Cosway? Nonsense —

the estate was going downhill for years before that. He drank himself to death. Many's the time when — well! And all those women! She never did anything to stop him — she encouraged him. Presents and smiles for the bastards every Christmas. Old customs? Some old customs are better dead and buried. Her new husband will have to spend a pretty penny before the house is fit to live in — leaks like a sieve. And what about the stables and the coach house dark as pitch, and the servants' quarters and the six-foot snake I saw with my own eyes curled up on the privy seat last time I was here. Alarmed? I screamed. Then that horrible old man she harbours came along, doubled up with laughter. As for those two children — the boy an idiot kept out of sight and mind and the girl going the same way in my opinion — a *lowering* expression.'

'Oh I agree,' the other one said. 'but Annette is such a pretty woman. And what a dancer. Reminds me of that song "light as cotton blossom on the something breeze", or is it air? I forget.'

Yes, what a dancer — that night when they came home from their honeymoon in Trinidad and they danced on the *glacis* to no music. There was no need for music when she danced. They stopped and she leaned backwards over his arm, down till her black hair touched the flagstones — still down, down. Then up again in a flash, laughing. She made it look so easy — as if anyone could do it, and he kissed her — a long kiss. I was there that time too but they had forgotten me and soon I wasn't thinking of them. I was remembering that woman saying 'Dance! He didn't come to the West Indies to dance — he came to make money as they all do. Some of the big estates are going cheap, and one unfortunate's loss is always a clever man's gain. No, the whole thing is a mystery. It's evidently useful to keep a Martinique obeah woman on the premises.' She meant Christophine. She said it mockingly, not meaning it, but soon other people were saying it — and meaning it.

While the repairs were being done and they were in Trinidad, Pierre and I stayed with Aunt Cora in Spanish Town.

Mr Mason did not approve of Aunt Cora, an ex-slave-owner who had escaped misery, a flier in the face of Providence.

'Why did she do nothing to help you?'

I told him that her husband was English and didn't like us and he said, 'Nonsense.'

'It isn't nonsense, they lived in England and he was angry if she wrote to us. He hated the West Indies. When he died not long ago she came home, before that what could she do? *She* wasn't rich.'

'That's her story. I don't believe it. A frivolous woman. In your mother's place I'd resent her behaviour.'

'None of you understand about us,' I thought.

Coulibri looked the same when I saw it again, although it was clean and tidy, no grass between the flagstones, no leaks. But it didn't feel the same. Sass had come back and I was glad. They can *smell* money, somebody said. Mr Mason engaged new servants — I didn't like any of them excepting Mannie the groom. It was their talk about Christophine that changed Coulibri, not the repairs or the new furniture or the strange faces. Their talk about Christophine and obeah changed it.

I knew her room so well — the pictures of the Holy Family and the prayer for a happy death. She had a bright patchwork counterpane, a broken-down press for her clothes, and my mother had given her an old rocking-chair.

Yet one day when I was waiting there I was suddenly very much afraid. The door was open to the sunlight, someone was whistling near the stables, but I was afraid. I was certain that hidden in the room (behind the old black press?) there was a dead man's dried hand, white chicken feathers, a cock with its throat cut, dying slowly, slowly. Drop by drop the blood was falling into a red basin and I imagined I could hear it. No one had ever spoken to me about obeah — but I knew what I would find if I dared to look. Then Christophine came in smiling and pleased to see me. Nothing alarming ever happened and I forgot, or told myself I had forgotten.

Mr Mason would laugh if he knew how frightened I had been. He would laugh even louder than he did when my mother told him that she wished to leave Coulibri.

This began when they had been married for over a year. They always said the same things and I seldom listened to the argument now. I knew that we were hated — but to go away . . . for one I agreed with my stepfather. That was not possible.

'You must have some reason,' he would say, and she would answer 'I need a change' or 'We could visit Richard'. (Richard, Mr Mason's son by his first marriage, was at school in Barbados. He was going to England soon and we had seen very little of him.)

'An agent could look after this place. For the time being. The people here hate us. They certainly hate me.' Straight out she said that one day and it was then he laughed so heartily.

'Annette, be reasonable. You were the widow of a slave-owner, the daughter of a slave-owner, and you had been living here alone, with two children, for nearly five years when we met. Things were at their worst then. But you were never molested, never harmed.'

'How do you know that I was not harmed?' she said. 'We were so poor then,' she told him, 'we were something to laugh at. But we are not poor now,' she said. 'You are not a poor man. Do you suppose that they don't know all about your estate in Trinidad? And the Antigua property? They talk about us without stopping. They invent stories about you, and lies about me. They try to find out what we eat every day.'

'They are curious. It's natural enough. You have lived alone far too long, Annette. You imagine enmity which doesn't exist. Always one extreme or the other. Didn't you fly at me like a little wild cat when I said nigger. Not nigger, nor even negro. Black people I must say.'

'You don't like, or even recognize, the good in them,' she said, 'and you won't believe in the other side.'

'They're too damn lazy to be dangerous,' said Mr Mason. 'I know that.'

'They are more alive than you are, lazy or not, and they can be dangerous and cruel for reasons you wouldn't understand.'

'No, I don't understand,' Mr Mason always said, 'I don't understand at all.'

But she'd speak about going away again. Persistently. Angrily.

Mr Mason pulled up near the empty huts on our way home that evening. 'All gone to one of those dances,' he said. 'Young and old. How deserted the place looks.'

'We'll hear the drums if there is a dance.' I hoped he'd ride on quickly but he stayed by the huts to watch the sun go down, the sky and the sea were on fire when we left Bertrand Bay at last. From a long way off I saw the shadow of our house high up on its stone foundations. There was a smell of ferns and river water and I felt safe again, as if I was one of the righteous. (Godfrey said that we were not righteous. One day when he was drunk he told me that we were all damned and no use praying.)

'They've chosen a very hot night for their dance,' Mr Mason said, and Aunt Cora came on to the *glacis*. 'What dance? Where?'

'There is some festivity in the neighbourhood. The huts were abandoned. A wedding perhaps?'

'Not a wedding,' I said. 'There is never a wedding.' He frowned at me but Aunt Cora smiled.

When they had gone indoors I leaned my arms on the cool *glacis* railings and thought that I would never like him very much. I still called him 'Mr Mason' in my head. 'Goodnight white pappy,' I said one evening and he was not vexed, he laughed. In some ways it was better before he came though he'd rescued us from poverty and misery. 'Only just in time too.' The black people did not hate us quite so much when we were poor. We were white but we had not escaped and soon we would be dead for we had no money left. What was there to hate?

Now it had started up again and worse than before, my mother knows but she can't make him believe it. I wish I could tell him that out here is not at all like English people think it is. I wish . . .

I could hear them talking and Aunt Cora's laugh. I was glad she was staying with us. And I could hear the bamboos shiver and creak though there was no wind. It had been hot and still and dry for days. The colours had gone from the sky, the light was blue and could not last long. The *glacis* was not a good place when night was coming, Christophine said. As I went indoors my mother was talking in an excited voice.

'Very well. As you refuse to consider it, *I* will go and take Pierre with me. You won't object to that, I hope?'

'You are perfectly right, Annette,' said Aunt Cora and that did surprise me. She seldom spoke when they argued.

Mr Mason also seemed surprised and not at all pleased.

'You talk so wildly,' he said. 'And you are so mistaken. Of course you can get away for a change if you wish it. I promise you.'

'You have promised that before,' she said. 'You don't keep your promises.'

He sighed. 'I feel very well here. However, we'll arrange something. Quite soon.'

'I will not stay at Coulibri any longer,' my mother said. 'It is not safe. It is not safe for Pierre.'

Aunt Cora nodded.

As it was late I ate with them instead of by myself as usual. Myra, one of the new servants, was standing by the sideboard, waiting to change the plates. We ate English food now, beef and mutton, pies and puddings.

I was glad to be like an English girl but I missed the taste of Christophine's cooking.

My stepfather talked about a plan to import labourers — coolies he called them — from the East Indies. When Myra had gone out Aunt Cora said, 'I shouldn't discuss that if I were you. Myra is listening.'

'But the people here won't work. They don't want to work. Look at this place — it's enough to break your heart.'

'Hearts have been broken,' she said. 'Be sure of that. I suppose you all know what you are doing.'

'Do you mean to say —'

'I said nothing, except that it would be wiser not to tell that woman your plans — necessary and merciful no doubt. I don't trust her.'

'Live here most of your life and know nothing about the people. It's astonishing. They are children — they wouldn't hurt a fly.'

'Unhappily children do hurt flies,' said Aunt Cora.

Myra came in again looking mournful as she always did though she smiled when she talked about hell. Everyone went to hell, she told me, you had to belong to her sect to be saved and even then — just as well not to be too sure. She had thin arms and big hands and feet and the handkerchief she wore round her head was always white. Never striped or a gay colour.

So I looked away from her at my favourite picture, 'The Miller's Daughter,' a lovely English girl with brown curls and blue eyes and a dress slipping off her shoulders. Then I looked across the white tablecloth and the vase of yellow roses at Mr Mason, so sure of himself, so without a doubt English. And at my mother, so without a doubt not English, but no white nigger either. Not my mother. Never had been. Never could be. Yes, she would have died, I thought, if she had not met him. And for the first time I was grateful and liked him. There are more ways than one of being happy, better perhaps to be peaceful and contented and protected, as I feel now, peaceful for years and long years, and afterwards I may be saved whatever Myra says. (When I asked Christophine what happened when you died, she said, 'You want to know too much.') I remembered to kiss my stepfather goodnight. Once Aunt Cora had told me, 'He's very hurt because you never kiss him.'

'He does not look hurt,' I argued. 'Great mistake to go by looks,' she said, 'one way or the other.'

I went into Pierre's room which was next to mine, the last one in the house. The bamboos were outside his window. You could almost touch them. He still had a crib and he slept more and more, nearly all the time. He was so thin that I could lift him easily. Mr Mason had promised to take him to England later on, there he would be cured, made like other people. 'And how will you like that' I thought, as I kissed him. 'How will you like being made exactly like other people?' He looked happy asleep. But that will be later on. Later on. Sleep now. It was then I heard the bamboos creak again and a sound like whispering. I forced myself to look out of the window. There was a full moon but I saw nobody, nothing but shadows.

I left a light on the chair by my bed and waited for Christophine, for I liked to see her last thing. But she did not come, and as the candle burned down, the safe peaceful feeling left me. I wished I had a big Cuban dog to lie by my bed and protect me, I wished I had not heard a noise by the bamboo clump, or that I were very young again, for then I believed in my stick. It was not a stick, but a long narrow piece of wood, with two nails sticking out at the end, a shingle, perhaps. I picked it up soon after they killed our horse and I thought I can fight with this, if the worst comes to the worst I can fight to the end though the best ones fall and that is another song. Christophine knocked the nails out, but she let me keep the shingle and I grew very fond of it, I believed that no one could harm me when it was near me, to lose it would be a great misfortune. All this was long ago, when I was still babyish and sure that everything was alive, not only the river or the rain, but chairs, looking-glasses, cups, saucers, everything.

I woke up and it was still night and my mother was there. She said, 'Get up and dress yourself, and come downstairs quickly.' She was dressed, but she had not put up her hair and one of her plaits was loose. 'Quickly,' she said again, then she went into Pierre's room, next door. I heard her speak to Myra and I heard Myra answer her. I lay there, half asleep, looking at the lighted candle on the chest of drawers, till I heard a noise as though a chair had fallen over in the little room, then I got up and dressed.

The house was on different levels. There were three steps down from my bedroom and Pierre's to the dining-room and then three steps from the dining-room to the rest of the house, which we called 'downstairs'. The folding doors of the dining-room were not shut and I could see that the big drawing-room was full of people. Mr Mason, my mother, Christophine and Mannie and Sass. Aunt Cora was sitting on the blue sofa in the corner now, wearing a black silk dress, her ringlets were carefully arranged. She looked very haughty, I thought. But Godfrey was not there, or Myra, or the cook, or any of the others.

'There is no reason to be alarmed,' my stepfather was saying as I came in. 'A handful of drunken negroes.' He opened the door leading to the *glacis* and walked out. 'What is all this,' he shouted. 'What do you want?' A horrible noise swelled up, like animals howling, but worse. We heard stones falling on to the *glacis*. He was pale when he came in again, but he tried to smile as he shut and bolted the door. 'More of them than I thought, and in a nasty mood too. They will repent in the morning. I foresee gifts of tamarinds in syrup and ginger sweets tomorrow.'

'Tomorrow will be too late,' said Aunt Cora, 'too late for ginger sweets or anything else.' My mother was not listening to either of them. She said, 'Pierre is asleep and Myra is with him, I thought it better to leave him in his own room, away from this horrible noise. I don't know. Perhaps.' She was twisting her hands together, her wedding ring fell off and rolled into a corner near the steps. My stepfather and Mannie both stooped for it, then Mannie straightened up and said, 'Oh, my God, they get at the back, they set fire to the back of the house.' He pointed to my bedroom door which I had shut after me, and smoke was rolling out from underneath.

I did not see my mother move she was so quick. She opened the door of my room and then again I did not see her, nothing but smoke. Mannie ran after her, so did Mr Mason but more slowly. Aunt Cora put her arms round me. She said, 'Don't be afraid, you are quite safe. We are all quite safe.' Just for a moment I shut my eyes and rested my head against her shoulder. She smelled of vanilla, I remember. Then there was another smell, of burned hair, and I looked and my mother was in the room carrying Pierre. It was her loose hair that had burned and was smelling like that.

I thought, Pierre is dead. He looked dead. He was white and he did not make a sound, but his head hung back over her arm as if he had no life at all and his eyes were rolled up so that you only saw the whites. My stepfather said, 'Annette, you are hurt — your hands . . .' But she did not even look at him. 'His crib was on fire,' she said to Aunt Cora. 'The little room is on fire and Myra was not there. She has gone. She was not there.'

'That does not surprise me at all,' said Aunt Cora. She laid Pierre on the sofa, bent over him, then lifted up her skirt, stepped out of her white petticoat and began to tear it into strips.

'She left him, she ran away and left him alone to die,' said my mother, still whispering. So it was all the more dreadful when she began to scream abuse at Mr Mason, calling him a fool, a cruel stupid fool. 'I told you,' she said, 'I told you what would happen again and again.' Her voice broke, but still she screamed, 'You would not listen, you sneered at me, you grinning hypocrite, you ought not to live either, you know so much, don't you? Why don't you go out and ask them to let you go? Say how innocent you are. Say you have always trusted them.'

I was so shocked that everything was confused. And it happened quickly. I saw Mannie and Sass staggering along with two large earthenware jars of water which were kept in the pantry. They threw the water into the bedroom and it made a black pool on the floor, but the smoke rolled over the pool. Then Christophine, who had run into my mother's bedroom for the pitcher there, came back and spoke to my aunt. 'It seems they have fired the other side of the house,' said Aunt Cora. 'They must have climbed that tree outside. This place is going to burn like tinder and there is nothing we can do to stop it. The sooner we get out the better.'

Mannie said to the boy, 'You frightened?' Sass shook his head. 'Then come on,' said Mannie. 'Out of my way,' he said and pushed Mr Mason aside. Narrow wooden stairs led down from the pantry to the outbuildings, the kitchen, the servants' rooms, the stables. That was where they were going. 'Take the child,' Aunt Cora told Christophine, 'and come.'

It was very hot on the *glacis* too, they roared as we came out, then there was another roar behind us. I had not seen any flames, only smoke and sparks, but now I saw tall flames shooting up to the sky, for the bamboos had caught. There were some tree ferns near, green and damp, one of those was smouldering too.

'Come quickly,' said Aunt Cora, and she went first, holding my hand. Christophine followed, carrying Pierre, and they were quite silent as we went down the *glacis* steps. But when I looked round for my mother I saw that Mr Mason, his face crimson with heat, seemed to be dragging her along and she was holding back, struggling. I heard him say, 'It's impossible, too late now.'

'Wants her jewel case?' Aunt Cora said.

'Jewel case? Nothing so sensible,' bawled Mr Mason. 'She wanted to go back for her damned parrot. I won't allow it.' She did not answer, only fought him silently, twisting like a cat and showing her teeth.

Our parrot was called Coco, a green parrot. He didn't talk very well, he could say *Qui est là? Qui est là?* and answered himself *Ché Coco, Ché Coco.* After Mr Mason clipped his wings he grew very bad tempered, and though he would sit quietly on my mother's shoulder, he darted at everyone who came near her and pecked their feet.

'Annette,' said Aunt Cora. 'They are laughing at you, do not allow them to laugh at you.' She stopped fighting then and he half supported, half pulled her after us, cursing loudly.

Still they were quiet and there were so many of them I could hardly see any grass or trees. There must have been many of the bay people but I recognized no one. They all looked the same, it was the same face repeated over and over, eyes gleaming, mouth half open to shout. We were past the mounting stone when they saw Mannie driving the carriage round the corner. Sass followed, riding one horse and leading another. There was a ladies' saddle on the one he was leading.

Somebody yelled, 'But look the black Englishman! Look the white niggers!', and then they were all yelling. 'Look the white niggers! Look the damn white niggers!' A stone just missed Mannie's head, he cursed back at them and they cleared away from the rearing, frightened horses. 'Come on, for God's sake,' said Mr Mason. 'Get to the carriage, get to the horses.' But we could not move for they pressed too close round us. Some of them were laughing and waving sticks, some of the ones at the back were carrying flambeaux and it was light as day. Aunt

Cora held my hand very tightly and her lips moved but I could not hear because of the noise. And I was afraid, because I knew that the ones who laughed would be the worst. I shut my eyes and waited. Mr Mason stopped swearing and began to pray in a loud pious voice. The prayer ended, 'May Almighty God defend us.' And God who is indeed mysterious, who had made no sign when they burned Pierre as he slept — not a clap of thunder, not a flash of lightning — mysterious God heard Mr Mason at once and answered him. The yells stopped.

I opened my eyes, everybody was looking up and pointing at Coco on the *glacis* railings with his feathers alight. He made an effort to fly down but his clipped wings failed him and he fell screeching. He was all on fire.

I began to cry. 'Don't look,' said Aunt Cora. 'Don't look.' She stooped and put her arms round me and I hid my face, but I could feel that they were not so near. I heard someone say something about bad luck and remembered that it was very unlucky to kill a parrot, or even to see a parrot die. They began to go then, quickly, silently, and those that were left drew aside and watched us as we trailed across the grass. They were not laughing any more.

'Get to the carriage, get to the carriage,' said Mr Mason. 'Hurry!' He went first, holding my mother's arm, then Christophine carrying Pierre, and Aunt Cora was last, still with my hand in hers. None of us looked back.

Mannie had stopped the horses at the bend of the cobblestone road and as we got closer we heard him shout, 'What all you are, eh? Brute beasts?' He was speaking to a group of men and a few women who were standing round the carriage. A coloured man with a machete in his hand was holding the bridle. I did not see Sass or the other two horses. 'Get in,' said Mr Mason. 'Take no notice of him, get in.' The man with the machete said no. We would go to police and tell a lot of damn lies. A woman said to let us go. All this an accident and they had plenty witness. 'Myra she witness for us.'

'Shut your mouth,' the man said. 'You mash centipede, mash it, leave one little piece and it grow again . . . What you think police believe, eh? You, or the white nigger?'

Mr Mason stared at him. He seemed not frightened, but too astounded to speak. Mannie took up the carriage whip but one of the blacker men wrenched it out of his hand, snapped it over his knee and threw it away. 'Run away, black Englishman, like the boy run. Hide in the bushes. It's better for you.' It was Aunt Cora who stepped forward and said, 'The little boy is very badly hurt. He will die if we cannot get help for him.'

The man said, 'So black and white, they burn the same, eh?' 'They do,' she said. 'Here and hereafter, as you will find out. Very shortly.'

He let the bridle go and thrust his face close to hers. He'd throw her on the fire, he said, if she put bad luck on him. Old white jumby, he called her. But she did not move an inch, she looked straight into his eyes and threatened him with eternal fire in a calm voice. 'And never a drop of sangoree to cool your burning tongue,' she said. He cursed her again but he backed away. 'Now get in,' said Mr Mason. 'You, Christophine, get in with the child.' Christophine got in. 'Now you,' he said to my mother. But she had turned and was looking back at the house and when he put his hand on her arm, she screamed.

One woman said she only come to see what happen. Another woman began to cry. The man with the cutlass said, 'You cry for her — when she ever cry for you? Tell me that.'

But now I turned too. The house was burning, the yellow-red sky was like sunset and I knew that I would never see Coulibri again. Nothing would be left, the golden ferns and the silver ferns, the orchids, the ginger lilies and the roses, the rocking-chairs and the blue sofa, the jasmine and the honeysuckle, and the picture of the Miller's Daughter. When they had finished, there would be nothing left but blackened walls and the mounting stone. That was always left. That could not be stolen or burned.

Then, not so far off, I saw Tia and her mother and I ran to her, for she was all that was left of my life as it had been. We had eaten the same food, slept side by side, bathed in the same river. As I ran, I thought, I will live with Tia and I will be like her. Not to leave Coulibri. Not to go. Not. When I was close I saw the jagged stone in her hand but I did not see her throw it. I did not feel it either, only something wet, running down my face. I looked at her and I saw her face crumple up as she began to cry. We stared at each other, blood on my face, tears on hers. It was as if I saw myself. Like in a looking-glass.

•   •   •

'I saw my plait, tied with red ribbon, when I got up,' I said. 'In the chest of drawers. I thought it was a snake.'

'Your hair had to be cut. You've been very ill, my darling,' said Aunt Cora. 'But you are safe with me now. We are all safe as I told you we would be. You must stay in bed though. Why are you wandering about the room? Your hair will grow again,' she said. 'Longer and thicker.'

'But darker,' I said.

'Why not darker?'

She picked me up and I was glad to feel the soft mattress and glad to be covered with a cool sheet.

'It's time for your arrowroot,' she said and went out. When that was finished she took the cup away and stood looking down at me.

'I got up because I wanted to know where I was.'

'And you do know, don't you?' she said in an anxious voice.

'Of course. But how did I get to your house?'

'The Luttrells were very good. As soon as Mannie got to Nelson's Rest they sent a hammock and four men. You were shaken about a good deal though. But they did their best. Young Mr Luttrell rode alongside you all the way. Wasn't that kind?'

'Yes,' I said. She looked thin and old and her hair wasn't arranged prettily so I shut my eyes, not wanting to see her.

'Pierre is dead, isn't he?'

'He died on the way down, the poor little boy,' she said.

'He died before that,' I thought but was too tired to speak.

'Your mother is in the country. Resting. Getting well again. You will see her quite soon.'

'I didn't know,' I said. 'Why did she go away?'

'You've been very ill for nearly six weeks. You didn't know anything.'

What was the use of telling her that I'd been awake before and heard my mother screaming '*Qui est là? Qui est là?*', then 'Don't touch me. I'll kill you if you touch me. Coward. Hypocrite. I'll kill you.' I'd put my hands over my ears, her screams were so loud and terrible. I slept and when I woke up everything was quiet.

Still Aunt Cora stayed by my bed looking at me.

'My head is bandaged up. It's so hot,' I said. 'Will I have a mark on my forehead?'

'No, no.' She smiled for the first time. 'That is healing very nicely. It won't spoil you on your wedding day,' she said.

She bent down and kissed me. 'Is there anything you want? A cool drink to sip?'

'No, not a drink. Sing to me. I like that.'

She began in a shaky voice.

> *'Every night at half past eight*
> *Comes tap tap tapping —'*

'Not that one. I don't like that one. Sing *Before I was set free.*'

She sat near me and sang very softly, 'Before I was set free.' I heard as far as 'The sorrow that my heart feels for —' I didn't hear the end but I heard that before I slept, 'The sorrow that my heart feels for.'

I was going to see my mother. I had insisted that Christophine must be with me, no one else, and as I was not yet quite well they had given way. I remember the dull feeling as we drove along for I did not expect to see her. She was part of Coulibri, that had gone, so she had gone, I was certain of it. But when we reached the tidy pretty little house where she lived now (they said) I jumped out of the carriage and ran as fast as I could across the lawn. One door was open on to the veranda. I went in without knocking and stared at the people in the room. A coloured man, a coloured woman, and a white woman sitting with her head bent so low that I couldn't see her face. But I recognized her hair, one plait much shorter than the other. And her dress. I put my arms round her and kissed her. She held me so tightly that I couldn't breathe and I thought, 'It's not her.' Then, 'It must be her.' She looked at the door, then at me, then at the door again. I could not say, 'He is dead,' so I shook my head. 'But I am here, I am here,' I said, and she said, 'No,' quietly. Then 'No no no' very loudly and flung me from her. I fell against the partition and hurt myself. The man and the woman were holding her arms and Christophine was there. The woman said, 'Why you bring the child to make trouble, trouble, trouble? Trouble enough without that.'

All the way back to Aunt Cora's house we didn't speak.

The first day I had to go to the convent, I clung to Aunt Cora as you would cling to life if you loved it. At last she got impatient, so I forced myself away from her and through the passage, down the steps into the street and, as I knew they would be, they were waiting for me under the sandbox tree. There were two of them, a boy and a girl. The boy was about fourteen and tall and big for his age, he had a white skin, a dull ugly white covered with freckles, his mouth was a negro's mouth and he had small eyes, like bits of green glass. He had the eyes of a dead fish. Worst, most horrible of all, his hair was crinkled, a negro's hair, but bright red, and his eyebrows and eyelashes were red. The girl was very black and wore no head hand-kerchief. Her hair had been plaited and I could smell the sick-ening oil she had daubed on it, from where I stood on the steps of Aunt Cora's dark, clean, friendly house, staring at them. They looked so harmless and quiet, no one would have noticed the glint in the boy's eyes.

Then the girl grinned and began to crack the knuckles of her fingers. At each crack I jumped and my hands began to sweat. I was holding some school books in my right hand and I shifted them to under my arm, but it was too late, there was a mark on the palm of my hand and a stain on the cover of the book. The girl began to laugh, very quietly, and it was then that hate came to me and courage with the hate so that I was able to walk past without looking at them.

I knew they were following, I knew too that as long as I was in sight of Aunt Cora's house they would do nothing but stroll along some distance after me. But I knew when they would draw close. It would be when I was going up the hill. There were walls and gardens on each side of the hill and no one would be there at this hour of the morning.

Half-way up they closed in on me and started talking. The girl said, 'Look the crazy girl, you crazy like your mother. Your aunt frightened to have you in the house. She send you for the nuns to lock up. Your mother walk about with no shoes and stockings on her feet, she *sans culottes*. She try to kill her hus-band and she try to kill you too that day you go to see her. She have eyes like zombie and you have eyes like zombie too. Why you won't look at me.' The boy only said, 'One day I catch you alone, you wait, one day I catch you alone.' When I got to the top of the hill they were jostling me, I could smell the girl's hair.

A long empty street stretched away to the convent, the con-vent wall and a wooden gate. I would have to ring before I could get in. The girl said, 'You don't want to look at me, eh, I make you look at me.' She pushed me and the books I was carrying fell to the ground.

I stooped to pick them up and saw that a tall boy who was walking along the other side of the street had stopped and looked towards us. Then he crossed over, running. He had long legs, his feet hardly touched the ground. As soon as they saw him, they turned and walked away. He looked after them, puzzled. I would have died sooner than run when they were there, but as soon as they had gone, I ran. I left one of my books on the ground and the tall boy came after me.

'You dropped this,' he said, and smiled. I knew who he was, his name was Sandi, Alexander Cosway's son. Once I would have said 'my cousin Sandi' but Mr Mason's lectures had made me shy about my coloured relatives. I muttered, 'Thank you.'

'I'll talk to that boy,' he said. 'He won't bother you again.'

In the distance I could see my enemy's red hair as he pelted along, but he hadn't a chance. Sandi caught him up before he reached the corner. The girl had disappeared. I didn't wait to see what happened but I pulled and pulled at the bell.

At last the door opened. The nun was a coloured woman and she seemed displeased. 'You must not ring the bell like that,' she said. 'I come as quick as I can.' Then I heard the door shut behind me.

I collapsed and began to cry. She asked me if I was sick, but I could not answer. She took my hand, still clicking her tongue and muttering in an ill-tempered way, and led me across the yard, past the shadow of the big tree, not into the front door but into a big, cool, stone-flagged room. There were pots and pans hanging on the wall and a stone fireplace. There was another nun at the back of the room and when the bell rang again, the first one went to answer it. The second nun, also a coloured woman, brought a basin and water but as fast as she sponged my face, so fast did I cry. When she saw my hand she asked if I had fallen and hurt myself. I shook my head and she sponged the stain away gently. 'What is the matter, what are you crying about? What has happened to you?' And still I could not answer. She brought me a glass of milk, I tried to drink it, but I choked. 'Oh la la,' she said, shrugging her shoulders and went out.

When she came in again, a third nun was with her who said in a calm voice, 'You have cried quite enough now, you must stop. Have you got a handkerchief?'

I remembered that I had dropped it. The new nun wiped my eyes with a large handkerchief, gave it to me and asked my name.

'Antoinette,' I said.

'Of course,' she said. 'I know. You are Antoinette Cosway, that is to say Antoinette Mason. Has someone frightened you?'

'Yes.'

'Now look at me,' she said. 'You will not be frightened of me.'

I looked at her. She had large brown eyes, very soft, and was dressed in white, not with a starched apron like the others had. The band round her face was of linen and above the white linen a black veil of some thin material, which fell in folds down her back. Her cheeks were red, she had a laughing face and two deep dimples. Her hands were small but they looked clumsy and swollen, not like the rest of her. It was only afterwards that I found out that they were crippled with rheumatism. She took me into a parlour furnished stiffly with straight-backed chairs and a polished table in the middle. After she had talked to me I told her a little of why I was crying and that I did not like walking to school alone.

'That must be seen to,' she said. 'I will write to your aunt. Now Mother St Justine will be waiting for you. I have sent for a girl who has been with us for nearly a year. Her name is Louise — Louise de Plana. If you feel strange, she will explain everything.'

Louise and I walked along a paved path to the classroom. There was grass on each side of the path and trees and shadows of trees and sometimes a bright bush of flowers. She was very pretty and when she smiled at me I could scarcely believe I had ever been miserable. She said, 'We always call Mother St Justine, Mother Juice of a Lime. She is not very intelligent, poor woman. You will see.'

Quickly, while I can, I must remember the hot classroom. The hot classroom, the pitchpine desks, the heat of the bench striking up through my body, along my arms and hands. But outside I could see cool, blue shadow on a white wall. My needle is sticky, and creaks as it goes in and out of the canvas. 'My needle is swearing,' I whisper to Louise, who sits next to me. We are cross-stitching silk roses on a pale background. We can colour the roses as we choose and mine are green, blue and purple. Underneath, I will write my name in fire red, Antoinette Mason, née Cosway, Mount Calvary Convent, Spanish Town, Jamaica, 1839.

As we work, Mother St Justine reads us stories from the lives of the Saints, St Rose, St Barbara, St Agnes. But we have our own Saint, the skeleton of a girl of fourteen under the altar of the convent chapel. The Relics. But how did the nuns get them out here, I ask myself? In a cabin trunk? Specially packed for the hold? How? But here she is, and St Innocenzia is her name. We do not know her story, she is not in the book. The saints we hear about were all very beautiful and wealthy. All were loved by rich and handsome young men.

'. . . more lovely and more richly dressed than he had ever seen her in life,' drones Mother St Justine. 'She smiled and said, "Here Theophilus is a rose from the garden of my Spouse, in whom you did not believe." The rose he found by his side when he awoke has never faded. It still exists.' (Oh, but where? Where?) 'And Theophilus was converted to Christianity,' says Mother St Justine, reading very rapidly now, 'and became one of the Holy Martyrs.' She shuts the book with a clap and talks about pushing down the cuticles of our nails when we wash our hands. Cleanliness, good manners and kindness to God's poor. A flow of words. ('It is her time of life,' said Hélène de Plana, 'she cannot help it, poor old Justine.') 'When you insult or injure the unfortunate or the unhappy, you insult Christ Himself and He will not forget, for they are His chosen ones.' This remark is made in a casual and perfunctory voice and she slides on to order and chastity, that flawless crystal that, once broken, can never be mended. Also deportment. Like everyone else, she has fallen under the spell of the de Plana sisters and holds them up as an example to the class. I admire them. They sit so poised and imperturbable while she points out the excellence of Miss Hélène's coiffure, achieved without a looking-glass.

'Please, Hélène, tell me how you do your hair, because when I grow up I want mine to look like yours.'

'It's very easy. You comb it upwards, like this and then push it a little forward, like that, and then you pin it here and here. Never too many pins.'

'Yes, but Hélène, mine does not look like yours, whatever I do.'

Her eyelashes flickered, she turned away, too polite to say the obvious thing. We have no looking-glass in the dormitory, once

I saw the new young nun from Ireland looking at herself in a cask of water, smiling to see if her dimples were still there. When she noticed me, she blushed and I thought, now she will always dislike me.

Sometimes it was Miss Hélène's hair and sometimes Miss Germaine's impeccable deportment, and sometimes it was the care Miss Louise took of her beautiful teeth. And if we were never envious, they never seemed vain. Hélène and Germaine, a little disdainful, aloof perhaps, but Louise, not even that. She took no part in it — as if she knew that she was born for other things. Hélène's brown eyes could snap, Germaine's grey eyes were beautiful, soft and cow-like, she spoke slowly and, unlike most Creole girls, was very even-tempered. It is easy to imagine what happened to those two, bar accidents. Ah but Louise! Her small waist, her thin brown hands, her black curls which smelled of vetiver, her high sweet voice, singing so carelessly in Chapel about death. Like a bird would sing. Anything might have happened to you, Louise, anything at all, and I wouldn't be surprised.

Then there was another saint, said Mother St Justine, she lived later on but still in Italy, or was it in Spain. Italy is white pillars and green water. Spain is hot sun on stones, France is a lady with black hair wearing a white dress because Louise was born in France fifteen years ago, and my mother, whom I must forget and pray for as though she were dead, though she is living, liked to dress in white.

No one spoke of her now that Christophine had left us to live with her son. I seldom saw my stepfather. He seemed to dislike Jamaica, Spanish Town in particular, and was often away for months.

One hot afternoon in July my aunt told me that she was going to England for a year. Her health was not good and she needed a change. As she talked she was working at a patchwork counterpane. The diamond-shaped pieces of silk melted one into the other, red, blue, purple, green, yellow, all one shimmering colour. Hours and hours she had spent on it and it was nearly finished. Would I be lonely? she asked and I said 'No,' looking at the colours. Hours and hours and hours I thought.

This convent was my refuge, a place of sunshine and of death where very early in the morning the clap of a wooden signal woke the nine of us who slept in the long dormitory. We woke to see Sister Marie Augustine sitting, serene and neat, bolt upright in a wooden chair. The long brown room was full of gold sunlight and shadows of trees moving quietly. I learnt to say very quickly as the others did, 'offer up all the prayers, works and sufferings of this day.' But what about happiness, I thought at first, is there no happiness? There must be. Oh happiness of course, happiness, well.

But I soon forgot about happiness, running down the stairs to the big stone bath where we splashed about wearing long grey cotton chemises which reached to our ankles. The smell of soap as you cautiously soaped yourself under the chemise, a trick to be learned, dressing with modesty, another trick. Great splashes of sunlight as we ran up the wooden steps of the refectory. Hot coffee and rolls and melting butter. But after the meal, now and at the hour of our death, and at midday and at six in the evening, now and at the hour of our death. Let perpetual light shine on them. This is for my mother, I would think, wherever her soul is wandering, but it has left her body. Then I remembered how she hated a strong light and loved the cool and the shade. It is a different light they told me. Still, I would not say it. Soon we were back in the shifting shadows outside, more beautiful than any perpetual light could be, and soon I learnt to gabble without thinking as the others did. About changing now and the hour of our death for that is all we have.

Everything was brightness, or dark. The walls, the blazing colours of the flowers in the garden, the nuns' habits were bright, but their veils, the Crucifix hanging from their waists, the shadow of the trees, were black. That was how it was, light and dark, sun and shadow, Heaven and Hell, for one of the nuns knew all about Hell and who does not? But another one knew about Heaven and the attributes of the blessed, of which the least is transcendent beauty. The very least. I could hardly wait for all this ecstasy and once I prayed for a long time to be dead. Then remembered that this was a sin. It's presumption or despair, I forget which, but a mortal sin. So I prayed for a long time about that too, but the thought came, so many things are sins, why? Another sin, to think that. However, happily, Sister Marie Augustine says thoughts are not sins, if they are driven away at once. You say Lord save me, I perish. I find it very comforting to know exactly what must be done. All the same, I did not pray so often after that and soon, hardly at all. I felt bolder, happier, more free. But not so safe.

During the time, nearly eighteen months, my stepfather often came to see me. He interviewed Mother Superior first, then I would go into the parlour dressed ready for a dinner or a visit to friends. He gave me presents when we parted, sweets, a locket, a bracelet, once a very pretty dress which, of course, I could not wear.

The last time he came was different. I knew that as soon as I got into the room. He kissed me, held me at arm's length looking at me carefully and critically, then smiled and said that I was taller than he thought. I reminded him that I was over seventeen, a grown woman. 'I've not forgotten your present,' he said.

Because I felt shy and ill at ease I answered coldly, 'I can't wear all these things you buy for me.'

'You can wear what you like when you live with me,' he said.

'Where? In Trinidad?'

'Of course not. Here, for the time being. With me and your Aunt Cora who is coming home at last. She says another English winter will kill her. And Richard. You can't be hidden away all your life.'

'Why not?' I thought.

I suppose he noticed my dismay because he began to joke, pay me compliments, and ask me such absurd questions that soon I was laughing too. How would I like to live in England? Then, before I could answer, had I learnt dancing, or were the nuns too strict?

'They are not strict at all,' I said. 'The Bishop who visits them every year says they are lax. Very lax. It's the climate he says.'

'I hope they told him to mind his own business.'

'She did. Mother Superior did. Some of the others were frightened. They are not strict but no one has taught me to dance.'

'That won't be the difficulty. I want you to be happy, Antoinette, secure, I've tried to arrange, but we'll have time to talk about that later.'

As we were going out of the convent gate he said in a careless voice, 'I have asked some English friends to spend next winter here. You won't be dull.'

'Do you think they'll come?' I said doubtfully.

'One of them will. I'm certain of that.'

It may have been the way he smiled, but again a feeling of dismay, sadness, loss, almost choked me. This time I did not let him see it.

It was like that morning when I found the dead horse. Say nothing and it may not be true.

But they all knew at the convent. The girls were very curious but I would not answer their questions and for the first time I resented the nuns' cheerful faces.

They are safe. How can they know what it can be like *outside?*

This was the second time I had my dream.

Again I have left the house at Coulibri. It is still night and I am walking towards the forest. I am wearing a long dress and thin slippers, so I walk with difficulty, following the man who is with me and holding up the skirt of my dress. It is white and beautiful and I don't wish to get it soiled. I follow him, sick with fear but I make no effort to save myself; if anyone were to try to save me, I would refuse. This must happen. Now we have reached the forest. We are under the tall dark trees and there is no wind. 'Here?' He turns and looks at me, his face black with hatred, and when I see this I begin to cry. He smiles slyly. 'Not here, not yet,' he says, and I follow him, weeping. Now I do not try to hold up my dress, it trails in the dirt, my beautiful dress. We are no longer in the forest but in an enclosed garden surrounded by a stone wall and the trees are different trees. I do not know them. There are steps leading upwards. It is too dark to see the wall or the steps, but I know they are there and I think, 'It will be when I go up these steps. At the top.' I stumble over my dress and cannot get up. I touch a tree and my arms hold on to it. 'Here, here.' But I think I will not go any further. The tree sways and jerks as if it is trying to throw me off. Still I cling and the seconds pass and each one is a thousand years. 'Here, in here,' a strange voice said, and the tree stopped swaying and jerking.

Now Sister Marie Augustine is leading me out of the dormitory, asking if I am ill, telling me that I must not disturb the others and though I am still shivering I wonder if she will take me behind the mysterious curtains to the place where she sleeps. But no. She seats me in a chair, vanishes, and after a while comes back with a cup of hot chocolate.

I said, 'I dreamed I was in Hell.'

'That dream is evil. Put it from your mind — never think of it again,' and she rubbed my cold hands to warm them.

She looks as usual, composed and neat, and I want to ask her if she gets up before dawn or hasn't been to bed at all.

'Drink your chocolate.'

While I am drinking it I remember that after my mother's funeral, very early in the morning, almost as early as this, we went home to drink chocolate and eat cakes. She died last year, no one told me how, and I didn't ask. Mr Mason was there and Christophine, no one else. Christophine cried bitterly but I could not. I prayed, but the words fell to the ground meaning nothing.

Now the thought of her is mixed up with my dream.

I saw her in her mended habit riding a borrowed horse, trying to wave at the head of the cobblestoned road at Coulibri, and tears came to my eyes again. 'Such terrible things happen,' I said. 'Why? Why?'

'You must not concern yourself with that mystery,' said Sister Maria Augustine. 'We do not know why the devil must have his little day. Not yet.'

She never smiled as much as the others, now she was not smiling at all. She looked sad.

She said, as if she was talking to herself, 'Now go quietly back to bed. Think of calm, peaceful things and try to sleep. Soon I will give the signal. Soon it will be tomorrow morning.'

PART TWO

S O IT was all over, the advance and retreat, the doubts and
hesitations. Everything finished, for better or for worse.
There we were, sheltering from the heavy rain under a large
mango tree, myself, my wife Antoinette and a little half-caste
servant who was called Amélie. Under a neighbouring tree I
could see our luggage covered with sacking, the two porters and
a boy holding fresh horses, hired to carry us up 2,000 feet to the
waiting honeymoon house.

The girl Amélie said this morning, 'I hope you will be very
happy, sir, in your sweet honeymoon house.' She was laughing
at me I could see. A lovely little creature, but sly, spiteful, malignant perhaps, like much else in this place.

'It's only a shower,' Antoinette said anxiously. 'It will soon
stop.'

I looked at the sad leaning cocoanut palms, the fishing boats
drawn up on the shingly beach, the uneven row of whitewashed
huts, and asked the name of the village.

'Massacre.'

'And who was massacred here? Slaves?'

'Oh no.' She sounded shocked. 'Not slaves. Something must
have happened a long time ago. Nobody remembers now.'

The rain fell more heavily, huge drops sounded like hail on
the leaves of the tree, and the sea crept stealthily forwards and
backwards.

So this is Massacre. Not the end of the world, only the last
stage of our interminable journey from Jamaica, the start of our
sweet honeymoon. And it will all look very different in the sun.

It had been arranged that we would leave Spanish Town immediately after the ceremony and spend some weeks in one of
the Windward Islands, at a small estate which had belonged to
Antoinette's mother. I agreed. As I had agreed to everything
else.

The windows of the huts were shut, the doors opened into
silence and dimness. Then three little boys came to stare at us.
The smallest wore nothing but a religious medal round his neck

and the brim of a large fisherman's hat. When I smiled at him, he began to cry. A woman called from one of the huts and he ran away, still howling.

The other two followed slowly, looking back several times.

As if this was a signal a second woman appeared at her door, then a third.

'It's Caro,' Antoinette said. 'I'm sure it's Caro. Carolina,' she called, waving, and the woman waved back. A gaudy old creature in a brightly flowered dress, a striped head handkerchief and gold ear-rings.

'You'll get soaked, Antoinette,' I said.

'No, the rain is stopping.' She held up the skirt of her riding habit and ran across the street. I watched her critically. She wore a tricorne hat which became her. At least it shadowed her eyes which are too large and can be disconcerting. She never blinks at all it seems to me. Long, sad, dark alien eyes. Creole of pure English descent she may be, but they are not English or European either. And when did I begin to notice all this about my wife Antoinette? After we left Spanish Town I suppose. Or did I notice it before and refuse to admit what I saw? Not that I had much time to notice anything. I was married a month after I arrived in Jamaica and for nearly three weeks of that time I was in bed with fever.

The two women stood in the doorway of the hut gesticulating, talking not English but the debased French patois they use in this island. The rain began to drip down the back of my neck adding to my feeling of discomfort and melancholy.

I thought about the letter which should have been written to England a week ago. Dear Father . . .

'Caroline asks if you will shelter in her house.'

This was Antoinette. She spoke hesitatingly as if she expected me to refuse, so it was easy to do so.

'But you are getting wet,' she said.

'I don't mind that.' I smiled at Carolina and shook my head.

'She will be very disappointed,' said my wife, crossed the street again and went into the dark hut.

Amélie, who had been sitting with her back to us, turned round. Her expression was so full of delighted malice, so intelligent, above all so intimate that I felt ashamed and looked away.

'Well,' I thought. 'I have had fever. I am not myself yet.'

The rain was not so heavy and I went to talk to the porters.

The first man was not a native of the island. 'This a very wild place — not civilized. Why you come here?' He was called the Young Bull he told me, and he was twenty-seven years of age. A magnificent body and a foolish conceited face. The other man's name was Emile, yes, he was born in the village, he lived there. 'Ask him how old he is,' suggested the Young Bull. Emile said in a questioning voice, 'Fourteen? Yes I have fourteen years master.'

'Impossible,' I said. I could see the grey hairs in his sparse beard.

'Fifty-six years perhaps.' He seemed anxious to please.

The Young Bull laughed loudly. 'He don't know how old he is, he don't think about it. I tell you sir these people are not civilized.'

Emile muttered, 'My mother she know, but she dead.' Then he produced a blue rag which he twisted into a pad and put on his head.

Most of the women were outside their doors looking at us but without smiling. Sombre people in a sombre place. Some of the men were going to their boats. While Emile shouted, two of them came towards him. He sang in a deep voice. They answered, then lifted the heavy wicker basket and swung it on to his head-pad singing. He tested the balance with one hand and strode off, barefooted on the sharp stones, by far the gayest member of the wedding party. As the Young Bull was loaded up he glanced at me sideways boastfully and he too sang to himself in English.

The boy brought the horses to a large stone and I saw Antoinette coming from the hut. The sun blazed out and steam rose from the green behind us. Amélie took her shoes off, tied them together and hung them round her neck. She balanced her small basket on her head and swung away as easily as the porters. We mounted, turned a corner and the village was out of sight. A cock crowed loudly and I remembered the night before which we had spent in the town. Antoinette had a room to herself, she was exhausted. I lay awake listening to cocks crowing all night, then got up very early and saw the women with trays covered with white cloths on their heads going to the kitchen. The woman with small hot loaves for sale, the woman with cakes, the woman with sweets. In the street another called *Bon sirop, Bon sirop,* and I felt peaceful.

.

The road climbed upward. On one side the wall of green, on the other a steep drop to the ravine below. We pulled up and looked at the hills, the mountains and the blue-green sea. There was a soft warm wind blowing but I understood why the porter had called it a wild place. Not only wild but menacing. Those hills would close in on you.

'What an extreme green,' was all I could say, and thinking of Emile calling to the fishermen and the sound of his voice, I asked about him.

'They take short cuts. They will be at Granbois long before we are.'

Everything is too much, I felt as I rode wearily after her. Too much blue, too much purple, too much green. The flowers too red, the mountains too high, the hills too near. And the woman is a stranger. Her pleading expression annoys me. I have not bought her, she has bought me, or so she thinks. I looked down at the coarse mane of the horse . . . Dear Father. The thirty thousand pounds have been paid to me without question or condition. No provision made for her (that must be seen to). I have a modest competence now. I will never be a disgrace to you or to my dear brother the son you love. No begging letters, no mean requests. None of the furtive shabby manœuvres of a younger son. I have sold my soul or you have sold it, and after all is it such a bad bargain? The girl is thought to be beautiful, she is beautiful. And yet . . .

Meanwhile the horses jogged along a very bad road. It was getting cooler. A bird whistled, a long sad note. 'What bird is that?' She was too far ahead and did not hear me. The bird whistled again. A mountain bird. Shrill and sweet. A very lonely sound.

She stopped and called, 'Put your coat on now.' I did so and realized that I was no longer pleasantly cool but cold in my sweat-soaked shirt.

We rode on again, silent in the slanting afternoon sun, the wall of trees on one side, a drop on the other. Now the sea was a serene blue, deep and dark.

We came to a little river. 'This is the boundary of Granbois.' She smiled at me. It was the first time I had seen her smile simply and naturally. Or perhaps it was the first time I had felt simple and natural with her. A bamboo spout jutted from the cliff, the water coming from it was silver blue. She dismounted quickly, picked a large shamrock-shaped leaf to make a cup, and drank. Then she picked another leaf, folded it and brought it to me. 'Taste. This is mountain water.' Looking up smiling, she might have been any pretty English girl and to please her I drank. It was cold, pure and sweet, a beautiful colour against the thick green leaf.

She said, 'After this we go down then up again. Then we are there.'

Next time she spoke she said, 'The earth is red here, do you notice?'

'It's red in parts of England too.'

'Oh England, England,' she called back mockingly, and the sound went on and on like a warning I did not choose to hear.

Soon the road was cobblestoned and we stopped at a flight of stone steps. There was a large screw pine to the left and to the right what looked like an imitation of an English summer house — four wooden posts and a thatched roof. She dismounted and ran up the steps. At the top a badly cut, coarse-grained lawn and at the end of the lawn a shabby white house. 'Now you are at Granbois.' I looked at the mountains purple against a very blue sky.

Perched up on wooden stilts the house seemed to shrink from the forest behind it and crane eagerly out to the distant sea. It was more awkward than ugly, a little sad as if it knew it could not last. A group of negroes were standing at the foot of the veranda steps. Antoinette ran across the lawn and as I followed her I collided with a boy coming in the opposite direction. He rolled his eyes, looking alarmed and went on towards the horses without a word of apology. A man's voice said, 'Double up now double up. Look sharp.' There were four of them. A woman, a girl and a tall, dignified man were together. Antoinette was standing with her arms round another woman. 'That was Bertrand who nearly knocked you down. That is Rose and Hilda. This is Baptiste.'

The servants grinned shyly as she named them.

'And here is Christophine who was my da, my nurse long ago.'

Baptiste said that it was a happy day and that we'd brought fine weather with us. He spoke good English, but in the middle of his address of welcome Hilda began to giggle. She was a young girl of about twelve or fourteen, wearing a sleeveless white dress which just reached her knees. The dress was spotless but her uncovered hair, though it was oiled and braided into many small plaits, gave her a savage appearance. Baptiste frowned at her and she giggled more loudly, then put her hand over her mouth and went up the wooden steps into the house. I could hear her bare feet running along the veranda.

'*Doudou, ché cocotte*,' the elderly woman said to Antoinette. I looked at her sharply but she seemed insignificant. She was blacker than most and her clothes, even the handkerchief round her head, were subdued in colour. She looked at me steadily, not with approval, I thought. We stared at each other for quite a minute. I looked away first and she smiled to herself, gave Antoinette a little push forward and disappeared into the shadows at the back of the house. The other servants had gone.

Standing on the veranda I breathed the sweetness of the air. Cloves I could smell and cinnamon, roses and orange blossom. And an intoxicating freshness as if all this had never been breathed before. When Antoinette said 'Come, I will show you the house' I went with her unwillingly for the rest of the place seemed neglected and deserted. She led me into a large unpainted room. There was a small shabby sofa, a mahogany table in the middle, some straight-backed chairs and an old oak chest with brass feet like lion's claws.

Holding my hand she went up to the sideboard where two glasses of rum punch were waiting for us. She handed me one and said, 'To happiness.'

'To happiness,' I answered.

The room beyond was larger and emptier. There were two doors, one leading to the veranda, the other very slightly open into a small room. A big bed, a round table by its side, two chairs, a surprising dressing-table with a marble top and a large looking-glass. Two wreaths of frangipani lay on the bed.

'Am I expected to wear one of these? And when?'

I crowned myself with one of the wreaths and made a face in the glass. 'I hardly think it suits my handsome face, do you?'

'You look like a king, an emperor.'

'God forbid,' I said and took the wreath off. It fell on the floor and as I went towards the window I stepped on it. The room was full of the scent of crushed flowers. I saw her reflection in the glass fanning herself with a small palm-leaf fan coloured blue and red at the edges. I felt sweat on my forehead and sat down, she knelt near me and wiped my face with her handkerchief.

'Don't you like it here? This is my place and everything is on our side. Once,' she said, 'I used to sleep with a piece of wood by my side so that I could defend myself if I were attacked. That's how afraid I was.'

'Afraid of what?'

She shook her head. 'Of nothing, of everything.'

Someone knocked and she said, 'It's only Christophine.'

'The old woman who was your nurse? Are you afraid of her?'

'No, how could I be?'

'If she were taller,' I said, 'one of these strapping women dressed up to the nines, I might be afraid of her.'

She laughed. 'That door leads into your dressing-room.'

I shut it gently after me.

It seemed crowded after the emptiness of the rest of the house. There was a carpet, the only one I had seen, a press made of some beautiful wood I did not recognize. Under the open window a small writing-desk with paper, pens, and ink. 'A refuge' I was thinking when someone said, 'This was Mr Mason's room, sir, but he did not come here often. He did not like the place.' Baptiste, standing in the doorway to the veranda, had a blanket over his arm.

'It's all very comfortable,' I said. He laid the blanket on the bed.

'It can be cold here at night,' he said. Then went away. But the feeling of security had left me. I looked round suspiciously. The door into her room could be bolted, a stout wooden bar pushed across the other. This was the last room in the house. Wooden steps from the veranda led on to another rough lawn, a Seville orange tree grew by the steps. I went back into the dressing-room and looked out of the window. I saw a clay road, muddy in places, bordered by a row of tall trees. Beyond the road various half-hidden outbuildings. One was the kitchen. No chimney but smoke was pouring out of the window. I sat on the soft narrow bed and listened. Not a sound except the river. I might have been alone in the house. There was a crude bookshelf made of three shingles strung together over the desk and I looked at the books, Byron's poems, novels by Sir Walter Scott, *Confessions of an Opium Eater,* some shabby brown volumes, and on the last shelf, *Life and Letters of* . . . The rest was eaten away.

Dear Father, we have arrived from Jamaica after an uncomfortable few days. This little estate in the Windward Islands is part of the family property and Antoinette is much attached to it. She wished to get here as soon as possible. All is well and has gone according to your plans and wishes. I dealt of course with Richard Mason. His father died soon after I left for the West Indies as you probably know. He is a good fellow, hospitable and friendly; he seemed to become attached to me and trusted me completely. This place is very beautiful but my illness has left me too exhausted to appreciate it fully. I will write again in a few days' time.

I re-read this letter and added a postscript:

I feel that I have left you too long without news for the bare announcement of my approaching marriage was hardly news. I was down with fever for two weeks after I got to Spanish Town. Nothing serious but I felt wretched enough. I stayed with the Frasers, friends of the Masons. Mr Fraser is an Englishman, a retired magistrate, and he insisted on telling me at length about some of his cases. It was difficult to think or write coherently. In this cool and remote place it is called Granbois (the High Woods I suppose) I feel better already and my next letter will be longer and more explicit.

A cool and remote place . . . And I wondered how they got their letters posted. I folded mine and put it into a drawer of the desk.

As for my confused impressions they will never be written. There are blanks in my mind that cannot be filled up.

◆   ◆   ◆

It was all very brightly coloured, very strange, but it meant nothing to me. Nor did she, the girl I was to marry. When at last I met her I bowed, smiled, kissed her hand, danced with her. I played the part I was expected to play. She never had anything to do with me at all. Every movement I made was an effort of will and sometimes I wondered that no one noticed this. I would listen to my own voice and marvel at it, calm, correct but toneless, surely. But I must have given a faultless performance. If I saw an expression of doubt or curiosity it was on a black face not a white one.

I remember little of the actual ceremony. Marble memorial tablets on the walls commemorating the virtues of the last generation of planters. All benevolent. All slave-owners. All resting in peace. When we came out of the church I took her hand. It was cold as ice in the hot sun.

Then I was at a long table in a crowded room. Palm leaf fans, a mob of servants, the women's head handkerchiefs striped red and yellow, the men's dark faces. The strong taste of punch, the cleaner taste of champagne, my bride in white but I hardly remember what she looked like. Then in another room women dressed in black. Cousin Julia, Cousin Ada, Aunt Lina. Thin or fat they all looked alike. Gold ear-rings in pierced ears. Silver bracelets jangling on their wrists. I said to one of them, 'We are leaving Jamaica tonight,' and she answered after a pause, 'Of course, Antoinette does not like Spanish Town. Nor did her mother.' Peering at me. (Do their eyes get smaller as they grow older? Smaller, beadier, more inquisitive?) After that I thought I saw the same expression on all their faces. Curiosity? Pity? Ridicule? But why should they pity me. I who have done so well for myself?

The morning before the wedding Richard Mason burst into my room at the Frasers as I was finishing my first cup of coffee. 'She won't go through with it!'

'Won't go through with what?'

'She won't marry you.'

'But why?'

'She doesn't say why.'

'She must have some reason.'

'She won't give a reason. I've been arguing with the little fool for an hour.'

We stared at each other.

'Everything arranged, the presents, the invitations. What shall I tell your father?' He seemed on the verge of tears.

I said, 'If she won't, she won't. She can't be dragged to the altar. Let me get dressed. I must hear what she has to say.'

He went out meekly and while I dressed I thought that this would indeed make a fool of me. I did not relish going back to England in the role of rejected suitor jilted by this Creole girl. I must certainly know why.

She was sitting in a rocking chair with her head bent. Her hair was in two long plaits over her shoulders. From a little distance I spoke gently. 'What is the matter, Antoinette? What have I done?'

She said nothing.

'You don't wish to marry me?'

'No.' She spoke in a very low voice.

'But why?'

'I'm afraid of what may happen.'

'But don't you remember last night I told you that when you are my wife there would not be any more reason to be afraid?'

'Yes,' she said. 'Then Richard came in and you laughed. I didn't like the way you laughed.'

'But I was laughing at myself, Antoinette.'

She looked at me and I took her in my arms and kissed her.

'You don't know anything about me,' she said.

'I'll trust you if you'll trust me. Is that a bargain? You will make me very unhappy if you send me away without telling me what I have done to displease you. I will go with a sad heart.'

'Your sad heart,' she said, and touched my face. I kissed her fervently, promising her peace, happiness, safety, but when I said, 'Can I tell poor Richard that it was a mistake? He is sad too,' she did not answer me. Only nodded.

·   ·   ·

Thinking of all this, of Richard's angry face, her voice saying, 'Can you give me peace?', I must have slept.

I woke to the sound of voices in the next room, laughter and water being poured out. I listened, still drowsy. Antoinette said, 'Don't put any more scent on my hair. He doesn't like it.' The other: 'The man don't like scent? I never hear that before.' It was almost dark.

The dining-room was brilliantly lit. Candles on the table, a row on the sideboard, three-branch candlesticks on the old sea-chest. The two doors on to the veranda stood open but there was no wind. The flames burned straight. She was sitting on the sofa and I wondered why I had never realized how beautiful she was. Her hair was combed away from her face and fell smoothly far below her waist. I could see the red and gold lights in it. She seemed pleased when I complimented her on her dress and told me she had it made in St Pierre, Martinique. 'They call this fashion *à la Joséphine*.'

'You talk of St Pierre as though it were Paris,' I said.

'But it is the Paris of the West Indies.'

There were trailing pink flowers on the table and the name echoed pleasantly in my head. Coralita Coralita. The food, though too highly seasoned, was lighter and more appetizing than anything I had tasted in Jamaica. We drank champagne.

A great many moths and beetles found their way into the room, flew into the candles and fell dead on the tablecloth. Amélie swept them up with a crumb brush. Uselessly. More moths and beetles came.

'Is it true,' she said, 'that England is like a dream? Because one of my friends who married an Englishman wrote and told me so. She said this place London is like a cold dark dream sometimes. I want to wake up.'

'Well,' I answered annoyed, 'that is precisely how your beautiful island seems to me, quite unreal and like a dream.'

'But how can rivers and mountains and the sea be unreal?'

'And how can millions of people, their houses and their streets be unreal?'

'More easily,' she said, 'much more easily. Yes a big city must be like a dream.'

'No, this is unreal and like a dream,' I thought.

The long veranda was furnished with canvas chairs, two hammocks, and a wooden table on which stood a tripod telescope. Amélie brought out candles with glass shades but the night swallowed up the feeble light. There was a very strong scent of flowers — the flowers by the river that open at night she told me — and the noise, subdued in the inner room, was deafening. 'Crac-cracs,' she explained, 'they make a sound like their name, and crickets and frogs.'

I leaned on the railing and saw hundreds of fireflies —'Ah yes, fireflies in Jamaica, here they call a firefly La belle.'

A large moth, so large that I thought it was a bird, blundered into one of the candles, put it out and fell to the floor. 'He's a big fellow,' I said.

'Is it badly burned?'

'More stunned than hurt.'

I took the beautiful creature up in my handkerchief and put it on the railing. For a moment it was still and by the dim candlelight I could see the soft brilliant colours, the intricate pattern on the wings. I shook the handkerchief gently and it flew away.

'I hope that gay gentleman will be safe,' I said.

'He will come back if we don't put the candles out. It's light enough by the stars.'

Indeed the starlight was so bright that shadows of the veranda posts and the trees outside lay on the floor.

'Now come for a walk,' she said, 'and I will tell you a story.'

We walked along the veranda to the steps which led to the lawn.

'We used to come here to get away from the hot weather in June, July and August. I came three times with my Aunt Cora who is ill. That was after . . .' She stopped and put her hand up to her head.

'If this is a sad story, don't tell it to me tonight.'

'It is not sad,' she said. 'Only some things happen and are there for always even though you forget why or when. It was in that little bedroom.'

I looked where she was pointing but could only see the outline of a narrow bed and one or two chairs.

'This night I can remember it was very hot. The window was shut but I asked Christophine to open it because the breeze comes from the hills at night. The land breeze. Not from the sea. It was so hot that my night chemise was sticking to me but I went to sleep all the same. And then suddenly I was awake. I saw two enormous rats, as big as cats, on the sill staring at me.'

'I'm not astonished that you were frightened.'

'But I was not frightened. That was the strange thing. I stared at them and they did not move. I could see myself in the looking-glass the other side of the room, in my white chemise with a frill round the neck, staring at those rats and the rats quite still, staring at me.'

'Well, what happened?'

'I turned over, pulled up the sheet and went to sleep instantly.'

'And is that the story?'

'No, I woke up again suddenly like the first time and the rats were not there but I felt very frightened. I got out of bed quickly and ran on to the veranda. I lay down in this hammock. This one.' She pointed to a flat hammock, a rope at each of the four corners.

'There was full moon that night — and I watched it for a long time. There were no clouds chasing it, so it seemed to be standing still and it shone on me. Next morning Christophine was angry. She said that it was very bad to sleep in the moonlight when the moon is full.'

'And did you tell her about the rats?'

'No, I never told anyone till now. But I have never forgotten them.'

I wanted to say something reassuring but the scent of the river flowers was overpoweringly strong. I felt giddy.

'Do you think that too,' she said, 'that I have slept too long in the moonlight?'

Her mouth was set in a fixed smile but her eyes were so withdrawn and lonely that I put my arms round her, rocked her like a child and sang to her. An old song I thought I had forgotten:

> 'Hail to the queen of the silent night,
> Shine bright, shine bright Robin as you die.'

She listened, then sang with me:

> 'Shine bright, shine bright Robin as you die.'

There was no one in the house and only two candles in the room which had been so brilliantly lit. Her room was dim, with a shaded candle by the bed and another on the dressing-table. There was a bottle of wine on the round table. It was very late when I poured out two glasses and told her to drink to our happiness, to our love and the day without end which would be tomorrow. I was young then. A short youth mine was.

I woke next morning in the green-yellow light, feeling uneasy as though someone were watching me. She must have been awake for some time. Her hair was plaited and she wore a fresh white chemise. I turned to take her in my arms, I meant to undo the careful plaits, but as I did so there was a soft discreet knock.

She said, 'I have sent Christophine away twice. We wake very early here. The morning is the best time.'

'Come in,' she called and Christophine came in with our coffee on a tray. She was dressed up and looking very imposing. The skirt of her flowered dress trailed after her making a rustling noise as she walked and her yellow silk turban was elaborately tied. Long heavy gold ear-rings pulled down the lobes of her ears. She wished us good morning smiling and put the tray of coffee, cassava cakes and guava jelly on the round table. I got out of bed and went into the dressing-room. Someone had laid my dressing-gown on the narrow bed. I looked out of the window. The cloudless sky was a paler blue than I'd imagined but as I looked I thought I saw the colour changing to a deeper blue. At noon I knew it would be gold, then brassy in the heat. Now it was fresh and cool and the air itself was blue. At last I turned away from the light and space and went back into the bedroom, which was still in the half dark. Antoinette was leaning back against the pillows with her eyes closed. She opened them and smiled when I came in. It was the black woman hovering over her who said, 'Taste my bull's blood, master.' The coffee she handed me was delicious and she had long-fingered hands, thin and beautiful I suppose.

'Not horse piss like the English madams drink,' she said. 'I know them. Drink drink their yellow horse piss, talk, talk their lying talk.' Her dress trailed and rustled as she walked to the door. There she turned. 'I send the girl to clear up the mess you make with the frangipani, it bring cockroach in the house. Take care not to slip on the flowers, young master.' She slid through the door.

'Her coffee is delicious but her language is horrible and she might hold her dress up. It must get very dirty, yards of it trailing on the floor.'

'When they don't hold their dress up it's for respect,' said Antoinette. 'Or for feast days or going to Mass.'

'And is this a feast day?'

'She wanted it to be a feast day.'

'Whatever the reason it is not a clean habit.'

'It is. You don't understand at all. They don't care about getting a dress dirty because it shows it isn't the only dress they have. Don't you like Christophine?'

'She is a very worthy person no doubt. I can't say I like her language.'

'It doesn't mean anything,' said Antoinette.

'And she looks so lazy. She dawdles about.'

'Again you are mistaken. She seems slow, but every move she makes is right so it's quick in the end.'

I drank another cup of bull's blood. (Bull's blood, I thought. The Young Bull.)

'How did you get that dressing-table up here?'

'I don't know. It's always been here ever since I can remember. A lot of the furniture was stolen, but not that.'

There were two pink roses on the tray, each in a small brown jug. One was full blown and as I touched it the petals dropped.

'*Rose elle a vécu*,' I said and laughed. 'Is that poem true? Have all beautiful things sad destinies?'

'No, of course not.'

Her little fan was on the table, she took it up laughing, lay back and shut her eyes. 'I think I won't get up this morning.'

'Not get up. Not get up at all?'

'I'll get up when I wish to. I'm very lazy you know. Like Christophine. I often stay in bed all day.' She flourished her fan. 'The bathing pool is quite near. Go before it gets hot, Baptiste will show you. There are two pools, one we call the champagne pool because it has a waterfall, not a big one you understand, but it's good to feel it on your shoulders. Underneath is the nutmeg pool, that's brown and shaded by a big nutmeg tree. It's just big enough to swim in. But be careful. Remember to put your clothes on a rock and before you dress again shake them very well. Look for the red ant, that is the worst. It is very small but bright red so you will be able to see it easily if you look. Be careful,' she said and waved her little fan.

One morning soon after we arrived, the row of tall trees outside my window were covered with small pale flowers too fragile to resist the wind. They fell in a day, and looked like snow on the rough grass — snow with a faint sweet scent. Then they were blown away.

The fine weather lasted longer. It lasted all that week and the next and the next. No sign of a break. My fever weakness left me, so did all misgiving.

I went very early to the bathing pool and stayed there for hours, unwilling to leave the river, the trees shading it, the flowers that opened at night. They were tightly shut, drooping, sheltering from the sun under their thick leaves.

It was a beautiful place — wild, untouched, above all untouched, with an alien, disturbing, secret loveliness. And it kept its secret. I'd find myself thinking, 'What I see is nothing — I want what it *hides* — that is not nothing.'

In the late afternoon when the water was warmer she bathed with me. She'd spend more time throwing pebbles at a flat stone in the middle of the pool. 'I've seen him. He hasn't died or gone to any other river. He's still there. The land crabs are harmless. People *say* they are harmless. I wouldn't like to —'

'Nor would I. Horrible looking creatures.'

She was undecided, uncertain about facts — any fact. When I asked her if the snakes we sometimes saw were poisonous, she said, 'Not those. The *fer de lance* of course, but there are none here,' and added, 'but how can they be sure? Do you think they know?' Then, 'Our snakes are not poisonous. Of course not.'

However, she was certain about the monster crab and one afternoon when I was watching her, hardly able to believe she was the pale silent creature I had married, watching her in her blue chemise, blue with white spots hitched up far above her knees, she stopped laughing, called a warning and threw a large pebble. She threw like a boy, with a sure graceful movement, and I looked down at very long pincer claws, jagged-edged and sharp, vanishing.

'He won't come after you if you keep away from that stone. He lives there. Oh it's another sort of crab, I don't know the name in English. Very big, very old.'

As we were walking home I asked her who had taught her to aim so well. 'Oh, Sandi taught me, a boy you never met.'

Every evening we saw the sun go down from the thatched shelter she called the *ajoupa*, I the summer house. We watched the sky and the distant sea on fire — all colours were in that fire and the huge clouds fringed and shot with flame. But I soon tired of the display. I was waiting for the scent of the flowers by the river — they opened when darkness came and it came quickly. Not night or darkness as I knew it but night with blazing stars, an alien moon — night full of strange noises. Still night, not day.

'The man who owns Consolation Estate is a hermit,' she was saying. 'He never sees anyone — hardly ever speaks, they say.'

'A hermit neighbour suits me. Very well indeed.'

'There are four hermits in this island,' she said. 'Four real ones. Others pretend but they leave when the rainy season comes. Or else they are drunk all the time. That's when sad things happen.'

'So this place is as lonely as it feels?' I asked her.

'Yes it is lonely. Are you happy here?'

'Who wouldn't be?'

'I love it more than anywhere in the world. As if it were a person. More than a person.'

'But you don't know the world,' I teased her.

'No, only here, and Jamaica of course. Coulibri, Spanish

Town. I don't know the other islands at all. Is the world more beautiful, then?'

And how to answer that? 'It's different,' I said.

She told me that for a long time they had not known what was happening at Granbois. 'When Mr Mason came' (she always called her stepfather Mr Mason) 'the forest was swallowing it up.' The overseer drank, the house was dilapidated, all the furniture had been stolen, then Baptiste was discovered. A butler. In St Kitts. But born in this island and willing to come back. 'He's a very good overseer,' she'd say, and I'd agree, keeping my opinion of Baptiste, Christophine and all the others to myself. 'Baptiste says . . . Christophine wants . . .'

She trusted them and I did not. But I could hardly say so. Not yet.

We did not see a great deal of them. The kitchen and the swarming kitchen life were some way off. As for the money which she handed out so carelessly, not counting it, not knowing how much she gave, or the unfamiliar faces that appeared then disappeared, though never without a large meal eaten and a shot of rum I discovered — sisters, cousins, aunts and uncles — if she asked no questions how could I?

The house was swept and dusted very early, usually before I woke. Hilda brought coffee and there were always two roses on the tray. Sometimes she'd smile a sweet childish smile, sometimes she would giggle very loudly and rudely, bang the tray down and run away.

'Stupid little girl,' I'd say.

'No, no. She is shy. The girls here are very shy.'

After breakfast at noon there'd be silence till the evening meal which was served much later than in England. Christophine's whims and fancies, I was sure. Then we were left alone. Sometimes a sidelong look or a sly knowing glance disturbed me, but it was never for long. 'Not now,' I would think. 'Not yet.'

It was often raining when I woke during the night, a light capricious shower, dancing playful rain, or hushed muted, growing louder, more persistent, more powerful, an inexorable sound. But always music, a music I had never heard before.

Then I would look at her for long minutes by candlelight, wonder why she seemed sad asleep, and curse the fever or the caution that had made me so blind, so feeble, so hesitating. I'd remember her effort to escape. (*No, I am sorry, I do not wish to marry you.*) Had she given way to that man Richard's arguments, threats probably, I wouldn't trust him far, or to my half-serious blandishments and promises? In any case she had given way, but coldly, unwillingly, trying to protect herself with silence and a blank face. Poor weapons, and they had not served her well or lasted long. If I have forgotten caution, she has forgotten silence and coldness.

Shall I wake her up and listen to the things she says, whispers, in darkness. Not by day.

'I never wished to live before I knew you. I always thought it would be better if I died. Such a long time to wait before it's over.'

'And did you ever tell anyone this?'

'There was no one to tell, no one to listen. Oh you can't imagine Coulibri.'

'But after Coulibri?'

'After Coulibri it was too late. I did not change.'

All day she'd be like any other girl, smile at herself in her looking-glass *(do you like this scent?)*, try to teach me her songs, for they haunted me.

Adieu foulard, adieu madras, or *Ma belle ka di maman li.* My beautiful girl said to her mother *(No it is not like that. Now listen. It is this way).* She'd be silent, or angry for no reason, and chatter to Christophine in patois.

'Why do you hug and kiss Christophine?' I'd say.

'Why not?'

'*I* wouldn't hug and kiss them,' I'd say, 'I couldn't.'

At this she'd laugh for a long time and never tell me why she laughed.

But at night how different, even her voice was changed. Always this talk of death. (Is she trying to tell me that is the secret of this place? That there is no other way? She knows. She knows.)

'Why did you make me want to live? Why did you do that to me?'

'Because I wished it. Isn't that enough?'

'Yes, it is enough. But if one day you didn't wish it. What should I do then? Suppose you took this happiness away when I wasn't looking . . .'

'And lose my own? Who'd be so foolish?'

'I am not used to happiness,' she said. 'It makes me afraid.'

'Never be afraid. Or if you are tell no one.'

'I understand. But trying does not help me.'

'What would?' She did not answer that, then one night whispered, 'If I could die. Now, when I am happy. Would you do that? You wouldn't have to kill me. Say die and I will die. You don't believe me? Then try, try, say die and watch me die.'

'Die then! Die!' I watched her die many times. In my way, not in hers. In sunlight, in shadow, by moonlight, by candlelight. In the long afternoons when the house was empty. Only the sun was there to keep us company. We shut him out. And why not? Very soon she was as eager for what's called loving as I was — more lost and drowned afterwards.

She said, 'Here I can do as I like,' not I, and then I said it too. It seemed right in that lonely place. 'Here I can do as I like.'

We seldom met anyone when we left the house. If we did they'd greet us and go on their way.

I grew to like these mountain people, silent, reserved, never servile, never curious (or so I thought), not knowing that their quick sideways looks saw everything they wished to see.

It was at night that I felt danger and would try to forget it and push it away.

'You are safe,' I'd say. She'd liked that — to be told 'you are safe.' Or I'd touch her face gently and touch tears. Tears — nothing! Words — less than nothing. As for the happiness I gave her, that was worse than nothing. I did not love her. I was thirsty for her, but that is not love. I felt very little tenderness for her, she was a stranger to me, a stranger who did not think or feel as I did.

One afternoon the sight of a dress which she'd left lying on her bedroom floor made me breathless and savage with desire. When I was exhausted I turned away from her and slept, still without a word or a caress. I woke and she was kissing me — soft light kisses. 'It is late,' she said and smiled. 'You must let me cover you up — the land breeze can be cold.'

'And you, aren't you cold?'

'Oh I will be ready quickly. I'll wear the dress you like tonight.'

'Yes, do wear it.'

The floor was strewn with garments, hers and mine. She stepped over them carelessly as she walked to her clothes press. 'I was thinking, I'll have another made exactly like it,' she promised happily. 'Will you be pleased?'

'Very pleased.'

If she was a child she was not a stupid child but an obstinate one. She often questioned me about England and listened attentively to my answers, but I was certain that nothing I said made much difference. Her mind was already made up. Some romantic novel, a stray remark never forgotten, a sketch, a picture, a song, a waltz, some note of music, and her ideas were fixed. About England and about Europe. I could not change them and probably nothing would. Reality might disconcert her, bewilder her, hurt her, but it would not be reality. It would be only a mistake, a misfortune, a wrong path taken, her fixed ideas would never change.

Nothing that I told her influenced her at all.

Die then. Sleep. It is all that I can give you. . . . I wonder if she ever guessed how near she came to dying. In her way, not in mine. It was not a safe game to play — in that place. Desire, Hatred, Life, Death came very close in the darkness. Better not know how close. Better not think, never for a moment. Not close. The same . . . 'You are safe,' I'd say to her and to myself. 'Shut your eyes. Rest.'

Then I'd listen to the rain, a sleepy tune that seemed as if it would go on for ever . . . Rain, for ever raining. Drown me in sleep. And soon.

Next morning there would be very little sign of these showers. If some of the flowers were battered, the others smelt sweeter, the air was bluer and sparkling fresh. Only the clay path outside my window was muddy. Little shallow pools of water glinted in the hot sun, red earth does not dry quickly.

◆　◆　◆

'It came for you this morning early, master,' Amélie said. 'Hilda take it.' She gave me a bulky envelope addressed in careful copperplate. '*By hand, Urgent*' was written in the corner.

'One of our hermit neighbours,' I thought. 'And an enclosure for Antoinette.' Then I saw Baptiste standing near the veranda steps, put the letter in my pocket and forgot it.

I was later than usual that morning but when I was dressed I sat for a long time listening to the waterfall, eyes half closed, drowsy and content. When I put my hand in my pocket for my watch, I touched the envelope and opened it.

Dear Sir. I take up my pen after long thought and meditation but in the end the truth is better than a lie. I have this to say. You have been shamefully deceived by the Mason family. They tell you perhaps that your wife's name is Cosway, the English gentleman Mr Mason being her stepfather only, but they don't tell you what sort of people were these Cosways. Wicked and detestable slave-owners since generations — yes everybody hate them in Jamaica and also in this beautiful island where I hope your stay will be long and pleasant in spite of all, for some not worth sorrow. Wickedness is not the worst. There is madness in that family. Old Cosway die raving like his father before him.

You ask what proof I have and why I mix myself up in your affairs. I will answer you. I am your wife's brother by another lady, half-way house as we say. Her father and mine was a shameless man and of all his illegitimates I am the most unfortunate and poverty stricken.

My momma die when I was quite small and my godmother take care of me. The old mister hand out some money for that though he don't like me. No, that old devil don't like me at all, and when I grow older I see it and I think, Let him wait my day will come. Ask the older people sir about his disgusting goings on, some will remember.

When Madam his wife die the reprobate marry again quick, to a young girl from Martinique — it's too much for him. Dead drunk from morning till night and he die raving and cursing.

Then comes the glorious Emancipation Act and trouble for some of the high and mighties. Nobody would work for the young woman and her two children and that place Coulibri goes quickly to bush as all does out here when nobody toil and labour on the land. She have no money and she have no friends, for French and English like cat and dog in these islands since long time. Shoot, Kill, Everything.

The woman call Christophine also from Martinique stay with her and an old man Godfrey, too silly to know what happen. Some like that. This young Mrs Cosway is worthless and spoilt, she can't lift a hand for herself and soon the madness that is in her, and in all these white Creoles, come out. She shut herself away, laughing and talking to nobody as many can bear witness. As for the little girl, Antoinetta, as soon as she can walk she hide herself if she see anybody.

We all wait to hear the woman jump over a precipice 'fini batt'e' as we say here which mean 'finish to fight.'

But no. She marry again to the rich Englishman Mr Mason, and there is much I could say about that but you won't believe so I shut my mouth. They say he love her so much that if he have the world on a plate he give it to her — but no use.

The madness gets worse and she has to be shut away for she try to kill her husband — madness not being all either.

That sir is your wife's mother — that was her father. I leave Jamaica. I don't know what happen to the woman. Some say she is dead, other deny it. But old Mason take a great fancy for the girl Antoinetta and give her half his money when he die.

As for me I wander high and low, not much luck but a little money put by and I get to know of a house for sale in this island near Massacre. It's going very cheap so I buy it. News travel even to this wild place and next thing I hear from Jamaica is that old Mason is dead and that family plan to marry the girl to a young Englishman who know nothing of her. Then it seems to me that it is my Christian duty to warn the gentleman that she is no girl to marry with the bad blood she have from both sides. But they are white, I am coloured. They are rich, I am poor. As I think about these things they do it quick while you still weak with fever at the magistrate's, before you can ask questions. If this is true or not you must know for yourself.

Then you come to this island for your honeymoon and it's certain that the Lord put the thing on my shoulders and that it is I must speak the truth to you. Still I hesitate.

I hear you young and handsome with a kind word for all, black, white, also coloured. But I hear too that the girl is beautiful like her mother was beautiful, and you bewitch with her. She is in your blood and your bones. By night and by day. But you, an honourable man, know well that for marriage more is needed than all this. Which does not last. Old Mason bewitch so with her mother and look what happen to him. Sir I pray I am in time to warn you what to do.

Sir ask yourself how I can make up this story and for what reason. When I leave Jamaica I can read write and cypher a little. The good man in Barbados teach me more, he give me books, he tell me read the Bible every day and I pick up knowledge without effort. He is surprise how quick I am. Still I remain an ignorant man and I do not make up this story. I cannot. It is true.

I sit at my window and the worlds fly past me like birds — with God's help I catch some.

A week this letter take me. I cannot sleep at night thinking what to say. So quickly now I draw to a close and cease my task.

Still you don't believe me? *Then ask that devil of a man Richard Mason three questions and make him answer you. Is your wife's mother shut away, a raging lunatic and worse besides? Dead or alive I do not know.*

Was your wife's brother an idiot from birth, though God mercifully take him early on?

Is your wife herself going the same way as her mother and all knowing it?

Richard Mason is a sly man and he will tell you a lot of nancy stories, which is what we call lies here, about what happen at Coulibri and this and that. Don't listen. Make him answer — yes or no.

If he keep his mouth shut ask others for many think it shameful how that family treat you and your relatives.

I beg you sir come to see me for there is more that you should know. But my hand ache, my head ache and my heart is like a stone for the grief I bring you. Money is good but no money can pay for a crazy wife in your bed. Crazy and worse besides.

I lay down my pen with one last request. Come and see me quickly. Your obt servant. Daniel Cosway.

Ask the girl Amélie where I live. She knows, and she knows me. She belongs to this island.

I folded the letter carefully and put it into my pocket. I felt no surprise. It was as if I'd expected it, been waiting for it. For a time, long or short I don't know, I sat listening to the river. At last I stood up, the sun was hot now. I walked stiffly nor could I force myself to think. Then I passed an orchid with long sprays of golden-brown flowers. One of them touched my cheek and I remembered picking some for her one day. 'They are like you,' I told her. Now I stopped, broke a spray off and trampled it into the mud. This brought me to my senses. I leaned against a tree, sweating and trembling. 'Far too hot today,' I said aloud, 'far too hot.' When I came in sight of the house I began to walk silently. No one was about. The kitchen door was shut and the place looked deserted. I went up the steps and along the veranda and when I heard voices stopped behind the door which led into Antoinette's room. I could see it reflected in the looking-glass. She was in bed and the girl Amélie was sweeping.

'Finish quickly,' said Antoinette, 'and go and tell Christophine I want to see her.'

Amélie rested her hands on the broom handle. 'Christophine is going,' she said.

'Going?' repeated Antoinette.

'Yes, going,' said Amélie. 'Christophine don't like this sweet honeymoon house.' Turning round she saw me and laughed loudly. 'Your husban' he outside the door and he look like he see zombi. Must be he tired of the sweet honeymoon too.'

Antoinette jumped out of bed and slapped her face.

'I hit you back white cockroach, I hit you back,' said Amélie. And she did.

Antoinette gripped her hair. Amélie, whose teeth were bared, seemed to be trying to bite.

'Antoinette, for God's sake,' I said from the doorway.

She swung round, very pale. Amélie buried her face in her hands and pretended to sob, but I could see her watching me through her fingers.

'Go away, child,' I said.

'You call her child,' said Antoinette. 'She is older than the devil himself, and the devil is not more cruel.'

'Send Christophine up,' I said to Amélie.

'Yes master, yes master,' she answered softly, dropping her eyes. But as soon as she was out of the room she began to sing:

> *'The white cockroach she marry*
> *The white cockroach she marry*
> *The white cockroach she buy young man*
> *The white cockroach she marry.'*

Antoinette took a few steps forward. She walked unsteadily. I went to help her but she pushed me away, sat on the bed and with clenched teeth pulled at the sheet, then made a clicking sound of annoyance. She took a pair of scissors from the round table, cut through the hem and tore the sheet in half, then each half into strips.

The noise she made prevented me from hearing Christophine come in, but Antoinette heard her.

'You're not leaving?' she said.

'Yes,' said Christophine.

'And what will become of me?' said Antoinette.

'Get up, girl, and dress yourself. Woman must have spunks to live in this wicked world.'

She had changed into a drab cotton dress and taken off her heavy gold ear-rings.

'I see enough trouble,' she said. 'I have right to my rest. I have my house that your mother gave me so long ago and I have my garden and my son to work for me. A lazy boy but I make him work. Too besides the young master don't like me, and perhaps I don't like him so much. If I stay here I bring trouble and bone of contention in your house.'

'If you are not happy here then go,' said Antoinette.

Amélie came into the room with two jugs of hot water. She looked at me sideways and smiled.

Christophine said in a soft voice, 'Amélie. Smile like that once more, just once more, and I mash your face like I mash plantain. You hear me? Answer me, girl.'

'Yes, Christophine,' Amélie said. She looked frightened.

'And too besides I give you bellyache like you never see bellyache. Perhaps you lie a long time with the bellyache I give you. Perhaps you don't get up again with the bellyache I give you. So keep yourself quiet and decent. You hear me?'

'Yes, Christophine,' Amélie said and crept out of the room.

'She worthless and good for nothing,' said Christophine with contempt. 'She creep and crawl like centipede.'

She kissed Antoinette on the cheek. Then she looked at me, shook her head, and muttered in patois before she went out.

'Did you hear what that girl was singing?' Antoinette said.

'I don't always understand what they say or sing.' Or anything else.

'It was a song about a white cockroach. That's me. That's what they call all of us who were here before their own people in Africa sold them to the slave traders. And I've heard English women call us white niggers. So between you I often wonder who I am and where is my country and where do I belong and why was I ever born at all. Will you go now please. I must dress like Christophine said.'

After I had waited half an hour I knocked at her door. There was no answer so I asked Baptiste to bring me something to eat. He was sitting under the Seville orange tree at the end of the veranda. He served the food with such a mournful expression that I thought these people are very vulnerable. How old was I when I learned to hide what I felt? A very small boy. Six, five, even earlier. It was necessary, I was told, and that view I have always accepted. If these mountains challenge me, or Baptiste's face, or Antoinette's eyes, they are mistaken, melodramatic, unreal (England must be quite unreal and like a dream she said).

The rum punch I had drunk was very strong and after the meal was over I had a great wish to sleep. And why not? This is the time when everyone sleeps. I imagined the dogs the cats the cocks and hens all sleeping, even the water in the river running more slowly.

I woke up, thought at once of Antoinette and opened the door into her room, but she was sleeping too. Her back was towards me and she was quite still. I looked out of the window. The silence was disturbing, absolute. I would have welcomed the sound of a dog barking, a man sawing wood. Nothing. Silence. Heat. It was five minutes to three.

I went out following the path I could see from my window. It must have rained heavily during the night for the red clay was very muddy. I passed a sparse plantation of coffee trees, then straggly guava bushes. As I walked I remembered my father's face and his thin lips, my brother's round conceited eyes. They knew. And Richard the fool, he knew too. And the girl with her blank smiling face. They all knew.

I began to walk very quickly, then stopped because the light was different. A green light. I had reached the forest and you cannot mistake the forest. It is hostile. The path was overgrown but it was possible to follow it. I went on without looking at the tall trees on either side. Once I stepped over a fallen log swarming with white ants. How can one discover truth I thought and that thought led me nowhere. No one would tell me the truth. Not my father nor Richard Mason, certainly not the girl I had married. I stood still, so sure I was being watched that I looked over my shoulder. Nothing but the trees and the green light under the trees. A track was just visible and I went on, glancing from side to side and sometimes quickly behind me. This was why I stubbed my foot on a stone and nearly fell. The stone I had tripped on was not a boulder but part of a paved road. There had been a paved road through this forest. The track led to a large clear space. Here were the ruins of a stone house and round the ruins rose trees that had grown to an incredible height. At the back of the ruins a wild orange tree covered with fruit, the leaves a dark green. A beautiful place. And calm — so calm that it seemed foolish to think or plan. What had I to think about and how could I plan? Under the orange tree I noticed little bunches of flowers tied with grass.

I don't know how long it was before I began to feel chilly. The light had changed and the shadows were long. I had better get back before dark, I thought. Then I saw a little girl carrying a large basket on her head. I met her eyes and to my astonishment she screamed loudly, threw up her arms and ran. The basket fell off, I called after her, but she screamed again and ran faster. She sobbed as she ran, a small frightened sound. Then she disappeared. I must be within a few minutes of the path I thought, but after I had walked for what seemed a long time I found that the undergrowth and creepers caught at my legs and the trees closed over my head. I decided to go back to the clearing and start again, with the same result. It was getting dark. It was useless to tell myself that I was not far from the house. I was lost and afraid among these enemy trees, so certain of danger that when I heard footsteps and a shout I did not answer. The footsteps and the voice came nearer. Then I shouted back. I did not recognize Baptiste at first. He was wearing blue cotton trousers pulled up above his knees and a broad ornamented belt round his slim waist. His machete was in his hand and the light caught the razor-sharp blue-white edge. He did not smile when he saw me.

'We look for you a long time,' he said.

'I got lost.'

He grunted in answer and led the way, walking in front of me very quickly and cutting off any branch or creeper that stopped us with an easy swing of his machete.

I said, 'There was a road here once, where did it lead to?'

'No road,' he said.

'But I saw it. A *pavé* road like the French made in the islands.'

'No road.'

'Who lived in that house?'

'They say a priest. Père Lilièvre. He lived here a long time ago.'

'A child passed,' I said. 'She seemed very frightened when she saw me. Is there something wrong about the place?' He shrugged his shoulders.

'Is there a ghost, a zombi there?' I persisted.

'Don't know nothing about all that foolishness.'

'There was a road here sometime.'

'No road,' he repeated obstinately.

It was nearly dark when we were back on the red clay path. He walked more slowly, turned and smiled at me. It was as if he'd put his service mask on the savage reproachful face I had seen.

'You don't like the woods at night?'

He did not answer, but pointed to a light and said, 'It's a long time I've been looking for you. Miss Antoinette frightened you come to harm.'

When we reached the house I felt very weary.

'You look like you catch fever,' he said.

'I've had that already.'

'No limit to times you catch fever.'

There was no one on the veranda and no sound from the house. We both stood in the road looking up, then he said, 'I send the girl to you, master.'

Hilda brought me a large bowl of soup and some fruit. I tried the door into Antoinette's room. It was bolted and there was no light. Hilda giggled. A nervous giggle.

I told her that I did not want anything to eat, to bring me the decanter of rum and a glass. I drank, then took up the book I had been reading, *The Glittering Coronet of Isles* it was called, and I turned to the chapter 'Obeah':

'A zombi is a dead person who seems to be alive or a living person who is dead. A zombi can also be the spirit of a place, usually malignant but sometimes to be propitiated with sacrifices or offerings of flowers and fruit.' I thought at once of the bunches of flowers at the priest's ruined house. *' "They cry out in the wind that is their voice, they rage in the sea that is their anger." '*

'So I was told, but I have noticed that negroes as a rule refuse to discuss the black magic in which so many believe. Voodoo as it is called in Haiti — Obeah in some of the islands, another name in South America. They confuse matters by telling lies if pressed. The white people, sometimes credulous, pretend to dismiss the whole thing as nonsense. Cases of sudden or mysterious death are attributed to a poison known to the negroes which cannot be traced. It is further complicated by . . .'

◆   ◆   ◆

I did not look up though I saw him at the window but rode on without thinking till I came to the rocks. People here call them Mounes Mors (the Dead Ones). Preston shied at them, they say horses always do. Then he stumbled badly, so I dismounted and walked along with the bridle over my arm. It was getting hot and I was tired when I reached the path to Christophine's two-roomed house, the roof shingled, not thatched. She was sitting on a box under her mango tree, smoking a white clay pipe and she called out, 'It's you, Antoinette? Why you come up here so early?'

'I just wanted to see you,' I said.

She helped me loosen Preston's girth and led him to a stream near by. He drank as if he were very thirsty, then shook himself and snorted. Water flew out of his nostrils. We left him cropping grass and went back to the mango tree. She sat on her box and pushed another towards me, but I knelt close to her touching a thin silver bangle that she always wore.

'You smell the same,' I said.

'You come all this long way to tell me that?' she said. Her clothes smelled of clean cotton, starched and ironed. I had seen her so often standing knee deep in the river at Coulibri, her long skirt hitched up, washing her dresses and her white shifts, then beating them against the stones. Sometimes there would be other women all bringing their washing down on the stones again and again, a gay busy noise. At last they would spread the wet clothes in the sun, wipe their foreheads, start laughing and talking. She smelled too, of their smell, so warm and comforting to me (but he does not like it). The sky was dark blue through the dark green mango leaves, and I thought, 'This is my place and this is where I belong and this is where I wish to stay.' Then I thought, 'What a beautiful tree, but it is too high up here for mangoes and it may never bear fruit,' and I thought of lying alone in my bed with the soft silk cotton mattress and fine sheets, listening. At last I said, 'Christophine, he does not love me, I think he hates me. He always sleeps in his dressing-room now and the servants know. If I get angry he is scornful and silent, sometimes he does not speak to me for hours and I cannot endure it any more, I cannot. What shall I do? He was not like that at first,' I said.

Pink and red hibiscus grew in front of her door, she lit her pipe and did not answer.

'Answer me,' I said. She puffed out a cloud of smoke.

'You ask me a hard thing. I tell you a hard thing, pack up and go.'

'Go, go where? To some strange place where I shall never see him? No, I will not, then everyone, not only the servants, will laugh at me.'

'It's not you they laugh at if you go, they laugh at him.'

'I will not do that.'

'Why you ask me, if when I answer you say no? Why you come up here if when I tell you the truth, you say no?'

'But there must be something else I can do.'

She looked gloomy. 'When man don't love you, more you try, more he hate you, man like that. If you love them they treat you bad, if you don't love them they after you night and day bothering your soul case out. I hear about you and your husband,' she said.

'But I cannot go. He is my husband after all.'

She spat over her shoulder. 'All women, all colours, nothing but fools. Three children I have. One living in this world, each one a different father, but no husband, I thank my God. I keep my money. I don't give it to no worthless man.'

'When must I go, where must I go?'

'But look me trouble, a rich white girl like you and more foolish than the rest. A man don't treat you good, pick up your skirt and walk out. Do it and he come after you.'

'He will not come after me. And you must understand I am not rich now, I have no money of my own at all, everything I had belongs to him.'

'What you tell me there?' she said sharply.

'That is English law.'

'Law! The Mason boy fix it, that boy worse than Satan and he burn in Hell one of these fine nights. Listen to me and I advise you what to do. Tell your husband you feeling sick, you want to visit your cousin in Martinique. Ask him pretty for some of your own money, the man not bad-hearted, he give it. When you get away, stay away. Ask more. He give again and well satisfy. In the end he come to find out what you do, how you get on without him, and if he see you fat and happy he want you back. Men like that. Better not stay in that old house. Go from that house, I tell you.'

'You think I must leave him?'

'You ask me so I answer.'

'Yes,' I said. 'After all I could, but why should I go to Martinique? I wish to see England, I might be able to borrow money for that. Not from him but I know how I might get it. I must travel far, if I go.'

I have been too unhappy, I thought, it cannot last, being so unhappy, it would kill you. I will be a different person when I live in England and different things will happen to me. . . . England, rosy pink in the geography book map, but on the page opposite the words are closely crowded, heavy looking. Exports, coal, iron, wool. Then Imports and Character of Inhabitants. Names, Essex, Chelmsford on the Chelmer. The Yorkshire and Lincolnshire wolds. Wolds? Does that mean hills? How high? Half the height of ours, or not even that? Cool green leaves in the short cool summer. Summer. There are fields of corn like sugar-cane fields, but gold colour and not so tall. After summer the trees are bare, then winter and snow. White feathers falling? Torn pieces of paper falling? They say frost makes flower patterns on the window panes. I must know more than I know already. For I know that house where I will be cold and not belonging, the bed I shall lie in has red curtains and I have slept there many times before, long ago. How long ago? In that bed I will dream the end of my dream. But my dream had nothing to do with England and I must not think like this, I must remember about chandeliers and dancing, about swans and roses and snow. And snow.

'England,' said Christophine, who was watching me. 'You think there is such a place?'

'How can you ask that? You know there is.'

'I never see the damn place, how I know?'

'You do not believe that there is a country called England?'

She blinked and answered quickly, 'I don't say I don't *believe*, I say I don't *know*, I know what I see with my eyes and I never see it. Besides I ask myself is this place like they tell us? Some say one thing, some different, I hear it cold to freeze your bones and they thief your money, clever like the devil. You have money in your pocket, you look again and bam! No money. Why you want to go to this cold thief place? If there is this place at all, I never see it, that is one thing sure.'

I stared at her, thinking, 'but how can she know the best thing for me to do, this ignorant, obstinate old negro woman, who is not certain if there is such a place as England?' She knocked out her pipe and stared back at me, her eyes had no expression at all.

'Christophine,' I said, 'I may do as you advise. But not yet.' (Now, I thought, I must say what I came to say.) 'You knew what I wanted as soon as you saw me, and you certainly know now. Well, don't you?' I heard my voice getting high and thin.

'Hush up,' she said. 'If the man don't love you, I can't make him love you.'

'Yes you can, I know you can. That is what I wish and that

is why I came here. You can make people love or hate. Or . . . or die,' I said.

She threw back her head and laughed loudly. (But she never laughs loudly and why is she laughing at all?)

'So you believe in that tim-tim story about obeah, you hear when you so high? All that foolishness and folly. Too besides, that is not for *béké*. Bad, bad trouble come when *béké* meddle with that.'

'You must,' I said. 'You must.'

'Hush up. Jo-jo my son coming to see me, if he catch you crying, he tell everybody.'

'I will be quiet, I will not cry. But Christophine, if he, my husband, could come to me one night. Once more. I would make him love me.'

'No *doudou*. No.'

'Yes, Christophine.'

'You talk foolishness. Even if I can make him come to your bed, I cannot make him love you. Afterward he hate you.'

'No. And what do I care if he does? He hates me now, I hear him every night walking up and down the veranda. Up and down. When he passes my door he says, "Good-night, Bertha." He never calls me Antoinette now. He has found out it was my mother's name. "I hope you will sleep well, Bertha"— it cannot be worse', I said. 'That one night he came I might sleep afterwards. I sleep so badly now. And I dream.'

'No, I don't meddle with that for you.'

Then I beat my fist on a stone, forcing myself to speak calmly.

'Going away to Martinique or England or anywhere else, that is the lie. He would never give me any money to go away and he would be furious if I asked him. There would be a scandal if I left him and he hates scandal. Even if I got away (and how?) he would force me back. So would Richard. So would everybody else. Running away from him, from this island, is the lie. What reason could I give for going and who would believe me?'

When she bent her head she looked old and I thought, 'Oh Christophine, do not grow old. You are the only friend I have, do not go away from me into being old.'

'Your husband certainly love money,' she said. 'That is no lie. Money have pretty face for everybody, but for that man money pretty like pretty self, he can't see nothing else.'

'Help me then.'

'Listen *doudou ché*. Plenty people fasten bad words on you and on your mother. I know it. I know who is talking and what they say. The man not a bad man, even if he love money, but he hear so many stories he don't know what to believe. That is why he keep away. I put no trust in none of those people round you. Not here, not in Jamaica.'

'Not Aunt Cora?'

'Your aunty old woman now, she turn her face to the wall.'

'*How do you know?*' I said. For that is what happened.

When I passed her room, I heard her quarrelling with Richard and I knew it was about my marriage. 'It's disgraceful,' she said. 'It's shameful. You are handing over everything the child owns to a perfect stranger. Your father would never have allowed it. She should be protected, legally. A settlement can be arranged and it should be arranged. That was his intention.'

'You are talking about an honourable gentleman, not a rascal,' Richard said. 'I am not in a position to make conditions, as you know very well. She is damn lucky to get him, all things considered. Why should I insist on a lawyer's settlement when I trust him? I would trust him with my life,' he went on in an affected voice.

'You are trusting him with her life, not yours,' she said.

He told her for God's sake shut up you old fool and banged the door when he left. So angry that he did not notice me standing in the passage. She was sitting up in bed when I went into her room. 'Halfwit that the boy is, or pretends to be. I do not like what I have seen of this honourable gentleman. Stiff. Hard as a board and stupid as a foot, in my opinion, except where his own interests are concerned.'

She was very pale and shaking all over, so I gave her the smelling salts on the dressing-table. They were in a red glass bottle with a gilt top. She put the bottle to her nose but her hand dropped as though she were too tired to hold it steady. Then she turned away from the window, the sky, the looking-glass, the pretty things on the dressing-table. The red and gilt bottle fell to the floor. She turned her face to the wall. 'The Lord has forsaken us,' she said, and shut her eyes. She did not speak again, and after a while I thought she was asleep. She was too ill to come to my wedding and I went to say good-bye, I was excited and happy thinking now it is my honeymoon. I kissed her and she gave me a little silk bag. 'My rings. Two are valuable. Don't show it to him. Hide it away. Promise me.'

I promised, but when I opened it, one of the rings was plain gold. I thought I might sell another yesterday but who will buy what I have to sell here? . . .

Christophine was saying, 'Your aunty too old and sick, and that Mason boy worthless. Have spunks and do battle for yourself. Speak to your husband calm and cool, tell him about your mother and all what happened at Coulibri and why she get sick and what they do to her. Don't bawl at the man and don't make crazy faces. Don't cry either. Crying no good with him. Speak nice and make him understand.'

'I have tried,' I said, 'but he does not believe me. It is too late for that now' (it is always too late for truth, I thought). 'I will try again if you will do what I ask. Oh Christophine, I am so afraid,' I said, 'I do not know why, but so afraid. All the time. Help me.'

She said something I did not hear. Then she took a sharp stick and drew lines and circles on the earth under the tree, then rubbed them out with her foot.

'If you talk to him first I do what you ask me.'

'Now?'

'Yes,' she said. 'Now look at me. Look in my eyes.'

I was giddy when I stood up, and she went into the house muttering and came out with a cup of coffee.

'Good shot of white rum in that,' she said. 'Your face like dead woman and your eyes red like *soucriant*. Keep yourself quiet — look, Jo-jo coming, he talk to everybody about what he hear. Nothing but leaky calabash that boy.'

When I had drunk the coffee I began to laugh. 'I have been so unhappy for nothing, nothing,' I said.

Her son was carrying a large basket on his head. I watched his strong brown legs swinging along the path so easily. He seemed surprised and inquisitive when he saw me, but he asked politely in patois, was I well, was the master in good health?

'Yes, Jo-jo, thank you, we are both well.'

Christophine helped him with the basket, then she brought out the bottle of white rum and poured out half a tumblerful. He swallowed it quickly. Then she filled the glass with water and he drank that like they do.

She said in English, 'The mistress is going, her horse at the back there. Saddle him up.'

I followed her into the house. There was a wooden table in the outer room, a bench and two broken-down chairs. Her bedroom was large and dark. She still had her bright patchwork counterpane, the palm leaf from Palm Sunday and the prayer for a happy death. But after I noticed a heap of chicken feathers in one corner, I did not look round any more.

'So already you frightened eh?' And when I saw her expression I took my purse from my pocket and threw it on the bed.

'You don't have to give me money. I do this foolishness because you beg me — not for money.'

'Is it foolishness?' I said, whispering and she laughed again, very softly.

'If *béké* say it foolishness, then it foolishness. *Béké* clever like the devil. More clever than God. Ain't so? Now listen and I will tell you what to do.'

When we came out into the sunlight, Jo-jo was holding Preston near a big stone. I stood on it and mounted.

'Good-bye, Christophine; good-bye, Jo-jo.'

'Good-bye, mistress.'

'You will come and see me very soon, Christophine?'

'Yes, I will come.'

I looked back at the end of the path. She was talking to Jo-jo and he seemed curious and amused. Nearby a cock crew and I thought, 'That is for betrayal, but who is the traitor?' She did not want to do this. I forced her with my ugly money. And what does anyone know about traitors, or why Judas did what he did?

I can remember every second of that morning, if I shut my eyes I can see the deep blue colour of the sky and the mango leaves, the pink and red hibiscus, the yellow handkerchief she wore round her head, tied in the Martinique fashion with the sharp points in front, but now I see everything still, fixed for ever like the colours in a stained-glass window. Only the clouds move. It was wrapped in a leaf, what she had given me, and I felt it cool and smooth against my skin.

◆　　◆　　◆

'The mistress pay a visit,' Baptiste told me when he brought my coffee that morning. 'She will come back tonight or tomorrow. She make up her mind in a hurry and she has gone.'

In the afternoon Amélie brought me a second letter.

*Why you don't answer. You don't believe me? Then ask someone else —
everybody in Spanish Town know. Why you think they bring you to this
place? You want me to come to your house and bawl out your business
before everybody? You come to me or I come —*

At this point I stopped reading. The child Hilda came into
the room and I asked her, 'Is Amélie here?'

'Yes, master.'

'Tell her I wish to speak to her.'

'Yes, master.'

She put her hand over her mouth as if to stifle laughter, but
her eyes, which were the blackest I had ever seen, so black that
it was impossible to distinguish the pupils from the iris, were
alarmed and bewildered.

I sat on the veranda with my back to the sea and it was as if
I had done it all my life. I could not imagine different weather
or a different sky. I knew the shape of the mountains as well as
I knew the shape of the two brown jugs filled with white sweet-
scented flowers on the wooden table. I knew that the girl would
be wearing a white dress. Brown and white she would be, her
curls, her white girl's hair she called it, half covered with a red
handkerchief, her feet bare. There would be the sky and the
mountains, the flowers and the girl and the feeling that all this
was a nightmare, the faint consoling hope that I might wake
up.

She leaned lightly against the veranda post, indifferently
graceful, just respectful enough, and waited.

'Was this letter given to you?' I asked.

'No, master. Hilda take it.'

'And is this man who writes a friend of yours?'

'Not my friend,' she said.

'But he knows you — or says he does.'

'Oh yes, I know Daniel.'

'Very well then. Will you tell him that his letters annoy me,
and that he'd better not write again for his own sake. If he
brings a letter give it back to him. Understand?'

'Yes, master. I understand.'

Still leaning against the post she smiled at me, and I felt that
at any moment her smile would become loud laughter. It was
to stop this that I went on. 'Why does he write to me?'

She answered innocently, 'He don't tell you that? He write

you two letters and he don't say why he is writing? If you don't know then I don't know.'

'But you know him?' I said. 'Is his name Cosway?'

'Some people say yes, some people say no. That's what he calls himself.'

She added thoughtfully that Daniel was a very superior man, always reading the Bible and that he lived like white people. I tried to find out what she meant by this, and she explained that he had a house like white people, with one room only for sitting in. That he had two pictures on the wall of his father and his mother.

'White people?'

'Oh no, coloured.'

'But he told me in his first letter that his father was a white man.'

She shrugged her shoulders. 'All that too long ago for me.' It was easy to see her contempt for long ago. 'I tell him what you say, master.' Then she added, 'Why you don't go and see him? It is much better. Daniel is a bad man and he will come here and make trouble for you. It's better he don't come. They say one time he was a preacher in Barbados, he talk like a preacher, and he have a brother in Jamaica in Spanish Town, Mr Alexander. Very wealthy man. He own three rum shops and two dry goods stores.' She flicked a look at me as sharp as a knife. 'I hear one time that Miss Antoinette and his son Mr Sandi get married, but that all foolishness. Miss Antoinette a white girl with a lot of money, she won't marry with a coloured man even though he don't look like a coloured man. You ask Miss Antoinette, she tell you.'

Like Hilda she put her hand over her mouth as though she could not stop herself from laughing and walked away.

Then turned and said in a very low voice, 'I am sorry for you.'

'What did you say?'

'I don't say nothing, master.'

A large table covered with a red fringed cloth made the small room seem hotter; the only window was shut.

'I put your chair near the door,' Daniel said, 'a breeze come in from underneath.' But there was no breeze, not a breath of air, this place was lower down the mountain almost at sea-level.

'When I hear you coming I take a good shot of rum, and then I take a glass of water to cool me down, but it don't cool me down, it run out of my eyes in tears and lamentations. Why don't you give me an answer when I write to you the first time?' He went on talking, his eyes fixed on a framed text hanging on the dirty white wall, 'Vengeance is Mine.'

'You take too long, Lord,' he told it. 'I hurry you up a bit.' Then he wiped his thin yellow face and blew his nose on the corner of the tablecloth.

'They call me Daniel,' he said, still not looking at me, 'but my name is Esau. All I get is curses and get-outs from that damn devil my father. My father old Cosway, with his white marble tablet in the English church at Spanish Town for all to see. It have a crest on it and a motto in Latin and words in big black letters. I never know such lies. I hope that stone tie round his neck and drag him down to Hell in the end. "Pious," they write up. "Beloved by all." Not a word about the people he buy and sell like cattle. "Merciful to the weak," they write up. Mercy! The man have a heart like stone. Sometimes when he get sick of a woman which is quickly, he free her like he free my mother, even he give her a hut and a bit of land for herself (a garden some call that), but it is no mercy, it's for wicked pride he do it. I never put my eyes on a man haughty and proud like that — he walk like he own the earth. "I don't give a damn," he says. Let him wait. . . . I can still see that tablet before my eyes because I go to look at it often. I know by heart all the lies they tell — no one to stand up and say, Why you write lies in the church? . . . I tell you this so you can know what sort of people you mix up with. The heart know its own bitterness but to keep it lock up all the time, that is hard. I remember it like yesterday the morning he put a curse on me. Sixteen years old I was and anxious. I start very early. I walk all the way to Coulibri — five six hours it take. He don't refuse to see me; he receive me very cool and calm and first thing he tell me is I'm always pestering him for money. This because sometimes I ask help to buy a pair of shoes and such. Not to go barefoot like a nigger. Which I am not. He look at me like I was dirt and I get angry too. "I have my rights after all," I tell him and you know what he do? He laugh in my face. When he finished laughing he call me what's-your-name. "I can't remember all their names — it's too much to expect of me," he says, talking to himself. Very old he look in the bright sunshine that morning.

"It's yourself call me Daniel," I tell him. "I'm no slave like my mother was."

'"Your mother was a sly-boots if ever there was one," he says, "and I'm not a fool. However the woman's dead and that's enough. But if there's one drop of my blood in your spindly carcass I'll eat my hat." By this time my own blood at boiling point, I tell you, so I bawl back at him, "Eat it then. Eat it. You haven't much time. Not much time either to kiss and love your new wife. She too young for you." "Great God!" he said and his face go red and then a kind of grey colour. He try to get up but he falls back in his chair. He have a big silver inkstand on his desk, he throw it at my head and he curse me, but I duck and the inkstand hit the door. I have to laugh but I go off quick. He send me some money — not a word, only the money. It's the last time I see him.'

Daniel breathed deeply and wiped his face again and offered me some rum. When I thanked him and shook my head he poured himself half a glassful and swallowed it.

'All that long time ago,' he said.

'Why did you wish to see me, Daniel?'

The last drink seemed to have sobered him. He looked at me directly and spoke more naturally.

'I insist because I have this to say. When you ask if what I tell you is true, you will ask though you don't like me, I see that; but you know well my letter was no lie. Take care who you talk to. Many people like to say things behind your back, to your face they get frightened, or they don't want to mix up. The magistrate now, he know a lot, but his wife very friendly with the Mason family and she stop him if she can. Then there is my half brother Alexander, coloured like me but not unlucky like me, he will want to tell you all sorts of lies. He was the old man's favourite and he prosper right from the start. Yes, Alexander is a rich man now but he keep quiet about it. Because he prosper he is two-faced, he won't speak against white people. There is that woman up at your house, Christophine. She is the worst. She have to leave Jamaica because she go to jail: you know that?'

'Why was she sent to jail? What did she do?'

His eyes slid away from mine. 'I tell you I leave Spanish Town, I don't know all that happen. It's something very bad. She is obeah woman and they catch her. I don't believe in all that devil business but many believe. Christophine is a bad woman and she will lie to you worse than your wife. Your own wife she talks sweet talk and she lies.'

The black and gilt clock on a shelf struck four.

I must go. I must get away from his yellow sweating face and his hateful little room. I sat still, numb, staring at him.

'You like my clock?' said Daniel. 'I work hard to buy it. But it's to please myself. I don't have to please no woman. Buy me this and buy me that — demons incarnate in my opinion. Alexander now, he can't keep away from them, and in the end he marry a very fair-coloured girl, very respectable family. His son Sandi is like a white man, but more handsome than any white man, and received by many white people they say. Your wife know Sandi since long time. Ask her and she tell you. But not everything I think.' He laughed. 'Oh no, not everything. I see them when they think nobody see them. I see her when she . . . You going eh?' He darted to the doorway.

'No you don't go before I tell you the last thing. You want me to shut my mouth about what I know. She start with Sandi. They fool you well about that girl. She look you straight in the eye and talk sweet talk — and it's lies she tell you. Lies. Her mother was so. They say she worse than her mother, and she hardly more than a child. Must be you deaf you don't hear people laughing when you marry her. Don't waste your anger on me, sir. It's not I fool you, it's I wish to open your eyes. . . . A tall fine English gentleman like you, you don't want to touch a little yellow rat like me eh? Besides I understand well. You believe me, but you want to do everything quiet like the English can. All right. But if I keep my mouth shut it seems to me you owe me something. What is five hundred pounds to you? To me it's my life.'

Now disgust was rising in me like sickness. Disgust and rage.

'All right,' he yelled, and moved away from the door. 'Go then . . . get out. Now it's me to say it. Get out. Get out. And if I don't have the money I want you will see what I can do.

'Give my love to your wife — my sister,' he called after me venomously. 'You are not the first to kiss her pretty face. Pretty face, soft skin, pretty colour — not yellow like me. But my sister just the same . . .'

At the end of the path out of sight and sound of the house I stopped. The world was given up to heat and to flies, the light was dazzling after his little dark room. A black and white goat tethered near by was staring at me and for what seemed minutes I stared back into its slanting yellow-green eyes. Then I walked to the tree where I'd left my horse and rode away as quickly as I could.

The telescope was pushed to one side of the table making room for a decanter half full of rum and two glasses on a tarnished silver tray. I listened to the ceaseless night noises outside, and watched the procession of small moths and beetles fly into the candle flames, then poured out a drink of rum and swallowed. At once the night noises drew away, became distant, bearable, even pleasant.

'Will you listen to me for God's sake,' Antoinette said. She had said this before and I had not answered, now I told her, 'Of course. I'd be the brute you doubtless think me if I did not do that.'

'Why do you hate me?' she said.

'I do not hate you, I am most distressed about you, I am distraught,' I said. But this was untrue, I was not distraught, I was calm, it was the first time I had felt calm or self-possessed for many a long day.

She was wearing the white dress I had admired, but it had slipped untidily over one shoulder and seemed too large for her. I watched her holding her left wrist with her right hand, an annoying habit.

'Then why do you never come near me?' she said. 'Or kiss me, or talk to me. Why do you think I can bear it, what reason have you for treating me like that? Have you any reason?'

'Yes,' I said, 'I have a reason,' and added very softly, 'My God.'

'You are always calling on God,' she said. 'Do you believe in God?'

'Of course, of course I believe in the power and wisdom of my creator.'

She raised her eyebrows and the corners of her mouth turned down in a questioning mocking way. For a moment she looked very much like Amélie. Perhaps they are related, I thought. It's possible, it's even probable in this damned place.

'And you,' I said. 'Do you believe in God?'

'It doesn't matter,' she answered calmly, 'what I believe or you believe, because we can do nothing about it, we are like these.' She flicked a dead moth off the table. 'But I asked you a question, you remember. Will you answer that?'

I drank again and my brain was cold and clear.

'Very well, but question for question. Is your mother alive?'

'No, she is dead, she died.'

'When?'

'Not long ago.'

'Then why did you tell me that she died when you were a child?'

'Because they told me to say so and because it is true. She did die when I was a child. There are always two deaths, the real one and the one people know about.'

'Two at least,' I said, 'for the fortunate.' We were silent for a moment, then I went on. 'I had a letter from a man who calls himself Daniel Cosway.'

'He has no right to that name,' she said quickly. 'His real name, if he has one, is Daniel Boyd. He hates all white people, but he hates me the most. He tells lies about us and he is sure that you will believe him and not listen to the other side.'

'Is there another side?' I said.

'There is always the other side, always.'

'After his second letter, which was threatening, I thought it best to go and see him.'

'You saw him,' she said. 'I know what he told you. That my mother was mad and an infamous woman and that my little brother who died was born a cretin, an idiot, and that I am a mad girl too. That is what he told you, isn't it?'

'Yes, that was his story, and is any of it true?' I said, cold and calm.

One of the candles flared up and I saw the hollows under her eyes, her drooping mouth, her thin, strained face.

'We won't talk about it now,' I said. 'Rest tonight.'

'But we must talk about it.' Her voice was high and shrill.

'Only if you promise to be reasonable.'

But this is not the place or the time, I thought, not in this long dark veranda with the candles burning low and the watching, listening night outside. 'Not tonight,' I said again. 'Some other time.'

'I might never be able to tell you in any other place or at any other time. No other time, now. You frightened?' she said, imitating a negro's voice, singing and insolent.

Then I saw her shiver and remembered that she had been wearing a yellow silk shawl. I got up (my brain so clear and cold, my body so weighted and heavy). The shawl was on a chair in the next room, there were candles on the sideboard and I brought them on to the veranda, lit two, and put the shawl around her shoulders. 'But why not tell me tomorrow, in the daylight?'

'You have no right,' she said fiercely. 'You have no right to ask questions about my mother and then refuse to listen to my answer.'

'Of course I will listen, of course we can talk now, if that's what you wish.' But the feeling of something unknown and hostile was very strong. 'I feel very much a stranger here,' I said. 'I feel that this place is my enemy and on your side.'

'You are quite mistaken,' she said. 'It is not for you and not for me. It has nothing to do with either of us. That is why you are afraid of it, because it is something else. I found that out long ago when I was a child. I loved it because I had nothing else to love, but it is as indifferent as this God you call on so often.'

'We can talk here or anywhere else,' I said, 'just as you wish.'

The decanter of rum was nearly empty so I went back into the dining-room, and brought out another bottle of rum. She had eaten nothing and refused wine, now she poured herself a drink, touched it with her lips then put it down again.

'You want to know about my mother, I will tell you about her, the truth, not lies.' Then she was silent for so long that I said gently, 'I know that after your father died, she was very lonely and unhappy.'

'And very poor,' she said. 'Don't forget that. For five years. Isn't it quick to say. And isn't it long to live. And lonely. She was so lonely that she grew away from other people. That happens. It happened to me too but it was easier for me because I hardly remembered anything else. For her it was strange and frightening. And then she was so lovely. I used to think that every time she looked in the glass she must have hoped and pretended. I pretended too. Different things of course. You can pretend for a long time, but one day it all falls away and you are alone. We were alone in the most beautiful place in the world, it is not possible that there can be anywhere else so beautiful as Coulibri. The sea was not far off but we never heard it, we always heard the river. No sea. It was an old-time house and once there was an avenue of royal palms but a lot of them had fallen and others had been cut down and the ones that were left looked lost. Lost trees. Then they poisoned her horse and she could not ride about any more. She worked in the garden even when the sun was very hot and they'd say "You go in now, mistress".'

'And who were they?'

'Christophine was with us, and Godfrey the old gardener stayed, and a boy, I forget his name. Oh yes,' she laughed. 'His name was Disastrous because his godmother thought it such a pretty word. The parson said, "I cannot christen this child Disastrous, he must have another name," so his name was Disastrous Thomas, we called him Sass. It was Christophine who bought our food from the village and persuaded some girls to help her sweep and wash clothes. We would have died, my mother always said, if she had not stayed with us. Many died in those days, both white and black, especially the older people, but no one speaks of those days now. They are forgotten, except the lies. Lies are never forgotten, they go on and they grow.'

'And you,' I said. 'What about you?'

'I was never sad in the morning,' she said, 'and every day was a fresh day for me. I remember the taste of milk and bread and the sound of the grandfather clock ticking slowly and the first time I had my hair tied with string because there was no ribbon left and no money to buy any. All the flowers in the world were in our garden and sometimes when I was thirsty I licked raindrops from the Jasmine leaves after a shower. If I could make you see it, because they destroyed it and it is only here now.' She struck her forehead. 'One of the best things was a curved flight of shallow steps that went down from the *glacis* to the mounting stone, the handrail was ornamented iron.'

'Wrought iron,' I said.

'Yes, wrought iron, and at the end of the last step it was curved like a question mark and when I put my hand on it, the iron was warm and I was comforted.'

'But you said you were always happy.'

'No, I said I was always happy in the morning, not always in the afternoon and never after sunset, for after sunset the house was haunted, some places are. Then there was that day when she saw I was growing up like a white nigger and she was ashamed of me, it was after that day that everything changed. Yes, it was my fault, it was my fault that she started to plan and work in a frenzy, in a fever to change our lives. Then peo-

ple came to see us again and though I still hated them and was
afraid of their cool, teasing eyes, I learned to hide it.'
    'No,' I said.
    'Why no?'
    'You have never learned to hide it,' I said.
    'I learned to try,' said Antoinette. Not very well, I thought.
    'And there was that night when they destroyed it.' She lay
back in the chair, very pale. I poured some rum out and offered
it to her, but she pushed the glass away so roughly that it
spilled over her dress. 'There is nothing left now. They trampled on it. It was a sacred place. It was sacred to the sun!' I
began to wonder how much of all this was true, how much
imagined, distorted. Certainly many of the old estate houses
were burned. You saw ruins all over the place.
    As if she'd guessed my thoughts she went on calmly, 'But I
was telling you about my mother. Afterwards I had fever. I was
at Aunt Cora's house in Spanish Town. I heard screams and
then someone laughing very loud. Next morning Aunt Cora
told me that my mother was ill and had gone to the country.
This did not seem strange to me for she was part of Coulibri,
and if Coulibri had been destroyed and gone out of my life, it
seemed natural that she should go too. I was ill for a long time.
My head was bandaged because someone had thrown a stone
at me. Aunt Cora told me that it was healing up and that it
wouldn't spoil me on my wedding day. But I think it did spoil
me for my wedding day and all the other days and nights.'
    I said, 'Antoinette, your nights are not spoiled, or your days,
put the sad things away. Don't think about them and nothing
will be spoiled, I promise you.'
    But my heart was heavy as lead.
    'Pierre died,' she went on as if she had not heard me, 'and
my mother hated Mr Mason. She would not let him go near her
or touch her. She said she would kill him, she tried to, I think.
So he bought her a house and hired a coloured man and
woman to look after her. For a while he was sad but he often
left Jamaica and spent a lot of time in Trinidad. He almost
forgot her.'
    'And you forgot her too,' I could not help saying.
    'I am not a forgetting person,' said Antoinette. 'But she —
she didn't want me. She pushed me away and cried when I
went to see her. They told me I made her worse. People talked

about her, they would not leave her alone, they would be talking about her and stop if they saw me. One day I made up my mind to go to her, by myself. Before I reached her house I heard her crying. I thought I will kill anyone who is hurting my mother. I dismounted and ran quickly on to the veranda where I could look into the room. I remember the dress she was wearing — an evening dress cut very low, and she was barefooted. There was a fat black man with a glass of rum in his hand. He said, "Drink it and you will forget." She drank it without stopping. He poured her some more and she took the glass and laughed and threw it over her shoulder. It smashed to pieces. "Clean it up," the man said, "or she'll walk in it."

'"If she walk in it a damn good thing," the woman said. "Perhaps she keep quiet then." However she brought a pan and brush and swept up the broken glass. All this I saw. My mother did not look at them. She walked up and down and said, "But this is a very pleasant surprise, Mr Luttrell. Godfrey, take Mr Luttrell's horse." Then she seemed to grow tired and sat down in the rocking-chair. I saw the man lift her up out of the chair and kiss her. I saw his mouth fasten on hers and she went all soft and limp in his arms and he laughed. The woman laughed too, but she was angry. When I saw that I ran away. Christophine was waiting for me when I came back crying. "What you want to go up there for?" she said, and I said, "You shut up devil, damned black devil from Hell." Christophine said, "Aie Aie Aie! Look me trouble, look me cross!"'

After a long time I heard her say as if she were talking to herself, 'I have said all I want to say. I have tried to make you understand. But nothing has changed.' She laughed.

'Don't laugh like that, Bertha.'

'My name is not Bertha; why do you call me Bertha?'

'Because it is a name I'm particularly fond of. I think of you as Bertha.'

'It doesn't matter,' she said.

I said, 'When you went off this morning where did you go?'

'I went to see Christophine,' she said. 'I will tell you anything you wish to know, but in a few words because words are no use, I know that now.'

'Why did you go to see her?'

'I went to ask her to do something for me.'

'And did she do it?'

'Yes.' Another long pause.

'You wanted to ask her advice, was that it?'
She did not answer.
'What did she say?'
'She said that I ought to go away — to leave you.'
'Oh did she?' I said, surprised.
'Yes, that was her advice.'

'I want to do the best for both of us,' I said. 'So much of what you tell me is strange, different from what I was led to expect. Don't you feel that perhaps Christophine is right? That if you went away from this place or I went away — exactly as you wish of course — for a time, it might be the wisest thing we could do?' Then I said sharply, 'Bertha, are you asleep, are you ill, why don't you answer me?' I got up, went over to her chair and took her cold hands in mine. 'We've been sitting here long enough, it is very late.'

'You go,' she said. 'I wish to stay here in the dark . . . where I belong,' she added.

'Oh nonsense,' I said. I put my arms round her to help her up, I kissed her, but she drew away.

'Your mouth is colder than my hands,' she said. I tried to laugh. In the bedroom, I closed the shutters. 'Sleep now, we will talk things over tomorrow.'

'Yes,' she said, 'of course, but will you come in and say goodnight to me?'

'Certainly I will, my dear Bertha.'

'Not Bertha tonight,' she said.

'Of course, on this of all nights, you must be Bertha.'

'As you wish,' she said.

As I stepped into her room I noticed the white powder strewn on the floor. That was the first thing I asked her — about the powder. I asked what it was. She said it was to keep cockroaches away.

'Haven't you noticed that there are no cockroaches in this house and no centipedes. If you knew how horrible these things can be.' She had lit all the candles and the room was full of shadows. There were six on the dressing-table and three on the table near her bed. The light changed her. I had never seen her look so gay or so beautiful. She poured wine into two glasses and handed me one but I swear it was before I drank that I longed to bury my face in her hair as I used to do. I said, 'We are letting ghosts trouble us. Why shouldn't we be happy?' She said, 'Christophine knows about ghosts too, but that is not what she calls them.' She need not have done what she did to me. I will always swear that, she need not have done it. When she handed me the glass she was smiling. I remember saying in a voice that was not like my own that it was too light. I remember putting out the candles on the table near the bed and that is all I remember. All I will remember of the night.

I woke in the dark after dreaming that I was buried alive, and when I was awake the feeling of suffocation persisted. Something was lying across my mouth; hair with a sweet heavy smell. I threw it off but still I could not breathe. I shut my eyes and lay without moving for a few seconds. When I opened them I saw the candles burnt down on that abominable dressing-table, then I knew where I was. The door on to the veranda was open and the breeze was so cold that I knew it must be very early in the morning, before dawn. I was cold too, deathly cold and sick and in pain. I got out of bed without looking at her, staggered into my dressing-room and saw myself in the glass. I turned away at once. I could not vomit. I only retched painfully.

I thought, I have been poisoned. But it was a dull thought, like a child spelling out the letters of a word which he cannot read, and which if he could would have no meaning or context. I was too giddy to stand and fell backwards on to the bed, looking at the blanket which was of a peculiar shade of yellow. After looking at it for some time I was able to go over to the window and vomit. It seemed like hours before this stopped. I would lean up against the wall and wipe my face, then the retching and sickness would start again. When it was over I lay on the bed too weak to move.

I have never made a greater effort in my life than I made then. I longed to lie there and sleep but forced myself up. I was weak and giddy but no longer sick or in pain. I put on my dressing-gown and splashed water on my face, then I opened the door into her room.

The cold light was on her and I looked at the sad droop of her lips, the frown between her thick eyebrows, deep as if it had been cut with a knife. As I looked she moved and flung her arm out. I thought coldly, yes, very beautiful, the thin wrist, the sweet swell of the forearm, the rounded elbow, the curve of her shoulder into her upper arm. All present, all correct. As I watched, hating, her face grew smooth and very young again, she even seemed to smile. A trick of the light perhaps. What else?

She may wake at any moment, I told myself. I must be quick. Her torn shift was on the floor, I drew the sheet over her gently as if I covered a dead girl. One of the glasses was empty, she had drained hers. There was some wine left in the other which was on the dressing-table. I dipped my finger into it and tasted it. It was bitter. I didn't look at her again, but holding the glass went on to the veranda. Hilda was there with a broom in her hand. I put my finger to my lips and she looked at me with huge eyes, then imitated me, putting her own finger to her lips.

As soon as I had dressed and got out of the house I began to run.

I do not remember that day clearly, where I ran or how I fell or wept or lay exhausted. But I found myself at last near the ruined house and the wild orange tree. Here with my head in my arms I must have slept and when I woke it was getting late and the wind was chilly. I got up and found my way back to the path which led to the house. I knew how to avoid every creeper, and I never stumbled once. I went to my dressing-room and if I passed anyone I did not see them and if they spoke I did not hear them.

There was a tray on the table with a jug of water, a glass and some brown fish cakes. I drank almost all the water, for I was very thirsty, but I did not touch the food. I sat on the bed waiting, for I knew Amélie would come, and I knew what she would say: 'I am sorry for you.'

She came soundlessly on bare feet. 'I get you something to eat,' she said. She brought cold chicken, bread, fruit and a bottle of wine, and I drank a glass without speaking, then another. She cut some of the food up and sat beside me and fed me as if I were a child. Her arm behind my head was warm but the outside when I touched it was cool, almost cold. I looked into her lovely meaningless face, sat up and pushed the plate away. Then she said, 'I am sorry for you.'

'You've told me so before, Amélie. Is that the only song you know?'

There was a spark of gaiety in her eyes, but when I laughed she put her hand over my mouth apprehensively. I pulled her down beside me and we were both laughing. That is what I remember most about that encounter. She was so gay, so natural and something of this gaiety she must have given to me, for I had not one moment of remorse. Nor was I anxious to know what was happening behind the thin partition which divided us from my wife's bedroom.

In the morning, of course, I felt differently.

Another complication. Impossible. And her skin was darker, her lips thicker than I had thought.

She was sleeping very soundly and quietly but there was awareness in her eyes when she opened them, and after a moment suppressed laughter. I felt satisfied and peaceful, but not gay as she did, no, by God, not gay. I had no wish to touch her and she knew it, for she got up at once and began to dress.

'A very graceful dress,' I said and she showed me the many ways it could be worn, trailing on the floor, lifted to show a lace petticoat, or hitched up far above the knee.

I told her that I was leaving the island soon but that before I left I wanted to give her a present. It was a large present but she took it with no thanks and no expression on her face. When I asked her what she meant to do she said, 'It's long time I know what I want to do and I know I don't get it here.'

'You are beautiful enough to get anything you want,' I said.

'Yes,' she agreed simply. 'But not here.'

She wanted, it seemed, to join her sister who was a dressmaker in Demerara, but she would not stay in Demerara, she said. She wanted to go to Rio. There were rich men in Rio.

'And when will you start all this?' I said, amused.

'I start now.' She would catch one of the fishing boats at Massacre and get into town.

I laughed and teased her. She was running away from the old woman Christophine, I said.

She was unsmiling when she answered, 'I have malice to no one but I don't stay here.'

I asked her how she would get to Massacre. 'I don't want no horse or mule,' she said. 'My legs strong enough to carry me.'

As she was going I could not resist saying, half longing, half triumphant, 'Well, Amélie, are you still sorry for me?'

'Yes,' she said, 'I am sorry for you. But I find it in my heart to be sorry for her too.'

She shut the door gently. I lay and listened for the sound I knew I should hear, the horse's hoofs as my wife left the house.

♦

I turned over and slept till Baptiste woke me with coffee. His face was gloomy.

'The cook is leaving,' he announced.

'Why?'

He shrugged his shoulders and spread his hands open.

I got up, looked out of the window and saw her stride out of the kitchen, a strapping woman. She couldn't speak English, or said she couldn't. I forgot this when I said, 'I must talk to her. What is the huge bundle on her head?'

'Her mattress,' said Baptiste. 'She will come back for the rest. No good to talk to her. She won't stay in this house.'

I laughed.

'Are you leaving too?'

'No,' said Baptiste. 'I am overseer here.'

I noticed that he did not call me 'sir' or 'master'.

'And the little girl, Hilda?'

'Hilda will do as I tell her. Hilda will stay.'

'Capital,' I said. 'Then why are you looking so anxious? Your mistress will be back soon.'

He shrugged again and muttered, but whether he was talking about my morals or the extra work he would have to do I couldn't tell, for he muttered in patois.

I told him to sling one of the veranda hammocks under the cedar trees and there I spent the rest of that day.

Baptiste provided meals, but he seldom smiled and never spoke except to answer a question. My wife did not return. Yet I was not lonely or unhappy. Sun, sleep and the cool water of the river were enough. I wrote a cautious letter to Mr Fraser on the third day.

I told him that I was considering a book about obeah and had remembered his story of the case he had come across. Had he any idea of the whereabouts of the woman now? Was she still in Jamaica?

This letter was sent down by the twice weekly messenger and he must have answered at once for I had his reply in a few days:

I have often thought of your wife and yourself. And was on the point of writing to you. Indeed I have not forgotten the case. The woman in question was called Josephine or Christophine Dubois, some such name and she had been one of the Cosway servants. After she came out of jail she

disappeared, but it was common knowledge that old Mr Mason be-
friended her. I heard that she owned or was given a small house and a
piece of land near Granbois. She is intelligent in her way and can express
herself well, but I did not like the look of her at all, and consider her a
most dangerous person. My wife insisted that she had gone back to Mar-
tinique her native island, and was very upset that I had mentioned the
matter even in such a roundabout fashion. I happen to know now that she
has not returned to Martinique, so I have written very discreetly to Hill,
the white inspector of police in your town. If she lives near you and gets
up to any of her nonsense let him know at once. He'll send a couple of
policemen up to your place and she won't get off lightly this time. I'll
make sure of that. . . .

So much for you, Josephine or Christophine, I thought. So
much for you, Pheena.

It was that half-hour after the sunset, the blue half-hour I
called it to myself. The wind drops, the light is very beautiful,
the mountains sharp, every leaf on every tree is clear and dis-
tinct. I was sitting in the hammock, watching, when Antoinette
rode up. She passed me without looking at me, dismounted and
went into the house. I heard her bedroom door slam and her
handbell ring violently. Baptiste came running along the veranda. I got out of the hammock and went to the sitting-room.
He had opened the chest and taken out a bottle of rum. Some of
this he poured into a decanter which he put on a tray with a
glass.

'Who is that for?' I said. He didn't answer.

'No road?' I said and laughed.

'I don't want to know nothing about all this,' he said.

'Baptiste!' Antoinette called in a high voice.

'Yes, mistress.' He looked straight at me and carried the tray
out.

As for the old woman, I saw her shadow before I saw her.
She too passed me without turning her head. Nor did she go
into Antoinette's room or look towards it. She walked along the
veranda, down the steps the other side, and went into the
kitchen. In that short time the dark had come and Hilda came
in to light the candles. When I spoke to her she gave me an
alarmed look and ran away. I opened the chest and looked at
the rows of bottles inside. Here was the rum that kills you in a
hundred years, the brandy, the red and white wine smuggled, I

suppose, from St Pierre, Martinique — the Paris of the West Indies. It was rum I chose to drink. Yes, it was mild in the mouth, I waited a second for the explosion of heat and light in my chest, the strength and warmth running through my body. Then I tried the door into Antoinette's room. It yielded very slightly. She must have pushed some piece of furniture against it, that round table probably. I pushed again and it opened enough for me to see her. She was lying on the bed on her back. Her eyes were closed and she breathed heavily. She had pulled the sheet up to her chin. On a chair beside the bed there was the empty decanter, a glass with some rum left in it and a small brass handbell.

I shut the door and sat down with my elbows on the table for I thought I knew what would happen and what I must do. I found the room oppressively hot, so I blew out most of the candles and waited in the half darkness. Then I went on to the veranda to watch the door of the kitchen where a light was showing.

Soon the little girl came out followed by Baptiste. At the same time the handbell in the bedroom rang. They both went into the sitting-room and I followed. Hilda lit all the candles with a frightened roll of her eyes in my direction. The handbell went on ringing.

'Mix me a good strong one, Baptiste. Just what I feel like.'

He took a step away from me and said, 'Miss Antoinette — '

'Baptiste, where are you?' Antoinette called. 'Why don't you come?'

'I come as quick as I can,' Baptiste said. But as he reached for the bottle I took it away from him.

Hilda ran out of the room. Baptiste and I stared at each other. I thought that his large protuberant eyes and his expression of utter bewilderment were comical.

Antoinette shrieked from the bedroom, 'Baptiste! Christophine! Pheena, Pheena!'

'*Que komesse!*' Baptiste said. 'I get Christophine.'

He ran out almost as fast as the little girl had done.

The door to Antoinette's room opened. When I saw her I was too shocked to speak. Her hair hung uncombed and dull into her eyes which were inflamed and staring, her face was very flushed and looked swollen. Her feet were bare. However when she spoke her voice was low, almost inaudible.

'I rang the bell because I was thirsty. Didn't anybody hear?'

Before I could stop her she darted to the table and seized the bottle of rum.

'Don't drink any more,' I said.

'And what right have you to tell me what I'm to do? Christophine!' she called again, but her voice broke.

'Christophine is an evil old woman and you know it as well as I do,' I said. 'She won't stay here very much longer.'

'She won't stay here very much longer,' she mimicked me, 'and nor will you, nor will you. I thought you liked the black people so much,' she said, still in that mincing voice, 'but that's just a lie like everything else. You like the light brown girls better, don't you? You abused the planters and made up stories about them, but you do the same thing. You send the girl away quicker, and with no money or less money, and that's all the difference.'

'Slavery was not a matter of liking or disliking,' I said, trying to speak calmly. 'It was a question of justice.'

'Justice,' she said. 'I've heard that word. It's a cold word. I tried it out,' she said, still speaking in a low voice. 'I wrote it down. I wrote it down several times and always it looked like a damn cold lie to me. There is no justice.' She drank some more rum and went on, 'My mother whom you all talk about, what justice did she have? My mother sitting in the rocking-chair speaking about dead horses and dead grooms and a black devil kissing her sad mouth. Like you kissed mine,' she said.

The room was now unbearably hot. 'I'll open the window and let a little air in,' I said.

'It will let the night in too,' she said, 'and the moon and the scent of those flowers you dislike so much.'

When I turned from the window she was drinking again.

'Bertha,' I said.

'Bertha is not my name. You are trying to make me into someone else, calling me by another name. I know, that's obeah too.'

Tears streamed from her eyes.

'If my father, my real father, was alive you wouldn't come back here in a hurry after he'd finished with you. If he was alive. Do you know what you've done to me? It's not the girl, not the girl. But I loved this place and you have made it into a place I hate. I used to think that if everything else went out of my life I would still have this, and now you have spoilt it. It's just somewhere else where I have been unhappy, and all the other things are nothing to what has happened here. I hate it now like I hate you and before I die I will show you how much I hate you.'

Then to my astonishment she stopped crying and said, 'Is she so much prettier than I am? Don't you love me at all?'

'No, I do not,' I said (at the same time remembering Amélie saying, 'Do you like my hair? Isn't it prettier than hers?'). 'Not at this moment,' I said.

She laughed at that. A crazy laugh.

'You see. That's how you are. A stone. But it serves me right because didn't Aunt Cora say to me don't marry him. Not if he were stuffed with diamonds. And a lot of other things she told me. Are you talking about England, I said, and what about Grandpappy passing his glass over the water decanter and the tears running down his face for all the friends dead and gone, whom he would never see again. That was nothing to do with England that I ever heard, she said. On the contrary:

> *A Benky foot and a Benky leg*
> *For Charlie over the water.*
> *Charlie, Charlie,'*

she sang in a hoarse voice. And lifted the bottle to drink again.

I said, and my voice was not very calm, 'No.'

I managed to hold her wrist with one hand and the rum with the other, but when I felt her teeth in my arm I dropped the bottle. The smell filled the room. But I was angry now and she saw it. She smashed another bottle against the wall and stood with the broken glass in her hand and murder in her eyes.

'Just you touch me once. You'll soon see if I'm a dam' coward like you are.'

Then she cursed me comprehensively, my eyes, my mouth, every member of my body, and it was like a dream in the large unfurnished room with the candles flickering and this red-eyed wild-haired stranger who was my wife shouting obscenities at me. It was at this nightmare moment that I heard Christophine's calm voice.

'You hush up and keep yourself quiet. And don't cry. Crying's no good with him. I told you before. Crying's no good.'

Antoinette collapsed on the sofa and went on sobbing. Christophine looked at me and her small eyes were very sad. 'Why you do that eh? Why you don't take that worthless good-for-nothing girl somewhere else? But she love money like you love money — must be why you come together. Like goes to like.'

I couldn't bear any more and again I went out of the room and sat on the veranda.

My arm was bleeding and painful and I wrapped my hand-kerchief round it, but it seemed to me that everything round me was hostile. The telescope drew away and said don't touch me. The trees were threatening and the shadows of the trees moving slowly over the floor menaced me. That green menace. I had felt it ever since I saw this place. There was nothing I knew, nothing to comfort me.

I listened. Christophine was talking softly. My wife was crying. Then a door shut. They had gone into the bedroom. Some-one was singing '*Ma belle ka di*', or was it the song about one day and a thousand years. But whatever they were singing or saying was dangerous. I must protect myself. I went softly along the dark veranda. I could see Antoinette stretched on the bed quite still. Like a doll. Even when she threatened me with the bottle she had a marionette quality. '*Ti moun*,' I heard and '*Doudou ché*,' and the end of a head handkerchief made a finger on the wall. '*Do do l'enfant do*.' Listening, I began to feel sleepy and cold.

I stumbled back into the big candlelit room which still smelt strongly of rum. In spite of this I opened the chest and got out another bottle. That was what I was thinking when Christo-phine came in. I was thinking of a last strong drink in my room, fastening both doors, and sleeping.

'I hope you satisfy, I hope you well satisfy,' she said, 'and no good to start your lies with me. I know what you do with that girl as well as you know. Better. Don't think I frightened of you either.'

'So she ran off to tell you I'd ill-treated her, did she? I ought to have guessed that.'

'She don't tell me a thing,' said Christophine. 'Not one single thing. Always the same. Nobody is to have any pride but you. She have more pride than you and she say nothing. I see her standing at my door with that look on her face and I know something bad happen to her. I know I must act quick and I act.'

'You seem to have acted, certainly. And what did you do before you brought her back in her present condition?'

'What did I do! Look! don't you provoke me more than I provoke already. Better not I tell you. you want to know what I do? I say *doudou*, if you have trouble you are right to come to me. And I kiss her. It's when I kiss her she cry — not before. It's long time she hold it back, I think. So I let her cry. That is the first thing. Let them cry — it eases the heart. When she can't cry no more I give her a cup of milk — it's lucky I have some. She won't eat, she won't talk. So I say, "Lie down on the bed *doudou* and try to sleep, for me I can sleep on the floor, don't matter for me." She isn't going to sleep natural that's certain, but I can make her sleep. That's what I do. As for what you do — you pay for it one day.

'When they get like that,' she said, 'first they must cry, then they must sleep. Don't talk to me about doctor, I know more than any doctor. I undress Antoinette so she can sleep cool and easy; it's then I see you very rough with her eh?'

At this point she laughed — a hearty merry laugh. 'All that is a little thing — it's nothing. If you see what I see in this place with the machete bright and shining in the corner, you don't have such a long face for such a little thing. You make her love you more if that's what you want. It's not for that she have the look of death on her face. Oh no.

'One night,' she went on, 'I hold on a woman's nose because her husband nearly chop it off with his machete. I hold it on, I send a boy running for the doctor and the doctor come galloping at dead of night to sew up the woman. When he finish he tell me, "Christophine you have a great presence of mind." That's what he tell me. By this time the man crying like a baby. He says, "Doctor I don't mean it. It just happened." "I know, Rupert," the doctor says, "but it mustn't happen again. Why don't you keep the damn machete in the other room?" he says. They have two small rooms only so I say, "No, doctor — it much worse near the bed. They chop each other up in no time at all." The doctor he laugh and laugh. Oh he was a good doctor. When he finished with that woman nose I won't say it look like before but I will say it don't notice much. Rupert that man's name was. Plenty Ruperts here you notice? One is Prince Rupert, and one who makes songs is Rupert the Rine. You see him? He sells his songs down by the bridge there in town. It's in the town I live when I first leave Jamaica. It's a pretty name eh — Rupert — but where they get it from? I think it's from old time they get it.

'That doctor an old-time doctor. These new ones I don't like them. First word in their mouth is police. Police — that's something I don't like.'

'I'm sure you don't,' I said. 'But you haven't told me yet what happened when my wife was with you. Or exactly what you did?'

'*Your wife!*' she said. 'You make me laugh. I don't know all you did but I know some. Everybody know that you marry her for her money and you take it all. And then you want to break her up, because you jealous of her. She is more better than you, she have better blood in her and she don't care for money — it's nothing for her. Oh I see that first time I look at you. You young but already you hard. You fool the girl. You make her think you can't see the sun for looking at her.'

It was like that, I thought. It was like that. But better to say nothing. Then surely they'll both go and it will be my turn to sleep — a long deep sleep, mine will be, and very far away.

'And then,' she went on in her judge's voice, 'you make love to her till she drunk with it, no rum could make her drunk like that, till she can't do without it. It's *she* can't see the sun any more. Only you she see. But all you want is to break her up.'

(Not the way you mean, I thought)

'But she hold out eh? She hold out.'

(Yes, she held out. A pity)

'So you pretend to believe all the lies that damn bastard tell you.'

(That damn bastard tell you)

Now every word she said was echoed, echoed loudly in my head.

'So that you can leave her alone.'

(Leave her alone)

'Not telling her why.'

(Why?)

'No more love, eh?'

(No more love)

'And that,' I said coldly, 'is where you took charge, isn't it? You tried to poison me.'

'Poison you? But look me trouble, the man crazy! She come to me and ask me for something to make you love her again and I tell her no I don't meddle in that for *béké*. I tell her it's foolishness.'

(Foolishness foolishness)

'And even if it's no foolishness, it's too strong for *béké*.'
(Too strong for béké. *Too strong)*
'But she cry and she beg me.'
(She cry and she beg me)
'So I give her something for love.'
(For love)
'But you don't love. All you want is to break her up. And it help you break her up.'
(Break her up)
'She tell me in the middle of all this you start calling her names. Marionette. Some word so.'
'Yes, I remember, I did.'
(Marionette, Antoinette, Marionetta, Antoinetta)
'That word mean doll, eh? Because she don't speak. You want to force her to cry and to speak.'
(Force her to cry and to speak)
'But she won't. So you think up something else. You bring that worthless girl to play with next door and you talk and laugh and love so that she hear everything. You meant her to hear.'
Yes, that didn't just happen. I meant it.
(I lay awake all night long after they were asleep, and as soon as it was light I got up and dressed and saddled Preston. And I came to you. Oh Christophine. O Pheena, Pheena, help me.)
'You haven't yet told me exactly what you did with my — with Antoinette.'
'Yes I tell you. I make her sleep.'
'What? All the time?'
'No, no. I wake her up to sit in the sun, bathe in the cool river. Even if she dropping with sleep. I make good strong soup. I give her milk if I have it, fruit I pick from my own trees. If she don't want to eat I say, "Eat it up for my sake, *doudou*." And she eat it up, then she sleep again.'
'And why did you do all this?'
There was a long silence. Then she said, 'It's better she sleep. She must sleep while I work for her — to make her well again. But I don't speak of all that to you.'
'Unfortunately your cure was not successful. You didn't make her well. You made her worse.'
'Yes I succeed,' she said angrily. 'I succeed. But I get frightened that she sleep too much, too long. She is not *béké* like you, but she is *béké*, and not like us either. There are mornings when

she can't wake, or when she wake it's as if she still sleeping. I don't want to give her any more of — of what I give. So,' she went on after another pause, 'I let her have rum instead. I know that won't hurt her. Not much. As soon as she has the rum she starts raving that she must go back to you and I can't quiet her. She says she'll go alone if I don't come but she beg me to come. And I hear well when you tell her that you don't love her — quite calm and cool you tell her so, and undo all the good I do.'

'The good you did! I'm very weary of your nonsense, Christophine. You seem to have made her dead drunk on bad rum and she's a wreck. I scarcely recognized her. Why you did it I can't say — hatred of me I suppose. And as you heard so much perhaps you were listening to all she admitted — boasted about, and to the vile names she called me. Your *doudou* certainly knows some filthy language.'

'I tell you no. I tell you it's nothing. You make her so unhappy she don't know what she is saying. Her father old Mister Cosway swear like half past midnight — she pick it up from him. And once, when she was little she run away to be with the fishermen and the sailors on the bayside. Those men!' She raised her eyes to the ceiling. 'Never would you think they was once innocent babies. She come back copying them. She don't understand what she says.'

'I think she understood every word, and meant what she said too. But you are right, Christophine — it was all a very little thing. It was nothing. No machete here, so no machete damage. No damage at all by this time. I'm sure you took care of that however drunk you made her.'

'You are a damn hard man for a young man.'

'So you say, so you say.'

'I tell her so. I warn her. I say this is not a man who will help you when he sees you break up. Only the best can do that. The best — and sometimes the worst.'

'But you think I'm one of the worst, surely?'

'No,' she said indifferently, 'to me you are not the best, not the worst. You are —' she shrugged '— you will not help her. I tell her so.'

Nearly all the candles were out. She didn't light fresh ones — nor did I. We sat in the dim light. I should stop this useless conversation, I thought, but could only listen, hypnotized, to her dark voice coming from the darkness.

'I know that girl. She will never ask you for love again, she will die first. But I Christophine I beg you. She love you so much. She thirsty for you. Wait, and perhaps you can love her again. A little, like she say. A little. Like you can love.'

I shook my head and went on shaking it mechanically.

'It's lies all that yellow bastard tell you. He is no Cosway either. His mother was a no-good woman and she try to fool the old man but the old man isn't fooled. "One more or less" he says, and laughs. He was wrong. More he do for those people, more they hate him. The hate in that man Daniel — he can't rest with it. If I know you coming here I stop you. But you marry quick, you leave Jamaica quick. No time.'

'She told me that all he said was true. She wasn't lying then.'

'Because you hurt her she want to hurt you back, that's why.'

'And that her mother was mad. Another lie?'

Christophine did not answer me at once. When she did her voice was not so calm.

'They drive her to it. When she lose her son she lose herself for a while and they shut her away. They tell her she is mad, they act like she is mad. Question, question. But no kind word, no friends, and her husban' he go off, he leave her. They won't let me see her. I try, but no. They won't let Antoinette see her. In the end — mad I don't know — she give up, she care for nothing. That man who is in charge of her he take her whenever he want and his woman talk. That man, and others. Then they have her. Ah there is no God.'

'Only your spirits,' I reminded her.

'Only my spirits,' she said steadily. 'In your Bible it say God is a spirit — it don't say no others. Not at all. It grieve me what happen to her mother, and I can't see it happen again. You call her a doll? She don't satisfy you? Try her once more, I think she satisfy you now. If you forsake her they will tear her in pieces — like they did her mother.'

'I will not forsake her,' I said wearily. 'I will do all I can for her.'

'You will love her like you did before?'

(Give my sister your wife a kiss from me. Love her as I did — oh yes I did. How can I promise that?) I said nothing.

'It's she won't be satisfy. She is Creole girl, and she have the sun in her. Tell the truth now. She don't come to your house in this place England they tell me about, she don't come to your beautiful house to beg you to marry with her. No, it's you come all the long way to her house — it's you beg her to marry. And she love you and she give you all she have. Now you say you don't love her and you break her up. What you do with her money, eh?' Her voice was still quiet but with a hiss in it when she said 'money.' I thought, of course, that is what all the rigmarole is about. I no longer felt dazed, tired, half hypnotized, but alert and wary, ready to defend myself.

Why, she wanted to know, could I not return half of Antoinette's dowry and leave the island — 'leave the West Indies if you don't want her no more.'

I asked the exact sum she had in mind, but she was vague about that.

'You fix it up with lawyers and all those things.'

'And what will happen to her then?'

She, Christophine, would take good care of Antoinette (and the money of course).

'You will both stay here?' I hoped that my voice was as smooth as hers.

No, they would go to Martinique. Then to other places.

'I like to see the world before I die.'

Perhaps because I was so quiet and composed she added maliciously, 'She marry with someone else. She forget about you and live happy.'

A pang of rage and jealousy shot through me then. Oh no, she won't forget. I laughed.

'You laugh at me? Why you laugh at me?'

'Of course I laugh at you — you ridiculous old woman. I don't mean to discuss my affairs with you any longer. Or your mistress. I've listened to all you had to say and I don't believe you. Now, say good-bye to Antoinette, then go. You are to blame for all that has happened here, so don't come back.'

She drew herself up tall and straight and put her hands on her hips. 'Who you to tell me to go? This house belong to Miss Antoinette's mother, now it belong to her. Who you to tell me to go?'

'I assure you that it belongs to me now. You'll go, or I'll get the men to put you out.'

'You think the men here touch me? They not damn fool like you to put their hand on me.'

'Then I will have the police up, I warn you. There must be some law and order even in this God-forsaken island.'

'No police here,' she said. 'No chain gang, no tread machine, no dark jail either. This is free country and I am free woman.'

'Christophine,' I said, 'you lived in Jamaica for years, and you know Mr Fraser, the Spanish Town magistrate, well. I wrote to him about you. Would you like to hear what he answered?' She stared at me. I read the end of Fraser's letter aloud: *'I have written very discreetly to Hill, the white inspector of police in your town. If she lives near you and gets up to any of her nonsense let him know at once. He'll send a couple of policemen up to your place and she won't get off lightly this time.* . . . . You gave your mistress the poison that she put into my wine?'

'I tell you already — you talk foolishness.'

'We'll see about that — I kept some of that wine.'

'I tell her so,' she said. 'Always it don't work for *béké*. Always it bring trouble . . . So you send me away and you keep all her money. And what you do with her?'

'I don't see why I should tell you my plans. I mean to go back to Jamaica to consult the Spanish Town doctors and her brother. I'll follow their advice. That is all I mean to do. She is not well.'

'Her brother!' She spat on the floor. 'Richard Mason is no brother to her. You think you fool me? You want her money but you don't want her. It is in your mind to pretend she is mad. I know it. The doctors say what you tell them to say. That man Richard he say what you want him to say — glad and willing too, I know. She will be like her mother. You do that for money? But you wicked like Satan self!'

I said loudly and wildly, 'And do you think that I wanted all this? I would give my life to undo it. I would give my eyes never to have seen this abominable place.'

She laughed. 'And that's the first damn word of truth you speak. You choose what you give, eh? Then you choose. You meddle in something and perhaps you don't know what it is.' She began to mutter to herself. Not in patois. I knew the sound of patois now.

She's as mad as the other, I thought, and turned to the window.

The servants were standing in a group under the clove tree. Baptiste, the boy who helped with the horses and the little girl Hilda.

Christophine was right. They didn't intend to get mixed up in this business.

When I looked at her there was a mask on her face and her eyes were undaunted. She was a fighter, I had to admit. Against my will I repeated, 'Do you wish to say good-bye to Antoinette?'

'I give her something to sleep — nothing to hurt her. I don't wake her up to no misery. I leave that for you.'

'You can write to her,' I said stiffly.

'Read and write I don't know. Other things I know.'

She walked away without looking back.

All wish to sleep had left me. I walked up and down the room and felt the blood tingle in my finger-tips. It ran up my arms and reached my heart, which began to beat very fast. I spoke aloud as I walked. I spoke the letter I meant to write.

'I know now that you planned this because you wanted to be rid of me. You had no love at all for me. Nor had my brother. Your plan succeeded because I was young, conceited, foolish, trusting. Above all because I was young. You were able to do this to me . . .'

But I am not young now, I thought, stopped pacing and drank. Indeed this rum is mild as mother's milk or father's blessing.

I could imagine his expression if I sent that letter and he read it.

'Dear Father,' I wrote. 'We are leaving this island for Jamaica very shortly. Unforeseen circumstances, at least unforeseen by me, have forced me to make this decision. I am certain that you know or can guess what has happened, and I am certain you will believe that the less you talk to anyone about my affairs, especially my marriage, the better. This is in your interest as well as mine. You will hear from me again. Soon I hope.'

Then I wrote to the firm of lawyers I had dealt with in Spanish Town. I told them that I wished to rent a furnished house not too near the town, commodious enough to allow for two separate suites of rooms. I also told them to engage a staff of servants whom I was prepared to pay very liberally — so long as they keep their mouths shut, I thought — provided that they are discreet, I wrote. My wife and myself would be in Jamaica in about a week and expected to find everything ready.

All the time I was writing this letter a cock crowed persistently outside. I took the first book I could lay hands on and threw it at him, but he stalked a few yards away and started again.

Baptiste appeared, looking towards Antoinette's silent room.

'Have you got much more of this famous rum?'

'Plenty rum,' he said.

'Is it really a hundred years old?'

He nodded indifferently. A hundred years, a thousand all the same to *le bon Dieu* and Baptiste too.

'What's that damn cock crowing about?'

'Crowing for change of weather.'

Because his eyes were fixed on the bedroom I shouted at him, 'Asleep, *dormi, dormi.*'

He shook his head and went away.

He scowled at me then, I thought. I scowled too as I re-read the letter I had written to the lawyers. However much I paid Jamaican servants I would never buy discretion. I'd be gossiped about, sung about (but they make up songs about everything, everybody. You should hear the one about the Governor's wife). Wherever I went I would be talked about. I drank some more rum and, drinking, I drew a house surrounded by trees. A large house. I divided the third floor into rooms and in one room I drew a standing woman — a child's scribble, a dot for a head, a larger one for the body, a triangle for a skirt, slanting lines for arms and feet. But it was an English house.

English trees. I wondered if I ever should see England again.

. . .

Under the oleanders . . . I watched the hidden mountains and the mists drawn over their faces. It's cool today; cool, calm and cloudy as an English summer. But a lovely place in any weather, however far I travel I'll never see a lovelier.

The hurricane months are not so far away, I thought, and saw that tree strike its roots deeper, making ready to fight the wind. Useless. If and when it comes they'll all go. Some of the royal palms stand (she told me). Stripped of their branches, like tall brown pillars, still they stood — defiant. Not for nothing are they called royal. The bamboos take an easier way, they bend to the earth and lie there, creaking, groaning, crying for mercy. The contemptuous wind passes, not caring for these abject things. *(Let them live.)* Howling, shrieking, laughing the wild blast passes.

But all that's some months away. It's an English summer now, so cool, so grey. Yet I think of my revenge and hurricanes. Words rush through my head (deeds too). Words. Pity is one of them. It gives me no rest.

Pity like a naked new-born babe striding the blast.

I read that long ago when I was young — I hate poets now and poetry. As I hate music which I loved once. Sing your songs, Rupert the Rine, but I'll not listen, though they tell me you've a sweet voice. . . .

Pity. Is there none for me? Tied to a lunatic for life — a drunken lying lunatic — gone her mother's way.

'She love you so much. She thirsty for you. Love her a little like she say. It's all that you can love — a little.'

Sneer to the last, Devil. Do you think that I don't know? She thirsts for *anyone* — not for me . . .

She'll loosen her black hair, and laugh and coax and flatter (a mad girl. She'll not care who she's loving). She'll moan and cry and give herself as no sane woman would — or could. Or *could*. Then lie so still, still as this cloudy day. A lunatic who always knows the time. But never does.

Till she's drunk so deep, played her games so often that the lowest shrug and jeer at her. And I'm to know it — I? No, I've a trick worth two of that.

'She love you so much, so much. Try her once more.'

I tell you she loves no one, anyone. I could not touch her. Excepting as the hurricane will touch that tree — and break it. You say I did? No. That was love's fierce play. Now I'll do it.

She'll not laugh in the sun again. She'll not dress up and smile at herself in that damnable looking-glass. So pleased, so satisfied.

Vain, silly creature. Made for loving? Yes, but she'll have no lover, for I don't want her and she'll see no other.

The tree shivers. Shivers and gathers all its strength. And waits.

(There is a cool wind blowing now — a cold wind. Does it carry the babe born to stride the blast of hurricanes?)

She said she loved this place. This is the last she'll see of it. I'll watch for one tear, one human tear. Not that blank hating moonstruck face. I'll listen. . . . If she says good-bye perhaps adieu. *Adieu* — like those old-time songs she sang. Always *adieu* (and all songs say it). If she too says it, or weeps, I'll take her in my arms, my lunatic. She's mad but *mine, mine.* What will I care for gods or devils or for Fate itself. If she smiles or weeps or both. *For me.*

Antoinetta — I can be gentle too. Hide your face. Hide yourself but in my arms. You'll soon see how gentle. My lunatic. My mad girl.

Here's a cloudy day to help you. No brazen sun. No sun . . . No sun. The weather's changed.

•   •   •

Baptiste was waiting and the horses saddled. That boy stood by the clove tree and near him the basket he was to carry. These baskets are light and waterproof. I'd decided to use one for a few necessary clothes — most of our belongings were to follow in a day or two. A carriage was to meet us at Massacre. I'd seen to everything, arranged everything.

She was there in the *ajoupa;* carefully dressed for the journey, I noticed, but her face blank, no expression at all. Tears? There's not a tear in her. Well, we will see. Did she remember anything, I wondered, feel anything? (That blue cloud, that shadow, is Martinique. It's clear now . . . Or the names of the mountains. No, not mountain. *Morne,* she'd say. 'Mountain is an ugly word — for them.' Or the stories about Jack Spaniards. Long ago. And when she said, 'Look! The Emerald Drop! That brings good fortune.' Yes, for a moment the sky was green — a bright green sunset. Strange. But not half so strange as saying it brought good fortune.)

After all I was prepared for her blank indifference. I knew that my dreams were dreams. But the sadness I felt looking at the shabby white house — I wasn't prepared for that. More than ever before it strained away from the black snake-like forest. Louder and more desperately it called: Save me from destruction, ruin and desolation. Save me from the long slow death by ants. But what are you doing here you folly? So near the forest. Don't you know that this is a dangerous place? And that the dark forest always wins? Always. If you don't, you soon will, and I can do nothing to help you.

Baptiste looked very different. Not a trace of the polite domestic. He wore a very wide-brimmed straw hat, like the fishermen's hats, but the crown flat, not high and pointed. His wide leather belt was polished, so was the handle of his sheathed cutlass, and his blue cotton shirt and trousers were spotless. The hat, I knew, was waterproof. He was ready for the rain and it was certainly on its way.

I said that I would like to say good-bye to the little girl who laughed — Hilda. 'Hilda is not here,' he answered in his careful English. 'Hilda has left — yesterday.'

He spoke politely enough, but I could feel his dislike and contempt. The same contempt as that devil's when she said, 'Taste my bull's blood.' Meaning that will make you a man. Perhaps. Much I cared for what they thought of me! As for her, I'd forgotten her for the moment. So I shall never understand why, suddenly bewilderingly, I was certain that everything I had imagined to be truth was false. False. Only the magic and the dream are true — all the rest's a lie. Let it go. Here is the secret. Here.

(But it is lost, that secret, and those who know it cannot tell it.)

Not lost. I had found it in a hidden place and I'd keep it, hold it fast. As I'd hold her.

I looked at her. She was staring out to the distant sea. She was silence itself.

Sing, Antoinetta. I can hear you now.

Here the wind says it has been, it has been
And the sea says it must be, it must be
And the sun says it can be, it will be
And the rain. . . ?

'You must listen to that. Our rain knows all the songs.'
'And all the tears?'
'All, all, all.'

Yes, I will listen to the rain. I will listen to the mountain bird. Oh, a heartstopper is the solitaire's one note — high, sweet, lonely, magic. You hold your breath to listen . . . No . . . Gone. What was I to say to her?

Do not be sad. Or think Adieu. Never Adieu. We will watch the sun set again — many times, and perhaps we'll see the Emerald Drop, the green flash that brings good fortune. And you must laugh and chatter as you used to do — telling me about the battle off the Saints or the picnic at Marie Galante — that famous picnic that turned into a fight. Or the pirates and what they did between voyages. For every voyage might be their last. Sun and sangoree's a heady mixture. Then — the earthquake. Oh yes, people say that God was angry at the things they did, woke from his sleep, one breath and they were gone. He slept again. But they left their treasure, gold and more than gold. Some of it is found — but the finders never tell, because you see they'd only get one-third then: that's the law of treasure. They want it all, so never speak of it. Sometimes precious things, or jewels. There's no end to what they find and sell in secret to some cautious man who weighs and measures, hesitates, asks questions which are not answered, then hands over money in exchange. Everybody knows that gold pieces, treasures, appear in Spanish Town — (here too). In all the islands, from nowhere, from no one knows where. For it is better not to speak of treasure. Better not to tell them.

Yes, better not to tell them. I won't tell you that I scarcely listened to your stories. I was longing for night and darkness and the time when the moonflowers open.

> Blot out the moon,
> Pull down the stars.
> Love in the dark, for we're for the dark
> So soon, so soon.

Like the swaggering pirates, let's make the most and best and worst of what we have. Give not one-third but everything. All — all — all. Keep nothing back. . . .

No, I would say — I knew what I would say, 'I have made a terrible mistake. Forgive me.'

I said it, looking at her, seeing the hatred in her eyes — and feeling my own hate spring up to meet it. Again the giddy change, the remembering, the sickening swing back to hate. They bought me, *me* with your paltry money. You helped them to do it. You deceived me, betrayed me, and you'll do worse if you get the chance . . . (*That girl she look you straight in the eye and talk sweet talk — and it's lies she tell you. Lies. Her mother was so. They say she worse than her mother.*)

. . . If I was bound for hell let it be hell. No more false heavens. No more damned magic. You hate me and I hate you. We'll see who hates best. But first, first I will destroy your hatred. Now. My hate is colder, stronger, and you'll have no hate to warm yourself. You will have nothing.

I did it too. I saw the hate go out of her eyes. I forced it out.

And with the hate her beauty. She was only a ghost. A ghost in the grey daylight. Nothing left but hopelessness. *Say die and I will die. Say die and watch me die.*

She lifted her eyes. Blank lovely eyes. Mad eyes. A mad girl. I don't know what I would have said or done. In the balance — everything. But at this moment the nameless boy leaned his head against the clove tree and sobbed. Loud heartbreaking sobs. I could have strangled him with pleasure. But I managed to control myself, walk up to them and say coldly, 'What is the matter with him? What is he crying about?' Baptiste did not answer. His sullen face grew a shade more sullen and that was all I got from Baptiste.

She had followed me and she answered. I scarcely recognized her voice. No warmth, no sweetness. The doll had a doll's voice, a breathless but curiously indifferent voice.

'He asked me when we first came if we — if you — would take him with you when we left. He doesn't want any money. Just to be with you. Because —' She stopped and ran her tongue over her lips, 'he loves you very much. So I said you would. Take him. Baptiste has told him that you will not. So he is crying.'

'I certainly will not,' I said angrily. (God! A half-savage boy as well as . . . as well as . . .)

'He knows English,' she said, still indifferently. 'He has tried very hard to learn English.'

'He hasn't learned any English that I can understand,' I said. And looking at her stiff white face my fury grew. 'What right have you to make promises in my name? Or to speak for me at all?'

'No, I had no right, I am sorry. I don't understand you. I know nothing about you, and I cannot speak for you. . . .'

And that was all. I said good-bye to Baptiste. He bowed stiffly, unwillingly and muttered — wishes for a pleasant journey, I suppose. He hoped, I am sure, that he'd never set eyes on me again.

She had mounted and he went over to her. When she stretched her hand out he took it and still holding it spoke to her very earnestly. I did not hear what he said but I thought she would cry then. No, the doll's smile came back — nailed to her face. Even if she had wept like Magdalene it would have made no difference. I was exhausted. All the mad conflicting emotions had gone and left me wearied and empty. Sane.

I was tired of these people. I disliked their laughter and their tears, their flattery and envy, conceit and deceit. And I hated the place.

I hated the mountains and the hills, the rivers and the rain. I hated the sunsets of whatever colour, I hated its beauty and its magic and the secret I would never know. I hated its indifference and the cruelty which was part of its loveliness. Above all I hated her. For she belonged to the magic and the loveliness. She had left me thirsty and all my life would be thirst and longing for what I had lost before I found it.

So we rode away and left it — the hidden place. Not for me and not for her. I'd look after that. She's far along the road now.

Very soon she'll join all the others who know the secret and will not tell it. Or cannot. Or try and fail because they do not know enough. They can be recognized. White faces, dazed eyes, aimless gestures, high-pitched laughter. The way they walk and talk and scream or try to kill (themselves or you) if you laugh back at them. Yes, they've got to be watched. For the time comes when they try to kill, then disappear. But others are waiting to take their places, it's a long, long line. She's one of them. I too can wait — for the day when she is only a memory to be avoided, locked away, and like all memories a legend. Or a lie. . . .

I remember that as we turned the corner, I thought about Baptiste and wondered if he had another name — I'd never asked. And then that I'd sell the place for what it would fetch. I had meant to give it back to her. Now — what's the use?

That stupid boy followed us, the basket balanced on his head. He used the back of his hand to wipe away his tears. Who would have thought that any boy would cry like that. For nothing. Nothing. . . .

PART THREE

'THEY knew that he was in Jamaica when his father and his brother died,' Grace Poole said. 'He inherited everything, but he was a wealthy man before that. Some people are fortunate, they said, and there were hints about the woman he brought back to England with him. Next day Mrs Eff wanted to see me and she complained about gossip. I don't allow gossip. I told you that when you came. Servants will talk and you can't stop them, I said. And I am not certain that the situation will suit me, madam. First when I answered your advertisement you said that the person I had to look after was not a young girl. I asked if she was an old woman and you said no. Now that I see her I don't know what to think. She sits shivering and she is so thin. If she dies on my hands who will get the blame? Wait, Grace, she said. She was holding a letter. Before you decide will you listen to what the master of the house has to say about this matter. "If Mrs Poole is satisfactory why not give her double, treble the money," she read, and folded the letter away but not before I had seen the words on the next page, "but for God's sake let me hear no more of it." There was a foreign stamp on the envelope. "I don't serve the devil for no money," I said. She said, "If you imagine that when you serve this gentleman you are serving the devil you never made a greater mistake in your life. I knew him as a boy. I knew him as a young man. He was gentle, generous, brave. His stay in the West Indies has changed him out of all knowledge. He has grey in his hair and misery in his eyes. Don't ask me to pity anyone who had a hand in that. I've said enough and too much. I am not prepared to treble your money, Grace, but I am prepared to double it. But there must be no more gossip. If there is I will dismiss you at once. I do not think it will be impossible to fill your place. I'm sure you understand." Yes, I understand, I said.

'Then all the servants were sent away and she engaged a cook, one maid and you, Leah. They were sent away but how could she stop them talking? If you ask me the whole county knows. The rumours I've heard — very far from the truth. But I don't contradict, I know better than to say a word. After all the house is big and safe, a shelter from the world outside which, say what you like, can be a black and cruel world to a woman. Maybe that's why I stayed on.'

The thick walls, she thought. Past the lodge gate a long avenue of trees

*and inside the house the blazing fires and the crimson and white rooms.
But above all the thick walls, keeping away all the things that you have
fought till you can fight no more. Yes, maybe that's why we all stay —
Mrs Eff and Leah and me. All of us except that girl who lives in her
own darkness. I'll say one thing for her, she hasn't lost her spirit. She's
still fierce. I don't turn my back on her when her eyes have that look. I
know it.*

In this room I wake early and lie shivering for it is very cold. At
last Grace Poole, the woman who looks after me, lights a fire
with paper and sticks and lumps of coal. She kneels to blow it
with bellows. The paper shrivels, the sticks crackle and spit, the
coal smoulders and glowers. In the end flames shoot up and
they are beautiful. I get out of bed and go close to watch them
and to wonder why I have been brought here. For what reason?
There must be a reason. What is it that I must do? When I first
came I thought it would be for a day, two days, a week perhaps. I thought that when I saw him and spoke to him I would
be wise as serpents, harmless as doves. 'I give you all I have
freely,' I would say, 'and I will not trouble you again if you will
let me go.' But he never came.

The woman Grace sleeps in my room. At night I sometimes
see her sitting at the table counting money. She holds a gold
piece in her hand and smiles. Then she puts it all into a little
canvas bag with a drawstring and hangs the bag round her
neck so that it is hidden in her dress. At first she used to look at
me before she did this but I always pretended to be asleep, now
she does not trouble about me. She drinks from a bottle on the
table then she goes to bed, or puts her arms on the table, her
head on her arms, and sleeps. But I lie watching the fire die
out. When she is snoring I get up and I have tasted the drink
without colour in the bottle. The first time I did this I wanted
to spit it out but managed to swallow it. When I got back into
bed I could remember more and think again. I was not so cold.

There is one window high up — you cannot see out of it. My
bed had doors but they have been taken away. There is not
much else in the room. Her bed, a black press, the table in the
middle and two black chairs carved with fruit and flowers.
They have high backs and no arms. The dressing-room is very
small, the room next to this one is hung with tapestry. Looking
at the tapestry one day I recognized my mother dressed in an

evening gown but with bare feet. She looked away from me, over my head just as she used to do. I wouldn't tell Grace this. Her name oughtn't to be Grace. Names matter, like when he wouldn't call me Antoinette, and I saw Antoinette drifting out of the window with her scents, her pretty clothes and her looking-glass.

There is no looking-glass here and I don't know what I am like now. I remember watching myself brush my hair and how my eyes looked back at me. The girl I saw was myself yet not quite myself. Long ago when I was a child and very lonely I tried to kiss her. But the glass was between us — hard, cold and misted over with my breath. Now they have taken everything away. What am I doing in this place and who am I?

The door of the tapestry room is kept locked. It leads, I know, into a passage. That is where Grace stands and talks to another woman whom I have never seen. Her name is Leah. I listen but I cannot understand what they say.

So there is still the sound of whispering that I have heard all my life, but these are different voices.

When night comes, and she has had several drinks and sleeps, it is easy to take the keys. I know now where she keeps them. Then I open the door and walk into their world. It is, as I always knew, made of cardboard. I have seen it before somewhere, this cardboard world where everything is coloured brown or dark red or yellow that has no light in it. As I walked along the passages I wish I could see what is behind the cardboard. They tell me I am in England but I don't believe them. We lost our way to England. When? Where? I don't remember, but we lost it. Was it that evening in the cabin when he found me talking to the young man who brought me my food? I put my arms round his neck and asked him to help me. He said, 'I didn't know what to do, sir.' I smashed the glasses and plates against the porthole. I hoped it would break and the sea come in. A woman came and then an older man who cleared up the broken things on the floor. He did not look at me while he was doing it. The third man said drink this and you will sleep. I drank it and I said, 'It isn't like it seems to be.' — 'I know. It never is,' he said. And then I slept. When I woke it was a different sea. Colder. It was that night, I think, that we changed course and lost our way to England. This cardboard house where I walk at night is not England.

One morning when I woke I ached all over. Not the cold, another sort of ache. I saw that my wrists were red and swollen. Grace said, 'I suppose you're going to tell me that you don't remember anything about last night.'

'When was last night?' I said.

'Yesterday.'

'I don't remember yesterday.'

'Last night a gentleman came to see you,' she said.

'Which of them was that?'

Because I knew that there were strange people in the house. When I took the keys and went into the passage I heard them laughing and talking in the distance, like birds, and there were lights on the floor beneath.

Turning a corner I saw a girl coming out of her bedroom. She wore a white dress and she was humming to herself. I flattened myself against the wall for I did not wish her to see me, but she stopped and looked round. She saw nothing but shadows, I took care of that, but she didn't walk to the head of the stairs. She ran. She met another girl and the second girl said, 'Have you seen a ghost?' — 'I didn't see anything but I thought I felt something.' — 'That is the ghost,' the second one said and they went down the stairs together.

'Which of these people came to see me, Grace Poole?' I said.

He didn't come. Even if I was asleep I would have known. He hasn't come yet. She said, 'It's my belief that you remember much more than you pretend to remember. Why did you behave like that when I had promised you would be quiet and sensible? I'll never try and do you a good turn again. Your brother came to see you.'

'I have no brother.'

'He said he was your brother.'

A long long way my mind reached back.

'Was his name Richard?'

'He didn't tell me what his name was.'

'I know him,' I said, and jumped out of bed. 'It's all here, it's all here, but I hid it from your beastly eyes as I hide everything. But where is it? Where did I hide it? The sole of my shoes? Underneath the mattress? On top of the press? In the pocket of my red dress? Where, where is this letter? It was short because I remembered that Richard did not like long letters.

Dear Richard please take me away from this place where I am dying because it is so cold and dark.'

Mrs Poole said, 'It's no use running around and looking now. He's gone and he won't come back — nor would I in his place.'

I said, 'I can't remember what happened. I can't remember.'

'When he came in,' said Grace Poole, 'he didn't recognize you.'

'Will you light the fire,' I said, 'because I'm so cold.'

'This gentleman arrived suddenly and insisted on seeing you and that was all the thanks he got. You rushed at him with a knife and when he got the knife away you bit his arm. You won't see him again. And where did you get that knife? I told them you stole it from me but I'm much too careful. I'm used to your sort. You got no knife from me. You must have bought it that day when I took you out. I told Mrs Eff you ought to be taken out.'

'When we went to England,' I said.

'You fool,' she said, 'this is England.'

'I don't believe it,' I said, 'and I never will believe it.'

(That afternoon we went to England. There was grass and olive-green water and tall trees looking into the water. This, I thought, is England. If I could be here I'd get well again and the sound in my head would stop. Let me stay a little longer, I said, and she sat down under a tree and went to sleep. A little way off there was a cart and horse — a woman was driving it. It was she who sold me the knife. I gave her the locket round my neck for it.)

Grace Poole said, 'So you don't remember that you attacked this gentleman with a knife? I said that you would be quiet. "I must speak to her," he said. Oh he was warned but he wouldn't listen. I was in the room but I didn't hear all he said except "I cannot interfere legally between yourself and your husband." It was when he said "legally" that you flew at him and when he twisted the knife out of your hand you bit him. Do you mean to say that you don't remember any of this?'

I remember now that he did not recognize me. I saw him look at me and his eyes went first to one corner and then to another, not finding what they expected. He looked at me and spoke to me as though I were a stranger. What do you do when something happens to you like that? Why are you laughing at me? 'Have you hidden my red dress too? If I'd been wearing that he'd have known me.'

'Nobody's hidden your dress,' she said. 'It's hanging in the press.'

She looked at me and said, 'I don't believe you know how long you've been here, you poor creature.'

'On the contrary,' I said, 'only I know how long I have been here. Nights and days and days and nights, hundreds of them slipping through my fingers. But that does not matter. Time has no meaning. But something you can touch and hold like my red dress, that has a meaning. Where is it?'

She jerked her head towards the press and the corners of her mouth turned down. As soon as I turned the key I saw it hanging, the colour of fire and sunset. The colour of flamboyant flowers. 'If you are buried under a flamboyant tree,' I said, 'your soul is lifted up when it flowers. Everyone wants that.'

She shook her head but she did not move or touch me.

The scent that came from the dress was very faint at first, then it grew stronger. The smell of vetivert and frangipani, of cinnamon and dust and lime trees when they were flowering. The smell of the sun and the smell of the rain.

. . . I was wearing a dress of that colour when Sandi came to see me for the last time.

'Will you come with me?' he said. 'No,' I said, 'I cannot.'

'So this is good-bye?'

Yes, this is good-bye.

'But I can't leave you like this,' he said, 'you are unhappy.'

'You are wasting time,' I said, 'and we have so little.'

Sandi often came to see me when that man was away and when I went out driving I would meet him. I could go out driving then. The servants knew, but none of them told.

Now there was no time left so we kissed each other in that stupid room. Spread fans decorated the walls. We had often kissed before but not like that. That was the life and death kiss and you only know a long time afterwards what it is, the life and death kiss. The white ship whistled three times, once gaily, once calling, once to say good-bye.

I took the red dress down and put it against myself. 'Does it make me look intemperate and unchaste?' I said. That man told me so. He had found out that Sandi had been to the house and that I went to see him. I never knew who told. 'Infamous daughter of an infamous mother,' he said to me.

'Oh put it away,' Grace Poole said, 'come and eat your food. Here's your grey wrapper. Why they can't give you anything better is more than I can understand. They're rich enough.'

But I held the dress in my hand wondering if they had done the last and worst thing. If they had *changed* it when I wasn't looking. If they had changed it and it wasn't my dress at all — but how could they get the scent?

'Well don't stand there shivering,' she said, quite kindly for her.

I let the dress fall on the floor, and looked from the fire to the dress and from the dress to the fire.

I put the grey wrapper round my shoulders, but I told her I wasn't hungry and she didn't try to force me to eat as she sometimes does.

'It's just as well that you don't remember last night,' she said. 'The gentleman fainted and a fine outcry there was up here. Blood all over the place and I was blamed for letting you attack him. And the master is expected in a few days. I'll never try to help you again. You are too far gone to be helped.'

I said, 'If I had been wearing my red dress Richard would have known me.'

'Your red dress,' she said, and laughed.

But I looked at the dress on the floor and it was as if the fire had spread across the room. It was beautiful and it reminded me of something I must do. I will remember I thought. I will remember quite soon now.

That was the third time I had my dream, and it ended. I know now that the flight of steps leads to this room where I lie watching the woman asleep with her head on her arms. In my dream I waited till she began to snore, then I got up, took the keys and let myself out with a candle in my hand. It was easier this time than ever before and I walked as though I were flying.

All the people who had been staying in the house had gone, for the bedroom doors were shut, but it seemed to me that someone was following me, someone was chasing me, laughing. Sometimes I looked to the right or to the left but I never looked behind me for I did not want to see that ghost of a woman who they say haunts this place. I went down the staircase. I went further than I had ever seen before. There was someone talking in one of the rooms. I passed it without a noise, slowly.

At last I was in the hall where a lamp was burning. I remember that when I came. A lamp and the dark staircase and the veil over my face. They think I don't remember but I do. There was a door to the right. I opened it and went in. It was a large room with a red carpet and red curtains. Everything else was white. I sat down on a couch to look at it and it seemed sad and cold and empty to me, like a church without an altar. I wished to see it clearly so I lit all the candles, and there were many. I lit them carefully from the one I was carrying but I couldn't reach up to the chandelier. I looked round for the altar for with so many candles and so much red, the room reminded me of a church. Then I heard a clock ticking and it was made of gold. Gold is the idol they worship.

Suddenly I felt very miserable in that room, though the couch I was sitting on was so soft that I sank into it. It seemed to me that I was going to sleep. But I imagined that I heard a footstep and I thought what will they say, what will they do if they find me here? I held my right wrist with my left hand and waited. But it was nothing. I was very tired after this. Very tired. I wanted to get out of the room but my own candle had burned down and I took one of the others. Suddenly I was in Aunt Cora's room. I saw the sunlight coming through the window, the tree outside and the shadows of the leaves on the floor, but I saw the wax candles too and I hated them. So I knocked them all down. Most of them went out but one caught the thin curtains that were behind the red ones. I laughed when I saw the lovely colour spreading so fast, but I did not stay to watch it. I went into the hall again with the tall candle in my hand. It was then that I saw her — the ghost. The woman with streaming hair. She was surrounded by a gilt frame but I knew her. I dropped the candle I was carrying and it caught the end of a table-cloth and I saw flames shoot up. As I ran or perhaps floated or flew I called help me Christophine help me and looking behind me I saw that I had been helped. There was a wall of fire protecting me but it was too hot, it scorched me and I went away from it.

There were more candles on a table and I took one of them and ran up the first flight of stairs and the second. On the second floor I threw away the candle. But I did not stay to watch. I ran up the last flight of stairs and along the passage. I passed the room where they brought me yesterday or the day before yesterday, I don't remember. Perhaps it was long ago for I seemed to know the house well. I knew how to get away from the heat and the shouting, for there was shouting now. When I was out on the battlements it was cool and I could hardly hear them. I sat there quietly. I don't know how long I sat. Then I turned round and saw the sky. It was red and all my life was in it. I saw the grandfather clock and Aunt Cora's patchwork, all colours, I saw the orchids and the stephanotis and the jasmine and the tree of life in flames. I saw the chandelier and the red carpet downstairs and the bamboos and the tree ferns, the gold ferns and the silver, and the soft green velvet of the moss on the garden wall. I saw my doll's house and the books and the picture of the Miller's Daughter. I heard the parrot call as he did when he saw a stranger, *Qui est là? Qui est là?* and the man who hated me was calling too, Bertha! Bertha! The wind caught my hair and it streamed out like wings. It might bear me up, I thought, if I jumped to those hard stones. But when I looked over the edge I saw the pool at Coulibri. Tia was there. She beckoned to me and when I hesitated, she laughed. I heard her say, You frightened? And I heard the man's voice, Bertha! Bertha! All this I saw and heard in a fraction of a second. And the sky so red. Someone screamed and I thought, *Why did I scream?* I called 'Tia!' and jumped and woke.

Grace Poole was sitting at the table but she had heard the scream too, for she said, 'What was that?' She got up, came over and looked at me. I lay still, breathing evenly with my eyes shut. 'I must have been dreaming,' she said. Then she went back, not to the table but to her bed. I waited a long time after I heard her snore, then I got up, took the keys and unlocked the door. I was outside holding my candle. Now at last I know why I was brought here and what I have to do. There must have been a draught for the flame flickered and I thought it was out. But I shielded it with my hand and it burned up again to light me along the dark passage.

Jean Rhys was born in 1894 in the Windward Islands, the daughter of a Welsh doctor father and a Creole mother, and spent her childhood there. At the age of sixteen, she came to England, where she lived during the First World War. She then married a Dutch poet and lived on the Continent for ten years. Her first book (*The Left Bank*, 1927) was published with a preface by her patron Ford Madox Ford, who recognized the "passion for stating the case of the underdog" and the "singular instinct for form" that were to place her among the finest writers of our time. She died in Devon in 1979.

Diana Athill has been a director of Jean Rhys's English publisher, André Deutsch, since the firm was founded in 1952. She is the author of an autobiographical book, *Instead of a Letter.*

Brassaï was born Gyula Halász in Brassó, Hungary (now Brasov, Romania), in 1899. After studying art in Budapest and Berlin, he moved to Paris in 1923, where he became first a journalist, then, in 1930, under the influence of André Kertész, a photographer. His most celebrated book, *Paris de Nuit*, containing sixty of his early photographs of Parisian nightlife, appeared in 1933 and caused a sensation. Brassaï also achieved recognition for his portraits of such artists as Picasso, Miró, Matisse, Giacometti, and Braque. He died at his summer home on the Côte d'Azur in 1984.

The text of this book was set in a film version of Baskerville. The display face used throughout is Kabel, with calligraphy by Ina Saltz.

Art direction by Neal T. Jones.

Typography and binding design by Joe Marc Freedman.